D1617512

M. Aurel Stein

RUINS OF
DESERT
CATHAY

PERSONAL NARRATIVE OF EXPLORATIONS IN
CENTRAL ASIA AND WESTERNMOST CHINA

BY

M. AUREL STEIN

IN TWO VOLUMES
VOL. II

DOVER PUBLICATIONS, INC.
NEW YORK

This Dover edition, first published in 1987, is an unabridged republication of the work originally published by Macmillan and Co., Limited, London, in 1912. For technical reasons, in the present edition the location of some of the illustrations has been changed; most particularly, Plates I–III of Volume One, Plates X, XII and XIII of Volume Two and all three maps now appear in a pocket attached to the inside back cover of Volume Two. The maps, the frontispiece of Volume One, Plates IV and V of Volume One and Plates VI–IX and XI of Volume Two, which all appeared in color in the original edition, are in black and white in the present edition. In many cases the illustrations have been further reduced, so that the scales given in the captions are somewhat relative.

Manufactured in the United States of America
Dover Publications, Inc., 31 East 2nd Street,
Mineola, N.Y. 11501

Library of Congress Cataloging-in-Publication Data

Stein, Aurel, Sir, 1862–1943.
    Ruins of desert Cathay.

    Reprint. Originally published: London : Macmillan, 1912.
    Includes index.
    1. Sinkiang Uighur Autonomous Region (China)—Description and travel. 2. Asia, Central—Description and travel. 3. Stein, Aurel, Sir, 1862–1943—Journeys—China—Sinkiang Uighur Autonomous Region. 4. Stein, Aurel, Sir, 1862–1943—Journeys—Asia, Central. I. Title.
DS793.S62S7 1987   915.1'6043   86-24374
ISBN 0-486-25351-1 (pbk. : v. 1)
ISBN 0-486-25404-6 (pbk. : v. 2)

CONTENTS

CONTENTS

CONTENTS

CHAPTER LXXXIV

CHAPTER LXXXV

CHAPTER LXXXVI

CHAPTER LXXXVII

CHAPTER LXXXVIII

CHAPTER LXXXIX

CHAPTER XC

CHAPTER XCI

CHAPTER XCII

ILLUSTRATIONS

ILLUSTRATIONS XVII

PLATES, PANORAMAS, AND MAPS

The pocket containing Plates X, XII and XIII and Maps II and III is attached to
the inside back cover of this volume.

CHAPTER L

A NUMBER of archaeological indications rapidly gathered in the course of that first day convinced me that the ruins I had passed, and those to be expected in continuation eastwards, belonged to an early system of frontier defence corresponding in character to the extant 'Great Wall' on the Kan-su border. That I should have to return to them for thorough exploration as soon as men and animals had recovered from their fatigues by a short rest at Tun-huang was quite clear to me. Yet no chances of getting more familiar with details of the old *Limes* were to be forgone in the meantime.

So on the morning of March 9th, 1907, while the animals were allowed to enjoy grazing a little longer and the men to take it easy over packing, I retraced last night's route until I came again upon the line of the wall. It was now seen to turn off north, and to run straight down at right angles to the shore of the small lake near the end of which we had camped. I was able to trace the layers of clay and fascines, so impregnated with salt as to look quasi-petrified, to within twenty-five yards or less of the salt-encrusted lake shore. That the level of the latter lay only four or five feet below the exposed base of the wall was an important observation. The extent of local desiccation since the wall was built could not have been great here. It was still more interesting to note how the lake had been utilized as a substitute for the strange wall elsewhere guarding the line. It was evident that those who laid down the line were eager to make the most of natural obstacles and thus to save building labour.

This conclusion was soon confirmed after we had started on the day's march. Having skirted the winding south shore of the lake for about a mile and a half, the track took us to the foot of a steep ridge which edged the lake on its east side. On the highest knoll overlooking the route there rose a massive square watch-tower, T. XI., surrounded by a crumbling wall of clay. The latter looked rough and of late origin. But a short scramble along the back of the ridge sufficed to reveal again the line of the old *Limes* wall with its characteristic reed fascines. It started from the lake shore opposite to the one where I had last traced it, and crossed the ridge down to another marsh basin.

As I noticed two more towers beyond the latter eastwards, I felt assured now that the line of the wall ran more or less parallel to the end of the Su-lo Ho drainage, and that the route we were following would keep within it and probably near it. The next tower was passed, indeed, after about five miles from camp near the southern end of that second basin; but the wall was not traceable there, evidently running farther north. For the rest of the day's march the succession of towers kept by our left above the grey horizon like a line of yellowish beacons. The stretch of scrubby desert or gravel Sai separating us from them was, however, too great to permit me to visit them without risk of losing touch with my caravan. Luckily the plane-table enabled us to fix their positions with precision from the route, showing that the distance from tower to tower averaged two to three miles.

At the end of close on ten miles by the side of a long-stretched depression full of luxuriant reed-beds and evidently containing springs, we came upon a small ruined fort of massive appearance, as seen in Fig. 154. Its walls, built of remarkably hard and well-laid strata of stamped clay, each about three inches thick, rose in very fair preservation to a height of nearly thirty feet. Fully fifteen feet thick at the base, they formed a solid square about ninety feet on each side. What splendid shelter they might give, not against human attack alone, but also against those cutting east winds, the very home of which we now seemed to approach! There was no trace of earlier quarters inside, and only scanty refuse from recent occupation by wayfarers. And yet, when I had climbed to the top by a rough staircase spared from the massive walls in a corner, and looked round over all this desolation, I felt sure that I stood on a structure which had braved man and nature for many centuries past.

The view enjoyed from the top was wide and impressive. To the south I could see the scrubby depression merging in a belt of Toghrak and tamarisk jungle. Beyond there rose an absolutely bare gravel glacis towards the equally barren foot-hills of a great range far away. To the north-east four towers lit up by the sun behind us could be made out echeloned in the distance, silent guardians of a wall line which I thought I could still recognize here and there in faint streaks of brown shown up by my glasses. What a fine position, I thought, this height of the fort wall must have been for a commandant to survey his line of watch-stations, and to look out for the signals they might send along it! But how long ago was that? Those sombre, barren hills of the Kuruk-tagh, now standing out clearly again on the northern horizon, had seen wall and towers first rise, and would see their ruins finally disappear before the blasts of the ages. But it would be like asking Death itself for an answer.

Somewhere between the foot of those hills and the line of towers the old drainage of the Su-lo Ho was bound to have cut its bed westwards. But even from that command-ing position I tried vainly to locate it. And yet, as our march continued across a sterile gravel plateau till the evening, I could see that the route was drawing nearer and nearer to a wide marshy basin, stretching east to west and manifestly part of the main Su-lo Ho valley.

We had been skirting its steep clay bank for a mile or so, and were approaching a roughly built tower standing near it, when I saw in the twilight a huge structure rising before me from the low ground which fringed the basin. Hurrying to inspect it before it became quite dark, I found there three palace-like halls, with a total frontage of over 440 feet, and walls of great thickness rising to about twenty-five feet (Fig. 156).   A natural clay terrace some fifteen feet high had been used as a base and added greatly to the appearance of height.   There were remains of a massive walled enclosure with high towers jutting out at the four corners as if guarding a palace court.   The sight of so imposing a building was doubly impressive for wanderers in the wilderness such as we had been for months, and the purpose of the grand ruin most puzzling. The position showed clearly that it could not have been intended as a fortified station.   And what could have been the object of a palatial structure which comprised only three vast halls and seemed wholly to lack accessory habitations?

The problem was not solved that night.   I found the men pitching camp near some springs about a mile farther east, close to some beds of dry reeds which seemed but to wait for a conflagration.   After an incipient one had, luckily, been extinguished, a shift of camp became unavoidable.   In the darkness it took time to find a spot where the bare saline soil would safeguard us from that danger. But the inevitable delay had manifestly affected the temper of the more excitable people in my party, already tried by the long desert marches, and a succession of squabbles and affrays between Ramzan, my worthless Kashmiri cook, Ahmad, the servant of Chiang, and, alas! honest Naik Ram Singh, too, kept matters lively till midnight.   As an offset to these petty worries, Hassan Akhun, the ever wide-awake camel-man, was able to hand me two copper coins which he had picked up in the evening while searching around the foot of the great ruin.   They proved to be of an early Han type, and thus furnished the first distinct indication as to the antiquity of the site.

Next morning in the bitter cold I examined the big ruin more closely, and soon ascertained all the main facts as to its plan and dimensions.   But there was no clue to the real character of the imposing erection.   The total absence of any other remains near by only added to the puzzle.   Straight north there extended a wide salt marsh where there was neither need nor possibility of continuing the wall line.   But both to west and east a succession of

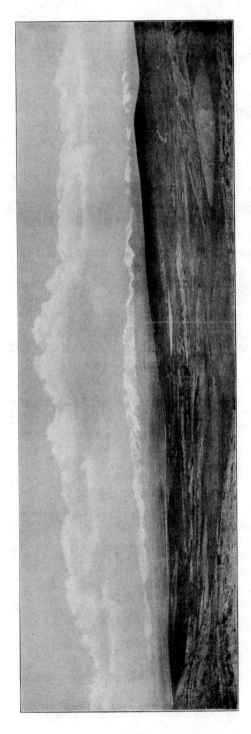

155. SHAGOLIN-NAMJIL RANGE, NAN-SHAN, SEEN FROM CAMP CCXV., ACROSS BASIN OF SU-LO HO HEAD-WATERS.

156. RUINS OF ANCIENT CHINESE MAGAZINE T. XVIII., TUN-HUANG *LIMES*, SEEN FROM SOUTH.

The figures of men standing at different points of the structure serve to indicate its size.

towers was in view, clearly showing where ran the line which was to be guarded. Through my glasses I could see quite distinctly that the nearest towers were all built on small isolated clay ridges, such as rose in numbers from the flat of the marshy basin. Thus the constructors of the line had duly appreciated and used the advantages here offered for a widened outlook.

But to me it was even more curious to notice the striking resemblance which these clay ridges and terraces, generally ranged in rows running north to south, bore to the eroded formations I had met in the dried-up basin east of Besh-toghrak. I could not have wished for a more exact reproduction of the aspect which that old terminal lake bed, and in all probability also the end of the ancient Lop-nor bed about Achchik-kuduk, might have borne at some earlier period. Another interesting illustration of physical conditions long past elsewhere was afforded by the rows of Toghraks which closely lined the lagoons and water-channels visible from afar within the wide marshy area. I thought of the lines of dead Toghraks I had crossed so often in the desert north of the present Lop-nor, and rejoiced at seeing the picture of the physical conditions I had conjectured as prevailing there before desiccation, now so faithfully materialized before my eyes.

My examination of the ruin delayed me while the caravan moved ahead, and as, according to our guide, a long march was before us I had reluctantly to renounce for the time all reconnaissances off the route. This now took us for miles through belts of fine jungle and scrub, filling a succession of big bays which the marshy basin sent south. The track we were following had since the previous day shown numerous cart ruts, old and new, a clear indication that Chinese from Tun-huang were in the habit of using it. The grazing, too, looked inviting. I had been wondering for some time at the utter solitude when at last, after some nine miles of march, I noticed a little group of my men gathered on a reed-covered hillock round two strange-looking figures. These proved to be Chinese herdsmen from Tun-huang, clad in queer, heavily padded rags, looking after some cattle and horses.

They were the first human beings we had seen for nearly three weeks past. Quaint specimens of humanity as they were, their appearance cheered up the spirits of my men greatly. I had never before had occasion to try my modicum of Chinese on people so humble in education and general intelligence, and that now, after repeated attempts, I succeeded in eliciting answers to some of my simple queries was felt by me no small encouragement. From them I learned that the place where we had met them was known as Shu-yu-t'ou, and that the cart tracks were those of people fetching timber and fuel to Tun-huang.

The route still continuing eastwards then crossed a succession of long-stretched gravel-strewn ridges, which from the glacis-like Sai on our right jutted out to the north like the fingers of a hand. The reed-filled depressions between them connected with a broad salt-covered basin north, manifestly containing a river course or lake bed, but too far off for close survey. After about six miles from Shu-yu-t'ou the narrow continuous ridges gave way to a wide bay bare of vegetation, and covered with rows of those characteristic clay terraces already familiar from the vicinity of lake basins dried up or undergoing desiccation. All the terraces had their long side stretching from north to south. There could be no possible doubt that they represented the remnants of earlier continuous ridges, such as we had just marched across, which the erosive force of the violent east winds and of the sand driven before them had slowly sawn through and broken up.

It was a very instructive illustration of a geological change still actually proceeding. The ridges themselves had evidently originated from the depressions between them having been scooped out by the drainage which during periods of much heavier precipitation came down from the foot of the mountains south, and cut up the clay sediments of a far more ancient lake bed. After another three miles of such ground we emerged on a level flat extending unbroken for three or four miles northward to the shore of a large sheet of dark blue water. At last we had come in sight of the Khara-nor lake, for which the map of Roborowsky and Kozloff had prepared us. But its extent was much larger than there shown, and the wide, salt-encrusted edges indicated that its level would at times rise still higher.

A number of small isolated clay terraces were seen scattered over the flat shore, manifestly the last survivals from terrace clusters and ridges which the relentless powers of erosion had long ago ground down and carried off. Two of them, not far from the present lake shore, could be seen crowned by watch-towers, for which they offered command-ing positions. But it was getting too late to approach them. Perched at the end of a long ridge projecting into the plain from the south there rose another ruined tower overlooking the route; which at this point turned to the south-east. One more great bay was crossed, filled with a succession of eroded clay terraces. There in the twilight we met for the first time a caravan, a big convoy of Keriya camels which had passed us at Miran at the beginning of February carrying the goods of some Khotan traders (Fig. 137), and which were now returning safely from Tun-huang. We did not envy the men their second desert crossing. Then the route led up a gently sloping alluvial fan, and at last in the dark, after a total march of some twenty-six miles, we pitched camp at a spring which our Abdal guide called Yantak-kuduk.

The water of the spring-fed pool proved perfectly fresh, and far better than any we had tasted for a long time. The thorny scrub close by just sufficed for the animals, and as the oasis now lay within a day's march, the morn-ing of March 12th saw the caravan start with unwonted alacrity. On a small knoll to the south where we fixed the plane-table I observed a novel sight, a miniature shrine built of clay and evidently cherished by Chinese wayfarers; for inside the tiny cella there lay votive offerings of papers and incense sticks. It served to remind me that we were approaching a region where Buddhism, or what figures as such in Chinese syncretistic belief, is still a religion in being.

Nothing else on that day's march indicated that we were moving towards a town of the living. For fully seven-teen miles we rode over a waste of gravel with practically no vegetation. There was nothing to intercept the view on this sterile alluvial fan, and looking back we could see the expanse of Khara-nor and the sombre hills beyond it quite clearly. Twice we crossed ancient river beds deep-cut, yet quite dry, marking probably an earlier delta of the Tang Ho. The second showed some growth of reeds, and evidently received subsoil water. Just before reaching it I caught the first distant sight of a line of trees marking the Tun-huang oasis, and after marching four miles onwards we found ourselves almost suddenly stepping from the barren Sai across the edge of cultivation.

The fine arbours and well-tilled fields, by contrast with the wastes we had passed through, looked inviting and neat, even in their wintry bareness. Half a mile onwards we came upon what looked like a dilapidated small fort now serving for cultivators' quarters. The Chinese occupants, after some parley with Chiang-ssŭ-yeh, allowed us to pitch our tents on the clean threshing-ground outside their high clay walls. It was evident that strangers were indeed a novel sight to them; for all the time that camp was being pitched and for hours afterwards we were watched with the utmost curiosity by every able-bodied man in the place and swarms of lively children.

There was a display of good nature all round, which was pleasing; and when I had managed somehow to make myself understood on a few simple matters by the jovial unkempt rustics, all doubts about the first welcome which might await us on true Chinese soil passed off. My own tent, as always, was kept at a good distance from the noise of the general camp. Just in front of it rose a clump of elms, and under them a picturesque little Buddhist shrine adorned with good wood-carving and some bold frescoes representing the 'Guardian divinities of the Regions.' All the surroundings breathed a novel air of well-ordered civilization; and when the crowd of good-natured watchers had dispersed with the falling darkness, I had reason to feel gratified with my first place of rest within the purlieus of a celestial population.

CHAPTER LI

On the morning of March 12th, 1907, we were prepared to make our entry into Tun-huang town. All the men had been looking forward eagerly to our arrival. But circumstances seemed to combine to deprive it of all state and even comfort. An icy gale was blowing from the east, and cutting as it was among the trees and houses, we congratulated ourselves inwardly that we had escaped it in the open desert. But what, somehow, seemed worse was that, though the town was said to be only some twenty Li, or about four or five miles off, no reply whatever was forthcoming to the elegant epistle which Chiang-ssŭ-yeh, at the very time of our reaching the oasis, had despatched to the Ya-mên, along with that imposing Chinese visiting-card of mine on red paper. It had announced our arrival within the magistrate's jurisdiction, suitably indicated my official rank and business, and expressed a request for the assignment of appropriate quarters. We knew from a letter received in December from my old friend P'an Ta-jên, Tao-t'ai at Ak-su, that he had duly recommended me to the authorities on the westernmost border of Kan-su.

Now that we were on the soil of a truly Chinese province, my excellent secretary seemed to feel more than ever his responsibility and his importance in serving my interests. He was not a little perturbed by this evident want of official attention, and showed his chagrin freely. In Turkestan the prompt appearance of a Beg or two from the Ya-mên would have been a matter of course, and even before their arrival village head-men would have shown themselves eager to attend. But here we had evidently to prepare for a different *milieu*. The few villagers about seemed to be sufficiently absorbed in their own business not to pay much heed to the Ya-mên, and only in the course of the morning did Chiang learn that a newly arrived magistrate had taken over the seal of his office the evening before. This great function, with all its attendant flutter in official dove-cots, would of course account, at least partly, for the neglect we had so far experienced.

So after some useless wait we set out for the town. Our atlases show it as Sha-chou, 'the City of Sands'; but to the local Chinese it is best known by its ancient name of Tun-huang, dating from Han times. The bitterly cold east wind and the dust haze would have befitted the shores of Lop-nor. But riding on I was struck by the abundant signs of careful cultivation and the substantial look of the buildings in the many isolated farms we passed. Of traffic on the road, such as enlivens the march near any Turkestan town or market, there was strangely little. We passed several large walled enclosures which looked like ruined forts, but in reality were only deserted villages once vainly defended, grim mementos of the terrible loss of population which Tun-huang, like all the other oases of Kan-su, had suffered during the last great Tungan rebellion.

At last we arrived by the river and found ourselves opposite the west face of the square-walled city. The river bed, then for the most part dry, was crossed by a dangerously rickety bridge, and then we rode through a ruinous town gate into the narrow main street of the place. Here, too, little life was stirring. In front of the outer gate of the magistrate's Ya-mên we met at last a small crowd of idlers, and directed by them, made our way past a couple of picturesque half-decayed temples with fine old wood-carving to the Sarai suggested for our residence. It proved a perfectly impossible place, so filthy and cramped that I decided at once rather to camp in the open. Among the people to whom this queer hostelry gave shelter we found several Turki traders from Kashgar and Hami. I was trying to elicit from them information about more possible quarters when at last a wretched-looking Ya-mên attendant arrived to offer help.

He seemed half-dozed with opium and utterly helpless; but stung into activity by Chiang's voluble language he served at least to establish official touch with headquarters.

I was already prospecting among gardens across the river for some suitable camping-place when there appeared on the scene the well-got-up 'Ta-i' of the magistrate, riding a lively donkey, and bringing profuse apologies from the newly installed dignitary. Local knowledge he had none to offer, having come with his master from another part of Kan-su. So I had to guide myself in the search. The few gardens to be found by the left bank of the Tang Ho were so small, and the pavilions or summer-houses adjoining them so ruinous, that I had before long to shift my reconnaissance back to the side of the present town.

There at last, half a mile or so from its south gate, I discovered a large orchard with a lonely house at one end which looked as if it had seen better days. On invading its precincts we found it still occupied, but luckily by people who were ready to find room for so big a party as ours. They were the widow of the late owner, apparently a petty landholder, and her mother, along with a number of small children. Round an inner court were grouped several small blocks of rooms and a hall, most of them unoccupied but for quantities of cranky ponderous furniture such as respectable Chinese families seem ever fond of accumulating. The cracked walls, broken paper windows, and other abundant signs of long-continued neglect, made a strange contrast with all the tinsel and gilding which covered the elaborate carvings.

I had hoped that, according to the custom prevailing in Turkestan, the women, after locking up their most cherished possessions, would clear out of the place and take shelter with relatives while the strange guests settled down in their house. But there was no such affectation of 'Purdah' on the part of our hosts. Cheerfully toddling about on their poor little bound feet the Chinese ladies huddled as much as they could of their household gods into one small block of rooms, while we were welcome to make what use we could of the rest. In a room close to them and chock-full of furniture Chiang managed to

effect a footing, his ever kindly and urbane presence being
evidently welcome as a set-off against the invasion of us
bearded barbarians.   He made friends at once with the
children, who were hugely enjoying all the unwonted
bustle.   Two large but ruinous rooms took in the Surveyor
and Naik, with honest Jasvant Singh, who was glad to do
his cooking under a roof even though half of it had fallen.

The spacious central hall ought to have offered me
shelter.   But there was no trace of a fire-place or stove to
warm it, and with gaping fissures in walls and roof it
would have been quite impossible to overcome the freezing
chill of the place.   So it was allotted for the keeping of my
boxes and the reception of official visits.   I myself vastly
preferred my cosy little tent outside among the leafless
fruit trees of the garden.   There was relative peace
and plenty of fresh air, with a chance of warming oneself
in the sunshine whenever the dust haze would allow this
to break through.   It was dusk before I could seek a
little peace and warmth in my tiny travelling homestead.
There had been trouble enough in settling down, quite
apart from the long search for quarters.   To secure the
badly needed supplies for men and beasts proved a serious
business.

We had indeed arrived in the centre of a prosperous
large oasis, but there was no obsequious Beg to take orders
and produce what we needed; nor was it of any use to
despatch the Ya-mên attendants to the town for what was
most urgently wanted, unless they were provided with cash
for immediate payment.   And what a trouble it took to
produce that cash in a form suited for local use!   Nobody
in Tun-huang would on any account take payment in
the coined silver of the 'New Dominion,' and all the
silver bullion I had brought consisted of big 'horse-shoes.'
The expedient of sending one of them to the blacksmith
to be cut up into chips for 'small change' did not dawn
upon us that first day.   At last one of the few Turki
traders came to the rescue by changing a few Taels of
silver into long sausage-like strings of copper 'cash' at a
rate which suited his fancy.

Even then it took hours before fuel, fodder, etc., arrived;

for the market, here held daily, had long been closed. My men, the Indians included, naturally grew impatient and annoyed at the endless delays caused by what they took for cussed contrariness in the 'heathen Khitai.' I myself felt plainly brought face to face with a great shift of the social background. Here in the very centre of Asia I seemed somehow forced into touch again with features of civilization familiar enough in the far-off West. It amused me to think what our experiences would have been, had our caravan suddenly pitched camp in Hyde Park, and expected to raise supplies promptly in the neighbourhood without producing coin of the realm !

Next morning the icy eastern gale was still blowing unabated. All the men not engaged over the scanty kitchen fires sought warmth and oblivion from discomforts past and present by a long day-sleep cuddled up in their furs. But it was a busy day for me. Early in the morning I had a long interview with a big deputation from the Turkestan traders settled in the town, who had come to pay their respects to me as a quasi-compatriot of official standing. The trade interests they represented were small, and it did not take long to realize that most of them had retired to Tun-huang from Hami, Charklik, Turfan, in order to find a safe refuge from inconvenient creditors or lawsuits. But the plentiful supply of camels which Tun-huang offered for hire had enabled them to extend their ventures far to the east and south. As long residence had made them familiar with local conditions in Kan-su, I was eager to gather from them as much as possible of the practical information needed for my immediate plans. It was interesting to learn that manufactured imports from Urumchi, Lan-chou, and Khotan seemed to compete here on approximately equal terms. The Mongol grazing-grounds in the high valleys and plateaus towards Tibet offered good customers for them in exchange for wool and skins.

Long before I started on this journey I had been struck by the geographically important position which the oasis of Tun-huang occupies near the point where the greatest old high road of Asia from east to west is crossed by the direct route connecting Lhasa, and through it India, with Mongolia and the southern portions of Siberia. Now, arrived on the spot, I was greatly struck to find that the region, the antiquities of which I was anxious to explore, had its modest marts impartially open to goods coming from China proper and its great ports in the East; to Russian manufactured produce brought *via* Kashgar or Urumchi; and even to British and Indian wares carried all the way from Khotan through the desert.

By noon I proceeded to the Ya-mên, where Ahmad, our Tungan interpreter, had previously carried in due form the announcement of my state visit along with the customary presents. Among the latter I had taken care to include the last piece of that fine yellow ' Liberty brocade' which I had before found most appreciated by Chinese recipients among my introductory offerings. I reached the magistrate's Ya-mên in the midst of a howling dust storm, and having to make my entry in my best ' Europe clothes,' black coat, sun-helmet, and patent leather boots, felt the cold pervading all its halls intensely. Naturally I should have liked under such conditions to make the first interview as short as I could. But Wang Ta-lao-ye, the ' Hsien-kuan,' at once proved an official so exceptionally cultured and pleasant that, over the lively talk about things learned and ancient which with Chiang's eager assistance ensued between us, I soon forgot the physical discomforts and the intention they had prompted.

The magistrate was a sparely built middle-aged man, with a face expressing keen intelligence (Fig. 209). There was something in his combination of courtly manners, scholarly look, and lively talk which recalled dear P'an Ta-jên. I heard in due course that Wang Ta-lao-ye had just managed to dig out from his predecessor's office records the elegantly worded epistle by which my Tao-t'ai patron had recommended me to the magistrate's attention. He was evidently impressed by its contents; and I instinctively felt that a kindly official providence had brought to Tun-huang just the right man to help me in my first work on these ancient Marches. Of course, I did not fail to make appropriate reference to my saintly guide and patron

Hsüan-tsang, and discovered to my delight that the Amban, as a scholar of wide reading, knew of the Hsi-yü-chi, the great pilgrim's genuine memoirs.

His apologies for our inadequate quarters were profuse, and evidently inspired by sympathy arising from similar experience. His own furniture and property had not yet arrived, and the reception hall of his Ya-mên looked terribly bare in spite of some elegant wood-carving on the walls and its much-faded gilding. As I looked round it struck me that the good people of Tun-huang could have but little attention to spare for their magistrate if they left him even for a short time without a brazier or a curtain to keep out the icy wind. It was a comfort to know that at least he could wear a succession of suits underneath his official robe to keep himself warm, whereas my own 'best clothes' strictly prevented similar protection and left me to feel the bitter cold.

The Buran was still raging when I rode back through the almost deserted streets and the great waste space which extended within the southern face of the town-wall. I hurried to get my half-frozen feet into big fur boots, and had just begun within my carefully-tucked-up tent to warm myself a little, when Wang Ta-lao-ye's return call was announced. There was nothing for it but to receive him in my inhospitable barn of a hall. However, etiquette having once been satisfied, I kept on my fur boots. Seated on a thick Khotan felt rug and with a charcoal fire kept going in the cauldron which served for my men's mess, I did not find the conditions quite so trying. From the mule trunks close at hand I brought forth specimens of ancient Chinese records excavated at Niya and Lop-nor, reproductions of earlier finds, and anything else that might be relished by the Amban's antiquarian eyes.

The effect was all I could wish for. Wang Ta-lao-ye thoroughly enjoyed the scholarly treat which my exhibits provided. With a kind of intuition, due no doubt to his interest in the subject matter, he generally managed to follow the archaeological queries and problems I ventured to submit to his judgment in my terrible Chinese jargon. I found him quite familiar with the geography of Eastern

Turkestan as it presents itself in the historical Annals and also to modern Chinese administration, though he had never served in that province. His knowledge was based wholly on books, and these, he frankly acknowledged, had told him nothing whatever about the ruined line of towers and wall I had traced in the desert.

Whether local information about it would be forthcoming from the people of Tun-huang remained to be seen. In a subdued conversation with Chiang-ssŭ-yeh he described them as very distrustful and rather awkward to handle. But he in any case would do his best to help me, whatever the difficulties might be about getting guides and labour for the desert. When he left us, after some hours of cheering confabulation, and more than one cup of tea, both Chiang and myself felt assured that for the work before us we could count on the genuine goodwill of a newly won scholar-friend.

Eager as I was to get ready for fresh explorations in the field, a number of practical obligations combined to prolong my halt at Tun-huang. Men and animals alike were much in need of a rest to recover from the preceding hardships. But though my body had its share in this enforced quiescence, there were plenty of urgent tasks to keep me very busy otherwise. Within thirty-six hours after our arrival I managed to pay off and dismiss to Charklik the whole of the donkey convoy which had helped us so effectively on the desert journey. It was a troublesome affair, for the animals belonged to different owners, and the payments had to be adjusted with regard to the services of the men who had looked after the donkeys, compensation for the six beasts which had died, etc. Then came the distribution of rewards among those men who had taken good care of their charges, and finally committal of the whole complicated account to Turki writing to assure faithful transmission of the moneys due at Abdal and Charklik. The men, well pleased with the sums I paid into their hands, were eager to set out on the long journey homewards. I, too, felt hearty relief when I saw the whole band gaily depart with the loads of maize I had presented as a *viaticum* for the donkeys.

Very soon afterwards I was able to despatch also my brave camels to a suitable grazing-ground where they were likely to gather fresh strength. This was an advantage gained through official support from another quarter. The very day after the exchange of visits with the prefect there called an officer sent by Lin Ta-jên, the military commandant at Tun-huang, to press upon me the assistance of some of his men to act as a camp guard, and to suggest through Chiang-ssŭ-yeh the propriety of mutual acquaintance. It was a wish which under any circumstances I would have been very glad to gratify. But here at Tun-huang it had not taken Chiang long to realize that the military was an element of far more consequence in the administration than we were accustomed to in "our own province of Hsin-chiang."

It appeared, in fact, that, since some earlier period which I was unable exactly to ascertain, these outlying westernmost districts of Kan-su had in their administrative organization retained some features recalling those of military frontier settlements. A number of Tun-huang agricultural families seemed to be in receipt of monthly stipends, paid on the understanding that certain members of them, able-bodied or otherwise, would be available for military service. Only a small proportion of the 600 men or so, supposed to constitute this corps of Tun-huang levies, were likely ever to have been embodied, and the few men who were actually seen about idling in the town on their turn of duty looked more harmless even than the 'soldiers' to be found in Chinese garrisons of Turkestan. But there could be no doubt that the Tun-huang people fancied themselves a bulwark of the Empire on what had been once an important frontier barrier, and was still a point of strategic importance. It became equally clear by and by that, owing to this organization of local levies, the military commandant at Tun-huang, having charge of all police arrangements, could play a hand in civil affairs, too, if he liked.

Lin Ta-jên, when I called at his Ya-mên, a fairly large and comfortable place, proved a cheery old warrior. He had a burly, active figure, of middle height, and a square-jawed face which expressed jovial good-nature and some character. At times he looked delightfully angular, like a figure from some early Flemish painting. His manners were pleasingly bluff and hearty, with just an occasional touch of quaint stiffness when he remembered what he owed to his present station and—prospects. His recollection of services went back to the time when he had tramped into Turkestan as a corporal in Liu Chin-t'ang's reconquering army. For many years he had remained a humble petty officer until the *débâcle* of 1900, when he had the good fortune to get attached to the Empress's escort, and riding by her chair on the flight to Hsin-an-fu to attract the imperial notice.

Promotion had been rapid since, and Lin Ta-jên seemed well pleased with himself and the way in which the world had treated him. He did not lay claim to much education nor to any particular interest in things dead and buried. But he seemed to cherish greatly the recollection of his early years spent in Turkestan, and would chat away gaily about such of his old haunts as Chiang and myself knew. He had read and heard a good deal about Japanese prowess in the late war, and seemed full of respect for the Westerners whose teaching had helped on their success. Our prolonged visit to the district was evidently welcomed by him as a pleasant diversion, and the help of his myrmidons which he pressed upon us as a safeguard against the obstructive indolence and occasional turbulence of the Tun-huang people in general, soon proved useful in more than one way. That Lin Ta-jên enjoyed more authority in his own sphere than Wang, the newly arrived civilian, did in his, was quite clear, and under the guidance of his men good grazing was soon secured for my camels. Luckily the two dignitaries were on excellent terms, and the magistrate was only too anxious to let me benefit by the predominant local influence of his military colleague.

From the Muhammadan traders there was information to be gathered about ruined sites in the vicinity of the oasis and along the great routes to the north and east. One among them, Zahid Beg from Urumchi, after many a venture north and south of the T'ien-shan, including

a Begship at Charklik, had sought here an asylum from
his Turkestan creditors.   Like the versatile person he
was, he had kept an eye open everywhere for 'Kone-
shahrs' with possible treasure.   So he was able to tell me
of ruins he had seen to the north-east of Tun-huang ; of a
walled town which lay half-buried under sand near Nan-
hu, to the south-west, and so on.   Vague as much of this
information necessarily was, it helped in forming my plans,
and was a perfect godsend when compared with the exasper-
atingly stolid and steadfast declaration of utter ignorance
which met every enquiry addressed to the Chinese of
Tun-huang.

But the most urgent task on hand was the preparation
of the detailed accounts which I owed for long months
past to the Comptroller of India Treasuries and the Indian
Survey Department, and which I was anxious to despatch
safely through the last of the Khotan Dakchis I had kept
by me.   Ever since the preceding summer there had been
no rest available for dealing with this accounts' incubus
which I had to face single-handed.   What its weight was
may be gauged from the fact that it meant not merely
extracting all and sundry items, however small, from my
general cash record into properly balanced 'Monthly Cash
Accounts' in due official form, as if I were my own
'Treasury Officer,' but also dividing all entries relating to
transport and the like according to whether they were to
be debited against the Government grant or the Survey of
India's subsidy meant for 'the Survey Party,' or, finally,
against my own personal purse, which would in due course
recoup them from authorized 'Travelling and Halting
Allowances.'   No wonder that for five or six days I felt
as if condemned to living more or less in the atmosphere
of an Indian Office room—though an uncommonly cold
one.

CHAPTER LII

IT was impossible to submit to this desk-work for long without a break while a site of exceptional interest was temptingly near, and awaiting as it were my first visit in fulfilment of a promise long made. Already in 1902 my friend Professor L. de Lóczy, the distinguished head of the Hungarian Geological Survey and President of the Geographical Society of Hungary, had directed my attention to the sacred Buddhist grottoes, known as the 'Caves of the Thousand Buddhas,' or Ch'ien-fo-tung, to the south-east of Tun-huang. As member of Count Széchenyi's expedition and thus as a pioneer of modern geographical exploration in Kan-su, he had visited them as early as 1879. I had been greatly impressed by his glowing description of the fine fresco paintings and stucco sculptures which he had seen there, and the close connection with early Indian art which he thought to have recognized in some of them without himself being an antiquarian student. It had, in fact, been a main cause inducing me to extend the plans of my expedition so far eastwards into China.

On the 16th of March I could at last pay my first visit to the famous cave temples to which my thoughts had turned for so long from afar. Chiang-ssŭ-yeh, Naik Ram Singh, and one of Lin Ta-jên's subordinates were to be my companions. The sky had cleared more rapidly than I could hope after those days of icy north-east wind and driving sand which greeted us on our arrival. It was a fairly bright morning, but still cold enough to make a wait trying. Yet, of course, we had to submit to that as an

inevitable feature of all work in these parts; for the
'Ya-i' who was to accompany us and carry the camera
had thought fit to requisition a pony instead of his usual
mount, a sturdy donkey, and so failed to turn up when
everybody else was ready.

At last by half-past eight our little cavalcade started
south-eastwards. Fringing the southern edge of the oasis,
the grey, dune-covered hills, which account for its later
name 'Sha-chou,' 'the City of the Sands,' loomed huge
through the leafless trees lining the roads. Most of the
route we followed through the oasis lay deeply sunk below
the level of the fields—an observation which brought back
memories of Khotan. But a glance at the fields would
suffice to remind me that Turkestan lay behind us. In
fine big plots they extended, ploughed and levelled with a
care which made them look as flat and smooth as billiard
tables. Of the irregular little embankments which for
irrigation purposes divide and terrace Turkestan fields,
there was no trace to be seen here.

After only a mile and half the road emerged on a bare
gravel glacis as uncompromisingly sterile as any I have
ever seen. Of dunes there were none, only a long, wall-
like stretch of sandy foot-hills stretching away on our right
to a hazy distance eastwards. An isolated small building,
rising on what looked like a 'witness' left on eroded
ground, proved to be, not a ruin, but a shrine with some
modest annexes for the priests. The dwellers were absent,
probably assisting in the celebrations which were reported
being held in the town in order to drive off an epidemic
attack described like influenza. The general look of the
morne hills south reminded me of the equally barren scarp
which the terrace-like offshoots of the Kun-lun about
Karghalik present towards the plains. Two ruined towers
suggested Pao-t'ais; but popular as the sacred caves no
doubt were from early times, their importance was not
likely to be indicated by the official marks of a high road.
And in fact no further towers were met with.

We were just approaching, after a total ride of some
nine miles, the shallow depression which marks the debouchure of the stream passing the sacred grottoes, when

there emerged from among the folds of the gravel-covered alluvial fan a lonely small shrine. It could not be very old; for the carved brickwork adorning the wall-tops and friezes showed tracery such as I had noted in the shrines of the city, and the bright yellow plaster looked recent. Yet, nevertheless, the whole bore every mark of premature ruin. The tiled roof with its fluted bricks was breached in more than one place, and that of an adjoining small cella had fallen entirely. But the coloured stucco images representing a Buddha, and some attendants whom I could not readily identify, were, in spite of missing limbs, still objects of worship. In front of them were the little sand-filled boxes which serve to keep lighted tapers upright. Red-coloured strips of paper inscribed with Chinese characters, probably short prayers or votive dedications, covered the base and wall surface.

Outside the gateway there hung from a stand a big bell, rusty and showing ominous cracks. About the closely packed Chinese characters which covered the outer surface, I could gather from Chiang's remarks only that they contained some Buddhist text. But more specific and satisfying was the indication that the inscription bore a date. It is true, it was not an old one, going back only to the first half of the last century; but it gave me the first assurance that the chronological precision so characteristic of Chinese ways was not ignored by Buddhist piety in these parts. How often have I wished that such sense for the value of exact dates might be met with among Indian worshippers!

The little Buddhist sanctuary, with its air of decay and desolation, was a fit preparation for the sights awaiting me at the sacred caves ahead. After less than a mile they came in view as we turned into the silent valley by the side of a shallow little stream just freed from the grip of winter. There was not a trace of vegetation on the curiously eroded grey slopes which the spurs of the low hill range eastwards send down to the debouchure of the stream (Fig. 157). But all thought of slowly dying nature reflected in these shrivelled barren ridges and hillocks passed from me when, on the almost perpendicular con-

157. BARREN HILL RANGE EAST OF CH'IEN-FO-TUNG VALLEY, SEEN FROM SOUTH END OF SITE.

158. MIDDLE GROUP OF 'THOUSAND BUDDHAS' GROTTOES (B) AND BEGINNING OF SOUTHERN GROUP (A).

glomerate cliffs rising on our right, I caught sight of the first grottoes.

A multitude of dark cavities, mostly small, was seen here, honeycombing the sombre rock faces in irregular tiers from the foot of the cliff, where the stream almost washed them, to the top of the precipice (Fig. 158). Here and there the flights of steps connecting the grottoes still showed on the cliff face. But in front of most the conglomerate mass had crumbled away, and from a distance it looked as if approach to the sanctuaries would be possible only to those willing to be let down by ropes or to bear the trouble and expense of elaborate scaffolding. The whole strangely recalled fancy pictures of troglodyte dwellings of anchorites such as I remembered having seen long, long ago in early Italian paintings. Perhaps it was this reminiscence, or the unconscious vision of rich rubbish deposits which such holy cave-dwellers might have left behind in their burrows, that made me in my mind people these recesses with a beehive of Buddhist monks, and wonder what awkward climbs they might have had when paying each other visits.

But the illusion did not last long. I recrossed the broad but thin ice sheet to the lowest point, where the rows of grottoes did not rise straight above the rubble bed, but had a strip of fertile alluvium in front of them ; and at once I noticed that fresco paintings covered the walls of all the grottoes or as much as was visible of them from the entrances. 'The Caves of the Thousand Buddhas' were indeed tenanted, not by Buddhist recluses, however holy, but by images of the Enlightened One himself. All this host of grottoes represented shrines, and I hastened eagerly to take my first glance at their contents.

The fine avenues of trees, apparently elms, which extended along the foot of the honeycombed cliffs, and the distant view of some dwellings farther up where the river bank widened, were evidence that the cave-temples had still their resident guardians. Yet there was no human being about to receive us, no guide to distract one's attention. In bewildering multitude and closeness the lines of grottoes presented their faces, some high, some low, perched one above the other without any order or arrangement in stories (Fig. 159). In front of many were open verandah-like porches carved out of the soft rock with walls and ceilings bearing faded frescoes. Rough stairs cut into the cliff and still rougher wooden galleries served as approaches to the higher caves. But many of these seemed on the point of crumbling away, and high up in the topmost rows there were manifestly shrines which had become quite inaccessible.

There was nothing to guide me in my first rapid sight-seeing. Some of the larger grottoes on the lowest floor had, indeed, elaborate wooden antechapels of unmistakably modern look to indicate restoration. But I soon found that even these shrines contained much that was manifestly old both in fresco work and statuary. As I passed rapidly from one cella to another my eyes could scarcely take in more than the general type of the frescoes and certain technical features of the stucco sculptures. The former, in composition and style, showed the closest affinity to the remains of Buddhist pictorial art transplanted from India to Eastern Turkestan, and already familiar from the ruined shrines I had excavated at Dandan-oilik and other old sites about Khotan. But in the representation of figures and faces the influence of Chinese taste made itself felt distinctly, and instead of the thin outlines and equally thin colouring there appeared often a perfect exuberance of strong, but well-harmonized colours. Where deep blues and greens preponderated there was something in the effect distinctly recalling Tibetan work.

I could not doubt for a moment that the best of these frescoes belonged to the times of the T'ang dynasty. In the rest, whether left in their original state or touched up by modern restorers, I could see that I had before me the work of painters who faithfully continued the artistic traditions of that period. The subjects and sizes of the mural paintings varied greatly in the different shrines, while the ground plan and arrangement of the latter showed much uniformity. From a kind of oblong antechapel, fully open to the light, but generally badly injured, a high and relatively wide passage led into a square, high-roofed cella hewn out of the rock, and as much as forty-five feet square. Within the cella was ordinarily to be found a group of images occupying either an elevated platform or else placed in a kind of alcove facing the entrance. All the wall faces were covered with plaster bearing frescoes. Those on the passage walls ordinarily represented rows of Bodhisattvas moving in procession or seated in tiers. Within the cellas the paintings were generally arranged in large, elaborately bordered panels, either singly or, where the wall surface was extensive, in a series. In the centre of these there appeared mostly figures of Buddhas, singly or in groups, surrounded by divine worshippers and attendants in many varied forms and poses. There were scenes from the Buddhist heavens, from legends in which Buddhas or saints figured, representations of life in their places of worship, etc. (Fig. 160).

But whether the wall decoration showed such pious compositions, or only that infinite multiplication of Bodhisattvas and saints in which Buddhist piety revels, all details in the drawing and grouping of the divine figures bore the impress of Indian models. In the figures of Buddhas particularly, the faithful preservation of the type of face, pose, and drapery as developed by Graeco-Buddhist art was most striking. In the subjects of the friezes and side panels, which often, apparently, reproduced scenes from the daily life of monks and other mundane worshippers; in the designs of rich floral borders, the Chinese artists seemed to have given free expression to their love for ornate landscape backgrounds, graceful curves, and bold movement (Figs. 203, 204). But no local taste had presumed to transform the dignified serenity of the features, the simple yet impressive gestures, the graceful richness of folds with which classical art, as transplanted to the Indus, had endowed the bodily presence of Tathagata and his many epiphanies.

Of the general style and merit of the sculptural remains it was more difficult to form a rapid impression; for much of this statuary in friable stucco had suffered badly through decay of its material, mere soft clay, and even more from the hands of iconoclasts and the zeal of pious restorers.   In almost all the shrines I visited, a seated figure of Buddha, sometimes of colossal proportions, was the presiding image ; but by his side there appeared regularly groups of standing Bodhisattvas and divine attendants more or less numerous (Fig. 161).

I could readily recognize representations of Dvarapalas, the celestial 'Guardians of the Quarters,' in the richly adorned and gaily dressed figures usually flanking the horse-shoe-shaped platform which bore the sculptured groups in the larger shrines, and here and there also images of the more prominent Bodhisattvas.   But for the rest, I realized from the first that prolonged study and competent priestly guidance would be needed.   But was there any chance that such guidance would be forthcoming at this sacred site which at the time looked wholly deserted ?   And how would my honest secretary, himself a stranger to all the intricate details of Buddhist mythology and iconography, succeed in correctly grasping and reproducing the technical explanations of the hoped-for cicerone ?   Indeed, in this as in so many other directions of enquiry since my arrival at Tun-huang, I had cause to regret bitterly my total want of Sinologist qualifications.

It was pleasing to note the entire absence of those many-headed and many-armed monstrosities which the Mahayana Buddhism of the Far East shares with the later development of that cult in Tibet and the border mountains of Northern India.   And still more reassuring was it to see everywhere the faithful continuance of the sculptural traditions as developed by Graeco-Buddhist art.   The heads and arms of most statues were, indeed, modern and very distant replicas, sadly inadequate attempts at restoration. But often the bodies and their rich drapery had sur-vived without change, and their exquisite colouring had escaped repainting.   The profusion of gilt images, I knew, was an early feature, and so also the frequency of colossal figures of Buddhas in a variety of poses.   The pious efforts of recent restorers seemed principally to have been directed towards these.   Hence the several giant images of sitting Buddhas, rising through caves with a

159. ROWS OF CAVE-TEMPLES, SHOWING DECAYED PORCHES, NEAR MIDDLE
OF SOUTHERN GROUP, 'THOUSAND BUDDHAS' SITE.

160. INTERIOR OF CAVE-TEMPLE CH. VIII., 'THOUSAND BUDDHAS' SITE,
SHOWING FRESCO DECORATION OF WALLS AND ROOF.

number of stories, had modern antechapels built in front, of gaily painted timber and profusely decked with Chinese inscriptions on scarlet paper.

Surely it was the sight of these colossal images, some reaching nearly a hundred feet in height, and the vivid first impressions retained of the cult paid to them, which had made Marco Polo put into his chapter on ' Sachiu,' *i.e.* Tun-huang, a long account of the strange idolatrous customs of the people of Tangut. " The Idolaters have a peculiar language, and are no traders, but live by their agriculture. They have a great many abbeys and minsters full of idols of sundry fashions, to which they pay great honour and reverence, worshipping them and sacrificing to them with much ado," and so on.

Tun-huang manifestly had managed to retain its traditions of Buddhist piety down to Marco's days. Yet there was plentiful antiquarian evidence showing that most of the shrines and art remains at the Halls of the Thousand Buddhas dated back to the period of the T'ang dynasty, when Buddhism flourished greatly in China. Tun-huang, as the westernmost outpost of China proper, had then for nearly two centuries enjoyed imperial protection both against the Turks in the north and the Tibetans southward. But during the succeeding period, until the advent of paramount Mongol power, some two generations before Marco Polo's visit, these marches had been exposed to barbarian inroads of all sorts. The splendour of the temples and the number of the monks and nuns established near them had, no doubt, sadly diminished in the interval.

As I passed hurriedly from grotto to grotto, faithfully followed by my literatus, we were at last joined by one of the local priests I had been looking out for. It was a young ' Ho-shang,' left in charge of the conglomeration of small houses and chapels which occupied a place amidst some arbours and fields facing the south end of the grottoes (Fig. 186). He was a quiet, intelligent fellow, quick at grasping what attracted my interest, and as unobtrusive a cicerone as one could wish for. His face showed scarcely any Chinese feature, and like so many physiognomies seen about Khotan curiously recalled Indian origin. But I had already seen enough of the people of Tun-huang to realize how thorough a mixture of races may be looked for at these ancient cross-roads between China, Tibet, and the quasi-Aryan settlements of the Tarim Basin.

Our guide readily took us to the temple containing a big Chinese inscription on marble which records pious works executed here in the T'ang period, and subsequently to the two shrines where smaller epigraphic relics dating from the Sung and Yüan dynasties are preserved. Alas! I had to leave the examination of them entirely to Chiang-ssǔ-yeh, who, with true Chinese delight in things palaeographical, was soon absorbed in a study of the finely engraved rows of characters. But it was a comfort to know that with one or two exceptions they had already been published by M. Chavannes from impressions brought back by M. Bonin.

At Tun-huang I had first heard through Zahid Beg vague rumours about a great hidden deposit of ancient manuscripts which was said to have been discovered accidentally some years earlier in one of the grottoes. And the assertion that some of these manuscripts were not Chinese had naturally made me still keener to ascertain exact details. These treasures were said to have been locked up again in one of the shrines by official order. In secret council Chiang and myself had discussed long before how best to get access to the find, and how to break down if necessary any priestly obstruction. I had told my devoted secretary what Indian experience had taught me of the diplomacy most likely to succeed with local priests usually as ignorant as they were greedy, and his ready comprehension had assured me that the methods suggested might be tried with advantage on Chinese soil too. The absence of the Taoist priest in charge of the manuscripts made it impossible to start operations at once. But the young monk was able to put us on the right track. So I soon let him be taken aside by the Ssǔ-yeh for private confabulation. From a rapid inspection of the southernmost caves, perched high up near the top of the cliff, I had just returned to the grotto containing the latest of the inscriptions, engraved about the middle of the fourteenth century, when Chiang joined me full of joy at the success of his investigation.

It was in a large shrine farther north, bearing on its walls evidence of recent restoration, that the deposit of manuscripts had been discovered. The entrance to the cave-temple had been formerly blocked by fallen rock-débris and drift sand. After this had been cleared out, and while restorations were slowly proceeding in the temple cella and its antechapel, the workmen engaged had noticed a crack in the frescoed wall of the passage between them. Attracted by this they discovered an opening leading to a recess or small chamber hollowed out from the rock behind the stuccoed wall to the right.

It proved to be completely filled with manuscript rolls which were said to be written in Chinese characters, but in a non-Chinese language. The total quantity was supposed to make up some cart-loads. News of the discovery ultimately reached provincial headquarters, and after specimens had been sent to far-away Lan-chou, orders were supposed to have come from the Viceroy to restore the whole of the find to its original place of deposit. So now behind the carefully locked door with which the recess had been furnished, these strange undeciphered manuscripts were said to be kept. The shrine, though full of Buddhist frescoes and sculptures, was in charge of a Taoist priest, the small fraternity of Ho-shangs or Buddhist monks, to which our guide belonged, peacefully sharing with him the guardianship of the site.

The priest was away in the oasis, apparently on a begging tour with his acolytes. Chiang had thus no chance to pursue his preliminary enquiries further. But, fortunately, the young Ho-shang's spiritual guide, a Sramana of Tibetan extraction, had borrowed one of the manuscripts for the sake of giving additional lustre to his small private chapel, and our cicerone was persuaded by the Ssŭ-yeh to bring us this specimen. It was a beautifully preserved roll of paper, about a foot high and perhaps fifteen yards long, which I unfolded with Chiang in front of the original hiding-place. The writing was, indeed, Chinese; but my learned secretary frankly acknowledged that to him the characters conveyed no sense whatever.

Was this evidence of a non-Chinese language, or merely an indication how utterly strange the phraseology of Chinese Buddhism is to the literatus brought up on a classical pabulum? However, a frequently repeated formula at once attracted our attention, containing the word 'Pu-sa,' the Chinese contraction of the Sanskrit term 'Bodhisattva.' This sufficed to show that the text must be Buddhist —enough to whet my appetite even more for the whole collection. The paper looked remarkably strong and fresh with its smooth surface and fine texture; but in a climate so dry and in a carefully sheltered hiding-place there was no judging of age from mere appearance. So I was obliged to put off all further speculation on this score until we should obtain access to the whole of the hidden library.

It was a novel experience for me to find these shrines, notwithstanding all apparent decay, still frequented as places of actual worship. But quite apart from the damage done by well-meant restorations, I reflected with some apprehension upon the difficulties which this continued sanctity of the site might raise against archaeological exploitation. Would the resident priests be sufficiently good-natured—and mindful of material interests—to close their eyes to the removal of any sacred objects? And, if so, could we rely on their spiritual influence to allay the scruples which might arise among the still more super-stitious laity patronizing their pilgrimage place or 'Tirtha,' to use the familiar Indian term? Only experience and time could show.

Meanwhile I was glad enough to propitiate the young Buddhist priest with an appropriate offering. I always like to be liberal with those whom I may hope to secure as 'my own' local priests or 'Purohitas' at sites of ancient worship. But, unlike the attitude usually taken up by my Indian Pandit friends on such occasions, when they could—vicariously—gain 'spiritual merit' for themselves, Chiang-ssŭ-yeh in his worldly wisdom advised moderation. A present too generous might arouse speculations about

161. STUCCO IMAGE GROUP, REPRESENTING BUDDHA BETWEEN DISCIPLES, BODHISATTVAS, AND DVARAPALAS, IN CAVE-TEMPLE CH. III., 'THOUSAND BUDDHAS' SITE.

possible ulterior objects. Recognising the soundness of his reasoning, I restricted my 'Dakshina,' or offering, to a piece of hacked silver, equal to about three rupees or four shillings. The gleam of satisfaction on the young Ho-shang's face showed that the people of Tun-huang, whatever else their weaknesses, were not much given to spoiling poor monks. As to Chiang, I thought I could in his attitude detect something closely akin to that mingled regard for the cult and self-conscious pity for its ignorant representatives, which in the old days never allowed of easy relations between my learned associates in Kashmir and the local priests at pilgrimage places we used to visit together for archaeological purposes.

It was getting dusk before I could tear myself away from this wonderful beehive of temples in its setting of barren rocks and sands. The route we followed when returning clambered up the riverine terrace by a steep detritus-covered slope, and then crossed the bare gravel plateau which edges the foot of the outer hills. The west wind which now swept it was piercing, and in the dust-laden atmosphere complete darkness soon overtook us. So there was nothing to interfere with the pictures full of vivid colour and grave pomp, all of ages long gone by, which that day's over-abundant sight-seeing had left impressed on my mind's eyes.

CHAPTER LIII

A DIFFICULT START FROM TUN-HUANG

AFTER the fascinating prospects that hurried excursion had opened before me, it seemed hard to continue my clerical toils unbroken during the days which followed ; but the tasks were so heavy that, busy as I was at my table from morning until midnight, the time seemed only too short. The departure of a Khotan trader, who was to start for Charklik by March 21st, offered a chance of sending off with him Kurban Niaz, the Dak man, the last safe link for my mails to Kashgar, India, and Europe, which I was likely to have for a long time. So the letter-bag I entrusted to him for what was bound to prove close on four months' transit, grew uncommonly heavy.

In the meantime I was able to think over and settle my immediate plans. I knew from my Taklamakan experiences what the climatic conditions in the desert of Tun-huang were likely to be when once the winter had passed. So I decided upon the exploration of the ancient frontier line as the first task of my new programme. It was quite impossible to calculate beforehand with any certainty what amount of time and labour excavations along it might claim. So with plans upon the ' Thousand Buddhas ' looming big before me, it seemed doubly important that I should start back to the ancient wall well provided in the matter of guides, diggers, and supplies, and thus prevent any needless delay in my proposed operations there.

It did not take me long to realize that the difficulties in all these respects would be serious. Of the ruins I was anxious to trace and explore in the desert nothing was known to our friends the magistrate and military commander, or to the other educated Chinese officials of Tun-huang, though they seemed interested in my work and ready to help. On the other hand, the deep-rooted secretiveness of the local Chinese population effectively prevented any offer of guidance from the herdsmen or hunters, who occasionally visit the nearer of the riverine jungles.

Still more serious was the trouble threatening about the provision of labour and transport. This was first brought home to me on the occasion when our military patron, Lin Ta-jên, and the learned magistrate jointly treated Chiang-ssŭ-yeh and me to a grand dinner-party. They had considerately waited until learning that the despatch of mails and accounts had at last set me free for a little diversion. The scene was laid in the guest-rooms of a finely situated temple on the north wall of the city. With only two other guests to share our Mandarin friends' hospitality it was easy to combine the discussion of scholarly and practical 'business' with enjoyment of the comforts provided.

It was a well-ordered little feast, and I frankly confess I greatly appreciated its setting. To find myself in neat and well-lit apartments, with an atmosphere pleasantly warm, was an experience which had not come my way since camping in Nar-bagh. The menu was ample and varied, and though I was not competent to judge of the dishes, and soon forgot even to keep count of them, it seemed a welcome change from the wearisome uniformity of the food my intractable Kashmiri cook was in the habit of preparing. Wang Ta-lao-ye had been thoughtful enough to cater for my intellectual appetite, too. He had brought a Chinese volume containing a kind of official gazetteer of the Tun-huang district and full of historical extracts. So during the preliminaries of the dinner I was able, with Chiang's help, to glean a good deal of interesting information about the history of the 'Thousand Buddhas'' site during T'ang times, as well as to ascertain how vague modern knowledge was in respect of the ancient routes leading westwards.

With the ruined line of wall we had traced in the desert of Tun-huang local Chinese scholarship had evidently never concerned itself, and later on Chiang, when at home, vainly searched the volume even for a mere reference. It was the old story of antiquaries, absorbed in their book-lore, not heeding to look for the realities of the past in the open. When I thought of the physical conditions prevailing on the desert ground I was eager to search, I could scarcely blame Chinese confrères for not having cared to explore it before me. Nor could I complain of any indifference on the part of my hosts when I explained to them the operations I was planning about those ruins. Chiang had told them a good deal since our first visits about my methods of work and the success which had rewarded them elsewhere, and with that historical curiosity which seems innate in every educated Chinaman, they were manifestly agreed that I should try my luck here too.

But when, in the course of our dinner talk, it came to discussing the practical arrangements needed for my proposed excavations, I realized that there were difficulties ahead such as on Turkestan soil no Amban had ever hinted at. Wang Ta-lao-ye gravely told me that he scarcely knew how to provide the dozen diggers I had mentioned as the minimum required for my first prospecting. Ever since the great devastations of the Tungan rebellion, the population of the oasis had remained very low, and the supply of agricultural labour extremely scanty. The cultivators owned their land. However small their holdings, to make them move out into the desert for digging would be a hopeless attempt, whatever the season and whatever pay might be offered; for Tun-huang people all loved their ease dearly, and having no struggle for existence to face were proof equally against official pressure and the desire of gain.

Besides, they were all and sundry confirmed opium-smokers, and as such most unwilling under any conditions to submit to a rough life in the open. It was the same with the few men available for hire as day labourers, a hopelessly inert set of wastrels, not likely to forsake easy employment about the town and hamlets for work in the dreaded 'Great Gobi.' In any case I should never get even these hapless loafers living from hand to mouth to accompany me into the wintry desert unless I took them there in carts. For me who knew what marching in waterless desert meant, the idea of my caravan moving with coolies on carts, like a snail with its shell, was comical and depressing beyond words.

But it was as well to have one's eyes fully opened to the radical difference in the relations between administration and people since we had exchanged Turkestan for these Marches of China proper. There, as the representative of a conquering power and set to rule over a race of inferior civilization, no Chinese Amban would have admitted any limits to his ability to order out labour, as long as the men were likely to receive a reasonable recompense. The task of collecting them would fall on the petty bureaucracy of Begs and village head-men, who had the will and traditional means of making their orders obeyed. Here among true celestial subjects all this was changed. As I realized more and more the farther we moved into Kan-su, the fundamental principle of administration appeared to be a sort of mutual toleration between nominal rulers and ruled, supported chiefly by that all-pervading factor, *vis inertiae*.

With this indolent but highly democratic public, practical experience must have taught the officials to restrict interference to the minimum compatible with the collection of such taxes as would suffice to keep the provincial machinery going and — to leave modest nest - eggs for the office incumbents on retirement. The people, while tolerating authority for the sake of tradition and general security, seemed to take good care to enforce such prudent reserve on the part of their administrators. What petty local officials we ever managed to get hold of invariably bore themselves more like representatives of defence unions of guilds and land-owning communities than as agents of the civil authority. That there was now in these westernmost parts of Kan-su practically no military force to back up the civil, became abundantly evident in the course of my

journey eastwards.   How little reliance could be placed on
the levies of Tun-huang in particular I was to learn in
good time by the tragic *dénouement* to be related hereafter, of which poor learned Wang himself became the
victim.

With such cares in the background, avowed or hidden,
it was natural that our conversation should turn to the
'New Dominion,' where there were still real rulers of
districts, and where a capable Amban need not take too
serious count of local opposition.   It was amusing to
watch how the mental atmosphere of our little official party
brightened with this change of topic.   Bluff and genial
Lin Ta-jên recalled stories of his own happy days of exile
in the newly reconquered province where any official of
sense could live without worries and make money.   Chiang
felt at once in his true element, and chattered gaily of all
the attractions which his adopted territory offered to men
in office and—to others who like his humble self were
trying to qualify for it.   To Wang Ta-lao-ye and the other
Kan-su guests Hsin-chiang, I could clearly perceive, must
have presented itself in the light of an Eldorado for literati
aspiring to the official's life.

I myself could not help sympathizing with them when
I thought what the reverse change would be like for any
of my Anglo-Indian civilian friends, say, from the charge
of a big district in the Punjab to the magistracy of some
slum-ridden Western centre full of highly advanced, though
ordinarily tame, Socialists.   So I was induced to expatiate
upon the many obvious points of contact between British
rule over India and the sort of paternal government which
Chinese state-craft has exercised since ancient times over
the *soi-disant* 'New Dominion' in Central Asia; and I
thought I found an appreciative audience in spite of the
crudeness of my best Chinese.   There could be no doubt
that we all felt united by sentiments of some common
official bond, and when our little party broke up I retained
the impression, not merely of some hours pleasantly spent,
but of a gain in good understanding.

I needed this assurance badly when on March 22nd
I was making my final preparations for returning to work

in the desert.   Men and animals had had a good rest now.
Ram Singh, the Surveyor, had completed inking and
tracing the winter's plane-table work, while the Naik had
made fair progress with the developing of my photographic
negatives.   I myself had managed to find time for re-
arranging the baggage, the bulk of which was to be stored
as a depot under Ibrahim Beg's care in quarters hired for
the purpose within the city walls.   But of the labourers
and hired camels I had asked for from the magistrate's
Ya-mên no sign appeared.   An informal call which he and
Lin Ta-jên paid me in the course of the day had given
me an opportunity of personally repeating my requests for
labourers who could walk on their own feet, and for camels to
carry the baggage and supplies for men and beasts.   They
promised to do their best, but looked much exercised over
the problem how to get Tun-huang people to follow me
into the desert and work.   I had told them that my start
was fixed for the morrow.   But though I was kept
busy until after midnight by many tasks, including the
settlement of accounts, which meant endless trouble of
weighing hacked silver and adjusting for differences of
scales, I waited in vain for either men or camels.

Next morning the wearisome wait continued.   But I
had decided to make a move in any case, just to show my
Mandarin friends that I was in earnest.   So my tent was
struck and the baggage which was to go with us made
ready for our own camels.   Hassan Akhun had over-night
brought them back safely from what even he, a fastidious
critic of all things in this infidel region, acknowledged to
have been splendid camel-grazing.   By and by there
appeared on the scene one of Lin Ta-jên's non-com-
missioned officers, a quiet, cheerful man, who was to
escort us with a mounted levy.   The Ya-mên attendants
had set out early to bring the promised camels and
coolies.   But hour after hour passed without their returning, and repeated reminders sent to the magistrate's Ya-
mên produced no result but apologies.   It was evident that
his good intentions were of little avail against indigenous
inertia and obstruction.   Long years of service in the
' New Dominion ' had accustomed Chiang to a different

procedure, and he freely displayed indignation at this open defiance of authority.

It was a pleasant contrast to note the civility shown by all those with whom our stay had brought us into contact. The ladies of the house which had given shelter to my people sent a dear little mite to wish me *bon voyage* and —to receive the rent. The levies who had kept watch over camp and animals showed exuberant gratitude for the *douceur* I sent them, though it was far from extravagant. However troublesome subjects the people of Tun-huang might be, want of manners was not among their chief faults.

I was sitting in the midst of the ready-packed baggage when there arrived a visitor to cheer me, whom here, far away in Cathay, I felt tempted to greet almost like a fellow-countryman. It was an enterprising Afghan merchant, Sher Ali Khan of Kabul, who traded at Khotan, and was just now returning from Kan-chou after a successful venture, partly with British fabrics imported through Kashmir and Yarkand. He was sending back his caravan *via* Charklik with tea and silk in return. My old haunts on the Indus and beyond were familiar places to him, and so too were Samarkand and Bokhara. As I looked at the tall, well-built man with a complexion like that of a Southern European, and thought of the thousands of miles he had covered on routes which were still very much as they must have been in the times of the ancient world, I needed no imagination to picture to myself those agents of 'Maës the Macedonian, also called Tatianus,' who eighteen hundred years ago had traded from Syria or Mesopotamia for the silk of the distant Seres.

At last, realizing that a further wait was useless, we set out by one o'clock, after Chiang-ssŭ-yeh had penned his poignantly polite epistle of protest to the Ya-mên on neat pink paper. My immediate programme was to move due north of the oasis, and to search there for the line of the ancient wall which I surmised to continue eastwards along the course of the Su-lo Ho. So we passed through the outer and inner walls of the town into its somnolent dirty streets, where pigs were more conspicuous

than people, and out again by the east gate. Just within
that a beautiful memorial arch in wood, of some age and
badly decayed, offered a pleasant relief to the eyes from
all the surrounding squalor.

We moved on through a well - cultivated tract with
orchards and scattered but substantial homesteads, but had
scarcely covered more than three miles when a mounted
messenger from the Ya-mên overtook me. He did not
bring news of the much - delayed transport and coolies,
but, to my great delight, telegraphic messages from
Kashgar and Peking. Immediately on my arrival at
Tun-huang I had taken care to send off Ibrahim Beg to
the town of An-hsi, four marches to the north-east, where
I knew the great high road from Turkestan to Kan-su to
pass and the telegraph line along it; messages entrusted
to him were to announce my arrival by wire both to Mr.
Macartney and to the Peking Legation. I was aware how
little reliable was that wire linking East and West, with
deserts between the rare stations, and with its constant
breakdowns lasting at times for a week or two. So my
joy at receiving replies within ten days was all the greater.

It was an exciting quarter of an hour as I sat by the
road-side deciphering the messages, which, like my own,
had, for the sake of reducing cost and risks of distortion,
been despatched in the Eastern Telegraph Company's
excellent code ' *Via* Eastern.' The news proved reassuring from both sides. Kashgar reported all well and a
big mail-bag having been started *via* Khotan. From
the Legation I heard that arrangements were completed
through the Chinese Foreign Office, allowing me to draw
6000 Taëls, equivalent roughly to £1000, from the Tao-
t'ai's treasury at Su-chou. It was a relief to have been
brought so rapidly into touch with the distant East and
West. But what I enjoyed most, perhaps, was the feeling
of living for the moment as it were in two widely different
periods. For travel or the transmission of letters the
distances separating me from Kashgar, and still more from
India or Europe, claimed an allowance of long weary
months such as Marco Polo would have found natural.
And now into this mediaeval perspective of time to which

I had become quite accustomed, there seemed to burst with the telegrams a flash of modern life.

This surprise would have sufficed to cheer me for the rest of the day. But the march too, short as it was, offered interest of its own. At several points we passed large bastioned forts with high and massive walls of clay which looked recent. Inside were only a few houses or farm buildings rarely tenanted. I now learned that these strongholds, so thoroughly mediaeval in look and reminiscent of the Pathan village forts, or ' Killas,' familiar to me from the Indian North-West Frontier, had all been built or repaired by the neighbouring villagers during the troubled times of the Tungan rebellion. Traditional Chinese notions had led the unfortunate settlers to seek safety behind high walls, however inadequate their defence was in numbers or spirit. So all these scattered places of refuge fell one after the other before the onslaught of the fanatical Muhammadan rebels, who spared neither women nor children. During the successive inroads of the great murdering bands there escaped only that portion of the population which had sought refuge in the town, and many died there of starvation.

Though over thirty years had passed since that time of horrors it was easy to note on all sides evidence of its lasting effects. The farther we passed from the town the more frequent became the sight of ruined houses and temples. Close by there were often quite substantial farms which had been reoccupied, and the land around was now under careful cultivation. But the population was manifestly still far from having made up its terrible losses in numbers. Gradually I noticed stretches of uncultivated ground appearing on either side of the canal we were following, while in the distance beyond them rows of trees marked other finger-like extensions of the oasis aligned along more canals. Abundant scrub attested that the soil of the intervening waste strips was quite fertile and only waiting to be brought under cultivation again.

Here and there the ruins of old homesteads could be seen rising amidst these abandoned fields, and troops of graceful small antelopes were now browsing there in peace.

Clearly the villagers were no hunters. But whether this
was due to surviving Buddhist feeling about the taking
of life, or to some special local superstition, or simply to
sheer indolence, I attempted in vain to find out.

The suspicious reticence of the people proved a terrible
barrier throughout. In time I learned to realize that even
the most reserved and shy of Turkestan 'Taghliks' were
almost loquacious when compared with these good people
of Tun-huang. No question I put about the reason which
caused these areas of fertile land to remain waste,
ever elicited any other answer beyond that impenetrable
'Pu chih-tao,' "I do not know." Was it really a diminution of the water-supply since pre-rebellion days, or rather
the want of adequate labour for more extensive irrigation? It seemed difficult to believe in the former as I
looked at the overflowing canal and the big range under
deep snow which came into full view on the south as the
ground got more open.

We camped in a tamarisk grove near the hamlet of
Shih-tsao, and before starting next morning were to my
relief joined by a small convoy of coolies and camels. The
eight men whom the Ya-mên attendants had managed to
scrape together looked the craziest crew I ever led to
digging—so torpid and enfeebled by opium were they;
but I was glad to have even them. So they were promptly
advanced a fair lump of silver to lay in provisions, and the
cart which had brought them from town was to be taken
along for their conveyance as far as the ground would
permit. Moving for some three miles northward along
the canal we came upon the crumbling homesteads of a
village left deserted since its sack by the Tungans. In the
midst of this desolation it was pleasant to find the decayed
fort tenanted by a number of baby camels, only a few days
old, which were being kept here out of mischief and the
biting wind while their mothers were grazing outside.
The antics of the quaint little beasts supplied a contrast
to the grim scenes of death and plunder which these walls
must have witnessed scarcely forty years before.

Then we turned off to the north-west across a
belt of scrub-covered waste where the lines of irrigation

channels, though dry since Tungan days, were still well preserved, and came to resumed cultivation near the flourishing little village of Chuang-lang. Its homesteads were
established mainly amongst the ruins of more substantial
dwellings built before the Tungan inroads. Most of the
trees in avenues and orchards were quite young, proving
recent reoccupation. But here and there big old ash
trees had survived the period during which this tract had
remained without people and its timber at the mercy of
wood-cutters from Tun-huang town.

After having crossed more stretches of waste land and
covered altogether eight miles, we arrived at the last
hamlet to which reoccupation has extended. Here the
recent colonists were still content with the shelter of mud
hovels and reed huts. To the west we were now within
view of the river bed of the Tang Ho, and immediately
to the north we had to cross a deep channel taking off
from it, which was manifestly an old canal of importance.
Beyond this there extended a wide steppe covered with
reeds and scrub, and cut up by numerous shallow channels
of water. Clearly this ground for its reclamation needed
drainage even more than systematic irrigation. And,
indeed, as we marched on we met a large party of poor
cultivators who had been engaged in reclaiming abandoned
fields for spring sowing. At last, after wading through
a good deal of flooded ground, I caught sight of the
' Kone-shahr' or ' old town' of which Zahid Beg had first
told me at Tun-huang. Shih-pan-tung, as our Chinese
companions called it, proved indeed a town, but its ruins
not older than the last Tungan rising. Nevertheless this
deserted site offered me a good deal that was instructive.

Within a square of crumbling clay ramparts, about
375 yards on each face, we found the remains of a
typical small Chinese town. It had been sacked by the
Muhammadan rebels about forty years before, and had
since fallen into complete ruin. The enclosing walls had
in many places decayed into a mere *agger* or mound. The
interior was for the greatest part filled with heaps of
débris ; but the usual alignment of streets at right angles,
somewhat after the fashion of a Roman castrum, could

still be made out quite clearly. Through the ruined gate in the centre of the southern wall face passed the main road towards a conspicuous temple ruin rising well above the débris-filled area and masking the north gate.

To the west of this road, and not far from the south gate, a small Ya-mên with a picturesque gateway still showed roofed rooms, but in a state approaching collapse. No timber had been removed here, and it looked as if some petty magistrate had occupied these quarters after the town was deserted, perhaps some official supposed to re-colonize it. Auspicious sentences penned on scarlet paper and similar flimsy adornments of official quarters still stuck to walls and posts. In the mellow afternoon light it was quite a picture of quiescent extinction. All other buildings within the walls, the couple of temples excepted, had been reduced to heaps of brickwork or bare walls, their timber having been removed long ago.

The main temple was a massive structure of true Chinese style, built in hard bricks with plenty of terra-cotta relievo work. It had a second story, formed by a separate shrine which was raised on a massive base of sun-dried bricks, about twenty feet high, at the back of the other. The stucco images, though all badly broken by vandal hands, were manifestly still objects of worship, and a large bronze bell was left *in situ* in spite of Tungan wrecking. Probably the raiding bands had neither time nor use for melting it down. In a smaller temple, too, crowning the centre of the west wall, there were traces of worship still clinging to the images, though they were reduced to a mere heap of clay fragments. Indeed, local cult dies hard. As I walked over the débris area, crossing more than one rubbish heap, I thought of the rich deposits likely to await some successor, say two thousand years hence. What antiquarian dainties might be gathered here—if only they became 'high' enough by the lapse of ages!

CHAPTER LIV

FROM the height of the town wall a watch-tower had been sighted to the north-north-east, and for that we set out on the morning of March 25th, with an icy wind sweeping down from the east. At first our progress was greatly impeded by the swampy condition of the ground, which was being purposely flooded for sowing. Large patches of the scrub-covered waste, once no doubt fields, had been cleared by burning, and water was now being brought to them in a rather erratic fashion by damming up channels which originally might in parts at least have been cut for irrigation. The camels and the men, now on foot, were forced to great detours and remained far behind.

But with a few of my people on horseback I struggled across to the 'Pao-t'ai,' which proved to be about four miles off. It was, as I had surmised from the first, a watch-tower of ancient construction. The material here consisted of hard lumps of salt-impregnated clay quarried from the low ridge on which the tower was raised; but any doubt as to its age was removed by observing in this strange masonry the same layers of reeds and tamarisk twigs at regular intervals which were characteristic of the towers guarding the old wall farther west. The whole formed a remarkably compact mass about twenty feet square at its base, and still over eighteen feet high, the permeating salts acting apparently like a sort of cement. Its solidity could be gauged from the fact that, though wind erosion had attacked and worn away the natural clay beneath the corners, the structure overhung there without any injury.

There was no trace of a wall line to be seen anywhere, and as the only landmark which might be a tower was seen in the distance north-eastward, I decided to follow a cart track which seemed to lead approximately in that direction. My intention was to push on first to the north and locate the course of the Su-lo Ho. If a crossing was possible, I would detach Ram Singh to survey the river along its northern bank down to the Khara-nor Lake. I myself, after seeing him safely across, would start eastwards for remains of the old wall near the left bank. The ground passed ahead was for some four miles covered with rich scrub and tamarisks, and by the side of our cart track I noticed two rough enclosures, built of remarkably hard lumps of salty clay, which bore the look of having been used at one time or other as sheep pens.

Then we encountered a low and narrow clay ridge stretching across our route, and from its top first sighted northward a wide marshy expanse suggestive of approach to the river. In the midst of it there could be seen rising a succession of clay terraces ranged in rows, all striking east to west. The sight of them reminded me at once of the eroded clay 'witnesses' we had passed in such numbers in the dry terminal basin of the Su-lo Ho and again in the vicinity of Lake Khara-nor. When, a mile or so farther on, we came upon the first fresh-water lagoon, and then had to ford a succession of shallow water-courses all flowing westwards and manifestly fed from the river, I could feel no doubt about the cause which had here determined the bearing of the rows of clay terraces. It was clearly the action of water which, working on the bottom of an earlier and wider fluvial bed, had first carved out ridges parallel to its own line of drainage from east to west. Then erosion by the winds blowing from the north-east had cut up these ridges into rows of terraces, and, no doubt, this scouring still continued. This combination of the erosive forces of running water and of wind was the very process by which I had conjecturally explained to myself the formation of those strange 'witnesses' in and near the dry lake basins previously met with. I felt no little satisfaction at seeing it now illustrated by actual observation on ground so near by and so closely corresponding.

Soon the cart tracks disappeared in a broad expanse of marshy ground where large areas were still covered by melting snow and ice cakes. For two and a half miles beyond the first clay ridge I pushed on with Naik Ram Singh and Tila Bai across the belts of boggy ground and the network of water-channels which extended between the chains of clay terraces. At last we forded with some difficulty a channel some twenty yards broad and four to five feet deep in which the icy water flowed briskly; but progress beyond was quite impossible for laden animals. A broad and long sheet of ice sighted to the north from the nearest ridge showed that the main course of the Su-lo Ho still lay ahead of us. Whether the ice would hold or not, there was nothing for us but to turn back. By the lagoon we had first met I halted for camp, and there the camels and coolies safely joined us in the darkness.

Next morning I retraced our route to the first clay ridge, and thence turned due east towards the tower we had sighted before. It took us nearly three miles to reach it across a reed-covered steppe where old fields with dry irrigation cuts were still clearly traceable. The tower built on a clay ridge rising about sixteen feet above the depression northward proved exceptionally massive and well preserved (Fig. 162). On a base twenty-six feet square it rose solid to a height of some twenty feet. On its top it bore a brick parapet, and within this a roofless cella open to the south, but provided with that peculiar masking wall which usually faces the street entrances to Chinese temples or mansions. The cella walls, some twelve feet high, still retained much of their plastering.

It was impossible to examine this crowning structure more closely owing to the disappearance of the ladder-like stairs which, judging from holes left for beams in the masonry, seem to have led up the west face. But a late origin, at least for the superstructure, was suggested by the peculiar way in which the bricks were set in alternately horizontal and vertical layers, such as I had never observed

163. FACE OF ANCIENT BORDER WALL, NEAR TOWER T. XXXV.,
TUN-HUANG *LIMES*, SHOWING CONSTRUCTION WITH
ALTERNATE LAYERS OF STAMPED CLAY AND FASCINES.

162. RUINED WATCH-TOWER T. XXV., NORTH OF TUN-HUANG OASIS,
SEEN FROM SOUTH-WEST.

Chiang-ssŭ-yeh at foot of tower.

164. REMAINS OF ANCIENT WATCH-TOWER T. XXVII., TUN-HUANG *LIMES*.

The ruin stands on a natural clay terrace of which the continuation is seen on right.
Naik Ram Singh in foreground.

165. REMAINS OF ANCIENT BORDER WALL, BETWEEN LOW DUNES, EAST OF TOWER
T. XXXV., TUN-HUANG *LIMES*.

The Chinese labourer on left stands on surface of low gravel mound.

on Chinese soil except in modern or mediaeval buildings. The bricks of the tower, too, differed in size from those observed in the watch-towers which I had examined along the ancient wall, being smaller and only two inches thick. I searched in vain for any traces of that wall with its characteristic reed-bundles, but found that a much decayed earthen rampart, about a hundred feet square, adjoined the tower on the south, evidently marking an enclosure. Had this served once as a place of refuge for some out-lying colony, and when had it been abandoned?

Not being able to sight any more towers, I felt rather puzzled how best to continue our search for the wall. However, I decided to march on farther east until we struck the track leading north across the Su-lo Ho towards Hami. Roborowsky and Kozloff, who had twice followed this route in 1893-94, had marked ruins of some sort on their map in a position south of the river, and I felt in any case bound to visit these whatever their age. So we moved on to the east across a level plain covered with thick scrub, and in one or two places with Toghraks of fair size.

Isolated clay terraces rose here and there, and after some four miles we fixed the plane-table on one of these. No tower came in view as we eagerly scanned the horizon; but luckily the Surveyor's sharp eyes sighted animals grazing in the distance. So we made for them quickly, and after a couple of miles to the east came upon a large flock of sheep, cows, camels, and ponies. We were met by a number of rather ferocious dogs (from which ' Dash,' my ever active little companion, had to seek shelter on Tila Bai's saddle), and by two truculent-looking herdsmen, mounted on wiry Mongolian ponies and carrying long flintlocks.

They proved to be Tungan nomads well acquainted with the riverine grazing-grounds on the Su-lo Ho and the high valleys and plateaus south of Tun-huang. Their rough looks and rather aggressive bearing would scarcely have inspired confidence in ordinary wayfarers. I could instinctively realize the loathing with which peace-loving Chinese, attached to their four walls, must regard such

rough, ever-roving customers. Whatever violence and
cruel deceit they might be prepared for in the rôle
of brigands and rebels, when occasion arose, these
Tungans had at least the saving grace of blunt, fearless
speech and pride in their local knowledge. When I
questioned them with Chiang's help about old 'Pao-t'ais'
in these parts, and offered a reward for showing me any,
the elder of the men, who claimed main ownership of the
flock, after some consultation with his brother, agreed to
guide us to a point where we might both obtain a sight of
some towers and find water for camping.

So led on by the Tungan we rode quickly ahead,
until after another three miles or so he brought us to
an isolated clay terrace some forty feet high on the edge
of a wide marshy belt stretching away towards the river.
I clambered up to the top, and looking south and south-
east could count not less than ten towers extending in a
line approximately east to west. The yellowish rays of
the sinking sun lit them up clearly in spite of the distance.
There could be no possible doubt about their marking the
alignment of the old wall, and my delight at this success
was great. The sturdy ruffian by my side had reason to
be satisfied with the reward of silver I gave him on the
spot without weighing. As he saw me gazing at the line
of towers through my prismatic glasses he without hesitation jerked out the information that this marked 'the old
Han road from An-shi to Lop-nor.'

It sounded like a strange confirmation of the surmise I
had nursed in my own mind for some time past. But
I had no means yet to decide whether the antiquarian hint
thrown out from this rough mouthpiece was correct, and
still less whether the Tungan's statement was derived from
a shrewd guess or the echo of a distant tradition. He did
not claim to have been much farther west along this 'old
Han road.' But an elder brother of his, now trading about
Hsi-ning-fu, had taken a strange 'Kuan' or official along it
to Lop-nor some seventeen years before. Judging from
the date indicated, I strongly suspect that this adventurous
traveller was the ill-fated M. Martin. As we know from
M. Grenard's account of the Dutreuil de Rhins expedition,

he was the first European in modern times to make his way across from Tun-huang to Abdal and Khotan, but did not live to record his story.

Beyond the river to the north-north-east, and a considerable distance away, my guide showed me a large group of ruined buildings, temples according to his statement. But the flooded condition of the river made them inaccessible for us now, and indications subsequently gathered make me inclined to believe that they were of relatively recent date, belonging to an abandoned road-side station on the route to Hami.

Gladly would I have kept my hardy Tungan for a guide in these regions, however obnoxious his presence might be to my Chinese entourage. But no fair words or offers would induce him to stay with me even for a day. He would not leave his flock in sole charge of others, and in all probability he preferred his sturdy independence to any service, however easy, which would bring him into constant touch with the despised 'heathen Chinee.' He left us soon, but promised to turn up in the morning with a sheep for which he was to be paid a good price. I hoped to get then at least a photograph of him ; but he never came, and the men I sent to fetch the sheep failed to find him. So the only man who could or would tell me of the old wall vanished from my horizon for good. I often wondered where the next Tungan rebellion, when it is due, will find him !

For me the day had closed with cheering promise, and the men found warm shelter in shallow cave-dwellings which some earlier occupants had excavated at the foot of the clay ridge. It was the more welcome as a cutting wind continued to blow from the east and the thermometer still showed twenty-five degrees of frost in the morning. Besides myself, only Naik Ram Singh, ever scrupulously clean and tidy about his person, preferred to stick to his little tent. The Chinese labourers were overjoyed at finding a nice den to huddle into ; but Hassan Akhun and the rest of my Turki followers, not liking the vicinity of the Tungans, tethered ponies and camels close by and kept a watch all night.

On the morning of March 27th I let the camp remain where it was, and set out with my assistants and half-a-dozen labourers to the east-south-east. I there hoped to strike approximately in the middle the line of towers I had sighted. Three miles across the scrub-covered plain brought us to another conspicuous clay ridge with a troglodyte dwelling occupied by a half-crazy wood-cutter. That he, being an orthodox Chinaman, expressed stereotyped ignorance about ruined towers and everything else was not a matter of consequence. Pushing onwards we passed through a belt of exceptionally thick scrub and low tamarisk cones, in which an inundation from the Su-lo Ho was steadily spreading. Nothing could induce our civilized slum-dwelling coolies to wade through the narrow channels. As they had each time to be mounted on ponies, one by one, progress was far too slow for my eagerness.

At last we emerged on a bare pebble Sai with much dead wood on the ground and isolated stunted Toghraks still living. The whole dreary ground bore the stamp of desiccation. But this was not the time for such observations. Right in front of me I saw rising the cone of an old watch-tower just of the shape and construction I had first seen in the desert westwards, and towards it I galloped as quick as 'Badakhshi,' my hardy pony, would bear me. Before reaching it I noticed a low mound composed of the familiar fascines and clay layers, stretching away across the bare gravel to the nearest tower on the east, and continuing also with a divergent angle south-westwards. There could be no longer any doubt: I was back again on 'my' wall!

The watch-tower, built entirely of regular courses of hard clay about four inches thick, with thin layers of tamarisk branches laid between them, still rose to over twenty-two feet. In order to give additional cohesion to the solid base measuring about twenty feet square, numerous wooden posts had been set in it vertically, and their ends were sticking out on the top. The wall once guarded by the tower had passed to the north of it, with a bastion-like projection at about six yards' distance.

Wind and driving sand had destroyed all but the lowest layer
of fascines, here all made up of tamarisk branches. But
this, with the overlying stratum of clay and gravel, cropped
out so clearly on the level flat that the line of wall which
it marked was easily followed by the eye far away. The
next tower on the east towards which this wall or *agger*
ran quite straight proved to be only one and one-eighth
mile distant. Beyond I could see three more 'Pao-t'ais';
but the examination of them had to be postponed.

Instead, I directed my attention to a close search of
the ground immediately adjoining T. XXVI., as I numbered the tower just described. Fortune for once seemed
inclined to encourage me at the outset. About four yards
from the south-east corner of the tower I noticed slight
refuse cropping out on the gravel surface. It proved the
last remnant of the rubbish once filling a small apartment
about eight feet square. Only traces of mud-built walls
with a plastered reed-facing survived. But within this
scant shelter and almost on the surface there turned up a
flat piece of thin wood, about one foot long and over an
inch broad, with Chinese characters neatly inscribed in
five columns. Dates such as I was eagerly asking my
learned secretary to look out for, were found neither in
this document, which Chiang took to be part of an account,
nor in another clearly written but incomplete Chinese
record of the 'slip' type, apparently referring to some
arms. But Chiang declared the writing to be of a strangely
ancient look, and in any case the discovery of records at a
spot at first sight so unpromising justified further hopes.
The labourers, somewhat roused from their torpor by the
prompt payment of a good reward, scraped the ground in
vain for remains in other quarters adjoining the tower.
The only find was two copper coins of the Han period.
But as this type had continued to circulate right down to
the early middle ages, they could not by themselves suffice
for the dating of a ruin even now within reach of people
from the oasis.

In order not to tax the tender feet of my Chinese
diggers too severely, I decided to turn next to the first
tower south-westwards, whence return to camp would be

nearer. For about three-quarters of a mile I could trace the line of the wall quite clearly, still rising in places to over three feet. Then we lost it on difficult ground, amidst tamarisk cones with soft eroded soil and dunes of fine drift sand between. The ruin which we reached after another mile and a half was undoubtedly that of a watch-tower, of the usual size, but badly decayed on some faces (Fig. 164). It had been built on a small clay terrace, which rose about seventeen feet above the eroded ground level on the south. On its west side the tower was adjoined by a mass of soft refuse about fifteen feet across, filling the remains of some poorly built structure to a height of three to four feet.

I had scarcely set the men to work when, on the southwest and almost on the surface, there were found three wooden slips inscribed with clear Chinese characters. They were quite complete, and showed the usual size, being about nine and a half inches long and half an inch wide (Fig. 119). Chiang at once recognized that two of them bore full dates, and our excitement was great. Presently three more inscribed narrow tablets emerged from under half a foot or so of rubbish in the middle of the heap, one of them being dated. Evidently we had struck a rich mine. But there was no time that evening to clear it with care; and as Chiang-ssŭ-yeh was unable to fix the 'Nien-haos,' or regnal titles in which the dates were recorded, I hastened to return to camp by sunset. We were both greatly exercised by conjectures as to the age which the date records, when identified, would reveal for the ruined wall and towers. Our high spirits were in a way shared by the labourers, who tramped after us pleased with the silver I had given in reward for the day's finds.

Arrived in camp by nightfall I almost grudged the time needed for a wash and hasty dinner before settling down with Chiang to search for those mysterious 'Nien-haos' in the chronological tables attached to Mayers' excellent *Chinese Reader's Manual*. It proved quite a thrilling hunt. In the absence of any definite clue, we had to search through the hundreds of regnal periods comprised within the possible limits from Han to Sung times. Of the reading of one ' Nien-hao,' Yung P'ing, Chiang felt quite sure.   But, alas! this proved to be represented several times, in the sixth as well as the third century A.D., and farther back I scarcely had the courage to look.   In the other ' Nien-hao,' Chien ——, my learned secretary was at a loss how to recognize the second character, though written quite clearly in two tablets.   Those who know something of the intricacies of Chinese script, with its tens of thousands of distinct ideograms and their palaeographic variation at different periods, will not wonder at his doubts.

I had vainly searched near the Yung P'ing periods already mentioned for a regnal title likely to give Chiang a clue to Chien ——, when at last in my despair I boldly took a jump of several centuries.   There was a Yung P'ing period commencing in 58 A.D.,—and just before it there stood the regnal title of Chien Wu.   Without a moment's hesitation Chiang recognized in it the character which had puzzled him so far.   It was the first title adopted by the Emperor who founded the Eastern Han dynasty in 25 A.D., and the twenty-sixth year mentioned in our two tablets corresponded to 50 A.D.   So the ruined frontier wall I had set out to explore went at least as far back as the first century of our era, and as proof I had in my hands the oldest written Chinese records so far known !

We both loudly rejoiced at this discovery, which put us at once on safe chronological ground for further researches.   Even ' Dash' was roused from below the blankets of my camp bed where he lay peacefully curled up for the night.   I wondered what he thought of the excitement displayed by his devoted Chinese friend and by his own master.   But, indeed, Chiang's historical sense was now keenly stirred, and I myself felt highly elated ; for I had all along put faith in the antiquity of this *Limes*, and now felt confidence in its successful exploration.

CHAPTER LV

NEXT morning broke with an icy north wind which later on shifted round to the north-west without losing any of its violence. My first business was to despatch one of the Ya-mên messengers with a letter to the magistrate asking for more labourers to push on excavations. Then I set out with every available man for the ruin sighted due south of our camp and next to the one prospected in the evening. The camp was to follow with a supply of water in tanks. It was essential to spare our handful of diggers all needless tramps to and fro; for I rightly suspected that with such shifty folk, all confirmed opium-smokers, the stimulus supplied by liberal rewards for finds would not hold out long, but only increase the craving for a good smoke and sleep in a warm den.

The watch-tower, for such it was, proved badly decayed; but thick layers of refuse covered the south slope of the low clay ridge on which as usual it had been built for the sake of better look-out, over some ten yards of length. At the foot of the slope they were fully three to four feet high. The chief ingredients were straw, twigs and bark of tamarisks, dung of horses—evidently mainly stable refuse of some watch and post station thrown down here. But from the very edge on the top there protruded the fragment of an inscribed Chinese tablet, and as more wooden records cropped up I promptly settled down to work here.

The harvest was abundant. Before mid-day two dozen or so of inscribed pieces had emerged, and the precious refuse heap was far from being exhausted. Chiang was indefatigable in exhorting and watching the coolies, pouncing upon and cleaning every dirt-encrusted ' tzŭ ' or writing with the utmost keenness. I could safely leave him and Naik Ram Singh to continue operations, while I myself set out for a preliminary inspection of the two remaining watch-towers visible south-westwards. By the time I returned from this reconnaissance the clearing of the whole of the refuse layers was completed, and the total number of inscribed pieces had risen to over seventy.

Only two of the records were fully dated, the year named corresponding to 75 A.D., and thus showing that the relics of this watch-station likewise went back to the Eastern Han dynasty. I could not doubt for a moment that the full interpretation of these records would need protracted study, and would tax the philological acumen even of so eminent a Sinologist as my friend M. Chavannes, for whom I destined them from the first. Chiang himself modestly disclaimed the capacity of solving the many puzzles in palaeographic features and in diction which the text of the tablets offered. Many of them, besides, were incomplete. Yet even his cursory examination sufficed to show that the records varied greatly in character. Brief reports on matters of military administration along the line of watch-stations ; acknowledgments of receipt for articles of equipment, etc. ; private communications ; fragments of literary texts ; even writing exercises seemed to be represented. But on all such points definite information came only through M. Chavannes' labours ; and for a general survey of the results which his unsurpassed learning and critical penetration secured from the materials discovered at this and other ancient stations along the wall, I must refer to a subsequent chapter.

It was far easier, of course, to become familiar on the spot with the external or stationery aspect of these mis-cellaneous ' papers,' to use an anachronism, the earliest of Chinese written records known till then. The most usual form was that of the thin wooden slip measuring when intact about nine to nine and a half inches long and from a quarter to half an inch wide (see Fig. 119). That some of the complete slips often contained over thirty Chinese characters (*i.e.* words) in a single vertical line will help to illustrate the remarkable neatness of the writing which prevails in these records.   Sometimes the writing was in several columns, or also continued on the back.   Among the woods used for these ' slips ' that of the poplar seemed most frequent, as at the sites I had explored in the Tarim Basin.   But, besides, there appeared a peculiarly streaked soft wood which the Naik recognized as belonging to some conifer.   It could not have grown in a climate so arid as the Su-lo Ho Basin must have had throughout historical times.   I conjectured it to have been brought from the slopes of the western Nan - shan, and there, in fact, I subsequently came across remnants of fir forest.   A still more distant import was represented by the neat slips of bamboo which turned up at other ruined stations.

But here in the refuse of tower T. xxviii. variety was imparted to the wooden stationery, also, by the plentiful ' fancy ' use of that abundant local material, the tamarisk. There were tamarisk sticks of varying length, roughly cut into polygonal shapes, and inscribed on a number of sides ; broad labels with rounded tops or peg-shaped, etc. Evidently convention was not so strict in the case of internal communications as about official correspondence, and for mere ' copy writing,' with which soldiers quartered at this and other stations had evidently beguiled their time, sticks of tamarisk cut on the spot were certainly good enough.   At the same time the number of ' shavings ' from regular slips (see Fig. 119, 14), and the fact of the latter being found often thinned down by repeated previous paring, showed that the supply of proper wooden stationery had its value, and was used over and over again.

Miscellaneous objects in wood also turned up among the refuse in plenty : such as small marked cubes apparently used for gambling or divination (Fig. 119, 15) ; tally sticks ; fragments of combs.   But what interested me most were two wooden seal-cases, evidently meant to be attached to some closed bag or other receptacle.   They showed the identical arrangement of three grooves for folds of string over which the seal was to be impressed in clay as I had first found on the envelopes of Kharoshthi documents at the Niya site. It was conclusive proof that I had been right years before in tracing all such details of that ancient wooden stationery of Turkestan back to earlier Chinese models.

No trace of the wall itself survived here, nor remains of the quarters sheltering those who had kept watch by the tower. Yet from the refuse thrown out by them it was possible to draw some conclusion as to their conditions of life. The line which the towers guarded must have already in the first century A.D. passed through desert ground. Wind erosion had, no doubt, progressed since; yet from the very position in which the undisturbed horizontal strata of rubbish were found, some ten feet below the level of the tower base, it was clear that the bare clay ridges rising above eroded ground had then already formed the characteristic feature of the site.

A curious indication of the remoteness of the guarded wall line from the inhabited area was supplied by the numerous fragments of coarse grey pottery, remarkably hard, which lay scattered in plenty on the surface, and often were found perforated on the edges with regular drilled holes. The discovery in the rubbish heap of several pieces still joined together by string of some rough vegetable fibre explained these holes (Fig. 172, 6), and bore witness to the value which the quondam owners had attached to their pots and jars however badly damaged. As the material was cheap enough, only the difficulty of transporting larger earthenware from the oasis would account for this continued use after the roughest mending.

On March 29th I took my men to the next tower south-westwards, which I had already reconnoitred. The distance proved to be only one and one-eighth mile. The tower, built of solid layers of stamped clay, rose in fair preservation to over twenty feet, and still bore on its top portions of a brick-built parapet below which horizontal rafters projected. No trace of stairs remained, but some holes on the south face had probably been utilized for a sort of ladder. Here, too, the tower had been built on a small clay ridge, no such advantage of ground being ever neglected by those who constructed the 'Wall.' A peculiar feature here was a relatively well preserved enclosure, about 107 feet square, of which the tower itself formed the north-west corner. Its walls, built of rough bricks and clay, with layers of tamarisk brushwood at intervals, still rose in one place to eight feet.

Whether this enclosure was coeval with the tower and the wall line it was meant to guard, I was unable to decide; for the accumulations of refuse found within its east face, and partly covering the floor and decayed walls of some rooms, yielded nothing but plentiful reed straw, cut brushwood, and dung of horses and camels. A large refuse heap some ten yards outside the south wall proved of similar composition. But here we came upon a fine jar, intact but for its mouth, and in shape resembling an amphora (Fig. 172, 5). Its height was nearly one foot, and its material a very hard dark brown stone-ware, with a mat slip burnt in. Within, traces of an oily substance survived. Small pieces of fine pottery, made of a very hard paste and with highly glazed surface, were picked up in plenty both within and around the enclosure. The glaze colours varied greatly; celadon green, ivory white, fine browns and black, an exquisite turquoise blue with several mottled tints, being all represented.

I was still wondering how to account for this unexpected abundance of superior pottery débris such as I had not yet come upon elsewhere in this region, when the clearing of a small ruined cella, previously noticed about fifty yards to the west, brought another surprise. It measured only eleven by thirteen feet outside, and with its entrance on the narrower side faced to the south. The walls, about two feet thick and built of fairly hard sun-dried bricks, rose nowhere above four to five feet. The interior was filled with débris of broken bricks, charred timber, and plastered reed wattle. When it was being cleared we came upon a platform built of bricks and running round all sides but that of the entrance. From the débris covering the platform to the north there came to light numerous fragments of stucco sculpture that unmistakably had once adorned a Buddhist shrine.

The fragments were all badly broken, but showed in

every detail close dependence on the models of Graeco-Buddhist art as transplanted to Central Asia.   There were portions of the arms of a statue somewhat under life size, modelled round cleverly dowelled wooden cores, bearing ornaments, and of well-shaped hands and fingers.   The blackened surface of the stucco, originally not baked, and the charred condition of the projecting core portions, showed that the statuary, like the little temple itself, had been destroyed in a conflagration.   One fragment of particular interest showed two small heads, one above the other, each only about three inches high, but excellently modelled (Fig. 273, 4).   While the upper one displays a look of placid contemplation, the lower one, with frowning brows and eyes and mouth wide open, cleverly expresses intense anger or passion.   As a third head is evidently missing below, it seems likely that one of those numerous 'Trimurti' representations of Buddhist divinities was intended, in which the 'angry' or demoniac form of the god usually plays a part.

However this might be, so much was clear, that the remains of the small Buddhist shrine here uncovered had some relation to the watch-station close by and the wall line which passed it.   But the style of the sculptured remains, though unmistakably old, seemed to speak against contemporary construction.   So I was led to conjecture that it was, perhaps, the tenacity of local worship—such as I had often seen exemplified elsewhere, and last among the ruins of deserted Shih-pan-tung—which had here caused a small shrine to be restored centuries after the wall was abandoned.   I did not realize until some time later that the direct route from the Tun-huang oasis towards Hami and the northern oases of Chinese Turkestan, passes even now in the vicinity of this old watch-station (T. XXIX.). Thus, if we may assume that already in ancient times it crossed the line of wall here, the existence of a small shrine near the gate station and its continued maintenance by pious wayfarers, say down to T'ang times, present nothing strange.   My subsequent discovery of a similar cult having survived on the old route westwards supplies an exact parallel.

But even in the immediate neighbourhood I made an observation which supports that assumption, though at the time I did not realize its true import. On the previous day's reconnaissance to the south-west, towards the next and last tower visible on that side, I had noticed, on the open salt-encrusted steppe intervening, and at a distance of less than a mile from T. xxix., some rough enclosures built of salt-impregnated clay lumps, and in the middle of one a miniature chapel, half-ruined, made up of the same coarse material. Looking back in the light of the indications since gathered, it now appears to me probable that this modest substitute for a shrine, manifestly of recent construction, represents the last lingering trace of the cult which those leaving or regaining the border wall of the Empire once paid to the sanctuary at this ' Gate.'

The westernmost tower extant on this part of the line proved less than two miles distant from T. xxix., and was a solid square mass of stamped clay. The small erosion terrace on which it was built made it a conspicuous landmark on this dismal salt-covered flat. No ancient remains of any sort except broken pottery could be traced near it, and far-advanced erosion had left neither trace of the wall nor any chance for digging. But I visited this tower (T. xxx.) again on my return march to Tun-huang, and then found that the deep-cut cart-track marking the route from the oasis to Hami actually passed between it and the tower T. xxix., which I now believe to have stood by the ancient gate through the wall. Though the view from the terrace of T. xxx. was open, no other ruin could be seen to the west except the tower T. xxiv., which I had already examined on my way north of Shih-pan-tung. It just showed its top over a maze of clay terraces to the west. So my survey in this direction was completed.

On March 30th, when we had a considerable fall of temperature down to thirty degrees of frost Fahrenheit, with the wind veering round to the west, I took my men back to the ruined watch-station (T. xxvii.) which had yielded the first dated records (Fig. 164). The débris adjoining the tower proved to belong to a room about

eleven by fourteen feet, partly cut out of the live clay of
the narrow ridge occupied by the tower. On clearing it
and a little terrace or loggia which faced it from the south,
we recovered two dozen more Chinese records on wood,
nearly half of them complete and in good preservation.
One of these, as we recognized with joy on the spot, showed
a clearly written date corresponding to 35 A.D. This
meant a farther step back in antiquity. Chiang was sure
that almost all the 'slips' referred to military posts or
individual officers, though he could not make out all the
details. So I concluded that the room by the side of the
watch-tower had served as quarters for some officer or
clerk attached to the troops guarding this part of the line.

M. Chavannes' analysis has since fully confirmed my
conjecture. One neatly written label, with a string still
attached, had evidently been taken from a bundle containing a soldier's outfit. From my learned collaborator's
translation I now know that it mentions the company
(*Hsien-wei*) he belonged to, as well as the locality (*Wan-
sui*) which he helped to guard. Over a dozen blank
tablets of the regular size evidently belonged to the
stock of stationery kept ready at this little office. Small
miscellaneous finds were abundant among the refuse within
the quarters and strewing the slope. Apart from remains
of cups of glazed stone-ware, spoons of wood, a broom, a
wooden seal, I may mention a fire-stick (Fig. 173, 3), exactly
conforming to the pieces found at the sites of Niya and
Endere as regards shape and arrangement of the holes in
which fire was produced by rubbing.

On the evening of that day we were joined by eight
fresh labourers sent with a Ya-mên attendant, and I was
heartily glad to get them; for the men of the first batch
already complained of exhaustion. Even the chance of
gaining rewards by lucky finds failed to retain them longer,
though at first it had appealed to them greatly as confirmed gamblers. Inwardly I could scarcely condemn them
altogether; for with the temperature falling that night
to a minimum of seven degrees below zero Fahrenheit,
the strong wind still blowing from the west made itself
felt intensely. Luckily fuel was abundant.

Whether it was mere reluctance to face the rigours of this desert 'spring' any longer, or disgust at the independent bearing of the Chinese labourers who were supposed to make themselves useful about camp fires, etc., but would not stand any of the bullying which my Kashmiri cook liked to indulge in, this worthy thought the time opportune first to go on strike and then to abscond with a pony in the morning. I knew that he could find his way back to Tun-huang, and that he would not fail to be stopped there as a suspected deserter. Still this incident did not add to the amenities of my Easter Sunday.

I used it to explore the remains of the wall as far as they were traceable eastwards. Moving back with my whole camp to the tower where the first tablets had been found, I then marched along the line marked by the four towers we had sighted before. The distances between them varied considerably, from one and one-eighth to three-quarters of a mile, though the ground was throughout a uniformly bare expanse of gravel. On it the line of the wall showed up quite clearly, both in the straight curtains between the towers and in the semicircular bastions by which the line curved round to the north of each tower. In many places the alternating layers of fascines and gravelly clay still rose to three feet or thereabouts. But even where this *agger* was reduced to nearly ground level, the layer of thick tamarisk branches used for a foundation was seen emerging on either side of the low gravel-covered swelling. There could be no doubt that it was the bearing of the line, nearly east to west, though not absolutely straight, which, being parallel to the direction of the prevalent winds, had helped to preserve this unbroken stretch of wall over five miles long.

The towers differed but little in construction, being built of solid layers of stamped clay about twenty feet square at the base and originally over twenty feet high. Those to the east had suffered more decay. Beyond this the position of a fifth tower could be traced only by a low débris heap and the bastion-like projection of the wall. Half a mile to the east of this last tower (T. xxxv.), we lost the line of the wall amidst dunes of drift sand, rising to about fifteen feet and evidently encroaching from the south.

But then it again emerged in patches, and at last on a broad gravel belt lined with dunes both to the north and south we came upon a remarkably well preserved bit of wall, quite unbroken for 256 yards, and rising in places to fully seven feet (Fig. 165). Its preservation was evidently due to a protecting cover of sand, though now the drift heaped up against the wall lay only three to five feet high. In the centre of this stretch the wall had a remarkably solid appearance. The sides showed scarcely any trace of erosion, except that the outer facing with fascines laid in the direction of the wall was missing.

Here the particular method of construction could be studied with ease. Layers of fascines, six inches thick, made up of mixed tamarisk twigs and reeds, alternated with strata three to four inches thick of coarse clay and gravel, as taken on the spot. Where I photographed the wall, as seen in Fig. 163, I counted eight double layers of fascines and stamped clay, respectively. I noticed that the reeds generally prevailed in a thin streak on the top of the tamarisk brushwood. This suggested that they had been specially inserted there in order to prepare a more level surface for the succeeding stratum of clay and gravel. It seemed to me highly probable that these latter layers had been regularly stamped, the water for the purpose being brought probably from the nearest lagoon.

The salts contained everywhere in the soil and water, and attested in the wall itself by a great deal of efflorescence, had given to the strange wall thus constructed a quasi-petrified consistency. In such a region it could hold its own against man and nature—all forces, in fact, but that of slow-grinding but almost incessant wind erosion. The thickness of the wall measured close on seven feet across the top, and allowing for the loss which the uppermost fascine layer had suffered on its edges through erosion, about one foot more at the base.

As I looked at the wall here rising before me still solid and with almost vertical faces, I could not help being struck by the skill with which the old Chinese engineers had improvised their rampart. Across an extensive desert area, bare of all resources, and of water in particular, it must have been a difficult task to construct a wall so solid as this, upon which even modern field artillery would make but little impression. The materials to which they had recourse, though of little apparent strength, were particularly well adapted to local conditions. I doubt whether any others within practicable reach could have stood better the stress of two thousand years and the constant onset of eroding forces.

I marched on for a mile and a half farther along and through low sand-dunes without coming upon any trace of the wall or sighting any more towers, though the view was open enough. Then regard for the animals, which needed water and grazing, obliged us to turn off northward in the direction of the river. We crossed in succession a belt of absolutely bare gravel; a dry river bed with Toghraks still alive; a zone where tamarisk growth was plentiful, but all dead; and finally, after seven miles from the wall, arrived at the deep-cut bed of the Su-lo Ho fringed by a riverine jungle of scrub and wild poplars.

Where we camped for the night, the river, or the branch we could see, was over fifty yards broad and certainly far too deep for fording. Its muddy water, carrying big ice cakes, flowed with a velocity of about two yards per second. The night was not so bitterly cold as the one preceding, but the wind steadily increased in strength until the atmosphere in the morning assumed a regular Buran hue. The haze was sure to last for days, and a further search for wall and towers eastward would have little or no chance under these conditions. Besides, it would have carried me to the town of An-hsi which I was bound to visit in any case later. The main object of my search was already secured. I had discovered that the remains of the ancient wall actually continued eastwards of Tun-huang, as I conjectured from the first. I also had been able to prove the occupation of this *Limes* in the first century A.D.

So I decided, on April 1st, to send the camp under the Surveyor's guidance back, to the conspicuous ridge where we had found the wood-cutter's troglodyte dwelling, and to make my way there myself with the labourers along the line of the wall.   It proved a more difficult matter than I had thought under the thick veil of dust which the gale raised.   Luckily we had our footprints to guide us across the gravel Sai, and then when we got among the dunes where there was much driving of sand, the remains of the wall served to direct us safely.   At each tower we searched whatever remains of quarters or refuse heaps could be traced.   But whether it was on account of the greater erosion to which they had been exposed on the open Sai, flat like a billiard table, or for some other reason, they proved decidedly scanty.   The finds of wooden records, all fragmentary, scarcely numbered half-a-dozen. However, we picked up several well-made triangular arrow-heads in bronze and a few coins belonging to the Han period.

It was a trying day's work, and I felt heartily glad when the force of the gale abated towards the evening, and we could move to the appointed camping-place in somewhat less discomfort.   The footprints of the track by which we had come from there to Tower T. XXVI. on March 27th were still perfectly distinct on the gravelly soil.   It was an interesting proof, thereafter often observed in a still more striking fashion, of how little deflation and the movement of fine sand affect the surface of such ground.   Nevertheless it was a relief when at last I saw the camp fires and was sure of the night's shelter and food.

The wind had now veered round to the north-west. From midnight until daybreak violent gusts of wind shook the tent, and when I stepped out of it in the morning slight snow-flakes were driving for some minutes.   The atmosphere was quite murky with a fog of fine sand, very irritating to throat, eyes, and nose.   We were now returning to the oasis, but before we reached it we had to pass through the bleakest and chilliest day experienced since Lop-nor.   The blizzard never slackened, and cut through our warmest furs.   The landscape was in lugubrious harmony.   Following a deep-cut track which carts had worn, and which in the end proved to mark the route coming from Hami, we reached after about six miles the westernmost ruined tower already referred to.

The area of scrub and sand had ceased before. We now crossed an absolutely bare, salt-encrusted steppe which fuel-collectors from the oasis had evidently long ago cleared of all dead tamarisks. But the cones which these had helped to form while alive, still rose to eight or ten feet. At last low scrub reappeared over dune-like formations, and then the first ragged outposts of cultivation in the shape of scattered fields and trees. We had covered close on twenty miles, and felt half-choked with dust and half-frozen when we arrived again at our old camping-place at Shih-tsao.

CHAPTER LVI

TO THE NAN-HU OASIS

Our march on April 3rd from Shih-tsao back to Tun-huang was short, and, I confess, we all felt glad for it. The prospect of shelter was pleasant after the icy blasts we had faced for the last week along that desolate 'Great Wall.' Whether it was the protection afforded by the trees of the oasis, or at last a sign of approaching spring, the air seemed warmer in spite of the continued north wind. Being with Chiang-ssŭ-yeh far ahead of the baggage, I could use the time gained before pitching camp for a visit to the large shrine which at the time of my start I had noticed near the west gate of the town. It boasted of a high pavilion-like structure, the first 'Pagoda' of the conventional type I had seen, and seemed in exceptionally good repair for this place of somnolent nonchalance. The frescoes of the outer gate showed that it was a Taoist temple, and by their new look prepared me for the inferior art of the decoration within. But there was compensation in the glimpse I unexpectedly gained here of one of the main schools of Tun-huang.

As soon as we had entered the inner court, a swarm of boys, mostly chubby and well clad, gathered around us. The teacher had repaired to his house in the town on some business, and his score or more of pupils were hugely enjoying the unearned recess. The halls on either side of the court bore so unmistakably the impress of scholastic use that for a moment I almost underwent the not altogether cheering sensation of having come for 'inspection duty.' There were lumbering big black desks near the windows, each covered with the 'copy-slips' and exercises of three or four pupils. The walls were hung appropriately with calligraphic specimens and 'moral sentences' penned evidently by the teacher or by select scholars on big rolls of red paper.   There was order about the whole place and an air of austere concentration on the school work which made me compare this establishment favourably with many a secondary school in the Punjab, where neither ample codes and inspections nor the supply of the latest appliances have succeeded in developing a sense of orderly arrangement.   How much did I feel my total want of philological preparation as I handled the much-thumbed and yet neatly kept primers and elementary classics of the several forms! The boys, big and small, showed good manners, and combined an alert air with such restraint on their youthful curiosity that I could not help mentally awarding a good note to the teacher for the 'tone' he had implanted in his school.

I had decided to restrict my stay at Tun-huang to a single day, April 4th, and knew well that it would mean anything but a rest for me.   Yet soon after my arrival at 'my' orchard I found that the time would have to suffice for a good deal more work than I had expected.   Sher Ali Khan, the enterprising Afghan trader who during my first stay had reached Tun-huang from a journey to Kan-chou, was to have despatched his caravan of forty camels laden with tea to Charklik and Khotan long before my return.   But with that truly Eastern disregard for exact dates and supposed urgency which for us Western people would at times be so useful a sedative, he now came to tell me that his camels had only started that morning, and that he himself would still remain longer ready for any service.   The opportunity of sending a mail safely to Kashgar and thus to my friends in Europe was as welcome as it was unexpected.   It is true none of the letters were as yet written.   But a messenger despatched by next morning would catch up the caravan easily, and I had an evening and if need be a night before me for filling my mail bag.

This catching of an unforeseen mail train was not made easy for me.   I had scarcely had time to wash the outer crust of dust off my face when, to my surprise, my inseparable local friends and protectors, Lin Ta-jên and Wang Ta-lao-ye, turned up for a visit. I had little doubt they were both glad to welcome us back at headquarters, and interested, too, to hear from our own mouths the story of our peregrinations and finds. But there was information, too, gathered as we passed through the town, to explain an increased display of official attention and support. It appeared that the telegraphic salutation I had sent to the Lan-chou Viceroy on arrival within the Kan-su borders had promptly been followed up by a telegraphic circular from that high dignitary to the Tao-t'ais of the several provinces, and through them to all the magistrates, strongly recommending me and my researches to official notice.

This explained the embarrassing haste of my friendly visitors. But for the length of their visit I had to hold my own finds to account. With the enthusiasm of a trained scholar Wang Ta-lao-ye could not forgo the pleasure of handling and *impromptu* deciphering those 'wooden letters' of the great Han times. Little problems which had baffled my 'field literatus' only incited his zeal. Tablet after tablet was scanned and commentated with a rapidity and ease which, despite my ignorance of Sinologist lore, enabled me to realize the sound learning of this Kan-su edition of P'an Ta-jên. Lin, his military colleague, wisely refrained from any pretence at equal scholarly qualifications. Yet I could see that his lively interest too was roused by the details of military organization on this ancient frontier, as revealed in those modest records from the posts once guarding it. I did not fail to use the opportunities offered by whetted appetites and by the support from higher quarters in order to impress my friends with the need of effectively combating local *vis inertiae* in the way of labour for excavations and adequate transport arrangements.

I was doubly glad for the diminished cold within the oasis; for it was 3 A.M. before I could close my mail that night, and with an icy gale blowing it would have been impossible to keep my tent warm enough for all the long writing. There was no time to make up for lost sleep; for from an early hour next morning arrangements for fresh supplies and transport, payment of labourers, etc., kept me busy. The weighing out of silver for all payments, big and small, proved as always a tantalizingly slow business. Patience is needed for supervising the process and subsequently for satisfying the recipients that they have been treated fairly. Tun-huang merchants, I was told, use three kinds of scales, with a view to profit by their slight differences when selling, buying, or exchanging big horse-shoes of silver for small pieces.

It was hopeless to battle with such refinement in a primitive system of currency. The simplest sacrifice was to accept the local traders' verdict, which made my scales brought from Charklik weigh about four per cent too light. What a story of fiscal experiments is disclosed by the queer fact that no Chinaman in these parts will ever accept coined silver or gold! Shapeless bits of metal are more readily trusted,—and yet I soon learned to be on the guard against pieces artfully loaded with lead. How difficult it would be for a future antiquary to believe the fact that a region sufficiently advanced to possess paper money is yet stolidly resisting all attempts to introduce the permissive use of coined silver!

By making all payments in silver even for petty items I certainly escaped reference to the daily varying rates of exchange between copper 'cash' and silver. But, naturally, the worry of finding pieces of hacked silver corresponding exactly to the amounts due, down to decimal fractions of an ounce, was great. Luckily I soon found that my zealous secretary was an excellent hand in adjusting such petty claims with that strangely archaic currency of bullion. Having read out to me the various amounts in the presence of the claimants, he would let me make up the total and weigh out the whole in a lump heap of small silver pieces, allowance being duly made for the difference of our own from the Tun-huang scales. He would next start distribution by squatting down on a little mat or carpet outside my tent and making the men sit in small groups. He then arranged these with infinite patience again and again, until the amounts due to the few people in each group could be accurately made up out of the available silver fragments lumped-up. Of course, I took care to supply him with a quantity of tiny chips to adjust slight differences. It took hours before such a settlement was completed. But I could go on with other business, and nobody else seemed much to mind about his own time. Everybody went away satisfied, but I wondered what further efforts it would cost each group to settle their mutual reckonings!

I scarcely could tell now how that single day's halt in Tun-huang, on April 4th, sufficed for all the manifold preparations for my main campaign on the remains of the ancient *Limes* in the desert westwards. But I managed somehow to raise a month's supplies, twelve fresh labourers, additional camels for transport, and even as many Ketmans as by fair words and high prices I could get hold of among the Muhammadan refugees at Tun-huang. Experience had shown me how much more useful for excavation those broad Turkestan hoes are than the spades and shovels of the Chinese settled in the oasis.

In the morning Ramzan, my faithless cook, turned up to make an unconditional surrender. His sudden return alone had, as expected, excited suspicion at Tun-huang, and he would have been obliged to await my own arrival under arrest at the Ya-mên had not Zahid Beg agreed to bail him out and keep watch over him. So the shifty, intractable Kashmiri realized that he had little chance of escaping from his contract even when near a great high road, and sulkily asked for his desertion to be forgiven as a sort of mental distemper brought on by the air of the desert. It was the story over again of Sadak Akhun, my queer cook in the winter of 1901, and the Jins of the Taklamakan. In the afternoon I spared time for return visits to the two Ya-mêns, and on my way, noting the excellent wood-carving and ornamental brickwork on the gates of dilapidated old houses, again rejoiced that Tun-huang town at least had escaped the utter havoc worked by Tungan ferocity elsewhere.

My plan was first to move south-west along the foot of the mountains to Nan-hu, a small oasis where Zahid Beg's information and Roborowsky and Kozloff's map indicated the existence of ruins. From there by going due north I would strike the line of the ancient wall in the middle. On April 5th, the day of our start, *more Cathaico*, neither camels nor men turned up until quite late in the forenoon. Since the first march along the Tang Ho was bound to be short, this luckily mattered little. Where we crossed the river just outside the west gate I found its water flowing in a channel about forty yards wide and three to four feet deep, with a velocity of about two yards per second. All the canals of Tun-huang, taking off well above this, were flowing over-full at the same time. There could be no doubt that at this season of the early spring irrigation the supply of available water more than sufficed for the needs of the present cultivated area.

On the left river bank we first skirted the crumbling clay walls of the old town of Tun-huang, a site said to have been occupied in T'ang times but now completely abandoned to fields and gardens. A subsequent measurement of the rectangular area enclosed by the walls, about 1500 yards from north to south and 650 across, showed that it was but slightly smaller than that of the present town, which is built within walls about 1100 yards square. Then we turned off to the south-west, and passing several well-kept temples, reached the edge of cultivation after a little over three miles. Here the ruins of a smaller walled town offered fresh proof of the destruction which followed the last great Tungan rising.

Beyond we followed the banks of an earlier river bed, now completely dry and flanked on each side by a network of wind-eroded clay terraces. After some five miles farther, and not far from a modern-looking ' Pao-t'ai,' I noticed ruined walls rising here and there above the bare gravel Sai westwards. Crossing the large canal which passes here close to the route, and conveys water for the western part of the Tun-huang oasis, I rode towards these walls and soon noticed that they invariably represented gateways to quadrangular enclosures which seemed completely decayed. The gateways, on the other hand, looked solid enough, rising in several cases to a height of about twenty feet and showing a thickness of eight feet. But these wall portions on either side of a wide entrance

measured only five or six yards in length.   Beyond this the
front of the enclosure as well as its other sides showed only
as low ridges of gravel.   They were made just perceptible
by the relief they presented in the slanting rays of the
setting sun.

While the 'gateways' showed fairly hard masonry of
coarse but unusually large bricks, I vainly searched on the
line of the enclosing 'walls' for any remains of brickwork
or even of reed fascines.   One of these strange quadrangles
measured seventy-five by seventy yards, having its entrance,
as usual, on the south.   The enclosing ridges were invariably orientated, though but roughly.   Within the enclosed
areas there were always to be found several low tumuli,
the largest facing the entrance from the north and the rest
scattered without any apparent arrangement.   Those in
the ruin just mentioned measured from fifteen to seven
yards in diameter, with a height not exceeding five feet.
Of course, the idea that these were ancient places of burial
soon occurred to me and to Chiang as well.   But neither
Chinese custom, nor what I knew of Buddhist and other
religious practices in Central Asia, seemed to offer any
clue.   And if the tumuli should prove to contain graves I
wondered how I should get Tun-huang people, particularly
orthodox in their superstitious awe of graves, to help in the
systematic opening.   But the site was anyhow within easy
reach of the oasis, and for the present I did not care to
delay on its account.

We found a convenient camping-place on a broad
grassy flat known as Tung-wei-chü by the left bank of the
river, and after a night when the thermometer still showed
a minimum of twelve degrees of frost, started for the march
to Nan-hu.   It proved close on thirty miles.   For the first
half of this distance the route led along the southern edge
of a gravel-covered plateau where it falls off with precipitous cliffs to the deep-cut bed of the Tang Ho.   It
was like the counterscarp of a deep fosse with a glacis
stretching away from its brink to the north.   Absolutely
barren outer hills, covered with dunes for the most
part, rose from the right bank of the river and were
fully in view throughout.   A few half-ruined Pao-t'ais of

no particularly ancient look and a couple of small brick
Stupas, well plastered and manifestly still receiving worship,
were the only objects to distract the eye in this dreary
landscape.

The route left the river not far from the point where
the Tang Ho valley turns sharply into the mountains south-
east, and was skirting the foot of a gradually rising ridge
when I first noticed what looked like a low dyke of gravel
and stones. It only rose four or five feet above the bare
Sai, and could easily have been mistaken for a natural
swelling, had it not stretched away steadily to the south
by west in a line absolutely straight. The route kept
close by it for upwards of five miles. As the dyke was
broad, measuring about twenty-four feet at its base, and the
surface on its top hard, it seemed to be used for preference
as a cart track. But what could its real purpose have been?
Without any trace of watch-towers or other structures, and
with nothing but absolute desert to right and left, it seemed
hard to imagine any defensive line of wall here. At last
the route diverged to the south-west while the puzzling
dyke could be seen running straight on towards a tower
just visible far away in the distance.

I was still searching in my mind for some explanation
of this strange work of man in the wilderness, when my
eye was caught by many curious low stone heaps rising on
the level flat of gravel. Of greatly varying sizes, they
were always circular in shape, and either had a straight
line of stones attached on one side like a handle, or else
faced small rectangular enclosures laid out with big
pebbles. The circular cairns—for such they seemed—
never rose more than three or four feet above the ground ;
but as they appeared on all sides in dozens, brought into
relief by the slanting light of the evening, the effect was
quite weird. Was this the desert cemetery of some
ancient population which had held the oasis we were
approaching before the Chinese occupation, or primitive
marks of cult left behind by some tribe which once had swept
through this region? I knew of no analogy by which to
guide my conjectures, nor could I stop there and then to
dig up some of the cairns.

But just as a dark patch of vegetation, seen westwards in the failing light, indicated approach to the Nan-hu oasis, I sighted not far from the track a brick-built gateway and an adjoining quadrangle marked by low gravel ridges, just like those I had met with the day before on the edge of the Tun-huang oasis. Within the quadrangle I could make out two circular tumuli of exactly the same shape as the 'cairns' I had just passed by in numbers. So anyhow it was clear that cairns and enclosures belonged to the same time and people. There was free scope for conjectures about them as I rode on in growing darkness amidst low dunes and tamarisk cones. At last the faint ripple of springs and then the glitter of a broad sheet of water assured us that the oasis was near. It was too late to search for houses. So we camped by the spring-fed stream, not a sound being heard from the village nor a soul coming near us. Dinner was an affair of midnight.

The search which I had to make next morning for a camping-place suited to a longer halt, soon showed what a pleasant little oasis Nan-hu is. Over two miles long from east to west, and nearly as wide across, its area was everywhere irrigated by delightfully limpid water from the great spring-fed reservoir or lake which we had skirted in the darkness, and which accounted for the name of Nan-hu, meaning the 'South Lake.' It had been formed by damming up the head of a broad and deep-cut flood-bed which meandered right through the oasis, and with its steep banks of loess and wide marshy bottom closely recalled the 'Yars' familiar from Khotan or other Turkestan oases. The water-supply was manifestly abundant; for, quite apart from the canals taking off at the artificial lake, there was a lively stream flowing in the middle of the Yar, and carrying its clear water to waste in the desert northward. A low but picturesque line of hills of red and yellowish sandstone, through which this stream had cut its way in a gorge, shut off the view towards the desert and gave to the whole oasis a pleasing air of seclusion.

The twenty-five to thirty homesteads or farms which

it comprised lay scattered about in tiny hamlets, sheltered by fine elms and ashes. All round them extended well-tilled fields with rows of big trees lining the irrigation channels. So carefully was all ground within the oasis utilized that, not wishing to camp in the middle of a ploughed field, I was at last grateful to find room for my tent in a little quiet grove occupied by graves. The good folk of Nan-hu must have thought it a queer taste, but had no objection to offer. They seemed a quiet, thriving set of farmers, endowed with delightful *insouciance* such as their comfortable conditions as regards arable land and water would foster.

About their pious zeal I could entertain no doubt when I found that this little settlement boasted of eight well-kept shrines 'in being' (Fig. 167), not counting the miniature chapels attached to almost every homestead and a number of small temples still in ruins, as the last Tungan inroad had left them. It seemed hard to think of that devastating tornado having swept across a place so placidly secluded as Nan-hu. Yet, according to the information we received, scarcely a man, woman, or child of the old population had then escaped with their lives. However this may be, those who had taken their places were now enjoying the ease resulting from under-population.

But it was the opportunity for archaeological observations of interest, not the rural attractions of this 'sleepy hollow,' which made me extend my stay to four days. At the first reconnaissance, guided by an elderly villager whom Lin Ta-jên's petty officer had secured for us, we found a number of remains throwing light on the history of the oasis. At a distance of only about one mile eastwards from the edge of the present oasis, and approached over ground which manifestly had once been under cultivation, there rose the broken clay walls of a small town built in the form of an irregular rectangle. Of the north face, measuring about 400 yards in length, the greater part still survived, half-buried under high dunes which had afforded protection. Of the east and west walls, too, considerable portions were still extant though cut through and broken up by wind erosion. Yet the 'masonry' of the wall,

166. RUINED HOMESTEAD, ABANDONED TO DESERT ABOUT SIXTY YEARS AGO, AT KUAN-TSOU, NORTH OF NAN-HU.

167. VILLAGE SHRINE AT NAN-HU, WITH SCHOOL-ROOM ON RIGHT.

Chiang-ssŭ-yeh in front of shrine.

carefully stamped clay in thin regular layers, was very solid, pointing to early construction. In places it still rose to eighteen feet, and it rested on a broad clay rampart raised at least another fifteen feet above the ground level.

The area enclosed showed no recognizable ruins, only some low mounds partly covered with drift sand. I was able to get trenches cut through these by the large number of men we obtained from the hamlets. But I may state at once that the only finds rewarding the work here were a few large bricks of extremely hard burnt clay, evidently left over from some structure of which the materials had been completely quarried and removed long before. That these fine black bricks were of great age was on the face of it probable. But on this point I felt more assured when the careful search I made along the exposed portions of the rampart brought to light coins all belonging to issues of Han times.

To the north and north-east of the ruined town I found an extensive area of the typical 'Tati' character, where the bare clay patches appearing between dunes big and small were abundantly covered with the usual hard débris of pottery, stones, etc. The people of Nan-hu called it 'the place for finding old things,' and, no doubt, searched it after great storms as keenly as Khotan 'treasure-seekers' their familiar Tatis. Repeated visits by Chiang and myself allowed us to collect here a good deal of bronze fragments, arrow-heads, small pieces of decorated stone-ware and the like. The latest of the numerous copper coins picked up proved to belong to issues of the T'ang dynasty, while on the other hand we failed to notice a single piece of porcelain by the side of such plentiful pottery. Thus the conclusion seems justified that the site was abandoned during the troubled period which followed the downfall of the T'ang rule in these parts, about the close of the eighth century A. D., and before porcelain became common under the Sung.

I cannot spare space to detail here a series of interesting observations as to the source from which this abandoned part of the oasis once received its irrigation, and as to the physical changes which have since taken place here. That desiccation had played a main part in bringing about the present conditions was clear. But in addition I could convince myself also of the destructive effect which occasional great floods might have had upon irrigation in such a position. I ascertained that the water-supply of the 'Tati' area must have been derived from a river bed now completely dry which skirts the belt of scrub and drift sand fringing the oasis on the east and north-east. It must have been the action of exceptional rain floods from the lower hills on the south, such as the villagers remembered in recent years, which had gradually turned this river bed into a deep-cut cañon-like 'Yar.' As such it passes close to the east of the old site, with some springs gathering in its marshy bottom fifty feet or so below the level of the Tati.

The water here rising had, until about fourteen years before my visit, been utilized for a small colony which existed some three miles lower down in this valley; it had as it were taken the place of the large settlement abandoned since the T'ang times. But a big flood, said to have occurred in the summer of 1893, had swept away irrigation channels and homesteads, and buried the fields under coarse sand. On visiting the spot I could still see clearly the effects of this catastrophe in the ruined houses and uprooted arbours, while the bed of the irrigating stream had been scooped out into a steep-walled 'Yar,' some twenty feet below the old level. What trees had been left standing were dead or dying, and gradually being cut down for fuel.

Curiously enough, it was information about another effect of this big flood which helped to clear up the mystery about that strange gravel embankment we had noted in the desert on our way to Nan-hu. I found that the tower towards which we had then seen it continuing rose on the edge of the gravel plateau which overlooks from the east the wind-eroded old site or Tati. Between this and the tower lay the deep 'Yar' or flood-bed just referred to. The tower was undoubtedly old in its solid clay portion, rising on a base about thirty-six feet square; but plentiful restorations in small bricks showed that it had been kept in repair until recent times. Close by was a small domed structure which our Nan-hu guide declared to have been tenanted until some seventy years ago by a guard watching the road from Tun-huang. He was quite positive about travellers even in his own recollection having followed the line of the embankment right up to the tower, and thence struck across the river bed and the Tati towards the oasis.

It was the flood of 1893 which, by cutting the bed into a sort of cañon, had made the direct road between the tower and Nan-hu impassable for carts, and had caused the diversion of the route southward. Clear traces of a cart track descending from the tower to the edge of the ' Yar ' and there suddenly ending, confirmed this statement. It thus became highly probable that the gravel embankment which the people of Nan-hu knew as the ' fêng-chiang ' or ' wind-wall,' had, as indeed our old guide thought, been intended as a road-mark across the desert, useful at times of dust storms and as a protection against the winds from the north and north-east. But it seemed equally clear that a work of such magnitude, the construction of a dyke for over eight miles through the desert, would never have been undertaken except at a period when the oasis of Nan-hu and its population were far greater than at present.

It was on the same day that I was able to investigate also those curious tumuli which had puzzled me on my first approach to Nan-hu. Going from the tower about a mile to the south-east we came upon the high brick-built gateway and adjoining rectangular enclosure then noticed. The flanking walls of the gate, about five feet thick and but little longer, still rose to fourteen feet or so, the material being coarse sun-dried bricks of a large size. The low lines of gravel enclosing the quadrangle were almost invisible while the sun stood high. The main tumulus which rose within, just facing the gate from the north, showed an annular shape and measured about eight yards across ; it was of loose stones and coarse gravel heaped up to a height of about three feet. By cutting through it and smaller tumuli close by we ascertained that these were the only materials used, and that the little mounds rested on the undisturbed gravel surface.

There could be no doubt that gate and tumuli were contemporary; but there was no clue to their origin and purpose. The people who built them were manifestly not Chinese nor of an advanced civilization. Was it possible to connect these modest cult relics with one or other of the small hill tribes, such as the Jô Ch'iang and the Little Yüeh-chih, to whom the Chinese Annals from Han times onwards make brief reference as dwelling along the slopes of the Altin-tagh west of Tun-huang, and whose grazing-grounds in those barren mountains and plateaus are now occupied by Mongol nomads?

I must refrain from touching here upon other points of historical and geographical interest which the observations gathered during this busy halt suggested in plenty. Nor can I discuss now the topographically important question, whether the ancient frontier station west of Tun-huang, which the Han Annals repeatedly mention under the name of 'Yang-kuan,' 'The Yang Barrier,' was really located at Nan-hu. The claim to this proud identification was put forward in a modern stone inscription, which some learned Tun-huang Mandarin of antiquarian tastes had set up in a small shrine between the south face of the ruined town and the lake. I think there is a good deal of topographical evidence to support it.

Whatever Nan-hu's ancient fame may have been, all of us were bound to appreciate the physical comforts which our stay in the little oasis offered. The days were unusually calm, and with the minimum thermometer rising for the first time above freezing-point, there was a spring-like feeling of warmth in the air, though as yet I looked vainly for a budding leaf or flower. Our hard-tried animals, too, felt refreshed, all but my enterprising little terrier who, while I was visiting a picturesque ruined temple above the gorge of the Nan-hu stream, picked up acquaintance with some half-wild shepherd dogs down below and absconded. After some hours of fruitless search he was recovered badly mauled. Having then to be kept chained up in my tent or carried on horseback until his wounds had quite healed, he had occasion to regret the results of his indiscriminating escapade. With his irrepressible spirits and pluck he was indeed far safer in the lifeless desert.

CHAPTER LVII

ANCIENT REMAINS FOR THE FUTURE

I was sorry to leave Nan-hu; for the abundant traces of ancient occupation, the quaint peaceful ways of Chinese village life, the picturesque half-ruined temples, and most of all the delicious clear water of its springs, had invested the little oasis with a peculiar charm. But the ruins along the ancient wall in the desert north were calling, and I knew that the days or weeks available for their exploration before the fierce heat would set in were numbered. So I reluctantly fixed April 11th as the time for our start. Ten men was the maximum contingent which the oasis could spare without injury to the spring labour now fully in progress in its fields. Their houses were almost all within shouting distance of our camp, and orders had been issued the day before. Yet it was nearly noon before the men were collected by the sleepy village elder. Men turning up without rations or spades and newly hired camels without ropes to tie their loads, all helped to extend the usual delay attending a start in these parts. The distance to be covered across the desert to the ancient wall by the Lop-nor route was too great for a single march. I had, therefore, decided to move that day only as far as the water of the Nan-hu springs reaches.

But even so far we were not destined to go. After the few warm days we had enjoyed in Nan-hu, a storm was gathering. It broke with full violence from the north-west just as the caravan had left the last fields of the oasis, and was toiling up the steep sand-covered ridge which borders it northward. I had ridden ahead to the ruined tower which crowns the ridge west of the picturesque gorge cut by the waters of Nan-hu, to get bearings for the plane-table. But scarcely had I reached it when the force of the gale enveloped us in a cloud of driving sand, which made it difficult to see farther than twenty to thirty yards, or even to keep one's eyes open. It was a true 'Buran' of the type with which I had become familiar in the Takla-makan during the spring of 1901 ; but from the difference of the ground it took a peculiar colouring.

Had the soil here consisted of the fine loess dust which prevails throughout the Khotan and Keriya desert, there would have been absolute darkness around us; for the force of the wind was so great that it could have carried this along in clouds of great thickness. But with the heavy coarse sand which forms most of the dunes about Tun-huang the effect was different. Looking up to the sky only a yellow haze screened us from the sun, while along the ground there was swept a hail of small pebbles and sand grains. The sensation to one's skin was distinctly more trying than that of the dust carried by a Turkestan storm. In order to gain some shelter we had to face the gale, and in spite of goggles and wraps I found it difficult to keep my eyes on the guide riding a few paces ahead.

I was still wondering what kind of camping-ground awaited us for the night, when I noticed trees looming in front, and fine dust instead of pelting sand whirling around. Two miles' march in the teeth of the storm had brought us down to a level plain, and to a small outlying hamlet of Nan-hu, known as Shui-i, the existence of which had previously been carefully concealed from me. To march on in the thick haze of dust would have been awkward on account of the risk of men and beasts going astray, and when after an hour's wait the storm showed no signs of abating I reluctantly gave the order for halting. I had reason to feel grateful to Shui-i for the shelter it gave us that evening. But the picture of the decay and squalor which its three farms presented still remains freshly impressed on my mind.

The larger of these dwellings where we had to seek quarters struck me from the first as half a ruin, only await-ing the advancing sand to be finally abandoned and buried.

The farm-house had been built originally in a substantial style, with large rooms arranged in orthodox Chinese fashion on three sides of an oblong court facing south. Now it was tenanted by several families of small cultivators. The walls in more than one place leant over in a dangerous fashion, and were for the time kept from falling by supports of roughly cut tree-trunks. Half the rooms had big holes in the roofing, the débris of timber and plaster which had fallen in filling the corners. Unspeakable litter was accumulated in the narrow court dividing the wings. It seemed too dirty a place even to my Turki followers for putting the ponies up. But there were plentiful tatters of coloured drawings and of inscriptions neatly penned on crimson paper decking the door-posts and half-broken window-screens, marks of former comfort and ease. It was not easy to get shelter here for my large party. But the driving dust outside and the howling gale made even the most critical among them settle down with contentment.

I had just given orders for my tent to be pitched behind the court wall of what looked a completely ruined building near by, when Tila, my observant Yarkandi follower, discovered in it a tiny room still tenanted and retaining its roof. The oldest of the cultivators, a quiet, white-haired man, had retired there with a half-crazy son on whom he seemed charitably to bestow his chief care. The old fellow looked eager to offer hospitality for the night; and when he saw my man surveying suspiciously the bundles of old clothes, etc., heaped up in a corner, he so promptly set about to clear out his belongings and tidy up his lair that I could not refuse so cordial a reception. The clouds of dust raised by the sweeping up of the half-ruined hovel were impressive even in this atmosphere of driving sand. After a clearing such as, I am sure, no place in the hamlet will ever receive before the desert overwhelms it, I moved in to relative comfort and shelter for the night.

I did not enjoy it long; for with some thirty-five miles of desert separating us from our goal, I was anxious to start early. By 4 A.M. I awakened the men, but it was close on 7 A.M. before the caravan with its contingent of Nan-hu labourers and camel-men not yet broken in

could be got to move off. In the meantime I was able
to survey the surroundings better. The storm had ceased
overnight, and only a light haze to the south remained to
mark its passage. Subsequently I had many occasions to
observe how much more transient than along the Taklamakan are the atmospheric effects of the storms which
sweep the coarse sands of the Tun-huang desert.

I could now see plainly that not the buildings alone,
but also the fields and arbours surrounding them, bore
every mark of approaching abandonment. Close to the
homestead we had occupied the fields were being overrun
by light drift sand. They are still being cultivated; but
irrigation fails to keep off the low dunes moving up from
the west, which had already enveloped the feet of the
trees of an avenue some 300 yards off, and threatened to
choke the shallow channels bringing water to them. A
small ruined shrine nearer to the main farm still showed
its painted gateway. But the beams of the roof had
fallen, and the drift sand caught within the walls had
almost completely smothered what remained of the clay
images.

Elsewhere I could see fields overgrown with thorny
scrub, threshing-floors edged round by low dunes, or
neatly-laid-out small orchards where the drift sand lay feet
deep along the fences, and the cuts needed for irrigation
were sadly neglected. An air of hopeless decay hovered
over the whole place, and my antiquarian imagination
found it easy to call up the picture it will present when the
desert shall have finally claimed it. Thus Dandan-oilik
or the Niya site may have looked during the last decades
preceding abandonment. I wondered to whose lot it will
fall to excavate 'the site' which is now preparing here,
and what that archaeologist, say, of two thousand years
hence will make of the scraps of English or Indian writing
which our stay over one night may have contributed to
the rubbish heaps accumulated at Shui-i. From consideration for that confrère far off in the ages, I purposely
refrained here from burning my waste paper!

Of course I did not lose the chance, with approaching
ruin so plainly written upon this small settlement, of

obtaining definite local opinion as to the cause. The villagers whom I questioned with Chiang's aid were ready to admit the far-advanced decay. But what they complained of was not want of water or uncertainty in its supply, but the difficulty of coping with the sand and the destruction caused by the troubles of the great Tungan rebellion. The day's march offered unhoped-for opportunities for studying the question, and proved in fact a most instructive antiquarian lesson.

The people of Nan-hu had before stoutly denied any knowledge of the route northward and of ruins eventually to be met with. We were following the lively stream, about twenty feet broad and one foot deep, which with a current of about one and a half yards per second carries the drainage of the Nan-hu springs down into the desert ; when after about a mile and a half I came upon a group of deserted houses, not far from its east bank and encircled by dunes. The drift sand was nowhere more than six to eight feet high ; yet the cut tree-trunks, and the dismantled condition of the ruins, showed that occupation had been definitely abandoned.

Chiang-huan, a well-to-do villager of Nan-hu, whom I had engaged to look after the labourers, now acknowledged that he knew quite well these deserted holdings of ' Upper Yen-chia' and those of ' Lower Yen-chia' sighted some one and a half miles farther on. They had been abandoned, he said, in consequence of the desolation wrought by the Tungan inroad of 1866, when Nan-hu was sacked and the greatest portion of its population killed. Since then the houses had furnished beams to the people of the oasis needing timber or dry fuel, and the trees once growing around them had been cut down for the same purpose. Yet the stream flowing past seemed still to carry water quite sufficient to irrigate these long strips of old cultivation. It was curious to note how the fine drift sand, evidently eroded clay or loess, had accumulated over them. It was retained probably by the trees, fences, and other obstacles, while to our left there stretched away the gravel Sai swept perfectly clear of all fertile soil.

When abreast with the ruins of Hsia (Lower) Yen-chia,

we passed a narrow sheet of water nearly a mile long which now receives this drainage of Nan-hu, wasting itself in the desert. But we soon found that canals within living memory must have carried water much farther to the north. The first dwellings of another abandoned small settlement were met with at seven miles from Shui-i. Our guide called it Kuan-tsou, and stated that it had been abandoned some sixty years ago. I was able to test here the accuracy of local tradition. Around the first farm I visited there were a few patches of ground not covered by sand, and among the small debris scattered over them my men soon picked up modern-looking potsherds and porcelain fragments, also some coins belonging to the regnal epoch of Ch'ien-lung (1736-96 A.D.). The isolated farm-houses were filled with drift sand to a height of six or eight feet, and owing to the greater distance from Nan-hu still retained most of their timber.

The trees once growing along the canals and irrigation cuts had all been cut down since cultivation was abandoned. But the trunks still emerging in a double row along what must have been the main channel, showed that its water was brought from the south-east, *i.e.* the now dry river bed I had traced east of the Tati forming part of the old Nan-hu oasis. Amidst the low dunes which had overrun what were once the fields of this hamlet, tamarisk cones had formed here and there up to a height of twelve feet. Everything showed that a typical 'site' was here in preparation to illustrate to posterity the conditions of Tun-huang village life early in the nineteenth century. The dwelling where I halted to take a photograph (Fig. 166) was more solidly built than the rest, and thus likely to attract the attention of some future archaeologist, say of 4000 A.D. So I could not forgo the temptation of depositing in a well-sheltered corner a dated 'Khat,' in the shape of a newspaper, for his eventual guidance and edification.

For over two miles farther north ruins of detached holdings were met with at intervals, all belonging to the same period, as frequent coin-finds proved. The last was a substantial homestead, with a thick refuse layer covering the courtyard (Fig. 168). A big dune, fully twenty feet high, rising close on the north, had with its concave slope buried part of the building. The farms lay all in one line and had, no doubt, like the final off-shoots of the Tun-huang oasis which stretch finger-like northward, been fed by a single canal. Here recent progress of desiccation seemed clearly established ; for the present water-supply from Nan-hu, even if united in a single channel, could scarcely be conducted so far.

All trace of human occupation disappeared beyond on the bare gravel plain. The only things living were scanty tamarisk bushes growing in shallow depressions cut out apparently by rare floods from the mountains. But after we had travelled some twelve miles from Shui-i there rose in this barren plain a tower of stamped clay, much decayed, but still standing to a height of about nineteen feet. Far away to the north my binocular showed another. In construction this ' Pao-t'ai,' or ' Tun ' as the Tun-huang people called them, did not differ from those we had become familiar with along the ancient wall. But its position seemed a puzzle, until the subsequent discovery of the subsidiary *Limes* running due south-south-east from the fort of Yü-mên, and bearing just in the direction of this tower, helped to explain it.

As we moved steadily on, a little to the west of north, the low but quaintly serrated hill range forming the eastern extension of the Kuruk-tagh rose clearer and clearer. To us who had seen it for days flanking our route from Lop-nor, it afforded assurance as to the relative proximity of the ancient *Limes*. But I could notice how our Chinese contingent, with the prospect of a camp in the waterless desert and no knowledge of the ground beyond, was getting fluttered and more and more straggling. So I detached Chiang-ssŭ-yeh and the Naik to form a sort of rear-guard. After a march of some twenty-four miles we struck a broad belt of tamarisk and other scrub ; but our map showed that we were still at least twelve miles from the road which skirts the marshes below Khara-nor. To reach it that evening with the tired caravan was out of the question. All I tried to get to was some reed-covered patch which might afford grazing. But after another three or four miles

spent in picking our way through the maze of tamarisk
cones, darkness forced us to halt in the first thicket of
Toghraks.

Small channels, which looked as if cut by running
water at no very distant period, here traversed the jungle
in plenty.   But of water, or of those reed patches which
usually denote its presence not deep below the ground,
there was none.   For the men this mattered little ; for in
our ' Mussucks' we had brought a plentiful supply; but I
was sorry for our ponies, which could not quench their
thirst after a long and warm march.   By 9 P.M. the Naik
arrived and reported that he had brought in the last
straggler, the man who had driven or rather dragged along
our three refractory sheep.   In the light of big bonfires
which the men lit, I discovered that close to my tent were
decayed huts dug out from the ground and covered with
rough tree-trunks.   No doubt herdsmen had once camped
here, and water could not then have been far off.   But
how long ago was it?   Here was an illustration of the
doubts ever besetting the student of things primitive and
devoid of chronology.

Rest came only after midnight, and before daybreak I
was aroused by the news that two labourers were missing.
My honest secretary was greatly excited about it.   He
knew that the two men were confirmed opium-smokers,
and feared that, having strayed from our track in the darkness or lagged behind surreptitiously to indulge in a
smoke, they would get hopelessly confused, and wander
about without aim, to succumb at last to thirst.   Vainly I
represented how difficult it would be for men possessed of
their senses not to see the light of our camp fires or to
trace our track in daylight.   While I resigned myself to
the belief that the men had taken the first chance to
decamp and were now moving back to Nan-hu, compensated by an unearned advance of money for whatever
trouble they might have in their wandering, Chiang's
imagination saw the hapless men already lying dead in
the jungle.

In any case we had to clear up the matter of their disappearance, and if they were really lost to bring them

assistance.   So Chiang-huan, the *soi-disant* guide, was
given a big gourd full of water and his pony a good drink,
and then sent back to track and bring in the missing men
if possible.   No blame could attach to Chiang and Naik
Ram Singh; for they were certain that no one had been
left behind on our route.   Nor was my own conscience
burdened, seeing that a responsible rear-guard had been
appointed, and had done its work as well as a tramp in the
darkness through desert and jungle permitted.

Our march on April 13th was short, but not without
further excitement.   Judging by the survey carried along
from Lop-nor (see inset *A* of Map I.), we were only about
seven miles in a straight line from the route then followed.
For about four miles we made our way through the belt of
thick tamarisk jungle, soon mingling with reed-beds, and
found tracks of wild camels and deer in plenty.   Curiously
enough we also came upon traces of old wheel-marks in
places where there were bare clay surfaces showing cracks as
if baked by the sun after some great soaking.   Then, crossing a narrow belt of gravel absolutely bare, we found ourselves in a depression filled with a salty marsh stretching
away to the south-east.   We had sighted before only a
single tower, and this did not suffice to fix our position
with certainty.   Down below by the marsh edge we could
not make out any definite landmark, and the marsh itself
had for some reason connected with the configuration of
the ground remained wholly unobserved when we first
moved along the route to Tun-huang.

In spite of the apparently hard salt crust covering great
parts of it, the marsh proved quite impracticable for the
animals, and threatened to cut us off for many a hot mile
from the fresh water we eagerly wished to reach.   But at
last we found a place where the boggy soil would bear
laden animals, and pushing up the gravel slope I arrived
at what could now be easily recognized as the tower I had
numbered T. xII. (Fig. 169).   The Chinese of our party
rejoiced greatly when they found themselves on the well-
worn cart-road, safely escaped as it were from the dreaded
'Gobi.'   They looked still more pleased when, marching
five miles west, we halted by the small reed-fringed lake,

168. RUIN OF FARM ABANDONED DURING LAST CENTURY, IN DESERT NORTH OF NAN-HU.

169. RUINED WATCH-TOWER, T. XII., ON ANCIENT CHINESE *LIMES*,
NORTH-WEST OF TUN-HUANG.

170. RUINED WATCH-TOWER, T. IX., ON ANCIENT CHINESE *LIMES*
N.W. OF TUN-HUANG.

our former camping-ground.   Here was water for all in plenty and the springs as fresh as before.

A few green shoots of young reeds were just showing on sheltered slopes of the marsh beds, the first sign of approaching spring in this desert region.   When the east wind dropped in the early afternoon, I found it quite close in my little tent.   It did not remain long where it was. Chiang, in his charitable thought for the missing labourers, had rather rashly started a great fire among the dry reed-beds, in the hope that the smoke and the light would guide them.   As the conflagration was spreading I was obliged to order removal of camp to the nearest patch of bare gravel, my Muhammadans and Indians naturally resenting the trouble which Chiang's care for two straying ' Khitai' had cost them.   His good intentions proved of no avail. The stragglers did not turn up, and when Chiang-huan rejoined us next day he reported having failed to find any trace of them.

In spite of this worrying mischance I felt elated on being at last back again by the old frontier wall which our rapid passage from Lop-nor had revealed here and there.   Only a few of the towers which mark its line had then been visited.   Most of them could be sighted only miles away. However much we strained our eyes, the existence of a wall connecting these towers had necessarily remained a conjecture.   How glad I felt now for the chance of fully exploring this old *Limes*!   Our discoveries since made along that section which continues it north-east of the Tun-huang oasis, had dispelled all possible doubts about the high antiquity of this frontier line.   The hope seemed now justified that among the remains of a fortified border line, which I knew to stretch away for at least fifty miles, there were more relics waiting to be gathered.   Yet little did I foresee how abundant the harvest would be.

CHAPTER LVIII

FIRST EXCAVATIONS ALONG THE WESTERN LIMES

At first the extent of the line to be explored was far from giving assurance. The party of labourers I had managed to bring along, even when reinforced by the contingent from Nan-hu, looked disproportionately small for the task, and the loss of the two missing men had still further weakened it. I had every reason to husband my time; for the mid-day heat of the last few days showed me that work on this desolate border was bound before long to become very trying. It was important to make the most of my resources. So, while the Surveyor was to move westwards and trace the line of towers as far as it might extend from the bend previously noticed near Toghrak-bulak, Ts'ao Ta-lao-ye, the officer of the Tun-huang levies whom Lin Ta-jên had attached to my camp, was hastily despatched to headquarters to bring up more labourers and supplies.

I thought it best myself to commence excavations on that part of the line which, owing to its distance from any suitable camping-ground, was likely to give most trouble. From Toghrak-bulak to our first lake camp the road had lain throughout over a gravel plateau destitute of water and fuel, and over these sixteen miles the old *agger* could be traced almost unbroken. About half-way I had then noticed some posts protruding from the pebble-covered slope of what looked like a small natural mound. Its position close to the inner side of the wall suggested, however, a ruin, and a little hurried digging had then shown that some structure was buried beneath. It was to this ruin (T. VIII.) that on April 14th I marched out my little band westwards.

The heat of the previous days had roused a violent east wind, and the atmosphere was hazy with dust. Yet as we moved along the low ridge of gravel which hides the remains of the wall, and stretches away quite straight over this barren desert soil, I was surprised to note that the footprints left as I had ridden past more than a month before, looked absolutely fresh. The gravel and coarse sand on the surface was evidently little affected even by such a succession of gales as had blown across the valley since. It was clear that, in spite of all the force of the winds, erosion, that greatest foe of ancient remains in practically rainless regions, could not exert its destructive power on the flat surface of such ground and on what was buried beneath it. I thus ceased to wonder at the remarkable state of preservation which the first two towers on this section of the wall line presented. The soil on which they stood had practically undergone no erosion, and since no undermining was possible, the winds of two thousand years had failed to shake down or seriously injure these heavy masses of brick and stamped clay.

Up to thirty feet or so they still rose, built solid on a base of over twenty feet square and tapering towards their top (Fig. 170). This had once borne a conning-room or a platform protected by a parapet; but the brickwork of the parapet had fallen, and the heavy timber of Toghrak which had been inserted to strengthen the top now lay bare. It was impossible to climb up; for these particular towers appear to have had no stairs, and the ladders or ropes which once may have given access had, of course, disappeared. On the east face of one of the towers I could still make out the holes in the brick-work which probably served as footholds. There were no remains of quarters or refuse indicating occupation near either of them. In order, probably, to command the ground better, these towers had been built on the very edge of tongues of the gravel-covered plateau, and little ravines had formed round them. If any structure less solidly built had ever adjoined them, its débris would inevitably have been washed down the steep slopes by either the winds or occasional rainfall.

It was at the completely ruined tower—for such the mound already referred to (T. VIII.) proved to be—that I first obtained a clear idea of the quarters which seem to have been built by the side of most towers for the accommodation of the soldiers keeping watch at these posts. The mound measured about forty-eight feet in diameter at the base and rose to ten feet above the ground. From the coarse gravel which covered its top and slopes, and gave it the appearance of a natural hillock, there emerged first masses of sun-dried bricks mixed with plentiful bundles of reeds. It was the débris of the tower, which in its fall had completely crushed and buried the walls and roof of the guard-rooms adjoining. To clear it away was heavy work for the men, and their own spades made little impression. Not being accustomed to the 'Ketmans' of Turkestan, which, warned by previous experience, I had with no small trouble obtained at Tun-huang, they got little work out of these otherwise ideal implements of the excavator. But the greatest hindrance, perhaps, was the little doses of opium which most of these Nan-hu men used to take in the midst of their labour. However, at last we got at what remained of the walls of the structure buried by the fallen masonry, and successive finds of broken wooden implements stimulated the men's hope of earning the liberal reward I had promised for the discovery of the first written record.

We had just cleared a small outer room on the north side, and were working our way into a somewhat larger one built against the solid masonry of the tower (Fig. 171), when this eagerly-looked-for find was made. It was a strangely puzzling object,—a solid block of wood, about twelve inches long and five broad, thick at one end but narrowing wedge-like at the other, and painted black all over (comp. Fig. 172, 4). On one of the faces of this wedge there appeared two large Chinese characters in red. Chiang could read them without difficulty, but vainly sought for their sense. That they were meant for a name seemed the most likely conjecture. But how to interpret the purpose of this queerly shaped 'tablet'?   The string still firmly fixed into the broad end showed plainly that this inscribed piece of wood was meant to be carried about or hung up.   But it was only weeks later, when several other watch-stations along the wall had yielded exactly similar objects, that the true explanation was hit upon by my Chinese assistant.

Elsewhere, too, these wedges had turned up singly, and marked with two characters which would give no proper sense except as names.   The size varied, but there was always the string.   So Chiang-ssŭ-yeh remembered how he had seen at Lan-chou and other garrisons soldiers from small detachments, when off duty and permitted to 'go to the Bazar,' as we should say in India, carrying about conspicuous pieces of wood inscribed with the initials or name of their commandant as tokens of their 'permit.'   Being large and easily distinguished by any passer-by, such a token would save the bearer any questions as to whether his absence from the post was authorized.   If provided for each detachment only in a single specimen it would also prevent too numerous applications for leave, just as in a school where only one boy at a time is allowed to leave the class-room.

This first find was soon followed by real records on wood: a large rectangular tablet with account entries, an inscribed seal-case, some broken 'slips' with the usual single line of characters.   Their material left no doubt as to the early date when the tower was occupied.   It was clear that this portion of the frontier line went back to the time of the Han dynasty, like the one explored eastwards.   Conclusive proof came to light next morning when, continuing the clearance of this room and of a sort of gate passage built against the east face of the tower, the men came upon more wooden slips of the orthodox shape, one of them dated in the third year of the Chü-shê period, corresponding to 8 A.D.   With such evidence of high antiquity, all the relics left behind in these humble quarters by their last occupants acquired increased interest (Figs. 173, 174).   There were plenty of quaintly carved wooden hooks, resembling the head and neck of some animal, with traces of bright yellow or red colour, which might possibly have served as pegs for hanging accoutrements or as handles for boxes ; a block of wood for holding lighted tapers ; curved pieces of wood which might have formed part of cross-bows or catapults, inscribed with the name of the regiment which had garrisoned this part of the *Limes* ; broken shafts of arrows, etc.

That the men stationed here had, after the good Chinese fashion, used their spare time for homely occupations was made clear by numerous wooden combs such as are still employed by rope-makers, by a wooden spindle-like instrument, and similar simple implements. A find, humble in appearance but of great archaeological value, was a foot-measure resembling in shape a bootmaker's foot-rule, and still retaining the string by which it was hung from the wall (Fig. 173, 2). Divided into ten inches, with further subdivisions on the decimal principle, it gives the exact value of the measures in use under the Han dynasty. It consequently enables us to determine accurately the equivalents of measurements given for different objects in records of that period. An interesting instance in which I was able myself to apply the test of this ancient foot-rule will be mentioned hereafter.

There were shreds of bright silk fabrics, perhaps left behind by officers or visitors of superior rank, and rags of coarse woollen stuff such as the soldiers might have worn. That luxuries were few and resources of civilized life carefully treasured was curiously illustrated by the pieces of several jars of hard grey pottery which had been broken, and then patched up again by means of leather thongs passed through neatly bored holes.

Surrounded as we were by these modest but telling relics of the hard life once led along this much-exposed frontier, the briefest information to be gleaned from the wooden records, as they passed from under the labourers' spades into Chiang-ssŭ-yeh's hands, acquired a significance which those who wrote them nineteen hundred years ago certainly never dreamt of. Among our first finds was a label evidently once tied to a bag, referring to a hundred bronze arrow-heads and naming a certain

**171. GUARD-ROOM BUILT AGAINST NORTH-EAST CORNER OF ANCIENT WATCH-TOWER
T. VIII., TUN-HUANG *LIMES*, AFTER EXCAVATION.**

On left is seen the narrow gate leading into the quarters of the watch-station, with sockets to hold bars of door ; on adjoining wall surface the rough outline sketch of a camel ; on extreme right steps of stairs once leading to roof of quarters and thence to top of tower.

**172. ANCIENT POTTERY AND IMPLEMENTS EXCAVATED FROM RUINED
WATCH-STATIONS ON TUN-HUANG *LIMES*.**

Scale, one-fifth.

1. Wooden beating-stick. 2. Broomstick of reeds. **3.** Iron hoe. 4. Wedge of wood inscribed with two Chinese characters. 5. Pottery jar. 6. Broken piece of pottery mended with leather thong passed through holes.

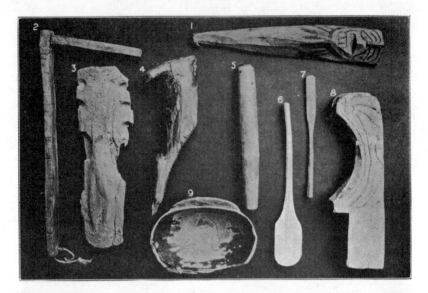

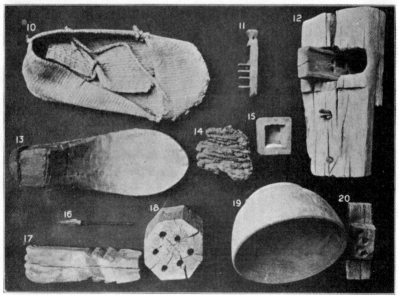

173, 174. ANCIENT IMPLEMENTS AND ARTICLES OF EQUIPMENT, EXCAVATED MAINLY FROM RUINED WATCH-STATIONS OF EARLY CHINESE BORDER LINE, TUN-HUANG.

Scale, one-fifth.

1. Ornamented wooden tent-peg. 2. Foot-measure with decimal division into inches. 3. Wooden fire-stick. 4. Polished wood handle. 5. Ivory-topped head of baton. 6, 7. Spatulas. 8, 17. Carved wooden hooks (see p. 95). 9. Bowl of lacquered wood. 10. Hemp shoe. 11. Wooden key. 12, 20. Parts of wooden locks. 13. Wooden boot-last. 14. Fragment of calcined reed fascine (see p. 110). 15. Wooden socket for attaching seal. 16. Bronze arrow-head. 18. Block of wood for holding tapers. 19. Wooden eating-bowl.

company of 'Yü-mên.' So at last I had found the name of that famous 'Jade Gate' which I had thought from the first was to be located somewhere along this westernmost part of the *Limes*. Again and again in the course of subsequent excavations I felt grateful for the *amor scribendi* which seems to have prompted these ancient 'military Babus'—like those whom one now meets in queer corners of the fortified posts scattered along the Indian North-West Frontier—to beguile their *ennui* and demonstrate their own importance by a constant flow of 'memos,' reports, store statements, and other documents so familiar to soldiering men in most regions.

But here, as at other watch-stations, records with a pleasant touch of actuality and personal interest were not wanting. How strange it seemed to hear my secretary explain the record left on the four sides of a roughly carved wooden stick, telling of a visit which three persons named had intended to pay to their friend stationed here, perhaps the petty officer in charge of the post. Finding him 'out' they had left their 'card,' scribbling down their regret at a missed chat on the best substitute for orthodox 'note wood' they could pick up from the fuel store. No doubt, they left it in the hands of the men on guard; hence they did not think of putting down the date for our benefit.

While Chiang delighted in scrutinizing the hand-writings, finding elegant penmanship here or execrably cursive 'grass script' there, I was gratified by a palaeographic discovery of my own of considerable interest. Among the peculiarities of the wooden stationery used for the Kharoshthi documents which I had the good fortune first to unearth at the Niya site, the cleverly fastened oblong envelopes (Fig. 94) had always seemed to me a specially ingenious device. Without definite evidence, but guided by a number of general considerations, I had in *Ancient Khotan* ventured to advance the opinion that this device, with other equally clever arrangements in the form and fastening of those Kharoshthi letters, might have been originally derived from Chinese models.

The discovery of a perfectly preserved wooden

'envelope,' about six inches by three, with the exact counterpart of the seal-socket and string-grooves familiar from those Niya finds, now placed my conjecture beyond all doubt. It is true, this particular 'envelope' had served to cover, not a tablet, but a box, as was proved by a small rim sunk on the under surface, and by the Chinese inscription in fine big characters, which indicated that the receptacle of which only this lid remained had been "the medicine case belonging to the Hsien-ming company." But seeing the radical difference between Chinese writing arranged in vertical columns and Indian script for which oblong material, whether birch bark, palm leaf, leather, or wood, was the traditional and most convenient form, the turning of the lid shape to use for a covering tablet was but a kind of intelligent adaptation.

In any case I had here the true prototype of my wooden 'envelopes,' but some three centuries older and used where everything else in the way of writing materials was purely and unmistakably Chinese. Subsequently, when clearing the great refuse heaps of T. xiv., I had the satisfaction of bringing to light Chinese records written on tablets exactly reproducing the shape of the Kharoshthi 'wedges' and dating in all probability from the first century B.C. Thus the Chinese origin of this kind of stationery, too, is placed beyond question.

The selection of this particular ruin for my first excavation proved fortunate also in respect of certain structural features which the protection offered by the adjoining debris made it possible to ascertain. Among these I may mention here only the existence of regular stairs which led up to the roof from the principal guard-room and thence probably to the top of the tower. Another feature was the abundant plastering and painting bestowed on the tower, probably with a view of making it better visible from a distance. On the east side we counted the layers left by four or five plasterings and more than a dozen coats of whitewash. The top coat bore the rough sketch of a camel (Fig. 171). As another curious detail I may mention that, on scraping the level ground south of the mound, we came upon two stout posts fixed in the soil at twenty yards' distance from each other, and upon remains of a thick rope of twisted reed which once joined them. It had manifestly been used for tethering horses after a fashion my own men often used when camping on absolutely bare ground.

By the evening of the second day the excavation of the ruins at the post T. VIII. had advanced sufficiently far for me to leave the completion of it to the care of Chiang and the Naik. All day a fierce gale from the east had been blowing, and eyes and throat suffered badly from the dust that rose from the dug-up quarters. It needed all the elation caused by the day's epigraphical finds to bear these atmospheric conditions cheerfully. They became more or less constant thereafter, and only left us at times to give way to equally trying heat and glare. As I rode the seven miles back to camp, the barren gravel Sai looking more desolate than ever in the dust-laden twilight, I was met to my surprise by a long string of camels. Seen from a distance across the absolutely level plateau where all perspective deceives, they suggested a phantom column moving along the old wall.

The season for travelling by the desert route to Lop-nor had now wellnigh passed. My surprise at meeting this belated caravan became still greater when it proved to be Sher Ali Khan's venture to which I had entrusted my letters so busily written at Tun-huang. I had thought them now safely nearing Abdal, and my disappointment was naturally keen when I found that this mail-bag, to which I had devoted almost the whole of a cold night, had managed to cover in eleven days less than eighty miles out of its four months' journey to Europe! The caravan men, a motley collection of Khotanliks, and people from Ak-su and Kashgar long exiled on the Kan-su border, crowded eagerly round me. It was a rueful tale they told of two valuable ponies, their only riding animals, which had strayed from a camp near the marshes to the east, and in spite of all search could not be recovered. None of the men, except the guide, had ever followed this desert track; and this worthy, upon whom they relied for a safe passage, was a young fellow who had first marched to Tun-huang as one of my donkey - men, and had proved the least intelligent of the lot.

Naturally enough, the camel-men felt apprehensive of what awaited them farther on. Remembering how easy it would be to lose one's way completely in that maze of clay terraces and dunes which intervenes between the terminal lake basin of the Su-lo Ho and Besh-toghrak, I congratulated myself at not being one of their party while dust storms of that day's violence were blowing. The whole party looked so forlorn that I forbore to complain about the delay caused to my mail, and only gave them what advice seemed needed to keep the 'guide' to the right track. When they told me that they would halt a day or two at Toghrak-bulak to give their camels a rest, I regretted more than ever to have entrusted my mail to such a terribly slow goods train.

I tried to exact compensation by asking the younger men to come back for that time to my ruin and help in the digging, "just to show those Khitai infidels how Mussulmans could wield their Ketmans." But I was not surprised when even the offer of magnificent wages and the chance of finding hidden treasure did not tempt the way-worn Seven. So I let them pass on with all my good wishes for their own and my mail-bag's safe journey. Two weeks later I found at Toghrak-bulak the carcass of one of their forty camels half devoured by wolves, and wondered how many more these luckless people would lose before reaching the green fields of Charklik. But they struggled through, and by the close of September my letters had safely arrived in England.

CHAPTER LIX

RECONNAISSANCES ALONG THE ANCIENT WALL

WITH Chiang-ssŭ-yeh and Naik Ram Singh once initiated in the work of clearing these ruined watch-stations, I was free to start on reconnaissance rides along the ancient wall. They were to show me in advance the task awaiting us at each ruin, and to enable me to select the most suitable camping-places. The latter consideration was important; for with so limited a number of labourers and with ruins so widely scattered, it would have been a serious loss to waste what little energy and strength the party possessed by long daily tramps to and fro.

Never did I feel more the strange fascination of this desolate border line than during the days I spent in thus tracing the remains of wall and watch-stations over miles and miles of gravel desert and past the salt marshes. There were, indeed, the towers to serve as guides from a distance. But when on the east of our first lake camp I began to search for the wall they were intended to guard, I soon found my task complicated by peculiar topographical features. Already before, when first following the Lop-nor route, we had noticed lakes and marshes in the depressions north of it. But only when I set out to visit each ruined tower we had seen rising far away to the north over what then looked a uniform dead level of gravel desert, did it become clear how broken the ground was over which those engineers of the Han times had here carried their frontier line.

What had seemed a plain extending to the very foot of those bare lifeless hills of the Kuruk-tagh now proved to be in reality a series of low gravel-covered plateaus separated by many winding depressions. A large-scale map would be needed to show properly this intricate configuration of the ground, which resembled a strongly developed coast line with flat tongues of land left between a complex system of bays and inlets. The larger depressions were partly filled by spring-fed marshes, in places over a mile broad. Dense reed – beds fringed the sheets of open water, and salt-covered bogs extended farther away in the line of the drainage north-westwards. Elsewhere all trace of water had disappeared from the surface; but tamarisk bushes and other hardy scrub mingling with thin reed growth, as well as the salt-efflorescence, showed that sub-soil water was near in these Nullahs. The marshes and salt-encrusted bogs were quite impassable for our ponies, and often détours of miles round their edges or over strips of less treacherous ground were needed to take us from one tower or mound to another.

Then, when these swamps had been successfully taken, like ditches in an obstacle race, came the still more exciting search for the remains of the old wall. This, I soon learned, had been carried unfailingly over every bit of firm ground capable of offering a passage for the enemy's inroads and right down to the edge of the marshy inlets (Fig. 176). In fact, I convinced myself from ample evidence that this alignment of the wall had been purposely chosen by the old Chinese engineers in order to supplement their line by natural defences, and thus to save labour of construction.

Where the soil was soft and scrub-covered, as near the marshes, the eye often failed at first to discover any trace of the *agger*; for the remains of the rampart constructed with alternating layers of earth and reed fascines had here decayed badly owing to the moisture rising from the ground. The remains were obscured besides by the coarse vegetation which finds nourishment in this salt-permeated soil. But when we had gained once more the bare gravel plateau, a search along its edges would soon reveal the familiar track of the wall.

Over considerable stretches the wall still rose to a conspicuous height, attracting the eye from afar (Fig. 175). Either some peculiarity in the constructive use of the materials, always layers of gravel and fascines, had secured greater consistency, or the direction, coinciding with the prevailing winds, and a sheltered position on lower ground had reduced the force of erosion.   Elsewhere, for some reason or other, the lapse of two thousand years and the violence of the winds, which rarely cease sweeping along this great desert valley, had wrought far greater havoc, and it needed a careful scanning of the ground to discover the low continuous swelling along the line which the wall had followed.   But even where the eye scarcely caught the alignment, the ends of the neatly laid reed bundles cropping out from below the gravel would supply a decisive indication ; and a single stroke with the Ketman would suffice to unearth the regular 'masonry.'   Tila Bai was usually my only companion on these reconnoitring rides, and grateful I felt for his keen eyes and power of intelligent observation which often enabled him to locate these faint traces of the wall from a distance.

Once we had hit the line on a particular plateau section, it was easy to follow it right through ; for straight it ran in the direction of the nearest watch-station eastwards. Nor was it difficult to locate these towers, since their position had invariably been chosen with a sharp eye for the advantages of ground commanding the nearest depressions.   What had lightened the task of the soldiers who once kept watch and guard here, now proved equally helpful to guide us to their ruined quarters.   However much decayed some of the towers were, and however broad the marshy depressions which broke the continuity of the wall and separated us from our next goal, the mass of broken masonry almost always sufficed for a guiding land-mark ; so well raised above the general level of the plateaus was the ground which it occupied.

Where the extent of wall line to be watched was great and the elevation afforded by natural features of the ground inadequate for the purpose, the towers had been built very massively to heights originally of twenty-five feet or more. Here the carefully set masonry or the hard clay stamped in regular layers was generally solid enough to hold out against all vicissitudes of the ages.   The original coating of thick plaster had, of course, fallen where not protected by the quarters which had been built against the foot of the tower, and often the erosive action of the winds had laid bare on the top the heavy Toghrak timber inserted to strengthen the masonry (Fig. 180). Where, however, the clay terrace or knoll selected for the watch-post assured by itself a commanding view, the towers had been built less high (Fig. 178). No doubt the reason is to be found in that intelligent aim at economy in efforts and means which is so characteristic a feature in all works of Chinese civilization. In cases where it was easy to provide access by means of a regular staircase, I found that the top was usually occupied not by a mere conning-platform, but by a small room affording better shelter to the men on guard.

The walls of such little watch-rooms had necessarily decayed far more than the tower below; but their débris made access to the top still practicable. As I sat there with my eyes wandering over this vast expanse of equally desolate marsh and gravel Sai, which was relieved only here and there by a narrow streak of Toghrak jungle or glittering sheet of salt water, it seemed easy to call back the dreary lives which had once been lived here. The setting of the scene—of this I had ample proof—could have changed but little as far as human conditions were concerned. The very materials of which wall and towers were built proved that the ground over which the troops of the Han emperors had kept border-guard, consisted then as now of nothing but bare desert, marshes, and such dreary scrub and reed thickets as could find nourishment in their salty water.

By contrast it seemed almost a pleasing picture when I raised my eyes to the long chain of barren brown hills which lined the horizon northward. Yet there, too, everything bore the impress of death-like torpor. Not a trace of vegetation survives on the detritus glacis sloping down to the wide desert valley, and the closely set ravines which furrow the bleak hill-sides looked as if scooped out by rain such as has failed to reach here for thousands of years. None of the valleys on this side of the Kuruk-tagh are now known to possess wells or springs. But there were at least the fantastically broken crests of the ridges, the view of rocky pinnacles peeping out above them from the unknown wilderness behind, and the many shades of colour, from light brown to deep purple, to engage the eye and to relieve it from the dreary uniform grey of the Sai and the trying glitter of the salt marsh.   No life of the present was there to distract my thoughts of the past ; not a sound in the air, nor a thing moving, but the hot air which vibrated above the ground and raised ill-defined wavy mirages on the horizon.

In such solitude it needed no effort to realize the significance of every relic of the distant past when this desert border knew permanent occupation.   Undisturbed by man or beast, or those far more destructive agents, moisture and driving sand, there lay at my feet the débris of the quarters which the guards had occupied, and often the more extensive rubbish heaps which had accumulated just outside.   With the freezing gales which blow over this desert for half the year and the torrid heat which beats down on it for the rest, little wonder that the men stationed here did not feel tempted to move far away from their towers.   So whatever they had no further use for found a safe resting-place in odd corners, or by the side of the tower and wall, to be recovered now with an ease such as I had rarely before experienced in my archaeological hunts.

The thinnest layer of gravel—and that, of course, the crumbling masonry supplied in plenty—sufficed to preserve in absolute freshness even such perishable objects as shreds of clothing, wooden tablets, arrow-shafts, straw, and chips.   Whatever objects had once passed under this protection were practically safe in a soil which had seen but extremely scanty rainfall for the last two thousand years, was far removed from any chance of irrigation or other interference by human agency, and had suffered on its flat surface but rarely even from wind erosion.   Often a mere scraping of the slope with my boot-heel or the end of my hunting-crop sufficed to disclose where the detachments holding the posts had been accustomed to throw their refuse.

With all the reports, statements, and enquiries which

a fully developed and, no doubt, scribe-ridden military organization had kept moving along this chain of border watch-stations for more than two hundred years, was it wonderful that I soon grew accustomed to picking up records of the time of Christ or before, almost on the surface ? Of course the harvest could not be reaped until my working party was brought to each of the ruined posts in succession, and Chiang-ssǔ-yeh was at hand eager to read out and interpret these 'waste papers' as well as he could at first sight. Curious it was then to hear of records which told of apprehended attacks, movements of troops brought up for reinforcement, inspection visits of high officers, or more frequently of such routine details as issue of fresh rations, arms and clothing. Just as along the telegraph lines of our Indian border, isolated small posts try to make up for the total dearth of local interests by keeping a constant flow of news from the busy world far away trickling over the wires as 'service messages,' so here, I thought, much of this correspondence was perhaps only a reproduction of orders meant originally for some headquarters and subsequently passed on to the lonely watch-stations.

But truly important was the steadily growing assurance, gathered from the dates which my indefatigable secretary's scholarly help allowed me to read with certainty, that this frontier line dated back to the end of the second century B.C., when Chinese expansion into Central Asia first began under the Emperor Wu-ti. As subsequently the date records receded farther and farther in antiquity, until we got to documents of the T'ien-han period commencing in 100 B.C., it became quite certain that the wall and the watch-stations along it were identical with the line of guard-houses planted at intervals, from Chiu-ch'üan (or Su-chou) to the Jade Gate. These the Han Annals record as having been constructed about 110 B.C., when attacks made by the Hsiung-nu on the Chinese political and commercial missions westwards forced the Emperor to despatch expeditions leading to the subjugation of Lou-lan and the establishment of Chinese military power in the Tarim Basin.

There could be no doubt that the main purpose of this *Limes* was to safeguard the territory south of the Su-lo Ho. This was indispensable as a base and passage for the Chinese military forces and political missions sent to extend and consolidate imperial control in the Tarim Basin and beyond. It was equally clear that the enemy, against whose irruptions from the north and north-west this base and line of communication had to be protected, were the Hsiung-nu, the ancestors of those Huns who some centuries later watered their horses on the Danube and the Po.

With this fact once established, how the horizon seemed to widen both in time and space ! The very existence of this *Limes* brought out the important geographical fact that the desert hill region north of the Su-lo Ho marshes, now quite impracticable owing to the absence of water, must then have been passable for small raiding parties. In historical perspective, too, it was stirring to think that this western-most end of the ' Great Wall ' had not been built for mere passive defence, a purpose so easily associated with every ' Chinese Wall,' but, like more than one Roman *Limes* within a century or so later, primarily to keep the route open for a vigorous strategic advance. But of such historical affinities and connections more anon.

Fascinating as it was to let my thoughts wander far away to Roman borders I had known, it was easier still to forget altogether the lapse of long ages, while the humble accessories of the life once led on this desolate frontier lay before my eyes seemingly untouched by twenty centuries. The men, indeed, had passed away, those who kept guard and those against whose raids the great line had been drawn right through the desert. Yet nature had changed scarcely at all, and on this ground its forces had failed to efface the work of man.

Never did I realize more deeply how little two thousand years mean where human activity is suspended, and even that of nature benumbed, than when on my long recon-noitring rides the evenings found me alone amidst the débris of some commanding watch-station. Struck by the rays of the setting sun tower after tower far away, up to ten miles' distance and more, could be seen glittering in a yellowish light as if the plaster coating of their walls were still intact to make them conspicuous. As they showed up from afar, with long stretches of the wall between them often clearly rising as straight brownish lines above the grey bare gravel desert (Fig. 175), how easy was it to imagine that towers and wall were still guarded, and that watchful eyes were scanning the deceptive plateaus and Nullahs northward with the keenness born of familiarity with a fleet and artful enemy !

The arrow-heads in bronze which I picked up in numbers near the wall and towers (Fig. 174, 16) were proof that attacks and alarms were familiar incidents on this border. Unconsciously my eye sought the scrub-covered ground flanking the salt marshes where Hun raiders might collect before making their rush in the twilight. How often had I amused myself on the Indian North-West Frontier with looking out for convenient lines of approach which our friends, Wazir or Afridi outlaws from across the border, might fancy ! Once across the chain of posts the road lay open for Hun raiders to any part of the Tun-huang oasis or the settlements farther east. It is true the barren desert stretching north of the wall might have proved a far more formidable obstacle than the line of watch-stations itself. But did not those hardy horsemen sweep across great deserts almost as forbidding before they reached the Danube plains to become the scourge of the tottering Roman Empire ? Just as the notion of time, so also the sense of distance, seemed in danger of being effaced when I thought how these same Huns, whom the Han emperors had struggled so long to keep away from their borders, were destined a few centuries later to shake the forces of Rome and Byzance.

But the slanting rays of the setting sun would reveal also things of the past far more real. The line of the wall showed then quite distinctly for miles and miles, even where it had decayed to little more than a low long-stretched mound with reed bundles sticking out (Fig. 176). It was at that time that the eye most readily caught a curiously straight furrow-like line running parallel to the wall and at a distance of some thirty feet within wherever there was a

175. STRETCH OF ANCIENT BORDER-WALL, BUILT OF LAYERS OF REED FASCINES AND CLAY,
EAST OF TOWER T. XIII., TUN-HUANG *LIMES*.

176. REMAINS OF ANCIENT BORDER-WALL ADJOINING SALT MARSH, TO WEST OF TOWER
T. XIV. A., TUN-HUANG *LIMES*, SEEN FROM SOUTH.

well-preserved stretch of it. Close examination proved that it was a narrow but well-defined track, worn into the coarse gravel soil by the patrols who had tramped along here for centuries. Again and again this strange, uncanny track reappeared along wall sections miles away from the caravan route, wherever the remains of the wall were high enough to offer protection against the coarse sand and pebbles driven by the north and north-east winds. Nevertheless I might have doubted this simple explanation, had I not had such abundant occasion to convince myself of the remarkable persistence with which this gravel soil retains all impressions such as footprints or wheel-tracks.

Frequently I came across the latter running to depressions which may at one time have afforded some grazing or fuel, but where both these inducements to visits on the part of the cart-loving Tun-huang herdsmen must have disappeared for many years past. Yet the tracks left even by a single vehicle which had thus crossed the Sai were usually quite clear and continuous. Then elsewhere I noted with surprise that the footprints which we ourselves and our ponies had left on the ground when first tracing the wall on our journey to Tun-huang, looked two months later absolutely as fresh as if we had just passed by. We knew by sad experience the force of the gales which in the interval had blown almost daily over this desert valley. I have since ascertained that exactly corresponding observations have been repeatedly reported by French and other travellers of experience from gravel areas of the Sahara.

An equally striking proof of the extraordinarily preservative power of this desert soil and climate was supplied by an observation which at first puzzled me greatly. At a number of the watch-stations examined on my first reconnaissances I had noticed a series of queer little mounds, arranged in regular cross rows *quincunx* fashion, wherever the ground adjoining the wall on its inner side afforded sufficient level space for such an arrangement. Closer examination revealed that these small structures, each about seven or eight feet square and up to seven feet in height, were built up entirely of regular reed fascines, laid crosswise in alternate layers.   Intermixed with them was a slight sprinkling of coarse sand and gravel; but whether this was done on purpose, or merely a result of the layers having caught and retained the sand and small pebbles driven against them by exceptional gales, it was difficult to determine.   Toghrak sticks driven vertically through the fascines were certainly intended to secure them when first stacked.

No strengthening of this sort was any longer needed; for through the action of the salts once contained in them and in the soil the reeds had acquired a quasi-petrified appearance and considerable consistency, though each reed, when detached, still showed flexible fibres.   The regularity with which these strange stacks of antique Kumush were laid out near the watch-towers, usually at sixteen or seventeen yards' distance from each other, made me think at first of their having served for some defensive purpose, like a zariba.   With such a supposition it would have been possible to reconcile, perhaps, the evident fact that some of them had been burned, their position being marked by plentiful calcined fragments (Fig. 174, 14).   But when I found subsequently that exactly similar structures were irregularly disposed over narrow ridges, where the ground near the towers was much cut up by ravines or otherwise restricted, this idea had to be abandoned.

The true explanation presented itself when I noticed similar though not so accurately measured bundles of Toghrak branches heaped up in the same fashion near the south-west extension of the *Limes*, where such timber abounded and had been largely used in the wall construction.   I then remembered that the dimensions of the neatly laid bundles, whether of reeds or branches, corresponded exactly to those of the fascines used in building the wall, and it dawned upon me that these queer mounds were nothing but stacks of the identical fascines kept ready at the posts for any urgent repairs in the wall. Thus breaches made in it could be quickly closed without having to collect and carry the required materials over a considerable distance.   They at once reminded me then of the stacks of wooden sleepers seen neatly piled up at a railway station.   If stacks of what after all is mere straw could without any special protection withstand the destructive effect of two thousand years, the climate and conditions of the Tun-huang desert may well be credited with preservative qualities of an exceptional order.   The use made successively of the stored materials would account for the greatly varying height of the stacks from one to seven feet still extant at the same watch-station.

But it still remained to explain why some of the stacks at different posts were found reduced by fire to calcined fragments.   It was easy, of course, to think of wilful damage done by raiders and the like.   But the most plausible explanation did not suggest itself until M. Chavannes' translations showed me how frequent are the references to fire signals in the records from the watch-stations.   No doubt such signals would ordinarily be lit on the top of the tower.   But when time was pressing, or perhaps a particularly big fire was needed to penetrate a murky night, it would be simpler to set a whole stack on fire.   The fact that the remains of burnt stacks were always found at points of the quincunx where the risk of igniting others was less, supports this interpretation.

CHAPTER LX

DISCOVERIES BY THE 'JADE GATE'

I SHALL not attempt to describe day by day the labours which kept me busy for fully a month along this ancient *Limes.* Every watch - station we cleared furnished its quota of antiquarian spoil, often in novel forms. Even where my task was merely to trace the old wall across desert and marshes, there was an abundance of interesting observations to record about the changes, if any, which the ground had undergone since the line was first planned. No better gauge could have been designed for showing to the geographical student what physical conditions had prevailed here in Han times. With daily growing experience the reading of these marks of earlier water-level, of character and extent of vegetation, of wind direction, etc., soon became for me a fascinating study.

That it claimed the attention of the antiquarian and geographer alike was the greatest attraction. Vividly do I remember all the peculiar features which this apparently dull and uniform desert ground offered along the hundred miles or so of the border surveyed in the end, and equally also the many little surprises and incidents to which the search for the relics of a long-passed age treated us in the midst of this desolate region. But space does not suffice to record them all here, and in order to give some impression of the work effected and the results it has yielded, I must restrict myself to a brief account of the most notable finds.

In order to be nearer to the reinforcements of labourers and fresh supplies I had called up from Tun-huang, I shifted my camp on April 17th to the vicinity of the small but well-preserved fort which I had passed before some twelve miles east of our first lake camp (Fig. 154). It lay conveniently central for a number of watch-stations to be explored; but it did not fall on the line of wall, and there was nothing exactly to indicate its antiquity or purpose. To the north-west stretched a broad marshy Nullah, fed by springs which supplied us with water. It was, alas! also a fertile breeding-place for mosquitoes and other insects, which now, as it grew warmer day by day, would issue in perfect clouds to make our evenings lively.

The first important discovery which gladdened my heart while encamped here, came from one of the towers that guarded a section of the wall some four miles to the west. A number of wooden records in Chinese, among them two with exact dates corresponding to the year of Christ's birth and 20 A.D., had already emerged from the débris of some rooms adjoining this tower (T. XII. A) (Fig. 177), when I had to leave the work for a fresh reconnaissance eastwards. As usual, I had left Chiang and Naik Ram Singh behind to supervise the final clearing. My own ride that day showed me a great many promising ruins; but still greater was my satisfaction with what my assistants brought back to camp when we met again in the evening.

In a long narrow passage, scarcely two feet wide, left between the massive tower base and a decayed wall of the watchmen's quarters, had been found a thick layer of rubbish, mostly stable refuse. From this emerged one small roll after another of neatly folded paper containing what was manifestly some Western writing. A few of these letters—for as such they could easily be recognized from their folding and tying—had been found wrapped up in silk, while others were merely fastened with string. None of them, of course, had as yet been opened, but a glance at the partly legible writing on the outside of some of the documents showed me the same unknown script resembling early Aramaic which I had first come across on that piece of paper from the Lop-nor site. The paper here was exceedingly thin and brittle; but when at last I had succeeded in unfolding one roll, there emerged a complete document neatly written in bold black characters, and measuring about fifteen by nine and a half inches.

I could not attempt a decipherment, nor more than conjectures about the language in which this and the other ten as yet unopened documents were written. But in the very fact of this Semitic writing turning up on the border of China and in the material used for it, there was enough to keep my thoughts busy. Were these papers perhaps in some Iranian tongue, and were they left behind by some early traders from Sogdiana, or still farther west, who had come for the silk of the distant Seres while the route was kept open for direct trade from China to the regions on the Jaxartes and Oxus? How had they found their way into the rubbish heap of a lonely watch-station far removed from the actual Lop-nor route?

No less curious was the chronological puzzle. From the position in which these papers had been found, close to Chinese records on wood, it appeared highly probable that they must have found their way into the rubbish heap approximately at the same period. Now, among the tablets, over a dozen in number, the two exactly dated ones belonged, as already stated, to the years 1 and 20 A.D.; among the rest there were several which by the dynastic style used in the designation of a certain military body proved clearly to date from the reign of the usurper Wang Mang (9-23 A.D.).

The early form of Aramaic script presented by the documents would agree well enough with such a dating. Yet how to account for the material on which they were written, considering that the first discovery of paper in China is attributed by reliable historical texts to the year 102 A.D.? An explanation might possibly be found, I thought, in the references which M. Chavannes has unearthed in early Chinese texts to 'silk paper,' introduced some time before the manufacture of real paper from rags and bark was invented. Curiously enough, as if to illustrate in a palpable fashion what these texts record of the use of silk fabrics as a still earlier writing material, the same refuse layer had furnished a small strip of cream-coloured silk inscribed with a fragmentary line in Kharoshthi. It

177. RUINED WATCH-TOWER, T. XII. A., WITH REMAINS OF ADJOINING QUARTERS AND STAIRS, TUN-HUANG *LIMES*.

178. REMAINS OF ANCIENT WATCH-TOWER, T. XX., OVERLOOKING LAKE WEST OF KHARA-NOR,
TUN-HUANG *LIMES*.

179. HILLOCK WITH REMAINS MARKING POSITION OF ANCIENT 'JADE GATE' STATION,
NEAR FORT T. XIV., TUN-HUANG *LIMES*.

seemed as if three civilizations from the East, West, and South had combined to leave their written traces at this lonely watch-station in the desert, and with them to demonstrate also the earliest writing materials.

Expert investigation effected by learned collaborators since my return to Europe has singularly confirmed these conjectures. Professor J. von Wiesner, the chief authority on plant physiology as connected with the history of paper manufacture, has proved by a microscopical analysis of the paper that the material used for those documents represents the earliest effort so far known at producing rag paper. I had reason to feel equally gratified after the publication of one of the documents by my learned friend Dr. A. Cowley, and its subsequent analysis by M. R. Gauthiot, an accomplished young Iranian scholar. These furnished conclusive evidence that the script was, indeed, of Aramaic origin, and the language an early form of that Iranian dialect which was spoken in ancient Sogdiana (the region of the present Samarkand and Bokhara), and of which the Sogdian manuscripts recently recovered from Turfan and Tun-huang have preserved us later specimens. The documents can be clearly recognized now as letters, and complete decipherment may reasonably be hoped for as a result of further researches.

The old fort (T. XIV.) near which my camp stood, has already been briefly described in connection with my first passage along this route. With its thick walls of stamped clay it was an imposing structure to behold (Fig. 154). But vainly did I search within it and along its walls for any definite indication of its age. Not even refuse was to be found inside, a curious fact, seeing how grateful travellers would feel for the shelter it offers against cutting winds. My men, too, had shunned the place; for, rightly enough, they suspected that it would swarm with those terribly aggressive little insect fiends, the 'Tsao-p'i,' as the Chinese called them, from which we had trouble enough to escape even in the open. This absence of any mark of ancient occupation at a ruin occupying so convenient a position by the high road to Lop-nor puzzled me greatly, and as soon as my reconnaissances farther afield were concluded, I set about to search the ground systematically.

It was not long before I discovered fragments of that hard, dark grey pottery with which my work at other watch-stations had made me familiar, at the foot of a hillock rising less than a hundred yards to the north of the fort (Fig. 179). While Chiang and the Naik were engaged at the nearest watch-tower to the west, I had retained with me the least indolent of our men for prospecting; and as I made him scrape the slope of the mound at different points, layers of straw and other stable refuse came to light quickly at more than one point below the cover of gravel. I was conducting this first experimental search near the top of the west slope when his spade laid bare a vertical cutting into the hard clay composing the hillock.

It proved to be the mouth of a little tunnel about two and a half feet broad and about as high, running into the mound and filled with drift sand and refuse. Before I could form any view about its purpose, two dozen Chinese slips had emerged among pieces of blank stationery, matting, bones, and similar rubbish. Soon my digger had burrowed out of sight while clearing the tunnel. After making his way in for some ten feet, he reported that it led to a room completely filled with sand. No further work was possible here until the other men came back from their day's task. But the spirits of my own 'prospector' had been roused by a liberal reward for his discovery, and quickly he set about scraping elsewhere. Not far from the tunnel, but lower down on the slope, he unearthed a platform cut into the soft rock, and here another score of tablets turned up in excellent preservation. Of course I had sent word to Chiang-ssŭ-yeh, and when he arrived from the tower then ' in hand' two miles off, an eager scanning of the last finds began.

Many of the narrow slips of wood were covered with minute but well-written characters in several columns, and great was my joy when the dated pieces among those unearthed on the platform proved to belong to the period 48-45 B.C. So at last we had got well back into the pre-Christian era. All the dated records found in that queer tunnel belonged to the first two decades after Christ, the reign of Wang Mang the Usurper.   In both sets the documents seemed to have been addressed to some superior officer.   The presumption was that here we had struck the site of some sectional headquarters for this part of the *Limes*.   It received support when I learned that at least one of the records certainly emanated from the general officer commanding at Tun-huang, while several others contained reports or orders to superior officers holding charge of ' the barrier of Yü-mên.'

All along I had surmised that this ancient frontier station of the ' Jade Gate ' must have been located during Han times at some point along the line we were exploring. But where was its exact position, and had this always been the same ?   It was impossible as yet to arrive at any definite answer.   But with the documents before me I now began to realize what advantages this site offered for a chief watch-station commanding the ancient route westwards, and how little reason there was for doubts about the antiquity and the purpose of the ruined fort at this point.

Well withdrawn behind the protective line of wall and towers, and defended to the north-west and south-east by impassable marshes, its position was admirably adapted to serve both as a *point d'appui* for the posts along this portion of the *Limes* and as a station controlling traffic along the main road.   Only the day before I had discovered that the fort lay exactly in the line of a secondary wall running due south from the main wall in the direction of Nan-hu, and, though badly decayed, still traceable on the Sai.   This secondary wall showed exactly the same manner of construction with alternate layers of gravel and fascines, but only a thickness of a little under five feet.   It seemed clear from the first that this transverse wall was a subsequent work ; for without the main wall beyond, it would have been quite easy to turn it from the north flank.

But what had been the true object of this cross wall ? I had first thought of an inner line built, not for defence, but for purposes of police control in order to prevent the unauthorized entrance of individual travellers into Chinese territory.   But evidence subsequently accumulating revealed the important chronological fact that, while east of this transverse line the records brought to light proved continuous occupation of the watch-stations, down to about the middle of the second century A.D., the records found west of it stopped short with the reign of Wang Mang, and in the case of the more remote stations with dates considerably earlier.

I was thus gradually led to the conclusion, that in the early decades of our era, during the troubled times of Wang Mang's reign or very soon after, there took place a retrenchment of the border line lying westwards. By abandoning the outlying portion of the wall an appreciable reduction was, no doubt, made in the difficulties about victualling, etc., which must always have been felt most in the case of those detachments pushed out far into the desert. At the same time this retrogression of the guarded frontier line would have been fully in keeping with a contemporary change in Chinese policy. This we know was then no longer concerned about imperial expansion westwards, but until the last quarter of the first century A.D. kept strictly on the defensive. It was for the purpose of replacing the flank protection which the lopped-off western end of the original *Limes* had offered, that I believe the transverse wall to have been built during, or soon after, Wang Mang's usurpation.

In any case it was easy to realize that the station at which the great caravan road passed through this wall must have been a point of importance. In fact, from the reasons above indicated and supplementary evidence which cannot be set forth here in detail, I soon felt convinced that the 'Jade Gate' of the Later Han period, roughly corresponding to the first two centuries of our era, had to be located at this site. So I was most eager to have the remains on that unpretentious hillock cleared with all expedition and thoroughness. But the day was oppressively hot; and in the afternoon a violent gale, sweeping down from the north-east put a stop to further work, the temperature inside my tent rising to ninety degrees Fahrenheit.

But on the morning of April 21st I was able to start

systematic excavation with the whole of my little band of
diggers. A couple of days earlier it had been unexpectedly
strengthened by the two lost Nan-hu labourers, who to
Chiang's and my own great relief turned up by the route
from the east, looking very woe-begone, but as sound as
their nature and opium would allow. As far as Chiang
could make out their tangled story, they had fallen asleep
after a little 'smoke' of their beloved drug, mistaken the
track when they woke up, and then aimlessly strayed in
the desert until, after two days' wandering without water,
they were guided to the caravan track by the smoke from
the camp fire of the herdsmen we had met on our first
approach to Khara-nor. At a later season—and even now
without the sustaining effect of their opium—these hapless
fellows would almost certainly have perished. So nothing
worse befell them than that the herdsmen, who rightly
suspected desertion, had forced them to rejoin us.

The hillock we had to clear measured some eighty
yards from east to west and nearly as much across, and
there was nothing on the gravel-strewn slopes to show
where to search for rubbish and ancient remains. So
parallel trenches had to be dug all along the slopes down
to the natural hard clay in order to make sure that nothing
at this important point should escape us. There was
plenty of work here for the men, and it took them fully
three days to complete it, though on the very first there
arrived a most opportune reinforcement in the shape of
twelve additional labourers whom Ts'ao Ta-lao-ye, Lin
Ta-jên's petty officer, had managed to bring up from Tun-
huang along with half a month's fresh supplies. What
with all the digging effected by the men—whom small but
prompt rewards for interesting finds kept up to the mark—
the little hillock soon suggested a kopje girt with shelter
trenches against modern gun-fire. The results were ample
and offered strange surprises.

One of these was provided by the narrow tunnel on
the north-west slope, in which we first discovered that
batch of wooden records from Wang Mang's reign. For
instead of forming a window to some subterranean
chamber, as I had at first suspected, it proved to be the

only access to a well or shaft, about five or six feet square, which we cleared to a depth of over twelve feet without reaching the bottom. The earth roof of the shaft had originally been supported by timber, but now fell in, luckily without smothering any one. Dozens of wooden documents turned up in the sand cleared out, almost all, alas! badly decayed through damp, but some still showing legible dates of the first decades after Christ ; and from these I concluded that this curious shaft had been filled up with refuse not very long after that period. Its original purpose seemed obscure, until Chiang and some of my Muhammadans rightly suggested that it must have been intended for a dungeon, the use of similar wells for the safe keeping of dangerous prisoners being still remembered in Chinese Turkestan.

In fact, I subsequently ascertained that such methods of burying prisoners as it were alive subsisted in the Central-Asian Khanats, too, until the time of the Russian conquest. The narrow side opening near the top of the well had, no doubt, served as an air-hole. I did not care at the time to think much of the horrors which this dungeon might have witnessed ; but the fact that one of the inscribed slips here recovered, contains, according to M. Chavannes' translation, an order about the burial of a man who had died after having been beaten, has since helped to recall them. Curiously enough, the well-preserved ancient beating-stick of the traditional shape, shown in Fig. 172, was found on this very mound.

Of the structures which the top of the hillock had once borne, nothing but the scantiest foundations were discovered. But deposits of ancient rubbish laid bare at different points of the slopes yielded records on wood in abundance. From one refuse area near the centre close on five dozen documents were recovered. As almost all the dated pieces belonged to the years 96 - 94 B.C., it became quite certain that the occupation of this site went back to the time when the *Limes* was first established.

That the station had then already been one of import-ance was proved by several documents emanating direct from the commandant of the 'Jade Gate Barrier.' Others too possess a distinct historical interest, *e.g.* one directing the issue of provisions to the escort of an imperial envoy to So-ch'ê, or Yarkand, counting eighty-seven men. In another again there is a reference to an ambassador sent to the imperial court by a chief of the great tribe of the Wu-sun, who played an important part in the early history of Central Asia and then dwelt in the mountains of the present Farghana. But of such records I shall have occasion to give some account later, when dealing with the results of M. Chavannes' decipherment.

A very curious find, but for the topographical facts explaining the peculiar character of this site, might have puzzled me at the time. It was a considerable number of large paper fragments inscribed with elegantly penned Chinese characters. They turned up from the floor of what I soon recognized to have been a small cella, about ten feet square, on the western side of the hillock. That the texts they contained belonged to Chinese translations of Buddhist canonical works I could with Chiang's help make sure of at once, as well as of the reference made in another fragment to the dedication of some Buddhist images. So, taking into account the evidence furnished by the use of paper and the style of the writing, I concluded that these were relics from some modest shrine which had somehow survived at this otherwise long-abandoned site down to T'ang times. Other relics of it were ex-votos in the shape of small miniature flags made up of silk rags such as I had found at ancient sites excavated on my first journey.

Next morning this conjecture received striking confirmation by the discovery of a small wooden bowl embedded below the reed flooring and containing some eighty copper coins. Excepting two which were older, all were issues of the regnal period 713-742 A.D., and showed scarcely any wear resulting from circulation. So the attribution of the Buddhist text fragments to the eighth century, when the route to Lop-nor had last been an important line of communication, became practically certain. One of the fragments has since been proved by M. Chavannes to belong to a Buddhist canonical text, which Hsüan-tsang himself is known to have translated between

645 and 664 A.D. A fitting tribute this to the memory of the pious traveller ; for I felt quite sure at the time that my patron saint on his return journey must have passed within a few yards of the débris-covered hillock.

But what was the reason for this strange survival of worship at a site which must then for long centuries have been in ruins? The explanation was not far to seek. A number of considerations, as already stated, had gradually led me to the conclusion that the fort and the débris-strewn mound of T. XIV. marked the position of the 'Jade Gate' during the first two centuries A.D. When the danger of raids disappeared with the migration of the Huns west-wards, and later on Chinese control over the Tarim Basin was lost for centuries, the whole line of the *Limes* west of Tun-huang was abandoned to the wilderness. But occasional caravans, as we know from Fa-hsien's travels, still continued to use the desert route, and, no doubt, wandering herdsmen and hunters still visited the grazing along the lakes and marshes of the terminal course of the Su-lo Ho.

So local worship had a chance of proving once more its tenacity. It clung to the site where those leaving the 'Jade Gate' of the 'Great Wall' for the difficult desert journey had of old been accustomed to put up ex-votos at the border shrine and pray for a safe return, just as Chinese travellers still do at Chia-yü-kuan, the modern equivalent of the 'Jade Gate.' What more conclusive proof of that tradition having survived to the present day could I have wished for than that presented by a small modern shrine which lay in ruins only a little over a hundred yards to the west of the hillock explored? The coarsely made clay images were all broken, perhaps the act of some truculent Tungans, and the roof and all woodwork had disappeared. But there was evidence of herdsmen still offering prayers at the ruin, and my own labourers from superstitious fear could not be induced to dig even near it. I was not altogether sorry for this, since the chance of finding any-thing of interest under the modern ruin seemed remote, and because this continued veneration was in itself an interesting archaeological asset.

CHAPTER LXI

THE GREAT MAGAZINE OF THE LIMES

I CANNOT stop to describe here various interesting minor finds which rewarded our laborious clearing of all the layers of ancient débris and refuse on the hillock once occupied by the Gate station. There were plentiful rags of cast-off clothing; remains of iron implements; well-made shoes in hemp and other stout materials; fragments of lacquer bowls showing tastefully designed scroll ornamentation in black on red ground—all relics which, insignificant in themselves, helped me to picture the life once witnessed by this important border post (Figs. 172, 174). A reconnaissance made from this point while the digging was still in progress had revealed extensive rubbish layers at a point about two and a half miles northward and at a short distance within the main line of the *Limes*; and thither I moved camp on the morning of April 24th.

At first sight there was nothing to attract attention to the spot, and without Tila Bai's keen eyes, which noticed a slight swelling on the edge of a bare plateau tongue, I should probably have passed it without heeding. The gravel-strewn little mound, only about two or three feet high and less than forty feet across, proved to contain the débris from some brick-built structure, too much decayed and too scanty for any determination of its original character. The dozen and a half of records on wood which we found in the débris ranged in date from 65 to 137 A.D. At the time I noted this indication of relatively late occupation with special interest; for the ruin lay just within the corner where the line of the secondary wall above mentioned would join the main wall, if continued across an impassable marsh in its direction from south to north.

But that this point must have been occupied far earlier by a post of some importance soon became evident when my search revealed extensive refuse layers not only on the slopes below the débris mound but also on others farther away. As inscribed pieces of wood recovered from the latter ranged from 61 B.C. onwards, it seems probable that this rubbish had been thrown out from some structures which existed earlier and have completely disappeared. These various refuse deposits yielded so rich a harvest of Chinese documents that from the first I could not doubt that they marked the position of an important post, probably the quarters of some sectional commandant. M. Chavannes' analysis and translation of the records recovered from this post (T. xv. A), altogether over 160 pieces, have fully confirmed this conclusion. They have also revealed the existence of so large a number of specially interesting pieces that I cannot refrain here from at least alluding to a few of them.

Foremost in importance from the philological point of view is a beautifully written and perfectly preserved triangular tablet about fourteen inches long, which contains the first chapter of a lexicographical work, the Chi-chiu-chang, famous in Chinese literature and the subject of much learned commentary. As it is known to have been composed between 48 and 33 B.C., and as the tablet discovered by me must have been written within a century or two later, the critical importance which it possesses for the history of the traditional text can be easily understood even by the non-Sinologist. In any case M. Chavannes, in a preliminary notice communicated to the Académie des Inscriptions, has declared this tablet to be the earliest authentic specimen of a Chinese literary text. The particular work has always been much in use among Chinese students; and the discovery of pieces from it, not here alone, but at other *Limes* stations, proves that the studious habits of the race were represented even among the soldiers exiled on this desolate border.

Another very curious find consisted of a batch of eleven neatly written bamboo slips, scattered but clearly marked by their identical shape and writing as originally belonging to a sort of medical note-book (Fig. 119, 8). Some of them contain 'case records' and prescriptions for particular patients, others general recipes for men or ailing animals, mostly with special mention of the physicians with whom they originated. As a sample, I may mention the record left by the medical attendant 'Mr. An-kuo' of his twentieth consultation in the sad case of 'Mr. An Tien-hui,' who, having been benumbed with cold and in consequence tumbled out of his car, had injured himself internally, and who even after thirty days of treatment still suffered in his chest and extremities.

Of the great mass of records, which comprise chiefly reports, orders, and miscellaneous memos of military administration along the *Limes*, it is impossible to mention here more than a few. Thus, in a 'circular to the posts of the Yü-mên Barrier,' a sectional commander regrets to acknowledge the absence of certain soldiers at the time of the official inspection, and gives due warning of the punishments to be awarded in such cases. The 'I-tsou Company' here specified appears to have garrisoned this post right through the period covered by the records. Elsewhere we hear of difficulties about effective signalling, the distribution of duties among the men at the actual watch-posts, and such like.

A very interesting find, the archaeological importance of which has only been realized since M. Chavannes' interpretation, was a narrow strip of strongly woven cream-coloured silk bearing a line of Chinese characters inked in. This states precisely the length, weight, and price of a bale of silk, from the edge of which it had been torn off. The name of the place of manufacture, Yen-ch'êng, a locality in Shan-tung, serves to fix the date of its production at the close of the first, or in the early part of the second, century A.D. But what I greeted with particular interest is the statement there made of the width of the silk piece, viz. two feet and two inches. We know that the Chinese foot, with its decimal division into ten inches, has varied very considerably under succeeding dynasties. But when at the British Museum I came to measure up this very strip of silk with the bootmaker's foot-measure discovered at the watch-station T. VIII. (Fig. 173, 2), the original width of the piece proved exactly two feet and two inches according to the standard of the Han period.

I next applied my ancient measure to the small bale of silk which, as related in Chapter XXXII., I had unearthed at the Lop-nor site, and to a piece of silk found in one of the ancient ruins at Miran. The result tallied again as closely as is possible in the case of fabrics which in the course of seventeen centuries were bound to shrink a trifle. On the other hand, if measured by the foot-measure found at the Lop-nor site and manifestly belonging to the Chin period (3rd-4th century A.D.), all these pieces would show a width of *circ.* one foot and nine inches. Thus, by the evidence of actual silk remains brought to light from three widely distant sites, we can now establish that the silk exported from China to Central Asia and thence to the classical West during the centuries immediately before and after Christ retained a uniform width, corresponding approximately to one foot ten inches British measure, while the measuring standard in China underwent a considerable alteration during that period.

But this end strip was not the only silk remnant of antiquarian interest preserved in the refuse layers of the station T. XV. A. It was there that I discovered a small silken envelope a couple of inches long, which must once have held a letter written on a rolled strip of silk and on which M. Chavannes has been able to read the address. Equally interesting from another point of view is a narrow strip of silk bearing a long line in Indian Brahmi characters of a type associated with the rule of the Indo-Scythian or Kushana emperors. It has not yet been deciphered; so we cannot conjecture how this easternmost specimen of a document in true Indian script found its way to the 'Great Wall.' Of a tablet showing 'unknown' characters by the side of Chinese writing I may make passing mention, as a further indication of the polyglot traffic which is likely to have been brought to the *Limes* by the ancient caravan route.

Among the miscellaneous finds of ancient rags,

broken utensils, old boots, etc., which had survived in the refuse practically as fresh as when they were thrown down there, I can single out only one for special reference. It was a small closely tied bundle containing the broken pieces of a feathered arrow with the barbed bronze arrow-head packed away amongst them. The most likely explanation was that, in accordance with a system still in vogue in certain military departments over-anxious to check petty defalcation, broken arrows had to be returned 'into store' before new ones could be issued.

Our rich haul at this station was completed by April 25th, a perfectly clear day, when after long hours of work in a blazing sun I enjoyed in the evening a glorious vision of the snowy range far away to the south. What a vivifying contrast it was to the level expanse of gravel and salt marsh and the dreary bleakness of the low hills northward!

On the following morning I moved camp to the large ruin, some five miles eastwards, which when we first passed it on the journey to Tun-huang, had struck me by its palace-like dimensions (Fig. 156). My reconnaissances had since shown that this huge structure, T. xviii., with a much-decayed watch-tower rising on the plateau edge immediately south of it, lay actually on the line of the *Limes* as well as on the old caravan route. An expanse of lakelets and impassable marsh land, some four miles long and two across, stretched on its north side and rendered defence by a wall quite unnecessary. But neither the familiarity I had gained with the general plan and arrangements of the *Limes* nor the close survey I now made of the imposing ruin could at first give me any clue as to its true character and purpose.

The building with its enclosing walls presented the imposing length of over 550 feet, and at first sight suggested a barrack or Ya-mên; yet the very proportions were enough to dispel such a notion. It consisted mainly of three big halls, each 139 feet long and $48\frac{1}{2}$ feet wide, which adjoined lengthwise and formed a continuous block facing due south. Their walls, five and a half feet thick and constructed of solid layers of stamped clay about three inches in thickness, rose on a terrace of hard clay which had been cut away to within ten feet or so of the outer wall faces to form a natural base. As the latter stood fully fifteen feet above the low-lying ground occupied by the enclosure, and as the walls of the halls in spite of their decay still rose in parts to twenty-five feet or more, the height of the whole ruin was impressive.

A wall of large sun-dried bricks had once formed an enclosure around, keeping with its sides parallel to the outer faces of the great structure but at different distances. While on the north this enclosing wall ran within fifteen yards of the base, on the south it receded to about 106 yards from it, leaving a wide courtyard for approach. Owing to moisture from the low-lying ground, the enclosing wall had in most places crumbled away into a mere mound. But at four points of it, diagonally facing the four corners of the great block of halls, there still rose massive watch-towers to heights of over twenty feet. The fact that these towers were built within the enclosure seemed to indicate that they were meant, not for defence, but as points of vantage for sentinels.

Owing to erosion under-cutting the base, the south walls of the halls had fallen for considerable stretches, and deep hollows had been scooped out in the floor and base by the drainage of occasional rainfall escaping on this side. This made it difficult to ascertain where the main entrances of the three big halls and the stairs once giving access to them had been situated. Large windows, such as halls of this great size would have needed for their proper lighting, there were none to be seen in the extant walls. But, curiously enough, the latter both to north and south were at irregular intervals pierced by triangular openings about three feet high, on a level flush with the floor as well as about fifteen feet above it. It was clear they could have been intended not so much for lighting as for ventilation. Of internal fittings or arrangements which might have thrown some light on the purpose of the whole building, I could trace no remains. A narrow platform or plinth which ran round the foot of the walls at a height of eight inches or so did not give any clue.

So all hope of solving this structural puzzle with any certainty rested upon what records or other finds excavation might yield. I lost no time about starting them, but at first with very scanty results. The search made in those portions of the great halls where the original floor still survived, proved fruitless, except along the foot of the north wall in the central hall. There we discovered half-a-dozen fragments of inscribed wooden slips. Some of them seemed to relate to individual soldiers, naming their places of origin far away in Ho-nan and elsewhere; but none of them gave dates or any hint as to the character of the ruin.

Then I had the whole of the fairly well protected narrow court on the north side searched, and was just beginning to wonder at the total absence of any refuse heaps when at last, on scraping the ground at the foot of the tower occupying the north-west corner, we came upon two-score inscribed pieces of wood and bamboo scattered amidst straw and ashes. Still more abundant were blank bamboo slips, all much worn and repeatedly scraped, evidently representing 'waste paper' which had been prepared for fresh use as palimpsest records. The inscribed tablets, too, had here for the greater part suffered badly from moisture, and it was not until the very last piece turned up that Chiang could recognize a precise date. As it corresponded to the year 52 B.C. it now became certain that the ruin dated back to the early period of the *Limes* occupation.

But the doubt about the nature of the ruin did not lift until Chiang, by such prolonged poring over these records as would have done credit to any Western palaeographer, made quite sure that two among them distinctly referred to a granary. In the course of these days the idea occurred to us both, as well as to Naik Ram Singh, independently, that this strange big building might have been erected for the purpose of serving as a supply-store to the troops stationed or moving along the wall. The structural peculiarities above noted; the small openings for ventilation;

the size of the halls quite unsuited for habitation; the choice of a building site conveniently accessible yet well raised above the adjoining ground; the arrangements for guarding the building, not against hostile attack, but against theft, all found thus their simple explanation.

But definite proof was supplied only by M. Chavannes' detailed analysis of the still legible records. One among them is an issue order for grain signed by three officials specifically named as in charge of the granary. Another is still more significant, because it is an acknowledgment for a large consignment of corn delivered from a specified area of cultivation in the Tun-huang oasis, evidently as its contribution towards commissariat requirements of the border. Elsewhere, again, we find an order for twenty suits of a particular sort of clothing such as a military magazine might store.

The advantages of an advanced base of supply on this desert border, both for the troops which guarded it and for the expeditions, missions, and caravans which passed along it, must be obvious to any one familiar with the difficulties of moving large bodies of men over such ground. As I looked towards this ruined magazine from the route edging the plateau, and twenty centuries ago the main artery for Chinese trade and political expansion westward, I could not help turning my thoughts back to the huge sheds and 'commissariat godowns' which the traveller must pass as he approaches Peshawar. They contain the military stores provided for an advance, if ever it be needed, by the one great route which connects India in its extreme north-west corner with Kabul and thence with Central Asia.

And yet what a smiling look even the most barren parts of the Khyber Pass bear when compared with the desert through which the Chinese once moved their troops to Lop-nor! In those days the great magazine must have seen busy scenes, and quarters for guards and administrative *personnel*, no doubt, existed near it. The remains of all such less permanent structures had disappeared before the attack of wind erosion or moisture, except on a clay terrace near the eastern enclosing wall, where we came upon layers of refuse, and below them a room partly dug

out of the solid clay.   The single record found here also
dated from 52 B.C.

But it was not merely the archaeological assurance
gained that cheered me while encamped at this ruin.
On exploring two ancient watch-stations north-eastwards
(T. XIX. and T. XX.), I had noticed from the top of the
high isolated clay terraces on which their ruins were
perched (Fig. 178), that the wall here reappearing rested
its right flank on a lake over two miles long, and that an
open channel of water apparently led into the latter from
the side of the Khara-nor and again left it westwards.   A
short reconnaissance north had shown me that it was a
real river, some twenty yards broad, and quite unfordable
at this point, flowing out of the lake with a velocity of
nearly a yard per second.   At the same time I convinced
myself that, between the lake on the east and the wide
marsh bed already mentioned as extending north of the
magazine, there stretched a tongue of firm ground with a
few isolated clay terraces.   This circumstance at once
accounted for the care taken to close this gap in the
natural line of defence.

The wall was clearly traceable eastwards to the very
edge of the lake's marshy foreshore, which showed a level
only five feet lower than the foot of the wall, and was
evidently still liable to periodical inundation.   This was an
important piece of evidence, agreeing with observations
made at other points where the wall abutted on lakes or
marsh beds, and proving that the difference here in the
water level of the present and ancient times could not have
been very great.   There was another curious fact pointing
to little change in the local conditions of soil and climate.
The whole area between the two towers and farther on to
the lake shore was covered with a luxuriant jungle of wild
poplars—just as it must have been two thousand years ago ;
for the wall here proved by exception to be constructed, not
with the usual reed fascines, but with layers of Toghrak
branches, the material still abundant on the spot.

The time to realize fully the geographical importance of
that observation about the lake outflow arrived when in the
evening Rai Ram Singh rejoined me from the prolonged

tour of reconnaissance on which I had despatched him a fortnight earlier to the westernmost extremity of the wall. After tracing a far-extending line of towers south-westwards, and a wide basin of salt marshes and lakes which lay in front of them, he had returned to the caravan route at the point known to us as Toghrak-bulak, in order to replenish his supply of fresh water. Where he expected to find a spring-fed marsh, as seen on our first journey towards Tun-huang, he discovered to his surprise a deep and rapid river flowing westwards. He recognized at once that such a volume of water could only come from the flood of the Su-lo Ho which, as I realized at the time of our first approach from the Lop-nor side, had once made its way into that dry eroded basin we traversed on the day before reaching Toghrak-bulak. I had specially asked him to re-examine the dry river beds then sighted near it. Now, after fording with difficulty the river which flowed in the Toghrak-bulak bed, he followed it downwards until he made quite sure that it emptied itself through a little delta into the south-eastern end of the basin which early in March we had found quite dry.

Since my return to the *Limes* I had myself looked out more than once for the old bed, dry as I supposed it would be, stretching west of the Khara-nor, and on the north side of the fortified line. Once or twice I had pushed some distance beyond the latter to what seemed the very foot of an unbroken glacis of gravel sloping up gently towards the Kuruk-tagh. My abundant archaeological tasks would not allow me to move beyond this. So for the time being I had been driven to the assumption that the dry beds noticed about Toghrak-bulak had their continuation to-wards Khara-nor only in the chain of isolated depressions, some dry, some still occupied by salt marshes, which we had come across both within and without the line of the wall.

In this case a direct connection between those old beds and the Khara-nor could not well have existed within historical times. But now the aspect of this puzzling question of drainage was completely changed by the dis-covery of an actual outflow from the lake which lay west of Khara-nor and was unmistakably connected with it, and also by Ram Singh's discovery of a river flowing through the Toghrak-bulak bed. It became certain that the Toghrak-bulak river was fed from the Khara-nor, and that the latter was not the terminal basin of the Su-lo Ho river, as had been assumed hitherto. But it still remained to determine whether the connection between those two lay, as I expected, through the series of minor lakes and marshes I had seen west of Khara-nor, or whether there was perhaps a channel carrying the water of the Su-lo Ho direct from the latter down to Toghrak-bulak.

This question, too, was finally answered when on the morning of April 29th I set out to track this connection. From our camp near the big magazine ruin we moved to the north-west, skirting the wide basin of reed-covered marsh and lagoons, until suddenly we came upon a narrow and deep-cut Nullah receiving the suspected outflow towards Toghrak-bulak. It was a regular river, over twenty-five yards broad, and flowing with a velocity of a little under one yard per second. In the middle the water was over six feet deep. Though drinkable, it tasted distinctly brackish from all the salt deposits which this spring flood was sweeping out of the lake beds. As I followed this continuation of the Su-lo Ho for some distance downwards, I fully understood how easily the river could here escape discovery owing to the very deceptive way in which its course is masked by what looks an unbroken glacis of gravel. I must have approached it before at another point, to within a quarter of a mile or so without noticing its existence. Yet for the time boats could have passed along it with ease.

On the same day I shifted my camp back to the site of the 'Yü-mên' fort, preliminary to a move for the exploration of the westernmost portion of the *Limes*, while Rai Ram Singh was sent eastwards for survey work about Kharanor. Then on April 30th, by a forced march over twenty-eight miles, I brought my straggling column of camels and men right across to the point where the line of the wall as marked by its watch-towers was seen to bend round to the south-west. The heat and glare on the bare gravel plateaus was most trying; and when in the evening we descended to the edge of the wide marsh-filled basin which stretched westwards as far as the eye could reach, we were assailed by clouds of mosquitoes and other insects. In order to secure some protection from this pest, and yet at the same time to keep reasonably near to the springs located by the Surveyor and to the grazing, I pushed for nearly two miles beyond the edge of the basin, here lined by a belt of luxuriant vegetation, to where a bold and broad terrace of clay promised a dry and airy camping-place. For, like the wild camels whose resting-grounds we had repeatedly come upon on the top of isolated clay ridges or plateaus, we soon realized that an elevated wind-swept position was the only means for escaping the worst onsets of those insect fiends.

The tents had scarcely been pitched in the darkness when I became aware that the choice of our camping-ground had given us protection from a far more serious danger. The labourers sitting down for a little smoke while waiting for the baggage, had lit fires in the jungle and carelessly left them smouldering. A strong north wind, which rose after dark, fanned these into a big con-flagration, spreading with amazing rapidity amidst the dry thickets of scrub and reed-beds. It was a wonderful sight to watch the broad array of flames over-running the leafless wintry jungle. It spread a glorious illumination on three sides of us, and burst into something like fireworks where-ever groves of large Toghraks were set ablaze. From the bare slope of our clay terrace we could watch the grand spectacle without serious apprehension. But when the first supply of water brought along from the springs was exhausted, Hassan Akhun found it no easy task to take the camels back to them by a circuitous route, and most of our animals did not get a drink until daybreak.

CHAPTER LXII

ON THE WESTERN FLANK OF THE LIMES

When on the morning of May 1st I set out to visit the neighbouring ruins and reconnoitre this new ground, I was obstructed not a little by the strange combination of water and fire. Most of the ground separating our camp terrace from the three watch-towers within view was marshy, and it cost much care and many détours to avoid hopeless bogs. At the same time, where the soil on the edge of the wide depression was firmer, the fire in the reed-beds was still smouldering, and a passage had to be picked with caution. All over the low ground salt efflorescence was abundant, and its contrast with the blackened tamarisks and Toghraks and the singed reeds very striking. It seemed cruel to see this hardy jungle vegetation, which had held its own amidst such deterrent conditions of soil and climate, succumb to fire just when it was preparing to greet its short-lived spring.

But physical drawbacks were soon forgotten over the absorbing antiquarian interest of the site. A careful survey of the ground soon convinced me that I now stood within the westernmost extension of the *Limes*. With that unfailing eye for topography and all its strategic bearings which the Chinese have proved again and again to possess, the engineers of the Emperor Wu-ti had carried their fortified border line right up to the point where it could rest its flank safely upon a huge depression—once, no doubt, a great lake basin and since historical times an impassable bog in most places. A look at Map I. and its inset *A*, much reduced as is the scale, will fully explain this ; but a much larger map would be needed to illustrate the details. Instead of taking the wall towards Toghrak-bulak, where the caravan route must have run then as now, the constructors of the *Limes* let it continue due west along a narrow and well-raised plateau tongue up to its extreme point.

There a tower (T. IV. B) built of carefully laid bricks, and still over twenty-three feet high, rose on the brink of steep clay cliffs some 120 feet in height, commanding an extensive view westwards and over scrub and gravel Sai to the north. No better look-out place could have been selected for this exposed portion of the fortified line. But the wall had been carried about one and a half miles farther west to an isolated clay terrace rising from the scrub-covered edge of the basin to a height slightly lower than the plateau end just mentioned (Fig. 181). The top of this terrace was occupied by a much-decayed tower in stamped clay (T. IV. A), which completely overlooked the low-lying ground all round. Here the wall took a sharp turn to the south, and could be traced as a low mound for a mile or so running in the direction of the terrace on which our camp stood. But as the soil there grew more and more marshy, the last faint indication of the *agger* soon disappeared entirely. It was clear that the very nature of the ground to the west, all spring-fed marsh and lagoons, had rendered defence by a wall needless on this flank farther on. But a line of towers visible far away to the south-west, perched at great intervals on headlands of the plateau, showed that the flank had been guarded all the same.

The ruined quarters adjoining the tower T. IV. B yielded a number of well-preserved Chinese records on wood and silk, on one of which Chiang thought he could recognize a date corresponding to the year 94 B.C. So my thoughts were carried back to near the times when this *Limes* had served the first political expansion of China westwards. As I looked round from the commanding position occupied by this tower, I wondered why its builders had not rested content to let the wall make its bend here. Then my attention was attracted by two straight lines of mounds rising above the scrub-covered ground in the direction of

180. RUIN OF ANCIENT WATCH-TOWER, T. VI. A., ON WESTERN FLANK OF TUN-HUANG *LIMES*,
SEEN FROM SOUTH.

The tower is built on an eroded clay ridge, and on right overlooks a depression with Toghraks and reed beds.

A   T. IV. C.

181. RUIN OF ANCIENT WATCH-TOWER, T. IV. C., ON WESTERN FLANK OF TUN-HUANG *LIMES*,
WITH VIEW TO NORTH.

On left an eroded clay terrace with deep-cut Nullah. Across depression with Toghraks and tamarisks is seen in
distance an isolated clay terrace (A), bearing remains of ruined watch-tower, T. IV. A.

182. REMAINS OF ANCIENT WATCH-TOWER AND QUARTERS, T. VI. B., TUN-HUANG *LIMES*, BEFORE EXCAVATION, SEEN FROM WEST.

183. RUBBISH-STREWN SLOPE BELOW RUINED WATCH-TOWER T. VI. B., IN COURSE OF EXCAVATION.

The splintered piece of timber held by labourer marks the spot where hundreds of Chinese records on wood, all of 1st century B.C., were discovered close to surface.

the last tower westwards.   They looked distinctly like
the remains of earth ramparts meeting at right angles,
and their position within the bend of the wall and near
its westernmost point at once suggested an entrenched
camp.

Naik Ram Singh, who had taken the labourers to the
ruin while I was reconnoitring, had already noticed these
curious lines.   Subsequently, on riding over the ground,
I found that in spite of much ' Shor,' or salt efflorescence,
scrub of various sorts and reeds were covering it in profusion ; and so it was difficult to follow the lines up.   But
rows of little mounds, eight to ten feet high, and thickly
covered with dead Toghrak trunks and branches, could
even thus be made out at what from above I had taken
for the south-west angle of the enclosed area.   On going
up a steep terrace a short distance to the north, the lines of
ramparts showed up again, forming an oblong about five
hundred yards long and half that across.   With its short
side on the north this oblong seemed to approach closely
the line of wall connecting the two westernmost towers
(T. IV. A and B).

Were these then the remains of an entrenched camp
established at some time at the very point where the
ancient route from the Tarim Basin passed within the
walled line of the *Limes*?   Would this not have been the
most likely position to select for the original ' Jade Gate '?
Here at the foot of the plateau there would have been some
shelter from bitter winds and no difficulty about reaching
water by digging.   A larger station for troops was here
justified by the risks to be guarded against at this exposed
corner.   At the same time its existence would furnish
adequate explanation both for the extension of the wall to
a point beyond the tower T. IV. B, and for the construction
of a third tower (T. IV. C, Fig. 181), which we found overlooking and guarding the site from a plateau tongue about
one and a half miles to the south-east.   For the complete
decay of the rampart and the total absence of structural
remains inside I could account by the vicinity of abundant
subsoil water.   In fact, eight months later I had occasion to
acquaint myself with the exactly corresponding results which

permeation with water had produced on ruined sites by the salt-impregnated shores of Lake Baghrash.

On May 2nd, while excavation at the towers continued under Chiang-ssŭ-yeh and the Naik, I made a long day's reconnaissance with a few mounted men along the ancient route to the north-west. It furnished definite proof that, though there had been no extension of the wall in that direction, yet the towers I passed on my first approach to Toghrak-bulak in March had been constructed at the same time as the *Limes* proper. Evidently these were meant for watch-posts from which fire signals, such as the records of the *Limes* so often mention, could be sent on in advance to the detachments guarding the wall. Their position suggested that the deep-cut old river bed, now completely dry, near which these outpost towers were built, had then still received water from the Su-lo Ho, or had, perhaps, served as its main flood-bed. Now the river was confined to the narrow Toghrak-bulak bed, filling it so completely that we had to descend some distance before we could find a place shallow enough to cross. Its width there was over forty yards, the water being close on three feet deep, and flowing with a velocity of about two yards per second.

The following days were devoted to the exploration of the line of watch-stations which stretched far away to the south-west along the edge of the great marshy basin. The distances at which they were placed from each other, ranging from four to six miles, showed clearly that they were meant mainly as signalling-posts along a line and not for the purpose of warding off inroads. The objects which the wall was intended to serve along the front of the *Limes* was here secured by the impassable nature of the marshes westwards. Yet even thus the links of the chain of posts could not have been kept so far apart, with the consequent saving in trouble and cost, had not the configuration of the ground offered ideal positions all along for conspicuous signalling-stations.

As a look at the inset map *A* shows, the bare gravel-covered plateau marking the foot of the glacis of the mountains here stretches out a succession of finger-like ridges of clay. These project into the wide marsh-filled

depression like promontories of a much-indented coast-line.
Rising with very steep faces to heights of 120 to 200 feet
above the intervening depressions and commanding extensive views, these ridges furnished excellent natural
bases for the towers, and the Chinese engineers did not
fail to make the most of them.   On this account it was
always easy for us to sight these towers from afar.   It was
curious to note, as the survey progressed to the south-west,
how much care they had taken to place their signalling
towers for a direct distance of more than twenty-four miles
in an almost straight line, as if they had fixed their positions
by sighting with a diopter!   But it would need a large-
scale map to discuss such details.

But, quite apart from the skill of this early military
engineering, there was enough of interest in certain physical
features of this forlorn region to reward attention.   As I
made my way slowly from tower to tower I found myself
skirting the coast-line of an ancient lake basin now partially
dried up.   While crossing in succession its bays and inlets,
all occupied by abundant Toghrak groves and reed-beds,
and then again the boldly sculptured clay ridges which
formed the headlands between (Figs. 180, 181), I could
not help noticing that the latter almost all ran in the same
direction from south-east to north-west.   Where the bays
were wider there could be seen within them strings of
isolated clay terraces exactly parallel to the ridges.   Elsewhere the latter had a continuation formed by similar clay
terraces projecting farther into the marshy basin and still
maintaining the same bearing.

The bays and intervening ridges clearly owed their
direction to the carving done by running water, which had
once descended from the foot of the distant mountains
and across that gravel glacis now so terribly dry.   This
became quite certain when, just below one of the ridges
crowned on its top, some 200 feet higher, by a conspicuous
watch-tower, I came upon a deep-cut dry river bed.   It
came from the south-east, and showed unmistakable signs
of having been washed by occasional floods at a relatively
recent period.   The banks were so steep that the camels
could not be got across without difficulty.   Elsewhere,

too, the Surveyor, in the course of his reconnaissance, came upon dry ravines cut by floods into the glacis. The springs which we found rising in marshy beds within the larger bays also supplied proof of such drainage.

But it was equally certain that in forming those curious strings of isolated clay terraces another powerful agent had been at work, wind erosion. Again and again I observed how the crest of the narrow but still continuous ridges was being gradually sapped and scooped by wind-cut trenches mainly starting from the north-east. It was, of course, the direction from which since the winter we had learnt to expect the most violent gales. The ridges, stretched more or less at right angles across the line of the prevailing winds, were thus bound to be gradually broken up into terraces by the cutting force of the wind and the grinding produced by the driven sand which it uses for its instrument. But as I looked at the towers and saw how relatively little their bases had suffered by erosion in the course of two thousand years, I could judge what countless ages were needed even for that powerful agent to carve out those terraces from the hard clay, and finally to plane them away altogether.

I had before me the clearest illustration of that interaction of water and wind erosion which must have produced the maze of detached clay terraces I had before encountered, both at the north-eastern end of the ancient Lop-nor lake bed, and again in the terminal basin of the Su-lo Ho, and around Khara-nor. In the light of the evidence here gathered I was able to understand better the powerful rôle which wind erosion had played in this region as a geological factor affecting surface formations. Its effects upon the work of man were marked with equal clearness. Again and again I noted, in the course of my surveys on the *Limes*, how relatively well preserved the wall often rose along those sections which lay parallel to the prevailing direction of the winds, while where the line had been drawn across and in any way barred the progress of dust and fine gravel, wind erosion had badly breached or practically effaced the rampart.

I had ample occasion to convince myself that the winds

which now blow over the desert with remarkable violence and persistence come mainly from the north-east and east. How often had Chiang and myself had reason to comment upon that terribly cutting wind which sweeps down the lower Su-lo Ho valley from the side of the Mongolian Gobi, and which, as he told me beforehand, Chinese travellers to and from Turkestan have learned to dread under the name of ' the wind of An-hsi ' ! The whole region seemed, indeed, a true home for Boreas and his sons. The extent and character of the damage which the wall has suffered in its various sections fully agreed with the evidence furnished, on a vastly larger material and chronological scale, by the jagged ridges and isolated terraces of this ancient lake shore.

This observation derives additional importance from the fact that the same prevailing winds make their effect felt even far away in the Tarim Basin, as I had ample occasion to observe in the climatic conditions and surface formations round Lop-nor. It is probable that many years will pass before that delectable region and the equally attractive desert tracts about Tun-huang are provided with their meteorological stations to supply exact data,—and to tax scientific devotion. But even without such data I may hazard the conjecture that a likely explanation for these prevailing winds is supplied by ' aspiration,' due to the higher temperatures which the atmosphere of the low-lying desert around and to the west of Lop-nor must generally attain as compared with the great barren plateaus of stone and gravel to the north of the Su-lo Ho depression.

For me there was something distinctly stimulating in the bigger physical features of this desert of gravel and marsh-land, and in the expanding horizon as we moved from tower to tower south-westwards. The great marshy basin with its glittering salt efflorescence looked at times as if it were still one big lake. On clear days—and of such we now had several—I thought I could distinguish high ridges of drift sand beyond it to the north-west, the easternmost offshoots of the Kum-tagh sands we had skirted from the Lop-nor side. From the southern edge of the basin the

bare gravel glacis was seen rising to the foot of an outer
chain of hills completely overrun by huge dunes and
presenting a truly formidable appearance.   This great
obstacle must have absolutely protected the end of the
Limes from being turned on the south.   Behind this at
times towered up a magnificent range of snowy mountains,
the watershed towards the north of the Tibetan plateaus
of Tsaidam.

The feeling of remoteness which the whole silent landscape breathed was evidently shared by the wild camels.
They were now sighted frequently, moving down to the
springs and the grazing in the bay-like depressions, or else
speeding away fleetly to their resting-places on the bare
gravel plateaus to seek protection from the myriads of
tormenting insects.   Smaller game seemed to do likewise.
Only we men had to stick to our ruins and camps close by
the spring-fed marshes, and suffered accordingly in spite
of big fires and all else we could do to ward off those pests.
Even the motoring veil I was now wearing day and night
failed to provide adequate protection.   The heat and glare,
too, had grown more and more trying.

I could scarcely wonder that under such conditions
the difficulty in retaining our somnolent labourers steadily
increased.   The vicinity of the caravan route had helped
somewhat to calm their apprehensions about being in the
desert.   Chiang's paternal kindness of treatment and my
constant care for keeping them well provisioned at my own
cost had also made some impression on these shifty, callous
fellows.   But now they evidently dreaded being led farther
and farther into the 'Great Gobi.'   What with the men
who for some ailment or other had to be invalided, and
others who took the opportunity to desert with them back
to the oasis, our column was now rapidly dwindling.
There was no track or other indication of this ground
having been frequented in recent times by herdsmen or
others, and this seemed to depress the remnant.   It was
useless to point out to them the cut stumps of trees we
found here and there on salt-encrusted soil amidst jungle
mostly dead.   For who might say how many centuries ago
this clearing was done?

On the evening of May 4th I arrived at a ridge tapering away as usual at its end into a line of isolated terraces. The fact that both the end of the ridge and the last outlying terrace were occupied by towers was bound to attract my attention. As the distance between them was only about two miles, the ruined tower to the east and within the line (T. VI. B) could not have been intended for a mere signalling-post. So the thought suggested itself of some controlling main station. The plentiful débris adjoining the tower seemed to indicate quarters somewhat larger than usual, and numerous refuse layers scattered over the gravel slopes near by furnished proof of prolonged occupation (Fig. 182).

The position, though not more than a hundred feet above the basin, seemed well chosen for a sort of *point d'appui* on this flank. It commanded a complete view of the southern and south-eastern shore of the lake basin, up to the foot of the hill chain covered with high dunes which was seen to come from the direction of Nan-hu and to bend round to the north-west. It was clear that, as any attack from the west and the Lop-nor route would have to keep between the shore of the marshy basin and the impassable high sands, the line of watch-posts thrown out almost to within sight of the latter and controlled from this station would effectively prevent the main *Limes* being outflanked by raiders.

That evening we made an experimental scraping of the gravel-strewn slope at a point where a few wooden posts protruded some twenty yards north of the tower, and soon brought to light about two-score inscribed Chinese tablets of the usual shape. Though many of them had their surface decayed through exposure, the find was encouraging. Next morning I sent Chiang back from camp to continue the search while I had to look after the sinking of a well. When I rejoined him an hour later I found him triumphantly guarding for me nearly a hundred fresh Chinese records on wood, almost all complete, and in spite of slight damage from moisture quite legible. It was a delightful surprise, and my satisfaction grew still further when I ascertained that the numerous dated pieces all ranged between 65 and 57 B.C. This fine haul all came from an area scarcely more than two to three feet square.

It was clear that a little office archive had been thrown down here on the rubbish-strewn slope; and it proved by no means yet exhausted. Clearing the thinner refuse stratum lower down on the slope until the hard gravel surface was reached, and subsequently excavating and sifting with care the refuse round the original find-place, we brought the total of inscribed pieces of wood to over three hundred. Of uninscribed slips and tablets where the writing had become effaced through exposure there were found over two hundred more. Fig. 183 shows the scene of this successful digging, and also how shallow the protecting cover of gravel and refuse was.

The rest of the rubbish heaps on the other slopes below the watch-tower, extensive as they were, added scarcely more than a dozen wooden records. But in the course of this search, which Chiang-ssŭ-yeh supervised with his unfailing zeal and patience, there came to light at one point a great mass of wooden 'shavings' covered with Chinese characters. As the writing was manifestly by the same hand, and the phrases constantly recurring, Chiang at once rightly concluded that these were chips from tablets which some officer or clerk, eager to improve his penmanship, had used again and again for writing exercises, planing them down with a knife each time to obtain a fresh surface. The material had been of the cheapest, roughly cut from tamarisk and Toghrak branches, which the jungle close at hand would furnish in plenty.

The number of accurately dated records had been so great at this station, and their range in time so restricted, that the assumption seemed fully justified of the ruined quarters built against the tower representing the state in which they were when last occupied about 57 B.C. So all constructive details about the rooms, plain as they were, presented points of interest. The plan reproduced in Fig. 184 will illustrate their arrangement, which differed in no essential from that elsewhere observed along the *Limes*. The thickness of the outer walls and the massive

wooden posts of the narrow entrance arranged to take
heavy bolts, plainly indicated that the need of defence had
been present to those who
first built the small post.

The remains of furniture
and equipment left behind
by the last occupants as of
no value showed the same
uniform simplicity befitting
a remote frontier. There
were curious carved handles
or hooks of wood, intended,
perhaps, as emblems or for
supporting stands of arms;
pieces of hard wood with
leather-lined grooves, which
seem to have belonged to
cross-bows or small cata-
pults; wooden tent-pegs
with rough design of a
human head on the top;
pieces of painted and
lacquered bowls in wood;
much-mended rags of silk
garments, and, more plenti-

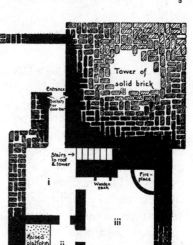

184. GROUND-PLAN OF ANCIENT
WATCH-STATION T.VI.B.

ful still, rope-soled shoes of coarse make (Figs. 173, 174).
Among the dozen or so of wooden records which had found
a safe refuge in a layer of refuse on the floor of an outer
room, there was one dated in the year 68 B.C. But after
all preceding experiences it scarcely needed this docu-
mentary evidence to convince me that, in a soil which had
seen extremely scanty rainfall for the last two thousand
years, and was far removed from any chance of interference
by human agency, nothing but wind erosion could prove
destructive even to the most perishable remains.

CHAPTER LXIII

RECORDS FROM AN ANCIENT WATCH-STATION

FASCINATING as it was to survey the ground along this most desolate of borders, and to study the actual remains of wall, towers, quarters, and arms, I found that it needed written records to restore a picture of the life once led here and of the organization which had planted this life in the desert. Chance could not have illustrated this better than by letting me light, at a post so modest in its extant structures, upon an abundance of wooden records thrown out from the commandant's office half a century before the birth of Christ. The fact that they all belong to practically the same period, and come from a station which lay off the main route and could not claim special importance, makes them all the more useful as typical evidence of the military administration then prevailing among the troops echeloned along the border. To M. Chavannes' critical acumen and unsurpassed powers of scholarly work I am indebted for full translations and notes of all documents found along the *Limes* that are still decipherable. Availing myself of the fruits of his labours I propose to give a brief summary of the chief topics of antiquarian interest which the records of this station illustrate, and to supplement them where desirable by general information gleaned from the rest of the documents.

From the first I had felt justified by Chiang's first rapid examination to hope that the records recovered would give us details as to the strength, distribution, and life of the troops guarding the border; their commissariat, equipment, and the like. This hope has been fully realized. In the introduction to his forthcoming volume

M. Chavannes shows that the troops on the border were composed of regular companies or 'tui,' organized under imperial edict and permanently attached to particular sections.   Now a large number of records found at the station T. VI. B mention the 'Ling-hu' (or 'barbarian-suppressing') company in such a way as to leave no doubt about its having garrisoned that station and had its head-quarters there.   Altogether some twenty companies are thus named in the records from the various stations, and in most cases it is still possible to determine the sections of the line which they guarded.   Curiously enough, a record found at T. VI. B distinctly quotes an imperial edict concerning the raising of the Ling-hu company and two others which seem to have been located near by, and directs the posting of the edict " in a place suited for general information."

Each company had a commandant who is frequently named as the recipient of orders sent from headquarters, and his station is always referred to as a 'T'ing.'   One of the documents specifies 145 soldiers as attached to this particular station, and M. Chavannes assumes this to have been the approximate number for each company. Under the company commandant the documents constantly mention the officers in charge of the watch-towers ('hou-chang') and the assistant attached to each of them.   To the soldiers placed under them, of whose number we are not exactly informed, but who must have been posted by reliefs, fell the duties of transmitting the fire signals, of patrolling the line, and furnishing the fatigue parties for collecting fuel, supplies, etc., to which our records so often refer.   Just as small groups of watch-towers were garrisoned by individual companies, so the latter formed sections of the ' barrier,' as the *Limes* is always spoken of, under superior officers.   Over the westernmost portion of the *Limes* control was exercised by 'the military commandant of the Jade Gate or Yü-mên,' who in turn depended, directly or indirectly, on the governor of the Tun-huang command.

In the files recovered from the office of the Ling-hu company we have ample illustration of the administrative routine which kept these links of the border hierarchy occupied. There are notifications of new appointments to sectional command or to charge of neighbouring companies; injunctions for the strict observance of previous regulations concerning the men, animals, and cars which passed through the 'barrier,' sometimes with the mention of specific dates, suggesting arrangements for convoys such as are in use, *e.g.* for caravan traffic through that 'Gate of India,' the Khyber Pass; instructions for the circulation of orders. Chiefs of companies are summoned to headquarters for discussion of particular questions, or detailed for the supervision of the granary. We have reports of cases of illness, of grants of leave, and the like, and here and there what evidently must have been quasi-confidential statements of the conduct of particular officers and of accusations against them.

Inspection visits along the 'barrier' by superior officers, in one case by the governor of the Tun-huang command, are announced in advance. It was a sensible precaution, to obviate—for the time being—awkward deficiencies in men, such as we find acknowledged with much contrition in a record from another watch-station. The frequency with which orders are addressed to 'indigenous functionaries,' apparently also entrusted with duties in guarding the line, is of interest; for it agrees exactly with Chinese policy as still maintained in the employment of such local auxiliaries for the guarding of outlying border posts, *e.g.* on the Pamirs and among the Kirghiz of the Kunlun. Our knowledge of the actualities referred to in such orders would, no doubt, be much more complete, were it not that in many cases the letters, though exactly indicating the functions of the sender and addressee, also the date and the person carrying the order, leave it to the latter to explain verbally the details of the message. Considering the intricacies of Chinese writing and official style, and the difficulty of providing an adequate clerical establishment for all the small detached posts, this procedure had, no doubt, much to recommend itself to officers in a hurry and dealing with non-Chinese.

Amidst the mass of correspondence dealing with

incidents of administrative routine and the still more numerous records concerning the internal economy of individual detachments, it is of special interest to come upon a few documents which give us a glimpse of the political power creating and protecting this border. The question how such documents, emanating, it appears, from the imperial chancellerie, should have found their way to an outlying military post is not easily answered. But M. Chavannes' scholarly analysis makes it certain that one of the records from the rubbish heap of T. VI. B has preserved for us an imperial edict directing the establishment of a military colony. Unfortunately there is no date given, and the tablet is not complete. Though the colony is evidently to be created in the territory of Tun-huang, the execution of the imperial order is entrusted to the governor of Chiu-ch'üan, corresponding to the present Su-chou. This important centre after its occupation in 115 B.C. seems to have served, in fact, as the main base for the political influence which China under the Emperor Wu-ti (140-85 B.C.) pushed farther and farther westwards. Two thousand soldiers raised from the garrison of the Tun-huang command, and some more troops from Chiu-ch'üan, under a complete staff of officers and accompanied by native functionaries, " were to proceed to the locality to be occupied and to establish there an agricultural colony." The governor in person was charged with the duty of " examining the configuration of the ground and selecting a suitable position. Utilizing natural obstacles, a rampart was to be constructed in order to exercise control at a distance."

This document, with its first-hand record of a phase in Chinese expansion on these marches, is full of historical interest ; but we can neither fix its exact date nor determine the location of the new military ' colony.' The reference to ' natural obstacles,' as well as the find - place of the document would, of course, make us think of some locality along the fortified border line. The skill with which the old Chinese engineers utilized the natural defences offered here by lagoons and marshes has been emphasized already more than once. But there remains the plain fact to be faced, that the physical conditions preclude all idea of agricultural occupation having been possible on this line during the Han period. Neither the marshy depressions which must have been, if anything, more extensive then than now, nor the absolutely bare gravel plateaus, well removed from all possibility of irrigation, could have furnished the fields needed for an 'agricultural colony.'

If the imperial edict really refers to the occupation of some part of the *Limes*, as we have now traced it west of Tun-huang, the only explanation would be that land for maintaining those troops might have been secured by an extension of the extant oasis and its produce allotted for the maintenance of the detachments by the wall. It is true that the records more than once refer to a 'delimitation' or clearing of 'celestial fields' as among the *corvée* duties imposed on the men of the stations. But in view of the local conditions it seems far safer to refer this expression to the clearing away of reed-beds and jungle, which must have seriously interfered with the safe watching of the border, than to the breaking up of desert soil for tillage, which had no chance without irrigation. I may mention here in passing that two more tablets from the same rubbish heap have proved to contain imperial decisions. The points on which they were issued cannot be made out with certainty; but the style of writing and expression used in conveying the Emperor's approval strictly accords with the formulas attested for the clerical etiquette of the period.

It is easy to understand that the records from the office of a small local commandant should yield more details about the soldiers he controlled, their condition of life and their duties, than about the policy and organization which kept them employed in guarding this route through the desert. It is of considerable interest that the records, where they name individual soldiers as recipients of articles of equipment, or otherwise, generally indicate with accuracy their origin, stating the canton, sub-prefecture, and province from which they had come. We are thus able to ascertain that the majority of these 'garrison soldiers,' to use their specific designation, were drawn from the distant provinces of Shan-hsi and Ho-nan, with a sprinkling of men from Kan-su, Ssŭ-ch'uan, and Tun-huang itself.

Most of the men must have served on foot; but horsemen, too, are referred to as well as mounted messengers. Numerous receipts and issue-warrants show that each soldier was entitled to about six-tenths of a bushel of corn *per diem*. In addition, he received pay calculated according to length of service. An elaborate system of reckoning was used to establish the total duration of the period for which pay could be claimed, with reductions for 'short months' of the luni-solar calendar, but also making allowance for the rule that two days of service on the border were to be counted as three, a significant indication of the hardships of service on such ground. In the case of a petty officer the daily rate of pay is stated in silver. A commissariat record at a certain station mentions provision for the feeding of watch-dogs, and proves that dogs were officially recognized as forming part of the regular establishment.

Numerous inventories show that the arms supplied to common soldiers by the Administration consisted of sword, cross-bow, and shield. In regard to the cross-bow care is usually taken to indicate its effective strength by stating the weight required to bend it. Thus cross-bows from three to six 'shih' are distinguished, a 'shih' being equivalent to 120 Chinese pounds. The greatly varying weight of the arrow-heads actually found by us bears out these distinctions as to the size and power of the cross-bows from which they were intended to be shot. When the strength had by age fallen below the nominal standard the fact was duly recorded. The regulation issue of arrows per man was 150, two kinds being mentioned, both with bronze heads. Quivers were provided for keeping them. In the case of shields the inventories repeatedly mention the factory in Ho-nan which supplied them and the date of their manufacture. Defects in the arms appear invariably to be stated in the inventory or record of issue.

Besides arms, clothing was furnished to the men free of charge. The inventories repeatedly mention tunics and dresses in black linen, for which the price paid by the company commander is duly recorded. The mention of an 'undress costume' of white silk in one soldier's kit agrees curiously with the abundance of silk rags of varying texture which the refuse heaps of the border-stations have yielded. The inclusion of a tent in the same list may help to account for the fact that the accommodation still traceable at the ruined watch-stations would have been quite inadequate to give shelter to the whole number of the garrison we may reasonably assume to have been quartered there. The Government store lists often include reserve strings of silk and hemp for cross-bows; axes, hammers, and other implements; and here I may mention that a big hammer of wood for tent pitching, which we found in the débris of the station nearest to T. VI. B, was in such perfect condition and so useful that I could not resist my men taking it into daily use for its original purpose during the rest of my journey.

There can be no doubt that the main duty of the detachments echeloned along the *Limes* was to provide guards for the watch-towers who would give timely alarm by signals to the rest of the line in case of the approach of raiders. The numerous wooden slips which accurately register the time and other details of fire signals received, or else refer to arrangements made for lighting them, would alone suffice to prove that this means of optic telegraphy was in regular use along the border. But the abundant information from early Chinese texts collected by M. Chavannes shows that the system of fire signalling was known and practised along the frontiers of the Empire long before the time of the Hans. The distinction which those texts indicate between signal fires visible at night and smoke signals intended for use by day is distinctly mentioned in one of the records on wood. In another, neglect to transmit such a signal received from one side of the line by immediately lighting a fire in turn is acknowledged as a grievous delinquency.

We are not informed by our records as to any devices by which such fire signals could be varied to convey more definite news along the guarded line. But since later texts quoted by M. Chavannes refer to a method of

marking the relative strength of the attacking force by corresponding repetition of the fire signals, it is likely that
similar devices were practised in Han times.   We read
elsewhere that General Ma Chêng, when reorganizing the
defences of the northern border in 38-43 A.D., placed the
fire-signal stations ten Li or about two and a half miles
apart; and this accords remarkably with the average distances observed from tower to tower on the earlier Tun-
huang *Limes*, due allowance being made for the varying
configuration of the ground.

No doubt such a system of optic telegraphy was in-
sufficient to assure the rapid transmission of warnings at
all times or for the communication of important particulars.
Hence the need for mounted messengers repeatedly
mentioned in the records, who by relays of horses kept
ready at the stations could cover distances at great speed.
The presence of such mounts was in fact attested by the
plentiful horse-dung we found at each tower, however
confined the accommodation near it.   A piece of ancient
Chinese poetry which M. Chavannes translates, though
referring to a part of the border much farther east, gives
so graphic a picture of such a scene that I cannot refrain
from quoting it : " Every ten Li a horse starts ; every five
Li a whip is raised high ; a military order of the Protector-
General of the Trans-frontier regions has arrived with
news that the Huns were besieging Chiu-ch'üan [Su-chou];
but just then the snow-flakes were falling on the hills along
which the barrier stretches, and the signal fires could raise
no smoke."

To keep watch and guard by the towers and the wall,
or ' to mount the barrier ' as the ancient Chinese expression
has it, did not exhaust the duties of the men posted at
these stations.   Numerous wooden records tell us of the
varied fatigue labours demanded from them.   Men were
ordered out to work on the construction of defences, a task
which along this westernmost *Limes* must have included
the preparation of the fascines forming the main materials ;
to collect fuel for the signal fires, not an easy matter where
the towers happened to be miles away from the scrub-filled
depressions.   At several stations we have also reckonings

of men employed in making bricks at the rate of 70 or 150 *per diem*, perhaps according to their size ; in shifting and piling up bricks ; in plastering walls of quarters, the work performed being accurately estimated in square feet. A considerable amount of *corvée* seems to have been absorbed by the carriage of supplies and materials needed at the several posts. In such cases an elaborate calculation informs us of the number of days spent, the daily distances covered, and the weight carried by each man. No payments to such fatigue parties are ever mentioned ; but careful record was kept, evidently for the purpose of making the distribution of tasks equitable.

The humdrum life of these petty garrisons must at times have been disturbed by serious incidents and alarms. Though the records of the main find at T. VI. B cover only a relatively short period (65-57 B.C.), they supply us with evidence of this. In one document, unfortunately for the greater part effaced, we have a report about "a barbarian horseman having been seen riding towards a watch-station with drawn bow ; on a discharge from the cross-bows he retired." But a serious attack was evidently anticipated, since "the chariots and horsemen are directed to keep on guard," and "the men at the watch-towers to keep a sharp look-out for fire signals and to keep the border clear." Elsewhere we have an earlier event referred to "when raiders burned and sacked the quarters of a battalion, exterminating two hundred people."

That the guarded line was incidentally used to prevent the escape of deserters or others 'wanted' within the border is made clear by notices relating to such offenders, In fact, we know from plentiful Chinese texts down to T'ang times that to pass the 'barrier' outwards required special authorization. Of private letters, too, there is a fair sprinkling ; but we must regret that, with their brevity and the exuberant indulgence in polite phraseology which Chinese epistolary style enjoins, they yield little of antiquarian interest. Yet short and formal as they are, it is impossible not to detect between their lines an expression of that feeling of weary exile which prolonged stay on this barren and trying frontier must have engendered.

And, indeed, compared to these desert stations the most forlorn outposts on our Indian North-West Frontier, which have become by-words for discomfort, would present themselves in the light of a veritable paradise.

Under such conditions of life, we should scarcely be justified in looking out for any literary remains. Yet there is interesting evidence to show that study of some sort was not altogether neglected. There are fragments of texts dealing with divination. But more numerous and interesting are fragments of lexicographical texts, among them eight pieces, found at different stations, of a famous treatise, the *Chi-chiu-chang*, composed between 48 and 33 B.C. and widely used in primary schools during Han times. They are the oldest manuscripts so far known of any Chinese literary work, and as they include a well-preserved large tablet with the first chapter complete, and showing some textual variation, their critical importance is in M. Chavannes' opinion bound to attract attention among scholars in China. The frequent recurrence of these fragments at various stations is significant of the popularity then enjoyed by that school-book, but it also proves that there must have been plenty of men among the scattered garrisons eager to 'improve their education.' Characteristically enough, there is found also in one tablet a reference to the *Biographies of Eminent Women*, an ancient work which has always enjoyed renown as a moral text-book.

With these literary fragments, modest in themselves yet of historical interest, must be classed the abundant remains of elaborate calendars yielded by the main refuse deposit of the Ling-hu company's station (T. VI. B). Written on tablets of a special size, over fourteen inches long, they indicate the cyclical designations of particular days in the month for each of the twelve months of the year. M. Chavannes, by a careful comparison of these data with those recorded in Chinese chronological works, has been able to prove that the calendars to which these tablets belonged were issued for the years roughly corresponding to 63, 59, and 57 B.C. They were indispensable for the correct dating of official correspondence, accounts, etc., which issued from the local headquarters. Without going into technical intricacies of the complicated cyclical system of reckoning, it must suffice to mention that these calendars possess considerable importance as records which help to control, and in a few instances to rectify, the traditional chronology of the Han period.

Up to May 7th I was busy clearing the station the records of which have just been passed in rapid review, and exploring the last watch-towers traceable westwards. The one which lay about two miles from T. VI. B was remarkable for the ideal position it occupied on the flat top of a small and completely isolated clay terrace fully 150 feet high. The precipitous wall-like slopes made access to the ruined tower quite impossible except from the east, where a steep ravine descended, and even there it meant climbing. The terrace, only about eighty yards long and less than half that in width, suggested a huge natural keep. From its top I looked across the great basin westwards, all salt-encrusted marsh with here and there large open sheets of water, and felt as if I were surveying a great lake from the highest deck of a steamer.

Here, too, the remains of the guard's quarters yielded relics of interest. The most curious among them was a remarkably well preserved tablet, about sixteen inches long, bearing at the top four short lines in the unknown script resembling Aramaic which we had found weeks before in the paper documents from the tower T. XII. A. The tablet looked like the right half of a larger piece cut through on purpose like a tally. I was already inclined to connect this writing with Western Turkestan, and the place of discovery, so far away from the ancient trade route, made me wonder at the time whether possibly men from that region had found service among the auxiliaries of the Chinese on this border.

In another way it was a strange observation to find a quantity of perfectly fresh-looking horse-dung and green reeds cut into straw under the débris of the small room or passage immediately adjoining the once heavily barred entrance to the quarters. The space measured only about seven feet square, and could barely have allowed the

horse to turn round.   Such tight quarters recalling life
on board ship were the best illustration of the need of
shelter which this inclement climate imposed even for
animals.

What with the heat and glare, the constant irritation
inflicted by the clouds of mosquitoes and other insects,
and the saltiness of the water, we were all suffering acutely
from the amenities of this desert climate in spring.   Little
wonder that the task of keeping our Chinese labourers
at work, all opium-smokers and of deep-rooted *vis inertiae*,
had grown more and more difficult even for the unfailing
tact and good-nature of my Chinese helpmate, Chiang-ssŭ-
yeh.   At last by May 8th, when supplies were beginning
to run low, owing to a fresh convoy having failed to reach
us, I was obliged to let most of them depart.   But by that
time the exploration of the extreme end of the *Limes* had
been completed.

The Surveyor had rejoined me three days earlier from
survey work about Khara-nor, and I had despatched him
with Naik Ram Singh and other mounted men to the
south-east, to reconnoitre the ground there, and if possible
push across the sand-covered hill range to the route leading
west of Nan-hu.   There or at So-mo-to, a little hamlet
nearer to the foot of the mountains, fodder would become
available for the ponies.   But by the evening of May 8th
Rai Ram Singh returned, after trying marches across the
barren waste, having been effectively baffled when nearing
the great sandy range by closely packed dunes which the
ponies could not surmount at this season.   I was glad he
gave up the attempt in time and brought back ponies and
men in safety.

I was not altogether sorry to find myself thus obliged
to make my way back to Tun-huang once more along the
Limes.   There were a number of smaller ruined stations
previously sighted eastwards remaining to be explored.
But though interesting finds of records on wood, rags of
patterned silk, etc., rewarded our search, I need not stop
now to describe it.   Nor can I do more than allude
here to what I was able to observe about the river
we discovered flowing out of Lake Khara-nor, and about

the natural barrage which accounts for the formation of the latter.

Already I had sent off in advance to Tun-huang my Indians and every man who could not be put to digging. After days made very trying by torrid heat and violent gales in turn, I was at last free to follow them with a good conscience. It was, indeed, high time to return to the oasis. The springs upon which we depended had always to be searched for by the marsh edge, and then wherever we camped the air was thick with mosquitoes and the ground swarmed with creatures equally bloodthirsty. So it was not without a feeling of physical relief that, on the evening of May 14th, I saw Lake Khara-nor disappearing behind me like a big sheet of chrysoprase colour, with the opposite shore merged in haze. A little earlier that day I had picked on marshy ground by the roadside my first flower of the season, a specimen of that hardy small iris-like plant which I knew and loved so well from the river banks of Kashmir. It gave welcome assurance that there were still pleasures left for the eye even in this dreary region.

Next day a long hot ride, diversified only by mirages playing over the glittering gravel waste, and with the temperature ranging somewhere about 150 degrees Fahrenheit in the sun, brought me back to the oasis. I shall never forget the delight of the first short rest I took on its very edge under fine shady elms, with a field before me where the blue of wild irises mingled in profusion with the bright green of young corn. How beautiful it all looked to my parched dust-filled eyes! Then I thought of what summer, when it came in full earnest, would be like by the desert border, and felt doubly elated in my heart at all the antiquarian spoil I was carrying back from its long-forgotten ruins.

That evening my little tent stood once more in the familiar old orchard of Tun-huang, with peach and pear trees close by to sprinkle it with their fresh blossoms.

CHAPTER LXIV

I HAD scarcely returned to the shelter of Tun-huang from the fascinations and trials of the ancient desert border when my eyes began to turn eagerly towards the cave temples of the 'Thousand Buddhas' at the foot of the barren dune-covered hills to the south-east. It was the thought of their sculptures and frescoes which had first drawn me to this region. But since my visit to the site in March, and the information then gathered about the great collection of ancient manuscripts discovered in one of the temples, the antiquarian attraction of the sacred caves had, of course, vastly increased. Eager as I was to commence operations at once, I had to contain myself in patience.

Just after my return to Tun-huang the annual pilgrimage to the shrines commenced, and it did not need the polite hints of my Amban friends to convince me that this was not the best time for a move to the site. The great fête, a sort of religious fair, was said to have drawn thither fully ten thousand of the pious Tun-huang people, and from the endless string of carts I saw a few days later returning laden with peasants and their gaily decked women-folk, this estimate of the popular concourse seemed scarcely exaggerated. I knew enough of Indian Tirthas to realize that such an occasion was better for studying modern humanity than for searching out things of the past.

So my start had to be postponed for five days. I found plenty to keep me busy in the meantime, what with adjusting accounts in that excruciatingly primitive currency of uncoined, and often far from pure, silver; with repairs to be effected in tents and kit, which those last weeks in the wind-swept desert had tried badly; and last but not least with a mail, for the despatch of which a petty trader's departure for Khotan by the route through the mountains offered a welcome opportunity.   Nor, to confess quite frankly, did I feel sorry for the short spell of physical ease which this delay gave me.   The oasis looked its best now, with its fields beautifully smooth and verdant like a well-kept lawn, and with little blue irises growing everywhere by the roadside.   The trees, too, mostly elms, were now refreshing to look at with their shady foliage; and the scattered homesteads which they sheltered seemed more than ever substantial in spite of the happy-go-lucky ways of these honest Cathayans.

If they were people hard to keep at work, especially in the desert, they were yet, when about their own fields and farms, jovial folk to talk to and wonderfully well mannered. Wang Ta-lao-ye, the learned magistrate, who had greeted my safe return and my rich harvest of ancient documents with something akin to enthusiasm, assured me that the people of Tun-huang were getting to like my ways, how-ever strange they had seemed at first.   Curiously enough, our queer set of slum-dwelling coolies proved mainly responsible for this change.   Though they had given much trouble by their hopeless indolence and their constant desire to desert, once safely returned from the wilds they appeared to have done their best to give us a good name, by stories about paternal care in administering rewards and medicine; about rations unfailingly provided and generously ignored in accounts, and the like.   Of course, I knew well that most of this unhoped-for credit had been earned through Chiang-ssŭ-yeh's kind-hearted care and inexhaustible patience with the humblest.

Never did I feel so strongly the old-world charm of this sleepy frontier of true Cathay as when I retired to the famous sanctuary of the 'Crescent Lake' for a day's peaceful writing.   It lay hidden away amidst high sands beyond the southern edge of the oasis and about three miles from the town.   For a desert wanderer there could be no more appropriate place of rest, I thought, than this delightful little pilgrimage place enclosed all round by sand-ridges rising to over 250 feet in height.   There was the limpid little lake, of crescent shape and about a quarter of a mile long, which has given to the locality its name and its sanctity.   Such delicious springs issuing between dunes of huge size and ever safe from being smothered by them, would have been worshipped in India as the residence of some great ' Naga' or spring deity.   No doubt, more than one Indian Buddhist passing through Tun-huang to China must have felt strangely at home here.

Near the eastern point of the crescent, where the lake has its outflow, there was room for small meadows where our ponies revelled in juicy grass such as they had never before tasted.   The southern shore of the lake was occupied by a number of picturesque modern temples, rising on terraces from the water's edge and decorated with a queer medley of Buddhist and Taoist statues and frescoes (Fig. 185).   Just in front of them and across the lake rose the famous resounding sand-hill, often mentioned in old Chinese records, about which the curious may read learned notes in Sir Henry Yule's translation of Ser Marco's book, where it deals with ' the Province of Tangut.'

I had ridden out to this secluded spot to enjoy undisturbed work ' in Purdah,' as our Anglo-Indian phrase runs. But Chiang, my only companion, though he had brought out work too, could not forgo the temptation of climbing to the top of the huge dune in his dainty velvet boots, just to make the sand slide down from there and hear the ' miraculous rumbling' it produced.   It was quite in keeping with his usual keenness to get at ' real truths.' We all duly heard the faint sound like that of distant carts rumbling, and Chiang felt elated to put it down in his Journal.

There was no other noise to disturb me all day.   In spite of its popular favour as attested by votive inscriptions in plenty, the whole place was deserted for the sake of the ' Thousand Buddhas'' fête-day.   Only one discreet figure moved about, a quaint, good-natured old priest, who remembered gratefully the little present I had left when paying my first visit here in March.   As I sat writing in the shady spacious hall, and watched him coming from time to time to have a good look at me, and then again retreating with the most silent of footsteps, it seemed as if familiar priestly figures from Indian shrines and tombs were trying to call me back to scenes and times of old.

When we sat down together in the evening to share tea and a simple repast *al fresco*, I told Chiang how grateful I felt to have spared this day of peaceful seclusion from the work awaiting us at the 'Thousand Buddhas.' He, too, had greatly enjoyed this outing; but full of mundane humour and keenly alive to any piece of sacred super-stition or folklore, he then gave an additional reason to justify the delay. He had picked up the story, that invariably after the annual fête the gods and local genii of Ch'ien-fo-tung sent a violent dust-storm to clean the sacred place of the refuse left behind after the multitude's pious picnic. So it would be better to wait until the divine sweeping was done. Considering the gales which rarely cease blowing down the Su-lo Ho valley for more than a couple of days at a time, one could readily take it for granted that the popular expectation would not be belied.

So it came about that when on May 21st I marched off to the sacred caves, we moved in a dust haze left behind by a storm of the previous night. Luckily these gales, sweeping westwards from An-hsi and down the desert ranges of the Pei-shan, have been at work with such constancy since early ages that there is comparatively little fine sand left for them to play with. So what in Khotan would have meant a choking Buran atmosphere was here only a pleasant protection against the heat of the sun. For, of course, *more Sinico*, we had to wait until nearly mid-day before carts were brought up and despatched with our heavy baggage. The two or three miles of ground we traversed to the edge of the oasis looked delightfully green, with young corn covering the big fields, and wild irises of bright blue still hugging in plenty the sides of the deep sunk roads. The cultivators seemed to find it hard to return to humdrum labour after their outing, and in front of most of the homesteads the women sat about in happy idleness still

185. TEMPLE COURT AT 'CRESCENT LAKE,' TUN-HUANG.

186. CLIFFS WITH MAIN CAVE-TEMPLES OF 'THOUSAND BUDDHAS' SITE, SEEN FROM WEST.

wearing their bright holiday dresses. I could never look at the poor crippled feet of these peasant women without a feeling of amazement at the power of fashion which here bows into cruel subjection even the humblest folk. What their well-to-do sisters in town may more easily forget must be a constant hindrance to these women of the country-side. It needs the iron grip of an ancient civilization to assure obedience to such conventions of self-inflicted torture.

Once beyond the edge of the oasis there was no trace of life stirring on the broad track which skirts the grey gravel waste at the foot of the sombre hill range, though thousands had passed here so recently. It remained the same when we turned into that strangely impressive desert valley and approached the point where the sombre conglomerate cliffs begin to be honeycombed with the gaping mouths of cave-temples big and small (Fig. 158). Long ages ago the little stream had carved out the valley, when there was still moisture to clothe these forbiddingly barren hills; but now it was dying away just here by evaporation on the thirsty rubble-filled bed. There was indeed gratifying shade beyond, where the narrow fringe of irrigated ground masked with its elms and poplars the approach to the main temple caves (Fig. 186). But otherwise the scene was not changed since my first visit in March, and I soon felt assured that the sacred site had once more resumed its air of utter desolation and silence.

There were special reasons for me to appreciate this assurance. The months passed since my arrival had provided abundant proof of the zeal with which the good people of Tun-huang remained attached through all vicissitudes to such forms of worship as represent Buddhism in the queer medley of Chinese popular religion. It scarcely needed the experience of the great annual fair just past to make it clear to me that the cave-temples, notwithstanding all apparent decay, were still real places of worship 'in being.' I knew well, therefore, that my archaeological activity at them, as far as frescoes and sculptures were concerned, would, by every consideration of prudence, have to be confined to the study of the art relics by means of photography, drawing of plans, etc., in short, to such work as could not reasonably arouse popular resentment with all its eventual risks.

Yet it was useless to disguise the fact from myself : what had kept my heart buoyant for months, and was now drawing me back with the strength of a hidden magnet, were hopes of another and more substantial kind.   Their goal was that great hidden deposit of ancient manuscripts which a Taoist monk had accidentally discovered about two years earlier while restoring one of the temples.   I knew that the deposit was still jealously guarded in the walled-up side chapel where it had been originally discovered, and that there were good reasons for caution in the first endeavours to secure access to it.   What my sagacious secretary had gathered of the character and ways of its guardian was a warning to me to feel my way with prudence and studied slowness.   It was enough that Chiang had induced Wang Tao-shih, the priest, who had come upon the hidden deposit, to await my arrival instead of starting on one of his usual tours in the district to sell blessings and charms, and to collect outstanding temple subscriptions.

I was glad that very first evening to find good quarters for all my people, as well as for the heavy baggage which had been brought up from its former place of storage at Tun-huang.   Fortunately the only two dwellings which Ch'ien-fo-tung boasts of, apart from its caves, were unoccupied, except for a fat jovial Tibetan Lama who had sought shelter here after long wanderings among the Mongols of the mountains (Fig. 190).   In one of the courts my Indians found rooms to spread themselves in, and the Naik a convenient place to turn into a dark-room.   In the other my Muhammadan followers secured shelter under half-ruined roofs of outhouses, while a hall, still possessed of a door and trellised windows, was reserved as a safe and discreet place of deposit for my collection of antiques—and its eagerly-hoped-for additions.

Better still, the narrow strip of cultivation extending in front of the caves for about half a mile (Fig. 186) offered just one little plot, grass-covered, where my tent could be pitched under the shade of some fruit trees.   My Mandarin friends

had insisted upon my taking along a petty officer and some
soldiers of the Tun-huang levy corps.   For them and the
Ssŭ-yeh there was ample room in the big verandahs and
halls built in front of the large caves just opposite our
camping-place.   Chiang himself had a delightfully cool
room at the very feet of a colossal seated Buddha reaching
through three stories, and with his innate sense of neatness promptly turned it into quite a cosy den with his
camp rugs.   Later on, when it got hotter, I myself used
the anteroom of another restored grotto close by for a
' Daftar.'   After what we had gone through during the
desert winter and spring we had all reason to feel ourselves in clover, in spite of the somewhat salt water of
the stream, which the Surveyor grumbled at much and
accused of reviving his rheumatism.

Next morning I started what was to be ostensibly the
main object of my stay at the site, the survey of the
principal grottoes, and the photographing of the more
notable frescoes.   Purposely I avoided any long interview
with the Tao-shih, who had come to offer me welcome at
what for the most of the year he might well regard his
domain.   He looked a very queer person, extremely
shy and nervous, with an occasional expression of cunning
which was far from encouraging (Fig. 187).   It was clear
from the first that he would be a difficult person to handle.

But when later on I had been photographing in one of
the ruined temple grottoes near the great shrine restored
by him, where the manuscripts had been discovered, I
could not forgo a glance at the entrance passage from
which their place of deposit was approached.   On my
former visit I had found the narrow opening of the recess,
locked with a rough wooden door; but now to my dismay
it was completely walled up with brickwork.   Was this
a precaution to prevent the inquisitive barbarian from
gaining even a glimpse of the manuscript treasures hidden
within?   I thought of the similar device by which the Jain
monks of Jesalmir, in their temple vault, had once
attempted to keep Professor Bühler from access to their
storehouse of ancient texts, and mentally prepared myself
for a long and arduous siege.

166 THE 'THOUSAND BUDDHAS' CH. LXIV

The first task was to assure that I should be allowed to see the whole of the manuscripts, and in their original place of deposit. Only thus could I hope to ascertain the true character and approximate date of the collection which had lain hidden behind the passage wall. In order to effect this Chiang had been despatched in the morning to another restored cave-temple where the priest had his quarters, and proceeded to sound him in confidential fashion about the facilities which were to be given. It proved a very protracted affair. Backed up by the promise of a liberal donation for the main shrine, the Ssŭ-yeh's tactful diplomacy seemed at first to make better headway than I had ventured to hope for. The saintly guardian of the reputed treasure explained that the walling up of the door was intended for a precaution against the curiosity of the pilgrims who had recently flocked to the site in their thousands. But evidently wary and of a suspicious mind, he would not yet allow himself to be coaxed into any promise about showing the collection to us as a whole. All that he would agree to, with various meticulous reservations, was to let me see eventually such specimens of the collection as he might conveniently lay his hands on. When Chiang, in his zeal momentarily forgetting the dictates of diplomatic reticence, was cautiously hinting at the possibility of my wishing, perhaps, to acquire 'for future study' one or other of those specimens, the Tao-shih showed such perturbation, prompted equally, it seemed, by scruples of a religious sort and fear of popular resentment, that my sharp-witted secretary thought it best to drop the subject for a time.

But after hours of such diplomatic wrangling he did not leave the priest's smoke-filled chapel and kitchen combined without having elicited an important piece of information. Statements heard at Tun-huang seemed to indicate that the great find of manuscripts had been reported at the time to the Tao-t'ai at Su-chou and thence to the Viceroy of Kan-su. Expression had been given also to a belief, of which we had no means of testing the foundation, that the latter had given orders for the transmission of specimens and for the safe keeping of the whole collection. If such

187. WANG TAO-SHIH, TAOIST PRIEST AT 'THOUSAND BUDDHAS' SITE,
TUN-HUANG.

188. CELLA AND PORCH OF WANG TAO-SHIH'S CAVE-TEMPLE, 'THOUSAND BUDDHAS' SITE, TUN-HUANG.

On extreme right the locked door leading to the rock-cut chapel, previously walled up, where the hidden library of MSS. was discovered. In foreground MS. bundles taken out for examination. The images on platform of cella are modern.

injunctions had really been issued and, perhaps, an official inventory taken, things would necessarily, from our point of view, become far more complicated.

Fortunately Chiang's apprehensions on this score were dispelled by what the priest, turning talkative at times like many nervous people, let drop in conversation.   A few rolls of Chinese texts, apparently Buddhist, had, indeed, been sent to the Viceregal Ya-mên at Lan-chou.   But their contents had not been made out there, or else they had failed to attract any interest.   Hence officialdom had rested satisfied with the rough statement that the whole of the manuscripts would make up about seven cartloads, and evidently dismayed at the cost of transport, or even of close examination, had left the whole undisturbed in charge of the Tao-shih as guardian of the temple.

But apart from this piece of information, the gist of Chiang-ssŭ-yeh's long report seemed far from justifying great hopes.   In spite of the optimistic tinge which Chiang's ever-cheerful disposition was apt to impart to his observations, there was much reason to fear that the priest's peculiar frame of mind would prove a serious obstacle.   To rely on the temptation of money alone as a means of overcoming his scruples was manifestly useless.   So I thought it best to study his case in personal contact.   Accompanied by Chiang I proceeded in the afternoon to pay my formal call to the Tao-shih, and asked to be shown over his restored cave-temple.   It was the pride and the mainstay of his Tun-huang existence, and my request was fulfilled with alacrity.   As he took me through the lofty antechapel with its substantial woodwork, all new and lavishly gilt and painted, and through the high passage or porch giving access and light to the main cella, I could not help glancing to the right where an ugly patch of unplastered brickwork then still masked the door of the hidden chapel (Fig. 188). This was not the time to ask questions of my pious guide as to what was being guarded in that mysterious recess, but rather to display my interest in what his zeal had accomplished in the clearing of the cella and its sacred adornment.

The restoration had been only too thorough.   In the

middle of the large cella, some forty-six feet square, there rose on a horseshoe-shaped dais, ancient but replastered, a collection of brand-new clay images of colossal size, more hideous, I thought, than any I had seen in these caves. The seated Buddha in the centre, and the disciples, saints, and Guardians of the Regions symmetrically grouped on his sides, showed only too plainly how low sculptural art had sunk in Tun-huang. But neither for this nor for the painful contrast these statues presented to the tasteful and remarkably well preserved fresco decoration on the walls and ceiling of the cella could the worthy Tao-shih reasonably be held responsible. His devotion to this shrine and to the task of religious merit which he had set himself in restoring it, was unmistakably genuine. As a poor, shiftless mendicant he had come from his native province of Shan-hsi some eight years before my visit, settled down at the ruined temple caves, and then set about restoring this one to what he conceived to have been its original glory.

The mouth of the passage was then blocked by drift sand from the silt deposits of the stream, and the original antechapel had completely decayed. When I thought of all the efforts, the perseverance, and the enthusiasm it must have cost this humble priest from afar to beg the money needed for the clearing out of the sand and the substantial reconstructions,—besides the antechapel there were several stories of temple halls built above in solid hard brick and timber, right to the top of the cliff, —I could not help feeling something akin to respect for the queer little figure by my side. It was clear from the way in which he lived with his two humble acolytes, and from all that Chiang had heard about him at Tun-huang, that he spent next to nothing on his person or private interests. Yet his list of charitable subscriptions and his accounts, proudly produced later on to Chiang-ssŭ-yeh, showed quite a respectable total, laboriously collected in the course of these years and spent upon these labours of piety.

It had not taken Chiang long to fathom Wang Tao-shih's profound ignorance of all that constitutes Chinese learning, and the very limited extent of his knowledge in general. So I knew that it would be futile to talk to him about my archaeological interests, about the need of first-hand materials for Chinese historical and antiquarian studies, and the like, as I was accustomed to do on meeting educated Chinese officials, ever ready to be interested in such topics. But the presence of this quaint priest, with his curious mixture of pious zeal, naïve ignorance, and astute tenacity of purpose, forcibly called to my mind those early Buddhist pilgrims from China who, simple in mind but strong in faith and—superstition, once made their way to India in the face of formidable difficulties.

More than once before, my well-known attachment to the memory of Hsüan-tsang, the greatest of those pilgrims, had been helpful in securing me a sympathetic hearing both among the learned and the simple. Wang Tao-shih, too, had probably heard about it. So surrounded by these tokens of lingering Buddhist worship, genuine though distorted, I thought it appropriate to tell Wang Tao-shih, as well as my poor Chinese would permit, of my devotion to the saintly traveller ; how I had followed his footsteps from India for over ten thousand Li across inhospitable mountains and deserts ; how in the course of this pilgrimage I had traced to its present ruins, however inaccessible, many a sanctuary he had piously visited and described ; and so on.

I confess, it never cost me any effort to grow eloquent on the subject of my ' Chinese patron saint,' whose guidance had so often proved fruitful for my own work. But now it was made doubly easy by the gleam of lively interest which I caught in the Tao-shih's eyes, otherwise so shy and fitful. As Chiang, in reply to interjected questions, elaborated details and made the most of my familiarity with Hsüan-tsang's authentic records and the distant scenes of his travels, I could read the impression made in the Taoist priest's generally puzzling countenance. Very soon I felt sure that the Tao-shih, though poorly versed in and indifferent to things Buddhist, was quite as ardent an admirer in his own way of ' T'ang-sêng,' the great ' monk of the T'ang period,' as I am in another.

I had ocular proof of this when he took us outside into

the spacious newly built loggia in front of the temple, and showed us with pride how he had caused all its walls to be decorated by a local Tun-huang artist with a series of quaint but spirited frescoes representing characteristic scenes from the great pilgrim's adventures (Figs. 189, 190). They were those fantastic legends which have transformed Hsüan-tsang in popular belief throughout China into a sort of saintly Munchausen. It is true they are not to be found in the genuine memoirs and biography. But what did that little difference in our respective conceptions of the hero matter? Gladly I let my delightfully credulous cicerone expound in voluble talk the wonderful stories of travel which each fresco panel depicted. Here the holy pilgrim was seen snatched up to the clouds by a wicked demon and then restored again to his pious companions through the force of his prayer or magic. Two queer-looking figures—one horse-, one bull-headed—were represented as his constant attendants. Elsewhere he was shown forcing a ferocious dragon which had swallowed his horse to restore it again, and so on.

But the picture in which I displayed particular interest showed a theme curiously adapted to our own case, though it was not till later that I appealed again and again to the moral it pointed. There was T'ang-sêng standing on the bank of a violent torrent, and beside him his faithful steed laden with big bundles of manuscripts. To help in ferrying across such a precious burden a large turtle was seen swimming towards the pilgrim. Here was clearly a reference to the twenty pony-loads of sacred books and relics which the historical traveller managed to carry away safely from India. But would the pious guardian read this obvious lesson aright, and be willing to acquire spiritual merit by letting me take back to the old home of Buddhism some of the ancient manuscripts which chance had placed in his keeping? For the time being it seemed safer not to tackle that question. Yet when I took my leave of the Tao-shih I instinctively felt that a new and more reliable link was being established between us.

189. MODERN FRESCOES IN LOGGIA OF WANG TAO-SHIH'S
TEMPLE, REPRESENTING ADVENTURES OF HSÜAN-TSANG.

Wang Tao-shih standing on left.

190. TIBETAN MONK IN LOGGIA OF WANG TAO-SHIH'S TEMPLE,
'THOUSAND BUDDHAS' SITE.

CHAPTER LXV

FIRST OPENING OF THE HIDDEN CHAPEL

I LEFT the Ssŭ-yeh behind to make the most of the favourable impression produced, and to urge an early loan of the
promised manuscript specimens. But the priest had again
become nervous and postponed their delivery in a vague
way 'until later.' There was nothing for me but to wait.

All doubt, however, disappeared in the end. Late at
night Chiang groped his way to my tent in silent elation
with a bundle of Chinese rolls which Wang Tao-shih had
just brought him in secret, carefully hidden under his
flowing black robe, as the first of the promised 'specimens.'
The rolls looked unmistakably old as regards writing and
paper, and probably contained Buddhist canonical texts;
but Chiang needed time to make sure of their character.
Next morning he turned up by daybreak, and with a face
expressing both triumph and amazement, reported that these
fine rolls of paper contained Chinese versions of certain
'Sutras' from the Buddhist canon which the colophons
declared to have been brought from India and translated
by Hsüan-tsang himself. The strange chance which thus
caused us to be met at the very outset by the name of my
Chinese patron saint, and by what undoubtedly were early
copies of his labours as a sacred translator, struck both of
us as a most auspicious omen. Was it not 'T'ang-sêng'
himself, so Chiang declared, who at the opportune moment
had revealed the hiding-place of that manuscript hoard to
an ignorant priest in order to prepare for me, his admirer
and disciple from distant India, a fitting antiquarian reward
on the westernmost confines of China proper?

Of Hsüan-tsang's authorship, Wang Tao-shih in his

ignorance could not possibly have had any inkling when
he picked up that packet of 'specimens.' Chiang-ssŭ-yeh
realized at once that this discovery was bound to impress
the credulous priest as a special interposition on my behalf
of the great traveller of sacred memory. So he hastened
away to carry the news to the Tao-shih, and, backed up by
this visible evidence of support from the latter's own
cherished saint, to renew his pleading for free access to the
hidden manuscript store. The effect was most striking.
Before long Chiang returned to report that the portent
could be trusted to work its spell. Some hours later he
found the wall blocking the entrance to the recess of the
temple removed, and on its door being opened by the
priest, caught a glimpse of a room crammed full to the roof
with manuscript bundles. I had purposely kept away
from the Tao-shih's temple all the forenoon, but on getting
this news I could no longer restrain my impatience to see
the great hoard myself. The day was cloudless and hot,
and the 'soldiers' who had followed me about during the
morning with my cameras, were now taking their siesta in
sound sleep soothed by a good smoke of opium. So
accompanied only by Chiang I went to the temple.

I found the priest there evidently still combating his
scruples and nervous apprehensions. But under the influence of that quasi-divine hint he now summoned up
courage to open before me the rough door closing the
narrow entrance which led from the side of the broad front
passage into the rock-carved recess, on a level of about
four feet above the floor of the former. The sight of the
small room disclosed was one to make my eyes open wide.
Heaped up in layers, but without any order, there appeared
in the dim light of the priest's little lamp a solid mass of
manuscript bundles rising to a height of nearly ten feet,
and filling, as subsequent measurement showed, close on
500 cubic feet. The area left clear within the room was
just sufficient for two people to stand in. It was manifest
that in this 'black hole' no examination of the manuscripts
would be possible, and also that the digging out of all its
contents would cost a good deal of physical labour.

A suggestion to clear out all the bundles into the large

cella of the cave-temple, where they might have been
examined at ease, would have been premature; so much
oppressed at the time was Wang Tao-shih by fears of
losing his position—and patrons—by the rumours which
any casual observers might spread against him in the oasis.
So for the present I had to rest content with his offer to
take out a bundle or two at a time, and to let us look
rapidly through their contents in a less cramped part of the
precincts.   Fortunately the restorations carried out by him,
besides the fine loggia already mentioned, included a kind
of large antechapel, having on either side a small room
provided with a door and paper-covered windows.   So here
a convenient 'reading-room' was at hand for this strange
old library, where we were screened from any inquisitive
eyes, even if an occasional worshipper dropped in to
'kotow' before the huge and ugly Buddha statue now set
up in the temple.

While the Tao-shih was engaged in digging out a few
bundles, I closely examined the passage wall behind which
this great deposit of manuscripts had been hidden.   The
priest had told us that, when he first settled at the 'Thousand Buddhas' some eight years before, he found the
entrance to this cave-temple almost completely blocked
by drift sand.   Judging from the condition of other caves
near by and the relatively low level of this particular
temple, it is probable that this accumulation of drift sand
rose to ten feet or more at the entrance.   Keeping only
a few labourers at work from the proceeds of pious dona-
tions, at first coming driblet-like with lamentable slowness,
our Tao-shih had taken two or three years to lay bare
the whole of the broad passage, some forty feet deep.
When this task had been accomplished, and while engaged
in setting up new statues in place of the decayed old
stucco images occupying the dais of the cella, he had
noticed a small crack in the frescoed wall to the right of
the passage.   There appeared to be a recess behind the
plastered surface instead of the solid conglomerate from
which the cella and its approach are hewn; and on widening
the opening he discovered the small room with its deposit
such as I now saw it.

Walled into the west face of the room had been found a large slab of black marble covered with a long and neatly engraved Chinese inscription.   It had subsequently been removed and set up in a more accessible place on the left-hand wall of the passage.   This inscription records imperial eulogies of a Chinese pilgrim named Hung-pien, who had visited India, and after returning with relics and sacred texts had apparently settled at these shrines to devote his remaining years to translating and other pious labours. As it is dated in the year corresponding to A.D. 851, it was clear to me from the first that the deposit of the manuscripts must have taken place some time after the middle of the ninth century.

But until we could find dated records among the manuscripts themselves there was no other indication of the lower date limit than the style of the frescoes which covered the passage walls.   According to the Tao-shih's explicit assurance, borne out by the actual condition of the wall surface around the opening, mural painting had also covered the plaster in front of the latter.   These frescoes, representing over-life-size Bodhisattvas marching in procession with offerings, were very well painted in a style met with again in numerous caves, the mural decorations of which had undergone no modern restoration, and appeared to me decidedly old.   On various grounds it seemed improbable that they could be later than the period of the Sung dynasty, which immediately preceded the great Mongol conquest of the thirteenth century.

So there was evidence from the first to encourage my hopes that a search through this big hoard would reveal manuscripts of importance and interest.   But the very hugeness of the deposit was bound to give rise to misgivings.   Should we have time to eat our way through this mountain of ancient paper with any thoroughness? Would not the timorous priest, swayed by his worldly fears and possible spiritual scruples, be moved to close down his shell before I had been able to extract any of the pearls? There were reasons urging us to work with all possible energy and speed, and others rendering it advisable to display studied *insouciance* and calm assurance.   Somehow we managed to meet the conflicting requirements of the situation.   But, I confess, the strain and anxieties of the busy days which followed were great.

The first bundles which emerged from that 'black hole' consisted of thick rolls of paper about one foot high, evidently containing portions of canonical Buddhist texts in Chinese translations.   All were in excellent preservation and yet showed in paper, arrangement, and other details, unmistakable signs of great age.   The jointed strips of strongly made and remarkably tough and smooth yellowish paper, often ten yards or more long, were neatly rolled up, after the fashion of Greek papyri, over small sticks of hard wood sometimes having carved or inlaid end knobs (Fig. 191).   All showed signs of having been much read and handled ; often the protecting outer fold, with the silk tape which had served for tying up the roll, had got torn off.   Where these covering folds were intact it was easy for the Ssŭ-yeh to read off the title of the Sutra, the chapter number, etc.

Buddhist literature lay wholly outside the range of Chiang's studies, as indeed it is nowadays beyond the ken of almost all Chinese literati.   I myself, though familiar to some extent with Buddhist scriptures in their original Indian garb, laboured under a fatal disadvantage—my total ignorance of literary Chinese.   So what Chiang could make out of the titles was of no guidance to me.   But on one point his readings soon gave me assurance : the headings in the first bundles were all found to be different.   So my apprehension of discovering here that inane repetition of a few identical texts in which modern Buddhism in Tibet and elsewhere revels, gradually vanished.   I set the Ssŭ-yeh to work to prepare a rough list of titles ; but as by and by the devout guardian of these treasures took more courage and began to drag out load after load of manuscript bundles, all attempt even at the roughest cataloguing had to be abandoned.   It would have required a whole staff of learned scribes to deal properly with such a deluge.

Mixed up with the Chinese bundles there came to light Tibetan texts also written in roll form, though with clearly marked sections, as convenience of reading required in the case of a writing running in horizontal lines, not in vertical columns like Chinese. I could not doubt that they contained portions of the great canonical collections now known as the Tanjur and Kanjur. In the first rapid examination Chiang failed to discover colophons giving exact dates of the writing in any of the Chinese rolls, and owing to their length a complete unfolding would have required much time. So I had reason to feel doubly elated when, on the reverse of a Chinese roll, I first lighted upon a text written in that cursive form of Indian Brahmi script with which the finds of ancient Buddhist texts at sites of the Khotan region had rendered me familiar. Here was indisputable proof that the bulk of the manuscripts deposited went back to the time when Indian writing and some knowledge of Sanskrit still prevailed in Central-Asian Buddhism. With such evidence clearly showing the connection which once existed between these religious establishments and Buddhist learning as transplanted to the Tarim Basin, my hopes rose greatly for finds of direct importance to Indian and western research.

All the manuscripts seemed to be preserved exactly in the same condition they were in when deposited. Some of the bundles were carelessly fastened with only rough cords and without an outer cloth wrapper; but even this had failed to injure the paper. Nowhere could I trace the slightest effect of moisture. And, in fact, what better place for preserving such relics could be imagined than a chamber carved in the live rock of these terribly barren hills, and hermetically shut off from what moisture, if any, the atmosphere of this desert valley ever contained? Not in the driest soil could relics of a ruined site have so completely escaped injury as they had here in a carefully selected rock chamber where, hidden behind a brick wall and protected by accumulated drift sand, these masses of manuscripts had lain undisturbed for centuries.

How grateful I felt for the special protection thus afforded when, on opening a large packet wrapped in a sheet of stout coloured canvas, I found it full of paintings on fine gauze-like silk and on linen, ex-votos in all kinds

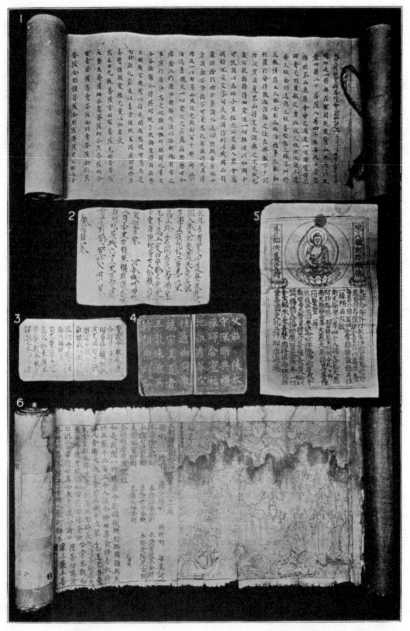

191. OLD CHINESE MANUSCRIPTS AND BLOCKPRINTS FROM WALLED-UP
TEMPLE LIBRARY OF 'THOUSAND BUDDHAS' SITE.

Scale, one-fifth.

1. Complete Buddhist manuscript roll, T'ang period. **2, 3.** Manuscripts of religious texts in book form.
4. Booklet made up of ink-rubbings from inscription. **5.** Block-printed sheet with Buddhist picture and prayer.
6. Roll of block-printed Buddhist text with frontispiece from wood-engraving, dated 864 A.D.

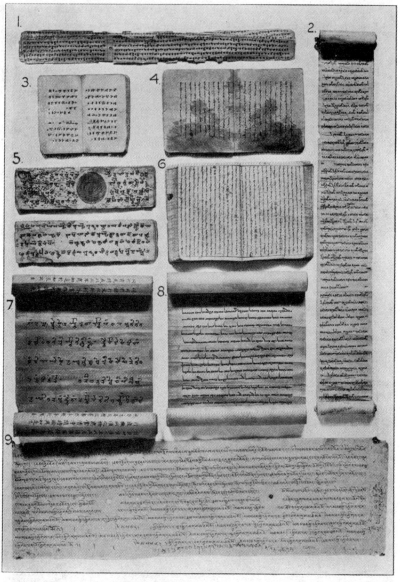

192. ANCIENT MANUSCRIPTS IN SANSKRIT, CENTRAL-ASIAN BRAHMI, SOGDIAN, MANICHAEAN-TURKISH, RUNIC TURKI, UIGUR, TIBETAN, FROM WALLED-UP TEMPLE LIBRARY, 'THOUSAND BUDDHAS,' TUN-HUANG.

Scale, one-seventh.

1. Sanskrit Prajna-paramita text on palm leaves. 2. Roll with Manichaean 'Confession of Sins' in early Turkish. 3. Book in Runic Turki. 4, 6. Uigur texts in book form. 5. Pothi in Central-Asian Brahmi script. 7. Text in cursive Central-Asian Brahmi written on reverse of Chinese MS. roll. 8. Roll with Sogdian text. 9. Leaf of Tibetan Buddhist Pothi.

of silk and brocade, with a mass of miscellaneous fragments of painted papers and cloth materials. Most of the paintings first found were narrow pieces from two to three feet in length, and proved by their floating streamers and the triangular tops provided with strings for fastening to have served as temple banners. These mountings made them look much more imposing when hung up. Many of them were in excellent condition, and all exactly as they had been deposited, after longer or shorter use.

The silk banners were usually found rolled up, and showed when unfurled beautifully painted figures of Buddhas and Bodhisattvas, almost Indian in style, or else scenes from Buddhist legend (Plates VI., VII.). There was no time then for any careful study. But of some external features I soon made sure. All the banners still retained, or originally had attached below, three or four long streamers of patterned or painted silk, which a lacquered or painted cross-piece of wood held in position at the bottom. From the triangular top, which was usually formed by a piece of brocade or painted silk edged with embroidery, there descended a broader streamer on either side. At the top and bottom of the oblong picture small 'strainers' of wood or bamboo helped to keep the banner in shape.

The silk used for these pictures was almost invariably a transparent gauze of remarkable fineness. As these banners floated in the air they would allow a good deal of light to pass through—an important point, since in order to be properly seen these paintings would have to be hung up across or near the porches through which alone the cellas of the temple caves would receive their lighting. For the same reason of transparency most of these banners appeared to have been painted on both sides. Some had undergone damage. This was the result, not of centuries of interment, but of use in the temples, as proved by the care with which rents had been repaired, or in a few cases the whole picture mounted on a backing of cloth or paper.

Whatever the technical advantages in the use of such a delicate material might have been, the attendant risks were evident when I came upon convolutes of silk paintings much larger in size, showing, as subsequently ascertained, dimensions up to six feet or more (Plate VIII.). Closely and often carelessly folded up at the time of their deposition, and much creased in consequence as they were, any attempt to open them out would have implied obvious risk of damage to the thin material which centuries of compression in the driest air had rendered terribly brittle. But by lifting a fold here and there I could see that the scenes represented were almost as elaborate as the fresco panels on the walls of the old grottoes. Greatly tempted as I was to search for votive inscriptions likely to contain dates, I had to leave the opening till later from fear of possible damage.

Nor was there time for any closer study, such as I should have loved to give there and then to these delicate, graceful paintings. My main care was how many of them I might hope to rescue from their dismal imprisonment and the risks attending their present guardian's careless handling. To my surprise and relief he evidently attached little value to these beautiful relics of pictorial art in the T'ang times. So I made bold to put aside rapidly 'for further inspection,' the best of the pictures on silk, linen, or paper I could lay my hands on, more than a dozen from the first bundle alone. I longed to carry away all its contents; for even among the fragments there were beautiful pieces, and every bit of silk would have its antiquarian and artistic value. But it would not have been wise to display too much *empressement*. So I restrained myself as well as I could, and put the rest away, with the firm resolve to return to the charge as soon as the ground was prepared for more extensive acquisitions.

To remains of this kind the priest seemed indifferent. The secret hope of diverting by their sacrifice my attention from the precious rolls of Chinese canonical texts or 'Ching' made him now more assiduously grope for and hand out bundles of what he evidently classed under the head of miscellaneous rubbish. I had every reason to be pleased with this benevolent intention; for in the very first large packet of this kind I discovered, mixed up with Chinese and Tibetan texts, a great heap of oblong paper leaves in the variety of Indian script known as Central-Asian Brahmi (Fig. 192).

They proved on arrangement to belong to half-a-dozen different manuscripts of the Pothi shape, some in Sanskrit, some in one or other of the 'unknown' languages used by Turkestan Buddhism. Several of these manuscripts were of large size, with leaves up to twenty-one inches in length, and some have since on arrangement proved to be complete. None of my previous finds in Brahmi script equalled them in this respect or in excellence of preservation. So that first day Chiang and myself worked on without a break until quite late, picking out sometimes stray leaves in Indian script even from regular bundles of Chinese or Tibetan rolls, or else Chinese rolls bearing on the reverse texts in a cursive form of Central-Asian Brahmi.

Flushed as I was with delight at these unhoped-for discoveries, I could not lose sight of the chief practical task, all-important for the time being. It was to keep our priest in a pliable mood, and to prevent his mind being overcome by the trepidations with which the chance of any intrusion and of consequent hostile rumours among his patrons would fill him. With the help of Chiang-ssŭ-yeh's genial persuasion, and what reassuring display I could make of my devotion to Buddhist lore in general and the memory of my patron saint in particular, we succeeded better than I had ventured to hope. I could see our honest Tao-shih's timorous look changing gradually to one of contentment at our appreciation of all this, to him valueless, lore. Though he visibly grew tired climbing over manuscript heaps and dragging out heavy bundles, it seemed as if he were becoming resigned to his fate, at least for a time.

When the growing darkness in the cave compelled us to stop further efforts for the day, a big bundle of properly packed manuscripts and painted fabrics lay on one side of our 'reading room' awaiting removal for what our diplomatic convention styled 'closer examination.' The great question was whether Wang Tao-shih would be willing to brave the risks of this removal, and subsequently to fall in with the true interpretation of our proceeding. It would

not have done to breathe to him unholy words of sale and
purchase; it was equally clear that any removal would
have to be effected in strictest secrecy.   So when we
stepped outside the temple there was nothing in our hands
or about our persons to arouse the slightest suspicion.

Then, tired as we all were, I took the occasion to
engage the priest in another long talk about our common
hero and patron saint, the great Hsüan-tsang.   What
better proof of his guidance and favour could I claim than
that I should have been allowed to behold such a wonderful hidden store of sacred relics belonging to his own times
and partly derived, perhaps, from his Indian wanderings,
within a cave-temple which so ardent an admirer of
'T'ang-sêng' had restored and was now guarding?   Again
I let the Tao-shih enlarge, as we stood in the loggia, upon
the extraordinary adventures of his great saint as depicted
in those cherished frescoes on its walls (Fig. 189).   The
panel which showed Hsüan-tsang returning with his animal
heavily laden with sacred manuscripts from India, was the
most effective apologue I could advance for my eager
interest in the relics the Tao-shih had discovered and was
yet keeping from daylight.

The priest in his more susceptible moods could not help
acknowledging that this fate of continued confinement in a
dark hole was not the purpose for which the great scholar-
saint had let him light upon these precious remains of
Buddhist lore, and that he himself was quite incompetent
to do justice to them by study or otherwise.   Was it not
evident, so Chiang pleaded with all the force of his soft
reasoning, that by allowing me, a faithful disciple of
Hsüan-tsang, to render accessible to Western students the
literary and other relics which a providential discovery had
placed so abundantly in his keeping, he would do an act of
real religious merit?   That this pious concession would
also be rewarded by an ample donation for the benefit of
the shrine he had laboured to restore to its old glory, was
a secondary consideration merely to be hinted at.

Whatever impression such and similar talks produced
on the mind of the good Tao-shih, constantly vacillating
between fears about his saintly reputation and a business-

like grasp of the advantages to be attained by accommo-
dating me in the matter of useless old things, the day
closed with a gratifying achievement.   In accordance with
his own advice, I had left the Ssŭ-yeh alone to tackle the
question of how to secure quietly the manuscripts and
paintings selected.   It was late at night when I heard
cautious footsteps.   It was Chiang who had come to make
sure that nobody was stirring about my tent.   A little later
he returned with a big bundle over his shoulders.   It contained everything I had picked out during the day's work.

The Tao-shih had summoned up courage to fall in with
my wishes, on the solemn condition that nobody besides us
three was to get the slightest inkling of what was being
transacted, and that as long as I kept on Chinese soil the
origin of these 'finds' was not to be revealed to any living
being.   He himself was afraid of being seen at night outside his temple precincts.   So the Ssŭ-yeh, zealous and
energetic as always, took it upon himself to be the sole
carrier.   For seven nights more he thus came to my tent,
when everybody had gone to sleep, with the same precautions, his slight figure panting under loads which grew
each time heavier, and ultimately required carriage by
instalments.   For hands accustomed only to wield pen and
paper it was a trying task, and never shall I forget the
good-natured ease and cheerful devotion with which it was
performed by that most willing of helpmates.

CHAPTER LXVI

A WALLED-UP LIBRARY AND ITS TREASURES

It would serve no useful purpose if I were to attempt to describe in detail how the search was continued day after day without remission, or to indicate in quasi-chronological order all the interesting finds with which this curious 'digging' was rewarded. From the first it was certain that the contents of the hidden chapel must have been deposited in great confusion, and that any indications the original position of the bundles might have afforded at the time of discovery, had been completely effaced when the recess was cleared out, as the Tao-shih admitted, to search for valuables, and again later on for the purpose of removing the big inscribed slab from its west wall into the passage outside. It was mere chance, too, what bundles the Tao-shih would hand us out.

Nor was that hurried search the time for appreciating properly the import of all that passed through my hands. The systematic study of the materials I was most eager to secure was bound to take years of specialist labour, and what this has so far revealed as regards the main classes of relics, I shall endeavour to sketch in a subsequent chapter. Here I must content myself with a rapid review of those discoveries which at the time struck me most and helped me to form conclusions as to the history of this whole *cache* of antiquarian treasures.

After the experience of the first day it was easy to recognize the special value of those bundles filled with miscellaneous texts, painted fabrics, ex-votos, papers of all sorts, which had evidently been stored away as no longer needed for use. By their irregular shape and fastening they could readily be distinguished from the uniform packets containing rolls of Buddhist texts in Chinese or Tibetan.   Fortunately their very irregularity had caused the Tao-shih to put them on the top when he built up the wall-like array of what I may call 'library bundles'; and the consequent ease with which they could be reached induced him now to bring them out in steady succession.

It was from those 'mixed' bundles chiefly that manuscripts and detached leaves in Indian script and of the traditional Pothi shape continued to emerge.   By far the most important among such finds was a remarkably well preserved Sanskrit manuscript on palm leaves, some seventy in number, and no less than twenty inches long (Fig. 192, 1). The small but beautifully clear writing closely covering these leaves showed palaeographical features which seemed to leave little doubt as to the manuscript going back to the third or fourth century A.D. at the latest.   This high age, not surpassed by any Sanskrit manuscript then known, made the text important, even though it has proved to be that of a work well known in the Northern Buddhist Canon. That the manuscript had been written in India itself was quite certain from its material.   But who was the pilgrim who had brought it to the very confines of China?

Like the manuscripts written in Indian script after the fashion of Pothis, so too the rolls with Indian Brahmi writing soon furnished a fine show-piece.   It was a gigantic roll of paper, over seventy feet long, and about one foot wide, entirely covered on its inner side with Brahmi writing in a fair upright hand of what scholars know as the Gupta type (Fig. 193).   A painting on the top of the outer side showed two cleverly drawn geese standing on lotuses and facing each other.   When hastily examining it in part, I could find only invocation prayers in corrupt Sanskrit of a kind familiar to Northern Buddhism, along with name lists of Buddhas, etc.   But the preliminary examination made by my learned collaborator Dr. Hoernle has since shown that, interspersed with these prayers, there are hundreds of lines with texts in that 'unknown' language which finds from sites about Khotan had first revealed to us, but without a key to its interpretation.

How this key was found since by Dr. Hoernle, with the help of two bilingual texts I brought away from the 'Thousand Buddhas,' will be related hereafter.

Apart from all philological interest, these texts in Indian script, whatever their language, possess historical value as tangible proofs that the monastic communities established at Tun-huang among a population mainly Chinese were, until a relatively late period, maintaining direct connection with their co-religionists in the Tarim Basin, from which Buddhism first reached China. That, in addition to this ancient connection with the 'Western Regions,' Tun-huang Buddhism had also been exposed at a certain period to a powerful influence from the south was attested strikingly by the abundance of Tibetan texts (Fig. 129, 9). From the first in the 'miscellaneous' bundles I had come upon leaves from Tibetan Pothis by hundreds, evidently representing large sections from works of the Buddhist Canon. The packets of leaves were usually mixed up in great confusion, but the greatly varying sizes, up to two feet and more in length, would help to restore order thereafter.

Besides these books of loose leaves, with their traditional string-holes but no strings to keep them together, I found out before long that there was a not inconsiderable proportion of packets with Tibetan rolls among the solid mass of 'library' bundles still left in the chapel. Not being a Tibetan scholar, I had no means to make sure whether these rolls contained different portions of that huge canonical collection, commonly known as the Tanjur and Kanjur, or mainly such endless repetitions of certain favourite texts and prayers as Tibetan piety still fondly cherishes. But I easily noticed that the paper of the Tibetan Pothis looked decidedly older than that of the rolls, and that in texture it also differed markedly from that of the Chinese texts. So the conclusion suggested itself that the Pothis represented mainly imports from Tibet itself, while the rolls had been written by Tibetan monks established locally.

But luckily it needed no conjectures to account for this conspicuous presence of Tibetan manuscripts in the walled-up library; nor could I be in doubt about the chronological

193. GIGANTIC ROLL OF PAPER, WITH SANSKRIT AND 'UNKNOWN LANGUAGE' TEXTS IN BRAHMI SCRIPT, FROM WALLED-UP TEMPLE LIBRARY, 'THOUSAND BUDDHAS,' TUN-HUANG.

Scale, one-fifth.

A shows the roll, which is over seventy feet long, partially opened.
B shows the silk painting on top of outer side.

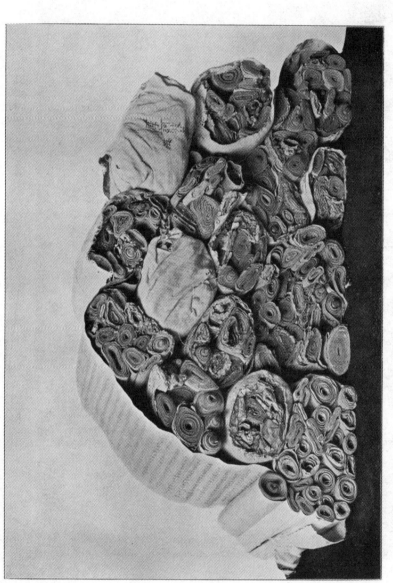

194. BUNDLES OF OLD MANUSCRIPT ROLLS, MAINLY CHINESE, IN ORIGINAL WRAPPERS, FROM WALLED-UP TEMPLE LIBRARY, 'THOUSAND BUDDHAS,' TUN-HUANG.

Scale, one-fifth.

evidence it afforded. From Chinese historical records, interpreted by M. Chavannes, including the fine Chinese inscription of the year 894 A.D. in one of the southernmost of the 'Thousand Buddhas' grottoes, I knew that the territory of Tun-huang, along with a great portion of Kan-su, had been conquered by the Tibetans about 759 A.D. But scarcely a century later, in 850 A.D., Chang I-ch'ao, the hereditary governor of Tun-huang, broke with the Tibetan power, and making his submission to the Emperor allowed the Chinese to re-establish a sort of suzerainty over these westernmost Marches. This must have ceased again during the troubles which followed the downfall of the T'ang dynasty at the beginning of the tenth century. When a Chinese envoy to Khotan about 938 A.D. passed through the territories corresponding to An-hsi and Tun-huang, he found them under Tibetan dependence, though the population remained mainly Chinese and the administration in the hands of a chief belonging to the great local family of the Ts'ao.

This Tibetan predominance at Tun-huang must have been at its height from the middle of the eighth to that of the ninth century, which is exactly the period when Tibet was a great power in Asia, holding in subjection vast tracts of Kan-su and even Central China. It was by way of Tun-huang that the Tibetans from about 766 A.D. onwards gradually overran the territories of Eastern Turkestan, and finally in 790 A.D. overwhelmed the isolated Chinese garrisons which had long struggled to maintain the imperial protectorate in the distant lands north and south of the T'ien-shan. Though the expansive strength of Tibet had largely spent itself by the latter part of the ninth century, its influence in the Tun-huang region evidently continued a good deal longer, and this political connection, directly attested for two centuries or so, made it easy to understand why Tibetan Buddhism was so amply represented among the literary remains of the walled-up cave.

But not from the Tibetan south alone had the old temple library received its foreign additions. Considering how flourishing Buddhism was throughout the powerful kingdom which the Turkish tribe of the Uigurs established after 860 A.D. in Turfan, Hami and the north-eastern portion of the Tarim Basin, and which in the tenth century extended even as far as Kan-chou, I was not surprised when Uigur manuscripts also cropped up in various bundles (Fig. 192, 4, 6). Some had the shape of small quarto volumes, being written on thin sheets of paper folded and stitched after the fashion of Chinese books and complete from cover to cover. Chinese glosses and rubrics found in a few of them clearly indicated Buddhist contents, a conclusion which has since been confirmed by the examination of my learned Orientalist friend, Dr. E. Denison Ross.

This ' Uigur ' script is a derivative of Syriac writing, and was already known to have been widely used for Turki writings before the spread of Muhammadanism among the Turkish populations of Central Asia. We found it also on the reverse of numerous Chinese rolls (Fig. 192, 8). From the first I noticed that in most of these the characters were distinctly less cursive and of a firmer shape than in the manuscript books and the specimens of Uigur texts I knew otherwise. But it was only after my return to Europe that I became aware of the language of these rolls. It is Sogdian, that Iranian dialect which Professor F. W. K. Müller's brilliant researches on manuscript finds from Turfan show to have been used for early translations of Buddhist literature in what is now Samarkand and Bokhara. What a large share this Iranian element must have had in the propagation of Buddhism along the old ' Northern route ' to carry its peculiar language and writing to these Marches of China proper !

I had further proof of the remarkable polyglot aspect which Buddhist religious places must have presented in these parts, when I came upon fragments of texts in that earliest Turkish script known as Runic Turki. Until a few years ago this had been known only from the famous inscriptions of a Turkish prince discovered on the Orkhon river in Southern Siberia and first deciphered by Professor V. Thomsen. Stranger still it seemed when there emerged from one of those miscellaneous bundles a narrow roll

(Fig. 192, 2), some fifteen feet long, showing a remarkably well written text in the peculiar form of Syriac script which recent discoveries at the ruined sites of Turfan have revealed as usually employed for Manichaean writings. What had this neat, almost calligraphic, manuscript to do in the Buddhist chapel, if it really contained some text of Mani's church which for centuries was a formidable rival to Buddhist and Christian propaganda alike throughout Central Asia ?

Less attractive at first sight, but in reality of special value, were the miscellaneous records in Chinese, such as letters, monastic certificates, and accounts, which filled those bundles of apparent ' waste paper.' Guided by the peculiar form of paper and writing, I soon learned to pick them out from among the masses of religious texts. They were likely to throw instructive light not only on details of monastic organization prevailing here during the centuries which preceded the walling up of the cave, but also on many aspects of political condition and private life. More important still was the chronological assurance I could derive from them at the time.

The Chinese, as people of culture and business habits, have always recognized the need of exact dates. So I soon was able to gather a considerable mass of dated documents, many quasi - official, from which to draw a definite conclusion as to the time when this great deposit of manuscripts and sacred relics was finally closed and forgotten. The great majority belonged to the ninth and tenth centuries of our era, and as those from the middle of the tenth century were frequent while only a few approached its end and none extended beyond the reign of the Emperor Chên Tsung (998-1022 A.D.), I was able to determine that the walling - up of the chamber must have taken place early in the eleventh century. There can be little doubt that the fear of some destructive invasion had prompted the act, and in view of the above chronological indication a connection naturally suggests itself with the conquest of Tun-huang by the rising power of the Hsi-hsia which took place between 1034 and 1037 A.D. The total absence of any manuscripts written in the special

characters which the founder of the Hsi - hsia dynasty
adopted in 1036 A.D., strongly supports this assumption.

But the small well-sheltered cave had in all probability
served for a long time previously as a place of deposit for
all kinds of objects sanctified by use but no longer needed
in the various shrines.   A clear indication of this was
supplied by many small and carefully packed bags which
I found containing tiny fragments of sacred texts, and
ragged remnants of silk paintings.   Such insignificant
relics would certainly not have been collected and sewn
up systematically in the commotion of a sudden emergency.
So much was obvious from the first, that the objects
deposited in this chapel must very often have been
already of considerable antiquity at the time when the
deposit was finally walled up.   Yet it was to me a very
gratifying assurance when in examining portions of our
Chinese collection, a year later, Chiang-ssŭ-yeh found a
series of manuscript rolls showing exact dates which seemed
to extend as far back as the third century A.D.   But even
then I realized that it would take protracted scholarly
labours in Europe before the date of the earliest pieces
could be definitely established.

As I worked my way in great haste through the
contents of the 'mixed' bundles,—we never knew how
long we might rely on the Tao-shih's indulgence—I felt
elated and at the same time oppressed by the constant
flow of fresh materials pouring down upon us.   Even in
the case of art relics and manuscripts which were neither
Chinese nor Tibetan, and of which I was able to estimate
the full interest, there was no chance of closer examination.   All I could do was to make sure of their being put
apart 'for further study,' as our polite convention called
removal.   But what obsessed me most at the time was my
total want of Sinologist training.   How gladly would I
then have exchanged one-half of my Indian knowledge
for a tenth of its value in Chinese!   Even with Chiang's
zealous help I could never be sure of not leaving behind
documents and texts of historical or literary interest
amidst the smothering mass of Buddhist canonical literature and the like.

Nevertheless in this tantalizing *embarras des richesses* I was able to catch a few encouraging glimpses. It was thus that, in a series of monastic records apparently issued under the seal of the abbot of the chief establishment, I lighted upon the old name of the Ch'ien-fo-tung site, which here figured as San-chieh-ssŭ, the ' Temples of the Three Regions.' Subsequently I found out that even now three divisions are distinguished among the cave-temples, though the old designation of the site seems quite forgotten. Then again I found complete rolls stamped with the die of the 'Temples of the Three Regions,' and thus clearly marked as having formed part of a general monastic library.

Greatly delighted was I when I found that an excellently preserved roll with a well-designed block-printed picture as frontispiece, had its text printed throughout, showing a date of production corresponding to 860 A.D. (Fig. 191, 6). Here was conclusive evidence that the art of printing books from wooden blocks was practised long before the conventionally assumed time of its invention, during the Sung period, and that already in the ninth century the technical level had been raised practically as high as the process permitted. Then again there were spirited drawings and woodcuts to be found in the midst of the Chinese text rolls, needing no specialist experience to recognize their artistic merit.

Five days of strenuous work resulted in the extraction and rapid search of all ' miscellaneous' bundles likely to contain manuscripts of special interest, paintings, and other relics which I was eager to rescue first of all. Fortunately when the Tao-shih had last stuffed back his treasures into their ' black hole,' these had been put mostly on the top or in other more or less accessible places, being, of course, less convenient building material than the tight uniform packets of Chinese and Tibetan rolls (Fig. 194). But my task was not ended while there still rose against the walls of the chamber that solid rampart of manuscript bundles. They would have to be cleared out, too, and rapidly looked through. It was bound to prove a troublesome undertaking in more than one sense, though discreet treatment and judiciously administered doses of silver had so far succeeded in counteracting the Tao-shih's relapses into timorous contrariness. The labour of clearing out the whole chapel might by itself have dismayed a stouter heart than that of our priestly 'librarian'; and what with this and the increased risk of exposure involved, Wang Tao-shih became now altogether refractory. However, he had already been gradually led from one concession to another, and we took care not to leave him much time for reflection.

So at last with many a sigh and plaintive remonstrance, and behind the outer temple gates carefully locked, he set to this great toil, helped now by a sort of priestly famulus whose discretion could be relied on. Previously I had sometimes feared that the little Tao-shih might get smothered under a tumbling wall of manuscript. Now I wondered whether the toil of pulling them out would not cause his slender physique to collapse. But it held out all the same, and by the evening of May 28th the regular bundles of Chinese rolls, more than 1050 in all, and those containing Tibetan texts had been transferred to neat rows in the spacious main cella of the temple (Fig. 188).

The bundles were almost all sewn up tightly in coarse covers of linen. But the ends were generally left open, and as Wang handed out bundle after bundle through the chapel door, Chiang and myself were just able to see hastily whether, amidst the usual rolls with Chinese texts, there were embedded any Pothi leaves from Brahmi manuscripts, folded-up pictures, or other relics of special attraction. Such we picked out and put aside rapidly. But there was no time even to glance at individual rolls and to see whether they bore anywhere within or without Indian or Central-Asian writing.

Perfunctory as the operation had to be in view of the Tao-shih's visibly growing reluctance, I had a gratifying reward for my insistence on this clearing in the discovery of several miscellaneous bundles at the very bottom. They had been used there by the Tao-shih to turn a low clay platform into a level foundation for the manuscript wall above. In spite of the crushing these bundles had undergone, I recovered from them a large number of exquisite silk paintings of all sizes, and some beautiful embroidered pieces. One of the latter was a magnificent embroidery picture, remarkable for design, colours, and fineness of material, and showing a Buddha between Bodhisattvas in life size, which I shall have occasion to discuss hereafter (Plate IX.).

Perhaps it was a lively sensation of the toil he had undergone and now longed to see ended, or else the fear that we were now touching those precious Chinese Sutra texts to which alone he seemed to attach any real value. At any rate the Tao-shih at this stage came to business, so to speak, by asking for a substantial 'subscription' (*pu-shih*) to his temple. At the same time he protested that any cession of sacred texts or 'Chings' was impossible. I myself was glad to take up the theme ; for I had recognized long before that it was my duty towards research to try my utmost to rescue, if possible, the whole of the collection from the risk of slow dispersion and loss with which it was threatened in such keeping.

But at the same time I could not close my eyes to the serious difficulties and objections. I was quite unable to form any definite estimate of the philological value of those masses of Chinese canonical texts which made up the bulk of the hidden library. Their contents were, no doubt, to be found in the complete editions of the Buddhist 'Tripitaka,' printed for centuries past in China, Korea, Japan. Still less was I able to select those texts which for one reason or other were possessed of antiquarian or literary interest. The removal of so many cart-loads of manuscripts would inevitably give publicity to the whole transaction, and the religious resentment this was likely to arouse in Tun-huang, even if it did not lead to more serious immediate consequences, would certainly compromise my chance of further work in Kan-su.

Nevertheless, I was prepared to face these risks rather than forgo the endeavour to rescue the whole hoard. Chiang-ssŭ-yeh, in spite of misgivings justified by his knowledge of the local conditions, loyally did his best to persuade the Tao-shih that removal of the collection to a 'temple of learning in Ta-Ying-kuo,' or England, would in

truth be an act which Buddha and his Arhats might
approve as pious.   He also urged that the big sum I was
prepared to pay (I hinted at 40 horse-shoes, about Rs.5000,
and was resolved to give twice as much, if need be, whatever the excess over my sanctioned grant) would enable
Wang to return to a life of peace in his native province,
distant Shan-hsi, if Tun-huang should become too hot for
him.   Or else he could allay any scruples by using the
whole sum for the benefit of the temple, which by his
restoration he could claim to have annexed as his own with
all its contents known or unknown.

But all in vain.   The prospect of losing his precious
'Chings' as a whole or in part profoundly frightened the
good priest, who had before resignedly closed his eyes to
my gathering whatever I thought of special artistic or
antiquarian value.   For the first time our relations became
somewhat strained, and it required very careful handling
and our suavest manners to obviate anything like a breach.
What the Tao-shih urged with all signs of sincere anxiety
was that any deficiency in those piles of sacred texts would
certainly be noticed by his patrons, who had helped him
with their publicly recorded subscriptions to clear and
restore the temple; that in consequence the position he
had built up for himself in the district by the pious labours
of eight years would be lost for good, and his life-task
destroyed.   He even vaguely reproached himself for
having given up sacred things over which his lay patrons
ought to have as much right of control as he himself, and
doggedly asserted the need of consulting them before
moving a step further.   And in the depth of my heart I
could bear him no grudge for these scruples and recrimina-
tions, or even gainsay them.

For two long days these discussions had to be carried
on intermittently with a view to gain time while my examination of the miscellaneous bundles was proceeding.   I
managed to complete this by the second evening.   But on
returning early next day to the temple in order to start the
close search of the regular Chinese bundles for Central-
Asian and other foreign text materials, I found to my
dismay that the Tao-shih in a sudden fit of perturbation

had shifted back overnight almost the whole of them to their gloomy prison of centuries. His sullen temper gave us further cause of anxiety. But the advantage we possessed by already holding loads of valuable manuscripts and antiques, and the Tao-shih's unmistakable wish to secure a substantial sum of money, led at last to what I had reason to claim as a substantial success in this diplomatic struggle.

He agreed to let me have fifty well-preserved bundles of Chinese text rolls and five of Tibetan ones, besides all my previous selections from the miscellaneous bundles. For all these acquisitions four horse-shoes of silver, equal to about Rs.500, passed into the priest's hands; and when I surveyed the archaeological value of all I could carry away for this sum, I had good reason to claim it a bargain. Of course, after so severe a struggle I lost no time in removing the heavy loads of Chinese and Tibetan rolls. Until now my devoted Ssŭ-yeh had struggled to my tent night by night with the loads of daily 'selections'; but to this task his physical strength would not have been equal. So help had to be sought on this occasion from Ibrahim Beg and Tila, my trusted followers; and after two midnight trips to the temple, under the screening shadow of the steep river bank, the huge sackfuls were safely transferred to my store-room without any one, even of my own men, having received an inkling.

The Tao-shih's nervousness had been increased by prolonged absence from his clients in the oasis; and now he hastened to resume his seasonal begging tour in the Tunhuang district. But a week later he returned, reassured that the secret had not been discovered and that his spiritual influence, such as it was, had suffered no diminution. So we succeeded in making him stretch a point further, and allow me to add some twenty more bundles of manuscripts to my previous selections, against an appropriate donation for the temple. When later on it came to the packing, the manuscript acquisitions needed seven cases, while the paintings, embroideries, and other miscellaneous relics filled five more. The packing of these was a very delicate task and kept me busy on the days when photographic

work was impossible in the caves.   There was some little
trouble about getting enough boxes without exciting
suspicion at Tun-huang.   Luckily I had foreseen the
chance and provided some 'empties' beforehand.   The
rest were secured in disguise and by discreet instalments.
So everything passed off without a hitch.

The good Tao-shih now seemed to breathe freely
again, and almost ready to recognize that I was performing
a pious act in rescuing for Western scholarship those relics
of ancient Buddhist literature and art which local ignorance
would allow to lie here neglected or to be lost in the end.
When I finally said good-bye to the 'Thousand Buddhas,'
his jovial sharp-cut face had resumed once more its look of
shy but self-contented serenity.   We parted in fullest
amity.   I may anticipate here that I received gratifying
proof of the peaceful state of his mind when, on my return
to An-hsi four months later, he agreed to let depart for
that 'temple of learning' in the distant West another share
of the Chinese and Tibetan manuscripts in the shape of
over two hundred compact bundles.   But my time for
feeling true relief came when all the twenty-four cases,
heavy with manuscript treasures rescued from that strange
place of hiding, and the five more filled with paintings and
other art relics from the same cave, had been deposited
safely in the British Museum.

CHAPTER LXVII

BUDDHIST PICTURES FROM THE HIDDEN CHAPEL

NEITHER at the time of that hurried 'excavation' and gathering at the 'Thousand Buddhas,' nor in the course of my subsequent explorations, was it possible to find leisure for any close examination of my novel 'finds.' I had to be content with knowing them safely packed and transported across the deserts and mountains. The year and a half which has passed since the unpacking of those precious cases at the British Museum has not sufficed for more than a preliminary sorting and survey of the contents. The *embarras des richesses* in materials has proved great, and the labours their proper arrangement and study will demand from my scholar-helpmates in different fields of research are likely to be protracted. So a succinct review of the main classes of remains undergoing elucidation is all that can be attempted at present; even this must needs be incomplete in various directions.

Of all the contents of the Tao-shih's cave the fine relics of Buddhist pictorial art impressed me most from the time when they emerged to the light, and in view of their artistic interest and importance I may give a brief account of them first. The great majority were painted on silk, while the rest had for their material either linen or paper. The prevailing use of fine silk gauze was a gratifying fact in itself; for it was reasonable to assume that to the superior material there would correspond also a higher degree of care and technique in the painting. Nor was this expectation disappointed. But I had not proceeded far in my search before I realized how much this very

fineness of the material added to the difficulties of immediate examination and safe transport.

A fair number, indeed, of the narrow painted banners
from the 'miscellaneous' bundles which a lucky chance
first placed in my hands, were found neatly rolled up, with
their silk material still so pliable and soft that they could
be unfolded without risk. The masses of ex-voto rags of
all sorts and crumpled-up paper amidst which they were
embedded had helped to protect the delicate fabric from
pressure and consequent hardening. But in other bundles
these pictures had fared worse, and those in particular
which I was able to pick out from among the heavy Chinese
rolls of regular 'library bundles' showed only too plainly
under what crushing weight they had suffered. They
were pressed into tight little packets, so hard and brittle
that no attempt at opening them was possible on the spot.

The big paintings on silk ranging up to over six feet
square, had naturally been affected even more by this
compression of some nine hundred years. I could not
venture to open out even those which appeared to have
been folded at the time of their deposition in a more or
less regular fashion, from fear of increasing the damage
undergone at the creases. But most of these big pictures
presented themselves merely as shapeless large parcels of
crumpled-up silk, of which it was quite impossible at the
time to determine the contents. There was abundant proof
in the shape of dirt-encrustation, backings with paper, and
other repairs to show that many of them had suffered from
long use, incense-smoke, and the like, perhaps for considerable periods before they were put away in such careless
fashion within their dark hiding-place.

The task of safely packing these convolutes of often
extremely brittle silk gauze was difficult enough. But
though they travelled quite safely, the proper opening out
and examination in the case of most of these paintings,
whether big or small, could not be commenced until they
had been subjected to a special chemical treatment under
expert hands in the British Museum. Though this labour,
requiring extreme care, has now proceeded steadily for
over a year in the Department of Prints and Drawings

under Sir Sidney Colvin's kind supervision, only about two-thirds of these precious packets have been dealt with.

The work has been attended by many surprises. From some of the least promising convolutes, when the crinkled and brittle silk resumed its original suppleness, there have emerged wholly unsuspected pieces of fine paintings, complete or fragmentary. Portions missing in some large compositions have been discovered in quite a different conglomeration. No exact estimate as to the total number of individual pictures can, therefore, be given at present; but it is probable that it will exceed three hundred. Still more difficult does it appear to estimate the extent of labour that will be needed for the permanent preservation of all these paintings. For the present we have to be content to strengthen the silk banners by getting them mounted on a fine gauze with large meshes, and subsequently fixed under sheets of glass, while the large compositions have been temporarily backed with thin sheets of Japanese paper, and thus made capable of being rolled in the traditional fashion of the Far East.

The primary task of recovery and safeguarding is still far from being completed. But the materials already available are sufficient to allow us to form an adequate idea of the general character and art value of these paintings. Their detailed study and interpretation was bound to offer puzzles, no less than points of novel interest. It was evident from the first that these relics from the 'Thousand Buddhas' of Tun-huang were separated by considerable intervals, both in time and space, from almost all hitherto known representations of Buddhist pictorial art. The great majority of these pictures and the corresponding frescoes of the caves undoubtedly belong to the T'ang period (7th to 9th century A.D.), from which scarcely any genuine specimens of Buddhist religious painting have survived in China or Japan. There were marks, too, of a distinct local influence which the art of these paintings must have undergone for a prolonged period, in spite of its close dependence on the models originally supplied by Indian and Central-Asian Buddhism. So I

had good reason to consider myself fortunate when my
old friend M. A. Foucher, a leading authority in Buddhist
iconography, kindly offered his collaboration for the study
of these remains. To him and my artist helpmate, Mr.
F. H. Andrews, I am largely indebted for the observations
upon which the following remarks and descriptions are
based. But seeing how succinct these must necessarily
be, I feel doubly glad that it has been possible to illustrate
the various classes of pictures by characteristic specimens
faithfully reproduced in colours.

The diversity of the material used does not reflect a
corresponding difference in subject or treatment. But a
closer examination of the pictures, whatever their fabric,
soon reveals an outward distinction which guides us to a
classification on broad lines. The smaller pieces, when
completely preserved, show mostly the shape of oblong
banners, provided with a triangular headpiece, and streamers
on either side, and attached below to 'strainers' of wood
or bamboo, as seen in Fig. 195.

The streamers are secured at the bottom by a weighting-
piece in lacquered or painted wood. This arrangement,
and still more the care with which the picture proper is
painted on both sides of the silk or linen, prove that the
banners were invariably intended to float in the air suspended from the vaults of cellas and porches, or from the
ceilings of antechapels. The larger pieces, being painted
on one side only and often provided with some backing
material, but never with streamers or other floating attach-
ments, were clearly meant to be hung up on temple walls
or gateways. The subjects represented in these are always
groups of divine figures or scenes from Buddhist heavens ;
but the banners are painted only with figures of single
divinities, or else with a succession of scenes from the life
of Buddha. The latter are the less numerous, but may
well claim the first place on account of the interest both
of subject and artistic treatment.

The scenes presented to us are just those which
Indian Buddhist art chose for its favourite subjects.
They are ordinarily borrowed from that period of
Buddha's life - story which preceded the Bodhi or final

195. PAINTED SILK BANNERS, OF T'ANG PERIOD, REPRESENTING BODHI-
SATTVAS, FROM WALLED-UP TEMPLE LIBRARY, 'THOUSAND BUDDHAS,'
TUN-HUANG.

Scale, one-sixth.

enlightenment. They show us the whole cycle of his nativity as Prince Gautama; the miracles of his childhood and youth; the life of pleasure in the princely seraglio; and, after the four pathetic encounters which arouse his vocation, the flight from the palace; the incidents which follow this renunciation of the world; the six years of austerities; and finally, the scene on the bank of the Nairanjana river which immediately precedes the illumination. "In short," as M. Foucher puts it, "we meet again with almost the whole catalogue of episodes which have remained classic since the Graeco - Buddhist school of Gandhara. The most important point to note is the frankly Chinese fashion in which these traditional subjects have been treated. Under the hands of the local artists they have undergone the same disguising transformation which Christian legend has under those of the Italian or Flemish painters."

The two banners reproduced in Plate VI. may serve to illustrate this interesting group of paintings. Both have lost their streamers, etc., but seem otherwise complete, except for tears and the like minor injuries. The one to the right, about two feet high in the original, shows at its bottom the straining piece of bamboo clumsily refastened, and a little higher an ancient tear, coarsely sewn up with red thread. In the upper panel we have a representation of the dream of Queen Maya, Buddha's mother, which figures in the legend concerning his conception. Below we see the queen being carried in a litter to the Lumbini garden where her son's birth was destined to take place. The rapid onward stride of the men carrying her is rendered with much skill.

Next follows the scene of Prince Gautama's miraculous birth from the side of his mother. It is pictured with scrupulous adherence to the traditional details; but we recognize a clever device, unknown to the Gandhara models, in the graceful use made of Maya's wide sleeve to screen the first appearance of the divine babe. It is repeated in other representations of this scene and had evidently become fixed in local tradition. At the foot of the banner we see the miracle of Gautama's first steps towards his mother, with lotuses springing up to mark the spots which the child's feet have touched. The landscape of the last three panels is treated with thoroughly Chinese taste in its setting, and the distances are cleverly adapted and balanced. In the bottom panel the cartouche is filled in with a Chinese legend setting forth the particular episode, whereas the corresponding cartouches above have been left blank, as only too frequently in these paintings.

The banner on the left of the Plate is bordered on its long side by a rich floral ornament, which I found frequently also in the decorative settings of the frescoes in the caves. The upper portion contains a spirited representation of the famous legend how Prince Gautama, wishing to free himself from all worldly bonds and temptations of the senses, as a preliminary to progress towards full enlightenment, leaves his palace at night while all the women and minstrels of his seraglio and the guards outside the gates are overcome by deep sleep. On the cloud above the battlemented wall we see the future ' Buddha' galloping towards freedom on his favourite steed, his faithful groom, Chandaka, keeping by his side. The deep blue tints over hills and forest shown below the riding figure skilfully symbolize the time when the escape took place. In the lower portion of the picture we see the four emissaries sent out by King Suddhodana, Gautama's father, to call back the princely fugitive; having failed to find him they are brought up for judgment before the king and his ministers. Their arms are bound at their backs, and two purple-robed executioners stand behind, carrying beating-sticks, exactly like the one which I excavated at one of the stations of the Tun-huang *Limes* (Fig. 172, 1).

However fascinating these scenes from Buddha's life-story are, on account both of the faithful reproduction of all features in the original Indian legends and of the artistic merit of their Chinese setting, I must pass on to the far larger group of banners which display single divinities of the Buddhist Pantheon. Their variety is truly bewildering; and as the figures are but rarely accompanied by descriptive cartouches, and even characteristic emblems often absent, the correct identification of them

PLATE VI. ANCIENT BUDDHIST BANNERS OF PAINTED SILK GAUZE SHOWING SCENES FROM THE LIFE-STORY OF BUDDHA. DISCOVERED AT THE 'CAVES OF THE THOUSAND BUDDHAS,' TUN-HUANG.

(CHAP. LXVII.   SCALE, TWO-SEVENTHS).

PLATE VII. ANCIENT BUDDHIST BANNERS OF PAINTED SILK GAUZE
SHOWING FIGURES OF BODHISATTVAS. DISCOVERED AT THE 'CAVES
OF THE THOUSAND BUDDHAS,' TUN-HUANG.

(CHAP. LXVII.   SCALE, TWO-SEVENTHS).

all will provide many a crux for expert authorities on
Buddhist iconography. But even before this detailed
analysis is attempted it is easy to recognize three broad
categories of the divine personages represented—Buddhas,
Bodhisattvas, and Lokapalas or 'Guardians of the Worlds.'

The very small number of pictures showing Gautama
Buddha or corresponding epiphanies in earlier or future
cycles cannot cause surprise ; for from an early period
other divine figures claimed far more attention in Buddhist
worship, especially in the Mahayana system which prevailed
from Gandhara right through Central Asia into China.
Its favourite objects were the Bodhisattvas or 'Buddhas
elect' in their inexhaustible multiplicity, and these we
find abundantly represented on our banners. Rich adornment in dress and jewelry is common to all these princely
incarnations of Buddhas past or future, with the single
exception of Kshitigarbha, who curiously enough figures in
the costume of a monk.

A certain number of the Bodhisattvas are presented in
a style plainly Indian, and can on account of their characteristic emblems and distinctive colours be easily identified
with the miniature figures in certain old Buddhist manuscripts from Nepal which M. Foucher first studied and
published. Thus we meet repeatedly with Manjusri on
his lion, Samantabhadra on the elephant, Vajrapani with
the thunderbolt, Maitreya with the rosary, and other well-
known creations of Buddhist imagery. Even more frequent are representations of Avalokitesvara, whom Chinese
Buddhism has gradually transformed into Kuan-yin, its
much-beloved 'Goddess of Mercy.' In all these the faithful adherence to the style in pose, features, and drapery,
as originally fixed by Graeco-Buddhist art, is obvious.
This tenacity of traditional type is a familiar feature in the
iconography of all religions. All the more interesting are
those numerous banners in which the representation of
Bodhisattvas has undergone unmistakable adaptation to
new standards developed in the later Buddhist art of
Central Asia, or quite plainly to Chinese taste.

From the artistic point of view these latter pictures of
Bodhisattvas are often distinctly superior in design and

execution; but the interpretation of them is in many cases very difficult. Some types, like the Bodhisattva with the censer or the one carrying a transparent bowl (Fig. 195), are manifestly new mythological creations. In others, again, we look vainly for any recognizable attributes. *Such are the two striking figures reproduced in colour, Plate VII., from silk banners which, except for the streamers, are practically complete. The Bodhisattva on the left, with its undulating line of figure and its elaborate dress and adornment, shows no essential divergence from the type to be met with in the frescoes and stucco sculptures of Eastern Turkestan ruins. The light pink robe hanging from the waist, the dark green chiton-like garment partly covering the breast, and the stole, purple outside and green inside, which is gracefully draped round shoulders, body, and arms, all correspond to the traditional garments of Indian Buddhist saints as Central-Asian painting and sculpture show them. Yet Chinese influence is strongly evident in the flowing ease of the draperies as they gracefully fall with studied carelessness, partly inside, partly outside the open lotus which serves as pedestal, in the hair festooned across the forehead and hanging in long tresses behind to below the elbow, as well as in a mass of details contributing to the picturesque effect of the whole.

The same qualities of freely sweeping line, of graceful movement, and harmoniously blended intense colours, are even more conspicuous in the fine figure of a Bodhisattva seen on the right. There is neither recognizable emblem nor any other mark which would allow us to identify him. The figure is seen in full profile striding forward in vigorous action. The right hand uplifted carries a pink object largely hidden by the elaborate head-dress, and its pose is cleverly balanced by the left hanging down to grasp the floating drapery. The movement of the body is admirably expressed also in the trailing masses of the rich red robe draped round the legs and feet, and in the gyrations of the stole or Uttariya at the back. It is reflected, too, in the swing of the jewelled tassels hanging from the canopy and in the curls of the flames which encircle the jewels on its top. The bold curving shapes

*In black and white in the present edition.

and elaborate bosses of the gold ornaments are distinctly suggestive of Chinese taste. Very curious is the profile representation of the halo, which is here indicated by a mere colourless disk instead of the usual multi-coloured circle.

The Chinese style of local art seems to have annexed altogether the images, represented with relative frequency, of the four Lokapalas or Guardian-kings of the four world-regions. They appear to have been popular objects of worship in Chinese Buddhism of the period, and the numerous pictures of them are often executed with much care. They are all represented in warrior guise, heavily armed from head to foot. The inscribed miniatures which a small illuminated Chinese manuscript gives of them enable us to identify with full assurance Vaisravana, king of the Northern Region, by his halberd; Dhritarashtra, of the East, by his bow or arrow; Virudhaka, of the South, by his club; and Virupaksha, who rules the West, by his sword.

Another group of minor divinities which figure with relative frequency among the banners, that of the Dharma-palas or 'Protectors of Religion,' also bear a distinctly Chinese look, though even here peculiar features of their presentation are foreshadowed in Graeco-Buddhist sculpture. As manifestations of Vajrapani in fury, they are made to display an exaggerated development of muscles; and thus, as M. Foucher observes, "they recall quite as much the athletic demons of Japan as the horrible apparitions of Lamaistic worship. It is only fair to point out, however, that they show as yet neither the extravagant multiplication of limbs nor the monstrous obscenities of the latter." Altogether, it is a relief to observe that among the images represented by these painters, whether on banners or in frescoes, very few are found of a form not simply human. Female divinities also are extremely rare. "The Pantheon which the paintings of Tun-huang reveal to us," so M. Foucher remarks with full justice, "was evidently composed for the benefit of donors reasonable in their tastes and under the direction of monks still heedful of decency."

CHAPTER LXVIII

LARGE PAINTINGS AND OTHER ART RELICS

WE find the general characteristics just indicated equally represented in that class of paintings, mostly of large size, which were meant for the decoration of walls, and which represent groups of divine beings in more or less elaborate composition. Among the many specimens of this class I may call attention first to the fine picture suc-
*cessfully reproduced in the coloured frontispiece of Vol. I.; for it is unmistakably an original work of exceptional artistic merit. It shows Vaisravana, the king of the Northern Region, moving on a cloud across the ocean, followed by a train of heavenly attendants and demons. From his left rises a small cloud supporting a miniature Stupa. His right hand carries the halberd, while bundles of flames shoot up behind his shoulders, expressive of rapid movement. His richly brocaded dress and elaborate golden armour are represented with exquisite care, to which reproduction on a scale necessarily so small cannot do full justice.

It is the same with the figures and adornment of his numerous host, among which variation of type and expression is introduced with remarkable skill. The individualizing touch bestowed on each demon's head seems to bring these fantastic figures nearer to human interest, as in a famous relievo of Graeco-Buddhist art representing the demon army of Mara. On the extreme left an aged demon-warrior is seen getting ready to shoot his arrow at a Garuda, half-man half-bird, who escapes to the heights of heaven. The big rolling waves of the ocean are rendered with a freedom and irresistible dash which

*In black and white in the present edition.

PLATE VIII. LARGE BUDDHIST PAINTING ON SILK, DATED 864 A.D., REPRESENTING GROUPS OF BODHISATTVAS, WITH PORTRAITS OF THE DONORS BELOW. DISCOVERED AT THE 'CAVES OF THE THOUSAND BUDDHAS,' TUN-HUANG.

(CHAP. LXVIII. SCALE, ONE-EIGHTH).

PLATE IX. ANCIENT EMBROIDERY PICTURE ON SILK, SHOWING BUD-
DHA BETWEEN DISCIPLES AND BODHISATTVAS, WITH THE DONORS
IN ADORATION BELOW. DISCOVERED AT THE 'CAVES OF THE THOU-
SAND BUDDHAS,' TUN-HUANG.

(CHAP. LXVIII.   SCALE, ONE-TWELFTH).

recalls Japanese art at its best. Far away in the background the mountains of Meru, the range representing the
Himalaya in Indian mythology, and appropriately assigned
to the 'King of the Northern Region,' close the scene.
The whole bears the impress of a master hand, and could
hold its own in any collection of Far Eastern art.

The silk paintings which represent scenes in Buddhist
heavens are particularly numerous; but as most of them
are large and crowded with figures, it is difficult to reproduce them adequately here. They usually show a Buddha
as their central figure seated on a lotus platform, with
an elaborate structure resembling the terraced gardens
which often adjoin Chinese temples, and surrounded by
a host of saints and heavenly attendants. Two or more
Bodhisattvas, distinguished by larger size and more lavish
adornment, are seated by his side or symmetrically enthroned in separate pavilions. On a series of elegantly
decorated terraces below we see crowds of haloed figures
representing Arhats or saints enjoying the divine presence,
and the scene is rendered festive by the dancing which
gracefully whirling girls perform to the music produced by
Gandharvis and other celestial entertainers. Lotus-filled
tanks are often shown between the terraces; and in the
background architectural vistas, sometimes of considerable
beauty, provide an appropriate setting to the amenities of
this heavenly revel.

It is difficult, without protracted research, to ascertain
which of the various heavens known to Buddhist mythological fancy is intended in each picture. Nor does it
much matter from the artistic point of view or that of the
student of religion. Whether it is Sukhavati, the heaven
far away in the extreme west of the world, or Maitreya's
paradise where dying Hsüan-tsang fondly hoped to be
re-born, it is clear that what the pious donors and painters
of these pictures looked forward to as the final goal of
bliss was a very human paradise not lacking the good
things of this world. However remote this conception is
from the true Nirvana, the Enlightened One's real goal,
we may appreciate the air of dignified repose and enjoyment which all these scenes breathe. Their architectural

decoration is unmistakably Chinese and not less interesting on that account. But there is good reason to believe that the general scheme, and the grouping of the divine figures, like their iconographic presentation, is a faithful reflex from Indian and Central-Asian models. However that may be, it is an interesting fact, brought out by comparison with the photographs I took of the frescoes in the 'Thousand Buddhas' caves,' that many of the larger pictures on silk are reproductions of these on a reduced scale.

A good idea of the colour effects of the pictures may be gained from the painting, close on five feet high, reproduced * in Plate VIII. Here we see on the right the Bodhisattva Manjusri riding on his lion, which a black Indian conducts. On the left is Samantabhadra, another Bodhisattva, riding on his elephant led by a similar figure. Above are shown in a row four standing Bodhisattvas, manifestations of an Avalokitesvara or 'Kuan-yin,' whom the Chinese legends by their side allow us to identify as 'The Very Compassionate.' At the foot of the painting we have portraits of the donors, some of them dressed as monks, and of female members of their families. A dedicatory Chinese inscription on the central panel acquaints us with the occasion when the gift of this picture was made, and supplies the welcome fact that it dates from the year 864 A.D.

Among a number of paintings which cannot be classed under any of the above categories, but yet will repay attention, I can only mention one. It is a long roll of paper with curious representations of scenes of judgment in Buddhist hells. In each two sinners are being brought up before the tribunal. They are condemned to wear the 'cangue' or wooden board, still a favourite implement of Chinese justice, while two figures attend them, carrying one an armful of sacred texts, and the other a statuette of Buddha, evidently to mark the means of grace and salvation.

I have left myself little space to discuss other works of quasi-pictorial art rescued by me from the walled-up chapel, though their interest from more than one point of view is great. I mean the embroideries. By far the most important among them is the magnificent picture, nearly * nine feet high, which Plate IX. reproduces in colours.

*In black and white in the present edition.

The central life-sized figure, with its rather hieratic look and severe archaistic pose, is Buddha himself; the indications of rock behind suggest that the scene is laid at the Gridhrakuta or 'Vulture grotto,' famous in Buddha's life-story. The two figures nearest to the Master on either side have suffered sad havoc, probably through want of care and protection before the cave was walled up. They seem to represent his earliest disciples, Kasyapa being still recognizable in the aged face on the right. Outside them we see two richly adorned Bodhisattvas in poses of worship. A similar grouping was observed in some of the oldest frescoes of the site. Above them two graceful Gandharvas on cloud-scrolls support the canopy over Buddha's head. Below we see the donors and their female relations grouped in adoration, on either side of a yellow central panel from which the inscription originally stitched in has unfortunately disappeared.

The colours of the silks used for the embroidery have survived in remarkable freshness and shimmer, far better than the reproduction, owing to unsurmountable technical difficulties, succeeds in showing. The work contained in this picture may be guessed from the fact that merely to stitch it on to a new backing of canvas, a task which was absolutely needed and which Miss E. A. Winter, a lady trained at the Royal School of Art Needlework, performed with great care and skill, took over two months. The damage which this fine piece of embroidery had suffered before its final deposition is shown by earlier attempts at repairs, and confirms the impression of its high antiquity derived from other indications.

A word of mention must be given to the fine embroidered cushion cover seen in Fig. 197. Its floral ornamentation and tracery is remarkable, both for its harmonious colours and for its close affinity to designs still common in modern embroidered work of Turkestan and China. Were it not for the ascertained date of the walling-up of the chapel, we should scarcely have suspected that this piece of domestic art went back to at least the tenth century A.D.

But questions even more curious in their antiquarian aspects are raised by the remains of woven art fabrics which have turned up among the finds of that wonderful cave. A number of triangular head - pieces, which were found detached from their painted banners, are composed either in their body or in their broad borders of pieces of fine silk damask. The multi-coloured patterns woven into them present a striking resemblance to the type which finds of patterned silk fabrics from Egyptian tombs of the early Christian and Byzantine period have made familiar to Western archaeologists, and which is usually known by the conventional designation of 'Sassanian.'

In one piece we see a gracefully designed pattern of rosettes and palmettes interspersed with symmetrically arranged figures of flying birds; in another an elaborate diaper of rings and quatrefoils in bright greens and pinks is decorated with pairs of horned deer or geese posed in profile. The quaint but effective modelling of the woven figures and their colouring recall so vividly the designs of ancient fabrics excavated in the early Christian cemeteries of Egypt and commonly classed as 'Coptic,' that, according to the opinion of Professor J. Strzygowski, a leading authority on the art history of the Near East, who has kindly undertaken the study of my materials, a close connection in origin may be considered certain. The same affinity of style is to be observed in a mass of fine damasks and brocades which have survived as mere strips and rags among the ex-votos plentifully deposited in the cave. The full reconstruction in drawing of the patterns which these torn pieces of fabrics once exhibited is a task of considerable interest that will necessarily take time.

The problem presented by these fabrics is made still more interesting by certain specimens of exceedingly fine silk tapestry which have been discovered among our 'finds' from the 'Thousand Buddhas.' One of them is contained in the hand - woven strips which form the converging borders of a beautifully painted triangular head-piece of a banner. The general idea of design, elaborate in spite of the minute execution, is a duck-pond surrounded by various delicately coloured plants; this, too, recalls motifs used in ancient Egypt and the Near East.

Another specimen is to be found on a perfectly preserved silk cover, about two feet long, intended for a
manuscript roll.   Its narrow bands of silk tapestry,
extremely fine in texture, show a richly and yet delicately
tinted pattern which consists of an adaptation of the
palmette and connecting scroll and bears an unmistakably
Chinese character.   As if this artistic manuscript cover
had been specially designed to bring home to us a fascinating problem, we find it decorated also with broad bands
of thick silk damask showing a pattern of pronounced
'Sassanian' type, winged lions facing each other with
curled tails.   The difference of styles thus brought into
closest juxtaposition by the hand which fashioned the
cover, is a most suggestive illustration of the widely
distant civilizations that once met at Tun-huang.

The question as to the origin of these silk damasks of
'Sassanian' pattern is as yet difficult to solve.   That the
designs represented in them are borrowed from Hellenistic
art as transplanted to Mesopotamia and thence to Iran,
must be considered certain.   But are we justified in
assuming that the fabrics themselves, showing this close
resemblance in style to the 'Coptic' finds in Egypt, were
manufactured in, and imported from, the Sassanian
dominions in Mesopotamia or Persia?   Whatever silk was
worked up there and in the Near East, until the first silk-
worms were introduced into the Byzantine empire about
550 A.D., must have been brought from China itself—or
from Khotan.   Can we reasonably assume that silk first
travelled all the huge distance to Persia from the 'land
of the Seres,' always the most important place of its
production, in order to be brought back again in the shape
of damask to Tun-huang, on the very border of China?
The aggregate journey for caravans would even now
amount to at least a year and a half, whereas the distance
from the nearest silk-producing provinces of China to
Tun-huang could be accomplished easily in less than
three months.   And the art of silk-weaving must have
reached a high standard in China long before Han times,
as my finds of fine silk and damask fragments along the
Tun-huang *Limes* conclusively prove.

Is it not possible that damasks with carefully copied 'Western' patterns were manufactured in China itself for regular export, just as Chinese porcelain factories produced 'China' with European designs for export to the West all through the seventeenth and eighteenth centuries? Or have we, perhaps, to look upon Khotan, an early home of transplanted sericulture, as the industrial centre which, being in close touch with the Oxus regions and Iran, was able to turn out fine silk fabrics in a style closely approaching the 'Sassanian' patterns? No definite answer can safely be attempted as yet. But all advance in research is bound up with problems, and so I feel glad that the 'finds' in that hidden temple cave have raised them in more than one direction.

196. MODERN STUCCO IMAGES IN CHINESE STYLE, REPRESENTING HSÜAN-TSANG AS AN ARHAT, WITH ATTENDANTS, IN A CAVE-TEMPLE OF THE 'THOUSAND BUDDHAS,' TUN-HUANG.

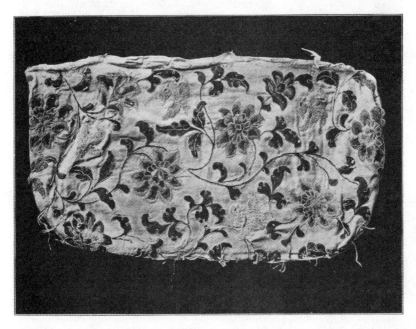

197. OLD SILK EMBROIDERY ON CUSHION-COVER FROM WALLED-UP TEMPLE LIBRARY, 'THOUSAND BUDDHAS,' TUN-HUANG.

198. RUINED BUDDHIST GROTTOES, NEAR WANG TAO-SHIH'S CAVE-TEMPLE, 'THOUSAND BUDDHAS,' TUN-HUANG.

The antechapels and porches of the cellas above have completely disappeared. The stucco images show recent restoration. Below are seen the porches, partially filled with sand, leading to other cellas.

CHAPTER LXIX

A POLYGLOT TEMPLE LIBRARY

THE interchange of influences from varied regions and races is also illustrated in characteristic fashion by the manuscript remains from the hidden temple library. A rapid review of them will suffice to bring out the large part played by Buddhist propaganda in linking civilizations right across Asia, and how much of its current must have passed through Tun-huang during successive periods.

Regard for the original home of Buddhist doctrine— and personal attachment to my old Indian field of work —induces me to mention in the first place the relics of Sanskrit manuscripts. They all belong to Buddhist religious literature. Though their number and extent are relatively modest, Professor L. de la Vallée Poussin, who has kindly undertaken the examination of them, has discovered texts of considerable interest for the critical history of the Sanskrit Canon of Northern Buddhism, which in India itself has been almost completely lost through the vicissitudes of the Buddhist church in the country of its origin. The large and well-preserved manuscript on palm leaves (Fig. 192, 1) which I had occasion to mention previously contains portions of a famous canonical work, and has on account of its great age and undoubtedly Indian production proved of particular value. Other manuscripts written on paper evidently represent text recensions which were current in Central Asia.

Far more numerous and of exceptional linguistic as well as palaeographical interest are the rolls and Pothis on paper written in several Central-Asian varieties of Indian Brahmi script but in non-Indian language (Fig. 192, 5, 7).

The character of the writing sufficed to connect these manuscripts with one or more of the 'unknown' languages once used in Eastern Turkestan, the study of which was commenced by my friend, Dr. A. F. Rudolf Hoernle, C.I.E., fully twenty years ago, after the first acquisition of ancient manuscript fragments from Kuchar and Khotan. It was, therefore, a special satisfaction to me to be able to place the new materials at the disposal of that veteran scholar, the true pioneer in this field of research. They are so abundant that even a preliminary analysis cannot be completed as yet. But the succinct notices so far published by Dr. Hoernle indicate a number of philologically important results and give every hope of further elucidations.

Most, if not all, of the texts so far examined have proved to be written in that 'unknown' language which, as previous researches seemed to show, was current in the Khotan region and the southern oases of the Tarim Basin both for religious literature and for secular record. Though the Indo-European character of this language had gradually come to be recognized, it could not be interpreted nor even its relation towards the Indian and Iranian language groups determined. It was hence a discovery of far-reaching importance when Dr. Hoernle was able to identify two well-preserved and practically complete books as literal translations of well-known Buddhist texts available in their Sanskrit originals, the Vajracchedika and the Aparamitayuh-sutra. So here were at last found the eagerly-hoped-for 'bilingual' texts, without which it seemed practically impossible to expect any real decipherment of the 'Southern unknown language.'

Even the elaborate tables of alphabet and syllabaries which are often found inserted before such Central-Asian texts written on the back of Chinese rolls, and which I was first inclined to treat lightly, have under Dr. Hoernle's expert examination proved of considerable palaeographical value. They have settled once for all the true readings of difficult ligatures, in the very cursive form of Central-Asian Brahmi script which was adopted with particular frequency for texts of that language.

We are taken to a field of Buddhist propaganda much farther in the West by a number of rolls and Pothi fragments written in a script which, like that used later by the Uigurs, was derived from the Syriac alphabet but here serves for the record of a language undoubtedly Iranian (Fig. 192, 8). To Professor F. W. K. Müller, of the University of Berlin and one of the most learned of living Orientalists, belongs the merit of having first recognized in fragments of similar script brought back from Turfan by Prof. A. Grünwedel's expedition remnants of that Sogdian language which was a branch of Middle Persian spoken in ancient Sogdiana, corresponding roughly to the present Samarkand and Bokhara. We knew already from Chinese and other sources that Buddhism had penetrated early to that region from India through what is now Afghanistan, and that it flourished there until the Arab conquest in the eighth century A.D. The Turfan fragments deciphered by Professor F. W. K. Müller established the fact that people from Sogdiana, both Buddhists and Manichaeans, were widely spread through the northern portions of what is now Chinese Turkestan, and that they continued to use there Sogdian translations of their respective scriptures.

The Sogdian manuscripts discovered among the contents of the hidden library at the 'Thousand Buddhas' now prove that this Iranian influence spread much farther eastwards and into China proper. As far as Professor Müller has been able to examine them, they contain translations from the canonical literature of Buddhism. The close agreement in outward appearance and paper suggests that they were mostly written in a region where Chinese influence prevailed, perhaps at Tun-huang itself. The interpretation of Sogdian texts, owing to the inadequacy of the language material hitherto available and to other causes, still presents great difficulties. Hence the philological value of these new and more extensive materials— one of the well-preserved rolls measures over seventeen feet—is bound to prove considerable.

It is in connection with these texts in Sogdian language that I may conveniently mention the discovery, so far isolated among the 'finds' from the 'Thousand Buddhas,' of a manuscript roll which takes us to a religion and literature originating even farther away in the West. This is a neat little book-roll, about four inches broad but close on fifteen feet long (Fig. 192, 2), written with great clearness in that peculiar form of Syriac or Estrangelo script which, since Professor F. W. K. Müller's brilliant discoveries among the finds of the German expeditions to Turfan, has been recognized as the characteristic writing of the Manichaeans.

The followers of Mani and his creed, that strangest of all syncretistic religions of the East, in which elements of Christian belief, Zoroastrian tenets, and Buddhist metaphysics were fused in an extraordinary medley, were widely spread through the whole of Central Asia and even into China during the later part of what in Eastern Turkestan may conveniently be designated as the Buddhist period. From Chinese historical sources we knew that Manichaeism counted many followers among the Uigurs, that Turkish tribe which, after the downfall of Chinese control over Eastern Turkestan at the close of the eighth century A.D., and the withdrawal of Tibetan occupation half a century later, established its power from westernmost Kan-su to the north-east of the Tarim Basin.

Turfan was for more than two centuries the main seat of Uigur power. It is therefore appropriate that the ruins there should have been the first to yield relics, both in Middle Persian and early Turkish, of that Manichaean literature which, until Professor Müller's discovery, was thought to have completely vanished. They apparently justify the belief that Manichaeism and Buddhism existed peaceably side by side among a population mainly Turkish, which, with a tolerance characteristic of the race, was ready to give a hearing to more than one system of salvation. It was probably much the same also on Chinese ground at Tun-huang; and thus we can account for the strange fact that, among sacred texts and relics deposited in a Buddhist shrine, there should have survived a manuscript of that church of Mani which had its chief ecclesiastical centre in Babylon and which, as plentiful passages in the Fathers of the Church show, was long a serious rival to Christianity on the shores of the Mediterranean.

But apart from this quasi-historical interest, the Manichaean relic from the 'Thousand Buddhas' has proved also of philological value.   Dr. A. von Lecoq, the distinguished Turkologist savant of the Royal Ethnographical Museum at Berlin and the successful leader of the second German expedition to Turfan, who was kind enough to undertake its publication, has shown in an annotated edition recently brought out in the Royal Asiatic Society's *Journal* that the Tun-huang manuscript contains the most complete text so far known of the 'Khuastanift' or Confession Prayer of the Manichaean auditores or laymen, in its early Turkish version.   Only about one-tenth of the text at the commencement has been lost, and this could fortunately be supplemented from fragments now at Berlin.   Without going into details it will suffice to mention, in Dr. von Lecoq's words, that "its excellent state of preservation and the fact of its being written in the clear unequivocal letters of the Manichaean alphabet render this manuscript a most valuable help to all interested in the study of the ancient Turkish speech."

For the same reason another unique 'find' from the walled-up library claims mention in this place.   It is a small manuscript book of over a hundred pages in that earliest Turkish writing designated Runic Turki, known until recently only from the famous Orkhon inscriptions. Some fragmentary leaves in the same script resembling in appearance the runes of the North had turned up at Turfan, and I myself had come upon a sheet of it in the ruined fort of Miran, as already related, as well as some fragments among the contents of the Tun-huang cave. But the little book just referred to is complete from beginning to end (Fig. 192, 3), and by far the largest literary text in that script.

Its value is much increased by the fact that, according to a communication of Professor V. Thomsen, who has honoured me by accepting the task of publishing it, the book is probably an original composition in Turkish and not a translation from some Buddhist or other imported religious text, as is the case with most early Turkish language remains so far recovered.   It contains a collection of short stories on men and animals, bringing out points of moral instruction for children and youths, and the author's own colophon records occasion, place, and time of writing.   Though the date given in the usual Turkish cyclical years cannot be accurately determined, it is improbable that the manuscript is later than the eighth century.

Old Turkish translations of Buddhist canonical works are represented by half-a-dozen books in the so-called Uigur script which developed from Syriac writing, and was in use already for Sogdian texts.   Several of these books are perfectly preserved volumes, counting hundreds of pages and largely interspersed with Chinese rubrics and glosses (Fig. 192, 4, 6).   My friend Dr. E. Denison Ross has been able to identify in at least two of these volumes translations of different portions of a commentary on the Abhidharmakosa, a famous Buddhist metaphysical work, which Hsüan-tsang was the first to transplant into Chinese from its Sanskrit original.   In spite of the difficult contents, there is reason to hope that a detailed study of these Uigur versions, such as Dr. Ross is now engaged upon, will materially enlarge our knowledge of the early Turkish vocabulary.

I have already explained how sadly I felt on the spot my total want of Sinologist training with reference to those masses of Chinese manuscript which formed the preponderating bulk both of the hidden library and of what I was able to bring away from it.   Helped by Chiang-ssŭ-yeh's zeal and intelligent interest I had, indeed, endeavoured, while any selection was possible, to secure Chinese manuscripts mainly from those 'miscellaneous' bundles in which documents and secular writings of various kinds seemed to be more frequent than among the closely tied packets of rolls with Buddhist canonical texts (Fig. 194).   But even if Chiang had been a scholar trained in Western methods of research, it would have been difficult for him to find time for any systematic selection under the conditions prevailing.   As for myself I had to rely almost solely on the assumption that miscellaneous papers showing signs of having been old and badly cared for, long before the final closing of the cave, were most likely to contain materials of historical and antiquarian interest.

It was hence a matter of relief to me when, subsequent to my return to England in 1909, I learned that M. Paul Pelliot, then Professor of Chinese at that great centre of Far Eastern research, the École Française d'Extrême Orient at Hanoi, and since appointed to a chair at the Sorbonne, one of the most distinguished Sinologists living, had in the course of the archaeological mission entrusted to his leadership by the Government and several learned bodies of France, visited Tun-huang about a year after my own stay and been able to search thoroughly all the masses of manuscripts I had been obliged to leave behind in Wang's precarious keeping.   Aided by his exceptional mastery of Chinese literature and bibliography, especially in its branches related to Buddhism, and by the well-merited respect which his learning gained for him everywhere among the Chinese, M. Pelliot succeeded in rapidly sifting the contents of those hundreds and hundreds of tightly packed bundles.   The Tao-shih, who seems to have been much reassured by the discretion maintained about our own little transaction, and by the absence of all awkward consequences, now showed greater indulgence.   No doubt duly rewarded, he allowed M. Pelliot to pick out and bring away whatever manuscripts he considered of importance for historical Chinese or philological studies.   The preliminary account of his labours shows how abundant has been his harvest, a result of competent gleaning.

So it was a particular satisfaction for me when M. Pelliot, after his own return early in 1910, expressed the wish to examine my collection of Chinese manuscripts from the cave, and eventually to undertake its catalogue.   The results of the first rapid scrutiny to which he was good enough to devote a fortnight of unremitting labour, were as gratifying as they well could be.   It showed that the total number of Chinese manuscripts amounted to over 9000, about one-third of these consisting of complete text rolls, and about two-thirds of detached records and fragmentary texts.

"The former in their great majority belong to works of Buddhist literature contained in the Chinese and Japanese editions of the Buddhist Canon.　Being the oldest manuscripts the complete rolls are, of course, very valuable for a future detailed study of those canonical texts; but on the whole they yield relatively little new information which can be immediately utilized.　It is very different with the detached records, acts of ordination, bans, accounts, etc., often exactly dated; these illustrate all the varied aspects of local life, and represent a category of documents of which, until the Tun-huang discoveries, practically no ancient specimens were known to exist.　Finally, it is among the fragmentary manuscripts that there are found most frequently those texts of secular literature, historical, geographical, lexicographical, etc., which are of the greatest importance for the advance of learned Sinologist research."

M. Pelliot's brief preliminary report, from which I have just quoted, gives assurance that philological instinct had guided me rightly when I fixed my attention from the first upon those bundles of 'miscellaneous' papers.　But I have even more reason to feel grateful for the fact that the intrinsic interest of the manuscripts thus secured has induced him to offer his labours for the preparation of a systematic inventory, a task for which no scholar living could possibly be better qualified by learning and critical experience.　It is a comfort to know that the publication of the inventory is assured by the Trustees of the British Museum, in which this portion of my collection is to find its final resting-place.

I have left mention of the Tibetan manuscripts (Fig. 192, 9) to the last because, owing to a variety of causes, including their great mass which is second only to that of the Chinese, no sufficiently extensive examination has as yet been possible.　But from what information I have been able to obtain through the kindness of my friend Dr. F. W. Thomas, the learned Librarian of the India Office, and of Miss C. M. Ridding, an accomplished Tibetan scholar, it seems safe to conclude that the vast majority, if not the whole, of the rolls and 'Pothis' contain texts from the Tibetan Buddhist Canon.   The frequent repetition of certain particularly cherished chapters and prayers, a quasi - mechanical process for acquiring spiritual merit which seems at all times to have had a fatal attraction for pious Tibetans, has confirmed the suspicions I entertained from the first.   But apart from those endless Prajnaparamitas, etc., there remains abundant material which will repay close study when the time comes for textual criticism of the vast literature of Tibetan Buddhism embodied in the Kanjur and Tanjur.   In the meantime these manuscripts, the oldest so far known that can be dated with certainty, are to be carefully catalogued for the India Office Library, their future place of deposit.

CHAPTER LXX

DECORATIVE ART AT THE 'THOUSAND BUDDHAS'

As long as all my efforts had to be devoted to the search among the treasures of the hidden chapel, there was no time to spare for the closer inspection of the hundreds of temple grottoes, big and small, which honeycomb the precipitous conglomerate cliffs on the left river bank above and below Wang Tao-shih's shrine. But on occasional strolls along their line extending for nearly a mile I managed to familiarize myself with the position and character of the larger and more important cave-temples. So when my immediate task of 'excavation' came to an end with the Tao-shih's departure on May 31st, and I was left free to turn my attention to them, there was some preliminary acquaintance to guide me in my survey of their artistic features.

It did not take long to convince me that this survey would necessarily have to be of an eclectic nature, if I was to retain a sufficient margin of time for my other archaeological and geographical tasks of that summer. The total number of separate grottoes, varying in size from big cellas up to fifty-four feet in depth, with antechapels and porches, to miniature shrines of very modest dimensions, amounts to over five hundred, as ascertained in the course of the general site plan which I got the Surveyor to make with the plane-table. They fall roughly into three main groups, the largest of which, to the south, comprises all the caves still visited for worship. The photograph (Fig. 158) shows to the left the lower end of this group, beyond Wang Tao-shih's shrine, and to the right part of the second and much smaller group.

199. ROWS OF SMALL BUDDHIST CAVE-TEMPLES SEEN FROM THE SHRINE OF A COLOSSAL BUDDHA, IN SOUTHERN GROUP OF 'THOUSAND BUDDHAS' SITE, TUN-HUANG.

200. STUCCO IMAGES OF BUDDHA WITH DISCIPLES AND BODHISATTVAS, PARTLY RESTORED, IN ALCOVE OF A SMALLER CAVE-TEMPLE, 'THOUSAND BUDDHAS,' TUN-HUANG.

The walls of cella show diaper decoration with rows of small stencilled Buddhas.

This and the third group still farther down comprises only small grottoes, practically retaining no traces of decoration and evidently inaccessible for long ages. The stream here washes the very foot of the conglomerate cliff, about 50 to 60 feet high in its lowest and most precipitous step, and much of the friable rock-face once containing approaches to the various cave chambers and passages between them has fallen and crumbled away completely. Of wooden galleries and stairs such as must once have served in addition for communication, no trace has survived here. It is probable that most of these small grottoes in the northern groups served as quarters for monks rather than as shrines.

In the southern and largest group, too, the caves are disposed in so irregular a fashion as to preclude all idea of systematic planning. The number of grottoes excavated one above the other varies according to their respective heights; and only for short distances, such as near the Tao-shih's temple (Fig. 198) and between the two shrines containing colossal seated Buddhas (Fig. 199), is it possible to recognize something corresponding to regular rows or stories. In front of many of the upper grottoes wooden stairs and verandahs, dating from the time of the last restoration, are visible, though generally far too decayed for use. Elsewhere their position can still be made out by the holes cut into the rock as supports for the rafters (Fig. 159). The varying stages of decay shown by these adjunct structures suggest that restoration has never quite ceased. The different styles of decoration displayed by the frescoes in parts of the same shrine as well as by the stucco sculptures confirm this conclusion. In fact, with so many grottoes left neglected and available for fresh consecration by any pious donor who would pay for their restoration, centuries are likely to have passed since any new excavation.

A number of archaeological indications show that most if not all the large cave-temples, usually situated on the ground level, date back to T'ang times or even earlier. There is strong reason to assume that the best work in their decoration belongs to the same period, though even then it is impossible to determine whether it was always contemporary with the original construction. The prevalence in the porches of many old shrines of a style of fresco decoration different from the manifestly older compositions in the cellas, but closely resembling that of the procession of large Bodhisattvas painted over the wall which hid the entrance to the Tao-shih's chapel (see Fig. 188), led me to conclude that at some period after the tenth century Ch'ien-fo-tung had seen another protracted spell of prosperity.   Perhaps it coincided with the reign of the great Mongol dynasty which for a century assured peace and flourishing trade through vast areas of Central and Eastern Asia.   But restorations must have been frequent also at certain other periods, as suggested by the marked variations in the character of the fresco work met with in the antechapels and porches where the plastered surface of the cave walls was most liable to suffer damage.

Photographs and exact ground-plans were the only available means for keeping some record of these remarkable shrines, and they, too, could be prepared only for a select series among those hundreds and hundreds of caves.   Fortunately the task of selection was lightened by the general uniformity in their architectural arrangement.   I have already described how the temple cella was in each case approached by a broad porch or passage which alone admitted light and air to the interior excavation. The openings of these porches are clearly seen in Figs. 159, 199.   Outside them the larger shrines have ordinarily antechapels, of the same width as the cellas but much narrower and often verandah-like, closed by wooden construction in front.   In the upper stories communication between the adjoining shrines was once maintained chiefly by passages opening from one antechapel into the other.

Within the cella, which usually is a little deeper than wide—*e.g.* that of Wang Tao-shih's temple measures fifty-four by forty-six feet—the larger shrines have generally a horseshoe-shaped platform facing the porch and elaborately decorated.   Its centre is occupied by a colossal stucco image of Buddha, at the back of which a kind of screen and canopy combined has been spared from the rock and

richly decorated with painting (see Fig. 160). By the sides
of the principal image are grouped statues, up to ten in
number, representing saintly disciples, Bodhisattvas, and
at the extreme corners Guardian-kings of the Regions.
But often only the lotus bases have survived to mark their
positions. Invariably a passage was left between the
platform and the cella walls for the worshippers to perform
the circumambulation prescribed by Buddhist worship after
its ancient Indian model. In the smaller cellas, which
ordinarily are exactly square in shape, the images similarly
grouped are placed on a platform within a broad niche or
alcove (see Fig. 200). In a few cases the centre of the
cella had been left unexcavated and the square block of
rock used as a backing for stucco images. In one of these
shrines the back wall of the cella is occupied by a colossal
representation of Buddha lying in death or rather Nirvana,
a scene quite rare at Ch'ien-fo-tung, and evidently not a
theme cherished by these Chinese artists.

The ceiling of the cellas is usually raised very high
in the shape of a truncated cone, with a coffer-like device
in the centre over a succession of receding steps, some
real and some cleverly painted in succession (see Fig. 160).
The dimensions of the truly colossal seated Buddha statues,
attaining a height of over eighty feet in two temples,
necessitated here a special architectural disposition, the
great height of the cella being lit through a succession
of antechapels on three or four stories which can be reached
over narrow, breakneck flights of stairs carved out from
the soft rock.

The sculptures of the cellas have suffered even more
than the pictorial decoration both from iconoclastic zeal
and from the hands of pious restorers. The fact of their
being modelled throughout in stucco of friable mud
accounts for the risks to which this statuary must have
been exposed at all times. An examination of the many
completely broken old images showed that there was no
essential difference between their make and the methods
of modelling which I saw used by a couple of Tun-huang
'hua-chiang,' or sculptors, who came during my stay to
execute some repairs. Just as I had noticed in the ruined

shrines of the Khotan region, the core of the statues was invariably formed by a rough wooden frame supplemented by broom-like reed bundles for the support of extremities. To this the wet clay was attached in rough clods, subsequently carved into shape with the help of wooden modelling tools, and finally richly painted over a succession of colour washes.

If the technical methods had remained the same, the steady course of deterioration in design and artistic execution was painfully brought home by the restorations old and new. Few statues likely to date from T'ang times had survived, and these only in their lower portions and without their original hands or feet. But wherever such old work had escaped, as seen *e.g.* in Fig. 161, the superior modelling of the limbs, the well-balanced pose, and the graceful arrangement of the drapery, would distinguish it at a glance from the stiff and clumsy additions of later restorers, or such coarse modern 'creations' as seen *e.g.* in Figs. 188, 201. The hideousness of the latter was scarcely redeemed by finding even here unmistakable traces of the influence which the traditional style, originally reflecting Graeco-Buddhist models, and imported through the Tarim Basin, had continued to exercise almost to the present day on local sculptural art however great its debasement.

Taking a general view, the preservation of elements derived from the Buddhist art of India and Central Asia was far more marked in the sculptural remains of these cave-temples, whatever their age, than in the corresponding pictorial work. It was just the reverse in respect of the purely Chinese elements. Conspicuous as the latter were in the frescoes, I found but few sculptures of such distinctly Chinese style as those reproduced in Fig. 196. And significantly enough, the principal figure here represented was Hsüan-tsang, the great Chinese pilgrim and 'Arhat,' to whom this temple was dedicated.

It is, however, in the frescoes or, to use a more accurate term, mural paintings in tempera that the influence which Chinese taste had upon Buddhist art transplanted to Tun-huang most clearly asserts itself. There can be no doubt that the most valuable artistic feature of the site

201. ALCOVE OF BUDDHIST CAVE-TEMPLE, 'THOUSAND BUDDHAS,' WITH MODERN STUCCO IMAGES OF BUDDHA WITH DISCIPLES, BODHISATTVAS, AND LOKAPALA.

202. FRESCO COMPOSITION ON WALL OF CAVE-TEMPLE, 'THOUSAND BUDDHAS,' TUN-HUANG, SHOWING SCENE IN BUDDHIST HEAVEN.

For details see ii. p. 226.

is the abundance and relatively good preservation of the large mural paintings, of which many probably go back to T'ang times. Nothing but careful copies in colour by the hand of an artist fully conversant with Eastern painting and Buddhist iconography could do justice to all the wealth of spirited composition, graceful design of figure and ornament, and harmonious colour effects which these frescoes display, and then it would need his devotion for many laborious months. The task of their exhaustive study or of securing the materials for it was beyond my power and that of my camera. But there was at least the comfort to know that these fine remains of pictorial art were protected by continued worship and local superstition against wanton vandalism, and any attempt at 'museum exploitation.'

As already stated, the best-preserved and manifestly oldest frescoes were to be found within the large cellas, and just there the conditions of lighting were such as to render photographing particularly difficult. Only during certain hours of the morning could adequate light be obtained for particular portions of the painted wall surfaces. Even then work was often seriously interfered with or stopped by the dust-haze left behind by the violent gales which after some days' interval used to blow up the desert valley from the north or north-east. Thus it cost no small amount of time and effort to secure the dozens of photographic negatives by which, in combination with detailed notes, I endeavoured to bring away some record of the most characteristic schemes of mural decoration to be found in these grottoes.

I shall not attempt to describe now the frescoes in each of the temple caves with which I thus made myself familiar. Instead of this, I propose to explain the typical features in a few decorative schemes which were of special frequency or interest, and for the partial illustration of which the reproductions here available will suffice. In the smaller shrines, where the image groups occupy a large niche or alcove, both walls and ceiling show a general diaper decoration with rows of small stencilled Buddha figures, all alike in outline and pose, and varied only in the

colours of dress, halo, etc. (Fig. 200). My excavations
at sites of the Khotan region had familiarized me with this
style of decoration, which must have been common throughout Buddhist Central Asia during T'ang times, and which
allowed even a very modest temple cella to boast of its
' Thousand Buddhas.' Elaborate and often very beautiful
floral ornament forms the borders of these great stencilled
wall surfaces and of the image alcoves. Within the latter
the walls are covered either with large figures of Bodhisattvas and other saintly personages (Fig. 191), or else with
fine floral tracery, cloud scrolls and the like, as seen in Figs.
200, 201. The rich halos with flame bundles painted at
the back of the principal figures are here often a specially
striking decoration. The ceilings of the alcoves usually
show a divine group, such as the Buddha enthroned among
Arhats, cleverly painted in perspective (Fig. 161).

The centre of the side walls in these smaller shrines
is ordinarily occupied by a large fresco panel representing
a crowded scene from some Buddhist heaven. I have
already had occasion to refer to such scenes when discussing
the larger paintings on silk which often look like reduced
copies of such panels (Chap. LXVIII.). In the one reproduced in Fig. 202 we see a Buddha seated on his lotus
throne between somewhat smaller figures of Bodhisattvas
and saintly attendants. Pavilions containing other divine
figures and shaded by rich foliage are disposed at the sides
and behind as an architectural setting. In front of the
terrace occupied by the main group are shown three
platforms rising from a lotus tank and connected by
bridges.

On the middle one, curiously recalling the central
marble terrace always found in the artificial lakes of the old
Moghul gardens so familiar to me from Kashmir and the
Punjab, there is seen a dancing girl performing a spirited
dance on a tesselated pavement. Rows of divine musicians,
probably representing Kimnaris, play on either side on
various instruments. On the side platforms two Buddhas,
with bowls and plates of fruit set before them, seem to
take their share in enjoying the divine ballet. In a few
panels of this class I found also figures of Nagas and

Naginis, half-human half-snake, represented as disporting themselves in the water.

No photographs could convey an impression of the charm which these compositions, and those to be described presently in the larger temples, derive from their rich and harmoniously blended colouring. In the design and grouping of the figures, in their drapery and general iconography, most of what is presented to us by these panels is a direct inheritance from Graeco-Buddhist art as developed in Central Asia. But when we come to examine the technique, even of these hieratic representations where regard for the traditional models was strongest, the difference in treatment is striking. Everywhere the free sweep of the brush so characteristic of Chinese pictorial art endeavours to assert itself over the delicate outline drawing which the same figures display in the frescoes and panels of ancient Khotan. With this change goes naturally a far greater attention to colour effect. The deep purples, browns, and blues which prevail, are set off very strikingly by the usual ground colour, a pale greenish blue most restful to the eye and probably first suggested by the lotus tanks amidst which these scenes of Buddhist paradise are so often placed.

Chinese style, which after all could only modify but not radically change the treatment of these hieratic scenes fixed by convention going back to Indian ground, found free scope in the smaller side panels and dados decorated with quasi-secular scenes of monastic life, husbandry, and travel. It is true that these little scenes, usually accompanied by cartouches filled in with Chinese inscriptions, or more often left blank, are in all probability meant to illustrate 'Jatakas,' or stories from Buddha's former births. But whether from the absence of Graeco-Buddhist models to guide, or on account of some other reason, the whole treatment here seems frankly Chinese. The result is work less effective from a decorative point of view, in fact often a little prosaic and confused, but full of quaint life and vivid movement.

The frescoes of some larger shrines show in places big panels of this type side by side with the conventional

heavenly scenes, and their juxtaposition, as seen in Fig.
203, helps to bring out the contrast. As an interesting
departure from the usual styles of wall decoration practised
at the 'Thousand Buddhas,' I may mention the paintings
found in a small cella to the north of the Tao-shih's cave.
Here the work seemed to be real fresco, not the usual
tempera on a plain stuccoed surface. The large figure
in the middle is that of Avalokitesvara represented as
'the most compassionate Kuan-yin' with many hands.
On either side haloed figures are shown in the act of
worship, while above floats on a cloud a beautifully designed
Gandharvi.

The photographs reproduced in Figs. 160, 203 may
convey some idea of the wealth of mural paintings in one
of the largest cave-temples (Ch. VIII. as I numbered it).
Its cella has retained most of its original wall decoration
and, judging from certain indications, appears to have
served as a model for several other grottoes. The screen
at the back of the chief image, which has completely disappeared and been replaced by a coarse modern Stupa in
plaster, is covered below with rows of colossal Bodhisattvas.
Above is painted a canopy with garlands of big flowers
resembling chrysanthemums. Behind the screen is seen
the rich decoration of the roof rising in the shape of a
truncated pyramid. The spandrels in the corners below,
where it springs from the side walls, are filled with four
grotesque figures of warriors painted in unmistakably
Chinese style and representing the Guardian-kings of the
Regions.

The cella walls are covered throughout with paintings,
all about twelve feet high, those on the north and south
sides being divided into five panels, each over nine feet
wide, while the rest show continuous compositions. The
panels contain scenes from Buddhist heavens cleverly
varied in their composition. The wall facing the entrance is
covered with crowded representations of stories, probably
taken from the 'Jatakas,' shrines, monastic dwellings,
and scenes of travel being distinguishable even in the
photograph (Fig. 204). The shorter walls on either side
of the entrance show above a royal procession, and below,

203. FRESCOES IN NORTH-WEST CORNER OF LARGE CAVE-TEMPLE
CH. VIII., 'THOUSAND BUDDHAS,' TUN-HUANG.

For details see ii. p. 228.

204. FRESCO COMPOSITION REPRESENTING BUDDHIST STORIES, ON WEST WALL OF LARGE CAVE-TEMPLE CH. VIII., 'THOUSAND BUDDHAS,' TUN-HUANG.

For details see ii. p. 228.

in a dado which unfortunately has suffered in parts, rows of female figures richly clad and carrying offerings. The head-dress of all of them is extremely elaborate, with huge pendants and bulb-shaped coiffures. Richer jewelry and somewhat greater stature evidently indicate distinctions in rank. A Chinese inscription on one of these dados, as interpreted on the spot by Chiang-ssŭ-yeh, and since confirmed by M. Chavannes, conveys the important information that this temple cave had been dedicated by a princess of Yü-t'ien, or Khotan. Full light on her date, as on so many details of these frescoes, may confidently be expected from M. Pelliot, who was able to study them carefully.

The fine frescoes on the walls of the broad passage or porch leading into this cella were exposed to far greater injury. But on the southern wall a large and very spirited piece of work has survived, curiously recalling some old Venetian picture by its rich colours and the stately pomp and free movement depicted (Fig. 205). It shows a colossal seated Buddha riding through the air on a richly decorated car which flying genii keep in rapid motion. His right hand is raised in the symbolic act of making 'the wheel of supreme sovereignty' revolve. A robe of pale pink covers his shoulders, while an under-garment of brilliant azure envelops the body from the waist downwards. Two gorgeous banners showing dragons on white ground strewn with green and blue fleurs-de-lys float behind, and mark the quick movement by their fluttering ends. A host of saints and armed attendants are shown flying by the side of and behind the car. Above float cleverly painted clouds on which small groups of saints stand or kneel.

I may conclude this rapid survey of the pictorial decoration of the shrines by a reference to a fairly large cave (Ch. XVI.) situated at the southern extremity of the site. The general scheme here corresponds closely to that of the Khotan princess's temple, and certain details of execu tion make it clear that the latter had served as the direct model. But what gave to this shrine a particular interest was the curious fresco composition which covers the whole of the back wall, some twenty-seven feet long. The legend represented appears to have been a favourite subject in this region; for I found it repeated both here and at the 'Caves of the Myriad Buddhas' subsequently visited; but I have not been able to trace its traditional interpretation.

The right-hand portion of the composition, seen in the photograph of Fig. 206, is remarkable for the vivid realistic way in which the effect of a powerful wind is depicted. In the centre we see a canopied tent-like structure in danger of being blown away. The curtains or tent-flies, along with the massive arrangement of tassels, are tossed up into the air in violent movement, while the richly dressed figure under the canopy, without a halo, and, perhaps, meant for a royal personage, bends forward as if to balance the threatened overthrow of the structure. Some bearded attendants, with their hair and clothes twisted by the wind, endeavour from a ladder to secure the canopy and its whirling curtains. Other groups of human figures seem to watch the scene in amazement, while in the corners, above and below, incidents are depicted which evidently form no part of the main story.

If we now turn to the opposite or left-hand end of the composition (Fig. 207), we find that wind-raised tumult balanced as it were by the calm, dignified presence of a Buddha or Bodhisattva, wearing apparently the patch-work robe of a monk and gently fanning himself with his right hand. An elaborately adorned canopy is steadily supported above his head by cloud-scrolls. In front and below the divine figure there are shown in detached groups persons undergoing painful operations: one has his head pressed down, another his arms tied behind, while a lamenting female turns her hands towards the Buddha as if to implore redress. Above a priestly figure seems about to strike a bell which is carried through the air, and some other figure close by holds out his arm as if pointing towards the effect produced at a distance. The middle portion of the fresco, which extended behind the screen of the central platform of the cella, and which in this confined position could not be photographed, likewise showed figures and objects violently tossed about by the wind.

Finding this scene pictured in much the same fashion elsewhere, I could not resist the conclusion that the theme which the artist in each case aimed at emphasizing was the contrast between the Holy One's gentle gesture of fanning and the violent storm shaking the royal tent far away in the distance. Was it a divine warning miraculously conveyed to an erring prince, or some similar legend, and had the wind-swept condition of this Tun-huang region perhaps something to do with the local popularity of the story? Whatever its true interpretation may prove to be, it is certain that the original designer of this composition commanded no small degree of artistic imagination and skill.

During these weeks of uninterrupted strenuous labour it was no small relief from the strain and anxieties which attended my tasks with Wang Tao-shih that there were such works of true art to claim my attention. My sole relaxation between the day's struggle with materials only too abundant and the note-writing which had to follow at night time, were strolls in the dusk up the wild gorge of rock into which the valley of the 'Thousand Buddhas' rapidly narrowed higher up. On my return from there one dust-laden evening a delightful surprise awaited me at my tent. Turdi, my faithful Dak-man, had arrived with two huge bags of mails. From Abdal quaint old Mullah had guided him along the high barren plateaus of the Altin-tagh, where water was almost scarcer than by the desert route, but, of course, no such trouble from heat. By a succession of forced rides on ponies hired from each little oasis Turdi had managed to cover the distance from Khotan within a month and a half.

It was a remarkably quick performance, considering that over most of the ground the ponies had to carry food supplies for themselves and their rider ; I could well imagine what Turdi's hardships had been from heat, sand-storms, and the frequent want of water. But stolid and close-tongued as usual, my trusty postman allowed little to be extracted from him besides bare dates and 'Salams' from all the Begs who knew me between Khotan and Charklik. Since the beginning of February I had sadly missed all

written news from India and Europe, and now after four
months' waiting the shower of letters which unexpectedly
descended upon me was refreshing like summer rain in the
desert.   That most of those from Europe went back as far
as the last month of the previous year scarcely affected my
joy at resumed touch with dear friends.   Notions of time
proved singularly elastic under changed conditions.   I sat
up till long after midnight opening and rapidly reading this
big budget of letters, close upon two hundred ; and when
it was finished at last, the violent gale blowing up the
valley prevented sleep—until it was daylight and time to
start for fresh work.

Soon afterwards another small diversion was brought
by a visit from Wang, the learned district magistrate.   It
came too late to affect my transaction with the Tao-shih,
nor did I doubt that secretly I might count on my Mandarin
friend's scholarly sympathy.   But I could not help feeling
uneasy when I learned confidentially through Chiang that
Wang Ta-lao-ye's visit had been caused mainly by instructions just arrived from the Lang-chou Viceroy, enjoining
him to dissuade me with all diplomatic politeness from any
attempt at excavation.   The idea apparently was that my
archaeological activity would necessarily turn towards
tombs, the only find-places of ancient remains known to
Chinese collectors of antiques, and that popular prejudice
thus aroused might expose me to personal risks—and the
provincial government to inconvenient trouble.

A report received from the Ya-mên of the Brigadier-
General commanding at Su-chou, and responsible for the
peace of this outlying portion of Kan-su, was said to have
started this official perturbation.   My prolonged stay in
the Tun-huang district had evidently given alarm.   But
since Wang knew better, and could in all honesty point out
the harmless nature of my work, which lay all ' in the Gobi,'
I could hope to avert that polite official obstruction which
might otherwise prove a far more serious obstacle to my
tasks than any chance of my exciting popular resentment.
Nevertheless I took care to send Chiang to town for a
couple of days, and to assure myself through him that the
report despatched to the Viceroy put my case in the right

205. LARGE FRESCO COMPOSITION ON SOUTH WALL OF PORCH IN CAVE-TEMPLE CH. VIII.,
'THOUSAND BUDDHAS,' SHOWING BUDDHA ON CAR.

For details see ii. p. 229.

light.   For all such gentle guidance of bureaucratic wheels
Chiang's help was invaluable.

While hindrance was safely averted on this score, I
learned through Chiang that there was reason for uneasiness at the local Ya-mêns from a far more serious cause.
For some years past there had been contention over a
matter of revenue assessment between the magistrate's
office and a section of the headstrong Tun-huang colonists.
The case had been finally decided against the latter
at provincial headquarters; but there was well-founded
apprehension in the official dove-cots that enforcement of
the judgment might provoke resistance among these *soi-
disant* protectors of the Empire's marches.   So Wang's
head rested uneasy on his cushions; and when breezy old
Lin Ta-jên, his military colleague, came out towards the
end of my stay to pay me a short visit, he confided that
they both deemed it prudent to put off any action until I
was safely out of the district.   I thought the hint very
considerate, and finally decided to move all my impedimenta
with me to An-hsi, instead of depositing them at the
friendly Tun-huang Ya-mên, as I had first intended, until
my return from the mountains.

By dint of great exertions my work at the caves was
completed on the 13th of June.   The camels had been
brought back from the mountains where they had found
precarious grazing, but well-deserved rest and coolness.
The heat of the plains precluded all idea of using them
for burdens or even of keeping them long there.   So I
was doubly glad when the five big three-horsed carts
needed for our transport arrived overnight from Tun-
huang.   It only struck me afterwards that the desire
to see us with all our belongings safely off before the
administrative tension had developed too far, might have
had something to do with this unusual promptness.   Next
morning I started the whole train off by the direct route
towards An-hsi, and after a hearty farewell to the Tao-shih
at his shrine, and a final visit to those caves which had
fascinated me most by their paintings, galloped off with
Chiang for Tun-huang.

The departure cost me a wrench; but the oasis looked

delightfully green and refreshing, and I greeted it like an anchorite set free from another Thebais. There I was kept busy all day with the last settling of accounts and farewell visits to my Amban friends. A pleasant hour was passed at Wang's cool and shady Ya-mên, where I had my last chat about local antiquities with that refined scholar friend. His grey-haired old mother, a dignified matron, had just joined him from Shan-hsi, and with her son and daughter-in-law sat for a peaceful family group (Fig. 209). How could I have foreseen the scenes of bloodshed and pillage which were soon to be witnessed here! Then a small but *recherché* meal united us at Lin Ta-jên's table.

The heat of the day had worn off when I finally rode away from the garden which had served as my Tun-huang camp. At the large temple outside the east gate of the town I found my Mandarin friends assembled with a large array of their officials, all in gala dress, to bid me a hearty farewell. It was a true scene from the ancient East, and the polychrome woodwork of the high temple portico made a striking frame for my last impression of Tun-huang. It was dark before I reached the edge of the oasis, and midnight by the time I rejoined my camp at a solitary road-side station in the desert. So there was plenty of time for thought of all that Tun-huang had yielded up to me. But the strain of these labours had been great, and my relief was equally great at being now free to exchange archaeological work in the torrid desert plains for geographical exploration in the mountains.

206. FRESCO COMPOSITIONS IN NORTH-WEST CORNER OF LARGE CAVE-TEMPLE
CH. XVI., 'THOUSAND BUDDHAS,' TUN-HUANG.

On left, representation of 'wind scene.' For details see ii. p. 230.

207. FRESCO COMPOSITION IN SOUTH-WEST CORNER OF LARGE CAVE-TEMPLE
CH. XVI., 'THOUSAND BUDDHAS,' TUN-HUANG.

In centre Buddha or Bodhisattva raising fan.   For details see ii. p. 230.

CHAPTER LXXI

AT AN-HSI, THE 'WEST-PROTECTING'

AN-HSI, the headquarters of the 'Independent Department' to which Tun-huang belonged, had seemed a convenient place for a depot and new base; for it lies at the point where the great road coming from Su-chou and China 'within the Wall' turns off towards Hami and Eastern Turkestan. Whatever shape my plans for the next winter's work in the Tarim Basin might take, I should have to pass through An-hsi, and there was the immediate advantage of my being able to strike due south to the snowy range of the westernmost Nan-shan by a route which promised to be of varied interest. Three hot and fairly long marches along the barren foot of a completely denuded outer hill range brought us by June 16th to the humble road-side station of Kua-chou-kou, which derives its designation from the ancient name of the whole oasis. Next day a fifteen miles' ride across the wide scrub-covered plain took me to the town of An-hsi. All the way strips of poor fields alternated with extensive waste lands, and the ruins of walled villages and towns, most of them said to have been destroyed during the great Tungan rebellion, were far more conspicuous than the scattered homesteads of present occupation.

So I was not altogether surprised by the air of neglect and stagnation which everything about An-hsi bore. The town boasted of the name, 'the West-protecting [garrison],' which once in the great times of the T'ang had been borne by the seat of the Chinese Governor-General controlling the whole of Turkestan. But it was now scarcely more than a straggling street within a big, desolate-looking oblong formed by the crumbling town walls. Compared with it Tun-huang seemed quite a thriving city. The town lies not far from the Su-lo Ho river, and at the eastern end of a compact stretch of cultivation, about a couple of miles wide, which forms the main oasis.

Luckily I was not obliged to seek shelter within its insalubrious precincts. Forewarned by Wang Ta-lao-ye of my tastes, En T'ai-tsin, the magistrate, had arranged for my quarters at a modest temple about half a mile outside the western gate. In its single hall I could store my cases in safety and seek protection from the fierce heat of the daytime, while a tiny orchard behind allowed my tent to be pitched in something like privacy to serve as my abode for the night. Close by was a tumble-down structure, which the good-natured priestly guardian of the temple kept usually under lock and key. It was full of coffins, big and small, with bodies awaiting transport to their ancestral homes in far-away provinces. Luckily I did not make the discovery until quite the end of my stay.

This, in spite of my eagerness to set out for the mountains, stretched out longer than I had first thought. The magistrate, a well-meaning though by no means brilliant person, quite exhausted himself in politeness, and in spite of a certain nervous air expressed himself ready to become responsible for the safe storage of my cases in his Ya-mên. But the provision of the transport needed for my move southward seemed a formidable affair, and I had not been long at An-hsi before I realised how very limited were the resources of the place in spite of its magistrate's high-sounding title. Apart from the struggling hamlets in the wide, scrub-covered plain, which was very slowly recovering from the terrible ravages of the Tungan inroads, the district in his immediate charge comprised but a few scattered villages far away in the foot-hills, where his orders had scant chance of being obeyed with promptness. I had also reason to believe that the Viceregal apprehension about the risks which I might cause by my excavations had, in spite of Wang's sensible representation of the true facts, left its impress on his timorous mind. I had avowed my intention of visiting on my way the ruins near the outlying village of Ch'iao-tzŭ, about which a Turki Muhammadan trader of An-hsi had given me information ; and this became an additional reason for delay in effecting the needful arrangements.

Fortunately I was able to use the six days which it cost to surmount these obstacles not only for many tasks of writing, but also for interesting archaeological observations in the neighbourhood. I had every reason to believe that the line of the ancient *Limes* which I had traced in April from Tun-huang to within thirty miles or so of An-hsi continued past the latter place eastwards. The large towers, which on approaching An-hsi we had sighted due west, proved of more recent origin. But when I subsequently inspected two smaller towers which the Surveyor had come across in the course of a reconnaissance tour, about four miles to the south-west of the new town, I soon convinced myself that in dimensions and method of construction they corresponded exactly to the watch-towers so familiar from the Tun-huang desert.

The remains of an *agger* connecting them and still rising in places to four or five feet furnished conclusive evidence of this being indeed the line followed here by that ancient *Limes*. The mound on being cut through showed the usual layers of Toghrak branches embedded in earth and gravel. The preservation of these traces of the Han wall was manifestly due to the bare gravel of which the ground just at this point consisted, while elsewhere, to the east and west of that stretch, it was scrub-covered loess. The moisture reaching the latter from the overflow of canals had sufficed to efface all traces of the wall, and when revisiting this neighbourhood in October I found, in fact, much of the broad belt of waste flooded. The extant towers of stamped clay stood at about one mile's distance from each other, and near them low mounds of clay seemed to indicate the position of quarters. But I vainly had the soil searched for any datable relics apart from ancient potsherds.

Curiously enough, where the line of the old wall still traceable in places strikes the present main road from Tun-huang to An-hsi, I found a much-restored tower with a small modern reception-hall built near it. It seemed very probable that the core of the tower was ancient, and that continuity of local tradition had something to do with selecting the spot where the road passed through the *Limes* for what Chinese custom treats as the conventional mark of a district headquarters boundary.

The ruined town, situated about two miles south-east of the present An-hsi on a barren waste of fine gravel, was also an interesting place to examine. According to local information it had been deserted towards the close of the eighteenth century, after repeated destruction by fire, and its interior was absolutely clear of buildings. The enclosing walls, solidly built in stamped clay of about fifteen feet thickness, formed a square of about 600 yards; but that they could not be of any great age was certain from many indications. All the more striking was the extraordinary effect which wind erosion had produced upon them. The east face, and to a somewhat lesser extent also the west face, had been breached at short intervals by deep fissures resulting from the scouring with driven sand. Many breaches thus effected reached down to within five or six feet of the ground, and at the north-east corner, as seen in Fig. 208, they had been carried down so low that the wall there has been razed off altogether.

The cuttings which had not yet advanced so far were always broader on the east than on the west face of the wall, and the scouring which produced these trumpet-shaped troughs could be studied with clearness at their bottom. One measured cutting of average size was thirteen feet deep and eight broad on the east side. The sand carried by the prevalent east and north-east wind through these troughs had accumulated under the shelter of the west or inner side of the eastern wall face in dunes up to eighteen or twenty feet. Outside this face but little drift sand remained. Whatever sand is carried through the breached east wall is subsequently driven across the open interior to repeat its work of destruction on the west wall.

While the east and west faces are thus gradually undergoing erosion which will ultimately efface them altogether, the town walls facing north and south parallel to the prevailing wind direction have escaped with relatively little damage.   What better illustration than this could I have desired to show why the east and west walls of the ancient Chinese station north of Lop-nor had completely disappeared while I could still trace those to the north and south ?   Curiously enough the semicircular bastion in front of the east gate of old An-hsi has nowhere been breached, though its foot has been under-cut by driven sand in a few places.   Evidently the sand not meeting here with absolute obstruction is diverted sidewise.

When I subsequently examined the walls of the present An-hsi town I found that the eastern face was in danger of falling from exactly the same cause, the onset of that relentless foe, the famous 'wind of An-hsi.'   In order to prevent breaching on the top, this particular wall face had been protected, apparently since the reconquest after the Tungan rising, with a solid stone parapet.   This had to some extent averted the attack above, though even thus I found that a dune fifteen to twenty feet high had formed on the inside.   But the drift sand baffled in its usual line of assault was now scouring the clay rampart below, and in many places the under-cut wall looked as if destined to tumble before long.   Yet at the same time I found scarcely any traces around An-hsi that wind erosion, with so much of its ready instrument, driven sand, close at hand, had produced those characteristic Yardang trenches of the Lop-nor desert, or lowered the ground level generally as at sites along the southern edge of the Taklamakan.   No doubt the cover of vegetation, scanty as it looked in places, was sufficient to afford protection to the soil.   That all trees and shrubs about An-hsi had a marked western bend in their growth is a point that scarcely needs emphasizing.

Our stay there was enlivened by a succession of dust-storms.   Yet in spite of them the heat continued oppressive. So it was a great relief when during the night of June 22nd brisk showers descended, followed by drizzling rain at intervals during great part of the next day.   It was the first real rain I had seen since those trying days of last August high up in the Karanghu-tagh mountains, and it seemed

quite a delightful experience. But it was also a reminder
that the conditions of practically unbroken dryness which had
favoured my search for antiquities as far as the Tun-huang
desert could not be expected to extend much farther east.
The carts by which the baggage was to move to Ch'iao-
tzŭ had been promised for that day. But when I saw the
water-logged condition of the fields and lanes under a sky
of true Europe hue, I was less inclined to chafe at the
inevitable Cathayan delay.

At last, on June 24th, I was able to leave An-hsi. The
transfer to the Ya-mên of all cases with manuscripts and
antiques, as well as of all stores and equipment which
could be spared till the autumn, had greatly reduced our
impedimenta. Three light carts sufficed for their transport,
and by 9 A.M. I saw them safely move off with the majority
of my party. I myself with Chiang-ssŭ-yeh had to pay
farewell visits at the Ya-mên, a welcome opportunity to
convince myself personally that the place of storage in the
magistrate's official quarters was as safe as human forethought could provide in this region. The obliging if
somewhat timorous Mandarin had allotted to them a room
airy and easily watched within his private courtyard.
Large beams had been laid over pillars of bricks to raise
the precious cases well above the ground, and Ibrahim
Beg was to see to it that once every week they were
carried out into the sun to prevent all possibility of damp
attacking the contents.

In spite of the exceptional rain which had fallen the
day before, there was in truth little fear on this score in
wind-swept and sun-parched An-hsi. But it was a convenient means to assure a frequent check by faithful
Ibrahim Beg of my precious deposit. The Amban had
accepted full responsibility for its safe keeping as far as
numbers and seals could show it, and Ibrahim's weekly
inspections would help to keep alive this sense of official
responsibility. Elaborate fastenings on each case, secured
by seals within wooden seal-cases copied from ancient
specimens, would effectively prevent 'unauthorized inspection' of the contents, if such an excess of antiquarian
curiosity—or greed—could be apprehended on the part of

the somnolent dwellers of An-hsi. The formal receipt drawn up in due style by Chiang on a sheet of brilliant scarlet looked imposing, and when it had been signed by Ên T'ai-tsin and stamped with his large official seal, my conscience could rest satisfied with the precautions taken against human risks.

My visit to the Telegraph Office was a less formal affair. Like the telegraph poles I first came upon here, ' Mr. Li, the Telegraph Commissioner' who looked after the single wire all the way from Su-chou to Hami, had been a novel feature in my stay at An-hsi. His letters received while near Tun-huang had been written in such excellent English that I was much surprised on arrival to find him quite unable to speak it. But his first visit had shown him as a very gentlemanly and scholarly person, and both Chiang and myself had greatly taken to him, especially as he showed keen antiquarian taste and knowledge. So I was eager to thank him once more for the unfailing care and accuracy with which he had managed my intercourse with Kashgar and Peking.

His neatly kept Ya-mên, with flower-beds in its court-yard and young trees in front of the gate, was a pleasing contrast to unkempt and desolate An-hsi. The delightfully clear atmosphere, due to the preceding rain, had exposed still more the utter decay of the place with its wind-breached wall and wide expanse of waste grounds now partly covered by pools. Within Mr. Li's quarters everything breathed an air of well-ordered activity. His modest reception room lined with neat rows of books, painted scrolls, and specimens of Chinese palaeography, as well as some ancient brasses brought from Kan - chou, plainly reflected the studious and artistic habits of this learned and yet business-like official.

His English training under the Lan-chou Mission and in the Telegraph Department's course had been gone through in less than a year. Yet judged by his ability to write a letter in plain English, and still more by the taste acquired for English reading and solid facts of Western knowledge, this very brief training had been attended by results which are rare in the case of Indian students who have painfully dragged themselves through a course six to ten times as long. This is not the place to discuss the causes which may explain the difference. For me at the time it was enough to have personal evidence how well the linguistic training needed for access to Western knowledge could find its place in a mind still fully imbued with the tastes and ideas of traditional Chinese culture.

Mr. Li's son, an intelligent, sturdy boy of ten, was summoned from the master who was introducing him and a few other boys from the local officials' families to the rudiments of Chinese classics. In neatness of dress and quiet, courteous manners he seemed the very replica of his father. I had nothing quite suitable to offer in return for the exquisitely written fan which Mr. Li presented to me as a parting gift. But I hoped that my An-hsi friend's taste would appreciate Dr. Bushell s *Handbook of Chinese Art*, with its cleverly chosen illustrations, when the copy I ordered from London should after a year or so have found its way to these cross-roads of Asia.

What with the officials' return visits, the distribution of *douceurs* to their myrmidons detailed for my camp, etc., it was 2 P.M. before I could set out for Ch'iao-tzŭ. I had not been able to gather any definite information about the position of the place; but from the vague indications of the Ya-mên attendant who was to serve as guide, it appeared that it lay somewhere beyond the low hills to the south-east and a long way off. So we hurried over the bare steppe which extends east of An-hsi town, though much hampered by the numerous shallow channels, in which the rain water from that weather-worn range had for once spread itself.

After some six miles we struck the canal which brings the water of the Su-lo Ho to the An-hsi oasis. There we left the bumpy track that figures as the imperial high road into Kan-su, and turned to the south towards the hill range which, though low and entirely barren, promised welcome coolness; for in the absolutely clear atmosphere the sun's rays burned fiercely. While crossing the desolate steppe some three miles broad to the foot of the hills, I noticed on a stretch of bare gravel two mounds of clay rising before us separated by a distance of about two miles. I was at once struck with the idea that they might mark ruined watch-towers of the ancient frontier line, such as we had previously failed to trace east of An-hsi, and as we passed between them this was strikingly confirmed. When near, it was easy to notice the low but continuous mound, the old *agger*, which connected the towers. Its line ran parallel to the river, as elsewhere. There was no time then to visit the badly decayed towers; but of their character there could be, no doubt, and I was glad to have ocular proof of remains of the old wall surviving so far eastward.

Close to a large deserted road-side station, ruined apparently as so many others during the havoc of the Tungan rebellion, we crossed a narrow belt of grass and jungle watered by a channel coming from the river, but now swollen to unusual size by surface drainage. The vivid green formed a pleasing contrast to the dark grey gravel of the glacis and the red and brown tinted hills in the background. The grey-haired old 'Ya-i' who was supposed to guide us knew no name for either stream or station. The ground now rose quickly, and within a mile or so the well-marked cart track brought us among the denuded cliffs and detritus slopes of a regular Wadi. The fantastically eroded hill-sides were so steep, and the winding gorge between them so narrow, that I was constantly wondering how the lumbering carts of this region could ever find a passage through them. But the gorge, in spite of the rock *coulisses*, never closed completely, and, if it did, a conveniently low ridge at the end of a side branch gave access to another passage.

As is so often observed among desert hills, which wind erosion even more than that of water has scoured and fissured, the eye could not always make out whether the particular bit of gorge was rising or falling. It was getting quite cool when we crossed a somewhat wider depression which I thought might be the watershed, at an approximate elevation of about 5700 feet, to plunge once more into a maze of small serrated ridges and gorges. Their cliffs, apparently coarse sandstone and shale, were

244 AN-HSI, THE 'WEST-PROTECTING' CH. LXXI

lit up brilliantly by the evening sun in red, yellow, and brown. Chiang, my lively companion, had not prepared himself for this coolness of the hills, and I could see him draw close around his breast the dainty silk robe and jacket he had donned for our state visits. There was some anxiety, too, about the inner man, when I heard him enquire again and again about the distance before us. Dismayed at the vague statement that it might still be fifty Li, about ten miles—or a good deal more—he confided that he had that day omitted the precaution of a substantial morning meal. Accustomed, however, to such incidents in travel, he would not accept my offer of the few rusks left over in my 'tiffin-basket.' Perhaps he remembered the hardness and plainness of this *pièce de résistance* of my travelling cupboard.

The next five miles were ascent and descent in rocky gorges, which as the first bit of hill travel after ten months on flat desert ground pleased me greatly; but at length we emerged on the broad valley beyond. This great basin was an impressive sight, fully fifteen miles wide, with three distinct ranges rising above it, the last snow-capped. But clouds were gathering quickly over the higher ones and hid them long before dusk. The whole valley looked strangely green to eyes accustomed so long to the grey and yellow of the desert. Large dark green plots far away marked tree-girt oases, while all the rest of the wide expanse was thickly covered with reeds, grass, and scrub. Much of it seemed marshy, and wherever the porous clods of the soil lay bare, it betrayed saline efflorescence.

Soon the narrow cart track which was to take us to Ch'iao-tzŭ became more like a ditch or continuous strip of bog. It was close on 7 P.M., and with the clouds now descending and threatening fresh rain we all began to look out eagerly for the oasis. Of the carts which had preceded us long before through the pass there was no trace to be seen, and I wondered how they could ever have been dragged over so boggy a road. In the dusk, hastened by drizzling rain, every large bush of tamarisk loomed big like a clump of trees, rousing deceptive hope of at last nearing Ch'iao-tzŭ. Our age-bent guide, trotting ahead on a diminutive donkey, had no explanations to offer. So to the pleasure of groping in growing darkness along a slippery, half-submerged rut, there was added uncertainty as to when and where we might again meet with our baggage.

At last about 10 P.M. loud barking told us that we were near some inhabited spot which proved to be an outlying farm of Ch'iao-tzŭ. Half-a-mile farther east our hapless ' Ya-i,' already half-overcome by fatigue, conducted us to a small group of homesteads which he declared to be the chief place of the oasis. It took time before we had aroused some men from their slumber, while a dozen or more of ferocious curs were yelping around us. The peasants had not seen or heard any carts pass, and with that persistent display of ignorance which seems to characterize these honest but wary folk on the Kan-su borders, refused to offer the slightest suggestion as to any other route the carts might possibly have followed under their far more intelligent guide supplied by the military commandant. Chiang would have gladly taken shelter then and there, in spite of the squalid look of the dwellings and his well-justified anger at the incompetence of the helpless representative of the civil powers.

But I was not prepared to give in so readily, and when Chiang had refreshed himself with my ultra-dry rusks— with satisfaction I watched him empty the little tin before he could realize in the darkness that there was nothing left for me—we set out for a fresh search. The rain had now stopped, but none of the drowsy villagers would act as guide. The ' Ya-i,' however, ransacking the dim corners of his memory, thought he had once in his younger days been to a part of the oasis known as ' South Ch'iao-tzŭ ' which might be worth searching. Alas! we had not got far in the darkness before the old man's flickering sense of locality gave out completely. Stumbling at a lonely farm which he pretended was ' Nan-Ch'iao-tzŭ, we received the not wholly unexpected information that nothing was known of our carts and people. So I resigned myself to spending the hours till daylight at what our ' Ya-i ' had hailed as the best quarters of Ch'iao-tzŭ.

It was midnight when we regained them. Round three sides of a small quadrangular court, which to touch and smell suggested a pig-sty, there were three single-roomed dwellings detached in the orthodox fashion. All three proved to be held in strength by cultivators, their women-folk and children sleeping the sleep of the just. But the head of the farm was still awake and politely now offered hospitality. It took time, however, before the centre room could be cleared of closely-huddled-up humanity. When I first peeped into it by the light of a small flickering oil lamp it seemed quite a Rembrandtesque picture—but the setting not exactly inviting. Luckily my camp chair had come with me from An-hsi to save me a night on the murky mud floor, or on the still dirtier rugs left behind on the sleeping platform, probably not without the usual live-stock. Tea was soon ready in kettle and cup from my little basket, and when I had got a couple of eggs boiled for this midnight 'dinner' I felt grateful for a rest in my not over-luxurious camp chair and under a dry roof.

208. WIND-ERODED WALLS AT NORTH-EAST CORNER OF RUINED TOWN, AN-HSI.

209. WANG TA-LAO-YE, MAGISTRATE OF TUN-HUANG, WITH HIS WIFE AND MOTHER.

210. WIND-ERODED GROUND AT FOOT OF GRAVEL GLACIS, EAST OF RUINED TOWN
OF CH'IAO-TZŬ.

211. GATE PAVILION OF OLD TEMPLE IN CH'IAO-TZŬ VILLAGE.
In front carts loaded with our baggage.

CHAPTER LXXII

THE RUINS OF CH'IAO-TZŬ

NEXT morning we were up long before the sun rose, and were just preparing to start on a fresh search for the missing baggage when reassuring proof came of its presence at no great distance. It was brought by a pony belonging to the cart which had been requisitioned to An-hsi from this very farm. The men at once rightly concluded that the animal had escaped from the place where our main party had put up for the night. It was a delightfully cool and fresh morning, with the luxuriant grass and reeds along the clear spring-fed stream still moist with the rain of the night. The sky above had cleared, but a light veil of mist and vapour clung to the bare hills north and south. It was long since I had felt so completely carried back to the soft colours and outlines of rural England.

I was almost sorry that the groups of fine shady elms scattered among fields only some two miles off to the south proved to mark 'South Ch'iao-tzŭ,' the goal we had vainly searched for the previous night. Great was my surprise when the screen of tall elms and willows unmasked a small walled town, the true centre of the oasis. Through a big half-ruined gate we reached the enclosed area, about a quarter of a mile square, but of irregular shape. Passing the high clay walls of an inner fort and the silent ruins of dismantled dwellings, we soon came upon a village of some thirty or forty houses hidden among the remains of a place once far more populous. Leisurely householders and numbers of lively boys were already about in spite of the early hour, and quickly we were guided to where a

group of picturesque temple halls, shaded by beautiful old
elms, had given shelter to my belated caravan (Fig. 211).

It was soothing to find all our belongings safely arrived
and quite dry. Like sensible men, Kao Ta-lao-ye, the
petty officer attached to my camp, and the cart drivers
had not attempted the straight route, which was hopelessly
bogged, but had skirted the marshes by a slightly circuitous
track through the outlying hamlet of P'ing-t'ou-shih. To
leave the choice of my own quarters even to circumspect
Tila Bai would ordinarily spell disappointment. But here
with plenty of room for all to spread themselves, he had
proved a wise quarter-master. I found my camp kit laid
out in the airy verandah of the temple which lay farthest
off the entrance, and near the south-west corner of the town
wall. So I was quite safe from the sonorous neighbourhood of followers, ponies, camels, *et hoc genus omne*.

There was peace in the grass-grown court in front of
'my' temple, with its big-eaved loggia facing north, and
in order to secure ease and comfort it only remained
to remove two huge coffins which graced the premises.
Fortunately these monumental receptacles owned by men
of substance at Ch'iao-tzŭ proved as yet untenanted, and
their transfer to another shrine was quickly effected
without risk of pious objections. Mats from the temple
school and felts from my baggage were soon fastened to
the paling in front of the open hall to give privacy.
Refreshed by a 'tub' and a meal that combined dinner
and breakfast, I almost enjoyed the remembrance of the
night's cheerless experiences.

The peaceful retreat I had found under the walls of half-
decayed, somnolent Ch'iao-tzŭ was made doubly welcome
by the plentiful tasks which helped to make my stay busy.
There was still much writing to be done for the long-
delayed mail bag which faithful Turdi was to take back to
Khotan, and then there was the old site which claimed
my attention with equal urgency. Fortunately the days
were so long that by riding out to the ruins at sunrise and
galloping back to my writing table when heat and glare
became strongest in the early afternoon, I managed to find
time for both.

The 'old town,' of which I had heard the vaguest of accounts at An-hsi, proved a large site and one highly instructive. It lay at a distance of about five miles due south of Nan-Ch'iao-tzŭ. It was separated from the extant oasis first by a belt of scrub-covered steppe, and then by a narrower strip of ground partly undergoing wind erosion and partly overrun by low dunes which reeds and tamarisks were binding. Here I found the conspicuous remains of a walled town of the usual Chinese type forming an irregular quadrangle. Outside it, and scattered over an area which covers at least half-a-dozen square miles, there rose ruins of clay-built towers, walled enclosures, and thick pottery débris marking the position of dwellings now completely eroded.

I soon saw that within the walled area there was little scope left for systematic excavation ; for the slow but sure destruction dealt by wind erosion and the depredations of villagers had spared nothing but massive walls of stamped clay, and here and there big mounds composed of potsherds, brick fragments, charcoal, and similar hard débris. At the same time the abundant tamarisk growth and the presence even of trees in depressions not covered by deep sand were indications of subsoil water with its destructive moisture relatively near. But the study of the physical changes which had come over the ruins and the adjoining ground since they had been deserted proved very instructive. Copper coins, of which plenty were picked up on soil swept clear by the winds, showed that the site must have been inhabited during the whole of the T'ang period and down to at least the twelfth century A.D. Yet, relatively short as the time passed since its abandonment may appear, it had sufficed to produce effects on the ruins as well as on the soil which vividly recalled to my mind the most striking features observed at the far more ancient sites in the desert north of Lop-nor.

The town and the once cultivated area near it occupy a flat stretch of fertile loess soil extending along the edge of the bare gravel glacis which slopes down from the hill range south. Left unprotected now by vegetation owing to want of surface water, this belt, stretching away to west and east for at least sixteen miles, has been scooped out and sculptured, by the same powerful east wind which we had seen at work in the Su-lo Ho basin, into innumerable small ridges and trenches invariably showing the direction east to west (Fig. 210). It was the desolate scene so familiar from the Lop-nor sites that I found reproduced here with surprising fidelity. Only the scourings of the ground were less deep, generally varying from two to five feet. This was obviously due to the fact that the time which had elapsed since the disappearance of the protecting vegetation was here fully a thousand years less. The corrosive action of the coarse sand carried down from the detritus-covered hill range must have powerfully aided deflation, *i.e.* wind erosion pure and simple. Yet none of this sand was left on the broad belt of eroded loess stretching away eastwards as far as the eye could reach.

But within the massive town walls, enclosing a quadri-lateral of about 530 yards on the east and west faces, 620 yards on the north, and about 500 yards on the south, the sand lay heaped up in almost continuous dunes covering the original ground in places up to twenty feet. The east wall, just as in the old town of An-hsi, had been cut through in a succession of huge breaches. But the dunes which had thus accumulated within the enclosed area had so far succeeded in protecting the west wall from similar breaching, though its top already showed incipient cuttings. When once these are carried to a sufficient depth, the wind will regain full play over the sand now filling the interior and quickly drive it out westwards. Then erosion will do its work within the walls as thoroughly as it already has outside, and of the enclosure now half-smothered under dunes nothing will be left but an eroded Tati with remains of the clay ramparts facing north and south. It was curious to note how little these two wall-faces, protected by their direction parallel to the destructive wind, had suffered so far, another striking illustration of the conditions observed at the ancient walled station of ' Lou-lan.'

Of the bastions, and other protective structures of So-yang-chêng, as the deserted town is still known to the people of Ch'iao-tzŭ, I need not give details here. They showed plainly that the art of fortification, as seen in the extant towns of this region, had practically remained unchanged since T'ang times or probably even an earlier period.   But, as a peculiar feature possibly accounted for by local conditions, it deserves to be mentioned that the town possessed two walls facing east, the inner built at a distance of about 200 yards from the outer.   The latter had to bear the full force of erosion and was traceable only as a line of badly decayed segments.   The inner had suffered many breaches, but its massive foundations were still continuous and the bastions and gate recognizable.   Is it possible that the inner east wall was raised for protection when the outer had been reduced by the relentless wind to a condition beyond hope of repair or defence?   The shrinkage in population which must have long preceded abandonment might also have recommended this expedient.

However this may be, there was evidence that desolation had come over this little town, not at once, but as a slow, lingering death.   On the top of the débris mounds emerging above the drift sand I found remains of poorly built dwellings manifestly of later date, and statements of villagers, whom curiosity drew out from the hamlets of Ch'iao-tzŭ to watch my proceedings, indicated that some of these had been temporarily tenanted even within memory of man.   Herdsmen grazing their ponies on the marshy steppe northward used to seek shelter there against the icy blasts of the winter.   Even at the present day the ruined town saw temporary residents in the shape of people coming to collect saltpetre from the soil once occupied by buildings.   In more than one place at the foot of the west wall I saw the little smoke-begrimed caves which these humble folk had dug out for quarters.

In front of the largest there rose, on what was plainly a worked-out rubbish heap, a tiny mud shrine such as I had often seen near detached farms or even by the side of fields in the oases.   Sticks of pine wood, commonly burned for incense, lay on the miniature altar, evidence that this modest sanctuary still saw worship.   But, luckily, no religious scruples had prevented Kao Ta-lao-ye, our active

252 THE RUINS OF CH'IAO-TZŬ CH. LXXII

military factotum, from carrying away from it a very
interesting small antique, which he rightly thought I
should value. It was the fragmentary arm of a statue
carved in wood, covered with elaborate relief ornaments
showing close resemblance in style to the Gandhara
designs which I had admired in the wood-carvings of
the Lop-nor sites. Remains of bright colouring still
adhered. There could be no doubt that the statue to
which this relic had once belonged was a work of early
date. But there was no clue to guide us to its original
place of discovery.

Excavations, carried out experimentally under the
supervision of Chiang-ssŭ-yeh at several débris mounds,
revealed neither written records nor other objects of special
antiquarian interest. But the fragments of pottery and
porcelain which came to light confirmed my conclusion as
to the date down to which the town was inhabited. An
elaborately decorated Stupa, which rose on a solid base of
clay about a quarter of a mile to the east of the town
(Fig. 212), still retained portions of its original coating
with hard yellow stucco. The mouldings and general
design suggested that it had been constructed during later
Sung times (eleventh to thirteenth centuries A.D.) when
the Hsi-hsia tribe ruled this part of Kan-su. Of the
temple which had once adjoined it on the south nothing
remained but small fragments of hard bricks, some bearing,
in beautiful green glaze, scroll ornaments in low reliefs.
These might have served as roofing tiles.

A big cutting in the brickwork of the Stupa showed
that treasure-seekers had followed the procedure so familiar
to me from Turkestan ruins. Their burrowing had not
spared the small Stupas, about ten to twelve feet in
diameter, which rose in a row north and north-east along
the edge of the terrace. Some had completely collapsed
in consequence of this operation. Those still upright
showed invariably a small interior chamber, only one or two
feet square, and in one case this was found filled with
hundreds of miniature Stupas modelled in clay and exactly
resembling those I had discovered at Khadalik. Evidently
these little clay Stupas, all produced from two or three

moulds, were intended by the pious donor to take the place of those sacred relics which every tower of this sort is by traditional theory supposed to cover.

On the opposite side of the walled town, about 400 yards from its north-west corner, and just outside what appears to have been an outer enclosure, two massive clay structures close together attracted my attention. They looked like small forts, forming squares with sides about sixty feet long. The walls, fully twenty feet thick, rose to a considerable height, but curiously enough showed neither a proper entrance nor any stairs or other arrangement for reaching their top. Making my way to the interior through a gap which had formed where the massive rampart had parted at one of the corners, I searched in vain for any remains to explain the purpose of these strange structures, until I noticed, lying loose on the sand which half-filled the enclosure, some fissured planks. Their length was just that needed for the boards of a coffin, and I had scarcely communicated my conjecture to the two Ch'iao-tzŭ men who were with me, when by scraping away the sand in one corner they laid bare similar planks still *in situ* enclosing a skeleton. It was clear that these extraordinarily massive walls had served to protect, not living people, but an abode of the dead; and an inspection of the ground outside, where left bare by drift sand and consequently eroded, soon showed that it had all once been used as a cemetery. Small fragments of human bones were all that erosion had spared of the graves.

The question as to the water-supply which the town and the cultivated area near it must have once commanded, presented, of course, a special interest. It could not possibly have come from the spring-fed marshes, the drainage of which now irrigates the Ch'iao-tzŭ oasis; for a look at the ground showed that these springs lay considerably below the level of the 'Tati' ground southward. The barren gravel glacis, as seen from So-yang-chêng sloping up for miles to the foot of the hill range, showed no clear trace of any stream. But as I rode over the strangely scoured ground east of the town, with its steep little clay terraces and intervening depressions recalling

the *hachure* of an etching, my eye was caught by a low
gravel-covered ridge running south-eastwards.

It proved, as expected, to be the line of a canal, with
the banks still clearly marked on the top of the pebble-
strewn ridge. The heavy gravel and coarse sand which
the water of the canal carried down in its course had helped
not only gradually to raise the canal bed, as noticed in
almost every oasis from Khotan to An-hsi, but also to
protect it from the force of the winds which have been
continually cutting up and scooping the loess ground on
either side ever since irrigation ceased. Thus it is easily
explained why the level of the canal banks now lies ten
feet or so on the average level above that of the ground
traversed by it. For fully three miles I followed the canal
to where a massive but shapeless mound of stamped clay,
evidently the relic of some watch-tower or small fort, rises
close by its side.

From here onwards the traces of the canal were lost on
ground completely furrowed by Yardangs (Fig. 210). But
in the distance to the south-east a line of white clay cliffs
seemed to indicate a river course now dry and sunk into
the gravel glacis. A gap seen south of this in the outermost hill range suggested that this course had served also
for the drainage of the next higher range which, though
without permanent snow, was likely to receive at times
a little more moisture. That it was this same drainage
which, finding its way underground, now came to light in
the marshes east and south-east of Ch'iao-tzŭ appeared to
me very probable. But in any case the total impossibility
of bringing surface water at present for the irrigation of
the old site was plain evidence of desiccation, whether
general or restricted to this region.

212. RUINED STUPA AT OLD TOWN OF CH'IAO-TZŬ, SEEN FROM SOUTH.

213. CAVE-TEMPLES OF THE 'MYRIAD BUDDHAS,' ON LEFT BANK OF SHIH-PAO-CHÊNG STREAM.

CHAPTER LXXIII

THE 'VALLEY OF THE MYRIAD BUDDHAS'

THE heat of the season and the consequent impracticability of employing our camels for transport precluded more extended surveys on this interesting but terribly arid ground along the foot of the outer ranges. So, after despatching honest Turdi under old Mullah's guidance with my heavy mail-bag to Tun-huang, whence they were to make their way across the mountains to Abdal, I started on the morning of the 29th of June for our expedition into the Westernmost Nan-shan. It seemed almost too soon to leave my cool and peaceful temple quarters at Ch'iao-tzŭ; but I thought of the huge mountain area which it was my intention to survey, and for which the next two months were all I could spare.

Our first march was very pleasant, taking us westwards through a delightfully green grassy plain to the oasis of T'a-shih. Like Ch'iao-tzŭ, it seemed to count about two hundred homesteads; but they were much scattered, and the numerous uncultivated strips of land within the oasis suggested want of water—or of people. I had by now learned enough of Chinese notions of life not to wonder at the total absence of cattle on the magnificent grazing we passed through. For had not all the people I had met since first reaching Tun-huang shown in many significant ways that the nation's traditional abhorrence of anything akin to the herdsman's semi-nomadic existence was as strong among these settlers of the border as it might be among the most town-bred folk farther east? So by sad experience I had learned that milk was never to be hoped for, however splendid the grazing, unless there were Chinese

Muhammadans or Tungans about; and in these parts none of these quondam rebels had been allowed to survive or to effect a fresh footing.

Yet T'a-shih had not escaped their fury during the times of the last great rebellion, as was shown by the quaint, only half-restored temple in which I found airy quarters outside the walled central village. Scarcely twelve years had passed since, as Lin, my warrior friend of Tun-huang, related, a large body of Tungan rebels, retreating from Hsi-ning, threatened T'a-shih with fresh destruction. The outer enclosure of the temple still displayed the loopholes and other defences then hastily improvised by the local troops sent up from Tun-huang to intercept them. We had struck now, in fact, the main route which connects An-hsi and the great road from northern Turkestan and Mongolia with Tibet and the Koko-nor region across the high plateaus of Tsaidam.

I knew that the Dalai-Lama in 1904, on his flight from Lhassa to Urga, had passed by this route, and that I might any day while along it meet pious Mongols or Buriats returning from their Tibetan pilgrimage. Yet with all these geographical facts before me, I never suspected that T'a-shih on the very night of my stay had given shelter also to the late Lieutenant Brooke, the plucky young English traveller, who some eighteen months later was to fall a victim of exploring zeal among the treacherous Lolos. Starting from the Hsi-ning side he had vainly attempted to make his way through to Lhassa, and, foiled by Tibetan obstruction, was forced to retreat by the very route which I was now about to survey up to the watershed of the Tun-huang river sources. I heard first towards the end of July of his passage at Su-chou, but did not learn until nearly four years later, when Mr. Fergusson published an account from his papers, that without knowing of each other's presence we had passed in such close proximity.

The fresh transport promised completely failed us at T'a-shih. However, on hearing that the route was just practicable for carts over a march which would take us to the cave-temples of Wang-fo-hsia, I managed, with much difficulty, to induce the men from Ch'iao-tzŭ to take us up so far; for I was now anxious to get into the mountains, where the greater coolness would make it possible to rely for a short time on our own camels without risk of a breakdown, even though their summer holiday was long due. We had followed the bed of the T'a-shih river, deeply cut into its own alluvial fan of Piedmont gravel, upwards for over ten miles, when, close to the point where the river debouches through the outermost hill range, we came face to face with a group of about ten small cave-temples cut into the conglomerate cliffs above the right bank. The place bore appropriately enough the name of the 'Little Ch'ien-fo-tung'; for the frescoes, though far less varied and extensive, showed exactly the same style in design and composition as those of the 'Thousand Buddhas.' In most of the little grottoes the paintings were badly effaced and in all of them the stucco sculptures recent.

So after a short halt I pushed up the picturesque river gorge to find there to my pleasant surprise a narrow but beautifully green expanse, with luxuriant shrubs and trees embedded between the most barren of hillsides. After a couple of miles this fertile strip, watered by the river, again gave way to uncompromising bareness of rock and detritus; and at a point where this contracted to a narrow winding defile, some fifteen miles above T'a-shih, I found the route defended by a massive stone wall extending across the valley bottom and for some distance up the steep slopes. It was a regular 'Klause' of unmistakably old appearance, and clearly suggested that the Chinese settlements on the ancient line of communication along the Su-lo Ho Valley had been exposed to attacks from the side of the Tibetan plateaus quite as much, perhaps, as to raids across the desert north and west.

A couple of miles ahead the valley expanded into a little basin filled with plentiful shrubs and trees, known as Mo-ku-t'ai-tzŭ, which promised excellent grazing for our brave camels if only we could spare them to take their badly needed 'long vacation.' Accordingly they were left behind, at least for the night, while we moved on with the carts over a steadily rising Sai on the right bank, until after another four miles we found ourselves above that point of the river gorge, now turned into a cañon, which is known as Wang-fo-hsia, or the ' Valley of [the caves of] the Myriad Buddhas.' I knew well that, in spite of its grandiloquent name, this sacred site could not compare in importance with the 'Thousand Buddhas' of Tun-huang; but the singular wildness of the scene rendered the first impression most striking. Along both sides of the deep rift, only about 200 yards wide at its bottom, which the river coming from the snowy range above Shih-pao-chêng has cut through the hard conglomerate, the almost vertical cliffs showed the openings of temple grottoes extending for a distance of over a quarter of a mile (Fig. 213). A narrow strip of orchard and cultivation raised along a tiny canal at the bottom only heightened by contrast the effect of those frowning rock walls, more than a hundred feet high, and of the dark cavities piercing them.

On descending the precipitous footpath I was welcomed by three cheerful and well-fed Taoist priests, and soon found excellent quarters in the verandah of a patio-like court in front of the grotto containing a colossal seated Buddha, which is seen on the extreme right in the photograph of Fig. 214. It took hours to get our baggage carried down, and I used the time in the dusk for a rapid look round. The numerous small shrines and Stupas scattered along a raised terrace at the foot of the cliffs of the right bank seemed kept in fair repair, and everything bore the air of a religious establishment quite 'in being' and relatively well off in the matter of pious support. The place had evidently escaped the usual havoc from Tungan rebel bands, and the vicinity of well-to-do Mongols grazing in the mountains south probably helped the priests towards getting comfortable sustenance. What with the delightful coolness of the evening—we had now risen to about 6200 feet above the sea—and the music of the stream tossing in its rocky bed, it was pleasant enough to wait for dinner till midnight.

The next two days were busily used for the examination and photographing of the shrines. Though executed on a distinctly smaller scale, and probably commenced at a somewhat later date, they resembled the cave-temples of

214. CAVE-TEMPLES OF THE 'MYRIAD BUDDHAS,' ON RIGHT BANK OF SHIH-PAO-CHÊNG STREAM.

On the extreme right is seen the court in front of the colossal Buddha shrine.   On the extreme left the grotto of the oldest of the resident priests.

215. FRESCOES IN THE ANTECHAPEL OF A CAVE-TEMPLE AT THE 'MYRIAD BUDDHAS' SITE.

The figures in the procession of Bodhisattvas on the right are over life-size.

Ch'ien-fo-tung so closely in all essential points of architectural disposition and artistic decoration that a summary
description will suffice. The principal caves are found on
the right bank, ranged in two stories as seen in Fig. 214,
one on a terrace about twenty feet above the river bed,
the other between fifty and sixty feet higher. The five
main caves below are rendered very dark by the verandahs
built in front of them, and comprise, besides the colossal
seated Buddha already referred to, an image of Buddha
recumbent in Nirvana, fully thirty feet long.

Owing to abundant restoration, all stucco images in
these caves bear a modern appearance, while the large
fresco panels in some of them show a style suggesting that
Tibetan influence had asserted itself upon the traditional
local art. These caves, and some five or six smaller
grottoes in the same lower story, seem to receive most
attention from the priests in residence and to attract most
gifts from pious visitors. The former all claimed to have
resided here for over thirty years, and one of them, a white-
haired old man, who had installed himself in the picturesque
little grotto on the extreme left of Fig. 214, was approached
with special reverence by our people from An-hsi and
Ch'iao-tzǔ. Even Chiang, usually so sceptical in regard
to saintly claims, was inclined to let him pass for a ' sage.'

The upper row of caves is approached near this holy
man's grotto by a rough staircase cut from the rock. Then,
crossing a deep fissure of the rock wall by a rickety bridge,
and passing by a cave of which the front part had fallen in,
we arrived at the northernmost of a flight of thirteen cave-
temples, communicating with each other. All of them consist of a cella square or nearly so, varying from twenty to
thirty-eight feet on each side ; of a high porch or passage,
sometimes twenty or thirty feet deep, admitting light and
air ; of an antechapel in front of the latter, as broad as the
cella, but narrow and opening towards the cliff face by a
big outer porch as seen in the photograph. Communication between the shrines was originally effected by narrow
passages leading from one outer porch to the other through
the facing part of the rock wall. But in places this had
crumbled away or become unsafe, and a rough tunnel

connecting the antechapels had been cut, evidently at a later date, as shown by the broken wall paintings.

All the walls of these cave-temples are decorated with frescoes, or, to use a more exact term, mural paintings in tempera. The walls of the porches ordinarily show processions of red - robed monks with broad - brimmed black hats, and facing them rows of nuns with elaborate head-dresses made up of flower pendants around a bulb-shaped cap. Exactly the same types had been seen by me at the 'Thousand Buddhas.' The walls of the cellas and antechapels display either processions of large Bodhisattvas, gracefully draped and adorned, or else a variety of panels with a Buddha enthroned among Bodhisattvas on lotus seats; scenes from a Buddhist heaven, with the spirited representation of a 'divine ballet and concert' in the foreground, as seen in so many frescoes of Ch'ien-fo-tung, and others. The photograph in Fig. 215 illustrates both themes of decoration. Even the curious 'wind scene' of the legend already discussed in Chapter LXX. is reproduced on the back wall of two cellas.

The frescoes generally showed great uniformity of style, and were evidently more or less coeval reproductions of the same prototypes. That these were to be looked for among the mural paintings of the 'Thousand Buddhas' appeared to me at the time to be beyond doubt, fresh as my recollection of the latter then was. The technique of the execution seemed generally inferior, and suggested either a somewhat later date or else employment of less skilful hands. In some cases the coarse washes replacing the carefully drawn outlines of the older work suggested extensive use of stencils.

I could not find inscriptional record of the date of construction for any of the shrines of the 'Myriad Buddhas.' But a large number of dated Chinese sgraffiti left behind by pilgrims on the walls of the caves helped to fix the lower date limit. Most of these seemed to belong to the close of the Mongol dynasty's rule, showing dates corresponding to 1331-67 A.D. By their side, but far less numerous, were to be found short sgraffiti in Uigur script, or its later Mongol form, and in Tibetan. There were one

or two lines in Central-Asian Brahmi script, a badly effaced
short entry in Arabic writing, and also some characters
which I thought might belong to the peculiar script used
by the Hsi-hsia in the eleventh to thirteenth centuries.

How long after the painting of the frescoes these
mementos of visitors had been left behind, it was impossible
to determine.   In any case the Chinese sgraffiti proved
that the temples must have been much visited by pilgrims
about the middle of the fourteenth century, and that their
appearance must have been then much the same as now.
Destructive invasions had probably affected this out-of-the-
way site in the hills far less than the sacred caves near
Tun-huang which had served as a model.   The caves on
the left bank number about ten, disposed in three irregular
groups, all at a considerable height above the river.   Their
frescoes seemed distinctly coarser in design and execution
than those on the right bank, and their irregular arrangement
may also be taken as an indication of relatively later origin.
Yet, here too, dated Chinese sgraffiti showed that the time
of construction lay before the fourteenth century A.D.

CHAPTER LXXIV

IN THE MOUNTAINS OF THE WESTERNMOST NAN-SHAN

THE picturesque seclusion and the cool air of the abode of the 'Myriad Buddhas' had been so delightful that I felt quite sorry to leave when after two days' busy work my tasks there were ended. Alas! there was no hidden library to explore—or, if ever there had been such a deposit, the rock walls of the caves had kept their secret. A few camels had been brought down from the Mongol grazing-grounds at the foot of the snowy range, and with their help and that of our own camels we resumed our journey to the latter by the morning of July 3. For two days we marched up by the river which flows past the 'Myriad Buddhas' and T'a-shih. First we ascended a steadily rising gravel plateau, and then passed through the narrow gorge in which the river has cut its way through the second barren hill range sighted from Ch'iao-tzŭ.

With its absolutely bare slopes fissured by a maze of ravines and its serrated crest-line frowning down from a height of over 10,000 feet, this range was sufficiently forbidding. But once we had passed through what looked like the apex of this outer hill chain, a great change occurred in the scene. A grand semicircle of mountains, carrying snow - beds and small glaciers on their most prominent peaks, rose suddenly before us in the distance, some thirty miles away to the south. A huge fan-like glacis, descending with unbroken slope from its foot, seemed to absorb all the drainage from the numerous valleys of the range and to discharge whatever was left of it into the gorge we had ascended.

A little above this point we reached the ruins of Shih-

pao-chêng, which Kozloff's map had led me to expect here.
They proved to be those of a small but relatively well
built fort, evidently recent in its extant construction.   It
overlooked broad riverine meadows and occupied an
excellent strategic position ; for the various routes
which crossed the high range before us from the south
naturally debouched towards the plains by the gorge the
fort guarded.   A massive clay tower about thirty feet
high, which occupied its north-west corner, formed a conspicuous landmark.   So we chose it as the station for our
astronomical latitude observation, while we camped some
distance below where there was grass and fresh running
water in a channel about ten yards wide and one and a half
to two feet deep.   Our camp here was about 7450 feet
above the sea, and all thought of heat now lay behind us.

The ground was singularly well adapted for starting
extensive and necessarily rapid survey work such as we
were bent upon in the Nan-shan.   Across the uniform
expanse of the great alluvial triangle we could at once
sight the whole amphitheatre of mountains bending round
an arc close on fifty miles long, and shape our movements
accordingly.   The landscape, barren in the extreme,
singularly combined the attraction of grand mountain
vistas with that feeling of freedom which wide Alpine
plateaus always seem to convey.   But the very uniformity
of its features, which enabled us in the course of six days
to survey an area of over 1200 square miles, will also
explain why I may endeavour to shorten my account by
avoiding a description of our work day by day.

The first two marches which took us south-westwards
to the vicinity of the Kashkar Pass sufficed to show me
the remarkable dryness which characterizes the western
extremity of the Nan-shan even along its most elevated
range.   Ascending the great alluvial slope to an elevation
of about 10,000 feet, we nowhere met with surface
water, and all the dry beds we found crossing it from the
mountains were quite shallow.   I soon convinced myself
that even at this season of melting snows the water
brought down by the valleys of the main range becomes
completely lost in the vast beds of rubble almost at their

very debouchure.   The difficulty of finding water by
which to camp was great, and only the help of some
Chinese whom we discovered grazing their camels near
the route to the Kashkar Pass saved us from serious
trouble.   The vast deposits of Piedmont gravel which form
the glacis to the very foot of the range were, it is true,
covered mostly with a thin layer of clay or loess.   But the
scrub and grass which grew on it was both scanty and
coarse, clear evidence of the extreme aridity in soil and
atmosphere.   What water we had seen leaving the glacis
by the gorge below Shih-pao-chêng was, no doubt, all
derived from springs in which the drainage absorbed
higher up by the beds of gravel came to light again.

Skirting the foot of the main range we then made our
way eastwards into the large valley known as Ta-kung-ch'a,
which receives its drainage from a big snowy massif rising
to close on 20,000 feet.   Leaving our camp on a small
grassy plateau above the river bed, which, though deep-cut
and over a quarter-mile wide, held only tiny courses of
water, we rode on July 8th up to the watershed.   For about
six miles our route lay in the broad stony bed of the river,
flanked first by conglomerate cliffs, and higher up by sandstone rocks in a variety of striking colours—purple, bright
red, and dark green.   A sturdy Mongol, whom we found
encamped with his flock on a grassy plot (Fig. 216), served
as guide.   He told me curious details about the Dalai-Lama
who had travelled down to An-hsi over the Kashkar Pass
on his flight in 1904, and whose cortège he had again
accompanied more recently when he journeyed back from
Urga to Hsi-ning.

We left the main valley at a point about 12,000 feet
above the sea where it turns eastwards, and continued our
ascent to the south-east by a steeper side valley which, by
slopes of shingle overlying greenish slate and gneiss rock,
brought us to the top of the pass after a total march of
some ten miles.   It proved over 13,400 feet in height,
and commanded a wide view to the south, but it was one
distinctly desolate.   A bleak basin-like valley lay before
us, fully six to eight miles broad, and bounded southward
by a long range of straggling hills, apparently none

216. MONGOL CAMP ON EAST SIDE OF TA-KUNG-CH'A VALLEY.

217. HASSAN AKHUN PACKING CAMEL AT SU-CHI-CH'ÜAN SPRING.

218. VIEW SOUTH-WEST TOWARDS SNOWY MAIN RANGE FROM CH'ANG-MA VILLAGE.

219. INTERIOR OF WALLED VILLAGE OF CH'ANG-MA, LOOKING TO NORTH-WEST.

The large temple near west wall served for our quarters.

higher than 14,000 or 15,000 feet.   Large glittering ex-
panses of salt in the centre marked dry lake beds.   Our
guide pointed to a pass leading over this low range to the
head-waters of the Tun-huang river and called it P'in-ta-
fan (Dawan).

The whole view before us looked thoroughly Tibetan
in type, and I was by no means surprised when a wild ass
approached us to within 300 yards or so.   A bitterly cold
north wind was blowing, suggestive of what the summer
breezes of these bleak uplands of northernmost Tibet are
like.   The position of the Ta-kung-ch'a Pass gave us a
chance of sighting the southern slopes of the main range
for some distance.   So I was able to convince myself that
the permanent snow-line here lay at an elevation of fully
18,000 or 19,000 feet, and thus even higher than on the
north side.   It all helped to confirm the impression of the
scanty moisture received by this westernmost part of the
Nan-shan.

All the more gratified did I feel when, on the day after
moving from Ta-kung-ch'a eastward, while encamped at a
small spring called Su-chi-ch'üan, we experienced the first
rain which, according to Mongol testimony, these mountains
had received that summer.   It was gentle, but sufficiently
steady to give one the feeling of being somewhere in the
Alps, and a little snow melting as it neared the ground
was thrown in as an extra.   When the sky cleared in the
afternoon of July 10th and I could take a stroll round, the
effect on the vegetation seemed like magic.   Where the
grass had before looked stunted and shrivelled, blades
were now sprouting rapidly.   For the first time I noticed
hardy edelweiss showing in large clumps, and a few white
flowers resembling Podophyllum.   It was such occasional
rain which accounted for the very thin but sufficiently
cohesive coat of vegetation clothing the lower slopes of
the range up to an elevation of about 11,000 feet, while
the absence of heavy rain or snow explained the fact that
it escaped denudation.

At this same camp we were joined at last by hired
camels sent up from the hill oasis of Ch'ang-ma.   I was
thus able to let our own hardy beasts depart under Hassan

Akhun's care (Fig. 217) for the fine grazing below Wang-fo-hsia, where they were to enjoy an unbroken and much-needed holiday until my return to An-hsi in the autumn. The presence of Ibrahim Beg at An-hsi and the neighbour-hood of the friendly priests at the 'Myriad Buddhas' had recommended that vacation-retreat for my camels, and I may say at once that I had no reason to regret it.

On July 11th we marched over easy but barren slopes to the north-east, and, just after crossing the almost imper-ceptible watershed between the great basins of Shih-pao-ch'êng and Ch'ang-ma, found a spring of slightly sulphurous water at the foot of the absolutely bare outer range known as Ying-tsui-shan. There we camped. The sky had become delightfully clear, and next morning a magnificent view revealed the glacier-girt main range rising to peaks over 20,000 feet high and draining towards Ch'ang-ma. The distance and relatively high elevation from which we saw these bold peaks, with the extraordinary contrast of the flat fore-ground formed by another huge gravel glacis sloping down towards Ch'ang-ma, made the panorama most impressive. Everything seemed on such a big scale, and there were no distracting details. A broad gap above the alluvial fan to the south-east marked the point where the Su-lo Ho on its way down to Ch'ang-ma breaks through the snowy range flanking it from the north.

For over fourteen miles we marched down over a stony steppe, showing but very scanty scrub and, in spite of numerous shallow flood beds, not a drop of water. Nor did we come upon any spring in the broad dry river bed we were at last following, until within half a mile of Sha-ho, the westernmost hamlet of the oasis. But from here onwards water abounded; it seemed as if all the under-ground drainage from the snowy range was here eager to get to the surface. Our surroundings seemed changed as if by magic, and the eleven miles' ride down the gradually broadening oasis of Ch'ang-ma was delightful.

There were marshy meadows full of springs along the left bank of the river, and in spite of canals taking off on the right, a short distance below Sha-ho the main channel was about fifteen yards broad with a depth of over two feet of deliciously limpid water.   Here at an elevation of over 7000 feet it was still spring, and the bright green of the foliage and young crops had an exquisite offset in the brick-red and purple tints of the low and barren ridges encircling the oasis on all sides.   Above those to the south-west and south, which I took for offshoots of the high To-lai-shan range farther east, the whole of the snowy main chain showed in overpowering grandeur (Fig. 218).   It was, no doubt, the contrast between the fertile open valley and the towering array of white peaks in the background which helped to recall so vividly my beloved Kashmir.

In the largest of the several walled villages or ' P'u-tzu ' (Fig. 221), as we got to know them, a big temple offered comfortable, if dim, quarters (Fig. 219).   The magistrate of Yü-mên-hsien, on which Ch'ang-ma depended, had been duly advised of our passage, and had sent up a petty official with some soldiers to receive us.   There was no want of attention ; but when I insisted on arrangements for guides and transport to take us through the mountains, to the Chia-yü-kuan gate of the 'Great Wall' all knowledge of such a route was stoutly denied.   That the Chinese of these parts have no love for the mountains I had learned long before ; and when I offered to act as guide myself, the want of ponies or mules which would be needed for any really rough track presented a formidable obstacle.   It cost great exertions to secure even camels ; and in order not to allow the opposition to the route I had planned to gather strength, I thought it advisable to set out with them at once on the afternoon of July 13th, however unwilling my caravan seemed to leave the flesh-pots of Ch'ang-ma.

I managed to move it that evening to the right bank of the Su-lo Ho, which flowed here as a vehement mountain river in a steeply cut bed some twenty yards wide.   The quantity of water carried down was great, as we could see when looking down upon the tumultuous turbid rush from the solid cantilever bridge which spanned the river.   But how much greater the river must have been during earlier periods, I could judge from the old bed still well defined across which we moved for fully a mile before reaching the bank of the present one. Its level lay about forty feet above the actual flood level, and its own banks were sharply cut to a depth of some fifty feet below the great alluvial plain occupied by Ch'ang-ma.

During the evening, while a cheerless camp was being pitched on the rubble bed by the river, I had the satisfaction to find a well-marked track leading off to the southeast where the Ch'ang-ma people had before professed the utmost ignorance of any route. So next morning we induced our camel-men after a good deal of trouble to follow it, instead of their beloved high road to the plain. It was a steady but easy ascent in a side valley coming from the western end of the To-lai-shan range (see Map III.). There was low scrub in plenty, but no trace of water, and I was heartily glad when, after seventeen miles, some of the Ch'ang-ma men with the transport reluctantly disclosed their local knowledge by turning off into a well-screened side gully where we found a tiny stream issuing below sandstone cliffs. Here at an elevation of close on 10,000 feet we camped, and in the course of the evening the local men barefacedly owned up to a knowledge of the route which was to take us to Chia-yü-kuan. All their previous protestations of ignorance had been lies intended to save them from a troublesome track.

After this frank avowal and the experience gained about finding water in this barren hill tract hitherto unexplored, I thought it best to let our unwilling 'guides' guide us. The route which they showed took us in two days across the Shui-ch'ü-k'ou Pass, and through a very narrow and picturesque valley where we came again upon water, down to the outermost hill chain. At two points, known as Yen-mên-tzŭ and Ku-lung-shan, where the valley contracts to a tortuous defile between very high and precipitous cliffs, we found ruins of walls and watch-posts built to close the route. But there was no water-supply to be traced near them now, and there were other signs of desiccation having affected this region.

From the little shrine of Ch'ing-t'sao-an-tzŭ, where we camped on July 16th, I looked down upon the wide valley, half barren gravel Sai and half scrubby waste, with its scattered small oases, through which the great route leads from Su-chou to Yü-mên-hsien. But I had determined, before proceeding to Su-chou, to visit the watershed of the northernmost chain of the Nan-shan at the Tu-ta-fan Pass where Obrucheff, the distinguished Russian geologist and traveller, had crossed it. Baffled by the difficulty about guidance and suitable transport in reaching the Pass from the south, I now made my way to it from the north.

One forced march along the stony glacis of the range and across the Po-yang Ho river carried us to the tiny hamlet of Po-lo-hu-tung at the opening of the valley coming from the Tu-ta-fan. While waiting till late at night for the arrival of the baggage, I learned a good deal of curious local information from the centenarian head of the family owning the central walled farm. Cultivation depended on a single spring at the mouth of the valley, and the extent of old abandoned fields seemed to suggest increasing scantiness of water. Yet the old man was loth to admit this, and dwelt more on the losses in men and labouring cattle which the raids of Tungan rebels had caused. He seemed not a little proud of the fine substantial coffin which filial piety was keeping ready in the best room of the house for his occupation. Owing to the elevation, well over 8000 feet, oats were the main crop, and the lateness of spring here was pleasantly attested by the little blue irises and other wild flowers recalling Tun-huang in May.

Next morning, on July 18th, I sent off the baggage to the neighbouring hamlet of Ta-han-chuang and set out with the Surveyor towards the pass. We found the narrow mouth of the valley, known as Ch'ing-tao-shan, defended by a small post of Mongol levies and a large empty entrenchment thrown up some twelve years before against Tungan rebels expected from the Hsi-ning side. Above this point the valley opened out rapidly, and as we rode up became greener and greener. There luxuriant grass such as I had nowhere yet seen in these mountains, and flowers, too, suggestive of an Alpine vegetation. It was a strangely refreshing sight for eyes which had almost forgotten to associate with mountains aught but rock, detritus, and snow.

My delight was still greater when I reached the broad grass-covered ridge which at an elevation of about 12,380 feet forms the watershed. A grand panorama spread out before us, comprising to the south and south-east a long line of snow-clad peaks which belong to the western To-lai-shan range, and with their drainage give rise to the Po-yang Ho (Fig. 220). The wide gravel bed of the latter spread itself in the valley below us. Some particularly striking massifs to the south-east, bearing big beds of snow on their slopes, proved subsequently to attain heights over 19,000 feet, as ascertained by clinometrical observation. Westwards we were particularly glad to be able to recognize a number of peaks of the To-lai-shan and of the northernmost range, which had been sighted from our plane-table stations above Ch'ang-ma. So it was possible for the Surveyor to complete the mapping of a good deal of interesting ground which so far had been entirely a cartographical blank.

Tu-ta-fan proved, in fact, quite an ideal 'hill station.' Amongst other orographical points, it permitted us to make certain that the Richthofen range of the Nan-shan, which with its snow-clad peaks dominates the plains between Su-chou and Kan-chou, has its direct continuation in the bold, but considerably lower, chain which runs north and east of Ch'ang-ma, and through which we had passed in the gorge of Yen-mên-tzŭ. But it was, as subsequent observations convinced me, not merely the lesser height of the western part of the range which would account for its utter barrenness as compared with the part we were now beginning to survey. The change in vegetation, first noticed in such striking fashion on my visit to the Tu-ta-fan, was but an indication of the altered climatic conditions of the whole region into which we were now about to pass near the plateau occupied by the 'Great Wall.' We were here leaving behind the extreme eastern limits of the great arid basin of innermost Asia, and were entering that portion of Kan-su which is affected in its

220. VIEW FROM TU-TA-FAN TO SOUTH-WEST, SHOWING A PORTION OF TO-LAI-SHAN RANGE.

221. FORTIFIED VILLAGE AT CH'ANG-MA OASIS, WITH VIEW TO SOUTH-EAST TOWARDS SU-LO HO.

climate by the increased moisture passing up from the Pacific drainage.

It was 6 P.M. when I regained the two lonely farms at the debouchure of the Ch'ing-tao-shan valley. The air was delightfully clear, and the setting sun brought out in bold relief the rugged ravines furrowing the slopes of a curious outer fringe of low hills which stretched along outside the big mountain rampart. The deep red and purple clays, which cropped out in layers alternating with white chalk rock and what looked like gneiss, made up quite a fantastic effect, and the two fortified farms in the foreground fitted in with it. It cost quite an effort to remember that these massive piles of clay were the home of harmless cultivators, not robbers' keeps.

Ta-han-chuang, where I had sent our camp ahead, seemed near enough as I looked down on the little spur behind which the hamlet was said to cluster. But to take a straight cut over the intervening five miles was impossible; deep ravines cut up the fertile loess slope and necessitated great détours. I did not feel sorry, since the track took me over two picturesque little plateaus each bearing terraced fields and a half-ruined fort-like farm. The air of decay was upon fields and buildings; the springs which bring verdure to the tiny oases of Ma-mi-t'u were scantier even than those of Po-lo-hu-tung, and most of the cultivable ground looked abandoned.

But more striking still than the ride close to that strange counterscarp of the mountains, so barren and yet so glowing in colours, was the view across the vast valley stretching away eastwards to Chia-yü-kuan. A lifeless steppe of brownish-green tints, fully twelve to fifteen miles broad, separated the fringe of the snowy Nan-shan from a terribly bare reddish range northward. Looking down from a height of close on 8000 feet I could see distinctly the low gravel ridges closing the valley at its eastern end, and above them a faint white line lit up by the setting sun—the long-expected 'Great Wall.' The distance separating me from it was still over twenty miles. Yet I thought that I could make out towers reflecting the slanting rays and beyond them a great expanse of dark ground, the fertile district of Su-chou. Thus at last I was within sight of the westernmost end of the true Middle Kingdom, China 'within the Wall.'

It was getting dark when I approached the little oasis of Ta-han-chuang. Outside its square fort-hamlet two petty officers with half-a-dozen red-cloaked soldiers were drawn up in line to receive me. It was an outpost of the garrison of Chia-yü-kuan, supposed to watch the mountain flank of the 'Great Wall.' Among the 'men' was a nice-looking child of some five years, bravely wearing the red jacket left him by his father, with sleeves almost sweeping the ground. I found my tent pitched by the side of a lively brook, amidst grassy terraced fields where the scent of flowers rose in the cool air of the evening. Many fine trees could be seen in the moonlight lining the bed of the little stream, and I almost felt as if I were pitching camp once more in some quiet nook of Kashmir.

CHAPTER LXXV

BY THE GATE OF THE 'GREAT WALL'

THE next morning, July 19th, did not change my pleasant impression of Ta-han-chuang. The meadows were bright with rich grass and flowers; for here, some 7700 feet above the sea, spring had not yet lost its freshness. Strolling up a little plateau while the baggage was being loaded, I found it occupied by the fort from which yesterday's military reception had come. There was at its north-west corner a big and ruinous watch-tower (Fig. 222), which when seen from afar looked as if carried away bodily from that desolate desert *Limes*. Crenellated walls adjoined it in a square enclosing the ramshackle quarters of the garrison. They turned out again promptly in their scarlet cloaks, the child-soldier included, as seen in the photograph. Small plots of vegetable gardens bordered the half-decayed post, and below to the east I found the springs which feed the life-giving stream, issuing on grassy patches within a broad and dry river bed.

The march to the great 'Gate' was long and weary; for on the bare stony Sai, supporting only the scantiest tufts of scrub, the sun beat down fiercely, and, with the ground sloping down eastwards and no wind, for once, stirring, the heat and glare increased steadily. The distant vista of the Chia-yü-kuan towers had vanished. Fata Morgana instead raised up on the eastern horizon long dark patches suggesting groves of trees, with the heated atmosphere below shining like a sheet of water. To the south rose chain above chain with glittering snowy peaks, more imposing even than those we had seen from Tu-ta-fan. The long barren range which flanks the high

273

road to An-hsi and Turkestan from the north drew nearer and nearer as we moved transversely over the valley, and eagerly I scanned it for traces of the ancient wall which might have followed its foot on the way to Yü-mên-hsien and the Su-lo Ho.   When after sixteen miles' straight march I struck at last the great route near the point where the gorge of Hao-shan-k'ou cuts through the south-eastern end of the range, three large towers perched on low spurs of the range came clearly into view.   In spite of their white plaster facing they might be of early date, remnants of the fortified line for which I was looking.   But they were too far off to be examined in the course of the day's march.

It did not need ruins to make me feel the historical importance of the narrow cart track by which we continued our march due east.   I knew that I was now treading the very ground over which all Chinese enterprise towards the 'Western Regions' had moved during more than two thousand years.   These terribly barren ridges, furrowed by a maze of narrow ravines, must have frowned down on the very first Chinese missions and expeditions which went forth to conquer Turkestan.   How many of those thousands and thousands of soldiers and administrators who passed by here to the lands of exile in Central Asia, had lived to see the day of their fondly-hoped-for return 'within the Wall'?

In the annals of the Han and later dynasties the military and official story of Chinese expansion westwards is amply chronicled.   But where are we to look for all that was of human interest and worthy of record in the lives lost during long centuries of struggle with Huns and Turks, Tibetans and Arabs?   As I thought of the dreary deserts which then as now must have made up nine-tenths of these much-disputed regions from the Oxus to the Kan-su border, the sacrifices in men and treasure which this policy of Central-Asian expansion had cost to the Middle Kingdom seemed great beyond all proportion.   But what would have been our knowledge of the past of those vast regions, of the great migrations which with their last waves shaped the destinies of Europe as well as of India, without the light transmitted through the records of those who during

222. WATCH-TOWER OF MODERN GUARD-STATION AT TA-HAN-CHUANG, AT FOOT OF NAN-SHAN.

A

223. SEGMENT OF ANCIENT BORDER WALL NORTH OF SU-CHOU.
The figure in Chinese costume above A is Father Essems.

224. THE CHIA-YÜ-KUAN GATE OF THE 'GREAT WALL,' SEEN FROM SOUTH-WEST.

225. PAVILION OVER INNER WEST GATE OF CHIA-YÜ-KUAN, WITH VIEW ACROSS INTERIOR
OF CIRCUMVALLATION.

long centuries kept open for China the routes to the distant West?

I was thus in the right mood to appreciate what Chiang was relating of the feelings which the gate of Chia-yü-kuan arouses in modern Chinese exiles. What sighs it must have heard from those whom duty, ambition, or more frequently *saeva paupertas* sends forth annually to the 'New Dominions'! Like many others, my good Ssŭ-yeh had here said good-bye to true China with tears in his eyes when he passed through seventeen years before. He was sharing now my elation at approaching the famous Gate again. But bravely as he carried himself, I could not help noticing an undercurrent of wistful regret; for he felt that this return *intra murum*, or 'kuan-li-t'ou,' 'within the Barrier,' as the Chinese phrase puts it, was not the final one. Fully three months' journey still separated Chiang from his Hu-nan home, where he had then left behind his wife and newly-born son; and with years still needed to raise his savings to the standard fixed for retirement, he had resolutely put aside all idea of returning to them until the period of exile had come to its appointed end.

Four miles of stony waste, slightly but steadily rising, brought us at last to the top of a broad plateau-like ridge which bears at its eastern edge the closing wall of Chia-yü-kuan. From a distance of about two miles the many-storied gate tower built in wood first became visible (Fig. 224); then, as we got nearer, the clay wall which stretches away on either side of the square fort guarding the great gate. On the south it was visible for a distance of some seven miles to the foot of a projecting buttress of the Nan-shan. Northward for over four miles the wall was hidden by the scarp of the ridge on which we stood. But on the slope of a rugged spur close to the eastern end of the Hao-shan-k'ou gorge I could again pick up its line lit up by the setting sun.

There could be no doubt that the position for a barrier, intended to close approach from the barbarian West to the oases along the north foot of the Nan-shan, had been chosen with true topographical sense. The broad glacis between the snowy mountains and the desert hills of the Pei-shan could nowhere be guarded with greater ease than here. But while the eye took in easily the purpose of the barrier here erected and the natural advantages of the position, I felt puzzled by an archaeological problem of obvious historical interest. What was the relation between this wall, so well preserved and manifestly of later date, and another surviving only in detached segments which I could see stretching away across the plain north-eastwards?

I knew well that all books and maps, whether Chinese or European, made the ancient 'Great Wall' which protects the northern border of Kan-su terminate in an imposing line of wall which bent round the westernmost part of the Su-chou oasis to the very foot of the Nan-shan. But the wall I could now see running in the direction from south-west to north-east was not a continuation of the barrier rising before me. It manifestly adjoined the latter at right angles, yet was so distant from its northern end that a different period of construction and a different purpose at once suggested themselves. It was useless to ply my posse of local people with questions. With that persistent pretence of utter ignorance which seems their favourite line of defence in the face of all strangers, they even refused to recognize any wall at all besides the one just in front of us.

There was enough to look at and enjoy that evening without antiquarian preoccupations. Outside the massively built gate with its imposing tower there awaited me a picturesque band of soldiers and officers whom the commandant of the Chia-yü-kuan garrison, Shuang Ta-jên, had sent out to greet me. A still more formal reception by this 'lord of the Gate' himself, as he would have been called in old Kashmir, had only been obviated by a polite remonstrance on my part sent ahead in the morning. As soon as we had done with this ceremony and had approached the 'Wall,' a pleasant surprise awaited me. Instead of the cluster of mud-hovels and rest-houses which I expected to find behind it, the view from the gravel ridge overlooking the wall showed a delightfully green expanse of tree-bordered meadows close to the south of the little fortified town guarding the great gate. A series of springs, which here issue at the eastern foot of the gravel ridge, accounts for this refreshing verdure as well as for the name of Chia-yü-kuan, 'the Barrier of the Pleasant Valley.'

To this inviting camping-ground I at once led my caravan through a big gap in the wall offering a convenient short cut. I had scarcely selected a shady clump of trees under which to pitch my tent, when Shuang Ta-jên emerged in great style from his stronghold. He proved an extremely pleasant old gentleman, full of genuine kindness. Though the constant flow of officials and others whom he must have seen passing through his Gate since taking charge some twelve years before, ought to have somewhat cooled his hospitable ardour, he would brook no excuse of mine meant to save him the trouble of a collation at his Ya-mên. Soon we were so absorbed in talk about the ancient frontier he was guarding that I forgot my longing for a 'tub' and change, and allowed myself to be carried off without further ado to the Ya-mên of the cheery old major.

The short walk through the gates and streets of Chia-yü-kuan was a treat for the eyes (Fig. 225). The high walls of reddish clay kept in fair repair, with their loop-holed battlements and numerous towers, took one back straight to the middle ages, or the East such as old travellers' sketches show it. Not less than three big vaulted gates had we to pass through before we reached the little *castrum* that hides behind these circumvallations. That the gates were all as wide open as the bars of certain London streets, and the armament of the place made up only of stones disposed in little heaps on the parapet, did not detract from the illusion. Within the second gate I passed a fine temple, said to date from Ming times, with a profusion of excellent wood - carving, and a roof of beautifully glazed green tiles (Fig. 227). The little town within the innermost wall looked sadly decayed, half the houses of its single broad street being roofless ruins. But the Ya-mên of the commandant was still a comfortable abode, and neat flower-beds in the inner courtyard relieved the faded colours of the woodwork.

How grateful I felt for the forethought of our kindly host who before treating us to a simple but neatly served repast had washing basins produced, with hot water, towels, and soap all complete! He had evidently made it his business to study the needs of the guests whom the great road made pass through his gates. The time passed quickly in talk about the history of these Marches and the vicissitudes to which the last great Tungan rebellion had reduced their people. Shuang Ta-jên had first come here with the forces which Liu Chin-t'ang led to the reconquest of Turkestan, and vividly he described the great efforts it had cost to provide for their passage through the desolate desert region between Chia-yü-kuan and Hami. When after an hour or so I walked back with Chiang to camp in the light of the young moon, I felt that I could not have found a more cheering welcome at the Western Gate of the Middle Kingdom.

My halt on July 20th was to be utilized for a close examination of the old walls. The start was delayed by a very early visit of Shuang Ta-jên, who came himself to bring the requested local guide. The sun had already risen high before I was free to ascend the great tower built over the west Gate, whence a distant view could be gained. From the height of the second story it was easy to follow the line of the much-decayed rampart and adjoining clay towers which stretched away across the vast plain eastwards. Most of the ground it traverses was now seen to be a bare stony Sai, with little patches of cultivation forming a thin chain. Soon I rode off north to survey the actual Chia-yü-kuan defences. That the massive clay wall which now closes the valley from south to north is built on low ground within a furlong or two of the high gravel ridge forming the natural barrier, seemed strange, until I realized to what extent the level of this ridge is broken by steep ravines. Overlooked though the wall is from the plateau crest, it was safe from being commanded in the days of arrows or matchlocks, and there was the supreme advantage of an ample supply of water from springs close at hand.

But the advantage of holding the ridge, too, had not been neglected by those who drew the line of the present wall; for the detached towers of clay surrounded by trenches and earth-walls, of which three rise between the gate stronghold and the end of the Hao-shan-k'ou spur northward, were manifestly built for this purpose.   Judging from the shape and arrangement of their sun-dried bricks, these advanced towers did not look of a very remote age.   Yet their state of decay and the signs of successive repairs plainly indicated that they were older than the wall extending behind them.   For the latter it seemed difficult to assume a greater antiquity than that of Ming times, as local tradition asserts ; so well preserved were the main wall itself and the enclosures of the towers which served as quarters and rallying-points for the men guarding it.

The disposition of the loopholes in the crenellated clay parapet suggested defence by firearms.   Otherwise these towers built inside the wall and adjoining it showed but little departure from the principles of fortification illustrated by the ancient *Limes* in the desert.   There was the same solid cone of stamped clay, some thirty-four feet square at the base, with a lightly built watch-room on the top.   A double line of foot-holes ascending one of the sides was intended to help the watchmen who had to climb up by a rope.   Within the enclosure, some sixty feet square, which guarded the tower, were small quarters for soldiers, now ruined.   The main wall showed at its foot a thickness of eleven feet, and with its parapet rose to sixteen feet.

It was at the very first of these towers of the wall, situated only some two miles beyond the great Gate, that I struck the remains of the far more decayed wall, previously referred to, running south-west to north-east.   Closer inspection at once proved that my assumption of a different, and probably far earlier, date of construction was correct. This wall, which had only a thickness of eight or nine feet on the ground and reached a height of ten or eleven feet, was also built of stamped clay.   But whereas the clay layers in the wall closing the Chia-yü-kuan valley were four or five inches in height, those in the older wall touching it here at right angles were fully ten to twelve inches thick. These measurements at once recalled the almost identical ones observed in the rampart north and west of Tun-huang, which my explorations of the spring had proved to be of early Han times.   The conclusion thus suggested received support also from the height of the wall and from the dimensions of the towers lining it at distances varying apparently from one and a half to two miles. The tower of this old wall which I subsequently examined showed clay layers of identical thickness and the dimension of twenty-five to twenty-six feet square so familiar from the *Limes* of Tun-huang.

I had gathered enough evidence to convince me that the wall stretching away from here to north of Su-chou and Kan-chou was in reality but the continuation of the frontier defence line which I had traced through the Tun-huang desert and then again near An-hsi. But the hope of exactly testing its date here by excavations had quickly to be abandoned. Cultivation extended to the very foot of the old wall and even in places beyond it, and, what with the moisture of the soil and man's destructive vicinity, the chance of any datable records surviving along its line was scanty indeed. In another direction, too, I had to resign myself. The old wall stopped completely where it strikes the Chia-yü-kuan barrier, and of the stretch of about a mile which would be needed to take it on to the precipitous slopes of the Hao-shan-k'ou ridge, I was unable to trace any distinct remains.

Along that ridge itself, which forms a formidable flanking defence for the great route west of Chia-yü-kuan, a wall was certainly needless. There was not sufficient time to try and fill the gap by a minute search of the barren stony glacis sloping up to the rugged spurs; for the continued survey of the other line of wall running northward was of importance. I followed it for another three miles or so to the small village of Huang-tsao-ying, which with its luxuriant fields nestles cosily at the debouchure of the Hao-shan-k'ou gorge. Beyond the stream which issues from the latter, the wall runs on for half a mile more and finally climbs up the slope of a rugged rocky spur for some 200 feet to where this becomes wholly unscalable.

It was interesting to examine how much care had been taken to defend also the triangular area formed by the mouth of the little valley outside the main wall. On the south a

short branch wall had been built from the latter to the
side of the steep spur which flanks the debouchure on the
right.   And when I followed the gorge upward for about
a mile I found it closed at its narrowest point, about 180
yards across, by a battlemented wall of similar construction
and manifestly of the same age as the main wall of Chia-
yü - kuan (Fig. 226).   The dark rock faces, apparently
schist, rise on either side very precipitously to heights of
300 or 400 feet, and the rugged nature of the hill range
effectively protected this 'Klause' from being turned.
With the gorge closed in front and the main wall behind,
the dwellers of Huang-tsao-ying might, indeed, feel safe
from raiders.   But it seemed very strange when, only
some hundred yards higher up in the gorge, I discovered
remains of a second wall, with its parapet facing east, just
opposite to the side on which it would be needed for the
defence of the village.   This second wall was massively
built of stamped clay over rough stones bearing a significant layer of rushes; with its parapet it still reached a
height of about eleven feet.

If the gorge had been situated somewhere on the
Afghan border, the fact of two fortified positions facing
each other at such close range would have had nothing
surprising; for where neighbours always see each other in
the light of enemies, actual or prospective, the maintenance
of defences in near *vis - à - vis* is a matter of common
prudence.   But here on the North - West Frontier of
China, where not internal feuds but common defence
against an ever-restless foe outside the Wall was the
settlers' constant preoccupation, the close proximity of
such inverse lines of defence was bound to have a different
significance.   It did not need prolonged thought to reveal
it.   The clay rampart facing eastwards was beyond all
doubt older, as proved by its far-advanced decay in spite
of massive construction.   What it was meant to protect
was not the gorge, which farther up offers no room for
cultivation of any value, but the safety of the great route
which passes south of the Hao-shan-k'ou ridge.

In this rugged hill chain nature had, as already noted,
provided an impassable barrier to attack from the north.

But this natural barrier was pierced in one place, the gorge debouching at Huang-tsao-ying, and for the safe keeping of the ancient border line held during Han times it became essential to bar this opening. When the *Limes* protecting the route to Tun-huang and hence to the 'Western Regions' was abandoned during the T'ang period, the closing of the Hao-shan-k'ou defile ceased to have any purpose. The old wall built across must have been a complete ruin by the time when the new 'Klause' was erected for the sake of purely local defence. Thus the existence of the two walls facing each other finds its simple chronological explanation.

In the Hao-shan-k'ou gorge I had in fact touched the point where the wholly distinct purposes of the line belonging to the old Han *Limes* and of the defensive line of Chia-yü-kuan reveal themselves in full clearness. The crumbling wall of stamped clay which I had seen starting from the latter at right angles, and which I subsequently traced along the whole northern border of the Su-chou and Kan-chou districts, proved to have been originally connected with the *Limes* of Tun-huang and An-hsi, and to date like that from the second century B.C. Its purpose was to protect the narrow belt of oases along the north foot of the Nan-shan which, since Chinese expansion westwards had commenced under the Han dynasty, was indispensably needed as a passage for commercial and political advance into Central Asia. The second line through which one now passes by the Chia-yü-kuan Gate, —the first western mention of it is to be found in the account of the embassy sent to the Ming Emperor's court in 1420 A.D. by Shah Rukh, the son of the great Timur —is of far more recent construction, and was built for the opposite purpose, that of closing the great Central-Asian trade route at a time when China had resumed its traditional attitude of seclusion from the barbarian West.

Of the border policy which Chia-yü-kuan served from the very beginning down almost to our own days, Shah Rukh's envoy has left us a characteristic glimpse. In his narrative, as excerpted by Sir Henry Yule, he records how

" on their arrival at a strong castle called Karaul (or 'guard station') in a mountain defile through which the road passed, the whole party was counted and their names registered before they were allowed to proceed.   They then went on to ' Suk-cheu ' or Su-chou."   An exactly similar account was given about 1560 by a Turkish Dervish to Gislen de Busbeck, Charles V.'s envoy at Constantinople. Starting from the Persian frontier, his caravan, after a fatiguing journey of many months, " came to a defile which forms, as it were, the barrier gate of Cathay.   Here there was an inclosing chain of rugged and precipitous mountains, affording no passage except through a narrow strait in which a garrison was stationed on the king's part.   There the question is put to the merchants, ' What they bring ? whence they come ? etc.' "

On my way back to the Gate I took occasion to visit a portion of the old wall some two miles away from its terminating point.   Everywhere cultivation actually touched the much-decayed clay wall and in places extended even beyond it.   In a soil kept moist by irrigation for centuries it would have been useless to look for relics of the early days when this border was first garrisoned.   Nor could they have survived on the towers themselves ; for the many repairs which these had undergone during the last thousand years were only too evident in the masses of recent brickwork filling rifts in the old clay and covering the top.

For excavations there was plainly no scope here.   But with the question as to the date and character of this part of the Great Wall solved, I did not feel much regret at this.   Nor could I feel sorry that my ride back to camp took me through fertile village lands instead of that usual setting of my archaeological work, a parched-up desert. The many opium fields, with their huge pink and purple poppies in full bloom, were a glorious sight.   How I longed for colour photography or better still a clever impressionist brush to retain the gorgeous colour effects of these fields of iniquity !   Everywhere throughout the oases of Su-chou opium is the favourite produce.   Sad were the stories I heard of how its cultivation first brought prosperity to the peasants and then invariably ruined them. For none of those who grow opium in these parts can long resist the temptation of personal use. Laziness, gambling, and other evil habits soon get firm hold of the cultivator, and in the end the mortgaged property passes out of his hands into the clutches of the town usurer.

226. HAO-SHAN-K'OU GORGE WITH RUINED WALLS INTENDED TO CLOSE PASSAGE.

On left, remnant of ancient wall (A) with parapet facing east ; on right, battlemented wall of later origin (B) facing west.

227. TEMPLE OF KUAN-YIN, OR AVALOKITESVARA, WITHIN EAST GATE OF CHIA-YÜ-KUAN.

228. PAVILION AND COLONNADE AT ENTRANCE OF CHIU-CH'ÜAN TEMPLE, SU-CHOU.

229. GARDEN AND TEMPLE COURT AT CHIU-CHÜAN, THE 'SPRING OF WINE,' SU-CHOU.

The group of trees on left hides the temple, used as 'my' reception hall.

CHAPTER LXXVI

My rapid survey of Chia-yü-kuan completed, I was free on the morning of July 22nd to set forth for Su-chou. The first large town we were to see within true Cathay was exercising a magnetic attraction on my people, and baggage and men were ready far earlier than usual. Yet even this early start did not prevent the kindly 'guardian of the Gate' from seeing me off in person. With an escort of ten mounted men, who had arrived the evening before as a special compliment from the Brigadier-General commanding at Su-chou, my cavalcade looked imposing. Two banners of large size and gay colours were being carried along by the little troop, and the huge straw hats with fluttering bands which the men wore added to the general quaintness. A carbine or two among their equipment looked strangely out of place in this mediaeval stage-mounting. But for the snowy peaks of the Richthofen range looking down upon us from the south there was little to distract the eye on the nineteen miles' march to Su-chou. By far the greatest part of it lay over a stony waste, which sorely tried our ponies' feet, already unshod from the last days' marches. Numerous canals from the left bank of the Pei-ta Ho were crossed *en route*; but the fertile loess belt which they irrigate lies miles away to the north.

The heat and glare were great, and we all felt relieved when by 3 P.M. the high walls of Su-chou came in view from the edge of unbroken cultivation near the west bank of the river. The many branches we forded held little water at the time, but the deeply cut loess banks on either side and the width of the rubble-filled bed itself, fully a mile across, attested the great volume of water carried down at times by the Pei-ta Ho.   Past rich fields of wheat and the omnipresent opium we rode to a little suburb outside the north gate of the city, where the former Ya-mên of Lin Ta-jên, the late Belgian Mandarin Springaert, had been prepared for my quarters.   It was a rambling structure of imposing dimensions, with several big courtyards and halls.   Although but few years had passed since the first occupant had left Su-chou and his office of Collector of Customs on the Turkestan high road, the whole place looked so shaky and tattered that the prospect of several days' stay in it was far from inviting.   Not even the sensible disregard of orthodox Chinese fashion which allowed the courts and main quarters to face northward could make up for the total absence of trees and needful shade.   So I quickly turned my back on this pretentious jerry-built mansion, with its wall-papers all in rags and its roofs swarming with bats, and rode round the north wall of the city to the only temple that was mentioned as a possible camping-place.

A delightful surprise awaited me at the end of the dusty ride.   On terraced ground, above a large reed-filled basin filled by the limpid water of a bubbling spring, I found a fine arbour and garden lined by temple halls and airy colonnades connecting them (Fig. 228).   For a moment I felt in doubt whether I had been suddenly carried back to the shore of a Kashmir lake or to an old Moghul country-seat in the Lahore Campagna.   Features of both these surroundings, which happy times of the past had endeared to me, seemed to mingle in the pleasantest fashion at Chiu-ch'üan, the 'Spring of Wine,' as this charming spot has been known since ancient times.   Once it gave its name to the city itself.

There was the cool clear spring in its stone-lined tank overgrown with mosses and maidenhair, a worthy brother of the Nagas, which lend charm and life to every favoured nook of Kashmir beloved by gods and men.   But the temple halls with their gaily painted stucco, the tumble-down galleries and belvederes built in timber, and the

jungle-like thickets of the garden seemed rather to belong
to one of those half-ruined villas once tenanted by Moghul
or Sikh grandees which during years gone by had furnished
me with cherished haunts in the country around Lahore.
In the end I decided that a kindly fairy had chosen for my
delectation to reproduce, in distant Cathay and in a climate
recalling Kashmir, that delightful old garden of Shah
Balawal, with its shady terraces and gaily stuccoed little
shrines, which was my favourite refuge during Lahore
times. Maharaja Sher Singh, with more than one of his
courtiers, had been murdered there, and old friends who
cheered me with their visits used to call it my 'tomb.'
Would that I could have greeted them also at this its
Cathayan replica!

On an airy terrace overlooking spring and lake as well
as much of the fertile land across the river, I had my tent
pitched. The roof of a small belvedere which had long
ago lost doors, windows, and other encumbrances of a
sedentary civilization, furnished welcome shade. A walled
garden behind, with thick clumps of fruit-trees, on which
the apricots were just ripening, secured desirable privacy.
Outside it to the west, under majestic old elms which
seemed to rival the plane-trees of Kashmir (Fig. 229),
was my reception hall, a large and elegant temple all in
wood, with a fine carved roof and gracefully curved eaves
over its verandahs. Its architect had evidently thought
more of providing a convenient place for social gatherings
than a home for divinities ; for whereas the images,
grotesque figures in stucco and of recent make, occupied
a modest alcove to the north, the main body of the
structure was given up to a large hall without any
religious use.

The whole was as airy as one could wish, the open-
work screens forming the sides having long lost their paper
covering and all doors their panels. The little garden
parterre, full of marigolds, sunflowers, and peonies, through
which the hall was approached, had suffered less from
neglect than the buildings and supplied a gay patch of
colours. A small dwelling by its side, half ruin half wood-
shed, accommodated Chiang-ssŭ-yeh, ever content with his

quarters as long as they offered a sleeping platform, while the Surveyor, who had refused the several temples put at his disposal as being too 'theatrical,' had his camp pitched in a shady arbour fronting the main temple court.

I had reason to feel specially grateful for the pleasant *milieu* in which my days at Su-chou were spent; for various difficulties caused my stay to drag out longer than I had intended. The six days which passed before I could set out for the mountains were both busy and pleasant. But space suffices only for the briefest account of them. Exchange of state visits with the chief dignitaries of Su-chou absorbed most of the first day. The Tao-t'ai who, under the arrangements made by the Peking Legation and the Wei-wu-pu or Foreign Office, was to act as my banker while in Kan-su, I found to be a quiet old gentleman, much bent by illness and the burden of years. Conversation with him was bound to lag a little; for his faint lisping talk was often difficult to catch even for Chiang's quick ear. The main point was that everything about my credit of 6000 Taels, or roughly £1000, was in due order.

Ch'ai, the Brigadier-General, proved a very different and far more imposing person. A fine presence, coupled with most cordial and wholly unaffected manners, drew one quickly to the old soldier. His flowing white beard, an object of pride not only to the General but to all his numerous *entourage*, quite captivated Chiang. He had long served in the northern garrisons of Chinese Turkestan; had travelled in Russia and apparently elsewhere in Europe, for he spoke of a visit to Fo-kuo (or France), described as a neighbouring country; and had brought back from these distant wanderings an evident liking for foreign ways. I could see that his apprehensive report about my intended excavations, which in April had stirred up uneasiness in official circles at Lan-chou, had originated only from good-natured caution, and not from any obstructive intentions. He was full of genuine interest for my antiquarian relics from the ancient Han frontier, and manifestly glad that the confidential objections from Lan-chou had in no way hampered my work in the desert—and elsewhere.

But, perhaps, the most interesting figure among the Su-chou dignitaries was Chin T'ai-tsin, the magistrate of the 'Independent Department' of Su-chou, a lively and witty man between fifty and sixty, full of culture and practical common-sense.   His very dress and the furniture of his Ya-mên betokened taste and refinement.   Clothed in dainty pale silks befitting the season, showing me with a connoisseur's joy his fine porcelain cups, flower-pots, and other 'things of merit,' he looked the very embodiment of a well-bred and cultured administrator.   Of his scholarly attainments he made no show, though they had earned him a rank superior to that of his Tao-t'ai, out of tactful regard for whom he never wore his proper hierarchical button. But from his questions and quick grasp of points of historical interest I could see how wide were his reading and his mental horizon.

The light collation to which he treated me when returning his visit, was far more entertaining than the great dinner jointly given by the three official 'chiefs' of Su-chou. Out of an excess of polite attention, they had fixed upon my 'own' temple hall as the scene of the symposium.   The very morning after I had pitched my camp at the 'Spring of Wine,' I had noticed with surprise the rapid, though, of course, very superficial, process of patching-up which the neglected old hall was undergoing.   When my hosts had gathered with all their following, filling the temple court with a gaily dressed crowd, huge umbrellas and other trappings of office, and I was duly invited to my own reception hall, I could scarcely recognize it in its refurbished elegance.

It was an imposing banquet, lasting to my dismay from 4 P.M. until nightfall.   I soon gave up counting the dishes with all their expensive and far-fetched dainties.   Chin T'ai-tsin, who, as the junior in the official trio, had charged himself with all arrangements—and, I fear, also with their expense—could be trusted to do things in style.   He and the genial General rivalled each other in enlivening the Petronian feast with amusing stories drawn for my benefit chiefly from their Turkestan experiences.   Even the meek old Tao-t'ai, who was allowed to sip his tea instead of the superior arrack presented to the rest of us, chimed in from time to time with a word of cheerful interest.

Yet this pleasant gathering did not end without leaving awkward doubts about the immediate tasks I had set my mind upon. In accordance with Chinese custom and guided by Chiang's advice, I utilized the last courses for 'talking business' with regard to my proposed expedition into the Nan-shan. I needed transport and guides, and local assistance towards securing them. I knew well that Kan-su people, officials and others, did not share my love for the mountains, and that apprehension of my contemplating a move into territory where Chinese authority was not respected, might raise difficulties. But I was not prepared to hear the assembled authorities, civil and military, declare, in unison and with the gravest air, that there were absolutely no routes to the head-waters of the rivers of Su-chou and Kan-chou which I wished to explore; that the mountains and valleys were all inaccessible owing to 'wild Tibetan robbers' and dangers of all sorts; and, finally, that not even the combined power of my influential hosts could ever induce Kan-su people to venture into that *terra incognita*.

It was useless to point out that the high valleys from which the rivers of the Su-chou and Kan-chou oases descend were well known to be within the Chinese administrative border; that Russian travellers had visited them in parts; and that peaceful Chinese were from time to time washing gold in several places. Nor would my honest assertion that Kan-chou and not Tibet was my goal, make any impression. If I had possessed my own pony transport I could have afforded to treat the objections of my official patrons with some equanimity, and relied on making my way into the mountains without local assistance. But I could afford neither the time nor the money to purchase the sixteen ponies needed for a trip of only about four weeks, and, consequently, the Su-chou dignitaries would only have to maintain their *non possumus* attitude in order to frustrate my long-planned explorations in these mountains.

No doubt their attitude was due solely to the wish of

escaping all responsibility for my safety. But this fact could not relieve my disappointment. It would have been out of place to press the matter further that evening. But next day I lost no time in sending Chiang to Chin T'ai-tsin's Ya-mên, armed with maps and the strongest representations I could make about the absurdity of the statements which had been brought up to confront my requests. The reply with which he returned was by no means reassuring; but at least the order for the supply of ponies on hire was issued. Whether I should get their owners to go where I wanted, seemed most doubtful, and bitterly I regretted my dependence on aid which in this case was so little in keeping with local interest. In order to provide for all eventualities I made it widely known that I was ready to buy ponies. But the animals brought for inspection were so few and ill-conditioned that the hope of gaining my end independently of the Ya-mên looked poor indeed.

It was a great comfort in those days of depressing uncertainty that I could again, after more than a year, enjoy pleasant European society. Father Essems, of the Belgian Missionary Congregation established in Kan-su, had come to Su-chou only a few months before; and as my enquiries at Tun-huang had revealed nothing of this new mission station, the receipt of his Chinese visiting-card came as a pleasant surprise. I lost no time in making my call at the neat little house which was being converted rapidly into a hospitable new 'residence' of the order, and found in Father Essems a very amiable young priest full of knowledge about things Chinese, and full of sympathy, too, with the people. The hours we spent together proved most instructive, and it was no small advantage to me to submit my impressions of what little I had seen of Kan-su to a keen Chinese scholar with years of experience in this region.

Much of our talk turned to Marco Polo, whose account of 'Sukchu' and 'Campichu,' Su-chou and Kan-chou, reveals so much accurate observation of local detail. Nor did I fail to give vent to my pious remembrance of brave Benedict Goëz, 'who had sought Cathay and found heaven.' Here at Su-chou, where he might well think himself near to his goal, and where, nevertheless, he came to be detained for sixteen weary months, the devoted Jesuit traveller succumbed in 1607 to disease and priva- tions. I had thought of him and his plucky perseverance at all the points—Lahore, Peshawar, the Pamirs, Sarikol, Yarkand, and Khotan—where I had touched the line of his wanderings. And grateful I felt now to Fate which had allowed me to reach the site of his tragic end. There is nothing to suggest even approximately the spot where his wearied limbs were laid to rest by the young Chinese convert whom the Jesuit fathers had despatched from Peking to his relief, and who arrived just a few days before all earthly trouble was ended. But I hope that when the Catholic Mission at Su-chou shall have built its permanent chapel, means may be found to recall to those who worship in it the memory of Benedict Goëz.

The city of Su-chou, rebuilt on a new site after the destruction caused by the last great Muhammadan rising, seemed a busy and flourishing place, but sadly deficient in those quaint old temples which abound at Tun-huang. Evidently the new settlers brought here from different parts of China were less ready for pious sacrifices than the people who had held out at that ancient outpost. The number of shops with goods brought from the seaports was large, and articles of Japanese manufacture were plentiful. But the attempt I made in them to pick up articles which might help to replenish my exhausted stock of official presents, proved a failure. Only the shoddiest productions of the West seemed to penetrate to what was once an emporium for China's Central-Asian trade.

Far more refreshing than this futile attempt at ' shop- ping' was a day's excursion to the ancient border wall which I made in Father Essems' company. We struck the remains of a wall at a point some eight miles in a direct line northward ; but the marshy nature of the ground intervening in parts obliged us to make a considerable détour. Cultivation still extends to the *Limes*, but only in detached belts. In the areas separating them I came repeatedly on traces of old fields now abandoned to coarse grass and scrub. Some perfect specimens of rudimentary dunes which we met on the swampy meadow land just south of the wall served to demonstrate how close is the vicinity of the Mongolian Gobi. The wall itself, extant only in broken segments (Fig. 223), showed exactly the same construction as where I had examined it north of Chia-yü-kuan. But it was interesting to note that the clay wall rested here not on the natural ground, but on a low earth mound, evidently needed for a foundation on soil which two thousand years ago was already liable to become water-logged.

Throughout the cultivated tract the appearance of the crops indicated a rich soil and abundance of water. The wavy expanse of green fields, with the many large patches of flowering red poppies and the frequent avenues of tall poplars and elms, made up a bright rural landscape. The mighty snow-crested range of the Nan-shan supplied an Alpine background. The day before clouds had gathered over it, and the discharge of rain caused a flood in the river by the time we returned. All over the broad bed there raced courses of muddy water. The force of the current was great, and the depth well over three feet, even where the channels were broadest.

The persistence with which I urged the necessity of my work in the mountains and my determination to obtain the needful transport, did not fail in the end to produce its effect on the Ya-mêns. The formidable objections on account of dangers were abandoned one by one, and by the fifth day Chiang could report that he had seen with his own eyes fourteen animals collected for me at the Magistrate's Ya-mên. I hastened to offer a promise of liberal payment greatly beyond the official rates of hire, as well as assurance of all possible care for the animals and their owners. But there remained grave misgivings how far transport raised under such pressure could be got to move into the mountains. All the Chinese of Kan-su seemed to be swayed by a perfect dread of the mountains, which to them remain a *terra incognita* beyond the outermost range. So there was widespread grumbling at this extension of the obligation of supplying transport which is

otherwise accepted for official journeyings in the plains as
a recognized corvée.

During those last days the telegraph had brought
grave news from Tun-huang, which made Tao-t'ai, General,
and Magistrate inclined to show additional caution.
Already at the 'Thousand Buddhas' I had heard of the
decision in a long-standing case about certain revenue
arrears due from Tun-huang cultivators. Trouble was
anticipated on its enforcement; and in order to avoid the
risk of its breaking out while I was still within the district,
Wang, my considerate Amban friend, and his military
coadjutor, Lin Ta-jên, were temporizing. Now news had
come that the attempt to enforce the fiscal claims had
resulted in a serious riot. After the chief agitator, a
literatus, had forcibly resisted arrest and been killed,
Wang's Ya-mên was attacked by the populace and partly
destroyed, over a dozen people being killed on both sides.

There was much doubt in official circles as to how far the
Tun-huang levies had upheld the cause of order. Rumour
asserted that they had opened the city gate to the rioters.
But there could be no doubt that Wang had faced serious
danger, and was asking for armed support from Su-chou.
From what Chiang could learn, there was far more disposition at the Ya-mêns to sacrifice him to the inevitable
viceregal censure than to vindicate impaired official
authority. The General was reported to deprecate the
despatch of military aid, on the ground that if he moved
out himself the troublesome people of Tun-huang might
be driven into desperate courses by fear of the terrible
consequences! The old Tao-t'ai, no doubt, could be
trusted to shelter himself from any responsibility. Chin
T'ai-tsin, the shrewd Magistrate, might well fear that, as a
result of his own reputation for administrative perspicacity,
he would himself eventually be ordered to undertake the
unenviable task of putting things straight at Tun-huang.
Was it then to be wondered at if the distant chance of
trouble arising from my tour in the mountains weighed
heavier on my Mandarin friends' minds than it would
otherwise have done?

So my relief was great when on July 27th the longed-for transport was brought to my quarters. The men looked decidedly sulky, and showed little disposition to take the ten days' hire I paid out to them, when it was explained that this was meant as an advance for the purchase of rations for themselves and their animals. In fact, they broadly hinted that they would take our baggage only to the foot of the mountains and no farther.

However, much was to be gained by the mere start from headquarters. So I purposely refused to pay attention to warnings of this sort. The same day I paid my farewell visits at the Ya-mêns. Here, too, it seemed the right policy to treat the complete execution of my programme in the mountains as a matter of course. How could Tao-t'ai, General, or Magistrate fail to respond to such unhesitating reliance on their willingness and power to help? But inwardly I confessed to misgivings when I heard that Chin T'ai-tsin, under the Tao-t'ai's orders, was to move out with me to Chin-fo-ssŭ, the last village at the foot of the mountains, and personally to superintend my start.

The return visits of these dignitaries in the evening coincided with a modest return, picnic-fashion, which I was paying on my terrace to Father Essems' hospitality. As my missionary guest was accompanied by his native coadjutor, and as Chiang, too, was of the party as a matter of course, regard for Chinese notions demanded a reasonable multiplication of dishes. My strictly limited camp service was thus put to no small strain. But the difficulty in serving up properly the various little 'confections' which my Kashmirian cook had contrived, grew more embarrassing when General and Magistrate also turned up and had to be invited. The confusion of Aziz, my Ladaki servant, was amusing. It had taken him years to learn how the simple camp dinner of a far from fastidious Sahib was to be put on the table. Now he was caught by the sudden ambition to do these things in true Chinese fashion, which he had never had a chance of observing closely. The result was a very funny muddle, in which we were expected to drink custard with chopsticks. Luckily none of my guests, expected or otherwise, was likely to be put out by such little *faux pas*. Level-headed Tila Bai was at hand, and soon grasped that visitors to a Sahib's camp, whether they were true Chinese or Europeans living in Chinese dress and fashion like Father Essems, could only be served after the Sahib's ways. So things righted themselves in the end, and, whatever the short-comings, all my guests enjoyed the view over the reed-filled lake and the cool refreshing air of the evening.

CHAPTER LXXVII

THROUGH THE RICHTHOFEN RANGE OF THE NAN-SHAN

ON the morning of July 28th the sixteen hired ponies and mules turned up late in spite of their having been kept under watch. By depositing at the Ya-mên whatever could be spared of stores and kit, I had greatly reduced our baggage. Yet it was not until 11 A.M. that the whole of the caravan was got under way. Fortunately the journey to the foot of the mountains south-eastwards could easily be divided into two marches. After only three miles through rich fields and along shady avenues lining the roads, near the large and already half ruined cantonment which had been established after the last great Tungan rising, we reached the bare gravel steppe which sloped gently down from the mountains.

The heat of the sun was fierce while we crossed this waste for upwards of six miles. But the sight of the great chain of snowy peaks, and of the fertile tract of San-chi-p'o which lined the horizon northwards, afforded relief. Numerous canals carrying water from the river which debouches from the Richthofen range east of the Pei-ta Ho, were crossed by the track. Then we entered a fan-like belt of rich red clayey soil; cultivation was here unbroken, yet the number of the fields evidently left long unsown suggested deficiency in either water-supply or population. Near Shih-hui-yao-miao, a large temple in course of construction, we pitched camp, a violent gale blowing down from the mountains all the evening. Without bringing a drop of rain to the plains, it cleared away all the clouds that had been hovering for days along the great snowy range.

The brilliantly clear atmosphere and the coolness which set in made the next day's march to Chin-fo-ssŭ, only some sixteen miles away to the south-east, quite delightful. With the exception of two strips of rubble-strewn Sai, the whole of it led through fertile village land, called Hung-shan, 'the Red Hills,' from a low chain of red foot-hills. The abundance of fine old trees, mostly elms, gathered in groves near the hamlets or scattered between the fields, was striking, and the harmonious blending of the colours, the light green in the fields, and the bright red of the bare soil, a constant joy to the eye. In one of the hamlets of Hung-shan I found the walled enclosure of a small and ruinous temple occupied by a perfect bee-hive of students, tucked away in a number of half-decayed temple quarters. Droning sounds of recitation in unison issued from the hovels of the different classes, and made it easy for the simple ' Hsien-shêng ' to control their progress without leaving his own little burrow, where a few more advanced students were receiving instruction in Confucian classics. Once again I was struck by the order and neatness which prevailed in this village school. Our intrusion, in spite of all the curiosity it excited, failed to draw the little ones from their writing-desks. The droning, by no means displeasing to the ear, proceeded peacefully to the accompaniment of the small bells on the gate-tower tinkling in the breeze.

The picturesque little fort-town of Kuei-yin-ssŭ, which we passed some four miles farther on, now completely de-serted, will also keep fresh in my memory. The massive clay walls, some 250 yards square, still rose thirty feet high ; but only a desolate temple and some old trees were left within. A few acres of ground along the walls were still irrigated ; but elsewhere there spread terraced fields abandoned to waste. That cultivation here had considerably receded was certain. But was this the result of diminishing water-supply, or of the devastation which had followed the last great rebellion ? Local enquiries, as so often among these secretive people of the border, proved useless.

Across a broad belt of sterile ground strewn with

pebbles and boulders, we reached the long-stretched fields of Chin-fo-ssŭ. They occupy the central part of the large alluvial fan at the mouth of the valley by which we were to enter the mountains. The small town which gives its name, meaning the 'Shrine of the Golden Buddha,' to this fertile tract showed high and well-kept walls bearing towers and battlements (Fig. 230). Outside its eastern gate I found a posse of petty officials with a handful of red-cloaked soldiers drawn up to receive me. But the squalid temple close by intended for our accommodation looked far from attractive, and still less so the prospect of getting our water from a slimy tank just in front.

Moving up the steadily rising ground towards the debouchure of the valley I soon found a shady camping place in a terraced fruit garden overgrown with luxuriant scrub. A high watch-tower behind, surrounded by a moat, and some farm dwellings adjoining, showed the same picturesque neglect. The canal which passed by the side of this orchard was dry ; but assured that water was to be let into it 'presently,' I decided to remain. Here, so close to the mountains, and about 6300 feet above the sea, the air was already much cooler. But the pleasant sensation grew fainter as hour after hour passed without the desired water arriving. When at last a few bucket-fuls were brought, smell and colour showed plainly that the water came from a tank and not a running canal.

During this weary wait, which was enlivened only by a good-natured crowd of curious villagers (Fig. 231), I had to receive Chin T'ai-tsin, who had just arrived from town to arrange for my safe start. His misgivings about the pony-men brought from Su-chou were but too well founded. After depositing our baggage they and their animals vanished completely. Next day was to show whether they could be caught again or replaced by transport locally raised. A day's halt was the least allowance I could make to my Mandarin friend for trying his diplomacy and suave pressure on the recalcitrant people from Su-chou. Late at night I heard that they had crowded into his quarters and declared that they were prepared to take the severest beating rather than move into those dread mountains. So the prospects were decidedly gloomy when I retired to rest about midnight. No water had come down our little stream, and I could not indulge in illusions about the liquor serving for my late tea and dinner.

Next day I lost no time in sending Chiang to the Magistrate's quarters. Long hours passed without either ponies or news turning up to relieve the strain. I used the time busily for a home mail which this time was to go eastwards, to the newly opened Imperial Post Office at Lan-chou, and thence *via* Tien-tsin and the Trans-Siberian railway. That those letters arrived in England by the first week of October speaks well for the working of the modern postal service established by the Chinese Customs Department. While my thoughts were travelling far away, things on the spot had taken a more promising turn. By mid-day Chiang arrived with the news that the Magistrate had managed to retain half of the Su-chou animals, and that great efforts were being made to raise the rest of the transport around Chin-fo-ssŭ.

But concessions were asked for on my part. It was easy to agree to double the rate of hire we had paid about Tun-huang and elsewhere. But more difficult was it to comply with the demand that each load was to be reduced by one-half. I had already at Su-chou deposited all equipment not likely to be needed for a month or two, and had now little to spare, except the bulk of the silver I had taken from the Su-chou Ya-mên. Fortunately two people of our party could safely be left behind. For Naik Ram Singh's services there was little use in the mountains, and with him I could send to Kan-chou also Ahmad, the interpreter. Assured of the help of a Chinese-speaking companion, the Naik greeted the temporary separation with equanimity if not satisfaction. A few weeks' stay in Kan-chou town would give him a good rest. There was also the attraction of cooking his meals after his own Jat tastes, which different caste rules had not always allowed to be followed in the common *ménage* with the Surveyor. In regard to sugar and clarified butter he had great arrears to make up, and I hoped that the resources of Kan-chou would allow him fully to use his *carte blanche*.

230. NORTH WALL OF CHIN-FO-SSŬ TOWN, WITH FOOT-HILLS OF RICHTHOFEN RANGE IN BACKGROUND.

231. CHINESE VILLAGERS AT CHIN-FO-SSŬ WATCHING MY TENT.

232. VIEW SOUTH FROM HOU-TZŬ PASS ACROSS DRY LAKE BASIN.

When at last after much sifting of baggage I could return Chin's visit in the evening I found him quite pleased with the success of his diplomatic efforts. The sixteen ponies and mules had now been secured without further lamentations or protests. Even the provision of twenty-four days' supplies for men and beasts had been faithfully promised by the village head-men, of course from the further advances of hire I was to provide. So with my mind relieved of the most pressing cares, I could indulge in a long chat about interesting local topics, the apparent decrease in cultivated land, the irrigation system, and much else. From the villagers it would have been futile to ask information. But in Chin T'ai-tsin I had an observant administrator to question, and from his statements based on official records I gathered that the amount of irrigation water, the basis for land revenue assessment in these parts, had even since the quelling of the last Tungan rebellion undergone a certain reduction.

I was interested, too, to see for once how a Chinese District Officer installs himself when 'on tour.' My Mandarin friend was a man of taste, and this was reflected even in his dainty camp tea-service and in the neat little baldachin of coloured silk which enclosed his travelling bedstead. When we returned to camp in the evening Chiang confided that the trouble taken by Chin T'ai-tsin personally to assure my safe start had its advantage for himself. The move to Chin-fo-ssŭ had greatly reduced the risk of his being sent off by telegraphic orders from Lan-chou to take charge of the troubled affairs at Tun-huang. It greatly amused me to think that Chinese officials, too, had found out the danger of being near a telegraph. But how different were their motives from those which might at times tempt administrators on the Indian Frontier to cut that troublesome wire from headquarters!

The morning of July 31st saw at last our start into the mountains. The animals did not arrive till 8 A.M., and it took two hours before they were laden. But in the joy of seeing the move made in earnest I did not much mind the delay nor the trouble which the weighing out of silver for advances to pony-men gave me. The loads containing supplies for men and animals had also to be inspected. Four donkeys were provided, in addition, to carry the pony-men's rations. In the midst of all this bustle I almost missed the farewell visit of the attentive Magistrate. The morning was delightfully cool, and as soon as the two miles of bare alluvial slope, with many traces of terraced fields now abandoned, had been crossed to the mouth of the valley, I found myself in refreshing verdure.

A picturesque tower guarded the entrance, and by its side a richly decorated temple, half in ruins, and a hamlet lay ensconced under big trees. A shop newly built by the roadside, and a gaily painted little shrine behind it, were evidently intended for the patronage of the miners who travel by this route to the gold-fields high up in the mountains. The luxuriant growth of grass and flowers which I noticed from the very debouchure was a striking contrast to the barrenness of the mountain gorges about Tun-huang and An-hsi. The far moister climate of this central part of the Nan-shan became evident at the first glance, and I greeted it with delight even though its welcome soon took the form of a steady and plentiful rain. It was so refreshing to see the steep slopes between which the gorge winds upwards clothed with true Alpine verdure, and even our many crossings of the clear stream gave pleasure.

After about six miles we passed the first of the coal-seams so abundant in these mountains. At present only scraped on the surface, they may yet prove for Kan-su the promise of a great industrial future. Two miles higher up the rough track led through a massively built wall, closing the gorge at a point where its precipitous rock sides approach within about 150 yards. A profusion of herbs and mosses covered the wall facing southwards; nowhere since leaving Kashmir had I seen the fertile powers of nature so busy at work in hiding and effacing the labours of man. Yet these remnants of a Klause looked decidedly old. A couple of miles farther on a charming little stretch of meadows, known as Ying-kao-ko, offered an excellent camping-place. The rain had stopped opportunely, and, while the tent was being pitched, I could

indulge in the long-missed pleasure of gathering Alpine
flowers by the handful, among them deep blue gentians
which I could greet as old friends.   In the rocky ravines
descending on both sides grew luxuriant brushwood, and
the men were soon drying themselves by huge fires such
as these poor folk of Su-chou could scarcely ever have
afforded to light.

I was just gleefully reflecting how our ponies would
revel in their Alpine pasture when Sahid Bai, my wild-
looking but quaintly tame pony-man from Yarkand
(Fig. 246), came up with alarmed mien to report that five
of the animals were standing about benumbed and refusing
to touch grass or fodder.   I at once suspected that they had
eaten of the poisonous grass which infests certain parts of
the Nan-shan, and about which old Marco has much to tell
in his chapter on ‘Sukchur’ or Su-chou.   The Venetian's
account had proved quite true; for while my own ponies
showed all the effects of this inebriating plant, the local
animals had evidently been wary of it.   A little bleeding
by the nose, to which Tila Bai, with the veterinary skill of
an old Ladak ‘Kirakash,’ promptly proceeded, seemed to
afford some relief.   But it took two or three days before
the poor brutes were again in full possession of their
senses and appetites.   The evening brought more rain,
and to my tent plentiful company.   Under the sides of its
outer fly there collected rapidly a dense crowd of humanity,
the pony-men fleeing thither from the elements.   How glad
I often felt thereafter for being able to offer this much-
appreciated hospitality!   The five soldiers from Chin-fo-ssŭ,
whom the Magistrate had insisted on sending along as
escort, had wisely brought their two tiny *tentes d'abri*.

Next morning I woke to a delightfully clear day; but
at first a heavy mist clinging to the higher slopes hid its
glory.   We had to wait until the bright sunshine had made
its way into the narrow valley and partially at least dried
men and tents.   The preceding day's ascent had been
steep and had brought us to a level of about 10,400 feet
above the sea.   Yet I scarcely suspected our first pass to
be so near as it actually proved.   As soon as we had
turned a rocky spur above the camp the valley widened to

a small amphitheatre, and an ascent of 1000 feet over steep
Alpine meadows brought us to a grassy plateau known
as Pan-t'o-pa. On its edge rose a watch-tower, built of
stamped clay with a wooden framework and similar in size
and construction to the watch-towers familiar to me from
the desert *Limes*. But what a change in the surroundings! Clay and woodwork both looked much decayed;
but with climatic conditions so different from those of the
plains no estimate of date could be hazarded.

Only one thing seemed clear. This tower and an
exactly similar one on the pass itself, together with the
little fort of which I found traces on the Chio-po-chia Pass
beyond, plainly proved that inroads had been feared from
these mountains. Who were the people who once threatened
the low lands from the now uninhabited valleys of the Nan-
shan? I thought of the 'Little Yüeh-chih,' remnants of an
ancient nomad race, who are mentioned in these mountains
by later Chinese records down to the tenth century A.D.
They are said to have been left behind here when their
kindred, the 'Great Yüeh-chih,' who under the name of
Indo-Scythians were destined to become the rulers of the
Oxus region and the Indian North-West, were forced by
Hun aggression in the second century B.C. to start on
their great migration westwards. If only the snowy peaks
which have ever looked down on these valleys and plains
could tell us the story!

The distance across the plateau to the Hou-tzŭ Pass
southward was only three-quarters of a mile; yet, small as
it was, it brought a surprise. A stream which came down
from a snow-capped peak on the right disappeared before
my eyes in a boulder-filled basin enclosed by grassy slopes
on all sides. Its water, no doubt, finds an underground
passage into the Chin-fo-ssŭ valley below. As soon as I
had reached the pass itself, about 11,350 feet high by the
aneroid, the same curious topographical feature presented
itself on a larger scale. Below a beautiful semicircle of
snowy peaks rising in the centre to close on 9000 feet
there extended a large level basin to the south foot of the
pass (Fig. 232).

At first glance it might have been taken for a lake;

for the moisture brought down by last night's rain was just rising in dense vapour as seen in the photograph. There was no visible outflow for the streams descending into this basin from the surrounding peaks and ridges; and when after a steep descent of some 300 feet I arrived at its edge, I found that the level bottom, fully two miles long from north to south, was completely clear of water. The fine sand covering the bottom showed plainly that the basin must at times still be under water, and a track leading well above the flat ground along the steep slope westwards confirmed this assumption. At the time of the snow's first melting a shallow sheet of water was said to extend where now we crossed dry-shod.

Just where the bottom of the basin began to show a gentle slope rising towards the main range, our track turned south-east to the first of the lateral passes by which we were to cross the high side spurs projecting from the main Richthofen range. The ascent to the Chio-po-chia Pass, about 12,600 feet above sea, led over rich mountain meadows and was easy enough. But from its narrow ridge, defended by a small ruined fort with a double rampart of rough stones and clay, we looked down into a deep-cut valley which with its many precipitous rock coulisses vividly recalled the trying Karanghu-tagh gorges south of Khotan. I was glad that the rough serpentine track which led down most abruptly had not to be negotiated by our baggage animals in the reverse direction. But even here, where erosion had exposed so much of the rock frame of the mountains, abundance of flowers delighted the eye. Edelweiss, gentians, and a host of Alpine flowers which, alas! I had never learned to name, covered the slopes of detritus. Wild rhubarb, for which the Nan-shan was famous in Marco Polo's days, spread its huge fleshy leaves everywhere.

The formation of the gorge, side ravines, and spurs was curiously alike to that seen so often in the poor desiccated Kun-lun ranges. Yet what a contrast there was in vegetation, colours, and true Alpine sensations! After three miles of a much-twisted course, the gorge suddenly debouched into a valley running parallel to that of Chin-fo-ssŭ, but quite impracticable in its lower part. A rapid

stream fed by the snows of the main range had to be forded
before we could reach our camping-ground, known as Lung-
kuo-ho, in the broad scrub-covered bottom of the valley.
Its height was only about 9900 feet, and with the valley
open to the day's bright sunshine the air felt distinctly
warmer.

The march of August 2nd was rather a trying one for
the animals. With the route skirting closer and closer the
north face of the great snowy range, no less than three
lateral spurs had to be crossed in succession. The ascent
to the first pass, called Chin-tou-an-shên, about 13,000 feet
above sea, was steep though leading over grassy ridges.
A small herd of cattle met here was the first and last sign
that the value of these valleys for grazing is not altogether
unknown to the Kan-su people.

How often thereafter had I occasion to wonder at the
absolute neglect of these splendid grazing-grounds in the
mountains! I need not dilate on the causes, probably
racial as well as cultural, which seem to make the Chinese,
where undiluted by other elements, so averse to life as
herdsmen. The fact remains that mountain tracts, which
could maintain tens of thousands of cattle during the
summer months, and to a sufficiently hardy race would
afford attractions for nomadic existence far superior to
those of the Pamirs or T'ien-shan, are at present absolutely
uninhabited, even during the warmest part of the year.
Again and again I thought of the fine herds of cattle,
horses, and sheep which Kirghiz or Mongols could raise
here. But perhaps the Chinese, unwilling themselves to
turn to account these opportuntites for nomadic prosperity,
are wise in keeping others out of them. If the nation has
suffered for many centuries from its neighbours in the
great plains northward, it could scarcely be expected to
cherish the presence of similar troublesome nomads to the
south of the long-drawn Kan-su border.

From a knoll rising to the south some two hundred feet
above the pass a grand panoramic view was obtained
towards the main range. From south-east to south-west
there rose above us a succession of bold snowy peaks
which, as the subsequent computation of the clinometrical

observations showed, reached heights up to close on 19,000 feet. Here on their north slope the snow-line descended to about 15,000 feet. As soon as survey and photographic work was completed we hurried on to the next pass, the Li-yüan-ta-fan, only about one mile off. From it a steep descent of over a thousand feet brought us to the junction of two streams draining the main range.

The track thence turned up the valley to the south-east, which, in strange contrast to the luxuriant scrub and grass met before, showed nothing but bare slopes of detritus. On the higher parts of the spur which we had to surmount the snow still lay in large beds to within a thousand feet or so of the pass. The latter, a narrow rocky saddle, over 14,000 feet above sea, bore not without reason the designation of Hsi-ta-fan, 'the Snow Pass.' After the steep pull up its west slope, there was compensation in an easy descent on the other side, over delightful mountain meadows and then through a picturesque gorge of gneiss rock. Less than three miles from the pass we emerged in the valley of the Ma-so Ho, which was to open a passage for us through the main range.

From Ch'ing-shui-k'a-tzŭ, where we had camped on a small plateau carpeted with Alpine flowers and over-looking some abandoned gold-pits by the river (Fig. 233), we set out on August 3rd on a glorious morning. A short thunderstorm the evening before had cleared the atmosphere; but with a minimum temperature falling to two degrees Fahrenheit below freezing-point and a heavy hoar-frost, it took time before the tents were sufficiently dried for a start. The track up the river led for ten miles almost throughout over gently sloping meadows; but in order to keep to such easy ground we had to cross the stream half-a-dozen times.

As its depth was nowhere more than two feet, 'Dash' alone felt the trouble, having each time to be caught and carried across on horseback. My little companion quite grasped that frequent swims of twenty or thirty yards in icy-cold water were not the right thing for him; but after the long months of desert marching he had forgotten the art acquired in the mountains south of Khotan of jumping up to the stirrup, and thence to the pommel of whoever was offering him a lift. Fortunately there were plenty of marmots, big red-haired fellows just as I knew them from Kashmir and the Pamirs, to afford him pleasant distraction. Sitting boldly upright over their burrows to sun themselves and shrilly whistling as we passed, they were distinctly provoking for so indefatigable a hunter as ' Dash.' But, of course, he never caught one napping.

Where the valley approached the south slopes of a broad snowy peak already surveyed from the opposite side, a bold spur from the watershed westwards made it bifurcate. The steep grassy end of this spur, over 13,000 feet high, furnished an excellent survey station. Our track led into the narrower valley south-westwards, and soon pleasing views of Alpine verdure gave way to bare slopes of detritus, and higher up to bleak cliffs of slate or schist rock. When a mile from the watershed the narrow defile opened out again, another striking change came over the scenery. After passing a gloomy rock gate I found myself among gently rounded downs of bare clay, a brilliant red-brick in colour. The snow appeared to have left them quite recently, and some pretty crocuses were just emerging.

On gaining the broad flat ridge, about 14,600 feet above the sea, which forms the Ch'iang-tzŭ-k'ou Pass, a grand and impressive panorama lay before me. To the north and north-east there stretched in a vast chain of snowy peaks the Richthofen range, with a crest-line falling nowhere, it seemed, below 16,000 feet. The only gaps visible for a distance of upwards of fifty miles were the valley far away to the north-west through which the Pei-ta Ho forces its way to the plains, and the Ma-so Ho Valley up which the day's march had lain. The whole view to the north was dominated by a grand peak, of about 18,600 feet, with a broad ice sheet descending to about the same level as where we had our 'fixing' above the pass.

But what gave true relief to this mountain panorama was the vast plateau stretching from north-west to south-east and separating the Richthofen from the next inner range, the To-lai-shan. Like a big mountain-girt basin it looked ; but the trend of the many shallow valleys furrowing

233. CAMP AT CH'ING-SHUI-K'A-TZŬ, ON LEFT BANK OF MA-SO HO.

234. TUNGAN GOLD MINERS FROM HSI-NING.

it showed that it belonged to two different drainage systems. Looking westwards I could see how all the streams draining these undulating red-clay slopes gathered in a big depression which the eye could follow for some twenty miles. There a transverse ridge made it turn off to the north as a gorge disappearing between rugged snowy peaks. The 'River of the Red Water,' Hung-shui-pa Ho, was the expressive name which I here heard applied to the stream which, after breaking through the Richthofen range, fertilizes a great part of the Su-chou oasis.

As my eyes wandered south towards the less serried To-lai-shan range, they soon caught a broad ridge of red clay forming the low watershed between the 'Red River' basin and a still greater one to the south-east. It was the head-waters area of the Kan-chou River. Some twenty miles broad at its head, the valley stretched away unbroken so far to the south-east that the snowy flanking ranges seemed almost to meet in the distance. Seen across such big basins and lying farther away from the pass, the To-lai-shan did not present the same appearance of a towering mountain rampart as did the range of Richthofen. But its individual snow-peaks stood out more boldly, and where they gathered far away to the south in a great massif of glittering ice and snow, the effect was sublime. What, however, I then rejoiced most to see was the well-defined character of the Nan-shan ranges and the open nature of the intervening valleys, of which this wide view first gave promise. It was bound to prove a great advantage for extending systematic survey work.

Though the rays of the setting sun were still passing freely down the great basins and along the ranges, heavy clouds had gathered above our heads. An icy wind played around us, and a shower of sleet soon followed. So we were glad when the surveying work was done and we could follow the baggage. We had now reached the area of gold-mining, up to which one or two men in our escort had confessed their ability to guide us. The network of shallow depressions into which we descended looked terribly bleak, with bare slopes of red clay or slaty detritus. Everywhere we passed abandoned pits of gold-washers and small channels dug to carry the needful water, Of the gold-washers' hovels nothing remained but small shapeless lines of rubble ; there was nothing to determine how long they had been deserted.

As we moved south towards the watershed between the Hong-shui-pa Ho and the Kan-chou River, the ground became more and more boggy. The snow had melted here but recently, and evidently the soil was unable to absorb all this moisture. At last, as it was getting dark, we arrived at the miners' camp known as Ta-pen-ko, at an elevation of over 13,400 feet. The pits, no longer worked, had been cut into the edge of the watershed. In their midst stood two hovels built of boulders and cut turf, giving shelter to some twenty men working pits lower down to the south. They were hardy Tungans from the Hsi-ning side, whom a more venturesome disposition made brave the rigours of this terribly exposed upland (Fig. 234). Our twenty odd Chinese quickly huddled up with them. The ground along the ridge was so spongy and peat-like that it took time before a spot sufficiently firm and dry could be found for my tent. A bitterly cold south-west wind had followed the shower of sleet, and my Turkestan followers were not without reason venting their feelings against the perversity of those 'heathen Khitais' who had brought us out of our way to this bleak spot.

CHAPTER LXXVIII

ACROSS THE TO-LAI-SHAN RANGE

NEXT morning, August 5th, a heavy white fog hid the whole of plateau and mountains until 7 A.M. But when the sun broke through, the vistas were inspiring. Near by the eye was refreshed by the sight of young flowers, among them many edelweiss, just appearing amongst the scanty tufts of grass and moss. The men needed the forenoon to dry their clothes in the sun and to cook their food for which fuel had been lacking in the evening, and I used these hours of brilliantly clear sky to ascend to a dominating point of the watershed, about 14,000 feet high. From there I secured a complete panorama of this strange amalgam of high ranges, bright red downs, and boggy uplands (Fig. 235).

When I returned to camp I found everybody, Surveyor and Chiang included, eager to turn their back upon this bleak spot. The miners' little stock of dry dung and other substitutes for fuel had given out completely. Of course, I had to pay for it handsomely. The Surveyor took the chance of investing a loan of twenty Taels, a little over three pounds, which he had asked from me, in gold dust purchased from the miners. The rate of exchange, 25 ounces of silver to one ounce of gold, seemed to him to promise a fair margin of profit on taking the gold to India. The question as to the purity of the gold was the speculative element in the transaction.

I had determined that for survey purposes we should follow the plateau separating the Richthofen and To-lai-shan ranges as far to the north-west as possible, and then make our way over the latter. Accordingly we marched down the Hung-shui-pa Ho to the debouchure of a side valley which drains the small glaciers of some To-lai-shan peaks. Here at an elevation of close on 12,900 feet scanty scrub could be collected for fuel, and a few wooden poles discovered in a deserted miner's hut made a very welcome addition. The spot, known as Hsiao-lung-k'ou, was apparently the lowest in the basin where gold had been washed from the detritus.

The evening brought drizzling rain, and during the night it poured so heavily that next morning, the clouds still hanging low and rain continuing at intervals, a start became impossible. I used the enforced halt for writing work and Chinese study. That day our little escort departed, having been relieved by a fresh batch of men sent from another post at the foot of the mountains. I could see no purpose in this relief by men who had practically started at the same time as ourselves, and who apparently had not even been warned of the length of time likely to be taken by my journey. But, as I had not asked for their services, the adequacy or otherwise of their food-supply would be their own look-out.

Next morning the heavy rain-clouds had drifted eastwards, and, the sun breaking through at last, we resumed our march westwards to the watershed of the Pei-ta Ho drainage. For about four miles we followed the Hung-shui-pa River, with its brick-red waters now considerably swollen, down to the point where, turning north, it disappears in a gorge quite impassable at this season. All along its course on flat ground deserted gold-pits abounded. Then we ascended for some six miles over grass-covered alluvial fans of streams draining large snow-beds of the To-lai-shan, and over undulating ridges, until we reached the Chu-lung-kuan pass, at an elevation of about 13,600 feet (Fig. 236). It commanded a very extensive view westwards, as far as a fine massif of snowy peaks we had seen weeks before from the Tu-ta-fan. Its highest point rose to over 19,000 feet.

On our left the To-lai-shan range showed little snow for some ten or twelve miles, but beyond rose again in a beautiful ice-clad ridge close to where the Pei-ta Ho

235. VIEW TO SOUTH-WEST FROM RIDGE ABOVE TA-PEN-KO, *CIRC.* 14,000 FEET HIGH, SHOWING PORTION OF TO-LAI-SHAN.

236. VIEW TO S.E. FROM CHU-LUNG-KUAN PASS, SHOWING PORTION OF TO-LAI-SHAN RANGE.

237. ON CREST ABOVE HUO-NING-TO PASS, LOOKING N.W. TOWARDS PEI-TA HO VALLEY.

238. VIEW DOWN THE PEI-TA HO VALLEY FROM LEFT BANK OF RIVER.

breaks through. The river had cut its bed too deep to
be visible; but the valleys of all its tributaries on this,
its middle course, lay before us in perfect clearness. The
march down the valley was delightfully easy. Its almost
flat bottom, about three miles broad, was covered with
plentiful coarse grass, and its slope was so gentle that,
when after eight miles or so we pitched camp in a
little amphitheatre of rich meadow-land at the foot of the
range northward, the aneroid still showed an elevation
of over 12,100 feet. Ever since crossing the watershed
we had seen many wild yaks grazing in the ravines just
below the snow-beds. Now we had good reason to
feel grateful for the relics left lower down of their presence
at other seasons; for the only fuel to be found was their
dung which abounded about our camping-ground.

The following day, August 7th, we crossed the To-lai-
shan range. I was anxious to make the passage as far
west as possible, and consequently felt much pleased
when the only man of our escort who had ever been
so far in the mountains confessed to knowing a pass
approached from a point farther down. He called it
Huo-ning-to. Grateful as I felt for the chance it eventually gave of completing the survey towards the Pei-ta Ho
without descending the valley farther, yet I should have
hesitated in taking this track had I guessed its difficulties.
We had scarcely left the down-like slopes of the main
valley and ascended for about a mile over steep grassy
meadows, when there came a succession of scrambles, most
trying for the laden animals along rugged cliffs where
the ravine debouched from the pass. It would have been
a good day's work for a sapper company to turn this
mile of rock ladders into a safe bridle-path. In the
stream bed itself huge boulders blocked the way. A
series of terraces, high above the stream on the left bank
and covered with luxuriant Alpine pasture, afforded a brief
respite to the animals. Then the ravine contracted again,
and we had to ascend by a breakneck track at its bottom.
At last after a mile and a half's ascent in the boulder-filled
bed, and then over precipitous shingle, we reached the
bare detritus slope at the head of the little valley.

Here at last the ground became safe for the animals. It was a terribly bleak nook of the mountains, closed in by rugged rock ridges. But the wild yaks evidently fancied it for its height and seclusion; for their droppings thickly covered the ground up to the narrow crest at which the gorge ended south - eastwards. From here a view opened eastwards into a maze of bare gorges, with rock slopes of deep red and yellow. The watershed was only reached after half a mile more of steady ascent along the narrow arête just mentioned. The pass proved a much-confined saddle, close on 15,000 feet high, cut into a line of serrated ridges remarkably steep. The crest-line of the range was here visibly lower than to the east, where it was formed by a chain of broad peaks clad with small glaciers. The ridges on either side of the pass showed but little permanent snow, and that only in shaded ravines northward. Yet, owing to the peculiar ruggedness of the rock faces produced by the withering forces of Alpine nature, the ground was far more difficult than we should have found it near one or other of the passes eastwards.

For the sake of getting a more commanding survey station, Ram Singh and myself climbed the crest of the watershed to the north-west over a staircase of huge fissured rocks (Fig. 237). On reaching the nearest pinnacle at a height of close on 15,500 feet a glorious *panorama rewarded us (Plate x.). The whole of the Richthofen range lay before us from the high needle-like peaks beyond the Pei-ta Ho to the great snowy domes first seen east of the Chiang-tzǔ-k'ou Pass. Due north there revealed itself a big massif girt with imposing glaciers, a buttress as it were of the range on its south side. Of the To-lai-shan Range, on which we stood, the neighbouring rocky ridges hid all but one snowy peak.

But of the next parallel mountain rampart southward, which its first Russian visitors, Obrucheff and Kozloff, have named the range of Alexander III., we enjoyed a vista extending probably over more than forty miles. Most of its peaks bore large snow-beds. To the south-east rose a grand array of glacier-clad mountains, more

---

*Plate x is in the pocket attached to the inside back cover of this volume.

like a range by itself, yet in the line of the same chain : clearly the Uge-shan group indicated in Obrucheff's sketch map. A depression due west of these peaks marked the approximate position of the pass by which Obrucheff first crossed the range. But for our own passage I preferred to seek a route due south of our point of survey, where a wide boulder-strewn river bed suggested a relatively easy access to the watershed.

I was anxious to strike the Su-lo Ho Valley, behind the Alexander III. Range, as low down as the obstacle now in full view would permit. So the sight of this promising route was specially welcome. Yet there was one feature which might have caused misgivings. Behind the snowy peaks just before us there rose others in the distance, evidently far higher and glittering under a mantle of ice. Should we have to make our way also past these, or did they belong to the fourth range which I knew to line the Su-lo Ho head-waters on the south, and which had been named by Obrucheff after the great Austrian geologist Suess? Nothing in the published cartographical sketches suggested that this last range, which I was anxious to survey, was higher than the Alexander III. Range. If the great ice-clad heights now sighted on the horizon really formed part of it, it meant an important modification in our conception of Nan-shan orography.

The atmosphere was delightfully clear, and with the pleasure of getting this chance for a photographic panorama I scarcely noticed the icy wind which played over our narrow arête. So wild was the confusion of its fissured rocks that to keep the camera secure and take exposures all round cost much trouble. So when the work was accomplished I was glad to hurry down to the pass which our baggage train had just crossed in safety. That only one animal had broken down *en route*—we never saw it again nor its owner, who promptly seized the chance of returning as soon as the donkeys sent back had relieved his beast of its burden—showed that our transport possessed unsuspected powers of endurance.

A steep descent of half a mile over shingle slopes brought us to Alpine verdure. The limit of vegetation

lay here fully 700 feet higher than on the north side, and
at 13,500 feet or so its growth was richer than at the
lowest point touched by us in the Chu-lung-kuan Valley.
The striking difference was manifestly due to greater
abundance of moisture. For the same reason denudation
and erosion of the slopes was far less advanced here than
at corresponding heights north of the watershed. The
same observation was repeated on our subsequent crossings
of these Nan-shan ranges. It formed a complete contrast
to the surface conditions with which I was familiar from
the Hindukush and the Kashmir Himalaya. There invariably the northern slope is clothed in richer vegetation, the
southern one being left relatively bare and consequently
more exposed to erosion. Two hours' brisk walking
brought us down close to where the narrow valley debouches into the down-like expanse of the upper Pei-ta
Ho basin. The track was so faint that its use must have
been rare for many years past.

There was luxuriant pasture and plentiful scrub where
we halted near the debouchure of the little valley, about
12,000 feet above sea. Beasts and men, too, deserved a
good rest after the trying pass. But soon after midnight
a violent gale blew, and in the morning I found about an
inch of snow on the ground. The minimum temperature
had fallen to six degrees Fahrenheit below freezing-point.
But the sun shone out brightly, and my eyes wandered
with pleasure over the gently sloping basin ten to twelve
miles broad, drained by the Pei-ta Ho (Fig. 238), which we
were to cross that day from north to south. It promised an
easy march, just such as our comfort-loving Chinese would
appreciate ; but human factors had decreed it otherwise.

We had just emerged from our little valley into the
great Pamir-like plain beyond, when I noticed that our
baggage train, instead of following us to where we
intended to cross the Pei-ta Ho, was moving away at an
unwontedly brisk pace by a track to the south-east. This
was roughly the direction of the Kan-chou river's head-
waters, and it was easy to guess that our pony-men would
have liked us to turn there straight away. But my own
plan was first to cross the range of Alexander III. and

then to explore the head-waters of the Su-lo Ho and of the river flowing to Ta-t'ung, the northernmost large tributary of the Huang Ho. The pony-men were soon overtaken, but proved more recalcitrant and sulky than usual. They protested that there was no route across the big range facing us on the south; that another pass like the one behind us would finish their animals; and that anyhow there was no one now to guide us farther.

The latter assertion was true enough; for the only man of the escort who had ever been in these mountains knew nothing beyond the Pei-ta Ho Valley, and professed a holy fear about crossing into the mountain desert behind it, haunted by 'wild Tibetans.' That a move was possible over ground unknown to their cherished 'guide' or 'ta-lu-ti,' 'the man of the high road,' as the Chinese term characteristically signifies, or in fact even over ground where there was no 'road' at all, was a lesson still to be learned by our Chinese. With a good deal of trouble we managed to head off the convoy in the right direction to the river. While the Surveyor kept in front to show the way and search for a likely ford, I myself with Chiang and trusty Tila Bai brought up the rear.

For nearly a mile we marched along the top of a low and narrow ridge clearly marked as the remnant of an ancient side moraine of the ice stream which once descended from the Huo-ning-to Pass. A mile and a half more of alluvial soil covered with rich pasture brought us to the right bank of the river. Its bed of gravel and mud was fully half a mile broad, and the two main channels filled by a rapid current of water, and each about forty yards wide, looked at first an awkward obstacle for the baggage.

So our obstructive transport men seized the opportunity of making a stand here. With a great deal of vociferation and gestures manifestly intended to express the ferocity of despair, they refused to advance a step farther. Leaving the Surveyor and Chiang by the bank to prevent a stampede, I went ahead with Tila Bai and after some searching up and down found a ford. The water was up to four feet deep in places and the current strong; but luckily the bottom was firm. In order to encourage the

Chinese, I sent Sahid Bai and his young acolyte Turdi ahead under Tila's guidance with our own lightly laden spare ponies, and having seen them safely across returned to fetch our main train.

Seeing us now in earnest the pony-men tried to drag the animals back from the river. They had been sullenly holding counsel while I was away and now attempted open resistance. By some pushing and beating three of them were induced to move ahead with their animals. Tila Bai, with many a Turki oath, was inconsiderate enough to secure a pig-tail, and its unfortunate owner could not help getting into the water. But the rest broke away and began to run back as if for life. But they had not thought of taking beasts and loads along in their flight, and thus their disappearance seemed almost a good turn. Batch by batch I got the animals taken across the first channel by my own men, and then returned to where Chiang was.

All this time the escort had lagged behind as if the whole affray in no way concerned them. I now called for the petty officer in command of the matchlock-men, a weak-kneed person whose looks had from the first given little promise of help, and told him that unless he brought back the fugitives and made them march where I wanted them, he and his men had better return to their post, but that I should take care that his conduct was duly reported. He and his myrmidons now realized that there was nothing to prevent our onward move, and that I was quite ready to dispense with their and the pony-men's services. When he saw that his plot had failed—for he himself, as we found out afterwards, dismayed at the prospect of further rough tours in the mountains, had fomented the little revolt—he promptly changed face and galloped with his soldiers after the runaway men.

I was too busy with getting our baggage animals safely guided across the second and deeper channel to pay much attention to the chase. But I was still by the left bank distributing the animals among the three men whom we had managed to keep by us, when our armed host turned up driving the deserters before them like a flock

239. SNOW-FIELDS AT HEAD OF VALLEY EAST OF PASS ACROSS ALEXANDER III. RANGE.

240. SNOWY PEAK SEEN EASTWARDS FROM PASS ACROSS ALEXANDER III. RANGE.
Ponies resting in foreground ; elevation *circ.* 15,200 feet.

241. VIEW TO EAST FROM ABOVE LEFT BANK OF SU-LO HO.
The snowy peaks in distance belong to the Alexander III. Range.   Rai Ram Singh at work on the plane-table.

242. LARGE DUNES ON MARSHY GROUND IN HEAD-WATERS BASIN OF SU-LO HO.
Elevation *circ.* 13,400 feet.   The glacier-crowned peaks in distance belong to Shagolin-Namjil range.

of captured sheep. Ching Ta-lao-ye, the worthy commander, now evinced a violent desire of making an
example, and as the culprits themselves prayed through
the indignant Chiang for instant punishment rather than
arraignment at the Ya-mên, I let the chief mischief-maker
play the avenging angel. It was a comical scene to see
the fat little man jump furiously up and down with his stick
behind the line of kotowing rebels. He was evidently
accustomed to the function, and as his dupes and victims
were all well equipped with thick wadded clothing, I could
watch the performance without feeling too acute a pity.
That I rewarded the three men who had kept with us,
whether willingly or otherwise, with pieces of silver,
seemed to impress the deserters.

It was a relief to see the whole caravan meekly move
off again, but there was fresh reason now for feeling
uneasy. The attempted rebellion had cost a delay of
hours. From above the Huo-ning-to Pass I had clearly
seen that the broad river bed leading, as I hoped, to a
depression in the range was absolutely dry. Possibly we
might have to approach the actual snow-beds before finding
water on the surface, and those I knew lay far beyond
a reasonable day's march. The Surveyor was urging a
halt by the river. But this would certainly have been
interpreted by our Chinese as a sign of indecision and
brought on fresh trouble for the morrow. So the risk of
not reaching water before nightfall had to be faced.

The gently rising steppe over which we were moving
was absolutely dry. Yet short grass covered it in plenty,
and the Kirghiz of the Pamirs would have found such
grazing luxuriant. Had the Yüeh-chih, the later Indo-
Scythians, once driven their flocks over these wide pastures?
Now the only sign of life was supplied by the abundant
droppings of kulans or wild asses. The difficulty about
water was brought home to us when after about six miles we
struck the right bank of the huge, but absolutely dry, river
bed descending from the pass. The vegetation on the grassy
slope above it, however, grew richer, and a couple of miles
higher up we discovered at the foot of a barren hill-spur a
small stream descending in a ravine. We pitched camp

on a strip of green sward below it, and all troubles of
the day were ended.

On August 9th, a brilliantly clear day, I allowed men
and animals a good rest while I reconnoitred the head of
the valley for a route across the range. I had followed the
broad winding bed of shingle for some five miles when I
noticed a track taking off to what looked like a gap in the
range. But its approach was so steep that I doubted its
being the right route until I had convinced myself that
the head of the main valley to the south-east was completely closed by big snow-fields, feeding two small glaciers
which came down to a level of about 14,200 feet (Fig. 239).
So next day I led my convoy along the track I had
discovered and found my confidence rewarded; for, after
ascending a very steep rocky spur which at first frightened
our Chinese greatly and almost caused a fresh attempt at
mutiny, we came within sight of the pass.

It proved a broad saddle close on 15,200 feet above sea
and relatively easy (Fig. 240). The view of the Suess
Range was confined to the south and south-west, yet grand
beyond expectation. There was an unbroken chain of big
snowy peaks, girt with conspicuous glaciers, rising far
back from the wide Su-lo Ho Valley. It impressed me at
once as a range far more massive and elevated than either the
To-lai-shan or the one which we were then crossing. The
general crest-line in this portion of the Suess Range seemed
nowhere to fall much below 19,000 feet, and the computation
of the clinometrical heights taken subsequently revealed a
number of peaks rising well above 20,000 feet.

The northern slopes passed on the ascent had been
quite bare of vegetation from about 13,800 feet upwards;
but on the south coarse grass and some hardy flowering
plants were met with about 14,400 feet above sea level.
On the other hand, the neighbouring peaks, which northward had displayed such large snow-beds, were almost
entirely clear of snow on the south. This gave to the
mountain scenery a bleak, monotonous look; it was
distinctly enhanced by the dirty streaks of coal-carrying
strata which cropped out on both sides of the valley
between about 12,900 and 14,200 feet. Our descent led

down into a remarkably steep valley, the rock faces of which, mostly slate or chalk, looked as if cut by some former glacier. The track kept to the narrow boulder-filled bed of a stream, and was in many places very difficult for laden animals.

But at last, after some seven miles, this trying valley debouched on a broad, undulating expanse above the right bank of the Su-lo Ho. There at an elevation of about 12,400 feet we pitched camp, this time in a more compact formation. Our Chinese, in addition to all their other fears, were now getting apprehensive of ' wild Tibetans ' ; and as Kozloff appears to have met with Tangut encampments at the head of the Su-lo Ho valley, it seemed wise to keep a look-out for these pilfering nomads. No humans came to disturb our peace, nor did we see traces of any until eight days after. But as Chiang reported later, all the Chinese were disturbed that night by the sound of—dragons!

CHAPTER LXXIX

FROM THE SU-LO HO SOURCES TO KAN-CHOU

It was a great boon for us all that our farther progress now lay for a time up the magnificently wide valley of the Su-lo Ho, recalling a true Pamir and affording excellent grazing. The next three marches, though relatively long, were thus made easy for the animals. The expanse of the valley, fully fourteen or fifteen miles across from the top lines of the grassy slopes, was so wide that, by keeping near its middle and utilizing the broad ends of the spurs which descend from the Alexander III. Range, we could secure splendid stations both for the survey work and for photo-graphic panoramas (Fig. 241). In order to get a good view also of the valley farther down to the north-west, where it contracts just like that of the Pei-ta Ho, we crossed and recrossed the river on the first day. It flowed in numerous branches, none over thirty yards wide and three feet in depth. Higher up, from the point where the great valley changes its direction from south-east to east, the river seemed to split up into a perfect network of shallow channels.

Here at the end of the second day's march the rise in level became so slight that the general aspect was more that of a great upland basin than of a valley. Some miles before reaching our camp of August 12th at an elevation of close on 13,200 feet, I first sighted the group of great glacier-capped peaks which flanks the head-waters basin of the Su-lo Ho from the south. A long-stretched low ridge separates it from the serried snowy peaks of the Suess range, of which it otherwise forms the natural continuation. The detached position of this eastern group of peaks,

243. VIEW TO WEST TOWARDS SHAGOLIN-NAMJIL PEAKS FROM SU-LO HO–PEI-TA HO WATERSHED.

244. VIEW FROM SU-LO HO–PEI-TA HO WATERSHED, CONTINUED TOWARDS SOUTH-WEST.

This view joins Fig. 243 at line **A B**, forming part of panoramic view of Su-lo Ho head-waters basin. Taken from an elevation of *circ.* 14,600 feet.

245. VIEW SOUTH FROM SHEN-LING-TZŬ PASS ACROSS KAN-CHOU RIVER VALLEY TOWARDS TO-LAI-SHAN.

the wide marshy expanse at its foot, and the size of its
glaciers, made the view truly imposing. Behind this
great semicircle of snows, for which the Russian travellers
Roborowsky and Kozloff heard the Mongol name of
Shagolin-Namjil, lie the drainage of Lake Kokonor and
the confines of north-eastern Tibet. But I knew well
that my plans could not extend to those regions.

All day on August 13th we skirted the great basin in
which the Su-lo Ho gathers its main sources, having
mostly to keep close by the foot of low side spurs to avoid
its spreading marshes. But scattered over this boggy
expanse there showed, near and far, glittering ridges of
drift sand, in the shape of big semi-lunes so familiar to
me from the desert. It was strange to meet this combination of dunes and marshes on a scene set with ice-crowned
mountains. But was it not the most fitting birthplace for
the river which was to end its course amidst those dreary
wastes of sand, gravel, and salt marsh which I had
surveyed beyond the westernmost end of the Tun-huang
Limes? At one point I managed to approach the nearest
chain of dunes, and found there a succession of big semi-
lunes or Barkhans, to use the technical designation,
running roughly from south-east to north-west with
intervals of 400 to 600 yards between them (Fig. 242).
The one I examined closely measured fully 330 yards
between the extreme ends of its receding horns, and
showed forty feet as its maximum height in the centre,
which with its convex side was pointed to the north-west.
The ground within the concavity of these Barkhans was
generally quite clear of sand and in places occupied by
small spring-fed marshes.

From the point where we halted for the night of
August 13th, close on 13,500 feet above the sea, we had a
majestic view of the Shagolin-Namjil group (see Fig. 155).
But clouds were now gathering above it, and a distinct
change in the weather on the following day prevented
the determination of the highest peaks rising above the
large glaciers. The next march took us over easy detritus slopes, boggy in many places, to the top of a long-
stretched flat ridge forming the lowest point of the

watershed towards the Pei-ta Ho head-waters.   There, at
an elevation of about 14,600 feet, we saw the whole basin
of the rising Su-lo Ho spread out before us, dotted with
chains of small lakes which the head-streams connect
and drain (Figs. 243, 244).

Mossy vegetation with a few flowers covered the saddle,
and three wild yaks of huge size were seen browsing on
it when we approached.   We were all eager to bag one
of them ; for the supplies of our Chinese had begun to run
very short by the time of our reaching the Su-lo Ho, and
the risk of their starving was imminent.   The few wild asses
we had encountered since this state of things revealed itself,
were too wary to give much chance for our carbines.   And
now, Tila Bai's and my own first shots having failed to hit,
we had the chagrin of seeing these fine yaks disappear
at a speed which, considering their bulk and the difficulty
of breathing at such an elevation, seemed truly amazing.

With the crossing of that nameless pass and the change
in the weather there began for us an altogether trying
time.   Steady rain set in as we descended to the Pei-ta
Ho, and when the river was reached in the evening we
were obliged to halt at a point where there was scarcely
any grass or scrub.   The difficulty about fuel was now
brought home to us by the yak dung, on which we had so
far relied, becoming soaked and useless.   But the discomfort ensuing from this cause was slight compared with
the risks now caused by the want of supplies among our
pony-men and escort.

Though we had been on the march now for not more
than fifteen days, and the pony-men had been told to
bring flour for twenty-four, they now reported their
stock exhausted, and an inspection of their belongings
proved this true.   It was the same with the escort.
To meet this serious difficulty caused by their own
improvidence, I had already collected whatever could
be safely spared from our own supplies.   But this would
have been soon exhausted had I not been able to supplement this improvised commissariat store with the barley
brought for our own ponies.   Luckily the excellent grazing
so far found had allowed us to husband this fodder, and

what remained of it proved most helpful in warding off
starvation and the immediate return to the miners' camp
for which all the Chinese were now clamouring.

At first, however, they persisted in refusing to touch
the barley, declaring that it was impossible food for humans.
The argument that I ate it myself daily as porridge made
little or no impression until Chiang-ssŭ-yeh's diplomacy
came to the rescue. He had done his best all along to
look after and cheer the refractory pony-men, and had
slowly acquired some mild influence over them. He now
explained to them gravely that I, whom they curiously
enough readily credited with a good deal of Chinese
learning—though I could not give adequate expression to
it in their colloquial dialect—had found a classical passage
declaring barley a permissible substitute for one of the six
orthodox food-stuffs. This made due impression on their
minds, permeated by time-honoured prejudices and conventions ; but Chiang had bravely to set an example by
eating it himself before they reconciled themselves to a
diet of roasted barley.

Altogether the natural difficulties unavoidable in such
inhospitable solitudes were considerably increased by the
helplessness of our Chinese pony-men, and what I may
politely call their deep-rooted 'aversion to taking risks.'
Now these dreaded mountains were to them full of risks,
imaginary as well as real ; and instead of using such
intelligence as plentiful opium-smoking had left them to
guard against these, they tried their best to run away from
them altogether. Chiang and myself used to talk of them
as our 'senile babies' (Fig. 247). Like aged men taught
to suffer by much hard experience they saw risks everywhere, from avalanches, quicksands, sudden floods, robbers,
even dragons ; yet they were like babes in a wood when it
came to obviating any of them.

Their helplessness in meeting the ordinary difficulties
of camp-life away from civilization often put me in mind
of the attitude which the average East End slum-dweller
might assume if suddenly forced by some irresistible chance
to take his share in the marchings and campings of a rough
campaign on the Afghan border. Their organized attempts

at desertion threatened again and again to leave us without transport, but luckily could be suppressed without frustrating our plans.   Hence I need not record them in detail.

The heavy rain, which during the night changed into snow, did not allow us to resume the march until the afternoon of August 15th.   But before this I had walked down the valley for a couple of miles and inspected a curious low transverse spur through which the river had cut its way in a rift.   The precipitous cliffs showed mighty seams of coal between strata of sandstone.   Then, the clouds still hanging low on the mountain slopes, we made our way up the Pei-ta Ho along gently rising and very soppy ground until nightfall.

Next day we set out for the watershed to the southeast, where I knew we should strike the head-waters of the Ta-t'ung River, the northernmost large tributary of the Huang Ho.   For nine miles we had to struggle across the plateau-like head of the Pei-ta Ho Valley, which proved an almost continuous bog and was most trying to the animals. Everywhere the ground showed small pools of clear water between more or less peaty strips of grassy soil.   Had it not been for the hard layer of detritus underlying at a depth of about two feet, this ground would scarcely have been traversable.   The water-logged upland plain ended with an abrupt edge above a deep-cut valley which sends its water eastwards to the Yellow River.

Here, at an elevation of about 13,600 feet, I had the satisfaction of knowing that I had touched at last the drainage area of the Pacific Ocean.   There was something inspiriting in the thought that quite close to this point, only hidden behind the rounded spur in which the Alexander III. Range dies away, lay the head-waters of the Su-lo Ho which once had made its way right down into the great Lop-nor depression.   Thus on the easternmost slopes of the Shagolin-Namjil group, as the map shows, the drainage areas of the Pacific and the great Central-Asian basin practically touch.

Apart from this thought the outlook was far from encouraging.   I could see that, in striking contrast to all the ground so far met south of the Richthofen Range, the

A   B

246. HEAD OF ALPINE VALLEY AT CAMP CCXXI., NORTH-EAST OF SHEN-LING-TZŬ PASS.
Turdi (A) and Sahid Bai (B), our Turki pony-men, in foreground.

247. MY CHINESE PONY-MEN SAFELY RESTORED TO THE PLAINS.
On extreme right our aged 'Ya-i' pointing with stick to the chief mutineer.

248. FIRST MONGOL CAMP MET WITH IN KHAZAN-GOL VALLEY.
Chiang-ssŭ-yeh on left ; fir trees on slopes in background.

249. CAMP ON LEFT BANK OF KHAZAN-GOL, PACKED FOR START.

head-waters of the Ta-t'ung River formed a maze of steep
and deep-cut gorges. Even if we could make our way
down while the flooded condition of the streams lasted,
there was every reason to fear increased difficulties about
getting back again across the To-lai-shan range to the
Kan-chou River the farther we descended. So I decided
to keep to a broad ridge which we saw jutting out to the
south from the To-lai-shan into the midst of those deep
gorges. It promised an excellent survey station; but we
had scarcely ascended it and set up the plane-table when
the clouds gathering since the forenoon began to descend
in a steady downpour of icy rain which changed before
long into sleet.

In addition, the top of the ridge turned out to be a
flat, bog-covered plateau, quite as bad as the uppermost
basin of the Pei-ta Ho, of which it had once perhaps
formed part. During the four miles' painful progress
over this trying ground we all got drenched to the skin.
Over bad shaly slopes we scrambled down at last into a
sodden little valley, where our despairing Chinese would
fain have settled down for the night though there was
neither grass nor fuel. However, I managed to drive
them on into a somewhat larger valley to the east, which
promised a better approach to some gap in the To-lai-shan
range. On the way we came upon a stretch of rich
grazing which had evidently been visited in recent years
by Tangut herdsmen with sheep and cattle. So the fear
of 'wild Tibetans' was added to the other sufferings of our
hapless Chinese on this miserable evening. We pitched
our camp in continuous heavy rain, and I was glad that I
could at least offer shelter to the men under the outer
fly of my tent into which to huddle. Fuel there was
practically none.

It proved a wet and dismal night, and though by 8 A.M.
the rain ceased and the men could begin to dry their
clothes, the outlook was far from reassuring. Our Chinese
had become so demoralized that, unless we managed to
get them, as promised, across the snowy range above
us and on to the open Kan-chou Valley, there was
every reason to apprehend their getting out of hand and

eventually attempting something desperate. With the food-supply running short there was time neither for rest nor for a needful reconnaissance.

So by noon we set out to ascend the valley at the head of which I hoped to find a practicable pass. But what if my professed assurance failed to be realized? Well, serious trouble would follow, and I prepared the Surveyor and Chiang for it. For a mile or so there was a well-marked track along the stream. But this disappeared where the grassy slopes ceased on the left bank. We continued in the broad stony river bed for three miles more, but found ourselves stopped where this contracted to a narrow rock chasm only about four or five feet broad, in which it was quite impossible to advance with the ponies. With great trouble we managed to drag them up a precipitous rock spur on the west, and to ascend in the detritus-filled gorge. The barren slopes above and the low-hanging clouds made up a very sombre picture.

At last we gained a saddle whence we viewed an easier slope with a small glacier at its back. The gorge still continued very narrow, and my relief was intense when on reaching the actual watershed, some 14,600 feet above sea-level, I found that the glacier kept just clear of the pass; though descending some 500 feet lower, it left us a steep but relatively easy slope to descend by on its side. Near its snout we caught sight of a wide green valley northward which could only be that of the Kan-chou River. Then the gorge widened, luxuriant grass appeared on its lower slopes, and at last, at an elevation of about 12,500 feet, we could pitch camp on a delightful Alpine meadow with abundant scrub to yield fuel. The sky, too, cleared in the evening, and even our Chinese pony-men showed signs of reviving hope.

Our march on August 18th down the Kan-chou River valley justified this good augury, and men and animals, now refreshed, found the ground doubly easy. Where the alluvial fan from our side valley merged in the broad riverine flat a large herd of wild asses was skilfully stalked by three men of the escort, who managed to bag one of

them.   Its meat provided a much-needed feast for all our
Chinese party.   So, in spite of drizzling rain which continued all the afternoon and evening, there was cheerful-
ness about the camp which we pitched on a thyme-scented
flat by the left river bank.

We were now on a well-marked track which people from
the Hsi-ning side used in going to the gold-pits which we
had seen about Ta-pen-ko.   But I knew that we could not
possibly expect to find a passage right down the valley to
Kan-chou, owing to the confined nature of the river gorge
lower down.   So I was eagerly scanning the crest of the
Richthofen Range rising above us for the pass over which
the route, first followed from Kan-chou by the Brothers
Grishmailo, and marked on the small-scale Russian Trans-
frontier map, was likely to cross the range.   A low ridge
we had sighted from our camp suggested its approximate
position on the watershed, and when after proceeding four
miles down the river we found a narrow track branching
off towards it, I did not hesitate to ascend it.

We found that the pass, for which subsequent enquiry
among Mongols elicited the name of Shen-ling-tzǔ, led at
a height of close on 14,000 feet over the bog-covered
shoulder of a broad peak still partly covered with snow.
In spite of the low hanging clouds, there was a magnificent
view to the south and west extending over some fifty miles
of the Kan-chou River valley and the long snowy rampart
of the To-lai-shan beyond (Fig. 245).   With a violent wind
sweeping the pass I just managed to bring away a photographic panorama before the rain came down.   Over bare
detritus slopes we followed the incipient stream down for
some five miles, and then, seeing it disappear in a gorge
amidst very bold rocky peaks to the north, were warned to
look out for the track which turned off eastwards.

There we crossed a broad bog-covered saddle of the
type with which we had grown familiar, and enjoyed from
it a glorious vista over a succession of lofty side spurs of
the Richthofen Range, one rising above the other.   The
sky had completely cleared when we descended into a
verdant flower-carpeted valley which recalled scenery of
the true Alps more than any I had seen since Kashmir

(Fig. 246). The Chinese seemed now assured that they were near their eagerly-prayed-for ' ta-lu,' or ' big road,' and had still morsels of their wild ass to fall back upon. We had no fodder left for the ponies, but on such splendid pasture they could well make shift without it.

The promise of this refreshing camp was more than fulfilled by the next day's march.   There was serious trouble at first with our half-mutinous pony-men when, at a parting of the now well marked track, I insisted upon taking the route leading up a precipitous ridge which held out hope for, and actually gave us, a commanding ' station ' for survey work. But there was reward in the impressive panorama we secured over the succession of rugged side spurs projecting northward from the main range, now behind us, and the deep-cut green valleys between them.   Then, as we descended the valley leading south-east over alluvial terraces clothed in rich Alpine vegetation, Tila Bai's sharp eyes were the first to discern ponies grazing lower down in the valley.   Some miles farther on, to our Chinamen's intense relief, we lighted upon a small camp of Mongols grazing yaks, cattle, and ponies on a delightful Alp (Fig. 248).

The aged Mongol couple we met there were the first human beings seen since we had left the gold-miners' camp nearly three weeks earlier.   It was pleasant now to be assured of guidance, and to know that the worst of their fears and tribulations were lifted from our ' senile babies.' But what I greeted with even greater joy was the sight of the luxuriant forest of firs which clothed the slopes of the valley facing north.   Not since leaving the Lowarai Pass had I seen real tree growth in the mountains, and now I could fancy myself again in Kashmir.   That day we marched down the Khazan-gol Valley for a good distance amidst equally lovely scenery, and halted near other Mongol encampments which supplied sheep and that long-missed luxury, milk (Fig. 249).

We had by no means yet finished with the mountains, and the succeeding marches gave plentiful opportunities for interesting observations as well as for trials of endurance for men and beasts.   But considerations of space

250. VIEW TO SOUTH FROM FIRST FOREST-CLAD RIDGE ABOVE KHAZAN-GOL.
The Khazan-gol is just visible in valley.   In distance snowy peaks of main Richthofen Range.

251. VIEW SOUTH FROM FÊNG-TA-FAN TOWARDS MAIN RICHTHOFEN RANGE, ACROSS
KHAZAN-GOL VALLEY.

252. MONGOL HEAD-MEN NEAR GRAZING-GROUNDS OF LAO-T'U-KOU.

forbid my attempting any detailed description. All the rivers draining this part of the Nan-shan make their way lower down to the plains through tortuous and deep-cut gorges quite impracticable at the time of the summer floods. So the only possible route, along which our Mongol guides took us, led in succession over high transverse spurs (Fig. 250). The first of these was crossed, at an elevation of over 13,000 feet, and led to a delightful series of Alpine uplands broken by a crest of red sandstone ridges (Fig. 251). Our Mongols who knew some Chinese called it Fêng-ta-fan.

From there we dropped down into the confined and picturesque defile of the Ch'iang-kan Ho, where the route throughout lay practically in the flooded river bed, causing serious trouble and risk. The luxuriant tree growth, now largely composed of non-conifers, was a strange treat for eyes so long accustomed to Central-Asian barrenness. Ascending the next spur we passed through a ruined 'Klause' designed to guard the route, and then from the broad ridge overlooking the La-kê-ta-fan obtained a magnificent panorama of the Richthofen Range extending from the bend of Kan-chou River valley for a great distance west.

Northward the ridge, still over 12,000 feet high, fell away to the plains in gently sloping plateaus covered with rich pasture, which were curiously reminiscent in their structure of the loess-covered outermost slopes of the Kun-lun south of Khotan. But what a difference of surface conditions the far moister climate of the central Nan-shan had created! It was impossible not to feel that this region was already under the fertilizing influence of the Pacific Ocean.

We found the upper slope of this outer spur furrowed by broad valleys full of splendid fir forest, recalling scenery familiar to me from the Eastern Alps. Here Mongol camps abounded, and I was welcomed in state by a jolly-looking young Mongol chief who had received warning from Kan-chou of our possible advent (Fig. 252). Gladly would I have remained for a short rest among these cheerful nomads whom Chinese civilization has in the course of centuries so thoroughly tamed and divested of those formidable qualities which once made them the rulers of all Asia and the terror of Europe.   But supplies fit for our Chinese were scarcely obtainable, and our much-tried 'senile babies' were ever clamouring for a speedy escape to their beloved slum nursery in the plains.

Late at night on August 23rd we entered the broad Li-yüan Valley, after having in our descent passed rapidly from Alpine verdure into the familiar stony wastes of the foot-hills.   Next forenoon we reached the small and pretty oasis of Li-yüan, where even our Chinese felt assured that all troubles and privations were ended. From my tent pitched in a picturesque ruined garden I watched with real relief men and beasts enjoying the great treat I had ordered for them.   Not a single animal had been lost in spite of all the hard marching at great elevations, and as the photograph taken of our 'babes' (Fig. 247) shows, they too had not suffered any lasting hurt.

A day's well-merited halt was passed in pouring rain, but was made pleasant by the hospitable attention of the local commandant, a hearty old warrior, who had been expecting us for weeks past.   Then on August 26th we started for Kan-chou through a tract studded with oases containing walled villages (Fig. 253).   The flooded state of the rivers, which after the heavy rains spread themselves like big torrents across the plains, obliged us to move to the high road, and, causing much trouble there also, delayed our arrival until the next evening.   Outside the walls of the large and populous city (Fig. 254) a grand array of Mandarins received me.   The honour was some-what embarrassing, considering the tattered condition of what clothing I had been able to take with me to the mountains.

Naik Ram Singh, who rejoined me before Kan-chou, had prepared quarters for us in a large temple-like structure outside the south city wall, and there I was welcomed by a huge bag of mails which a messenger from Mr. Macartney had brought after a sixty days' ride from Kashgar.   A three months' thirst for news kept me awake for most of the night, and when sleep would not come after all the letters were read, I had the consoling thought of much work safely accomplished. The total of the mountain area covered by our plane-table survey between An-hsi and Kan-chou, with the additions subsequently effected on our return journey, amounted to close on 24,000 square miles.

CHAPTER LXXX

FROM KAN-CHOU TO THE T'IEN-SHAN

My six days' stay at Kan-chou, though made busy by a number of practical tasks, afforded welcome rest, and I was able to get many interesting glimpses of the conditions of life in a typical large Chinese city (Figs. 255, 256). Owing to the successful resistance which this important administrative seat and trade emporium had offered to the Tungan rebels, many quaint old buildings survive here uninjured. But I cannot pause to describe them nor to mention more than one of my personal experiences.

When on the morning after my arrival I set about to allot quarters to my various followers, who complained of want of space, I was not a little surprised to find that the large rambling structure which Naik Ram Singh had made us occupy at nightfall was crammed in almost every part with coffins duly tenanted. The sight of them here and there when we hastily settled down at night had not attracted special attention. But now it was soon revealed that what my honest Indian helpmate, eager to please me with a quiet camping-place outside the town, had taken for a temple was in reality a sort of residential coffin club. It was the building set apart by a guild of traders from distant provinces where deceased members might find quarters for periods more or less prolonged, until their families could arrange for transport to their ancestral homes.

Naturally enough my Muhammadans did not much relish sharing such quarters with their rightful occupants; and I myself, after attempting to camp in the shady garden, and finding next morning that my tent had been

253. FORTIFIED VILLAGE OF SHA-CHING-TZŬ, WITH TEMPLE GATE, ON ROAD TO KAN-CHOU.

254. CENTRAL GATE TOWER AND MAIN STREET IN KAN-CHOU.

255. MEMORIAL GATEWAY, BUILT ABOUT A.D. 1825, OUTSIDE WEST GATE OF KAN-CHOU.

256. ORNAMENTAL GATEWAY IN FRONT OF COMMANDER-IN-CHIEF'S YA-MÊN, KAN-CHOU.

pitched with a time-worn coffin tucked under its outer fly, felt obliged to seek another place of shelter, this time in a real temple not far off. Subsequently I learned with some amusement that the local official responsible had pointed out to Naik Ram Singh this little objection to his choice, but had politely given way when the innocent Indian assured him, through Ahmad the interpreter, that this was just the kind of quarters most acceptable to his ' Sahib ' !

Kan-chou was from the first intended to be the easternmost goal of my journey, and when on September 3rd I again set out from it westwards, it was with the distinct feeling that my return to India and Europe had begun. But the immediate purpose of the long journey then begun was to take me back to the Tarim Basin for my second winter campaign.   Several considerations, archaeological as well as practical, obliged me in the main to follow the great trade route which leads by way of Su - chou and An - hsi across the Pei-shan desert to Hami and thence to Turfan.   The fact that this high road between China and Turkestan has been repeatedly followed by recent European travellers does not detract from its historical or geographical interest, since the greater part of it leads along a line to which Chinese expansion westwards has clung since ancient times.   But many considerations oblige me to shorten my narrative from this point, and the fact that my return journey from Kan-chou to Kara-shahr in the north-eastern corner of the Tarim Basin lay over relatively well known ground is a special reason for succinctness.

After starting from Kan-chou I devoted a day to the examination of the ruined site of Hei-shui-kou, which the great route passes some ten miles to the north-west.   I found it to consist of an extensive débris area of the regular Tati type, covered with small fragments of pottery, and showing, where clear of dunes, abundant signs of wind erosion.   But this had lowered the ground level only by two or three feet at the most, and the plentiful débris of porcelain and the coin finds showed that the date of abandonment of this site was late, certainly subsequent to Sung times.   For systematic excavation there was no

scope, as all buildings had long ago been destroyed by
people from the neighbouring oases in search of building
materials, while the eroded ground was constantly being
searched for small objects. Three small circumvallations
of manifestly late date still raised their clay walls to a fair
height, evidence that the winds exercised much less erosive
force here than in the An-hsi region.

From Sha-ho I let Rai Ram Singh proceed by the
route of the southern oases in order to complete the survey
along the foot of the Richthofen Range, while I myself
followed the main road to Su-chou. I was thus able to
keep near the line of the 'Great Wall' which flanks it, and,
by reconnaissances pushed northward to examine in several
places the much-decayed clay rampart which marks this
portion of the ancient Kan-su *Limes*. In constructive
character it shows closest resemblance to the 'Great Wall'
seen north of Su-chou and Chia-yü-kuan.

After a short excursion to the outlying oasis of Chin-t'a
and the desert beyond, I reached Su-chou by September
13th. Another brief but pleasant halt at the 'Spring of
Wine' allowed me to bid farewell to my kind Mandarin
friends and to thank them for all the help afforded. It
was a little pathetic to meet also Wang Ta-lao-ye, the
learned magistrate of Tun-huang, whom administrative
weakness—and policy—had sacrificed to popular resentment after the outbreak already related. He had been
suspended from office and was now awaiting a formal court
of enquiry. I did my best to show at Su-chou what I
thought of the attempt to make my old friend and helper
the scape-goat for official irresolution. But I learned
behind the scenes that the whole trial was merely a sham
intended to conciliate popular feeling.

When, subsequently, on our way to Yü-mên-hsien we
met the witnesses against Wang who were being brought
up under escort, Chiang-ssŭ-yeh shrewdly guessed that
probably none of them would ever be allowed to see their
homes in Tun-huang again. Thus the sacrifice of Wang's
tenure of office would be appropriately compensated by the
non-official punishment of the popular witnesses (*recte*
rioters). In my farewell letter to the Viceroy sent later on

from Hami, Chiang made me put in a good word for Wang. I do not know what attention, if any, was paid to it; but before I left Turkestan Chiang heard the cheerful news that Wang had been finally exonerated and given a fresh magisterial charge elsewhere.

We left Su-chou on September 16th, and after passing again through the gate of Chia-yü-kuan lost all trace of the 'Great Wall' until we reached the small district town of Yü-mên-hsien five days later. There was good reason to believe that the road we had followed was already in ancient times the main line of communication. But the *Limes* intended to safeguard it had evidently been constructed farther north, where the rugged desert range first touched at Chia-yü-kuan offered the advantage of a strong natural rampart. I had subsequently the satisfaction of finding this assumption verified. On a reconnaissance made from Yü-mên-hsien to the north, I discovered a line of ancient towers just beyond the hamlets appropriately named Shih-tun ('Tower x.') and Shih-êrh-tun ('Tower xii.'), and on closer search I was able to trace unmistakable remains of the wall once connecting them.

Far-advanced decay had been caused by the proximity of marshy ground liable to inundation from a branch of the Su-lo Ho, whose great westward bend lies close by. Yet my archaeological conscience as to the connection of these scanty remains with the ancient *Limes* of Han times was assured when, on scraping the somewhat higher ground near one of the towers, I came upon those significant fascines, here composed of half-petrified twigs, so familiar from the Tun-huang border. The very name of Yü-mên-hsien, 'the town of the Jade Gate,' was manifestly borrowed from that *Limes*, though its transfer to a point so far east could certainly not have taken place until long after T'ang times.

On the second day after leaving Yü-mên-hsien for An-hsi I again sighted the old wall with its line of towers stretching along the north bank of the Su-lo Ho. It here afforded protection to the string of small oases which extend south of the river on both sides of the large walled town of Bulunjir; this is now but for a tiny garrison almost deserted. Some twelve miles west of Bulunjir I was able to fix the point where the old engineers of Han times, with their unfailing eye for the military advantages of the ground, had utilized the passage of the river between two low hill spurs for bringing their border line from the right to the left bank. Thence I traced it to the remains of the wall which I had already discovered in the summer south of An-hsi.

On my arrival at An-hsi I had the great satisfaction of finding my precious deposit of antiques quite safe. It was a pleasure also to be greeted by my old surveying companion Rai Lal Singh, whom the Surveyor-General of India, in response to an appeal despatched nine months before from Lop-nor, had kindly deputed to relieve Rai Ram Singh. The latter, in spite of his rheumatic troubles of the preceding winter and spring, had been able to render very valuable services in the Nan-shan. But his health was manifestly unequal to facing the hardships of a second winter campaign in the desert, and it was wise that he should now leave me to regain India *via* Khotan. I was particularly glad to have Rai Lal Sing once more by my side; for I had learned to appreciate the worth of his training and character on my trans-border expedition to Mount Mahaban, in 1904. He was soon to give me again splendid proofs of exceptional zeal and fitness for surveying work under trying conditions, as tested before by many an expedition from the Yemen to Eastern China.

Advantage was taken of Rai Ram Singh's journey to get an accurate survey of the more circuitous mountain route leading from Tun-huang to Charklik along the Altin-tagh. But before his departure tracings had to be made for safety's sake of all the plane-table sheets which he was to carry back to India, and this sufficed to keep both Surveyors busy for over a week. I myself was kept hard at work during my twelve days' stay at An-hsi with preparing the full report to Government on my previous operations, and with detailing the proposals which were to secure the time and means to record their results after my return.

In addition, my hands were kept full with manifold

preparations for our respective journeys.   On October 3rd
I was at last able to let Rai Ram Singh start on his return
to India, which he reached safely three months later after
rapid and almost continuous travel *via* Khotan, Sarikol,
and Gilgit.   A little earlier Rai Lal Singh had been
sent out to survey the remains of the Wall north of the
Su-lo Ho.

He had scarcely returned when there arrived also
Chiang-ssŭ-yeh, whom I had despatched on a secret
mission to Wang Tao-shih, bringing with him in the
stealth of night four camels heavily laden with more
manuscripts from the 'treasure cave.'   A written proposal
for further 'selections' sent through a trusty messenger
had met with a cautious response ; but in order to avoid
all suspicions I was obliged to remain away from the scene
and to entrust the execution to my ever-zealous secretary.
How he had managed to secure the timorous Taoist monk,
and to induce him for a very reasonable recompense to
hand out at night over two hundred additional bundles of
Chinese texts, was quite a dramatic story.   The whole
was managed most discreetly.   Ibrahim Beg with Hassan
Akhun and his camels, now refreshed by a long holiday in
the mountains, furnished the transport.   They had carefully kept clear of the high road on their way to the
rendezvous at the caves, and marching only at night on
their return escaped all inquisitive eyes.

Having secured this addition to my archaeological
impedimenta, I was glad to leave behind me by October 8th
that dreary *carrefour* of Asia, An-hsi, and to be quit for a
time of wearisome report-writing and accounts.   Eleven
long marches carried us and our big caravan north-
westwards to Hami through the barren hills of the
Pei-shan.   It was a wilderness of gravel and crumbling
rock which we crossed here, a true stony 'Gobi' with a
width of over two hundred miles.   With none of the
successive ranges through which the route leads rising
much above 6000 feet, there is little to observe here for
the traveller who is not a geologist.   But I knew that,
ever since Chinese power first asserted itself at Hami,
about 60 B.C., this 'Northern road,' with the few alternative

tracks practicable on the east and west of it, had formed an important line of communication to the oases on both sides of the T'ien-shan and to the Tarim Basin. In fact, since the more direct route from Tun-huang to the region north of Lop-nor had to be abandoned after the fourth century A.D., this Northern road became practically the main channel for trade and military operations alike.

So as we passed from one wretched little road-side station to the other, with its mud-built hovels, scanty well, tiny post of soldiers, and occasional road-side temple (Fig. 257), it was of interest to observe conditions of traffic which could have changed but little since old times. The difficulties of getting a sufficiency of reed straw, and in places even of water, for a large number of animals must always have hampered military movements along this line. I could therefore appreciate the efforts it must have cost the Chinese, after the crushing of the last great Tungan rebellion, to assemble at Hami the large force which overawed and quickly extinguished Yakub Beg's rebel dominion in Turkestan. Without the retention of Hami as a *point d'appui* the task might have proved impossible even for such an organizer as Tso Tsung-t'ang. At the same time my journey through a desert which still possessed occasional wells and some scattered grazing allowed me to realize better how in ancient days parties of raiding Huns could push their way south for attacks on the Tun-huang *Limes* before the desert of the western Pei-shan became wholly impassable through desiccation.

To Chiang-ssŭ-yeh this weary desert journey recalled associations of a more personal nature. At the wretched station, appropriately named ' K'u-shui ' after its more than usually brackish water, he related quite humorously how he had been returning to his native Hu-nan some nineteen years before, and how his travelling companion had here fallen ill and died. He packed up the corpse in what felts he could raise at these hovels and took it along in his cart to An-hsi. He had previously performed the funeral rites and taken the precaution to burn a well-penned prayer to the dead man's spirit, asking him to preserve the corpse in fair condition for a week and to prevent a breakdown of

257. TEMPLE NEAR STATION OF HSING-HSING-HSIA, ON ROAD FROM AN-HSI TO HAMI.
Barren Pei-shan hills in background.

258. GORGE ABOVE SU-BASHI, ON ROAD FROM TURFAN TO KARA-SHAHR.

259. RIDGE WITH RUINED BUDDHIST SHRINES IN WANG'S ORCHARD AT ARA-TAM, HAMI.
Seen from ruined temple cellas south-west.

260. RUINED VAULTS AND CHAMBERS NEAR WEST WALL OF CHONG-HASSAR, TURFAN.
A marks approach to ruined Buddhist cella.

their cart. The prayer proved efficacious. The corpse
travelled safely to An-hsi, where Chiang secured a sound
coffin. Then he carried his late companion's body faithfully all the four or five months' journey to Hu-nan and
delivered it to his relatives. With no word did Chiang
allude to the inconvenience he had suffered himself by his
pious action.

CHAPTER LXXXI

AT THE HAMI OASIS

In the desert, which only knows extremes, the weather had already been getting wintry, with occasional icy blasts. But after reaching, on October 19th, the oasis of Hami, or Kumul as the Muhammadans call it, I was glad to find that its sheltered position at the foot of the easternmost T'ien-shan still promised a few bright days of autumn, in spite of the high latitude of forty-three degrees. So I could not but prefer the fresh air of my tent to the quarters offered in one of the dingy Bazars of the town, and after a long search found a pleasant camping-place in Zahid Beg's garden beyond the spring-fed stream which flows past the west side of the Chinese town. Recommendations from Mr. Macartney and my old friend P'an Ta-jên had preceded my arrival, as was soon shown by the greetings and presents of welcome which poured in from the different Ya-mêns.

Next morning it was a novel experience to commence the round of my official visits with a call on a local Muhammadan chief. Mahsud Shah, the ruling 'Wang' or prince of Kumul, still retained a good deal of power over the Turki Muhammadans of the district. It seemed a genuine survival of the system by which Chinese rule contented itself with leaving the administration of Turkestan in the hands of hereditary chiefs ; some recent disturbances, which had caused bloodshed among the Wang's subjects, and of which I had heard through the wire at An-hsi, were directly attributed to his oppression. As I rode under the big vaulted gates of the Wang's stronghold, the presence of a crowd of armed retainers within a wide, shady space in front of the palace marked an appropriate change from the stereotyped Ya-mên setting.

The reception I was given by the chief on entering the large outer hall was Chinese in ceremonial ; but it was a relief to be able to talk homely Turki, and to look into a face that was almost European in features and expression. I noticed all round the inner hall, where we sat during the interview, evidence of a care for comfort and appearance which befitted the residence of a ruler. The Wang pleased me greatly by his gentlemanly ease, combined with a certain quiet dignity. A recent visit to Peking, where he had proceeded to pay homage to the sovereign, had manifestly enlarged his horizon. But I wondered whether the ideas of progress, *i.e.* comfort, which he had brought back, together with a few score of Mauser rifles, would not put the fiscal resources of Kumul to a severe strain.

From the Wang's fort I rode to the walled Chinese town eastwards which contains the several Ya-mêns and quarters for the garrison now much reduced. The well-kept walls and the clean and regular streets of this castrum were a refreshing sight after all the half-ruined 'Ch'êngs,' with their refuse-choked thoroughfares and waste areas, with which I had become familiar in Kan-su. At the Ya-mên of Colonel Yang, commanding the garrison, Chiang-ssǔ-yeh found an old acquaintance. The jovial commandant had much to relate of his experiences in the recent *émeute*, producing the red-tasselled hat which a 'rebel' bullet was supposed to have grazed. But what interested me more was the unmistakable *camaraderie* which seems to link all Chinese dignitaries in the 'New Dominions,' whether big or small. Hearing my Ssǔ-yeh talk about common friends in 'the service,' I realized how the whole provincial administration is looked upon as a family affair by these official exiles from Hu-nan. The civilian Amban of Hami, a sort of Resident attached to the Wang for his guidance, and likewise acting as local magistrate for the Chinese part of the population, proved a man of unmistakable learning. It was pleasant to find my references to the old foes of China in these parts promptly met by accurate mention of all the tribes from the Huns and 'Great Yüeh-chih,' or Indo-Scythians, downwards.

I was busy in the afternoon with the closing of a long-deferred mail, when my men announced with great anima-tion the visit of a European. During the morning I had heard rumours of the arrival of a Cossack officer. But to my pleasant surprise my visitor now proved Mr. Cecil Clementi, Assistant Colonial Secretary of Hongkong. He had passed through Russia to Kashgar, and when he told me of the pleasant days he had spent at Chini-bagh as recently as August, all sense of distance seemed effaced. Mr. Clementi had travelled extensively through different parts of the Chinese Empire, and the various illuminat-ing observations which he could relate brought home to me most forcibly the advantages possessed by those who can study things and men in this strange world of Cathay with a full knowledge of language and traditional ways. There was much to learn and tell, and the hours sped quickly. Of course, it did not take us long to dis-cover that we had common friends both in Oxford and India.

After another long confabulation Mr. Clementi continued his journey to Hongkong, and I let my exceptionally heavy mail bag depart for Kashgar, little foreseeing the risks to which it was exposed through the wiles of its Kashgari carrier, an unworthy namesake of Turdi.

Two more days passed in a whirl of practical occupa-tions. The winter equipment of all my people had to be attended to ; and as the resources of half-Chinese Hami in the matter of fur coats, moccasins, etc., such as honest Muhammadans would need, were decidedly scanty, the trouble of meeting all reasonable demands—and of resisting others—was great. What a relief it was to be able to effect payments without constant resort to that archaic instrument of torture, scales for weighing out silver! The adjustment of the longest pay rolls seemed positively child's play compared with what I had gone through when grappling with Chinese accounts and those ever-recalcitrant pieces of hacked silver. This does not imply that every-thing was plain sailing in matters of currency. 'Ak-tangas,' or coined pieces of silver, were, indeed, freely circulating and readily taken at Hami ; but the real medium of exchange was still the small Chinese copper 'cash,' and the discount between a Tael in this copper coin and in silver was considerable enough to require attention. I soon found out that fully twenty per cent could be saved by making all payments by means of local bankers' notes. Of course privileged people like my own followers could claim their dues in coined silver.

By the morning of October 24th I could at last commence my short tour in the district. Enquiries about old remains had elicited that certain ruins to be found west of Hami had already been partially explored by German archaeologists, Dr. A. von Lecoq and Professor A. Grünwedel, working from the side of Turfan. So, as survey work was to be done in the mountains, I decided first to visit the remains of some old 'Karauls' and shrines at the foot of the Karlik-tagh, that easternmost rampart of the T'ienshan. Guided by a pleasant old Beg whom the Wang had attached to my camp, I started off with a light equipment. The day's march led almost due north, and for the whole length, close on twenty miles, over the bare gravel of a great alluvial fan.

Almost as soon as we emerged from the dirty Bazar of the Chinese town this dreary waste was entered. The green marshy Nullahs, in which the water of the snow-fed streams comes to light again in the form of limpid springs, were soon left behind. Far away to the west the ruins of some abandoned forts showed clearly above the flat horizon. There was nothing in this dead plain to distract the eye from the long snow-capped range northward. Its last massive offshoot to the east had looked quite imposing from Hami. Though its height does not much exceed 13,000 feet, perpetual snow-beds and even small glaciers streaked the slopes of the main peaks, and were lit up in rosy tints by a blazing sunset. The length of the twilight reminded me how far northward I had moved since the previous autumn.

Some fourteen miles from Hami we reached the big lonely tower known as Akchik Karaul, which was guiding us on the way to Töruk.　It is reputed to be of great age, and the massiveness of the central pile, some forty feet square and probably quite as high, seems to lend that tradition support.　A roughly built enclosing wall was manifestly of later date, though far more decayed.　Against what marauding bands from the north was this forlorn post meant to offer shelter?

After a long and weary march by moonlight, which lay partly up the wide stony bed of a dry river course, we caught a glimpse of water, and after descending into a deeply cut bed to the right, found ourselves by the long-stretched fields of Töruk.　The little village of some fifteen households was wide-awake to receive us in spite of the late hour.　The rubble-built quarters of the village head-man where I was to put up proved to contain quite a comfortable guest-room, little suspected behind the exterior of this hovel.　To be able to pass the long wait for the baggage in a room which had a real fireplace, felt rugs on the floor, and a display of simple household treasures on shelves and cupboards around the walls, was cheering.　After all the bare, monotonous rooms I had seen in Chinese Ya-mêns and inns, this evening in a Turki homestead struck me like the first step back to Europe.

The Un-bashi was away in the mountains; but his wife, a homely matron of about forty, took care that hospitality should be full.　It seemed as if old nomad habits still lingered among these honest peasants at the foot of the mountains.　Scarcely had I been seated before the quickly kindled fire when a large bowl with milk was produced and a tray with delicious white wheat loaves. My hostess, passing in and out with that quiet unconcern of the true mistress of her home which I had often noted among Kirghiz women, assured me that it was customary for people in their position to keep a good store of tempting food ready for guests.　Once more I noted with pleasure how little adaptation to Chinese ways, so common among the Muhammadans of Hami, has as yet affected their women-folk.　Whereas the men had taken to various articles of Chinese dress, and in some cases even to pig-tails, the women's apparel was, but for the prevalence of bright red colours, practically the same as I had seen it far away in the west of Turkestan.

I was eager to reach Ara-tam, the object of my trip, in good time on the next day. So we were all astir early. The animation of the little village street was great, and in front of every hovel there was gathered a cluster of brightly clad children and women. Their merriment was a pleasant contrast to the stolid curiosity of a Chinese crowd. The route led us close to the foot of the mountains eastwards. We passed one alluvial fan after another spreading its rubble-strewn cone down to the endless gravel glacis southwards. But of all the narrow rocky defiles which had poured out these streams of boulders and detritus, only one still sees a permanent flow of water. The small village of Kara-kapchin which is irrigated from it looked delightfully green against the rugged cliffs of red sandstone. Where we crossed, the water still rushed with a limpid flow in a narrow bed lined by bushes. But only a mile or two farther down it disappeared in the rubble beds, to feed after a long subterranean course the eastern-most springs of the Hami oasis.

After some fifteen miles' march a narrow streak of vegetation with some pencil-like poplars showed far away on the eastern horizon. The Wang's Beg pointed out these first signs of his master's famous orchards of Ara-tam. As we drew nearer bright streaks of yellow and red could be distinguished against the bleak grey of the Sai. They were the fruit trees of the Ara-tam gardens in the full glow of their autumnal foliage. Not since I had made my way a year before through the terminal jungles of the Niya River, had my eyes been treated to such a feast. The tree belt descended for nearly two miles along a lively stream cascading in numerous small channels. A road lined by low walls of boulders led upwards through rows of fruit trees, blazing in every tint from bright yellow to pink and purple. In the background rose the steep serrated ridges of reddish sandstone illuminated by the setting sun. Through it the snow-fed stream of Bardash breaks in a narrow tortuous gorge to create all this luxuriance at its debouchure. The sky above us was still of a deep blue, and the effect of all these gorgeous colours was dazzling.

Nowhere in Turkestan had I seen a wood of such size and fruit trees in such delightful luxuriance. For nearly a mile the road turned and twisted among thick clumps of apple, apricot, and peach trees, and stately yellow-leaved walnuts. No landscape gardener in far-away England could have laid out his drive with more cunning, nor could any gardener's art produce such strangely varied fantastic shapes of trees. The handiwork of man seemed completely effaced here. Growing up among the rocks and boulders which some huge flood seemed to have scattered broadcast over the slope, every tree looked as if it had fought its own way down to the fertile bed of earth. Over the whole enticing wilderness of trees lay the peace of the evening, that great beautifier of the shelter awaiting the wanderer.

But the Wang's old country seat, to which this road of glowing colours led, did not need such embellishment. From a wide outer court, lined by a row of majestic elms still retaining their thick foliage, I passed into a smaller one fronted by a large open hall with an abundance of quaint massive wood-carving on roof, pillars, and beams. On either side of this hall there opened terraces with painted screens, and behind them whole suites of apartments which looked airy and inviting. In those to the right the chief was said usually to take up his quarters, and here felts and gay Khotan carpets had been spread out for me. But their northern aspect and shaded position, qualities which doubtless formed their special attraction during the heat of the fruit season, were not exactly suited for a chilly autumn evening. So I set out to search further for an abode in the main block of the building.

Crossing a grand hall, light and airy behind its movable screens of fretwork and paper, I discovered two sets of apartments opening direct on the Wang's private orchard and garden. Their arrangement suggested that they were meant for the ladies of the Zenana. Time and neglect had left their mark here too; the gaily painted panels of the roof, showing roses and flowery twigs in a style half-Chinese, half-Persian, were broken in more than one place, and rough boarding had replaced missing folds of the neatly carved window screens. But I soon found a cosy little room looking out on the garden. How Western all its shelves and cupboards appeared to me, unaccustomed to such luxuries ever since leaving Chini-bagh !

Then while a carpet and some small felts were being spread, I hurried out into the garden to look for the ruins there promised. After traversing a few hundred yards of terraced orchards I found myself suddenly before a series of cellas, carved from the live rock of a bold little ridge, which had once contained colossal images (Fig. 259). The stucco masses in which the latter were sculptured had almost completely collapsed ; but in one of the shrines which still retained part of its roof vault, at a height of nearly fifty feet, the outlines of a colossal seated Buddha had survived. The remains of fresco decoration in the corners of the stuccoed walls showed close resemblance to the designs familiar to me from the Ch'ien-fo-tung shrines. It was clear that the ruined shrines dated from the time of Uigur dominion (9th-12th century A.D.), when Buddhism had flourished here.

Eagerly I explored the less imposing remains of brick-built cellas and dwellings which covered the north face and the top of the little ridge. But when I was proceeding to extend this first hurried inspection to the ruins rising boldly on the crest of a higher ridge to the west of the orchard, the Beg now playing the cicerone raised so meek and plaintive a protest that I felt ashamed for having in my antiquarian eagerness quite forgotten the bodily cravings of a pious Muhammadan pining for food after the daily fast of the Ramazan. So reluctantly I left the ruins as dusk was setting over the prettiest bit of scenery that has ever offered me a chance of archaeological work. The impressions of that evening, so rich in glowing colours, haunted me as I wrote by the cheerful fire of my princely quarters till a late hour.

Alas ! the ruins did not prove as fruitful for the excavator as their picturesque setting would to the artist. Even in the ruins of two large cellas which I found occupying the top of the ridge westwards, the clearing effected in the course of the next two days brought to light only scanty fragments of a Buddhist image in stucco and badly perished wood-carving.   Destruction by fire, digging for timber, and the effects of moisture, which had evidently been more abundant until a period not very distant, had worked sad havoc all around.   Apart from remains of fresco decoration showing diapers of small Buddha figures, on the topmost wall portion, nothing survived in the five cellas which had been cut into the lower conglomerate ridge, and which now lay fully exposed owing to the collapse of the front walls.   But the close agreement in drawing and colouring with the mural decoration of the 'Thousand Buddhas'' caves was striking.   The same observation applied to the architectural arrangements both here and in some smaller much-ruined shrines still traceable on the north side of the same ridge.

That we found not a scrap of writing was scarcely a surprise.   Evidence of occasional rain was to be seen on all sides, and local information asserted that it was still plentiful in the valleys north, and had in 'old times' been so too at the foot of these mountains.   On the other side of the range, in the Bar-kul district, cultivation was said to be possible in many places without irrigation, and grazing even in the plains abundant.   All this agreed with what I knew of the totally different climatic conditions prevailing north of the T'ien-shan.   Those were the regions which had served for the migration westwards of one nomad race after the other.   But interesting as they are for the student of Central-Asian history, there was little to tempt the archaeologist as long as there were sites to explore within and around the parched-up Tarim Basin.

My eagerness was great to reach the latter in time for a fresh winter campaign in the desert.   So when the digging at Ara-tam and my anthropometrical work among the people of the neighbouring village were completed, I left 'my' delightful country seat and returned to Hami. There the great loads of manuscripts brought away from the Tao-shih's cave just before my start from An-hsi could at last be safely packed in twelve solid wooden cases. This task was scarcely completed when Rai Lal Singh rejoined me from a successful survey in the mountains. In spite of deep snow already covering the passes towards Bar-kul, he had managed to make his way to the watershed. An icy dust-storm raging through Hami had served to remind me, too, that winter was now quite near.

On the following day, November 2nd, we started from Hami on the journey which was to take us to Turfan. Various considerations obliged me to keep to the rather circuitous high road which for the sake of wells hugs the foot of the T'ien-shan. We managed, however, to cover the 195 miles to Pichan, the easternmost of the Turfan oases, by seven marches. Up to Togucha, our first stage, there extended patches of cultivated ground with ruined forts, attesting the prolonged struggle which the Chinese holding Hami had here fought against Yakub Beg's troops.

From Togucha, where I halted for two days, I was able to visit the ruins of some Buddhist temples near the little stream of Ili-kul. There the German expedition under Professor Grünwedel one year before had brought to light interesting remains, apparently dating from the period of Tibetan occupation. In a broad, gravel-strewn depression descending from Togucha south towards the oasis of Lapchuk, I surveyed a number of small ruined shrines. These evidently belonged to the latest Buddhist times, which, as attested by a record of Prince Shah Rukh's envoy to the Chinese Emperor, extended at Hami as well as at Turfan down to the very end of the fourteenth century. Neither these ruins nor the remains of a small ruined town at the northern end of the Lapchuk oasis seemed promising enough to justify the sacrifice of time needed for their clearing.

But on a long ride down the open fertile valley, where the cultivation of Kara-döbe continues that of Lapchuk down to a point about fifteen miles from Togucha, I could gather a good deal of geographically interesting observations regarding the curious and partly subterranean system of drainage coming from the T'ien-shan, which accounts for these pleasant oases in the midst of a stony wilderness. Fresh as I was from my wanderings on Chinese soil where the innate suspicion and reticence of the people had hampered any kind of enquiry, I could also appreciate the hospitable and open - hearted reception we met with everywhere among the Turki settlers after leaving Hami. Yet I wondered how long these pleasant features among the rural gentry would hold out against the influence of 'civilized' Chinese ways which is manifestly spreading in these parts—if that influence is destined to last.

CHAPTER LXXXII

GLIMPSES OF TURFAN RUINS

SIX rapid marches across a wearisome succession of low and absolutely barren spurs with almost equally dreary depressions intervening brought me by 10th November to the fertile oasis of Pichan. During the short halt there necessitated by topographical work, I was able to settle a provisional programme for my visit to the ruined sites of Turfan and for our surveys around them.

Exceptional conditions made it specially important to turn my available time to best use. Since 1897 an archaeological reconnaissance effected by Dr. Klementz on behalf of the Russian Academy of Sciences, and itself first suggested by Captain Roborowsky's observations, had drawn attention to the abundance of ancient ruins in the small but fertile Turfan tract. This, the Chü-shih of early Chinese records, is known to have been one of the chief seats of Uigur power after the downfall of T'ang supremacy. The facts reported by Dr. Klementz, and indirectly also the results attending my explorations in the far-off Khotan region during 1900-1, led to the despatch of a German expedition under Professor A. Grünwedel, Director of the Royal Ethnographic Museum of Berlin, and a high authority on Buddhist art, which in 1902 visited Turfan from the side of the Siberian railway for the purpose of serious excavations.

Its discoveries of art and literary remains of all sorts proved so important that provision was promptly made by the Prussian Ministry of Education, under the special patronage of the German Emperor, for the systematic continuation of the work by means of scientific expeditions, first under Dr. A. von Lecoq, a distinguished Orientalist, and then again under Professor Grünwedel. Their excavations which had been carried on with the help of abundant State means almost uninterruptedly from 1904 until about half-a-year before my arrival, had, as I knew, been attended with well-merited success.

It could not be my object, during the few weeks I could spare for Turfan, to attempt supplementing these protracted labours by digging at sites upon which the German savants had already been able to bestow ample time, unbounded scholarly zeal, and a thorough local experience. But I was anxious to familiarize myself as well as I could with the constructive peculiarities of the ruins, the art remains left *in situ*, and what else might help me to understand better the significance of the Turfan finds, and to use their evidence for the interpretation of my own. Even more, perhaps, was I attracted by the wish to study on the spot those peculiar topographical and archaeological facts which might throw light on the ever-fascinating subject of desiccation.

On this account I had already, on the last march to Pichan, greeted with special interest that characteristic feature of Turfan cultivation, the 'Karez' or underground irrigation channel. I knew it to be mainly responsible for the present flourishing condition of the oases in Turfan; for they are situated in a depression which is watered by no rivers of any size, and suffers from terrific heat during the greater part of the year. The cause of this heat, as Roborowsky first established, is to be sought in the fact that the lowest portion of this drainageless basin sinks well below the level of the sea.

This geographical interest induced me to start my tour at the south-eastern end of the basin. There Roborowsky's map marked the ruins of 'Chong-Hassar,' 'the Big Castle,' not far from the terminal marshes of the whole depression, and on ground which I was told was now desert. My archaeological predilection for the latter naturally influenced the choice, and I had no reason to regret it. Directing the heavy baggage train to proceed to Turfan town, I moved with the Surveyor on November 13th down the valley from Pichan to Lukchun. The twenty miles' ride down the broad bed in which the stream of Pichan soon completely lost itself acquainted me with two striking features of the Turfan depression. On the right we had the barren hill chain of red sandstone which divides the lower portion of the basin from the great gravel glacis sloping down from the snow-capped mountains northward. On the left there extended huge ridges of dunes, recalling the sand-covered foot-hills of Tun-huang, and evidently like the latter heaped up by the desert winds from the alluvium which the high range sent down.

The contrast with these barren surroundings presented by the rich fields and orchards of Lukchun farther on was most noticeable. The substantial dwellings and the crowds seen along mere village lanes at once gave an idea of the prosperity brought here by intensive cultivation. As elsewhere throughout the district, cotton is the most paying crop, and where adequate water is available, this is followed by cereals like maize, which was then just being gathered. Fruits of all sorts abound, and in the big country house of the Beg, which offered me shelter for the night, I found a year's provision of vegetables drying on the flat roofs.

As far as this point irrigation was derived from the stream of Lamjin, which, itself fed by springs at the foot of the great gravel glacis, breaks through the outer chain in a cañon-like gorge at the head of the Lukchun oasis. But proceeding next morning over the steadily sinking plain to the south-west, we left behind this area of old cultivation after a couple of miles and entered ground where the Karez was now the chief feature. On right and left we could see the lines of these underground channels marked on the bare clay surface by the little circular heaps of earth which the diggers had thrown up mole-like at the mouth of each successive well. Starting at ground level from the area to be irrigated, a low, narrow channel is tunnelled from well to well up the natural slope of the basin, but at a gradient less inclined than its surface, until a sufficient supply of water is tapped. The wells were said to range here to depths of over fifty feet; but the diggers are so expert that, working in parties of four or five men, they could complete an average Karez within half-a-year at a cost rarely exceeding twenty pounds.

The land which a single Karez could irrigate might be purchased originally for about fifty pounds ; but so rich is the return for this outlay, the cost of the annual cleaning of the Karez notwithstanding, that such newly cultivated land would within a few years sell for three times the money originally invested. I was told that since the re-establishment of Chinese rule not less than seventy new Karez had been dug by the people of Lukchun. But, characteristically enough, the lands thus irrigated were all situated within an area which had before been under cultivation, but where, owing to the deficiency of the canal water then used, the fields were sown only every third year in rotation. Whereas cultivation here under the older system had been precarious, and often failed through inadequacy of canal water in years of diminished snow-fall in the mountains, the Karez-served fields could be kept under intensive cultivation year after year.

The change taking place was connected by my informants with the great increase in the population of Turfan, following the re-establishment of peace and prosperity after the Chinese reconquest. At the same time it was generally acknowledged that the Karez construction was an innovation dating back only a century or so, and introduced from Iran. In agreement with this was the fact that none of the old Chinese accounts of Turfan, which are numerous and often detailed, ever alludes to the Karez system, though nowadays it is famous throughout Eastern Turkestan as the most characteristic feature of the district.

All these observations combined strongly impressed me as signs that the difficulties about irrigation must have increased in this region, and I may add that what I subsequently saw of the ruined towns of Turfan strengthened my belief that the district must have been able to maintain in ancient times a far larger population than now. I had not to wait long for definite evidence that desiccation had played a great share in this change. A seven miles' ride from our Lukchun quarters brought us to the farm of Besh-tam, with the last patches of Karez-cultivation. Beyond we came upon fields long abandoned, and then upon a shallow bed in which the water of the Lukchun canals, when left unused in the winter, endeavours to make its way down to the terminal lake bed. During the spring and summer, what with evaporation and absorption in the soil, not a drop of water would reach this point. Across this temporary overflow-bed there extended a wide sandy plain, with plentiful thorny scrub growing amidst rudimentary dunes ; where the ground was left clear of drift sand the erosive action of the winds, here chiefly from west to east, had commenced to furrow small trenches and Yardangs.

To me it seemed but a petty desert, and I was rather surprised when less than four miles of it sufficed to bring us to the ruins of 'Chong-Hassar,' which the Lukchun people had declared to be a place very trying to stay at. The remains of the fortified townlet or village I found there exhibited several typical features of Turfan sites. Within an irregular oblong, about 140 yards from east to west, and about 100 yards at its widest, there was a perfect rabbit warren of small vaulted chambers and casemates crowded against the enclosing rampart (Fig. 260). Massive masonry abounded, and the débris of sun-dried bricks choked the rooms often to their vaulting. In places the chambers had been built in irregular tiers one above the other. It was not difficult to realize from what I saw in the extant towns and villages, that this peculiar construction was needed for protection from the excessive heat of the summer and the violence of the dreaded winds of the spring. Extremely massive construction with walls up to seven feet thick characterized also a large vaulted pile rising like a keep in one corner of what looked an inner fort.

To clear the whole of these vaults and cellars would have cost many weeks of labour. So I was not surprised to find that the digging done during the flying visit paid to the site by one of the German expeditions was confined to a partial clearing of the cella of a small Buddhist shrine which could readily be distinguished near the west wall of the inner fort. From the débris left undisturbed in the outer passages, and still more from the refuse layers covering the floor of a room on the top of the rampart not far off, I recovered a number of manuscript fragments and documents all written in Uigur script. They sufficed to prove that the site had continued to be occupied until towards the close of the Buddhist period. From many indications it seemed safe to conclude that the area of scrub-covered desert around, now showing incipient wind erosion, was then under cultivation.

From the height of the ruined fort I could clearly see southwards the glittering end of the salt-encrusted lake bed which receives whatever of Turfan drainage escapes evaporation. Above it rose the gravel glacis of the low Chöl-tagh range towards Singer. During my three days' stay at Chong-Hassar I sent Rai Lal Singh on reconnaissances to south and east to survey this end of the basin, while careful observations made at Chong-Hassar with the mercurial barometer showed its level to be depressed fully 360 feet below the sea. The salt-encrusted bed of the lake was boggy and impassable on horseback, whereas the ground north of it was covered with ' Shor ' in hard cakes and lumps of salt, clear evidence that the extent of the lake had been shrinking within recent periods.

I myself examined the ruins known as Kichik-Hassar or the ' Little Castle,' two miles off to the north-east, and finding that the group of small Buddhist shrines and Stupas (Fig. 261) had never been touched by the archaeologist, took occasion to have them thoroughly cleared with the help of a band of labourers easily obtained from Besh-tam. Besides fragments of well - executed fresco work, we recovered remains of delicate paintings on linen, and a small but well-preserved statue of a Buddha in carved wood. Manuscript pieces and fragments of prints in Uigur, Chinese, and Tibetan proved that worship at these shrines continued at least as long as the occupation of Chong - Hassar. The fact that a route to Singer passes close by may account for the detached position of these shrines, which, as the photograph shows, are now being invaded by dunes.

261. RUINS OF SMALL BUDDHIST STUPA AND SHRINE AT KICHIK-HASSAR, TURFAN.

Tila Bai standing on top of dune.

262. RUINED SHRINES AND CAVE-TEMPLES ON WEST SIDE OF TOYUK GORGE, TURFAN.

263. CENTRAL MAIN STREET IN RUINED TOWN OF YAR-KHOTO, TURFAN, SEEN FROM NORTH.

The high structure in foreground is a temple ruin.   On the left the trees of Yar-khoto village, beyond
the eastern 'Yar,' show in the distance.

264. PORTION OF RUINED TOWN OF YAR-KHOTO SEEN FROM NEAR ITS SOUTH END.

On November 18th I divided my party, sending off Lal Singh for survey work along the foot of the main range, and Chiang with Ibrahim Beg to Turfan to secure for us quarters and fresh transport. I myself commenced a series of rapid excursions which was to acquaint me with the well-known sites of the Turfan district. The area into which they are crowded, mainly along the outer hill chain separating the gravel glacis of the mountains from the depressed basin, scarcely covers more than thirty-five miles from east to west, with a greatest width of about ten miles. Yet so numerous and extensive are the ruins that their rapid survey kept me busy till the close of the month. For the same reason I cannot find space here for more than a few general observations.

Starting from the east, I first visited the cañon-like gorge above the picturesque little township of Toyuk, where the steep cliffs of reddish sandstone on either side are honeycombed by numerous small caves, or show ruined temples built on their ledges (Fig. 262). Much in the situation and general aspects recalled the 'Caves of the Thousand Buddhas,' though on a reduced scale. There was unmistakable resemblance, too, in what survived of the fresco decoration *in situ*. But its condition attested only too plainly the destructive effects produced by the immediate vicinity of a large community of good Muhammadans, whose iconoclastic zeal could find ready vent here, especially after the first conversion. A different religious spirit had prevailed in Uigur times; for among the numerous finds of manuscripts which rewarded the German archaeologists, there were fragments of Manichaean and even Nestorian texts in early Turki and Sogdian. Other finds, too, in the Turfan region show that Christians and followers of Mani then lived peacefully among a population that was preponderatingly Buddhist.

The close association of the ruined past with the thriving life of the present, to me a novel experience, was even more striking when I visited the remarkable ruins of the Turfan capital of Uigur times at Kara-khoja, some seven miles to the west of Toyuk. Here a cluster of populous villages surrounds, and is partly built into, the massive clay walls which enclose nearly a square mile full of imposing ruined structures now scattered amidst cultivation. The areas once occupied by private dwellings have gradually been levelled into fields—a work in which irrigation deposits have doubtless aided. The massive ruins of big temples and monasteries, and of a fortified palace, are steadily being dug down by the villagers for the débris accumulated between their walls, which is much prized as manure. Old ' Khats,' *i.e.* manuscript fragments, are constantly turning up in the course of these operations, which are usually carried on during the winter months, and these used to be thrown away or utilized for papering window screens, until Russian travellers commenced to purchase such ' refuse.'

With so much destruction proceeding, and amidst such an *embarras des richesses* of remains, the archaeological exploitation of these ruins must be confronted by its own particular difficulties. I was not surprised at the number of the structures where it was impossible to distinguish the results of systematic excavation from the burrowings of manure - digging peasants. Nor was it easy to ignore the doubts of a chronological nature necessarily arising at a site which was never completely deserted, and where many of the buildings probably continued to be tenanted in one way or other long after their original use had ceased.

But in spite of these drawbacks the ruined town had proved a very rich mine, and I only wondered how the means might be found to assure the complete clearing of it before it was too late. To me personally, as I remembered the conditions of last winter's campaign in the desert, there was something both alluring and strange in the thought that everywhere about Turfan one's labourers could always return to their homes for a night's meal and shelter. Was it not like excavating in one's own garden or park to be able to carry out the tasks without constant care about food, water, and transport? The same was true of the interesting ruins of Buddhist shrines and cave - temples dotting the sides of the narrow picturesque valleys close above Kara-khoja. There in the recently cleared grottoes of Bezeklik I was still able to study a style of mural painting closely resembling that of the ' Thousand Buddhas,' though big gaps on the plastered wall showed where the best panels had been cut out to become treasures of the Berlin Ethnographic Museum.   How much greater would be the chance for the survival of these art remains *in situ* if only Turfan still held such a pious image-loving population as Tun-huang ?

When I subsequently transferred my headquarters to Turfan, the chief modern town of the district, I could see *en route* plentiful evidence of the severe struggle for water which now proceeds on this ground.   Most of the barren steppe we crossed below the gravel Sai of the outer range was being overrun by big dunes.   Yet the Karez, in spite of the fact that their pit mouths are exposed to the smothering drift sand, are pushed right across this broad zone over a stretch of eight miles to the head wells in order to secure water for part of the Turfan oasis.   Everywhere we saw abandoned Karez which had run dry or collapsed and been replaced by others.   The total number of pits on a single Karez was said to reach 200 in some cases, while the cost might rise to over £300.   The level of subsoil water was declared to have sunk within recent times, and consequently the cultivation dependent on Karez had shifted farther south.   The result was visible in the numerous abandoned farms we passed when approaching the old canal-irrigated part of the oasis.

Only exceptional fertility assured by climate and soil could account for so expensive a system of cultivation, and of that there was ample proof in the brisk trade which kept the Turfan Bazars ever filled with produce and throngs. Cotton, which is eagerly bought up and exported to the Siberian railway *via* Urumchi and Tarbagatai, is, no doubt, the chief factor of Turfan commercial prosperity.   But also for all surplus produce in food-stuffs and fruit there is a convenient market in Urumchi, the provincial capital, and the other large settlements north of the T'ien-shan.   The resulting return trade in imports from the Russian side is most striking.   Nowhere in the Tarim Basin or in Kan-su had I seen ' Europe' goods so widely brought into use.   What with kerosene lamps, chintz-covered ceilings, occasional glass windows, and the like, which I found in the houses of the hospitable Begs, I might almost imagine myself on the very edge of what I call 'Demi-Europe.' It all helped to explain that close connection in early times with what is now Russian Turkestan which the antiquities from Turfan ruins attest.

During the week spent at the oasis of Turfan proper most of my time was claimed by the remarkable ruined site usually known as Yar-khoto, which marks the capital of Turfan down to T'ang times. Just beyond the western edge of the present cultivation there rises between two deep-cut broad ravines, drained by spring-fed streams, a long and narrow clay terrace which nature itself has designed for a strong position. From the point of junction of the two 'Yars,' which have given the place its modern Turki name as well as its old Chinese designation 'Chiao-ho,' 'between the streams,' to where a broad cross ravine cuts off the north end of the terrace, the length of the terrace is a little over a mile. Its width is everywhere under a quarter of a mile.

The island-like area thus formed rises with precipitous cliffs of clay more than a hundred feet above the bottom of the flanking ravines, and is covered for about three-fourths of its length with closely packed ruins. Of the strange appearance of the whole the photographs (Figs. 263, 264) will help to convey some impression. The plateau is ascended by a steep ramp from the south. Thereupon caves and walls cut out from the live clay strike the eye on all sides in what at first seems utter confusion. Only gradually can narrow passages between them be made out, all alike leading towards two open spaces which traverse longitudinally most of the ruined area, and which had served as its chief streets.

It was, indeed, a dead town that lay spread out before me. But, alas! in spite of all the desolation it was only too evident how sadly its ruins lacked that protection which only a great natural catastrophe, as at Pompeii, or the isolation of the desert can assure to the relics of a life that has long been extinct. There was no drift sand here to cover up what objects might have escaped removal after

265. MY CAMP AT THE RUINS OF 'MING-OI,' NEAR SHIKCHIN, KARA-SHAHR.

The photograph shows the western and middle lines of ruined shrines as seen from north.　Hoar-frost covers scrub.

266. INTERIOR OF RUINED BUDDHIST CELLA MI. XVIII., AT 'MING-OI' SITE,
KARA-SHAHR.

The richly painted stucco image of a seated Bodhisattva, like the fine image-base by its side,
were found up-turned.　The shrine was once vaulted.

occupation had ceased, and the constant digging for soil to be used as manure had laid bare the natural hard clay floor in most of the smaller dwellings. The ruins of shrines usually rose on high bases spared from the original soil (Fig. 263), and still retained a good deal of débris between their walls ; among these partial excavations for antiquities had manifestly been effected.

Without systematic clearing it was impossible to make sure how much these ruins still contained, and still less to form any idea as to the chances of interesting finds in the numerous cellars and other underground places which implied centuries of construction on the part of the half-troglodyte dwellers of this town. Nothing but a sacrifice of long months of labour and corresponding expenditure would avail here, and, since even then results would largely depend upon luck, I wondered who would be fortunate enough to command the leisure and means for attacking Yar-khoto on the right scale. But there were plentiful observations of interest to reward the several visits I paid to this fascinating site and to the small rock-cut grottoes in the adjoining ravines. Most of these had evidently served as tombs ; and, since the finds of the German expeditions have proved the presence of Nestorian settlements at Turfan, imagination was free to recognize a resemblance between these resting-places and pictures of early Christian tombs in desert valleys of Egypt or Palestine.

CHAPTER LXXXIII

KARA-SHAHR AND ITS OLD SITES

In spite of all the interest of its ruins I was glad by December 1st to set out again from Turfan; for now the increasing cold warned me that it was high time to regain the basin of the Tarim for the winter's work in the desert. Rai Lal Singh was sent due south to Singer in the heart of the Kuruk-tagh in order to explore some desert plateaus and hill ranges hitherto unsurveyed westwards, while I myself covered in eight rapid marches the 180 odd miles to Kara-shahr.

As soon as we had descended from the gorges of the barren hills (Fig. 258), connecting Kuruk-tagh and T'ien-shan, into the great scrub-covered plain which encircles the northern shores of Lake Baghrash, ancient sites of some size could be traced near several points of the route. But the vicinity of subsoil water, generally impregnated with salts, and the effects of a climate evidently less dry than in other parts of the great Turkestan basin, had completely destroyed all structural remains, and reduced even the clay-built town walls to mere shapeless mounds of earth. This difference in climate had, as I soon found, left its mark also ethnically upon the Kara-shahr region, the Yen-ch'i of early Chinese records; for, attracted, no doubt, by the more abundant grazing, not only were there Mongols in the higher valleys, but small settlements of them had taken to semi-nomadic life involving temporary cultivation in the great plain watered by the Kara-shahr River. This, together with the numerous colonies of Tungans brought here since the rebellion, gave quite a peculiar aspect to the population of the district headquarters.

A

267. GENERAL VIEW OF RUINED BUDDHIST SITE OF 'MING-OI,' KARA-SHAHR, FROM SOUTH.

Parts of western and middle lines of southern group of ruins seen in foreground. The shrine Mi. xiii. marked by A was the chief find-place of small stucco relievos as seen in Figs. 270, 271. Behind it, in distance, cave-temples and ancient watch-tower.

268. RUINED BUDDHIST SHRINES IN CENTRE OF 'MING-OI' SITE, KARA-SHAHR, SEEN FROM NORTH.

Kara-shahr looked a small and poor town ; yet in recognition, no doubt, of the manifest strategic and administrative importance of the district as the geographical link between the Tarim Basin and the Turkestan territory north and east, it boasted of a full-blown prefect.   Being a subordinate of my old friend, the Tao-t'ai P'an Ta-jên, and forewarned of my coming, he gave me the kindest welcome. His help proved particularly useful when, after a rapid examination, I decided upon systematic excavations at the extensive collection of Buddhist shrines situated near Shikchin, some fifteen miles to the south-west of Karashahr, and known to the Turki-speaking Muhammadans as ' Ming-oi,' ' the Thousand Houses.'   The ruins lie only about four miles away from the little station of Chorchuk on the high road, and have been repeatedly visited by European travellers.   Yet there had been no digging except by Professor Grünwedel's party, which, as I had learned at Turfan, had been able to stay but a few days and had confined its attention mainly to some small cave-temples a short distance to the north of the main site.

The ruins of the latter dot a series of low rock terraces jutting out from the last spur of the hill range which flanks the valley of the Kara-shahr River on the south.   A desolate waste of sand and scrub stretches around without a trace of ancient occupation, and the recent settlement of half-nomad Mongols a few miles to the north-east was too small to involve any risk to the ruins.   Fortunately a little spring of fairly drinkable water rises at the foot of one of the rocky ledges.   So by the evening of December 11th I was able to pitch camp at once in the midst of the ruins (Fig. 265).

It was easy to realize that the disposition of the ruins in long rows of detached cellas, varying in size but similar in plan and construction, and all in close proximity, would facilitate the employment of a large number of labourers, and thus help me in making the most of my time. Fortunately, too, there was the populous village tract of Korla only some twenty miles off to supply willing contingents of Turki Muhammadans who knew how to use their Ketmans. The efficient staff of village head-men which the prefect's care had provided made it easy to keep my bands at work from the bitterly cold hours of dawn until nightfall, and to have relays of men ready to relieve them as soon as the effect of long days of such strenuous work under conditions necessarily involving exposure began to tell upon them.

The photographs reproduced in Figs. 267, 268 will give some idea of the general aspect and irregular distri- bution of the shrines. Their total number at the main site amounted to close upon a hundred. The dimensions varied greatly, from miniature cellas of four to six feet square to massive rectangular piles of brickwork measuring up to eighty-five feet on one side. But, whatever the size, much uniformity prevailed in types of construction. Besides the simple cellas provided with a porch outside, there were many which had either passages all round or a vaulted room behind the wall facing the entrance, thus permitting the traditional circumambulation of the main image-group within (Fig. 266). Domes built on the principle of the true arch appear to have originally roofed most of the cellas, and in a few cases still survived over the smaller ones. A peculiar and probably late development of the Stupa was represented by circular structures, resting on polygonal bases and covered by flat domes, which in their inner chamber seemed to have afforded shelter to funeral deposits. Many such deposits in the form of urns and little wooden boxes full of calcined bones were also dug up along the foot of square towers, recalling Buddhist funeral monuments in Ladak.

That all the exposed portions of the structures had suffered from the destructive effects of rain and snow was easy to observe at the first glance. But the excavations had not proceeded far before it became certain that most of the shrines had been subjected also to a great conflagration. Since none of the numerous finds of Chinese copper coins, originally deposited as votive gifts, were later than the close of the eighth century A.D., it seemed reasonable to connect this burning with the earliest Muhammadan invasions. But in spite of all the destruction due to iconoclastic zeal and atmospheric influences, plentiful spoil rewarded our systematic clearing.

The deep débris layers filling the interior of the larger shrines yielded a great quantity of fine relievo sculpture in stucco, much of it fragmentary and small in size, yet of great artistic merit. In all cases of good preservation the stucco (*recte*, mud plaster) was quite hard, a result evidently due to the effective firing which these pieces had undergone when the shrines were burnt down. In the same shrines some larger relievo figures, as seen in Fig. 269, had escaped more or less from the effect of the conflagration through their position low down in sheltered corners. But these had owing to damp become so soft and rotten that any attempt to remove them would have caused complete collapse. So I learned to feel grateful for the catastrophe which had helped to preserve the rest for us.

The remarkable abundance of delicately carved heads, busts, or torsos, as seen in Figs. 270, 271, which came to light from the débris of certain cellas—I gathered them by the hundreds—was due to the fact that the decoration there had largely consisted of relievo friezes running round the walls at some height. The rows of holes for the wooden supports of these friezes could still be discerned in places, as seen at the top of Fig. 269. The burning of the timber and other inflammable materials within the shrines had quickly calcined these friable relievos where they stood ; and by the time the projecting stucco masses fell away, the débris on the floor had accumulated sufficiently to mitigate the fall and protect the fragments. To attempt any reconstruction of the scenes which might have been represented in those friezes would be hazardous at the present stage. But the pieces reproduced in Figs. 270, 271 from the spoil of one or two of the cellas, will give some idea of the striking variety of types and the strongly marked classical influence displayed in their style.

Some of the heads, indeed, are as classical in modelling and expression as any to be found among the Graeco-Buddhist sculptures of Gandhara (Figs. 270, 272). Thus, the bearded heads are unmistakably derived from the representations of Satyrs in Roman and Hellenistic art. The head-dress and ornamentation in most of these relievos point to the extreme North-West of India or the Kabul Valley as the region where this adaptation of Hellenistic models to subjects of Buddhist imagery originally took place. But apart from the types common also to the Buddhist art of Gandhara, there are others which distinctly presuppose a local development of that art. There is, for instance, a curious naturalistic feeling, strangely recalling phases of Gothic art, in almost all the heads reproduced in the top rows of the two plates, and in the shrouded head in the middle of Fig. 270, 4, emotion being expressed with a freedom that is rare in Graeco-Buddhist art.

These reminiscences of post-classical European art will have nothing very startling for those who have followed the result of recent research. Professor Strzygowski has drawn attention to the pregnant influence which the Orientalized Hellenistic art of the Near East exercised through Byzantine mediation upon the early mediaeval art of Europe. As an instance of the very close connection existing between these relievos of Kara-shahr and the art of Buddhist Khotan, I may mention that the grotesque head so frequent as a plaque on the terra-cotta vases from the site of the ancient Khotan capital occurs in exact reproduction on several miniature shields in stucco from the 'Ming-oi' site (see Fig. 274), and is thus proved to be directly derived, as I long ago conjectured, from the model of the classical Gorgo's head.

The comparatively late occupation of the site would be difficult to reconcile with the survivals of early Graeco-Buddhist art, especially when these were executed in such friable material, were it not certain from manifold evidence that much of the plaster work was reproduced, and if necessary restored, from moulds which might be far older than the shrine itself. It was curious to find direct proof of this also in the case of some well-modelled architectural tiles (Fig. 274), which were hardened at the outset by burning, and of which numerous 'cast' specimens were discovered in an oven built close to one of the smaller shrines. But a number of delicately carved relievos in wood dis-

269. RELIEVO IMAGES IN STUCCO REPRESENTING BODHISATTVAS, IN RUINED
BUDDHIST SHRINE MI. XI., 'MING-OI' SITE, KARA-SHAHR.

The foot-measure serves as scale.

270. STUCCO HEADS, SHOWING GRAECO-BUDDHIST ART INFLUENCE, FROM
RUINED SHRINES, 'MING-OI' SITE, KARA-SHAHR.

Scale, one-third.

1. Bearded head of classical type with Indian headdress. 2, 3. Grotesque heads. 4. Shrouded head. 5. Grotesque head, derived from Gorgo on miniature shield (see ii. p. 368). 6, 9. Heads probably of Bodhisattvas. 7. Head of Naga type. 8. Satyr-like head.

271. STUCCO HEADS AND BUSTS FROM RELIEVO DECORATION OF RUINED
BUDDHIST SHRINES, 'MING-OI' SITE, KARA-SHAHR.

Scale, one-third.

1. Helmeted head. 2, 3. Heads in naturalistic style. 4, 6, 7. Female busts. 5. Divine male bust.

272. STUCCO HEAD IN HIGH RELIEVO, PROBABLY REPRESENTING A BODHI-
SATTVA, FROM RUINED SHRINE MI. XV., 'MING-OI' SITE, KARA-SHAHR.

Scale, one-half.

covered in the débris of different temples (Figs. 273, 275), which from the very nature of their material could not have been mechanically reproduced, show that art work of older date and decided merit was also represented among the votive deposits of this site.

Most remarkable among these specimens is, perhaps, the little detached panel in wood, a kind of miniature stēlē (Fig. 275, 3) about one foot high, which in the two upper stories shows a story from Buddha's legend, while on a projecting base worshipping figures are represented. The style of the modelling and the general disposition are so closely akin to those prevailing in the Graeco-Buddhist relievos of Gandhara that the idea of actual importation from the confines of India strongly suggests itself. In the same way the curved panel, perhaps originally forming part of a large halo carved in wood and richly gilt, which is decorated with five seated Buddha figures, could easily be matched in the stone-cut relievos of Buddhist Viharas in the Peshawar valley. Yet there can be no doubt that this piece, like other decorative wood-carvings of which a few specimens are given in Figs. 273, 275, must have been produced locally.

An interesting contrast to all this evidence of predominant Graeco-Buddhist influence is supplied by the excellently modelled little statuette in wood (Fig. 275, 4), which represents a 'Guardian-king of the World,' probably Vaisravana, in the best Chinese style of T'ang times. It helps to remind us that here, as at Khotan, local art during the last centuries of the Buddhist period must have been exposed to a reverse current of influence from the Far East.

This Chinese influence makes itself felt also in the mural paintings of the site. Those on exposed wall surfaces had suffered almost complete effacement; but in the vaulted passages behind the cellas timely burial had occasionally saved them from both fire and moisture. A large series of fresco panels illustrating scenes in the life of Buddha have survived almost complete. The panels were just big enough to be cut out and safely removed. It was a hard task, for the plaster adhered so closely to the wall that Naik

Ram Singh had to chisel off the brickwork behind before the panels could be secured. The specimen reproduced in Plate XI. A shows Buddha in the unusual act of writing, with disciples holding Pothi leaves and what is evidently intended for a brush such as used in Chinese script. The rich and harmonious colouring used throughout these frescoes is distinctly superior to the drawing, and the same observation applies to the painted votive panels of wood which had escaped the effects of fire and damp. The damp had dealt badly with manuscript remains ; but enough of fragmentary leaves in Indian and Central-Asian Brahmi and in Uigur script survived to help in confirming my approximate dating of the site.

The frequency with which cinerary urns and boxes were found around some of the shrines was a curious feature of the site ; but of traces of the abodes of the living there were none. Was the great plain stretching eastwards already in old days the same desolate scrub-covered waste which it is now, notwithstanding the relative ease with which it could be brought under irrigation by canals from the large Kara-shahr River ? Everywhere in this north-eastern corner of the Tarim Basin I was struck by the thinness of the population in relation to the abundance of cultivable land and of water to irrigate it, and many indications suggest that the conditions were not essentially different in ancient times. Had the peculiar position of Kara-shahr, which exposes it to attacks from all sides, something to do with this ?

As if to remind me of this local feature, there rose on the height of a barren ridge, and just above the caves already mentioned, half a mile to the north, a solid watch-tower built of bricks with thin layers of reeds between. In construction it was closely akin to those towers of the Han border with which I had become so familiar. Since corresponding watch-towers have been traced by Hedin and others along the west foot of the Kuruk-tagh on a line which the ancient route from Lop-nor must have followed, this similarity may have its significance. As a matter of fact, I subsequently came across another tower of this type at the foot of the range skirted by the direct route to

Korla, but had no opportunity to trace the connection farther.

During the fortnight spent at the Shikchin ruins we worked under quite Sarmatian conditions. Minimum temperatures down to 42 degrees Fahrenheit below freezing-point I should not have minded so much, had we been saved those chilling vapours sent forth by the great Baghrash Lake south. Day after day an icy mist enveloped ruins and camp. The nightly hoar - frost practically amounted to a light snowfall, and continued to cover the ground even when the sun fitfully struggled through at last. For some days I almost despaired of getting adequate light for the needful photographs, and the hoar-frost is conspicuous in most of them. Fortunately there was shelter of some kind for the men among the small cellas still retaining part of their vaulting.

Such climatic conditions made it easier to understand the relative frequency of grazing and water which Rai Lal Singh reported having found in the westernmost valleys of the Kuruk - tagh. After moving from Turfan south to Singer over a succession of barren plateaus, he had made his way by seven long marches across previously unmapped ground to Korla, whence he hastened to rejoin me, bringing welcome help for the digging.

CHAPTER LXXXIV

FROM KHORA TO KUCHAR

THE conditions of work at 'Ming-oi,' under what seemed to me Cimmerian gloom, had been so trying, that it was a great relief for all when the completion of the tasks I had set myself at the site allowed us just before Christmas to move up to the cold but sunny mountains of Khora. There, some twenty miles up the broad Kara-shahr Valley, information elicited with much trouble from reticent Mongol shepherds led to the discovery of Buddhist remains hitherto unnoticed. It was a collection of much-decayed little temples and Stupas perched boldly on low but steep rock spurs (Fig. 276). Below them a spring, now spreading itself under a glittering ice sheet, allowed of a few fields being occasionally cultivated by Mongols.

The picturesque seclusion of the site vividly brought back to my mind old Buddhist ruins once explored in the hills of far-off Swat and Buner. It had not saved the shrines from the fury of iconoclastic invaders, and moisture too had caused damage. Yet the clearing of them revealed interesting remains of their once rich decoration, including well-carved relievos in wood (Fig. 273, 2), and a large panel with an encaustic painting on gilt ground, alas! badly scorched. While I myself, refreshed by the delightfully clear atmosphere, spent busy Christmas days over these excavations, Rai Lal Singh profited by the opportunity for useful surveys on the range dividing the Kara-shahr Valley from the great Turkestan plains.

Then we moved down through the grim defile by which the green waters of the river which drains Lake Baghrash have burst their way into the Tarim Basin. How delightful

274. RELIEVO TILE IN TERRACOTTA AND MINIATURE SHIELDS IN STUCCO FROM RUINED SHRINES, 'MING-OI' SITE, KARA-SHAHR.

Scale, three-tenths.

8. Miniature shield with wooden stick supporting it.   9. Grotesque head on shield, from Gorgo model.   10. Tile showing head of Buddhist divinity.

273. MISCELLANEOUS WOOD-CARVINGS AND STUCCO RELIEVO FROM SITES OF 'MING-OI,' KHORA, 'THOUSAND BUDDHAS,' AND TUN-HUANG *LIMES*.

Scale, one-third.

1. Floral ornament in wood, 'Ming-oi.'   2. Grotesque relievo in wood, from painted panel, Khora.   3. Buddha image in wood, 'Thousand Buddhas.'   4. Stucco heads from Trimurti image, T. xxix., Tun-huang *Limes* (ii. p. 59).   5. Miniature Stupa in wood, 'Ming-oi.'   6. Relievo in Gandhara style from wooden casket, 'Ming-oi.'   7. Grotesque wood-carving, 'Ming-oi.'

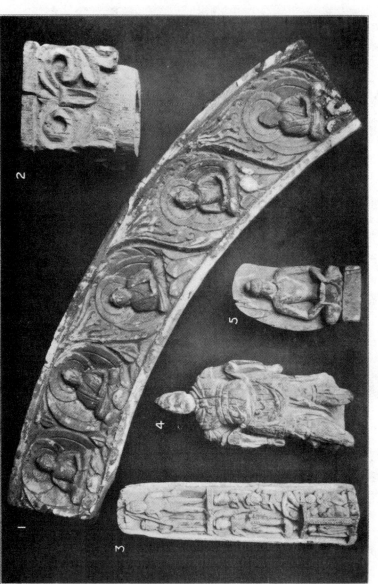

275. RELIEVOS AND DECORATIVE CARVINGS IN WOOD, FROM RUINED BUDDHIST SHRINES, 'MING-OI' SITE AND KHORA.

1. Relievo panel, gilt, showing small seated Buddhas. 2. Miniature Indo-Corinthian capital. 3. Miniature stélé in Graeco-Buddhist style with relievo scenes from Buddhist legend. 4. Statuette in Chinese style representing a Lokapala. 5. Relievo of seated Buddha, Khora.

it seemed from its debouchure to look down upon the oasis of Korla and, sighting the unlimited horizon of the yellow 'sand-ocean' beyond, to feel that there was but a single watershed far away left between me and the Indus! The short halt which detained me at Korla until New Year's Day of 1908 was pleasant though full of work. It was cheerful to find myself again among homely Turki folk of the true type, and to enjoy the comfort of such a clean and spacious room as the local Beg was able to offer me, boasting even of a papered window. It was a pleasant experience, too, to behold an oasis which enjoyed the rare boon of having an unfailing supply of water for irrigation, far in excess of the actual needs of its people. But foremost in my feelings was the satisfaction of having here, close to the north-east end of the great sandy desert, returned once more to my own ground.

This old fascination of the Taklamakan induced me to test the persistent reports about an 'old town' half-buried amidst the dunes, which Korla people declared they had seen in the desert south-westwards. The information which reached me while at 'Ming-oi' had sounded rather vague and romantic when gathered from the fear-bound tongues of labourers. But it took a more substantial form when at last fat and jovial Tahir Beg (Fig. 277), whom the Amban had deputed to act as my local factotum, acknowledged that he, too, knew of the 'old town.' His own cousin Musa, the 'Haji,' he told me, had some five years before come upon the ruins while hunting in the desert west of the Konche Darya, as the river from the Baghrash Lake is called below Korla.

The detailed account of the place which was described as a small ruined fort with a conspicuous gate, was confirmed in essential particulars by the discoverer himself, a gaunt, weatherbeaten figure, when he was brought into Korla (Fig. 280). He declared that he had not seen the ruins again, a dust-storm immediately after the discovery having prevented return, but was prepared to guide me. As the existence of some ruined 'Gumbaz,' or domed structures, was attested independently by a number of persons in the jungle belt of the Inchike Darya which lay in the same direction, I decided to give Musa Haji his chance, and started on New Year's Day south-westwards with light baggage and a small band of labourers. All Korla took it to be a real 'treasure quest,' and in spite of the winter cold recruits offered themselves in numbers.

After two short marches across excellent grazing-lands and then luxuriant riverine jungle, we crossed the hard-frozen Konche Darya and moved up along the flood-bed which occasionally receives water from the west, and is known as the Charchak Darya. The short expedition thus effected into the unsurveyed desert belt between the Inchike and Charchak river beds proved interesting geographically, showing in typical form the changes brought about by shifting river courses and general desiccation (Fig. 279). But after several days' close search in the desert, Musa Haji, whom I had taken care to keep accompanied by level-headed Daroghas, had to confess his inability to locate the 'old town' which he still swore he had seen and approached.

On the strength of equally positive assertions made by two other hunters, we subsequently pushed a net of systematic reconnaissances into the desert north of the Charchak river bed, but in vain. In the end I was able to establish with certainty that those elaborate reports had no more substantial foundation than the existence of early Muhammadan tombs and of rude shepherd huts amidst the dead jungle belts of earlier river beds. We succeeded in accurately tracing these remains after much trouble caused by the very deceptive ground. At the same time, the close study of the physical conditions convinced me that no per-manent cultivation on any scale could have existed on this ground within historical times.

For some time I was puzzled how to account for the conduct and psychological motives of my several *soi-disant* guides (Fig. 280). They all seemed quite genuine in their own way, and stuck stoutly to their story of what they believed they had seen, though differing as to the location of their respective 'old towns.' Most puzzling thing of all, I could not discern any reason for conscious imposition, considering that no reward for their guidance had been

276. GENERAL VIEW OF BUDDHIST TEMPLE RUINS, KHORA, FROM NORTH-EAST.

Tahir Beg in foreground.

278. BAKIR, PLAYER OF RABAB, ON DESERT MARCH.

277. TAHIR BEG AND AHMAD YÜZ-BASHI, OF KORLA.

asked or offered in advance. At last, after much careful
sounding, I fathomed the folklore belief which furnished the
clue to the mystery. All the Korla people had grown up
under the influence of the old tradition, which elsewhere also
haunts the outskirts of the great desert, about 'old towns'
buried by the sands, and full of hidden treasure. This
tradition was firmly coupled with a belief that such ruins
were guarded by demons, which prevented them ever
being seen a second time by those who were lucky enough
to discover them.

It was but a survival of the popular legend of which
Hsüan‑tsang, the great pilgrim, had already heard a
localized form between Khotan and Keriya, and which I
had occasion to relate in the narrative of my former
journey. Musa Haji and his fellow‑hunters had tried
their luck in searching for the ruins of their local ' Kötek-
shahri,' on different occasions and in different desert
areas. They had *bona fide* offered their guidance in the
fond hope that my supposed magic would be powerful
enough to overcome the evil genii hiding the walled
town of which their own imagination had before let
them only catch a glimpse—apparently in a dust-storm !
They now felt sorry for the failure of my ' Wilayet arts'
to secure them a chance of discovering all those hidden
treasures.

After marching up the Inchike Darya, Lal Singh and
myself separated on January 12th, 1908. While he was
to follow the hitherto unmapped river course right through
to Shahyar, I myself struck by forced marches through
the broad belt of unsurveyed desert north-westwards, and
after reaching the great northern caravan route at Bugur,
made my way to Kuchar. At this great and ancient
oasis I utilized a week's halt for visits to the interesting
ruins close by, which had during the preceding five years
been searched successively by Japanese, German, and
Russian archaeological parties, and had finally been cleared
with a thoroughness and method deserving of all praise
by the French mission under Professor Pelliot. Kuchar,
situated at the foot of the T'ien-shan, and watered by two
large rivers which debouch here, may by reason of its

geographical position and historical importance claim to
be a worthy *pendant* of Khotan in the south. So the
rapid survey I was able to make of the ruins, and especially of the old Buddhist temples and grottoes which survive
in a much-decayed condition at the mouth of the two river
gorges, proved very instructive.

Apart from these archaeological visits there was much
to keep me busy during my halt at Kuchar. It was there
that I finally had to settle all plans and arrangements for
the journey which was to take me through the desert to
the southern edge of the Taklamakan. Already while
near Korla I had learned from a letter of Rai Ram Singh,
received *via* Kashgar, that the enquiries set on foot under
my instructions from the side of Khotan had resulted in
the tracing of several unexplored sites in the desert below
Keriya and Khotan. This was confirmed in detail by a
letter from Badruddin Khan, my old Afghan friend and
factotum at Khotan, which a trader delivered to me at
Kuchar.

I was anxious to visit these sites before the heat and
sand-storms of the spring made work on that ground
impracticable, and to reach them if possible by the most
direct route. The heavy convoy of antiquities which
had followed after me from Korla by the caravan road
could safely be despatched by the well-known route which
leads along the dry bed of the Khotan River right through
the desert to the Khotan oasis, the prospective base for
my labours of the spring and summer. Once freed from
the care of these precious but embarrassing impedimenta,
I myself could strike due south from Kuchar to where the
Keriya River dies away in the sands. It was a march
beset with serious difficulties and risks. But Hedin's
pioneer journey of 1896 showed that it was practicable
under certain conditions, and seeing that there were ruins
to be visited near the Keriya River course, I decided to
try this 'short cut' and save time. Yet I must confess
that, even without this specific reason, I might have found
the chance of once more crossing the very heart of the
desert too great an attraction to resist.

A sky heavy with snow clouds made the dark and

confined quarters in Kuchar city which the hospitality of
Sabat Ali Khan, the kindly old Ak-sakal of the local
Afghan traders, had pressed upon me look doubly
gloomy. So I was glad when by the morning of January
25th the great division of my caravan was completed.
After blocking traffic in the narrow street for hours, the
heavy goods train of antiques on twenty-four camels was
started on its long journey to Khotan in charge of Chiang-
ssŭ-yeh and Tila Bai, the most reliable of my Muhammadans. My own caravan, including the party of Rai
Lal Singh who had rejoined me at Kuchar, seemed quite
handy and light in comparison. Our own seven brave
camels would have amply sufficed for our much-reduced
baggage. But I knew what heavy loads of supplies,
fodder, and water (*recte*, ice) would have to be added
before the desert march was begun, and wondered whether
by adding only eight hired animals I was not cutting the
margin too fine.

Through a grey misty afternoon, with slush on the road
and past snow-covered avenues of trees, we made the short
march to Char-shamba, near the edge of the Kuchar oasis.
On the next day a long ride over scrub-covered ground
which bore quite a homely European look, thanks to a
light fall of snow, brought us to Shahyar. The surroundings
of this small town, recently made the headquarters of a
separate little district, looked bleak, nor did its crowded but
dingy streets dispel this impression. But the attentive
magistrate, Chang Ta-jên, the same whom in 1906 I had
missed at Tash-kurghan, had provided a very hospitable
welcome. Begs and other local dignitaries rode out to
meet me, and everything for our onward journey was
reported in readiness.

But after I had settled down for the night under the
modest shelter of a trader's house at a safe distance from
the noisy Bazar, it did not take me long to ascertain that
the report about available guides was wrong. None
of the Shahyar hunters brought to me while I waited for
the arrival of the camels floundering in the soft snow, had
ever seen the route I was anxious to follow across the
desert. What these alleged 'guides' knew only was the

well-known track leading along the Tarim and then up the Khotan river bed.

That I should have to abandon all hope of getting local experience for the journey became certain when next morning the fountain-head of all Shahyar topographical knowledge was produced in the person of an age-bowed hunter named Khalil.   He was a quaint, withered little man, well over eighty, credited with many expeditions after wild camels, and a great deal of jungle experience.   But he had never been across the real desert, and stoutly denied even hearing of a route to the Keriya River.   Khalil, still glib of tongue and quick-witted for a person of his age, hobbled along with difficulty, but once lifted into the saddle could do his day's march with ease.   So he agreed to guide us at least to the point in the forest belt of the Tarim where Hedin had first touched a shepherd encampment.   This, I thought, would now serve as the safest starting-point in the reverse direction.

279. DUNES IN DRY RIVER BED NEAR CHARCHAK DARYA.

280. MUSA HAJI BETWEEN TWO OTHER HUNTERS FROM KORLA.
Seekers for the fabled sand-buried 'old town.'

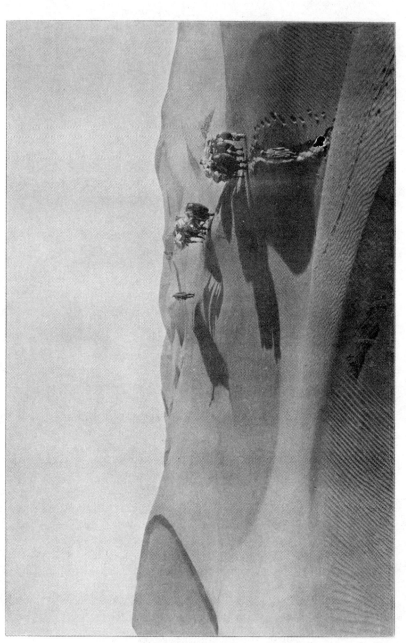

281. MY CARAVAN MARCHING OVER HIGH DUNES IN TAKLAMAKAN, SOUTH OF TARIM RIVER.

Hassan Akhun and Turdi with the camels ; Naik Ram Singh behind on left.

CHAPTER LXXXV

IN THE 'SEA OF SAND'

Had I known in Kuchar that guides were not to be secured from Shahyar I might, perhaps, have hesitated before attempting to strike right across the desert to the Keriya River; for without such guides I could not for a moment hide from myself the serious difficulty of the task and its inherent risks. Hedin, coming from the south, had left the end of the Keriya River with the certainty of striking the broad goal of the Tarim right across his route at some point or other, if only he kept long enough to an approximately northern course. For us coming from the north the case was essentially different. Our hope of reaching water within reasonable time depended solely on our ability to steer correctly across some 150 miles of high dunes towards a particular point—the termination of the Keriya River which flowed, not right across our route, but practically in the same direction; it involved also the assumption that the river still actually sent its water to where Hedin had seen it.

Now I knew well by experience the difficulty of steering a correct course by the compass alone in a real sea of sand devoid of all directing features. Nor could I overlook the fact that, however justified my reliance in Hedin's careful mapping was, differences in longitude deduced from mere route traverses were bound to be considerable on such ground, and in our case all depended on the assumed longitude being right. If we failed to strike the river end in the confused delta of dry beds which the river has formed since early periods in its death-struggles with the sands, our position was certain to be dangerous. There would be nothing to indicate whether the actual bed, in which we might hope to find at least subsoil water by digging wells, lay to the east or west. If we continued our course to the south there would be great risk of our water-supply getting completely exhausted, and of animals—if not of men, too—succumbing through thirst long before the line of wells and oases at the foot of the Kun-lun could be reached.

Against these objections there were to be reckoned the loss of time and other drawbacks which any change of plans would involve. After careful consideration I decided to stick to my programme and to guard, within the limits of human prevision, against the risks lying before us. An adequate supply of food and water was essential to assure safety. So I took special care to verify that all my people had actually provided themselves with supplies for one and a half months as ordered. The small contingent of labourers I wished to take along from Shahyar was to be equally provisioned, and also equipped against the rigours of the desert winter. I decided to limit this contingent to eight men, just sufficient for help with well-digging and loading *en route*, and as a nucleus for prospective excavation work at the other end.

The selection and equipping of the men during the one day's halt at Shahyar proved no easy affair; for the rumours about our expedition had been sufficiently deterrent to make it hard for the village head-men who had to furnish their quota to find acceptable men. At first they tried to pass off helpless persons, physically unfit for such a journey or else without adequate clothing and food supplies. The men picked out at last were sturdy enough in body; but, in spite of ample advances and the assurance of very liberal wages, they were so dismayed at the prospect that, when their district officer came to pay me his ceremonial visit, they all fell to praying on their knees for release from dreaded sufferings and certain disaster.

Luckily the energetic young Mandarin was a man of the right stuff. He reassured them by emphasizing my proved knowledge of desert travel and my determination to look after their comfort and safety, and in addition promised to exempt their families from all corvées for the year. Chang Ta-jên spoke Russian quite well—he had learned the language during a long stay at Mukden—and could make out with ease my intended route from the Russian map of Turkestan I showed him. Perhaps it was as well that he could form no adequate idea of its difficulties.

In spite of all my efforts and those of my energetic factotum Ibrahim Beg, the multifarious preparations were not completed until late at night. But the morning after that busy day's halt saw the fully equipped caravan started. The fifteen camels we took with us were by no means too many, considering that six weeks' food supplies had to be carried for a party counting altogether twenty men, and that at least eight animals would be needed for the carriage of ice to provide a reserve of drinking water. Once in the desert everybody had to walk, though I had rather rashly agreed to take four ponies along in order to assure greater mobility for my Indian assistants and myself after we should have reached the Keriya River.

Our route lay first in the tract of Chimen, where for nearly thirteen miles we passed through patches of cultivation alternating with scrubby steppe of equally fertile soil, but left untilled owing to want of water. Abandoned fields and canals corroborated the local statements that irrigation had become increasingly difficult over this area during the last ten or fifteen years. The people of Chimen assured me that the increase of 'new land' in the south-western part of the Kuchar oasis, with the consequent greater demand for canal water, was the chief cause why the river flowing from that side towards Shahyar now failed to fill their old irrigation cuts. It was curious to learn how the Chimen farmers had fought these adverse conditions, partly by shifting their fields to areas which the canals can feed even at a lower level, and partly by converting arable ground into pasture. As we approached the riverine belt of the Tarim, fenced sheep-runs, which I had seen nowhere else in Turkestan, became frequent.

Then behind a narrow line of dunes we struck the big bed of the Tarim. The river, hard frozen, now filled two channels 300 and 120 yards across; but the total width of the bed was nearly three miles, attesting the enormous volume of the summer floods. After a few miles along the right bank lined with fine Toghrak jungle, we halted for the night at the few scattered houses of Peres where some graziers live in comparative comfort. These homesteads, the last I was to see before Keriya, seemed a good illustration of the difference in economic conditions prevailing north and south of the Taklamakan. The sheep-farmers here had adopted an almost settled mode of life, while the nomadic herdsmen in the south had scarcely as yet learned to seek shelter in reed-huts. I did not grudge my servants their warm quarters in the head-man's best room, fitted with plentiful felts and quilts, and boasting even of a tasteful cotton-print dado. But for my own part I found pleasure in the thought that it would be more than 300 miles to the nearest house south.

From there we marched on January 29th under old Khalil's guidance south-westwards, and after moving all day through a belt of luxuriant Toghrak jungle and reed-beds reached after nightfall the shepherds' camp known as Samsak-daryasi, which was to serve as our starting-point. Wild as the place looked in the light of our bonfires, it offered a welcome supply of dried green reeds for the camels and ponies, the last treat of any sort they were to enjoy for a long time. The purchase of four sheep, by no means as fat as one might have expected in such fine jungle grazing, completed our commissariat arrangements.

Next morning we began the journey southwards ; but the time had not yet come when we should have to steer by the compass only. A broad belt of jungle watered at times by floods from the Tarim still separated us from the desert, and here we had to take the supply of ice which was an essential safeguard for the crossing before us. After covering about ten miles through forest and strips of tamarisk-covered sand, Tokhta, Khalil's thick-headed son, who was at this point acting as our guide, turned off to the south-west, and by nightfall brought us to the promised pools in a net-work of deep-cut dry river beds. The spot was called Luk-chikte by the shepherds who, as broad sheep tracks showed, resort to it regularly while grazing flocks in these arid jungles.

The pools, fully twenty-five feet or so below the level of the surrounding ground, did not look very inviting, with shores of black hard-trodden mud and a tangled mass of decayed reeds. But the water in a rough well constructed by their side proved quite fresh, and the supply of ice was abundant. Flood-water did not appear to have reached this point for long years ; yet the water left behind in this deepest part of the ravine had not dried up or turned salt. The explanation, no doubt, lay in the pools being fed periodically by underground drainage.

The cutting of ice went on all through the night and early morning, and it was not till 10 A.M. that we could set out with eight huge bags duly filled and loaded on as many camels. All the camels received here their last watering, six to eight bucketfuls making up the regulation 'drink' in winter before a long journey through waterless ground. Tokhta's rôle as guide had come to an end ; for we now shaped our course by the compass due south until we should strike the Keriya River delta. After about six miles we emerged from the last strip of forest upon an old river bed, narrow and winding, known as Achchik Darya. It held no ice where we passed it, only luxuriant beds of Kumush. From old Khalil, who caught us up in the morning, and who insisted upon accompanying us so far, I learned that until about ten years before the bed had been filled by flood-water from the Tarim. Now it no longer reached it, and the flourishing lines of wild poplars were likely to turn before many years into dead forest or 'kötek.'

A short halt enabled Khalil to give us his last farewell and blessing. He gave it with more ceremony than I should have expected for the occasion, turning towards Mecca in a long prayer, and the men all joining loudly in the 'Aman.' From Khotan to Lop-nor I had made more than one start into desert quite as forbidding, without ever witnessing such a display of emotion. But along the Tarim even reputed hunters are rather tame people, unaccustomed to the wilds, and the Shahyar men showed plainly how afraid they were of the venture. I could not instil into their timid souls that adventurous curiosity which had so

often secured me willing followers from the southern edge
of the Taklamakan. But I felt grateful for the fatalistic
submission which made them accept the situation without
further remonstrance, in spite of all misgivings.

Once across the dry river the dunes were not slow to
appear, but scattered Toghraks and plentiful scrub grew
between them. I was surprised to note the numerous fresh
tracks of wild camels. Evidently they were not much
afraid of the prowess of the Shahyar hunters. Where
the zone of occasional reed growth seemed to end we
decided to halt for the night, so as to give the camels their
last chance of some grazing. There was not a man in the
party with professional desert experience. So it fell upon
me to look out for a likely spot where water might be
reached by digging. Below a tamarisk cone the soil felt
damp, and a well sunk here through unfrozen clay reached
subsoil water at only five feet. It tasted salt, as was to be
expected so close to the riverine belt, but was just drinkable
for the ponies.

I had warned our camel-men against the risk of the
animals straying where wild camels and more tempting
grazing were so near, but in vain. The baggage was
ready for lading before 8 A.M., but the hired camels had
absconded about dawn, and their owner was late in pursuing
them. I had to send out wily Hassan Akhun to help in
the tracking, and even with his help the fugitives were not
brought back for three hours. The day's march was thus
short, but proved tiring. The dunes rose rapidly to over
twenty feet, and we had not yet got accustomed to long
tramps in soft sand. After we had surmounted a great
ridge of sand stretching from east to west, the height of
individual dunes sank, and on bare patches of ground between them the hardy Sagsag plant showed itself frequently.

Then came a fresh belt of closely packed dunes now
forty to fifty feet high, which would have been still harder
to cross had not their crest-line been also the direction of
our advance. The convex side of the dunes generally faced
to the west, a proof of the prevailing east winds. The
camels under their heavy loads could not on such ground
cover more than a mile and a half per hour. So after a

short march of only a little over ten miles we were obliged
to pitch camp in the midst of towering dunes. Luckily
here, too, depressions showing damp soil were frequent, and
the well we dug in one of them yielded water at five and a
half feet, somewhat less brackish than at the previous camp,
but too scanty to save much of our ice.

Next day, February 2nd, we had a desolate march
under a grey sky heavy with clouds, amidst high bare
dunes rolling on all sides like the waves of a 'choppy'
sea. The first five miles lay over a regular Dawan of
closely packed ridges rising to fifty and eighty feet above
the rare depressions. It was well that I could encourage my
men by pointing to signs of moisture in the latter. With
some relief, too, we sighted towards the evening two big
Dawans to the south-west and south-east, perhaps marking
the last offshoots of the high ridges of sand which flanked
the course of the Keriya River. The dunes grew perfectly
bare after about ten miles, and the apprehension about fuel
obliged us to stop at the first dead tamarisk cone we
encountered. In a crater-like depression a well was dug
which at a depth of only five feet gave us water sufficient
for the men and ponies with only a slight taste of saltness.

Next morning, after three miles' weary tramp along the
crests of huge dunes (Fig. 281), we emerged upon a broad
belt of living poplars and tamarisks. It was a strange
sight, this strip of vegetation stretching away to the north-
north-east for at least six miles, and for two more to south-
south-west. It took us nearly a mile to cross it. The
trees were all growing on small sand-cones, as I had seen
them often in the desert beyond the Niya and Endere
Rivers. The dunes between were like dwarfs by the side
of the mighty swellings of bare drift sand we had just
crossed. The direction of this jungle belt was clearly the
same as that of the lowest Keriya River.

After we had crossed it, a thin line of living trees still
remained in view both on our right and left, though at a
distance. They helped to keep up the spirits of our hapless
Shahyar men, who no longer believed that they were being
led to their doom, but fondly fancied the Keriya River to be
quite near. It cost me some effort to undeceive them.

After we had crossed a small area of Toghraks here all dead, the dunes rose once more to over thirty feet, but tamarisks grew plentifully between them. So when we halted in the evening by the side of a big tamarisk-covered cone we had fuel in plenty.

The well I had dug led through hard-frozen damp sand to water at a depth of only three and a half feet, and the water was now perfectly sweet. So there was contentment throughout the camp. There was nothing to eat for the camels, except bits from some huge cakes of bread I got baked for them. This emergency treat was repeated subsequently whenever we got water enough for the purpose. It was amusing to watch how fond my burly camels grew of their bread. By giving them the pieces with my own hand I made a rapid advance in their friendship. Willingly they would now let me stroke them instead of meeting my friendly attentions, as so often before, with surly grunts and unmannerly spitting.

Our march on February 4th seemed easy; for the dunes soon sank to a modest height, eight to ten feet, and only two Dawans were encountered on the fourteen miles' march to the south. Even over them there was good going. Up to the middle of the march moist depressions showed here and there amidst the dunes, and wells could have been dug with ease. Dead Kumush showing on bare patches of ground close to living tamarisks also seemed a hopeful sign. But as we marched on, the number of dead trees and bushes increased, while living Toghraks were now rarely within view. The ground, where clear of dunes, had changed to hard clay, and I was not surprised when at the place where the dusk obliged us to halt, our attempt to reach water by digging proved fruitless. The well was sunk at the most likely spot, in a hollow below a big Toghrak still living; but after a shaft had been sunk to a depth of fully fifteen feet the sand still felt so dry that the work had to be abandoned. Evidently the subsoil water from which the roots of this veteran drew their nourishment was still far below this level. So the Shahyar men once more grew despondent.

Next morning by daybreak I marched off ahead of the

caravan with a few men in order to dig a well *en route* as
soon as favourable ground should offer.   But the eagerly
desired chance failed completely.   The dunes kept high
and closely packed all day long.   Even dead poplars were
rarely met with ; but in the few groups we passed, they
stood in a clear line from north to south just as they would
grow along a water-course having that bearing.   Eroded
banks of clay which cropped up here and there on
ground not smothered by dunes invariably showed the
same direction.   There could be no doubt that the waters
of the Keriya River had at an early age reached this point
and determined their bearing.

But vainly did I look out for any sign of our nearing the
actual river delta.   From a Dawan some fifty feet high I
made out a line of scattered Toghraks still alive, far away
to the south.   When we reached them after a total tramp
of fourteen miles, the sand around proved so high that
well-digging was hopeless.   Droppings of wild camels
near the trees were plentiful ; but they seemed old, as were
also the few tracks of camels we had come across since
the previous day.   The grazing-places of these animals
were manifestly still distant.

It was sad to watch the depressed look in the men's
faces as they came up two hours later and found that my
advance guard's halt meant no water.   Only sturdy and
experienced Lal Singh kept up reliance in our route and
refrained from any sign of anxiety.   Of course, when we
were moving ahead and far from the others we did not hide
from each other that things were beginning to look serious
for our poor ponies.   A mile and a half more was covered
that evening, and then we had to halt for the night amidst
dismal dunes rising to thirty feet and more.   The last
night's temperature had dropped to twenty-eight degrees
of frost.   So we were glad to have at least plentiful fuel
in the débris of ancient poplars, fallen who could say how
many centuries ago.   Our water-supply had now been
reduced to three large bags and two galvanized iron tanks
full of ice.   Still, with all care for economy, I thought it
right to let each of the ponies have a pint of water.

It was a poor night's rest for me, for the anxiety to

wake the men in good time for an early start kept me from
sleep after 2 A.M.   The packing and loading was done in
darkness.   After going for a couple of miles over heavy
dunes we were just approaching a broad Dawan some sixty
feet high when the frequency of living tamarisks attracted
my attention.   One bush was growing almost on the surface
of a bare patch of clayey soil, without the usual cone, and
close to it was a hollow to a depth of ten feet below the
ground level.

More with a wish to divert the gloomy thoughts of the
Shahyar men than from any real hope I set them to work
here.   After clearing away some two feet of drift sand, blue
clay was struck which felt heavy, with the faintest suggestion
of damp.   The sand below this layer, of about one foot,
felt cool and another stratum of clay beneath it distinctly
clammy.   So nine Ketmans worked away for all their
wielders were worth.   With the last two days' scanty water
rations we all felt thirsty.   At a depth of five feet the sand
grew distinctly damp.   How eagerly the clods thrown out
from the bottom were weighed by us who watched the
work!   At last the strokes of Muhammad, the best of the
Shahyar men, who was digging away at the bottom, gave a
clicking sound suggestive of increased moisture, and at ten
feet depth the damp sand changed into mud.   Two feet
more, and water began slowly to gather under the man's
feet.   It was deliciously fresh, but gathered quite slowly.

I had sent all the camels except one ahead under Lal
Singh's steering.   The ponies were kept back by the well.
They seemed to realize for what purpose, and eagerly
pricked their ears at every click of the Ketmans in the mud.
At last we could let them have their first sorely needed
drink, a kettleful of muddy water for each animal.   Then
the filling of four skins or 'Mussucks' began, intended to
replenish our store of water.   It was terribly slow work,
as the sides of the well at the bottom where the sand had
been drained of its moisture, kept falling in and necessitated fresh clearing again and again.   But how elated we
all felt by the sight of this precious water!

This relief from immediate anxiety was doubly welcome,
since the distant view which opened from the Dawan just

beyond the well was more desolate than any previously encountered. A perfect sea of high and absolutely barren sand stretched southwards, bordered only by huge Dawans to the south-east and south-west. Leaving Ibrahim Beg behind with a few men to complete the filling of the Mussucks and to bring them into camp later, I hurried ahead to catch up the caravan. In the midst of high dunes I passed a broad hollow where Kumush white and brittle with age covered the banks of clay in profusion. It was manifestly an ancient terminal lagoon. But how many centuries might have passed since it last held water? Three or four days' marching would certainly be needed before we could hope to reach the actual death-bed of the river. Yet as a greeting from the belt of vegetation which lines it, the winds had carried towards us the delicate hair-like spores of living reeds. I remembered how on the march through the Lop-nor Desert this floating 'Pakawash' had been the first sign of 'nearing land,' and took it as a good omen that little flakes of it had gathered underneath almost every dead reed stalk now encountered.

The track which Lal Singh had followed under my instructions to S. 190° W., kept steadily rising over broad rolling dunes, and after about ten miles ascended the shoulder of a mighty ridge of sand culminating at a height of about three hundred feet. I caught up the camels just as they were rounding the ridge only a hundred feet or so below the bold line of its summit, and almost at the same time saw to my delight a broad valley-like belt of dead forest and living tamarisks stretching away below to south-south-west. The high sands we had just crossed and this continuous stretch of dead jungle agreed well with the description Hedin had recorded of the ground where on his march from the south he had finally lost touch with the dry river bed marking the former extension of the river. I felt, indeed, almost assured of having hit the very point which his map shows as Camp XXIV.

It seemed like a triumphant vindication of the accuracy of Hedin in mapping and of our own steering; yet as I look back to it now, it was too accurate to be true. The mere sight of the dark belt of vegetation put fresh heart

into the men.   Our hapless 'Yol-begi' ('road-master'), as
the Shahyar people euphemistically styled him, Khalil's
weak-kneed son, who ever since the previous vain search
for water had kept bewailing 'Atam, atam' ('Father,
father'), as if he were a mere boy instead of a man of forty-
five, now revived like a half-withered sprig put into water.

When we had descended from the Dawan there was,
indeed, good cause for rejoicing.   Amidst low dunes and
tamarisk cones we came upon a regular grove of fine old
Toghraks, some living, some dead.   Here camp was pitched;
and before dusk had settled, Hassan Akhun, whom I had
told off to search what unmistakably was an old river bed
marked by eroded clay banks, came back with hysterical
shouts of elation.   At a point some eleven feet below the
level of the nearest bank, the surface of the sand was in
truth hard frozen, and when this had been hewn through
with some trouble it needed only digging to a depth of
scarcely more than four feet to give us water.   It tasted
delightfully fresh, but once again it gathered but slowly.

However, we had a whole night to fill kettles and
buckets.   Contentment was great that evening throughout
the camp.   It seemed as if our main troubles were now
ended.   I had a huge dead tree turned into a bonfire to
guide Ibrahim Beg, and warmed myself by its blaze until
I could retire to my little tent.   The night promised to be
cold, under a sky at last perfectly clear of clouds, and, in
fact, I registered next morning a minimum of thirty-seven
degrees of frost.   My chief treat that cheerful evening was
a 'wash,' such as I had been sadly obliged to forgo for
days.   From the men's camp fire came sounds of a 'Rabab'
they had brought along from Shahyar to console themselves with in the wilderness (Fig. 278).   Under the stress
of the last week's marches its merry strings had remained
silent.

CHAPTER LXXXVI

IN A DEAD DELTA

OUR journey was resumed in good spirits on the morning
of February 7th. If we were right in the position assigned
to our camping-ground we ought to reach the grazing-
ground of Koshlash, where Hedin found the river ending,
in three days. Shaping our course upon this assumption
we steered west-by-south, and after passing for some five
miles through regular thickets of dead trees between high
bare ridges, emerged on more open ground, where dunes
were quite low and live tamarisks plentiful.

Here we picked up a dry river bed, well defined in
some places, but elsewhere again completely smothered by
drift sand (Fig. 282). After a few miles it became continuous, its width varying from sixty to a hundred yards,
and its depth from twenty to thirty feet. For a distance of
eleven miles we steadily followed this winding river course,
and then tried to cut off a great bend by going due south.
The result was that, after some three miles' progress
through dead forest, we found ourselves between two huge
accumulated ridges of drift sand, with no trace of the river
bed that was to guide us, and not a single living tree in
sight.

We were, by the showing of our plane-table, still a long
way north of latitude 39°, where the waters of the river
lose themselves in the sand, and our chance of getting
water by wells depended entirely on following some dry
bed receiving the drainage from the terminal river course.
The safest plan was to regain the old river bed we had
left, before it was too late. So with beasts and men much
fatigued—even the hard-marching Lal Singh had dropped

behind this day—the high Dawan to our right was climbed.
The view from the top in the evening light was depressing.
To east, west, and south alike there extended with bewildering uniformity vast stretches of dead forest, tamarisk cones,
and intervening ridges of sterile sand.

It was clear that we were now in the ancient dried-up
delta, which had once seen the death-struggle of the
Keriya River.   But which of the many dry beds that lay
hidden in this strangely oppressive wilderness of dead
jungle was the one leading to the actual river end ?   My
secret apprehension that our real trouble would begin on
reaching this dead delta was about to be fully verified.
It was as if, after navigating an open sea, we had reached
the treacherous marsh-coast of a tropical delta without
any lighthouses or landmarks to guide us into the right
channel.   With these doubts weighing heavily on my mind
I descended south-westwards in the hope of again striking
the bed we had followed during the morning.   But growing
darkness obliged us to halt before we could locate it.

The following morning opened more hopefully after
a night of worrying doubts.   When day broke it was
found that the depression where we had camped formed
part of the old river bed we had tried to regain, and which
we decided to follow southward.   For about three miles
we succeeded, as its course, though buried in places under
heavy sand, could generally be made out by the rows of
dead Toghraks lining the banks (Fig. 283).   But farther on
all trace of it vanished in a maze of dunes and dead forest.
The landscape was singularly flat and open.   But as far as
the eye would carry there extended the same desolate grey
screen of dead jungle.   To the south it seemed thicker
than behind us ; but this difference soon proved an optical
illusion, due to the shadows cast northward by the shrivelled
trees and bushes.   Only to the west far away there
showed ridges of bare sand ; their bright yellow was almost
a relief to the eye wearied by the dismal greyish brown of
the dead scrub.

With nothing to guide us in this never-ending delta
I was particularly anxious to make sure at least of our
latitude.   A mid-day observation was the simplest process

282. CARAVAN ON MARCH NEAR DRY RIVER BED AT END OF ANCIENT KERIYA RIVER DELTA.

283. HALT ON MARCH ACROSS DUNES AND DEAD JUNGLE OF DRIED-UP DELTA
OF KERIYA RIVER.

284. HALT AMIDST DEAD JUNGLE ON LEFT BANK OF DRY RIVER BED IN ANCIENT DELTA OF KERIYA RIVER.

Jasvant Singh and myself in foreground.

to ascertain this, and luckily all clouds had now disappeared for some days past. So Lal Singh was left behind with the theodolite near a row of tamarisk-covered hillocks we passed at 11 A.M., while I pushed on to the south. The Shahyar men had again become very downcast, and the increasing frequency of wild camels' droppings failed to rouse confidence. Luckily the going was easy, the dunes being quite low. After nine miles from our last camp I found myself suddenly on the left bank of a wide river bed, cut to a depth of twenty or thirty feet and only partially filled by dunes. Its breadth was more than 150 yards.

Deep hollows showed here and there at its bottom below banks of hard mud, and one of these tempted me to try digging a well. The camels were far behind, and thus no time would be lost if we failed. To my delighted surprise the men after a few feet struck what felt like damp sand, and as the digging continued with vigour in spite of the threatening vicinity of a big dune, water was at last reached at a depth of fourteen feet. But it oozed out very slowly, and the sand of the sides for several feet from the bottom kept falling in. The whole of the well led through fine river sand, and I kept wondering how long this would hold under the pressure of the dune which towered above the mouth at the distance of only a few feet. The subsoil water thus reached was some forty feet below the level of the nearest bank.

The caravan was, of course, halted in spite of the shortness of the day's march, for such a chance was not lightly to be missed. Not till late in the evening had water gathered sufficiently for the immediate need of all; and, in spite of men being kept at work in batches all through the night, only four half-filled Mussucks were ready by daybreak, and the ponies got but a few glassfuls.

Our march on February 9th opened hopefully. The discovery of water seemed to justify confidence in our dry river bed as the right guide; and the imposing width with which it stretched ahead, two to three hundred yards broad, and for some miles almost straight, gave a sense of space and freedom (Fig. 284). The tracks of wild camels frequently crossed the flat sands filling the bed. But more

curious was the finding of a worked flint on a patch of bare
clay.   It was a clear proof that this desolate region had
known human beings at least in the Stone Age.   The
river vanished after some four miles under smothering
dunes ; but passing through dead forest and low tamarisk
cones due south we found ourselves suddenly back again
on its bank.   As we followed it farther living poplars
increased in such number by its banks that even the low-
spirited Shahyar men began to believe in our nearing the
real river end.   The appearance of dead reeds in thick
beds was greeted with elation, and one of the Shahyar men
triumphantly picked up a piece of charred wood, the first
proof, we thought, of man's near presence.

Yet this glimmer of confidence did not last long.
When after crossing a great bend of the river through
dead forest we touched it again on the east bank, the look
of the bed was more desolate than ever.   We had now
closely approached the latitude where, according to Hedin's
map, the actual river with its jungle belt ended.   Yet vainly
did we look out for the live reeds and scrub which our
camels were needing so badly.   Huge dunes rolled across
the deep bed of the river, fully four hundred yards across
where we halted, and the patches of clay emerging between
them were perfectly dry.

The attempt to dig a well proved fruitless.   The hired
camels were showing signs of exhaustion.   Our own were
far bigger and better adapted for desert work,—were they
not bred in the Keriya jungle, and probably distant kindred
of the wild camels with the tracks of which we were now
so familiar ?   Yet even they felt the pinch, and used to
approach me with pathetic appeals for bread.   How glad
should I have been to afford them a really good treat of this
cherished luxury !   But a ten-pound loaf disappeared only
too quickly among these seven hungrily gaping mouths,
and our supply of flour and water for baking with was
getting too low for such additional customers.

February 10th was a day full of anxious uncertainty.
After little more than a mile on our march southward the
river bed, so imposing before, became completely buried
under big dunes.   As we moved on all trace of living

vegetation vanished. Even the tamarisks on their sand-cones were all dead. The approach of sterile and forbidding ridges of sand from the east decided me, after some four miles, to steer to the south-west. This brought us, after a time, back again to living tamarisk scrub in a depression. But this was so closely hemmed in by big sand-cones that it looked like a veritable trap in this treacherous dead delta. The thought struck me in this sombre maze how much better it would be to face a sea of dunes, barren but open, if our supplies and the animals' strength should give out before water was reached.

In a gloomy hollow between two high tamarisk cones the men thought they could discover traces of moisture in the sand. So a party was left behind under Ibrahim Beg's direction to try and dig a well. I myself had my hopes roused far more by the wide view which from the top of a high ridge suddenly opened over sandy jungle to the south. We had only covered eleven miles, when the sight of many fine Toghraks still alive made the camel-men eagerly plead for a halt. The heaps of dry leaves beneath the trees would offer some grazing for the poor beasts. There could be no doubt that the spot was a regular feeding-ground for wild camels. Their tracks were exceedingly frequent among the trees, and some looked perfectly fresh. Most were pointing southwards, and there, we concluded, must be the water whence the animals had come from. But how far might it be yet?

For our ponies and camels the need of water was now pressing. So Naik Ram Singh and myself set out in different directions to seek for likely places to dig a well. The rows of big Toghraks all aligned from north to south gave a park-like look to the sandy jungle; but though I struck another broad river bed before I had gone a mile or so southward, no damp spot could be found anywhere at its bottom. From a high tamarisk cone on the bank I was scanning the horizon dark with scrub and Toghraks, and yet without any encouraging sign, when I heard the Naik shouting from a distance. He had an exciting tale to tell when he came up panting. His search for moist sand had been as futile as mine; but, going to the south-east, he had come across what seemed almost better—the footprints of two men.

I hastened, of course, back with the Naik, and soon verified his discovery. There could be no doubt that we had before us the track of two men, faint or effaced in some places, but clear enough where scrub or low dunes had afforded shelter. The footprints led to a high cone commanding a wide view of the jungle. The hunters—for clearly such the men must have been—had ascended it for a look-out, since their footsteps turned thence sharply to the south-east. They now followed closely the track of some camels, no doubt the game they had been looking out for.

It was getting dark before we could trace their tracks much farther. But I had seen enough to convince me that we could not do better on the morrow than try and follow the footprints back to where the hunters must have camped. The only question was: had they come from a well or the river, or had they brought ice to their last camping-place. There were no questions of this sort to damp the joy of our people in camp. Ibrahim Beg had just brought in the men who had vainly laboured at a well down to a depth of sixteen feet. The great news we could give was the best antidote for the resulting dejection. Some had, evidently, made up their mind that they would never reach the abode of men—or water—again in life! Only the poor ponies, for which we could spare no drink from the half-filled Mussucks of our last well, remained without cheer that evening.

Unusual alacrity prevailed on the morning of February 11th throughout the camp, and by rousing Ibrahim Beg at 4 A.M. I managed to get the camels to move off before sunrise. The hillock which the two hunters had ascended was soon reached, and taking the cleverest of the party ahead we set out to track the footprints along the route they had come. It proved an exciting and by no means easy task. Wherever they led along the crest of dunes or on the lee slope, the traces had become faint and often completely effaced. Some two miles to the south they disappeared in a tangle of dead brushwood. The tracks of wild camels were here exceedingly numerous, and as most of these seemed to come from the south or south-south-west, parallel to the river bed, we thought it best to continue in that direction. We had not gone more than a mile when shouts from some of the men who had spread out in line for a wider search told us that the track had been picked up again. This time the footprints led close along the traces of two camels, and as the camels' feet had left depressions in the sand less easily effaced, the tracking once more became easier. So the chase went on quite merrily for miles. The camels and their pursuers had followed no straight line, but crossed the old river bed again and again. The dunes which had in most places smothered this made heavy going; and what with the many climbs up steep slopes of sand and the hard marching of so many days with scant rations of water, our human pack became sadly straggling. Only Ibrahim Beg kept steadily up with me.

A curious change in the colour of the dunes in and along the river bed, now more greyish than yellow, at first roused hopes that the real river was near. Just thus the high sand had looked near Kara-dong and along the Khotan Darya near Rawak. But this illusion vanished as the number of live Toghraks steadily decreased on the banks. Amidst the dead forest extending on the east bank we came at last upon a sign of life, but of life which might have passed away long centuries ago. Three Toghrak stems roughly cut as if for supporting a roof probably marked an old shepherd's shelter. But the posts were quite white and fissured with age and exposure. Close by the men discovered on a patch of ground, left bare of sand, what seemed to be cow dung. But there was no antiquarian test to gauge the age of such relics and the period when herdsmen had lived here.

After about nine miles we again came upon a group of fine old Toghraks still alive. Here we lost the hunters' footprints, and when my breathless human pack had spotted them again, the track to our dismay took a decided turn to the south-east amidst barren dunes. There was no 'Kötek' here to shelter the footprints, and the search for them became so difficult, and the look of the sandy waste so discouraging, that after a couple of miles we decided to resume our southward course as the safest. Over high ridges of sand we regained the bed followed during the morning. But shortly afterwards all traces of it disappeared under heavy dunes.

The Shahyar men, now that the hopeful excitement of the morning had worn out, trudged on more heavily than ever. I, too, felt the depressing effect of the death-bound waste through which we now steered by the compass. High sand-cones, with dead tamarisk clumps on the top, closed in around us. Nowhere a living bush or tree. Vainly I climbed up the sand cones and ridges to catch a glimpse of the river bed which we had been following. Yet suddenly, when the sun was setting and I had almost abandoned all hope of securing a few living Toghraks for our poor camels to feed upon, the screen of dead tamarisk cones opened, and we emerged once more on a short reach of open river bed. Was it the same we had followed in the morning or another channel of this confusing desert delta? Little enough it mattered as things now stood. A look at the few patches of hard clayey soil exposed in the bed showed that there was no hope of reaching water here. Yet the men, driven by thirst, settled down in sullen despair to digging a well. After eight feet or so no trace of moisture appeared, and the work was stopped.

CHAPTER LXXXVII

SALT MARSH OR ICE?

It was a dismal camp. There was nothing for the camels to eat but the branches of a few old Toghraks still alive by the banks. Glad I was that the patient, hardy animals, upon the strength of which our safety depended, took kindly to the twigs I had cut for them! No doubt the sap in the latter was refreshing. Even our hard-tried ponies, which had tasted no water for three days, munched this strange fodder greedily.

The time had now come when a final effort became imperative to locate the actual river and reach water. The only safe course open was to reconnoitre straight through to the east and west, and with a view to this I made our arrangements for the next day. We should march due south for another eight miles or so, and after a sun-observation for latitude Lal Singh and myself would set out in opposite directions with food for three days and practically no kit. By hard marching we could hope to extend our reconnaissances some twenty-five miles to east and west, and return within forty-eight hours to the camp where the men and animals were to rest. Then the whole party would move to wherever we might have found water in river or well.

Three much-reduced bags and two iron tanks of ice represented our available water-supply, sufficient to see us humans through six more days if rations, as for some days back, were kept limited to about one pint per diem for each man. It was a small enough allowance, considering that food, too, had to be prepared with it. With some self-restraint it just allayed the worst of thirst. But how was one to preach restraint to weary and improvident people like our Shahyar men? Some of them quaffed off their water ration almost as soon as it had been poured into their gourds. I felt more pity for the poor dumb ponies which now showed signs of real distress, and was glad when we managed to squeeze out of the frozen Mussucks a glassful of muddy liquid for each of them—all that was left of the water brought away from the last well. For 'Dash,' alert and unconcerned as ever, a saucerful spared from my cup of tea was fortunately quite sufficient, and this faithful companion caused me no special anxiety. But the ponies would soon succumb if water was not reached, and I counted the cartridges in the holster of my revolver to make sure of the means for putting them out of pain if the time came.

It was an anxious night for me. The disposition of the Shahyar men had grown so disquieting that special precautions seemed advisable to prevent a rush upon our ice-supply. The ice-bags had been carefully sewn up and stacked with the iron tanks close to Lal Singh's tent. Twice before midnight I approached to make sure that the precious store was safe, and had the satisfaction of being challenged by the ever watchful and resolute Surveyor. That I had an assistant so energetic and cheerful by my side was a comfort for which I never felt so grateful as during this trying time.

I was awake soon after 3 A.M.; and long before day-break we might have started, had not despair and unreasoning fear driven the Shahyar men into an attempt at ill-disguised mutiny. When the camels ought to have been loaded, they crowded before me and in menacing tones declared their refusal to march with us any farther. Thought of flight northward had been tempting them for days past into what was bound to prove their destruction. This I knew only too well, and explained that they could not possibly find their way back to the Tarim in safety, and threatened to use force against any one attempting such foolish desertion. Amongst other arguments I told them that it was only in their own interest that I refused to discharge them; for otherwise we should profit by their departure, as our ice-supply would last much longer without them. Whether it was some comprehension of the justice of my arguments, or merely the fear of force, the men fell to their tasks again, but with sullen looks betraying something akin to desperation. Tokhta, old Khalil's son, cut the most miserable figure of all.

I had decided to again steer due south, and a conspicuous ridge of high sand sighted the previous evening in that direction served as a useful landmark. Leaving Naik Ram Singh and Jasvant Singh, both armed, in charge of the baggage and of all the men except two needed for the plane-table and cyclometer, I pushed ahead with Lal Singh. After two miles or so the dry bed dropped away to our right. Tracks of hares had been frequent among the Toghraks, all coming from the south. Was it thither that the animals went for water? But our hopes had been disappointed too often for us to put faith in such signs.

Then we emerged on a wide depression covered with low bare dunes. Here in long rows stood small Toghraks which had died while still young, just as I had seen them seven years before near the site of Kara-dong, along side channels which the Keriya River had deserted at no distant period. The sight of some trees still living, not on the usual sand-cones, but growing on almost level ground, instilled in me for a moment something like hope. But soon the outlook became more depressing than ever. Big barren dunes rose before us in a chain running approximately south-west, and only at rare intervals there emerged between them the dreary cones with a tangle of dead tamarisk.

I had hoped against hope that the ridge once ascended would show us ground where I could leave our camp with some chance of subsistence for the camels which had practically fasted for a fortnight. But the view which opened before me was of oppressive desolation. Wide, indeed, it was, extending to a broken chain of Dawans far away on the eastern horizon with a vast valley-like depression in front. But in it the eye caught nothing but rolling dunes of yellow sand and grey patches of eroded clay soil. A light haze hung over this forbidding landscape and strangely fused its colours into death-like paleness. It looked as if we had now neared the extreme edge of this awful sand delta which had held us fast so long. Was it to any purpose to reconnoitre the absolute desert east-wards?

But the high ridge of sand which had guided us so far now rose quite close on our right, and was too good a survey station to be missed. Fully 300 feet high it seemed, and the expanse of bare clayey ground at its foot, overrun only by low dunes, made it look still more imposing. The crests of the big dunes forming its base rose up steeply, with curves of beautiful sharpness. We clambered up in haste to the first shoulder; but the view obtained here at about 150 feet above the plain was so unpromising that Lal Singh, who needed time to prepare for his latitude observation at mid-day, descended in dismay. I ordered him to move the caravan back for camping to where we had left the last living Toghraks, and then alone with 'Dash' hurried up to the summit of the steep slope for the sake of assuring my conscience.

From the top the panorama was grand, but also desperate at first sight. I was searching the ground with my prismatic glasses for indications of living jungle, when suddenly to the south-south-east some narrow bands of white caught my eye. Looking more closely through the binocular I could scarcely believe my eyes when they showed me in four distinct places glittering streaks of what could only be ice—or else salt efflorescence. The distance was fully four miles.

What joy rose in my mind at the chance of finding water thus suddenly revealed! It might be that these were the four small salt lakes which Hedin had heard of from shepherds as situated at the very end of the eastern branch of the river. But however undrinkable their water, they would, if frozen, give us fresh ice. And even if they had since dried up completely, they would at least enable us to ascertain our position and guide us in the right direction. So in haste I shouted the order to Ibrahim Beg below to let the caravan move on. When after taking careful bearings of those saving streaks of white I ran down the steep sand slopes and joined the men, all were in high-strung excitement. I could not restrain myself from announcing the hope of finding ice, but I also let them know at once that it might prove but a thin sheet over salt water. With the terribly barren desert before us it seemed almost a mockery to call up visions of pure water, and I did my best to prepare myself and the rest for disappointment.

The whole caravan was now moving ahead at a pace such as it had never attained since we entered the desert. Even the slowest of the men mounted to the top of every high dune which might offer a glimpse. But it was only after two miles or so that their impatient rush was rewarded by the sight of a streak of what now looked decidedly like ice, and could not be a Fata Morgana. Yet the sand was as barren as ever, and no trace of vegetation showed ahead except a few scattered Toghraks of great age. Why should a lakelet, however salt, be without the fringe of reeds and scrub which we had invariably found about the salt springs and marshes of the Lop-nor region? And then we noticed in the sand plentiful footprints of a small bird which the men knew as living near fresh water.

A mile farther ahead a halt had to be made to unload the theodolite needed by Lal Singh for his mid-day observation. So restless and eager were the men now that I had to exert my authority to assure a sufficient number remaining to help the Surveyor with the reloading. We had scarcely moved ahead more than a few hundred yards when a figure was seen running frantically towards us. It was young Turdi, my second camel-man, who had previously broken ahead in his eagerness to make sure of the water. What he waved in his hands was soon recognized as a big cake of ice, and joyful shouts rose at once all along the hurrying line of men.

It was ice, a big sheet of ice, Turdi reported as soon as he had recovered breath for articulate speech, and flowing through it a current of fresh water! It was the real river, then, we had struck, changed to a new bed in this desolate desert. Half a mile farther ahead we should reach it.

Quickly all the men were munching the bits of the ice cake
which Turdi distributed with no small satisfaction.   There
was relief now from all doubts, and shining contentment on
the faces of the mutineers of the morning.

The dunes in front of us were so high that we did not
realize the full width of the river until we almost dropped
down over the last steep sand slope on to its ice.   In
a glittering sheet of clear ice from one hundred and
sixty to two hundred yards broad it stretched away to
the north.   For the greatest part the ice formed only a
thin sheet resting directly on the mud of the bottom.   But
where the current had cut into our bank the water, a couple
of feet deep, flowed in an open channel about twelve feet
broad at the rate of about half a yard per second.   The
men rushed down to the brink, and bending down on
hands and knees took time over their drinks as probably
never before (Fig. 286).

Moving down the river I soon found a little bay where
the dunes had left patches of ground bare, with dead scrub
and trees, attesting that here, too, the river had once flowed
long before its latest migration.   Here my tent was pitched
in what I called my dead arbour (Fig. 287).   Ponies
and camels all seemed full of life in sight of the glorious
water, and after having been given a good rest to cool
down were allowed to drink *ad libitum*.   What a joy it
was to watch them as they took their long, long draughts
until they swelled visibly!   Then the poor hard-tried
ponies, which had been thirsting for three days, fell greedily
to the dry leaves collected for them from the few live
Toghraks around.

For the camels, which had marched so bravely without
once tasting water during the last thirteen days and under
heavy loads (Fig. 285), there was, alas! but the scantiest
fare within reach.   The Toghraks were too few to satisfy
their hunger with dry foliage, and even of that hardiest of
scrubs, the yellow ' Kamghak,' which made its appearance at a sheltered inlet, not enough could be found for
even a pretence of grazing.   Camels, otherwise so little
discriminating, do not ordinarily touch this terribly dry
and thorny plant, growing in curious ball-like masses.

285. CAMELS WAITING FOR THEIR FIRST DRINK AFTER ARRIVAL AT KERIYA RIVER.

286. SHAHYAR LABOURERS SLAKING THEIR THIRST AFTER REACHING ICE OF KERIYA
RIVER END.

287. MY TENT AT FIRST CAMP AFTER REACHING THE KERIYA RIVER END.
Ibrahim Beg in foreground.

288. BY THE NEW BED OF THE DYING KERIYA RIVER.
On right Ibrahim Beg and labourer with cyclometer.

But now, Hassan Akhun assured me, they greedily fell upon it.

As to my own treat, it came when after six days of missing ablutions I could indulge in a tub. At first it seemed an unholy procedure to use precious water in so lavish a manner. But when I could at last sit down to my modest ' Tiffin ' and breakfast combined, the big cups of tea tasted doubly refreshing for the liberal wash bestowed upon the outer man.

CHAPTER LXXXVIII

AFTER the sixteen days' continuous tramp across dunes a short halt was imperative for both man and beast. So the 13th of February was spent in enjoyable rest at our river camp (Fig. 287). There was plenty for us all to do, writing up notes for me, and for the men much mending, from the camels' 'Shotas' to worn-out boots, my own included. Delightful peace prevailed, and now that we were not ourselves on the move the total absence of life was more than ever impressive. Since we left the Tarim I had seen no living creature and had grown accustomed to a quasi-dead world. Here, too, by the side of life-giving water flowing past us in abundance, the banks were silent and dead. It was quite clear that the ever errant river had formed a new bed, and that the sands through which it flowed had not yet had time to lose their sterility.

Now that the river had been found, the best course seemed to follow it upwards. It was sure to bring us sooner or later to the belt of living forest where grazing would be available for camels and ponies. The Surveyor's astronomical observation had shown that we were still some way to the north of the latitude of the Kara-dong ruins. But there was nothing to indicate whether the old river bed lay to the east or west of our position. By making reconnaissances in both directions we could, no doubt, soon clear this up ; but this would have immobilized the caravan and entailed further fasting for the poor camels. So by daybreak of February 14th we set out for the south by the left bank of the river. Its bed made many bends, and the high dunes which lined it almost all the way made heavy going.

Vegetation, one might have thought, would quickly follow the presence of water.   Yet not a trace of it could be seen until, after some six miles, behind a transverse ridge of dunes we came upon a lake-like widening of the bed (Fig. 288).

It was evident from its formation that when the river had first taken this new course, probably with only a part of its volume, its waters had got dammed up here for some time.   Then when the level of the small lake thus formed, about half a mile long and a quarter wide, had risen sufficiently, the opposing ridge of dunes was quickly worn through and an outlet found to the north.   The cutting led through dunes fifty to sixty feet high, and the slopes were still very steep.   In the lake bed with its soft curving shores some small islands of sand had been left, protected by old tamarisk growth.   And here we came upon the first few stalks of living Kumush.   I had promised for days past a reward to whoever should sight it first, and was glad enough to pay it to Mullah, our carpenter and scribe combined, who always kept well ahead.

But the hope of jungle near at hand was disappointed. For the rest of the march the banks grew, if possible, even more sterile.   Not a single live Toghrak came in view, and barren ridges of sand limited the horizon.   Towards the end of the day's march small winding inlets or wholly detached pools became more frequent.   Judging from the plentiful tracks, they seemed the favourite drinking-places of hares, foxes, boars, and other dwellers in the riverine jungle.   Here a few birds flew past us, the first living creatures we had seen for more than a fortnight, and just as we halted for camp a flight of wild duck came into view keeping northward.   Were these hardy winter sojourners, or the advance-guard of flocks migrating from Sub-Himalayan marshes?

Around our camping-place large dead Toghraks abounded.   But for the camels there was still nothing to feed upon but thick tufts of Kamghak.   It was time to push on to more nourishing pasture.   The hired camels were getting terribly thin, and one of them, though carrying only a nominal load, was not brought in till a late hour. Next morning, on climbing a high ridge of sand a couple of miles farther on, where the river was turning to the south-west, we saw at last thick groves of living poplars eastwards across the river, amongst ice-covered lagoons and river-branches.   There was no trace of reeds to tempt a crossing.

On descending we found that the Toghrak jungle extended for a short distance to our side of the river. Here we saw signs, too, of the visits of shepherds, lopped branches of poplars, and old sheep droppings.   But after we had passed for less than a mile through the edge of a sandy jungle area, the river once more entered a zone of absolutely barren dunes.   The many lake-like inlets of the river here began to be troublesome.   The ice was now fast thawing, and though we could with care just pick our way across the lagoons, the camels were forced to great détours.   From another high sand ridge we ascended I made out what looked like a continuous belt of Toghraks running south at some distance from the right bank of the river.   It seemed worth while to abandon our course for this, if only reeds and scrub could be found there for the camels.   So in order to prospect we pushed across to the right bank.

The bed here was fully 300 yards broad, and the ice had mostly melted along the banks where the water could be seen flowing in channels ten to twelve feet broad and about three feet deep.   Before attempting to cross with the camels I was anxious to make sure of the ground ahead.   So I hurried eastwards with Ibrahim Beg and a few men.   After covering scarcely a mile between dunes and cones with live tamarisks we came upon a second bed, some 150 yards wide and with an open channel of water. We crossed this by wading.   But when after a few hundred yards more we emerged on a third river bed nearly half a mile broad and with the nearest channel of running water at least four and a half feet deep, I realized that to trust our camels and baggage to this tangle of newly formed courses with possible quicksands would mean too great a risk.   So after wistfully longing for water we now began to feel annoyed by its over-abundance.

As we resumed our march south the view of the river

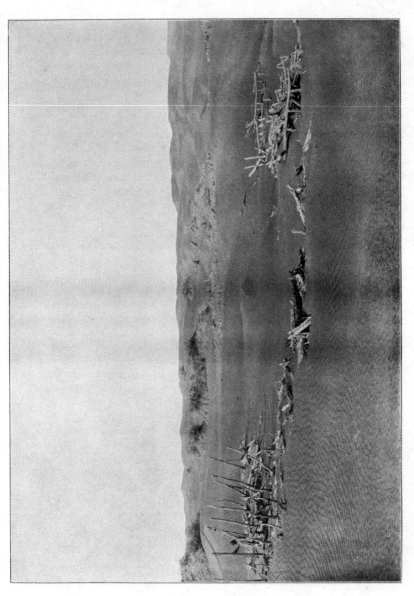

289. ANCIENT QUADRANGLE PARTIALLY BURIED UNDER DUNES, KARA-DONG SITE.

On left Tila Bai standing amidst timber remains of south-west corner.

290. ANCIENT DWELLING NEAR SOUTH END OF KARA-DONG SITE BEFORE EXCAVATION.

291. THE SAME ANCIENT DWELLING OF KARA-DONG SITE IN COURSE OF EXCAVATION.

grew quite imposing. Soon we came to a point where, from the top of a ridge covered with living tamarisks, we could overlook the parting of no less than three distinct branches. The main bed above their junction seemed fully three-fourths of a mile broad, and its ice-sheet shone rosy in the setting sun. What a glorious spot for skating this would have made a week or so earlier, if I had given in to my secret wish and burdened my baggage with a pair of skates! The ground on our side now seemed to grow more open. Amidst the low dunes tamarisk bushes were seen growing without the usual cones, and live poplars became more and more frequent. Where they first gathered into a grove we decided to halt for the night and to give our poor beasts the benefit of the dry leaves.

The morning of February 16th was close and cloudy, the minimum temperature of seventeen degrees of frost appearing quite warm. We now saw the river some miles ahead bend to the south-east and disappear between two high ridges of sand. After skirting big lagoons for about two miles we came at last upon the first beds of living reeds. How the ponies relished the high waving stalks in spite of their dryness! A short distance beyond we crossed an old dry bed joining in from the south-west, and among the Toghraks on its sides the tracks of sheep became numerous.

Suddenly on ascending the sandy bank a sound struck me as of bleating at a distance. None of the men with me had heard it. Yet in their frantic eagerness to come into touch with man again they rushed ahead. Soon the Mullah was shouting that he had seen sheep. But no other pair of eyes could discern them. The men were wavering between hope and despondency when on a distant sand hillock I sighted a little black figure. The sharp eyes of Ibrahim Beg, whose attention I called to it, at once recognized that it was a man.

A shout of joy went up from the men, and now began a wild chase which threatened to frighten our game away. How should a lonely shepherd of the Keriya River jungle, shy folk as I knew them, not be frightened by the sudden rush of such a crowd of people as was never seen in this region? The black figure descended the hillock as if to run away, then halted again as we shouted, ducked, and re-appeared ; but no command or friendly appeal would induce the man to advance and meet us. At last the men were upon him like dogs upon their prey, and approaching with my pack I found a lusty-looking young herdsman, in the quaint semi-savage get-up I remembered so well, goat-skins for shoes and leggings, a rough sheep-skin thrown over the body, and the head surmounted by a huge fur cap. The tame men from Shahyar might have been frightened if they had met such a figure alone. But under the uncouth appearance a good Muhammadan greeted them. To me, too, no 'Salam alaikum' had ever sounded more welcome.

My first question, of course, was as to where we were. When the man gave the name of Yoghan-kum for his grazing-ground our position at once became clear. Already the day before I had told the Surveyor and Ibrahim Beg that, judging from our plane-table work as checked by the last mid-day observation, we must be close to the latitude of Tonguz-baste. There, as I had observed in 1901, the river which had so far flowed in a well-defined bed first showed a tendency to strike off into branches. I remembered Yoghan-kum well as the name of a high ridge of sand lining its west bank just above the point where various old beds spread out like fingers.

Thus, after all, the old river course which Hedin had followed, and which I myself had seen in 1901 still full of water, lay to the east of the route we had moved by. At first look this was rather disconcerting, since according to our plane-table we were still a good deal east of the longitude previously assumed for Tonguz-baste. But luckily no such discrepancy, whatever its explanation, could affect our position. I knew that we had now reached the luxuriant jungle lining the Keriya River along its old bed, and that all troubles and doubts of this desert crossing were ended.

Guided by the young shepherd, whom a liberal present made forget his fright, we crossed the river a few miles higher up where it flowed still under a sound cover of ice. Marching down to the shepherd camp of Tonguz-baste, I was able to ascertain the exact point where the river, some four years earlier, had broken through the high sand ridges of Yoghan-kum to the north and formed the head of its new bed. The diversion had caused much trouble to the shepherds; for the vegetation lower down on the old bed was steadily drying up, and water along the former grazing-grounds was obtainable only from deep wells.

The river bed I had seen in 1901 was completely dry, but no dunes had yet gathered over it. This and the fact that no vegetation whatever had sprung up as yet by the new bed were significant proofs of the time needed to mature the full results of these riverine changes. That these changes were produced by the gradual silting up of the beds, which forces the river after a period to seek a new channel or to turn back into one long abandoned, could be seen here quite clearly. No less than four large river courses, all dry, diverged above Tonguz-baste, and, no doubt, all in succession had taken generations to develop their belts of jungle, whether now dead or still struggling with the withering dryness. It all helped in forming some estimate as to the length of the ages which had seen the growth of the terrible desiccated delta now happily left behind us.

CHAPTER LXXXIX

MORE TAKLAMAKAN RUINS

THE ground we had passed through had its own fascination, and survey work on it offered considerable geographical interest. Yet I was glad when, after a day's much-needed rest, I could by February 19th, 1908, resume archaeological labour at the Kara-dong site, which the river by its latest change has again approached after long centuries.

On my first visit in March 1901, a succession of sand-storms prevented a complete examination of the site. The shifting of dunes had since laid bare a number of small ruined dwellings (Figs. 290, 291), then deeply buried beneath the sand, half-a-mile or so to the south of the large quadrangle previously explored (Fig. 289). The excavation of them, now effected with the help of my Shahyar men and a small contingent raised from among the shepherds, furnished definite evidence that a small agricultural settlement, and not merely a frontier guard-post, had existed here far away in the desert at some period during the early centuries of our era.

Since none of the shepherds and hunters we got hold of knew anything of old remains farther down, I decided to move up the river in order to meet as early as possible the party of my old 'treasure-seeking' guides from Khotan whom, by an arrangement effected with Mr. Macartney's kind help *via* Kashgar, I had ordered up before starting from Kuchar. By February 25th I had the satisfaction of seeing this concentration across a vast space of desert duly achieved; for on this day a dozen familiar Khotan 'Taklamakanchis,' under the direction of Roze, old Turdi's quondam acolyte, joined me near my old camping-ground at

293. MENDICANT PILGRIM OR 'DIWANA' AT BURHANUDDIN'S
DESERT SHRINE, KERIYA RIVER.

292. PULLAT MULLAH AND IBRAHIM OF KHOTAN,
'TREASURE-SEEKERS.'

294. BUDDHIST SHRINE ON TAMARISK CONE AT SITE OF FARHAD-BEG-YAILAKI,
IN COURSE OF EXCAVATION.

295. REMAINS OF BUDDHIST SHRINE AT KARA-YANTAK, NEAR DOMOKO, IN COURSE
OF EXCAVATION.

Kochkar-öghil.   My joy at again greeting these experienced
searchers of 'old things' (Fig. 292) was much increased by
the exact local information they brought, in addition to my
mail bag from Khotan.   The men from Shahyar were now
discharged, well pleased with their liberal wages and an
ample *viaticum* in silver with which to make their way to
Khotan, and thence by the trade route homewards.   Alas!
by the time I revisited Keriya a month later I heard how
most of these shifty fellows had used the first opportunity
to gamble away with the dice what they had earned by
their trying tramp through the sands.

After a hearty welcome from my old friends, the aged
Sheikhs of Burhanuddin's desert shrine, and a quaint
mendicant pilgrim they sheltered (Fig. 293), I marched
with my band of 'treasure-seekers' by a new route to the
desert belt north of the oasis of Domoko.   There, in the
deceptive zone of tamarisk-covered sand-cones, they had succeeded in tracking an extensive but scattered series of ruined
dwellings with several Buddhist shrines, which had escaped
our search when in 1906 we worked at Khadalik, some
eight miles farther south.   The ruins of this site, which
from an adjoining jungle grazing-ground we called Farhad-
Beg-yailaki, had suffered much through the vicinity of
'Old Domoko,' a village which, as described in my former
narrative, was occupied until sixty or seventy years ago.
Yet the excavations which I was able to effect rapidly
during the first half of March, with a relatively large
number of labourers easily recruited from Domoko, were
rewarded by valuable finds of well-preserved manuscripts
in Sanskrit, painted panels, and tablets inscribed in the
language of old Khotan.   The time of abandonment here,
as at Khadalik, proved to have been the second half of
the eighth century A.D.

Some of our best finds at this site were made within
a small Buddhist shrine which occupied a quite unusual
position, emerging from the side of a tamarisk-covered sand-
cone about forty feet high (Fig. 294).   The relatively
well preserved cella with its massive walls of clay must have
been built when this cone was much lower; for the sand
of the latter now rose fully eighteen feet above the floor.

Among the frescoes covering the walls inside was the fine panel reproduced in Plate XI. B, the subject of which M. Foucher has identified with Hariti, the Indian goddess of smallpox. In full accord with the euphemistic conception exemplified by a well-known Graeco-Buddhist statue from Gandhara, the dread goddess, the destroyer of children, is represented as a kindly, richly dressed matron with young boys playing around her arms and shoulders. Her worship was probably quite as popular in the Tarim Basin as in ancient India, and shows features which have earned for her from M. Foucher the designation of a ' Buddhist Madonna.' The resemblance is close enough in the case of a picture of Hariti, excavated by the German expedition of Dr. von Lecoq at Turfan, to have at first caused some thought of a Christian Madonna being intended.

The fact of this cella having been originally built on the top of a tamarisk cone supplies us with two indications of geographical interest. It gives an exact gauge for the rate of growth here of these curious sand formations. It also proves that the ground upon which the village site of Farhad-Beg was established within or before the eighth century A.D., then already showed physical features closely akin to those now observed here and at other points near the border line between the cultivated area and the scrub-covered edge of the Taklamakan.

As if to illustrate the change which might be brought about along this line by human activity, without any very marked change in the climatic conditions, I found that irrigation was now being rapidly extended from the new colony of Malak-alagan, first visited by me in 1901, towards the deserted village of ' Old Domoko.' At Khadalik the site of the ruins I had excavated had since 1906 been actually brought under cultivation for spring crops, and villagers were already prospecting about Farhad-Beg for suitably level spots to which surplus water could be conducted off from the lower reach of the Domoko Yar. My work at both places had thus been accomplished just in time.

I had occasion subsequently, at the two oases of

PLATE XI.A. FRESCO SHOWING SCENE FROM THE LIFE OF BUDDHA; FROM RUINED BUDDHIST TEMPLE EXCAVATED AT 'MING-OI' SITE, SHIKCHIN, KARA-SHAHR.

(CHAP. LXXXIII. SCALE, ONE-SIXTH).

PLATE XI.B. FRESCO REPRESENTING HARITI, THE INDIAN GODDESS OF SMALL-POX; FROM RUINED BUDDHIST SHRINE EXCAVATED AT FARHAD-BEG SITE, DOMOKO.

(CHAP. LXXXIX. SCALE, ONE-SIXTH).

Domoko and Gulakhma, to note ocular proofs of expand-ing cultivation and increasing prosperity. Since my visit of 1906 a large Bazar had sprung up at Domoko, entirely through local enterprise, and the belt of scrubby desert with tamarisk cones separating the two village tracts was being rapidly reduced by newly levelled fields ready for irrigation. And yet there were complaints of the summer floods having been generally below the mark during the last ten years. I have little doubt that increased pressure of population and other economic factors play an important part in these changes affecting what otherwise would be ideal ground for watching ' pulsatory desiccation' at work.

The remainder of March was spent in supplementary archaeological labours at a number of old sites, like Kara-yantak (Fig. 295), Ulugh-Mazar, and others along the desert which fringes the interesting area shown in the inset map of ' Oases of Chira, Gulakhma, Domoko,' and thence westwards to Khotan. The photograph reproduced in Fig. 296 shows my helpmates and myself, as united at the end of this winter campaign in the desert. My short halt at Khotan during the first days of April was made most pleasant by the welcome my old friends gave me, and by the satisfaction I felt at seeing all my antiques sent from Kuchar now safely stored in Akhun Beg's house.

But, perhaps, the greatest pleasure of all was that my dear old host was there to receive me in person (Fig. 52), safely home from that distant pilgrimage to Mecca for which he had so pluckily started a year and a half before. The portly old gentleman looked more cheerful than ever after all he had gone through during long days by rail across Russia and on the tossing seas. What a much-travelled man Akhun Beg had become in this short span of time, with his quaintly told experiences ranging from Samarkand to Stambul and Mecca the Holy, and from the Red Sea to Bombay, Kashmir, and the Kara-koram passes! And yet, as I camped in his garden, flushed with the short-lived glory of Turkestan spring-time, I could appreciate how proud and glad he was to be back again at his bright home in this thriving oasis. The plum and apricot trees, just in full bloom, were strewing my tent and the garden around with their blossoms as with fresh snow.

During my brief stay at Khotan I had to occupy myself, besides other immediate tasks, with arrangements for my return journey to India. But there was still a considerable programme of work to be finished northward, and I knew how soon the rapidly increasing heat would put a stop to all operations in the desert. So by April 5th I said good-bye again to old friends and familiar surroundings at Khotan, and started on the journey which in the end was to take me to Ak-su and the foot of the T'ien-shan. My first goal was supplied by certain ruins which my 'treasure-seeking' guides had succeeded in tracing near the northern-most outskirts of the Khotan oasis. I had taken care to have their exact position fixed beforehand by Rai Lal Singh while he was completing our surveys around Khotan. Thus near Kara-sai, a new outlying colony to the north-west, I recovered from a much-eroded site a number of small Buddhist relievos finely worked in true plaster of Paris, and remarkably well preserved in spite of the total decay of the building (Fig. 76, 8).

On my move there I could let Islam Beg, my old factotum of 1900, have the eagerly claimed satisfaction of affording me hospitality for a night in his newly built country house at Altunche. My recommendation, in return for zealous and effective services, had earned him six years before from P'an Ta-jên an appointment to the office of 'Mirab,' or canal charge, of his native canton of Kayash. By good administration he had managed to retain his official employment, and since my second visit in 1906 he had gained promotion to the office of Beg. It was a pleasure to see how well my old protégé had prospered, and to have local proof, too, with what wise moderation he had used his opportunities.

The sight of expanding cultivation which greeted me everywhere was most cheering. A big new canal, dug along the left bank of the Kara-kash River when my old friend P'an Ta-jên was Amban, had brought verdure over what was before a belt of sandy waste, and now formed the canton of Bogar-ming, for nearly a day's march north-

296. MY COMPANIONS AND MYSELF AT ULUGH-MAZAR, IN THE DESERT NORTH OF CHIRA.

From left to right, sitting: Chiang-ssŭ-yeh, myself with 'Dash,' Rai Bahadur Lal Singh.   Standing : Ibrahim Beg, Jasvant Singh, Naik Ram Singh.

297. RUINED FORT AND WATCH-TOWER ON MAZAR-TAGH RIDGE SEEN FROM WEST.
Below, in background, wide flood-bed of Khotan River.

298. DIGGING UP ANCIENT DOCUMENTS FROM REFUSE LAYERS BELOW RUINED FORT
OF MAZAR-TAGH.

ward. My visit to Ak-su was largely prompted by the wish
to see again the scholarly Mandarin who had helped me so
effectively as Tao-t'ai. So it was doubly gratifying to hear
his praises sung by all the cultivators who had come here
as hopelessly poor folk, and were now beginning to feel
themselves veritable ' Bais ' or men of substance.

Then I crossed eastwards the strip of absolutely sterile
desert which separates the Kara-kash and Yurung-kash
Rivers. At a most unpromising-looking spot near Mayak-
lik I came upon the remains of a large Buddhist temple
completely buried under high dunes. After a day's hard
digging there emerged walls decorated with colossal fresco
figures and inscribed stucco relievos of large size. Everything clearly indicated that this temple, like the great
Rawak Stupa on the opposite bank of the Yurung-kash,
belonged to the early centuries of our era. Unfortunately
here, too, as at Rawak, subsoil moisture due to the vicinity
of the river had caused all the woodwork to perish. It also
had softened the clay of the walls and relievos to such an
extent that the frescoes on the former collapsed one after
the other soon after exposure. As continued excavation
would have resulted in complete destruction, I had to be
content with photographs and the removal of some smaller
frescoes.

We then set out northward for Ak-su by the desert
route which leads down the Khotan River bed, at that
season practically dry. From Tawakkel onwards I had
the benefit of having my caravan guided by Kasim Akhun,
the experienced hunter, who with his father Merghen
Ahmad had accompanied me seven years before on my
expedition to Dandan-oilik. The hardy old man, alas! had
passed away some months earlier. I had already heard
vague reports about the existence of old remains on the
curious desert hill of Mazar-tagh, which, as the last offshoot of a low and almost completely eroded range from
the north-west, juts out to the left bank of the Khotan
River.

On April 16th I reached the hill, which rises with its
gaunt and barren cliffs of reddish sandstone some two
hundred feet above the wide river bed and the sandy

wastes by its side. My satisfaction was great when I
found its top occupied by the ruins of a small and relatively
well preserved fort (Fig. 297). This had clearly been built
to guard the route leading by the river. Half-way up on
the steep scarp overlooking the river a collection of staffs
with votive rags marked the supposed resting-place of
a saint, from which the hill takes its present name. The
whole made up a striking picture of desert scenery, the
death-like torpor of the red rocks and yellow sands being
heightened by the heat and glare which brooded over all.

The little fort, looking down from its precipitous height
like a true robbers' stronghold, had been burnt out long
ago ; yet its siege, or rather that of its rubbish heaps, kept
us busy for three long and hot days. Tibetan records on
wood and paper cropped up with miscellaneous relics when
we cleared out the few still traceable halls and quarters
inside. But their yield was trifling compared with that of
the masses of refuse thrown down by the occupants in the
course of long years on to the steep rock slopes below the
east face (Fig. 298). The conditions had been exceptionally favourable for their preservation. Not a particle of
moisture could rise from the river below to the height of
this barren sandstone ridge which was clear of any trace of
the humblest vegetation. An outlying and somewhat lower
ridge kept off dunes and prevented erosion by driving
sand.

It seemed like another Miran, with all the unspeakable
dirt which these old Tibetans seem to have accumulated
wherever they held posts, and with all its peculiar con-
comitant odours still fresh in my recollection. Buried in
the thick refuse layers lay Tibetan tablets and papers by
the hundreds, along with documents in Chinese and Brahmi
script, and rarer pieces in Uigur and some unknown writing.
The Tibetan records greatly predominated, pointing, as in
the case of Miran, to the period of Tibetan invasions during
the eighth and ninth centuries A.D. As far as yet examined
by my learned collaborator, Dr. A. H. Francke, they seem
to contain military reports, requisitions, and the like.

The dating has been fully confirmed by finds of coins
and the Chinese documents. Among the latter some large

and well-preserved sheets have, under M. Chavannes' examination, proved to contain an exact daily record of
expenses, very interesting in its details, kept by the monks
of a Buddhist establishment. The constant references
made to outlays on creature comforts and luxuries un-
thinkable in such a desert locality, indicate that this
curious monastic account must have found its way here
from a distance. Whatever the origin of this particular
piece may have been, it is certain that this lonely frontier
post in the desert, just like the ruined fort of Miran, serves
to mark the wide extent of Tibetan predominance after
Chinese control of the Tarim Basin was lost in T'ang times.

While I was busy with the digging I let the Surveyor
make a reconnaissance along the geologically interesting
hill range stretching away north-westwards. He was able
to follow it for over twelve miles, and saw it continuing
beyond for at least as great a distance. Considering the
bearing of this curious low range and the similarity of its
geological structure with that of the chain of rugged, isolated
hills subsequently visited near Maral-bashi and Tumshuk
beyond the Yarkand River, it appears very probable that it
forms the last remnant of an ancient mountain system
which jutted out south-eastwards into the Tarim Basin from
the outermost chain of the T'ien-shan. The never-ceasing
wind erosion of countless ages has reduced this remnant to
its present insignificant dimensions, and has so completely
broken its connection with those apparently isolated rock-
islands that Hedin, when crossing in 1896 the great area
of drift sand from the side of the Yarkand River, saw no
trace of its line.

CHAPTER XC

On April 20th I started from Mazar-tagh down the dry bed of the Khotan River for Ak-su. During the eight rapid marches which carried us north to the river's junction with the Tarim we suffered a good deal from the increasing heat of the desert and a succession of sand-storms. Such conditions made me realize with full intensity the experiences of Hedin on his first disastrous crossing of the Taklamakan in May of 1896. Kasim, who had met him afterwards during his enforced rest at the shepherd camp of Böksam, was able to show me the pool of fresh water, some twenty miles lower down on the right bank, which had proved the great traveller's saving when he struggled through from the 'sea of sand' exhausted by thirst. The constancy of these pools, found at considerable intervals along that side of the river bed where the current sets, and the delicious freshness of their water, furnish proof that there must be a steady flow of subsoil water making its way down the bed of the river, often over a mile wide, even at the driest season.

Lower down we passed for days through a network of old and new river beds where Kasim's guidance was welcome. Yet, when my thoughts went back to that terrible dried-up delta of the Keriya River, our route here, with plentiful water and grazing at the end of each hot day's march, seemed quite a luxurious line of progress. The only incident of the journey was provided by a tiger which prowled round our camp the night before we reached the Tarim, evidently on the look-out for a pony or donkey. 'Dash,' otherwise the soundest of sleepers, awakened me

299. MY CAMP IN A BEG'S GARDEN AT AK-SU.
In foreground Haji Abid, the Beg's son.

300. CROWD IN BAZAR STREET AT AK-SU.

301. P'AN TA-JÊN, TAO-T'AI OF AK-SU, MY OLD PATRON AND FRIEND.

by some furious barks; but nobody gave heed to his warning until next morning we came upon the huge footprints of the beast, which could be traced for over six miles along the caravan track from the Tarim.

We crossed the latter by a shepherds' ferry on the evening of April 27th, and after a heavy thunderstorm during the night were regaled next morning by a glorious vision of the big snowy range far away to the north of Ak-su. A huge ice-clad massif towering above the rest was, on the strength of the Russian map, identified by us as Khan-tengri, the highest known peak of the T'ien-shan, some hundred and thirty miles away in a straight line. It was a most refreshing welcome from the great 'Mountains of Heaven'; but within a few hours it vanished for good in the dust haze.

During the three long marches which carried us to the 'New Town' of Ak-su, I had ample opportunities for studying the striking contrast between the abundance of water available for irrigation in the big snow-fed river of Ak-su and the scanty and careless cultivation carried on in the narrow village belt along it. Here the undeveloped condition of what might become a series of flourishing oases had manifestly nothing to do with inadequate water. The difference between Khotan and Ak-su was brought home to me also by the strong 'Tartar' look and the churlish ways of the people (Fig. 300). A strong infusion of Kirghiz blood was subsequently proved by my anthropometrical observations.

At the district headquarters of Ak-su I found an excellent camping-place in the shady garden attached to a Beg's suburban mansion (Fig. 299), and next day had the great joy of greeting again my old Mandarin friend, P'an Ta-jên, the Tao-t'ai (Fig. 301). He looked as hale and was as kindly and simple in manners as when I last saw him at Khotan seven years before, and his scholarly interest in all my explorations remained unabated. The dignified but peaceful post at Ak-su just suited his learned habits and serenely disinterested ways. For him there was no chance of becoming a Nabob in any administrative charge, and I often wondered inwardly how a man of his honesty and single-mindedness could have made his way up the official ladder.

It was a satisfaction to me to thank my dear old friend in person for all the help he had extended to me from afar, and my stay, which I prolonged for his sake to five days, passed most pleasantly. During our daily forgatherings there was so much to tell him about the results of my two years' explorations, and so many cheerful reminiscences of old Khotan days to revive. I had brought a few specimens of my finds from the Tun-huang *Limes* and elsewhere for P'an Ta-jên's benefit, and to see him reverently handle and study those Han relics was a treat. It was the same with the advance copy of my *Ancient Khotan* volumes which I was able to show him.

The practical objects of my Ak-su visit were obtained at the same time. Through the kind help of P'an Ta-jên I secured the local assistance which Rai Lal Singh needed for the continuous survey he was to carry through the outer T'ien-shan range as far as the passes north of Kashgar. My Surveyor was most keen on this chance of independent work before our return to India; for twenty-four years of hard service all over Asia from Arabian deserts to Mongolia had in no way blunted his energy and ardour.

Honest Chiang-ssŭ-yeh, too, well deserved a special effort on my part. P'an Ta-jên's friendship was to be utilized in order to obtain for Chiang the chance of official employment he had vainly striven for ever since he first came to the New Dominion some twenty-five years before. So a detailed report on his former services and all he had done for me was drawn up for submission to the Fu-t'ai or Governor-General at Urumchi, nominally in my name and ending with a recommendation for the grant of official rank. I myself did not expect success from such a document from a mere 'outsider,' and a foreigner in addition. But P'an Ta-jên thought well of Chiang's plan, and even took the trouble of revising the letter with his own hand. He also agreed to send it up to the fountain-head of official favours under his own seal and cover. So Chiang, ever sanguine, was buoyed up by hopes of thus gaining his way into the official hierarchy, even though he could not raise enough money to buy rank forthwith at Peking. For weeks after his anecdotes and little indiscretions about that quaint ' Civil Service' of the New Dominion which he knew so well, with all its glitter and foibles, were more lively than ever.

It was very hard to say good-bye to P'an Ta-jên for good. So I, too, indulged in a sort of sanguine self-deception by promising to return once more when my Mandarin friend will himself be Fu-t'ai at Urumchi! It is not for me to foresee what official wisdom may yet hold in store for P'an Ta-jên. But can I hope for the freedom to fulfil my part of the promise?

After sending off Lal Singh to the mountains due north I moved up the valley of the Taushkan Darya, the main feeder of the Ak-su River, and after three pleasant marches through almost continuous cultivation (Fig. 311) reached by May 8th the picturesquely situated small town of Uch-Turfan. I found it full of interesting Kirghiz folk from the valley higher up, and from the grazing-grounds on the high T'ien-shan range overlooking it (Fig. 303). The latter forms the boundary towards Russian territory around the Issik-kul Lake, and is crossed here by the Bedel Pass, over which since ancient times an important route has connected the Tarim Basin and Western Turkestan. I had here the satisfaction of visiting the last bit of ground in Chinese Turkestan trodden by Hsüan-tsang, my patron saint, which I had not previously seen. In addition I was able to use a brief stay here for interesting anthropometrical work among the Kirghiz, who have supplied so important an element to the racial composition of the present population in the Tarim Basin, especially in its north-western portion.

From Uch-Turfan I made my way south across barren and yet remarkably picturesque hill ranges, practically unsurveyed before, to the little-known oasis of Kelpin. In the Uch-Turfan Valley I had heard vague stories about ruins of some mysterious town which was said to be sighted on clear days far away in the mountains, but to disappear whenever search for it was made. When on May 11th a thirty-five miles' march in a broad and arid valley took me up to the encampment of the Kirghiz Beg Mangush (Fig. 302) and into Alpine coolness, it was easy for me to ascertain that these legends had their origin in the remarkable appearance presented by a high and fantastically serrated portion of the range towering above the valley from the south. Its peaks, curiously recalling the Dolomites of the Tyrol, though lacking the charm of ice and snow, rose above the Kara-shilwe side valleys to heights over 13,000 feet, and with their extremely bold pinnacles and precipitous rock walls bore a striking resemblance to ruined castles and towers.

I found that the Kirghiz knew the line of these peaks by the name of Kaka-jade, and regarded them with super-stitious awe. The stories they told me of dragons supposed to dwell among them and to issue forth at times in the shape of clouds raining hail and fire, correspond curiously to the legends, heard by the early Chinese pilgrims, of the Nagas dwelling on the heights of the Pamirs and above the Hindukush passes. But I was still more interested when information reached me, elicited with some difficulty through my keen-witted camel-man, Hassan Akhun, about the existence of a stone image to be found high up on the southern slope of that range.

We crossed the range over the Saghiz-kan Pass, some 9000 feet high, and felt glad to have our baggage on hardy Kirghiz ponies fit for such stony tracks. Leaving camp at Shait-kak south of the pass, where water was available in a natural rock cistern, I proceeded on May 13th in search of the image, guided by Mangush Beg. It was a delightful excursion, though of trying length and over ground which none but Kirghiz ponies could have covered in a day. Passing over high plateaus close below those towering peaks, I realized their strange fascination, and understood why old legends had placed in them the enchanted strongholds of wicked kings, full of wonderful treasures.

At last, after a seventeen miles' ride, we reached the Kirghiz grazing-ground of Chal-koide, right under the frowning crags of the eastern end of 'Kaka-jade's town,' or the 'town of the T'ang prince,' as the Chinese at Uch-

302. KIRGHIZ WITH FELT TENT BELONGING TO MANGUSH BEG, AT ILACHU.

303. KIRGHIZ FROM GRAZING-GROUNDS OF UCH-TURFAN.

304. IN CAÑON OF KORUM-BOGUZ RIVER NORTH OF KELPIN.

Mangush Beg, with pony, in foreground.

Turfan called it. There, to my surprise, I found the rough stone enclosure of a regular 'Ziarat' crowning the top of a small rocky knoll, and within it the stone image reported. It proved to be a stēlē-shaped slab about three feet high, rudely carved in flat relievo with the representation of a male figure holding a curved sword. The carving, though too rude for any safe dating, was manifestly old. That the image, whatever it was meant to represent, went back to Buddhist times was made clear by the discovery by its side of a small block of granite roughly carved into the miniature representation of a Stupa.

But the most curious feature to me was to see the enclosure around filled with all the usual votive offerings of orthodox Muhammadan shrines—horse-skulls, horns of wild goats, rags fastened on staffs, and the rest. It was manifest that worship was here very much a thing of the present, however sorely the 'idol' image must have scandalized the Uch-Turfan Mullahs of whose protests Mangush Beg told me. Never had I seen so unabashed a survival of an earlier local cult among good Muhammadans, such as all these Kirghiz herdsmen have been for many generations. The carved figure was supposed to represent the wife of some ancient hero called Kaz-ata, whose image pious eyes recognize in an inaccessible rock pinnacle high up on the crest of the range. This connection clearly indicates that the curious shrine here surviving must owe its origin to the worship of some striking natural feature such as is common in the folklore of India, ancient and modern, and for which Buddhist local cult has always been ready to find room.

On our return ride in the evening we had a great treat of milk at a Kirghiz 'Aul' below the Sar-bel Pass, and saw the joyful home-coming of a thousand sheep and lambs. It was difficult to understand where they found adequate grazing ; for the peaks above these narrow plateaus carry very little snow, and throughout these mountains the consequent want of water is a serious trouble for the few Kirghiz herdsmen who still cling to them. Here, and in the equally barren outer ranges, I could gather many useful observations about obvious desiccation.

The study of the extant conditions in these hills, where springs are now extremely rare, and all travel depends on an exact knowledge of the water-supply obtainable from natural cisterns or 'Kaks,' was to me of special interest; for very similar conditions may be supposed to have prevailed in the now absolutely waterless hills of the Pei-shan south of Hami during the period when bands of Hun raiders could still make their way through them towards Tun-huang and the great Chinese route to the west. In fact, Kirghiz raids of a corresponding character, effected from the T'ien-shan valleys upon the Ak-su-Kashgar high road in the plains, are still a matter of living recollection, and might yet be revived in practice if the hold of the Chinese administration were relaxed.

The route down to Kelpin led through narrow gorges and wild cañons (Fig. 304) cut into rock-walls of glorious hues by rivers which have long ceased to flow except after rare rain. How I longed for geological knowledge to interpret correctly the wonderfully twisting strata, of sand-stone and gneiss it seemed, which these deep cuttings had laid bare! In the broad open valley of Kelpin, edged on the south by the lowest of the outer T'ien-shan ranges, I found a cluster of some dozen hamlets subsisting on the water of springs which issue at the debouchure of several barren stony valleys draining the range to the north. The oasis lies so far off the main roads that the whole population had turned out to see the 'Firang.'

During my short halt at this pleasant oasis I could convince myself how inadequate was the water available for irrigation to meet the needs of a rapidly increasing population, in spite of the intensive cultivation here practised. Yet permanent emigration was unknown, and even Ak-su with its abundance of water and arable land could not tempt the men of Kelpin to more than seasonal visits as labourers. Their eyes were ever wistfully looking out for an additional water-supply, and I heard the old Beg guiding me lament that they had no rulers like the 'Firangs' capable of bringing water right through the mountains from the Taushkan Darya. Was this a reflex of stories, told perhaps by Mecca pilgrims, of the great Swat Canal tunnelled

below the Malakand, which is soon to bring fertility to parts
of the Peshawar Valley that have lain more or less waste for
long centuries?

The remains of old settlements which I traced close to
the edge of extant cultivation were too uncertain in date
and character to give definite indications of the former
extent of Kelpin. But information opportunely secured
through 'treasure-seekers' subsequently enabled me to
trace extensive débris areas marking ancient settlements
in the wide belt of absolute desert between the arid outer
hill chain of Kelpin and the lower course of the Kashgar
River. The intense heat and the difficulty of carrying water
at this season—our camels had to be spared all work after
Ak-su and could no longer help us—made exploration very
difficult on this ground. So it was, perhaps, as well to find
that far-advanced wind erosion had left little or no remains
for excavation at the central site to which our guides
brought us after a total march of some forty miles from
Kelpin.

It proved to be that of a fortified station surrounded by
a large 'Tati' with plentiful small débris of hard materials,
coins, and the like. The ample archaeological evidence
gathered here showed that this tract, now wholly abandoned
to drift sand and erosion, had been occupied from Han times
down to the eighth century A.D. by populous settlements.
Canals, still traceable in parts, once carried water to them
from the Kashgar River, now dying away much farther
south. I was also able to ascertain the line of the ancient
Chinese high road to Kashgar, which could still be traced
by a succession of ruined watch-towers.

A curious illustration of the pitfalls which beset the
archaeologist's field-work may find passing mention. The
time of abandonment for this ruined station was so
clearly indicated that I felt greatly puzzled when several
copper and silver pieces of the eighteenth and nineteenth
centuries were picked up in my presence from the same
ground. The riddle was solved only after my arrival
at the village of Tumshuk on the present high road, when
the aged Karaul-bashi, or commandant of the local police
post, related how about 1876 a rebel force had been routed

by Yakub Beg's son Hakaullah at Yaide some two marches by the road north-east. Many of the fugitives had sought escape by turning into the desert, and miserably perished there through heat and thirst under an August sun. People from Kelpin subsequently searched the desert for the money and valuables of the victims and buried the corpses. How could an antiquary, say of 3000 A.D., be expected to divine the true origin of those modern coins I picked up at the old site?

Quite apart from the much-decayed ruins of Buddhist shrines near Tumshuk, which former travellers had seen and M. Pelliot had systematically cleared, the whole of the ground to the north of the present high road was full of interest to me. Cultivation from the Kashgar River had extended in ancient times much farther than now, and canals as well as terminal beds, with the familiar dead forest, could be traced far away into the desert. How I longed for a few weeks of winter to follow up the whole of the old route to Kashgar! But the excursions I made northward from the present line of small oases near the Kashgar River end, between Tumshuk and Maral-bashi, showed that prolonged surveys were impossible at this season.

As it was, I spent a terribly hot time on these long rides, between thirty and forty miles daily, through barren steppe or tamarisk jungle. There was room also for interesting topographical work; for I discovered in this previously unsurveyed desert belt a series of low parallel ranges which were clearly connected geologically with the curious rugged hills cropping out like rock islands about Tumshuk and Maral-bashi, and which once, as indicated above, had their continuation to the south-east right into the Taklamakan.

In spite of the heat, glare, and thirst which attended work at this season, I found it hard to turn my back upon it. But the thought of the many heavy tasks still before me imperatively called me back to Khotan. From Maral-bashi the road lay open to both Kashgar and Yarkand, and, considering how little a five days' journey is reckoned in Turkestan, it cost me some effort to turn my face from the

former.   I longed to see the Macartneys again after nearly
two years' absence, and to tell my old friend in person of
the deep gratitude I felt for all the unceasing help and
support he had given me from afar.   But I knew that he
and Mrs. Macartney were soon to start for an amply earned
furlough to England, and could realize what preparations
and cares such a journey with small children implied.

I, too, could ill spare the time which the détour *via*
Kashgar would have cost.   So I took the direct route to
Yarkand.   The hundred and thirty odd miles were covered
in five rapid marches, not without some physical trouble ;
for my plane-table work obliged me to travel in the full heat
of the day.   There was profit to reap here too from exact
survey work ; for it taught me a good deal of the physical
conditions which affect irrigation along the Yarkand River,
and which account for curious fluctuations in the cultivated
area of these straggling oases.   The impression I gained
was that a stream of gold could be caught here, as in
some other parts of the Tarim Basin, if only there were a
a régime permitting of systematic irrigation schemes after
Punjab or Egyptian models.

At Yarkand, where I had the great pleasure of again
seeing Mr. and Mrs. Raquette of the Swedish Medical
Mission, I was obliged to halt for a few days, mainly in
order to dispose of my brave camels from Keriya.   It
seemed hard to part with these sturdy companions which
had served me so well during nearly two years' desert travel.
But they could not be used for the journey across the
mountains to India, and Yarkand, where the currents of
trade from the north and south meet, seemed the right place
to get a good price for them.   Since our Taklamakan crossing of the winter, the fame of my beasts had spread far
along the caravan routes, and, of course, nothing was lost
in the telling of the terrible deserts they had faced and
their long weeks of toil without food or water.

So when my intention of selling was made known there
were traders on the look-out to secure them.   The animals
were in excellent condition, though the spring clipping to
which Hassan Akhun had subjected them before leaving
Ak-su had left them rather naked and gaunt and without

their stately good looks (Fig. 305). The heavy season of traffic to the Indian and Russian sides was approaching, and when the owners of camel caravans had convinced themselves that I was in no hurry to sell, the offers, ridiculously low at first, began to rise steadily.

At last they topped my own estimate, and then with a secret pang I had to let my faithful beasts pass into the possession of an Afghan trader. The price he paid down in hard rolls of silver amounted to 51 Taels, or roughly 130 rupees per animal, and yielded a net profit of 70 per cent on the original cost—for the benefit of the Indian Government. For the last few days my camels had been feasting on bundles of fragrant dry lucerne and on young foliage around 'my' garden palace of Chini-bagh. Now for a farewell treat they had a huge loaf of bread from my own hands, and took it almost as eagerly as when I fed them in the heart of the desert. Have they ever since wished to be back with their master—as I have often wished to travel again with them ?

305. FAREWELL TO MY BRAVE CAMELS FROM KERIYA.

306. CARPENTERS AT WORK ON PACKING-CASES FOR ANTIQUES, IN COURTYARD OF NAR-BAGH.

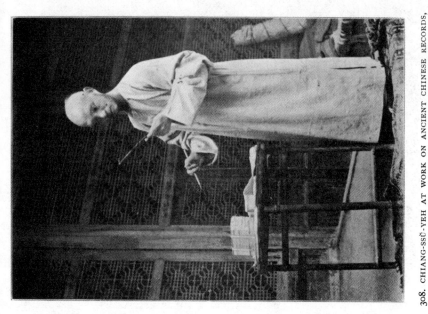

308. CHIANG-SSŬ-YEH AT WORK ON ANCIENT CHINESE RECORDS,
IN NAR-BAGH.

This photograph shows my devoted secretary just recovered from a short
attack of illness.

307. TURDI, MY DAK-MAN FROM KHOTAN.

The saddle-bag across Turdi's shoulder served to carry small mails.

CHAPTER XCI

PREPARATIONS AT KHOTAN

FROM Yarkand a rapid journey brought me back to Khotan by the 9th of June. It was done mainly by night marches to avoid the worst heat, and made specially delectable by a succession of sand-storms. On the way at Pialma I fell in with Satip-aldi Beg, the hardy old head-man of the Kirghiz on the upper Kara-kash River, and was able to arrange with him all details about the transport I should need in September for the journey across the Kara-koram to Ladak.

At Khotan I settled down in the shelter of Nar-bagh, my favourite old garden palace, not without some trouble this time; for the chief Mullah who owned it had died since my stay in 1906, and the large suburban residence with its garden and annexes had been divided among a number of inheritors. The airy central pavilion which made such desirable summer quarters had fallen to the lot of the head widow, a formidable old lady; and poor Badruddin Khan, the Afghan Ak-sakal, and my devoted local factotum, had to suffer grievous hurt from her sharp tongue before he was allowed to dislodge the silkworm nursery the dowager had thought fit to set up where once Niaz Hakim Beg, Yakub Beg's famous governor, used to sit in state. Old Akhun Beg was only too eager to offer hospitality again; but his house, even if I had allowed him to vacate it entirely, would not have afforded room for all the work before me.

The many cases deposited in the spring were soon joined from Kashgar by the cart-loads of antiques which Mr. Macartney had taken care of since 1906-7. With them came a big consignment of tin plates for packing which he had secured for me, thereby draining the whole Turkestan market of that much-prized commodity.   Then followed six weeks of constant toil for me, absorbed entirely by the sorting and packing of my archaeological collections.

Never, perhaps, has the oasis seen such making of cases and tinning, as went on in the courtyard of my old palace during those long hot weeks (Fig. 306).   There were, indeed, some leisurely ' Ustads ' to direct in a more or less casual fashion the labours of the dozens of men who were sawing up seasoned tree trunks and planing boards for cases.   But the actual repacking of the antiques in the tinned cases had to be done entirely by my own hands. The strengthening of the frescoes from Miran and elsewhere by a backing with glued strips of cotton and then the tight repacking between layers of reeds, as already described, cost weeks.   The results of my minute care and manual pains then taken have been gratifying indeed ; for those ancient relics, even when composed of the most brittle and friable materials, have safely survived all the risks to which they were exposed on a total journey of some 8000 miles, while being carried across high mountain ranges on camels, yaks, and ponies, and subsequently travelling by cart, rail, and steamer.   But it was a wearisome time while I toiled thus during the hottest season day after day without any interruption from daybreak ; only at dusk seeking a little refreshment in walks or rides along the dusty roads through the village tracts northward.

At the close of March I had deputed Naik Ram Singh from Chira for a supplementary task, mainly photographic, at Miran.   Before I had been long at Khotan he returned from his distant journey eastwards suffering from complete loss of eyesight.   No news whatever had reached me from him since we parted, and the shock was great when I saw my poor 'handy-man,' once so stalwart and strong, brought to me helplessly blind.   He had left me in what seemed good health.   While travelling rapidly to Charklik with Ibrahim Beg, the most efficient and experienced of my Turki followers, he was attacked by severe pains in the head.   Nothing before had suggested the approach of that fell disease, glaucoma. But during his stay at Charklik the pains in the head increased, and he was suddenly struck with blindness in one eye.

With heroic doggedness, a characteristic feature of his race, Naik Ram Singh clung to his task, and left the oasis for that trying desert site of Miran. There, while he was getting the larger temple cleared again under Ibrahim Beg's supervision preparatory to fresh photographic work, blindness descended on his second eye also. Undismayed by this terrible calamity, he persisted in waiting for some days by the side of the Miran stream hoping for an improvement and a chance of doing his work. Blindness did not loosen its grip, and after another week at Charklik he at last consented to rejoin me. Ibrahim Beg conducted him back with all possible care and expedition, travelling by the cooler hill route from Charchan to Keriya. I may mention as a significant trait in Ram Singh's dogged Sikh character, that though blind he would insist on cooking his food himself to avoid any infraction of caste rules, in spite of all trouble from burns and other accidents.

It was a pitiful story, and my heart ached at the thought of the poor fellow's sufferings. He was bearing himself most bravely, full of hope for ultimate recovery, and expressed touching gratitude for whatever little I could do to secure him comfort. I was quite unable to recognize the disease, but was all the more anxious to obtain professional exam- ination and help as early as possible. So after engaging the first Hindu who had settled at Khotan, a Shikarpuri usurer, to act as cook, I hastened to send Ram Singh on to Yarkand by Chinese cart with all possible care for his comfort. There the Rev. Mr. Raquette of the Swedish Medical Mission diagnosed the incurable disease, but was able to relieve the pains in the head which had aggravated the Naik's misery. Deeply distressed as I felt at Mr. Raquette's report received three weeks later, which left no hope of recovery for Ram Singh, there was at least some comfort in the assurance he gave me about the character and origin of the disease. It might have come on just as well if Ram Singh had never volunteered for this journey, and nothing but a timely operation could have saved his eyesight,—if ever there had been a chance of recognizing premonitory symptoms which often escape even the practised medical man.

The remainder of this sad story may be briefly told here. By the advice of Mr. Raquette, who all through showed the kindest interest in Ram Singh, I arranged to have the poor sufferer conveyed to Ladak, as soon as the Kara- koram route opened, and thence to India. All possible provision was made for his comfort and safety, Daud Beg, a particularly reliable Khotan petty official whom the Naik knew and liked well, being sent off to accompany him, besides two Hindu traders to whose care he was entrusted from Yarkand. Thanks to these arrangements the un- fortunate Naik travelled without any mishap or discomfort to Ladak. Thence after a good rest Captain D. G. Oliver, the British Joint Commissioner, saw him safely through to Kashmir.

My old friend Dr. A. Neve, of the Srinagar Mission Hospital, whose fame as a surgeon has spread all through the North-West Himalayas, could only confirm the sad Yarkand verdict. So poor Ram Singh was taken by his brother to his native village near Firozpur in the Punjab. Thence he came to meet me in December when I passed through Lahore. The signs of far-advanced mental decay which I then noticed in the poor fellow made the meeting doubly distressing. The substantial accumulations of the Naik — his emoluments while on duty with me were calculated at a rate amounting to about five times his ordinary pay—were entrusted by me to the safe keeping of his regimental authorities. During my visit to Calcutta I did my utmost to urge in the proper quarters the claims of this faithful companion to special consideration, and some months afterwards I had the relief to know that the Government of India had generously provided for his and his family's needs by the grant of a special pension. He did not live long to benefit by it; for before the end of 1909 gentle death had relieved him from all further pain, physical and mental. But as a well-deserved act of grace the greater part of the pension was continued by Govern- ment as a compassionate allowance to the widow and son.

309. BADRUDDIN KHAN, INDIAN AK-SAKAL AT KHOTAN, WITH HIS SONS
AND A TRUSTED SERVANT.

310. KHUDA-BERDI (YÜZ-BASHI) AND CULTIVATORS OF YOTKAN.

Khuda berdi sits on extreme left ; the figures stuck in his belt serve for easy reference in anthropometrical list.

312. MOSQUE AT RUKNUDDIN MAZAR, YOTKAN.

311. VILLAGE MOSQUE AT AK-YAR, ON ROAD TO UCH-TURFAN.

It may well be imagined how much these anxieties and efforts added to the strain thrown upon me by my exacting tasks at Khotan. There was no one to lighten the burden ; but it was a great comfort to have Chiang-ssŭ-yeh near me and to feel the genuine sympathy with which he shared my cares and sorrow about poor Ram Singh. He himself was busy from early morning until late at night over learned labours (Fig. 308), the preparation of a rough slip catalogue for at least a portion of the Chinese manuscripts from the 'Thousand Buddhas,' and the decipherment and transcription of the ancient Chinese records from the 'Wall.'

In addition to all labours of packing I had to bestow much care and trouble on the preparations for my long-planned expedition to the sources of the Yurung-kash River. My previous explorations in the Karanghu-tagh mountains had convinced me that the Yurung-kash head-waters were quite inaccessible through the narrow and deep gorges by which the river cuts its way westwards. So the fresh effort upon which I had decided long before was now to be made from the east, where that wholly unexplored mountain region adjoins the extreme north-west of the high Tibetan table-land. Thence I proposed to make my way to the uppermost Kara-kash Valley along the unsurveyed southern slopes of that portion of the main Kun-lun Range which feeds the Yurung-kash with its chief glacier sources. Climate and utterly barren ground were sure to offer great obstacles in that inhospitable region. So the arrangements about transport and supplies for this concluding expedition claimed the utmost care.

The difficulties presented by the transport problem looked formidable enough. It was certain that the explorations contemplated could not possibly be effected in less than forty days, counting the period from leaving Polur, the last inhabited place at the foot of the Kun-lun, to the highest point in the Kara-kash Valley where the Kirghiz of Satip-aldi Beg could keep a depot of supplies ready against our arrival. Now during the whole of this period the maintenance of ourselves and our animals could be provided for only by the supplies we carried with us. There would be no dependence on grazing for the ponies and donkeys, the only available beasts of burden.   Yet none of these would on such high ground be able to carry more than their own fodder-supply for forty days.   Thus our seven saddle ponies and the ten needed for our indispensable baggage and food supplies would require to be supplemented by an equal number of animals to carry fodder.   These fodder-carrying beasts would again have to be fed with fodder brought by other beasts, and so on and so on.   Thus the transport calculations would go on swelling *ad infinitum* until the thought of them oppressed me like a nightmare.

The only escape seemed to lie in the plan to send back the animals in detachments as their loads of supplies became exhausted, and to trust to their making their way back without fodder.   For facing great privations on such tracks as we should have to follow in those forbidding mountains, hardy donkeys would prove more suitable, besides requiring a smaller number of men to look after them.   So I decided to use donkey transport for the main stores.   There were plenty of ' Kirakash ' about Khotan accustomed to serve traders with ponies and donkeys on hire.   But they dreaded work in the unknown mountains ; and in spite of the pressure exercised from the Ya-mên and the lavish rates of hire I felt compelled to offer, the collection of sound and sufficiently strong animals proved a long and difficult business.   I had every interest to secure beasts which would last us to the very end of the expedition, whereas the owners of the transport, being paid a hire which practically covered the cost of good animals, would be indifferent to losses if they could but manage to palm off inferior beasts upon us.

In these troublesome transport tasks, which generally filled my weary evenings, I appreciated more than ever the devoted help which my old friend Badruddin Khan, the Afghan Ak-sakal, gave me from his life-long experience as a trader.   For weeks he took up his abode in one of the outer courts of Nar-bagh, together with his sons and servants, in order to be near at hand.   How he found time to look after his own trade affairs was a mystery to me, just as much as the way he managed to get all his accounts and correspondence done by his young son of thirteen or so (Fig. 309), who alone in the family was able to read and write. It is true that the long letters he used to send me through this youthful scribe had sorely tried learned Mullahs all along my route from Tun-huang to Yarkand, and that the disentanglement of his accounts of expenses incurred on my behalf was a business which I had learned to dread from sad experience.

In the midst of all these distracting concerns it was a real relief when on July 20th my energetic Surveyor, Lal Singh, rejoined me after a separation of nearly three months. Injury to a level of the theodolite, which at the time could not be repaired, had prevented the hoped-for triangulation from Ak-su to Kashgar; but he had succeeded in effecting very useful surveys with the plane-table along the T'ien-shan range up to the watershed north of Kashgar. Then he had travelled to Guma by a route different from the high roads already surveyed, and had thence succeeded in mapping, as directed, the last portion of *terra incognita* on the northern slopes of the Kun-lun between the Kilian and Middle Kara-kash valleys. Our routes since Ak-su had crossed only at one point, the oasis of Abad north of Yarkand; and it was no small satisfaction to me to find that, though the distance covered by me from our common starting-point, Ak-su, amounted to over 350 miles, the position shown for Abad by my own plane-table survey differed from that of Lal Singh by only one mile in longitude and about two in latitude. Just about that time there arrived also Muhammadju, my old Yarkandi follower, invalided home from Abdal, but now ready to serve me again with his knowledge of the Polur route and the Kara-kash Valley.

A week later the final completion of packing allowed me to take my first day of relative quiet by paying a farewell visit to Yotkan, the site of the ancient Khotan capital. The annual washing for gold in the 'culture strata' deeply buried beneath the layers of fertile alluvial soil had already begun, and while staying during the heat of the day with my old host, the Yüz-bashi, I was able to acquire from the villagers a fair collection of terra-cotta grotesques, and other small antiques brought to light since 1906. Besides I could take typical Khotan 'heads' (Fig. 310). Here on historic soil, where cultivation has effaced all traces of past greatness, I said good-bye to the charms of rural Khotan with its homesteads nestling in orchards and its quaint mosques shaded by huge old trees (Fig. 312).

On August 1st I was at last able to despatch my heavy convoy of antiques, making up over fifty camel-loads, to Sanju. There, under the care of Tila Bai and one of Badruddin Khan's trusted caravan men, it was to wait until the subsiding of the summer flood in the river would allow it to proceed in safety to Suget on the upper Kara-kash, where I hoped to rejoin it towards the close of September for the crossing of the Kara-koram.

After two more days spent in busy work, the time came for myself to set out for the foot of the mountains south-eastward. Chiang-ssŭ-yeh, whose labours for me were now ended, and also Badruddin Khan insisted upon accompany-ing me for the first march. Other Khotan friends saw me off by the bank of the Yurung-kash, which now rolled its huge summer flood in numerous beds, the two widest passable only in boats. The crossing with baggage was not without its risks, in spite of the large number and skill of the 'Suchis' or water-men detailed to guide men and animals. Dear old Akhun Beg, who bade me a touching farewell, remained behind to pray for our safe passage, and I still saw his venerable figure standing upright by the river bank when the whirling ferry-boat had carried me across the main bed. It took long hours before our three boat-loads of animals and baggage had been safely brought to the right bank (Fig. 313).

Then through the smiling fertile lands of the cantons of Yurung-kash and Sampula we rode to Kotaz Langar, where the night was passed by the edge of the bare gravel Sai. Next morning the baggage and the train of unladen animals intended for the mountains were sent ahead, while I remained behind to struggle with Badruddin Khan's last accounts and bid farewell to my devoted secretary and helpmate. It was a sad parting, and poor Chiang, at other times ever bright and cheerful, felt its pang quite as

313. LANDING BAGGAGE FROM FERRY-BOAT ON RIGHT BANK OF YURUNG-KASH RIVER.

314. VIEW EASTWARDS FROM ABOVE KAR-YAGDI, IN POLUR GORGE.
The peak in background, above glacier, rises to 20,080 feet.

315. OUR ADVANCE PARTY EMERGING FROM POLUR GORGE NEAR
KHAN LANGAR.

Rai Bahadur Lal Singh standing in middle.   'Badakhshi,' my pony, being held on the left.

deeply as I did. I had, indeed, the comfort of having through Mr. Macartney's kindness obtained for him the richly deserved appointment as Chinese Munshi of the British Consulate at Kashgar. But would this justify hope that I might ever see again the kindly face of the most devoted and capable helper Asia had ever given me? Even little ' Dash ' seemed to feel the emotion of the moment, and cuddled up to his Chinese friend with an exceptional display of affection. Honest Badruddin Khan, too, had tears in his eyes when we parted. Then, as I rode on, the quivering glare and heat of the desert seemed to descend like a luminous curtain and to hide from me the most cherished aspects of my Turkestan life.

CHAPTER XCII

FIVE long marches brought me from the edge of the Khotan oasis to the mountain village of Polur, where the western-most route from Tibet debouches. We were now steadily ascending in a diagonal line the great gravel glacis which slopes down from the northern main range of the Kun-lun (see Map II.), and I felt with delight how each night's halt gave increased coolness.

On August 5th we struck at Hasha the first of those submontane oases, narrow but long-stretched, which line the beds of a succession of glacier-fed rivers where they debouch from the foot-hills. At Hasha, as well as at Chakar and Nura, cultivation had evidently not yet reached the limits of the available water. Yet attentive Muhammad Yusuf Beg, who since 1906 had been transferred to this 'Hill' district from Niya, told me that the official reckoning of households in the whole of this wide tract had multiplied about nine-fold since the re-establishment of Chinese rule in 1878. Earlier changes of this kind in the extent of cultivation were indicated by remains of a small roughly built town of uncertain date which I found near Hasha, between two steep-scarped river beds in a position recalling Yar-khoto, and by a débris area, manifestly of Buddhist times, below Nura. It was at the latter place that the magnificent line of snowy peaks to the south first showed itself in full glory.

At the pretty cluster of little oases known as Imamlar I visited the well-shaded shrine, famous as a pilgrimage-place throughout the Tarim Basin, where pious belief has located the resting-place of four of those legendary Imams, or early warrior prophets of Islam, who are such popular figures in Khotan tradition.   I wondered whether we should ever learn to which Buddhist shrine this local worship traces its origin.   We were here some 7300 feet above sea, and a minimum temperature of thirty-seven degrees Fahrenheit under a perfectly clear sky felt delightfully refreshing.   On the same day, August 8th, after marching along the crest of the high Pomaz spur, which gave a grand view of the mountains, we reached Polur, nestling low in the valley.

This large village proved an excellent base of supplies, thanks to the ample arrangements made by Muhammad Yusuf Beg under the orders of the new Keriya Amban, whose help I had taken care to enlist in March.   Stores of flour, fodder, etc., were ready to be taken over, as well as a dozen sheep which were to supply us with meat during the long wanderings in the mountains.   Extra transport, too, had been collected to help in moving these stores up to the nearest Tibetan plateau; for I knew well the difficulties to be expected on the route immediately above Polur, and was anxious to lighten the task of our Khotan transport as long as possible.   My only regret was that the yaks I had hoped to obtain for this auxiliary transport column proved quite unaccustomed to loads, and after careering wildly through the one long village lane had to be exchanged for more donkeys.   I found later that, owing to the absence of grazing, yaks would have been of little use.

All these arrangements cost time and labour; and what with abundant accounts, the despatch of a last big mail-bag *via* Khotan, and anthropological measurements among these 'Taghliks,' who interested me by their type so different from the people in the plains, the start could not be effected until the morning of August 12th.   The whole of Polur was assembled to see us off; for though this route to Western Tibet had been used about half-a-dozen times by European travellers since the 'Pandits' of the Forsyth Mission first traversed it in 1873, the novelty of such an event had not worn off.   But I confess that I was more impressed by the farewell to honest Turdi, the Dak-man, who was to take my mail-bag for the last time back to

Khotan (Fig. 307).   I thought of how he had managed to
find me that Christmas Eve in the heart of the Lop-nor
Desert, and how another time I had sent him off from the
foot of the Nan-shan for a weary ride of months.   But
whatever the occasion, there was nothing to read in his
face but calm unconcern and a sort of canine devotion.

The difficulties began early as we made our way through
the confined gorges above Polur towards the high plateaus
beyond the northern main Kun-lun Range (Fig. 314).   It
took us three trying days of toil before we reached easier
ground at the point known as Khan Langar, over 13,000
feet above sea, where the Polur stream in its descent enters
the cutting it has effected through the ice-clad summit
portion of the range (Fig. 315).   Yet the track twisted and
turned so much that the total distance covered from Polur
village to this point amounted only to about twenty-one
miles.   Most of it was done by scrambling over boulders
and rocky ledges in narrow gorges half-filled by glacier-
fed torrents.   Bad as the going was for us men, the trouble
of getting our baggage and supplies safely through was a
far more serious business.   There were continuous crossings
and recrossings of the greyish-white tossing water which
our little donkeys had much trouble to negotiate at all times,
and, of course, could not ford at all when the daily flood
from the melting glaciers at the head of the gorges had
once commenced in the early afternoon to come down.

The track was impressively bad, whether winding
amidst slippery boulders below, or scaling precipitous slopes
of rock or detritus above when the bottom of the gorge
became quite impassable for man or beast (Fig. 316).
Through the Amban's care some attempt had been made
by the Polur head-men to improve the worst places, and
we had, fortunately, the help of some twenty hill-men for
the laden animals.   At a number of points where rocky
ribs projected from steep slopes of unstable shale, all loads
had to be taken off and carried round the dangerous corners
by the men.   It all involved a great deal of care and strain,
and when we had safely passed the particular precipices
where so careful and experienced an explorer as Captain
Deasy had lost ponies in 1898,—according to Polur tradition

316. TRACK IN POLUR GORGE NEAR SARIK-KORAM, VIEWED FROM SOUTH.

317. PASA, OF KERIYA, HUNTER OF WILD YAKS, AND OUR GUIDE.

also mule-trunks 'full of silver,'—and one of his men too, I knew I had reason for relief.

On August 15th we marched up a broad barren valley amidst mountain formations of slate and sandstone, strikingly different from those passed through in the gorges below, and then crossed the watershed by an easy pass some 16,500 feet high to a wonderfully wide and barren plateau. From a steep ridge above the pass which I climbed with Lal Singh, I enjoyed a glorious view both of the towering range behind us and the great wall of snowy mountains which flanks the Yurung-kash River sources. It was a grand panorama, but it was hard to photograph it with an icy gale from the north benumbing one's fingers. It was, no doubt, the continuation of a big Buran which was scouring the desert plains; but the accompanying dust-clouds could not pass over the great mountain wall rising to peaks well over 21,000 feet, and the view kept delightfully clear.

A ten miles' descent over gentle slopes of absolutely barren gravel brought us to a group of small lakelets with fresh water, where we camped, the icy gale pursuing us all the way. All round them the ground bore plain indications of being the dried-up bed of a lake once much larger than the present Seghiz-köl basin to the east. It was curious to observe here the same wind-eroded clay ridges and banks which are so characteristic of the Su-lo Ho's terminal basin; but their height rarely rose above ten feet, the direction of the eroded banks running generally east to west. The elevation was close on 15,000 feet.

Very few of the donkeys had managed to come in that night, and as the minimum temperature fell to twenty degrees below freezing-point, I felt doubly glad when the following morning broke deliciously still and sunny. Fringing the lake shore in patches there was a very coarse sort of grass, yellowish in colour, and appropriately known as 'Sarigh-ot' to the Keriya hunters who alone visit these parts. So when the poor hard-tried donkeys had straggled in during the forenoon, I could enjoy the sight of them peacefully browsing on these hardy tufts, or else lying lazily stretched out in the sun, which at mid-day showed a temperature of fully 130 degrees Fahrenheit. It was a good place to give the animals a short rest, and to form a base from which we might effect our expedition into the unexplored valleys of the uppermost Yurung-kash.

From the very careful trigonometrical survey which Captain Deasy effected in 1897 along this part of the Polur-Ladak route, I knew that the easternmost point of the Yurung-kash head-waters lay due south of Seghiz-köl. So Lal Singh, active as ever, set out on August 16th to reconnoitre the ground in that direction, and to start a fresh net of triangles with the help of Captain Deasy's points. Yet, I confess, I felt oppressed by doubts how we should be able to penetrate into that region of difficult deep-cut valleys for which my Karanghu-tagh experiences of 1900 and 1906 had prepared me. Considering the limitation of our supplies and means of transport, a false move at the start and consequent loss of time might prove fatal to all my plans.

Fortune for once played me a good turn by bringing into my hands a guide such as I had vainly searched for among all those reticent and wily hill-men of Polur. Lal Singh on his reconnaissance had fallen in with one of a small party of Keriya people hunting for wild yaks, and I promptly despatched Niaz Akhun, the energetic Darogha who had accompanied us from Khotan, to fetch them from their camp near Seghiz-köl. Half-frozen he turned up next morning bringing the whole party of hunters—Pasa, an experienced if shifty-looking fellow (Fig 317), with three equally ragged companions half-Tibetan in appearance. Pasa, after some cross-examination, confessed that there were gold-pits still worked by small parties of Keriya people in a side valley of the Yurung-kash known as Zailik, to be reached by a couple of marches. When I explained why I wanted to get to the river's easternmost sources by a route different from that leading south of Seghiz-köl, he acknowledged that he knew tracks by which we might make an almost complete circuit of the uppermost Yurung-kash head-waters.

Of course Pasa very soon caught the infection of pretended ignorance from our unwilling and contumacious

Polur people, who previously, when I noticed abandoned gold-pits in the upper Polur gorge, had stoutly denied all knowledge of any actual gold-digging in this region. But it was too late then, especially as Pasa was not particularly clever at lying, and evidently too hard-up not to be tempted by the promised rewards. So after much trouble we prevailed upon him to act as guide and to show us a track to the uppermost Yurung-kash gorge from the north-west. Discharging most of the Polur men and donkeys, I arranged to leave behind a depot of all supplies for men and beasts not immediately needed, as well as the majority of our hired donkeys. Ibrahim Beg, with the less active of the transport men, was to move his depot to the Ulugh-köl lake, one march to the south-west, on the route to Ladak, where some grazing was to be found, and to await our return there.

Then on August 18th we set out west with much-reduced baggage under Pasa's guidance, and after ascending the wide barren basin to the north-west, and crossing a relatively easy pass at some 16,200 feet above sea, reached by the evening of the following day the deep-cut valley of Zailik (Fig. 325). All knowledge of it had previously been denied by the secretive hill-men of Polur. There we found extensive gold-pits dug into the precipitous cliffs of conglomerate just above the gneiss of the stream-bed and evidently worked for long ages. Our irruption into this terribly tortuous and gloomy gorge of Zailik was quite a romantic event for the four dozen or so of gold-seekers who try to exploit what is left of auriferous layers. To us, too, it seemed a wonderful place—this long, rock–bound valley, where from an elevation of about 14,500 feet downwards all the steeply cut faces of conglomerate deposits are honeycombed with galleries and pits often in almost inaccessible places (Fig. 318).

It was difficult to guess how far back in the ages poor wretches had toiled here under all the hardships of a semi-arctic climate and practical slavery. Graves spread over every little bit of level ground which the gorge affords in its twelve to thirteen miles' course down to the junction with the Yurung-kash Valley, and on all sides the roughly

walled-up mouths of abandoned pits showed where many
more of the victims had found their last rest.   In the
days of the 'old Khitai rule' and of Yakub Beg, that
soi-disant liberator, when the digging was carried on by
forced labour, this rugged gorge, with its inclement climate,
must have seen more human misery than one cares to
think of.   Among all the desolate places of the earth to
which *auri sacra fames* has led men, this forbidding ravine,
cut between the most barren of mountains, with its atmosphere of Rider Haggard sensations, might well compete
for the front rank.

To us the discovery of this gloomy gorge proved of
great value.   Leaving our camp at a small grassy plot near
the central point of the present mining activity, some
13,600 feet above the sea, I managed with Lal Singh first
to descend by breakneck paths to the cañon-like valley of
the Yurung-kash (Fig. 320), and on subsequent days to
climb commanding points on a series of high spurs coming
straight down from the main Kun-lun Range northward.
By establishing our survey stations in full view of its crest-
line, here showing an average height of over 20,000 feet,
we managed to map with theodolite, plane-table, and
photographic panoramas, the greater portion of the in-
expressibly grand and wild mountain system containing the
unexplored eastern head-waters of the Yurung-kash.   On
the south, for a distance of over sixty miles, we could see
them flanked by a magnificent range of snowy peaks, rising
to over 23,000 feet, and all clad with glaciers more extensive
than any I had so far seen in the Kun-lun.

Among the peaks to the south-west we could, fortunately,
recognize several of a small group which had been triangulated over forty years earlier from high stations on the
Tibetan uplands to the north of Ladak, and thus exactly
determine our position.   I was all the more grateful for
this as, in spite of the clear weather which had set in after
light snow showers, clouds enveloped the glacier-girt
peak of the great Muz-tagh peak westwards which had
formed so dominating a landmark for our surveys about
Karanghu-tagh.

From the ridges we thus climbed above Zailik there

318. ABANDONED GOLD PITS IN CONGLOMERATE CLIFFS OF ZAILIK GORGE.

319. GROUP OF ZAILIK MINERS WHO SERVED AS CARRIERS.

320. VIEW UP THE YURUNG-KASH RIVER GORGE FROM DEBOUCHURE OF ZAILIK STREAM.

opened out panoramas more impressive and grand than any I had so far seen. As my eyes ranged over that amazing maze of ice-crowned spurs and deep-cut valleys enclosed between the two great Kun-lun ranges and drained by the Yurung-kash, it was an inspiriting thought that the whole of this grim mountain world was unexplored ground, and that in all probability human gaze had never rested so long on it. Who among hunters or miners would climb such high points always exposed to icy winds and beyond the scantiest vegetation which this arid region affords? Everything seemed on such a vast scale, and I wondered how many months or summers it would take to explore all this wonderful and forbidding Alpine world in detail. The long hours we spent at our stations over work with theodolite, planetable, and camera were made most trying by the icy blasts sweeping the crests of the ridges, and our fingers were benumbed while handling the instruments.

The poor miners, too, whom we engaged to carry our instruments (Fig. 319) felt the exposure badly even while the sun shone brightly, and the man whom I had to keep crouching between the legs of the camera stand, to steady it, while the panoramic work slowly proceeded, had to be changed every ten minutes or so to afford relief to his half-frozen hands. But our reward was ample, and to the miners, too, their well-paid exertions afforded a welcome change from their wretched burrowing in dark pits. In the end I gained their confidence sufficiently to obtain information about certain gold-pits which were once worked at points lower down by the precipitous banks of the Yurung-kash, and also about a difficult route, long suspected by me, which led to the latter right across the main range from the head-waters of the Genju River. But we had neither time nor supplies to waste over a descent down the valley, where the river still in full flood would make any crossing impossible.

The Zailik mines, accessible only during a few summer months, are now almost deserted, the total annual production of gold raised with difficulty by the Amban's contractor amounting to about 300 ounces. The small groups of miners toiling in this gloomy gorge are practically all bond-slaves of the contractor, who advances their supplies, clothing, and other necessaries.   Fortunately we were able to secure among them eight or nine porters, without whom it would have been quite impossible to transport our indispensable baggage and instruments over the very difficult ground before us.   Our queer guide Pasa, the yak-hunter, had told me that the tracks by which we were to make our way to the glacier sources of the Yurung-kash would be practicable only for men and possibly donkeys.   So I had the baggage cut down to the barest minimum, leaving everything the ten donkeys with us could not carry to be taken back by the ponies to our Ulugh-köl depot.

CHAPTER XCIII

TO THE YURUNG-KASH GLACIER-SOURCES

On August 25th we set out by a very steep side valley to the south, and crossed the rugged spur between the Zailik and main Yurung-kash Valleys by a pass over 17,700 feet high, leading over what manifestly had once been old névé beds. From a ridge just above the Shalgan Dawan, as Pasa called it, we could obtain once again a glorious panorama (Fig. 321). Here, and in the narrow valley beyond, the decay of all rocks was most striking. We camped about a thousand feet below the pass, and next day had a most trying descent in a steep gorge choked with big boulders and manifestly scooped out by glacier action. Lower down, where the gorge widened somewhat, I noticed old moraines, though the range above now showed only scanty snow-beds. Before the gorge joined the Yurung-kash defile we were surprised by coming upon a patch of ground covered with brushwood. There were indications that the Zailik miners used once to repair here for the sake of burning charcoal.

The view presented by the Yurung-kash Valley, where we reached it at an elevation of a little over 13,000 feet, was singularly impressive in its desolation (Fig. 322). On both banks of the river, which here rolled its greyish-white glacier water in a bed some hundred yards wide, there was nothing to be seen but absolutely bare cliffs of red or yellow sandstone and detritus slopes below them. For over two miles our faint track wound along these dead slopes of rubble. Then it had to drop into the actual river bed to turn a huge projecting rock-wall, and behind it we suddenly

449

found ourselves at the debouchure of a small stream which Pasa called Mandar-kol.

We camped there for the night, and the main valley farther up making a great bend and becoming quite impassable, we had to ascend next day to the top of a high spur eastwards. The pass was about 17,000 feet in height, and once again fortune was kind; for Pasa's track proved to pass quite close to a well-isolated peak making an ideal survey station. So, on August 28th, leaving camp in a small moss-covered ravine at the foot of an old glacier (Fig. 323), we climbed the peak and were rewarded by a magnificent panorama on the top of the highest rock pinnacle. Triangulation subsequently showed its exact height as 18,612 feet. For an hour or two heavy clouds were drifting over the snowy range south; but they lifted about mid-day and a truly grand view was then revealed of the latter.

A huge massif, covered with a continuous mantle of ice and snow, feeding the easternmost sources of the Yurung-kash, came now fully in view to the south-east. But the aspect of the range with its many fine glaciers to the south and south-west of us was almost as imposing, and the distance less (Fig. 324). I did my best to record by camera and copious notes the many interesting orographical features which presented themselves from this glorious station above Tar-kol; but this is not the place to discuss them. Only one striking observation may be mentioned. Whereas on the north slopes of the main range before us the snow-line descended to approximately 17,500 feet, on the slopes of the great spur behind us which faced south it lay certainly as high as 19,500 feet.

Our march of August 29th took us over a succession of somewhat lower side spurs, on the slopes of which traces of wild yaks were abundant, and brought us by nightfall into the little valley of Tüge-tash. There, at an elevation of about 15,000 feet, we spent a miserable night in snow and rain, but next morning had the satisfaction of descending at last to the main Yurung-kash Valley where Pasa declared it to become practicable for further progress. Fantastically eroded rock-faces, composed of shiny slate,

321. VIEW SOUTH TOWARDS SNOWY RANGE FROM RIDGE ABOVE SHALGAN DAVAN, *CIRC.* 17,700 FEET HIGH.

322. VIEW DOWN THE YURUNG-KASH RIVER GORGE FROM DEBOUCHURE OF
HASIB CHAP.

323. VIEW TOWARDS MAIN KUN-LUN RANGE, SOUTH OF YURUNG-KASH RIVER, FROM
CAMP BELOW TAR-KOL PASS.

The elevation of this camp was *circ.* 16,000 feet.

rose wall-like to 2000 feet or more on either side of the Tüge-tash stream, and also lined the right bank of the Yurung-kash where we reached it at last (Fig. 329).

We were now quite close to the huge array of glaciers which cover the north face of the big watershed range towards the Tibetan uplands; but at our elevation of about 14,000 feet we were too low down to get more than glimpses of their snouts protruding between the steep rocky buttresses of the range, 1500 feet higher. For about two miles above the Tüge-tash debouchure the wide rubble-strewn river bed offered easy progress, such as our poor donkeys badly needed after all their hard climbs and scrambles. Then a rugged promontory forced us to ford the river to the right bank. Fortunately it flowed now in two branches, about forty and twenty yards wide, and owing to the cloudy weather and the increasing cold which affected the glacier melting, its depth was nowhere over two feet. Once across we could follow our upward march by the river for a couple of miles over broad alluvial slopes deposited by the streams which came down from the glaciers above. In one place I observed the perfectly formed fan of an ancient terminal moraine, half a mile across, which the Yaghelik-sai glacier must have once pushed right down to the river.

That day's relative ease was a great boon for our patient donkeys; for the most trying day's work on this trip was still before us. Setting out after another miserable night with rain and snow at intervals, we had scarcely moved for a mile and a half up the river when we were brought up by a big glacier stream at a point where the main river makes a sudden bend to the north-east. The stream carried the drainage from at least three huge glaciers we had clearly sighted from the Tar-kol peak, and its volume seemed but little inferior to that of the main river from the east. The vehemence of the tossing greyish mass of water was great as it rushed past between big boulders, and for over an hour we vainly searched for a safe crossing amidst the whirls and cataracts. Yet the day's ice melting had scarcely begun. At last, by posting groups of men near convenient boulders and by the use of ropes, we got the donkeys safely across the thirty yards of seething icy water, three to four feet in depth. Most of the loads, though carried by the men, got thoroughly drenched, the instruments luckily escaping.

A short break in the gusts of driving snow had scarcely allowed the half-benumbed men and animals to warm themselves a little, when we had to start scaling a narrow and extremely steep rock promontory which raised its fantastic crags in the angle between the two valleys. I never quite understood how the donkeys with their loads, light as they were, managed to scramble up here some 500 feet. Then we found ourselves at the top of a narrow rock couloir leading down to the main river branch at an angle of some forty-five degrees (Fig. 326). The step-like ledges of the slaty rock, which in spite of the slippery condition facilitated descent for us men, were too narrow and the turns too sharp for the animals. So they had to be dragged down in the débris-filled centre of the couloir, where the rock fragments, ever giving way under their feet, came down in small avalanches. Several of the poor donkeys lost their balance and tumbled down in somersaults; it seemed a miracle that none of them was seriously injured.

After this descent we had still most difficult ground to face. The river from here upwards rolled its tossing waters, now of a light greenish tint, through a tortuous bed rarely wider than sixty to eighty yards at the bottom (Fig. 327). On the right bank the rock-walls were quite impassable; on the left precipitous cliffs and dangerous slopes of unstable shingle had to be crossed alternately. What track could be made out here and there was that pioneered by wild yaks, which, in fact, with occasional visits from half-tame hunters like Pasa, were alone responsible for the 'route' we had followed since Mandar-kol. The track, less than a foot wide, needed careful clearing where it wound along difficult rock-faces, before the much-shaken donkeys could pass. The precipitous slopes covered with big rock fragments, which looked as if shaken down from the wall-like spur above by some earthquake or landslip, were almost as risky. It took us fully six hours to clear the first two miles in this wonderful gorge above our crossing.

Then after passing a small waterfall the track, though very steep and rocky, presented less danger. On our left across the gorge there was a succession of perfectly wall-like spurs with deep chasms between ; but in front of us there showed at last long rounded ridges of detritus. As we ascended towards these the frowning spur above us assumed fantastic shapes of towers and huge battlemented walls. Decomposition had created here a striking *pendant* to the ' T'ang prince's town ' above Uch-Turfan. The Zailik men at once recognized the ' Kone-shahr ' I pointed out to them, and the sight at once set their ' treasure-seeking ' imagination in motion. How could they doubt that I had really come to this forbidding mountain region in order to search for hidden riches ?

At last we emerged on broad detritus slopes, the four and a half miles from camp having taken us some nine hours of toil. Very soon it became evident that we were moving across the huge terminal moraines, now buried under detritus, of what must once have been a perfect mantle of ice descending from a big spur of over 21,000 feet. Then we passed within less than a mile the end of a still extant glacier flanked by huge moraines. How grateful we felt for the easy going which the bare sodden ground of this fan provided ! We had now reached an elevation of about 15,500 feet, and the rarity of the air was more noticeable.

Under the heavy grey clouds which all day had treated us to showers of snow and sleet, it was soon getting dusk ; but this made the mighty panorama in black and white still more impressive. Fresh snow streaked all the less steep slopes, while to the south the peaks and glaciers rose in unblemished white splendour. But the precipitous rock-walls of the great gorge through which the Yurung-kash has carved its passage loomed in blackness. It seemed as if we had left behind us the dark gate of that wild maze of deep-cut inaccessible valleys, and entered a land of barren downs set amidst ice-clad ranges, the fringe of true Tibet. At last we found shelter for the night in a narrow gorge cutting through the glacier-ground talus slope, and were glad to rest our weary and cold limbs by a camp fire.

Next morning, on September 1st, we marched under a clear sunny sky to the north-east, and after less than four miles had the relief to find the ponies with my tent and much-needed supplies arrived from the Ulugh-köl depot, as previously arranged, under the guidance of one of Pasa's companions, and grazing at a grassy spot near the river's left bank. There we halted at an elevation of 15,600 feet, and let men and donkeys enjoy a day's much-needed repose in the sunshine. We had now reached the great elevated basin where the main feeders of the Yurung-kash meet, coming down from a perfect amphi-theatre of glacier-girt peaks. It was very interesting ground geographically and geologically, with abundant evidence that the glaciers had in a relatively recent period extended over many square miles of what is now a huge rolling plateau covered with glacier mud and ice-carried boulders. I thought of my ancient sites in the desert, and how the recession of all these glacier feeders must have affected their fate.

On September 2nd I climbed with Lal Singh an easy but well-isolated ridge to the north-west, which at its top, about 17,400 feet above the sea, revealed the panorama re-*produced in Plate XII. The view was gloriously clear and wide, and showed to the south and south-west an unbroken line of ice-clad peaks extending in direct distance to upwards of sixty miles. How delighted I was to greet once again all our newly won friends, familiar from our earlier 'stations,' bold snowy peaks with triangulated heights reaching up to over 23,000 feet, and glaciers no less imposing because they had no names! The sight of the great mantle of ice enveloping the big spur just in front of us to the south was truly glorious. Its glaciers seen at a near distance formed a broad glittering rim to the big basin stretching away southward to the uppermost sources of the river. These could be located at an enormous glacier which was visible up to its head at some twenty miles' distance. But the snowy massif from

*Plate XII is in the pocket attached to the inside back cover of this volume.

which this ice-stream descends in the innermost angle of
the range was clear of clouds only at intervals.

It is impossible to describe here all the features which
gave overwhelming grandeur to this panorama, and which
no photograph can adequately render. But I may allude
to the sharp, needle-like peaks I saw rising in groups to
the north-east above the long bare ridges separating us
from the Ulugh-köl depression. They formed part of the
northern main Kun-lun where it is broken through by
the Keriya and Niya rivers ; in the gaps between them
my gaze wandered down to those parched plains beyond
hidden under yellowish haze.

It seemed hard to forsake this immense mountain
horizon, and harder still to forgo all endeavour at more
detailed exploration of the Yurung-kash sources. But I
had now succeeded in tracing the river's course to its very
head, and been able to form a true idea of the unfailing
stores of ice which supply the Khotan River with its
enormous summer flood, and enable it for a few months to
carry its waters victoriously right through the thirsty
desert. The report received from Ibrahim Beg about the
fodder supplies still available at our depot showed that
there was not a day to be lost in the start for the Kara-
kash head-waters.

So on September 3rd we set out for Ulugh-köl, and
after marching over flat detritus plateaus bearing abundant
traces of former glaciation, crossed the stripling Yurung-
kash just where its bed turns sharply south (Fig. 328).
Then an easy ascent over rubble beds past the snout of
the much-torn Gügrüge glacier took us up to a grass-
covered saddle, less than 16,000 feet above the sea, where
the Yurung-kash drainage was left behind almost before we
became aware of it. That evening we found our depot
not far from the southern end of the Ulugh-köl, and camped
once more on ground typically Tibetan, looking flat and
tame after the rugged world of ice and rock we had passed
through.

CHAPTER XCIV

ACROSS TIBETAN PLATEAUS

A busy evening and morning at Ulugh-köl were spent over selecting the fittest of the spare donkeys, and making up reserve loads of supplies and baggage. It was encouraging to note how well the brave donkeys, which struggled through with us, had stood all their trials. The less fit-looking animals were sent back to Polur, as twenty donkeys would now suffice for the reduced stores; for these and the hired ponies we retained the five sturdiest of the 'Kirakash' men. The little band of gold-miners who had proved so helpful were discharged to Zailik with ample reward and adequate food for the journey. Of all the motley company there were to remain with us only Pasa and one of his fellow-hunters, the former newly equipped with a good fur-coat which I bought for him as a present off the back of a returning pony-man.

Then we started, on September 4th, under the farewell blessings of those who were glad to escape the hardships still before us. My object was to follow the great snowy range, which flanks the Yurung-kash head-waters on the south-east and south along its southern slopes westwards, until we reached the uppermost valley of the Kara-kash River, and thus to complete our survey of what had now proved to be the true main chain of the Kun-lun. For this purpose we had first to march by the Polur-Ladak route to the elevated basin, more than 17,000 feet above the sea, where the Keriya River rises.

The five marches we made along this route took us over ground already surveyed by Captain Deasy, and my account of them may, therefore, be brief. On the first

324. VIEW SOUTH-WEST TOWARDS MAIN KUN-LUN RANGE, FROM TRIANGULATED PEAK ABOVE TAR-KOL PASS.

The elevation of this peak, used as a survey station, is 18,612 feet.

326. DONKEYS DESCENDING ROCK COULOIR FROM SPUR ABOVE
HEAD GORGE OF YURUNG-KASH RIVER.

325. ZAILIK GORGE BELOW SAGHIZ-BUYAN, VIEWED FROM WEST.

day we struck the actual route by a short cut over a
spur west of it, and there obtained a parting view of the
Yurung-kash head-waters (Fig. 330).   That night we had
a fairly heavy fall of snow, and its cover was promptly
used by the wily Pasa to decamp with his comrade.   He
had shown so much experience of these mountains and
such resourcefulness that I had been eager to enlist his
help as a hunter and 'guide,' even though he protested
never to have been beyond the uppermost Keriya River.
His taking French leave in this fashion without waiting
for his wages was a proof both of his half-savage slimness
and of the dread which he, too, hardened as he was by his
roving life in the mountains, entertained for the wastes
before us.   Yet I felt so grateful for his previous guidance that in the end, disregarding this desertion, I sent a
well-earned reward through Badruddin Khan to his home
near Keriya.

Both Lal Singh and Jasvant Singh had followed the
route before.   So we had not much difficulty, in spite of
repeated snow-showers, about finding the track to the
Baba Hatim Pass, which at an elevation of about 17,600
feet gives access to the Keriya River.   But the descent
from it proved unexpectedly trying.   The last few days'
rain and snow had sufficed to turn the steep but otherwise
easy gorge into a perfect couloir of loose boulders intermixed with sliding mud.   It took long hours to get the
ponies down, and our poor donkeys could not be brought
in till late at night.   Even then half their loads were left
behind in the gorge to be recovered next day.

From that bleak and wind-swept spot we made our
way south in two marches to the head of the great elevated
basin, at an altitude of about 17,200 feet, where the
Keriya River rises at the foot of a line of great glaciers.
The range from which they descend proved identical with
the easternmost part of the ice-clad range confining the
Yurung-kash sources.   Our passage up to the Keriya River
head-waters, and for days after, was greatly impeded by
trying weather.   Frequent snow-storms swept across the
high plateaus and valleys, and the slush they deposited,
slight as it was each time, soon converted the gentle

slopes of detritus into veritable bogs, very difficult to cross
for animals already suffering from the effects of great
altitude, exposure, and an almost total absence of grazing.

Such conditions made the march, on September 7th,
along the broad basin of the Keriya River sources extremely
tiring, even though most of the ground was a level plain
(Fig. 331). Whenever the sun broke through between
the snow-storms my eyes could revel in the glorious glacier
array to the west, with wonderful bluish tints in its
shadows. There were plenty of interesting geographical
features to observe here, *e.g.* about the wholly impassable
gorge by which the infant Keriya River, like the Yurung-
kash, escapes from the cradle of its birth. But however
stimulating these impressions, they could not let me forget
the misery of that night's camp. The exhaustion of the
animals obliged us to halt by the side of a long lagoon.
The ground was so sodden that men and animals alike
felt glad to huddle on a narrow ridge of sand fringing the
shore. An icy gale, driving snow at intervals, passed
over us all the night. Apart from their rations of oats
there was absolutely nothing for the animals to eat. No
wonder that next morning the first victim remained behind
at this dismal camp. It was a poor pony, unable to move,
which a carbine bullet put out of pain.

That day, too, most of our efforts had to be spent in
extricating tired animals from foundering in the detritus
mud, and in finding tracks round impassable bogs. It
was almost a relief to have to climb up a spur close on
18,000 feet high, which crossed our route, as it meant
temporary escape from these miseries. Curiously enough
we had already crossed below it the almost imperceptible
watershed which divides the Keriya River drainage from
that of Lake Lighten. The wide valley beyond the spur
had so level a bottom that even Lal Singh's experienced
eye at first mistook the direction in which it was trending.

It was a great relief for us all when at last the flood-
beds meandering over the sodden plain united in a well-
defined channel and a sandy plateau came in sight.
There were wild asses grazing on the scanty tufts of
'yellow grass,' and when by nightfall we pitched camp

there, it must have seemed like paradise to our weary animals. Unfortunately the severe cold of the night, with a minimum temperature of seventeen degrees Fahrenheit below freezing-point, kept them from much enjoyment of the grazing, such as it was. We humans luckily now had the roots of the hardy scrub known to Tibetans as Burtze to fall back upon for fuel.

Here on the morning of September 9th we left the Ladak route in order to turn south-west to Lake Lighten. From there we should have to start our exploration of the ground westwards, which in atlases generally figures as a high plain with the name of 'Ak-sai-chin desert,' but which the latest Trans-frontier map of the Survey of India rightly showed as an unsurveyed blank. The valley we continued to follow was itself unknown ground; but after a long day's march it proved to drain into the lake, as I had assumed from the first.

The sky had now cleared, and the going was easy, but the ground was very barren. For four days the animals had had hardly any grass; so that the outlook began to be serious. Fortunately after twenty miles we came upon sparsely growing 'yellow grass,' just where the glittering sheet of water was first sighted. There was no fuel of any sort to cook with. But it was inspiriting to look northward to the high snowy peaks crowning the watershed towards the Yurung-kash head-waters, with a still higher ice-sheeted cone to the north-west. So I at least found it easier to forget the loss of a dinner. The whole scene, with the far-stretching lake and the rampart of snowy mountains above it, looked strangely majestic and lonely.

As the lake had before been sighted only from one corner in the south, I decided to follow a route by its north shore. It took us at first across a wide delta of detritus deposited by streams coming from the snowy peaks, but now completely dry, and then over low plateaus forming the foot of spurs which descend with easy slopes from the main range. Old shore lines and lagoons almost cut off by sandy peninsulas from the main lake showed that the expanse of the latter was shrinking. Yet with a length of over twenty miles and an average width of four or five, it was an imposing and beautiful sight (Fig. 332). Its hues ranged from light green to purple, and the relatively low but very bold range which stretched along its south shore, being entirely covered by fresh snow, provided a most effective setting. Hypsometrical readings gave a height of close on 16,100 feet for the lake.

Towards the middle of the day's march we passed clearly recognizable old moraines in a valley stretching down from a side spur which was now quite clear even of snow. A line of big ice-worn boulders showed that the longest of the peninsulas projecting into the lake was but a continuation of those moraines. So at some period glaciers from the north must have pushed their tongues right into the lake. The latter, with its glorious colours and numerous bays and inlets, looked most inviting for a cruise. But the solitude of its waters and shores was complete.

From a broad plateau crossed after thirteen miles' march a splendid view spread before us to the north and north-east. The line of great snowy peaks above the Yurung-kash and Keriya River sources rose in a grand amphitheatre, distant but none the less impressive. The spurs descending from it, for twelve to fifteen miles from the lake showed slopes singularly easy. Broad valleys stretched up between, in striking contrast to the tortuous deep-cut gorges which separate the spurs descending from the same range northward to the Yurung-kash. The higher slopes were all under snow, but no glaciers were to be seen. Altogether it was evident that the natural obstacles to the detailed exploration of the watershed range would be far less from this side. But, alas! our supplies and the strength of our animals were limited, and we could not linger.

A speedy passage to the Kara-kash drainage was now urgent. So it was reassuring when from that plateau we sighted the western end of the lake, and could recognize beyond it the commencement of a depression which seemed likely to open to us the hoped-for route westwards. In the wide valley to which we then descended there were extensive patches of coarse grass, and herds of wild yaks and asses could be seen grazing higher up. Brilliant

327. VIEW DOWN THE HEAD GORGE OF YURUNG-KASH RIVER, FROM AN
ELEVATION OF *CIRC.* 15,000 FEET.

328. VIEW SOUTH TOWARDS GLACIERS OF MAIN KUN-LUN RANGE FROM
HEAD-WATERS BASIN OF YURUNG-KASH.

329. SLATE CLIFFS RISING ABOVE RIGHT BANK OF YURUNG-KASH, NEAR
DEBOUCHURE OF TÜGE-TASH STREAM.

sunshine still intensified all the colours of the scene when we pitched camp here, and it was refreshing to see our hard-tried animals revel in the pasture, such as it was, while the warmth of the setting sun lasted. But their treat did not last long, for by nightfall a snow-storm was again sweeping down from the mountains.

On September 11th we started under a sky grey with snow-laden clouds for the western extremity of the lake. A bluff rocky promontory soon stopped progress by the shore, and forced us to ascend a valley behind it in the hope of finding a passage practicable for the animals higher up. The western bearing of this valley tempted us to follow it right up to its head, which promised a 'short cut' towards the great depression expected beyond the lake. We reached the previously sighted saddle, about 17,700 feet above sea, without serious trouble early in the afternoon; and in spite of the driving sleet and the snow which covered the ground, could have made good our object if only our baggage train had followed us. But the faint-hearted drivers, afraid of the pass, had preferred to lag behind, deceiving Ibrahim Beg with a forged message. By the time we had gone back to fetch them it was too late to cross the pass, and we had to descend again into the valley for the night's camp. It meant practically the loss of a day, and the icy gale which howled all night did not help to raise our spirits.

Next morning we discovered a passage practicable for laden animals over the low but precipitous ridge fringing the lake shore. The descent was made, and after six miles we reached a low spur which overlooked the westernmost inlet of the lake. Wild asses were grazing here in small groups, but with their usual shyness effectively evaded our rifles. As soon as we turned the spur a great change took place in the landscape. We found ourselves in a wide depression edged on the south by a low range of red hills, apparently sandstone, stretching far away westwards and on the north by the foot of the great snowy range behind which lay the Yurung-kash Valley. Here at last I felt assured about our hoped-for route. Undismayed by repeated snow-showers and an icy gale, our column moved on steadily over this easy ground until we struck a huge alluvial fan of bare gravel streaked by small channels mostly dry.

It was the debouchure of a big side valley, at the head of which a number of glaciers showed, evidently fed by the eternal snows of the Yurung-kash watershed. After a twenty miles' march we halted by the side of a small hillock rising island-like above this vast delta of detritus. A gloriously clear evening revealed once more all the splendours of the great chain to the north. Above the big valley there rose a majestic ice-girt peak, 23,490 feet high, which by the look of its double cone and its position we could clearly identify as one already sighted by us from our 'hill station' above Tar-kol. Glaciers of great size filled the heads of all the valleys here descending from the main range. The vista from our hillock was one of quasi-arctic grandeur, and the silent solitude all round heightened the impression of vastness. That we could not afford even a day's halt for triangulation caused a pang to both Lal Singh and myself.

On the morning of September 13th, when the minimum thermometer showed seventeen degrees Fahrenheit below freezing-point, a cloudy sky had effaced the more distant vision. Pursued by a succession of icy gales and showers of snow we crossed an almost imperceptible watershed towards a second large flood-bed draining the range north. Fitfully the sun broke through for short intervals, allowing us to sight again some fine snowy peaks already triangulated by us from the other side. We were moving over bare gravel wastes; and it was curious how soon a spell of sunshine would produce in the rarefied air Fata Morgana visions of blue lakes and hillocks raised into the air. But the ground seemed to grow if anything more dismal. At last, after a march of over twenty miles, we came upon a small stream, and finding some hardy patches of grass could camp by its bank. The baggage animals straggled in with ominous slowness. The bitterly cold night added to their suffering, and next morning two donkeys being found quite unable to move had to be shot when we started.

Our march that day led mainly westwards above the wide depression in which the bed of the stream, now practically dry, seemed to descend. We skirted the foot of some low barren spurs trending from the north ; but since the snowy main range now took a decided turn to the north-west we soon lost sight of its peaks. The increased distance from its life-giving snow and ice expressed itself in the absolute barrenness of the ground, even near flood-channels, in the diminishing moisture there, and the absence of all animal life. The view to the west was still encouragingly open; but I looked out in vain for any distinct sign of the great salt lake which early in the 'sixties pioneers of the Indian Trigonometrical Survey had roughly located in this region, and which by our bearings I thought we ought now to be nearing.

Under a burning afternoon sun we crossed a wide alluvial fan and found the flood-channels over its expanse absolutely dry. This was a new difficulty. There was no chance of getting water here, though dead Burtze roots showed that running water must have been near once. So I turned off to the north-west towards the foot of a low spur. The shallow Nullah we there met held no stream. But there were some grass-covered patches in the dry bed. Just as if we were in the Taklamakan, we took to digging a well at a spot which felt moist, and at a depth of three feet came upon fresh water. So men and beasts got a drink at least after the twenty miles' tiring march over ground still about 15,500 feet above the sea. But the violent east wind made the bitterly cold night very trying for the men who had difficulty in collecting enough fuel, and for our poor animals which vainly searched for shelter. Next morning another pony succumbed after having stood motionless behind my little tent all night.

Some relief came on the morning of September 15th, when in crossing a low saddle some four miles from camp, I sighted a glittering sheet of salt efflorescence stretching far away in the distance. It marked the bed of the large salt lake which was now for the most part dry. Its total length proved upwards of sixteen miles, and only

when approaching its western portion did we notice that
a long stretch along the south shore still held water.   The
ground over which we had to move skirting this much-
shrunken lake bed to the north-west was more depressing than any before.   The detritus of the slopes
we descended was so soft that one's feet sank in deep.
Along the shore of the dried-up marsh this soil was broken
up by large holes full of 'Shor.'   There was no sign of
life, plant, or animal to be seen anywhere except a big
vulture which kept sailing above us for a long time,
evidently in expectation of another victim.   I wondered
which of our poor mute companions it would be.

At last in the evening, after crossing a low barren
spur, we found ourselves on the east edge of a broad
desolate valley coming straight down from the main snowy
range.   For a short time the clouds lifted and allowed
me to sight again a few of the bold ice-capped pyramids
last seen from above Karanghu-tagh.   But even more
keenly did we scan the wide gravel bed of the valley
for any trace of running water by which to camp.   There
was none, and the outlook was gloomy indeed.   With Lal
Singh I hurried ahead of the lagging caravan across the
detritus waste, and at last came upon a strip of ground
supporting scanty tufts of 'yellow grass.'   On arrival I
set the despondent pony-men to work at a well, which,
luckily at a depth of some four feet, yielded very muddy
but drinkable water.   How strange it seemed to have to
re-enact familiar desert scenes on these Tibetan uplands!
The ponies I had sent to a large lagoon visible near the
lake shore in the hope of their getting an adequate drink
earlier ; but at night they were brought back without having
touched a drop of its brackish water.

330. DISTANT VIEW OF GLACIERS FEEDING THE YURUNG-KASH SOURCES, FROM PASS EAST OF ULUGH-KÖL.

331. GLACIERS OVERLOOKING THE BASIN OF THE KERIYA RIVER SOURCES FROM WEST. Elevation of basin *circ.* 17,200 feet.

332. VIEW ACROSS SOUTH-WEST END OF LAKE LIGHTEN.
Elevation of lake *circ.* 16,000 feet above the sea.

333. 'WITNESSES' IN WIND-ERODED DRY LAKE BED NEAR CAMP OF SEPTEMBER 16TH, 1908.
Aziz standing on a witness, Ibrahim Beg riding behind another.   Elevation *circ.* 15,300 feet above the sea.

CHAPTER XCV

ON AN OLD MOUNTAIN TRACK

THE salt lake skirted on our march of September 15th was manifestly the same which is shown, though with very different outlines, in the sketch map illustrating the route Johnson followed in 1865 on his plucky journey from Ladak to Karanghu-tagh and Khotan. This observation confirmed me in my original intention to try and make my way to the upper Kara-kash Valley by keeping a north-westerly course until we struck Johnson's route. I did not disguise to myself nor to trusty Lal Singh that as we were now situated, with our animals more or less on their last legs and the fodder supplies nearing exhaustion, this plan involved considerable risks. I knew from previous experience that Johnson's route sketch done under special difficulties could not be trusted for details; and even if we could discover his track, probably still two marches off, it was doubtful whether the ground he had passed with yaks would be practicable for our worn-out animals. However, I felt that the die was cast.

There was little encouragement when, on September 16th, after a weary ascent of eight miles we gained the saddle of a low barren range to the north-west, at an elevation of about 16,800 feet. Before us lay a huge basin absolutely sterile and showing a series of dry salt-encrusted lagoons disposed somewhat in the shape of a horseshoe. The total area of the dismal depression over which our eyes ranged could scarcely be less than four hundred square miles. Where should we find here vegetation, such as it is on these Tibetan plains, or even drinkable water? Death-like torpor lay over the whole region ; no living creature could be sighted nor even the track of one.   The thought then struck me vividly whether this was not a foretaste of what the surface of our globe might become in a distant future, after all moisture had departed and the rocks of the great ranges crumbled away under climatic extremes.   It all seemed as lifeless and hopeless as a landscape in the moon.

Along gentle slopes of detritus and crossing an absolutely dry river bed fully four miles wide at its debouchure, we descended towards the centre of the basin.   The salt-impregnated soil we struck in the evening while facing a snowy gale caused serious misgivings about water ; for on such soil well-digging would be useless.   But when I set out in the twilight to reconnoitre the ground to the west, I came upon a well-marked dry lake bed and to my surprise and relief upon a small stream with water just drinkable meandering in the midst of this salt waste.   Glad enough was I to bring my camp there, though there was no trace of vegetation dead or living to be found anywhere.

At this miserable spot I had the great grief to lose my hardy Badakhshi pony which had carried me ever since I entered Turkestan, except when I worked in the desert, and had never shown any sign of distress, even when crossing the Taklamakan on the scantiest allowance of water.   He was always equal to the hardest of fares, and would cheerfully chew even ancient dead wood if nothing more nourishing was in reach.   He had been ailing only since the morning, exactly from what, the united wisdom of my men, familiar as they all were with horseflesh, had failed to make out.   But when he was brought into camp his case already looked most serious.

I did all I could in that wilderness to procure comfort to my faithful comrade of twenty-seven months' travel, wrapping him in whatever felt and blankets could be spared during that bitterly cold night and giving him almost the whole of the bottle of Port I had kept for emergencies, mixed with hot water.   We had brought along some Burtze roots from the last camp just sufficient to cook our tea and meal.   But all endeavours to save 'Badakhshi' proved in vain.   When I got up before daybreak to look after him—men had in turn watched over him during the night—my poor companion lay in convulsions. Yet he recognized me when I stroked him, and on my holding some oats close to his mouth he struggled to get on his legs. Then the end came suddenly and brought relief from all pain.

I felt 'Badakhshi's' loss most keenly; for in the course of such long travels and hardships in common I had grown very fond of my brave and spirited mount, with his shapely head like an Arab's and his love of the wilds. Often I had pictured to myself our joint delight when I might let him taste on a Kashmir Marg what real grass and Alpine flowers were like. But the Gods had willed it otherwise and let him succumb, when the goal seemed so near, in the dreariest waste I had seen.

Our start that morning, September 17th, was made under the gloomiest aspects. So far careful rationing had allowed us to give each pony four to five pounds of oats daily and each donkey about half that amount. Grazing there had been practically none for the animals since September 12th, and now the remaining fodder store would just suffice for a day's feed at half rations. Yet no vegetation could be hoped for until we had descended to the Kara-kash Valley, and as we were unable to locate our position with reference to Johnson's rough route sketch, the distance thither remained very uncertain. The spirits of the men were very low, and the strength of the animals evidently giving out. I, too, felt it difficult to bear up against the depressing influence of nature.

We first trudged across sodden ground with occasional dry lagoons to the north-west until increasing marshiness obliged us to turn due north. There we struck a curious elongated dry lake bed undergoing wind erosion, and with its isolated clay terraces exactly reproducing on a small scale the characteristic features of the terminal Su-lo Ho basin (Fig. 333). The terraces, only six to ten feet high, displayed plain lacustrine stratification and clearly indicated that erosion was proceeding by winds striking west to east. Some large pools of brackish water lay quite close to the west of the 'Yardangs.'

As we skirted these swamps on their north side we again struck the winding bed of the stream by which we had camped, but found that its water, now extremely sluggish in flow, had turned too salt for drinking. Our onward route lay along the foot of bare spurs covered with reddish detritus. Up to a level of eighty to one hundred feet above the present marsh bed they all showed well-marked old shore lines; in places eight or ten of them could be clearly distinguished. When the water of the lake had stood so much higher, it probably communicated with a big extension of the basin which was visible westwards beyond a line of broken ridges fringing the extant salt marsh. The march along the detritus terraces was most depressing. Not a sign of life showed, and my thoughts turned back to the description of a big subterranean lake which had much impressed me in one of Jules Verne's stories read when I was a child. The valley which the day before I had sighted in the north-west corner of the basin, and which I fondly hoped would give us access to the Kara-kash drainage, seemed ever to retire farther.

At last after rounding a beautifully regular alluvial fan, some ten miles from camp, below an amphitheatre of small barren Nullahs, there suddenly opened a big valley due north. From its debouchure, fully one and a half miles wide, some snowy peaks showed, perhaps of a spur near the main range. The sight encouraged me to hope that at last we might be nearing the valley from which Johnson's sketch showed the " Kitai diwan Pass " leading north-west across to a feeder of the Kara-kash. But certain features, due as it proved afterwards to erroneous sketching, still effectively interfered with any clear identification. Confirmation appeared unexpectedly in the shape of two small stone-heaps I noticed close to the debouchure, half-buried under coarse sand and gravel. These were manifestly meant to mark a route coming from the south, and the first trace left by human hands we had seen since the Baba Hatim Pass.

Half a mile farther up my eye caught straight lines of stones laid on a level expanse of sand at the foot of some cliffs. They proved to belong to a small oblong platform for Muhammadan prayer and to what may have been intended to symbolize a rest-house. There could no longer be any doubt ; we had struck the old route, forgotten for more than forty years. By it Haji Habibullah, chief of Khotan at the commencement of the last Muhammadan rebellion, tried to open up direct communication with Ladak and India, while the Kara-koram route was in Yakub Beg's hold. Over this route that ill-fated ruler's envoy took Johnson in 1865 on his adventurous visit to Khotan as already related in Chapter XVII. Haji Habibullah had probably ordered the construction of shelters along this difficult route, such as I had seen at Khushlash Langar near Karanghu-tagh, and his subordinates naturally contented themselves with laying down rough slabs for the ground plan !

Desolate as was the place they had chosen for this symbolic 'Langar,' water would have to be near it. So we were not surprised after another half-mile to come upon a small shallow stream lost farther down in the wide gravel bed. The soil near it was so spongy that we might have found the crossing difficult had not a line of white horse-skulls guided us across the bog. All the men rejoiced at having been rightly led to a route which human feet had trodden before. Yet the valley was as barren and salt-encrusted as the basin behind us, and apprehensions about the night's camp had become serious when at last, four miles above the first cairn, we saw the first stumps of dead Burtze cropping out. A couple of miles higher up living specimens of that hardy plant survived in scattered clumps, and as this would help our half-starving transport, we gladly pitched camp there at an elevation of over 15,700 feet. Reconnoitring farther up, I discovered that we were within one mile of the mouth of a side valley marked by stone-heaps and evidently leading up to the ' Khitai Dawan ' meant by Johnson.

All through the evening and night a violent west wind howled, chilling one to the bone in the open and threatening to bring down the tents. Luckily we had fuel in plenty. But the poor animals must have felt it badly in spite of their felts, and two more donkeys had to be shot in the morning. Then we moved on into the side valley to the north-west, and near a cairn at its mouth found a store of Burtze roots white with age but still serviceable.

The pass in front proved nearer and lower than Johnson's sketch map had led me to expect. A well-marked track led up to it, and the animals crossed without much additional exertion. The elevation was just about 16,500 feet. At the top was a large and well-built cairn in perfect preservation, and the sight cheered my Khotan men greatly; they now felt convinced that we were on a 'Padshah's high road,' and had only to stick to it to get back to human beings. It was a characteristic proof of the dryness of the climate even on this high elevation that the cairns, the stacks of Burtze roots stored for fuel, and other small relics, such as a horseshoe, left behind here by those who followed this route during the few years it was last in use about 1864-66, had survived almost intact.

The descent was delightfully easy over broad detritus slopes, where the old track, not trodden by man for over forty years, was perfectly well defined. Officious—or could it be timorous?—hands had taken the trouble to mark it with small stone-heaps at intervals of only a few hundred yards. After six miles or so from the pass we halted near rows of big slate blocks laid out as if to mark Tibetan 'Obos.' Some small birds which had taken shelter among them lay dead. Had the frost stopped them in their flight to the warm South?

Some three miles lower down, our valley joined a still wider one, showing a good deal of coarse grass and gently trending south. It probably drained into the unsurveyed basin seen westwards on the preceding day's march. But what interested us far more was to find that the gap which we had noticed from above by the side of a high range facing us, and by which we hoped to effect our passage to the Kara-kash drainage, was not a pass but a wide and almost flat saddle, about 16,000 feet above the sea. As we marched over it to the north, passing a scarcely perceptible watershed, there appeared before us two parallel valleys separated by a rocky ridge and descending westwards. Both were overlooked by a towering snow-capped range. It was clearly a part of the main Kun-lun watershed behind which lay Karanghu-tagh, and the valleys before us could only drain to the Kara-kash. So no further effort need be exacted from our weary animals, and the relief this gave me was great.

As we descended in the nearer valley, which for a mile or so had more the appearance of a narrow flat-bottomed basin, we found its bed of soft detritus traversed by numerous tracks of wild yaks and asses. Suddenly my eyes caught recent-looking footprints of two men. Were these Kirghiz who had come to hunt or—to look out for us? Lower down, the valley narrowed and a deep-cut ravine in its centre disclosed on its right side the remains of a huge moraine. The masses of ice-worn granite boulders lay bare to a height of over one hundred feet.

A fairly good track wound along them, marked with well-preserved cairns, and brought us down to the junction with the second valley, which contained a swift snow-fed stream. This, spreading out amidst a flat boulder-strewn space at the junction, gave life to a modest amount of vegetation, and just below the confluence we found a roughly built shelter formed by walls of unhewn stones around some big overhanging rocks. It could not be anything else but the ' Haji Langar ' which old Satip-aldi, the Kirghiz Beg, had mentioned as having been built by Haji Habibullah's order where his route crossed the Kara-kash valley.

So after all hardships the goal of our expedition was safely reached, just when we had no more fodder to offer to the much-tried animals. But it was bitter to think of brave ' Badakhshi ' lying stiff and cold in that forbidding dead waste of salt, as I watched the other ponies raven-ously enjoying the grazing, limited as it was. Of course, we stopped here for the night, and the men, comfortably sheltered from the icy wind blowing up the valley, blessed the memory of ' Haji Padshah ' who had built this Langar to succour weary wayfarers.

I, too, felt grateful to the rebel ruler who, during his brief spell of power, had taken such trouble to mark the

approach to that forgotten route across the main Kun-lun
Range which I had tried hard to trace from the Karanghu-
tagh side.   No doubt it was the same by which the tyrant,
Aba Bakr, early in the sixteenth century, had made good
his escape to Ladak.   For long centuries it was probably
known to the wily hillmen as a track to be used in emergencies, a difficult loophole to safety for desperate men.   But
before Haji Habibullah, no Khotan ruler had attempted
to turn it into a trade route of his own to India.   The
effort had been as short-lived as Khotan's last independence.
Yet for me there was a sort of pathetic interest in finding
myself linked even beyond the ice-covered Kun-lun with
the historical past of Khotan.

On the morning of September 19th we started early
down the valley in order to reach, if possible, Abdul-
Ghafur-tam, the highest point in the main Kara-kash
Valley, where there was adequate grazing, and where I
expected Satip-aldi Beg's men to be awaiting us with
yaks and fresh supplies.   For over a mile the old route,
carefully lined with cairns, led along the edge of a barren
alluvial plateau, and I noticed marks of improvement at
places where it crossed broad torrent beds draining small
side valleys.   Then the line of cairns was seen running
straight across a huge alluvial fan to the north-west
towards the mouth of a valley coming down from the main
range.   It thus became certain that Johnson's 'Yangi
Dawan,' which led across the high range above Karanghu-
tagh, and for which I had looked out so long, would have
to be searched for somewhere at the head of that valley.

We continued to march down by the side of our
steadily widening river bed in which all water had now disappeared amidst rubble.   At last, after nine miles, we came
opposite to the point of junction with the main branch of
the Kara-kash River where it breaks through the flanking
range from the south, and I was relieved to find that
its vast bed of rubble, fully a mile broad, held at least a
few small and shallow channels of running water.   Of
vegetation there had been no trace since we left Haji
Langar, and the animals were now again showing plain
signs of exhaustion.   At last some five miles lower down

narrow banks of grass began to line the foot of the cliffs on either side of the flood-bed, and there we were obliged to halt, the baggage not coming in till much later.

In the evening I despatched Muhammadju on the strongest of the ponies down the valley to carry news of our arrival to the Kirghiz at Abdul-Ghafur-tam, which I knew could not be far off, and thence to Tila Bai whom I hoped he would find safely arrived with our convoy of antiques at Suget Karaul, some eighty miles farther down. It was a delightful surprise when three hours later a commotion in camp announced the arrival of Satip-aldi Beg in person. The faithful old Kirghiz, with his yaks and men, had been waiting for us a fortnight, and the arrangements, too, I had ordered months before for our onward journey across the Kara-koram had all been effected in good time. I received also welcome assurance of the safe arrival of Tila Bai's convoy at Suget Karaul, and felt quite in touch again with the world when Satip-aldi Beg handed me a letter from Captain Oliver dated early in August which held out full promise of help from the Ladak side. The old Beg rode off the same night with a letter to be sent on ahead to Captain Oliver, specifying the approximate date when we should need yaks for the route beyond the Kara-koram. Then for the first time after what seemed like long months, I could take my rest without anxious cares.

CHAPTER XCVI

THE SEARCH FOR THE YANGI DAWAN

On the morning of September 20th there arrived five sturdy Kirghiz with yaks and a few camels bringing the badly needed supplies of fodder for our animals, and of flour, butter, and sheep for us men. The day passed peacefully, giving rest for my men and a chance of quiet work on notes and plane-table for myself and Lal Singh. It also allowed me to make arrangements for the only exploratory task still remaining. This was to trace Haji Habibullah's route up to the point where it crossed the main Kun-lun range above Karanghu-tagh, and at the same time to determine the position of the ' Yangi Dawan ' with reference to our surveys of 1900 and 1906 which had been effected from the other side. Light snow fell overnight ; but on the following morning the sun shone out brightly, and leaving all our own animals and spare baggage behind, we set out with yaks and two lightly laden camels to return to Haji Habibullah's route. The yaks marched splendidly, and by noon we had gained the debouchure of the valley we had previously sighted leading to the pass. The aneroid showed here the same approximate elevation as for Haji Langar, 14,700 feet above the sea.

For about five miles the route up the valley led over broad detritus plateaus along the right bank of a wide drainage bed, absolutely dry. Small cairns, looking as if built yesterday, marked the track all along. Then it crossed a deep gorge coming from the west, where regular walls of rough stones had been built to facilitate descent in zigzags along the steep banks. I could see no trace of erosion having damaged the inclines thus supported. It was strange to come upon this bit of road-making on a long-forgotten route. How long would it last? Beyond, the track ascended at the bottom of a boulder-filled gorge coming from the range north. After a mile we passed a small stone enclosure under a shelter-ing rock wall, and in front of it found a large heap of mouldering Burtze roots, just as the last travellers must have left it over forty years before. On all sides was evidence of the extraordinary dryness of this region.

At about six and a half miles from the debouchure we passed what proved the last cairn, and higher up the bottom of the gorge considerably narrowed, being hemmed in by huge cliffs of what looked like gneiss. A short distance farther on the gradient became steep, and just there two ravines met, one coming from a glacier snout visible about a mile and a half off to the north, and the other from a snow-filled side valley opening towards the east. The ridges above the latter showed no marked depression and seemed to rise to fully 20,000 feet. Proceeding up the northern ravine we soon came to a spot where it widened slightly, receiving branches from the north-west and north-east, and there we pitched camp in a grim wilderness of rock, detritus, and snow, at an elevation of close on 16,700 feet.

Two of the Kirghiz told us that about sixteen days before, when sent by Satip-aldi Beg to look out for us, they had of their own accord reconnoitred the glacier above in search of the 'Yangi Dawan' they knew of by tradition. After a steep ascent along the rocks flanking the glacier from the west, they had found the surface of the ice practicable and, with its gentle snow-covered slope, apparently affording a possible approach to the watershed; but snowy weather had prevented them from ascending to this.

The description of the Kirghiz, plain and matter-of-fact like their persons, lent support to the belief that the depression they had seen in the range was really the looked-for pass. Apart from the necessity of settling this point, several considerations made me anxious to reach the watershed. It was my only chance to clear up a number of interesting questions which the orography of the ice-clad spurs south and south-west of Karanghu-tagh still presented, and which were made particularly puzzling by certain features of Johnson's route sketch. Nor did there seem any other hope of linking up our recent surveys with our previous mapping from the north side, and for fixing our position accurately with reference to triangulated peaks, two of which I knew ought to be looked for quite near our valley.

So I determined to make the ascent on the morrow if the weather would permit. Besides Musa, the Surveyor's hardy follower, four of the Kirghiz were to accompany Lal Singh and myself, and they all readily agreed. Accustomed as these Kirghiz are to hunting yaks in glacier-filled valleys, they fully appreciated the use of the roping I indicated as a necessary precaution against crevasses. An icy wind from the west had brought snow showers in the evening. But the sky was perfectly clear when I rose before 4 A.M., and though a restless night, due to an attack of colic, made me feel somewhat below par, I decided not to miss this rare chance for survey work. There was, in fact, only the choice between making the ascent that day or abandoning the attempt at the watershed altogether ; for there was absolutely nothing for the yaks to eat, and after a second or third day's fast they would not have been equal to giving that help on the high snow-beds which the Kirghiz insisted upon if they themselves were to carry up our instruments. So we started soon after 5 A.M., all of us mounted on yaks.

After less than a mile's scramble over piled-up boulders, we reached the narrow snout of the glacier and then took to a huge moraine on the west from which the ice had receded. The cold was so bitter, and a light layer of frozen snow had made the moraine débris so slippery, that I soon preferred to climb ahead on foot. On our right was an ice wall fantastically fissured, and rising in places to an almost perpendicular height of over 150 feet : on our left the masses of rock were often impracticable. But dodging between them we reached by 8 A.M. the point

previously attained by the Kirghiz at an elevation of about
18,000 feet. There the glacier widened to about half a
mile, and a solid rock terrace protruding into its side
allowed us to get on to the ice. After leaving behind a
load of fuel for emergencies, and most of the yaks under
the care of a Kirghiz, we now continued the ascent on the
glacier. Its surface seemed deeply covered with fresh
snow, and as long as this kept firm enough for a few yaks
to be driven before us their track saved us the need of
roping. But the power of the sun from a speckless sky
and through the rarefied air soon made itself intensively
felt, and the yaks, unable to push on in the softening snow,
had to be abandoned.

Roped together now to guard against crevasses, of the
presence of which we were made aware again and again
by the leading man sinking in almost to his arm-pits, we
toiled on. From a distance the far-reaching snow-covered
slope had seemed uniform and relatively gentle. But now
when we were painfully struggling up it, distinct shoulders
appeared which it took hours to conquer. Each time we
fondly hoped that the snow-ridge before us would give us
a view of the watershed, and each time our hope proved
false. The snow was now so soft that the leading man at
each step sank in thigh-deep, and those behind him had to
struggle from one snow-hole to another. Our ascent on
the Darkot in May 1906 seemed easy by comparison; for
the snow had then kept hard all the way up, and we
had not to contend with such trouble in breathing as the
much higher elevation now caused. But the Kirghiz, very
different from their Pamir brethren, stuck to their task
manfully, and cheerfully responded to my exhortation to
let us reach the crest-line, for which I promised a liberal
reward.

I had long realized that a glacier climb like this could
not possibly lead to a pass practicable within modern times.
But at last a far longer and easier slope, reached after 1 P.M.,
showed that we were now on névé beds, and probably
nearing the watershed. So I resolved to push up to it and
secure this chance for the plane-table, though the ' Yangi
Dawan' lay elsewhere. Lal Singh seemed to feel the

great elevation badly, but stout in spirit would not give in as long as his Sahib continued. As, however, his need of halting after every ten to fifteen steps caused delay, I decided, now that the risk of crevasses had practically ceased, to let the three Kirghiz pass on ahead while I put myself with Musa on the rope before the Surveyor and helped him by pulling. Fortunately there was no discernible danger from avalanches, owing to the width of the topmost névé beds and the distance of the great snowy ridge we saw towering above us on the right. The advance of the hardy Kirghiz in front of us continued steadily, and at last there came an encouraging shout that they had reached the crest. After what now seemed a short time we were by their side. But it was 3 P.M., and it had taken over seven hours to cover the approximate distance of four miles from where we first got on to the glacier.

The Kirghiz had stopped close to the brink of a snowy precipice falling away many hundreds of feet to the névé beds of a big valley north. Having reason to apprehend snow cornices, I moved up to a slightly higher knoll of snow which stood farther back from the edge. The panorama * before me was overwhelmingly grand (Plate XIII.). Straight to the north stretched a glacier - filled valley hemmed in by bold snow-covered spurs. Above the spur to the right I could see rising a fantastically serrated massif, which at once recalled to my mind groups of peaks I had seen two years before above the Nissa Valley. Beyond in the distance the view ranged over a maze of rugged snowless ranges, no doubt the barren eroded mountains overlooking the lower Kara - kash Valley. Even the brilliant white of the eternal snows all round us and the deep blue of the sky above could not efface the striking yellowish hue of the far-off horizon northward. It was clearly the dust-haze ever hovering over the familiar desert of Khotan, and it was the Taklamakan which thus sent me its greeting.

Our Survey aneroid, which had kept remarkably reliable as long as we could check it by the mercurial barometer, indicated for our position a height of close on 20,000 feet,

*Plate XIII is in the pocket attached to the inside back cover of this volume.

and the hypsometrical reading subsequently confirmed this.
But it would have sufficed to look at the snowy grandeur
of the peaks and ridges close to us on the west and north-
west to make me realize how high was the col on which
we stood. Though many of the exposed slopes faced
south, huge masses of permanent snow covered them
everywhere. It was a picture of Alpine majesty such
as I had nowhere beheld so close in the Kun-lun. Some
miles on our left the crest-line of the main range took
a sharp bend to the north, and thus much increased the
array of great snowy heights visible from our position.
Within a mile to the west rose a beautiful snow dome to
a height manifestly over 21,000 feet. But it was over-
topped by the huge crest flanking our col and glacier from
the east. The highest visible part of this could only be
got within the panorama by raising the lens considerably,
though it seemed distinctly farther off than the more
shapely dome west.

We could not see the northern slope of this culminating
massif of the range, nor make sure whether the top of the
ridge as we saw it was really its highest point. Subsequent
consideration of topographical points has convinced me that
we stood here below the western shoulder of the great peak
which rises at the head of the Nissa valley's largest glacier,
and for the highest point of which our triangulation of 1900
indicated an elevation of 23,071 feet.

To the south-east and just by the slope of the great
ridge referred to, there showed a well-defined snowy
pyramid, in which, by the indication of the plane-table,
we thought we could recognize the peak K_1 triangulated
long ago from the Ladak side with an accepted height
of 21,750 feet. It was clear now that the route to the
Yangi Dawan lay in one of the narrow valleys of which
the lowest parts were just visible from our col, leading
up to a part of the watershed situated north of K_1 and
hidden from us by the great ridge. This would agree
with the relative bearing indicated by Johnson's sketch
map between the pass and K_1, while the considerable
correction in distance which our survey demonstrated
would help to solve the main puzzle as to the line followed

by Johnson's route north of the watershed. A reference to Map II. will explain details.

But the view which most impressed me by its vastness extended to the south. There the eye ranged across the valley of Haji Langar to the great dead upland basins we had skirted, and to a seemingly endless vista of barren mountains beyond. On this succession of ranges the crest-lines seemed only at rare points to exceed our altitude, and thus it was likely that those farthest away to the south send their drainage to the Indus. The world appeared to shrink strangely from a point where my eyes could, as it were, link the Taklamakan with the Indian Ocean. It was a fit place for closing the exploratory work of this long journey; and the difficulties we had overcome, almost against hope, on this final climb only heightened my elation.

Even now, when looking back from a distance of time and sad experience, I can understand why the mind's feeling of triumph at the successful completion of our task let me forget what I owed to the body. This claimed rest and refreshment after the exhausting fatigues we had gone through; but there was too much work to be done. The plane-table was set up first, and it took time before, by a careful identification of previously sighted peaks south and of triangulated points supplied in Indian Survey tables, we could definitely fix and check our position. Then the spurs and valleys revealed northward had to be examined closely in order that we might correctly determine their relation to the previously explored orography of this region.

It is only thus that I obtained the data which finally convinced me that the glacier below us belonged to the feeders of the Panaz Darya, an important affluent of the Kara-kash, which Ram Singh had crossed in 1906. The necessity of specially guiding the plane-table work of Lal Singh, to whom the northern slopes of this part of the Kun-lun were quite new, delayed the start on my own photographic work. This, again, took much time, owing to the bitter cold and the deep snow, in which it was very difficult to secure the stability and correct levelling of the camera requisite for a panoramic series.

It was half-past four before this trying task was concluded, in a temperature of 16 degrees Fahrenheit below freezing-point with the sun still shining. I scarcely had time to eat a few mouthfuls of food before the Kirghiz insisted upon starting downwards. No doubt, they had good reason to fear our getting benighted on the glacier. But their precipitate departure deprived me of the chance for a change in my foot-gear which I had wished to effect. My mountain boots in the course of the ascent had got wet through and through, and during the long stay on the col with a rapidly sinking temperature they must have become frozen. But I felt no pain then in my feet, and attributed the trouble I had in descending with Lal Singh and Musa to the preceding fatigue and the deep holes of the track through the snow to which we kept for safety's sake.

Thus the descent, too, was painfully slow, and it was dark by the time we had struggled down to the rocky terrace by the side of the glacier where the Kirghiz awaited us with the yaks. No halt was now possible from fear of getting altogether benighted, and knowing that on the treacherous moraine slopes below, with their piled-up boulders and thin ice-coating, progress on yaks would be far safer than on foot, I followed the example of the Kirghiz and mounted. Alas, I forgot that my feet had no such protection as their felt moccasins would offer while drying.

The yaks were as sure-footed as ever but terribly slow, and this part of the descent in the dark seemed endless. I tried to keep my feet in motion but felt too weary to realize their condition. Where even the yaks could not negotiate the jumbled rocks without our dismounting, I struggled along with difficulty. I felt painfully the want of sure grip in my feet, but attributed it wrongly to the slippery surface instead of their benumbed state. At last, when we came to easier ground above camp and the difficulty of walking continued, I began to realize the full risk of defective circulation in my feet. I hurried down as quickly as the yak would carry me to where the camp fire promised warmth and comfort, hobbled into my little tent, and at once removed boots and double socks. My toes felt icy cold to the touch, and a rapid examination showed that they had been severely injured by frost-bite.

I immediately set about to restore circulation by hard friction with snow, Musa and Aziz, my Ladaki servant, doing their best to help. A rapid reference to my medical manuals showed that this was the safest course to persist in. On my left foot the toes under this vigorous treatment gradually recovered some warmth, though I could see that the skin and the flesh below was badly affected in places. But on the right foot the end joints of all toes remained quite insensible. At last I had to seek warmth and rest in bed, applying to the injured feet what dressing I could get from my invaluable little medicine chest of 'Tabloid' make which had so often served to relieve the pains of others.

Thus a day of hard-achieved success closed in suffering. It was bad luck, indeed; but I was glad all the same that our exploratory tasks had been carried through to their end, and that all my companions were safe.

CHAPTER XCVII

FROM THE KUN-LUN TO LONDON

NEXT morning, September 23rd, I found myself suffering from severe pains in my feet, and quite unable to move. The serious results of my accident and the urgency of surgical help were only too evident. I could not disguise from myself the symptoms which made it probable that the frost-bite had affected not merely the flesh but the bones, too, in some of the toes, at least on the right foot. My mountaineering manual, in which the subject was discussed at some length, plainly indicated that in such cases gangrene would set in, and recommended that "the aid of an experienced surgeon should be sought at once."

The advice was excellent but scarcely reassuring. For how could I secure such aid in these inhospitable mountains — and meanwhile might not gangrene spread further? So all my thought and energy had now to be concentrated on a rapid journey to Ladak. For only one day could I halt in that bleak camp under the frowning rock-walls to gather a little strength. I used it for sending Lal Singh to reconnoitre the gorge eastwards where we now located the approach to the Yangi Dawan. But he found it after a very short distance completely choked by snow and ice, and had to return. Evidently the advance of a glacier had here obliterated all trace of the old route.

The pains in my feet had increased, and next day when the start was made back to our main camp, I found that riding on a yak, owing to the low position of the feet, caused cruel suffering. The Kirghiz, whom many generations of life under conditions of constant hardship have made rather callous, absolutely refused to lend a hand in carrying me on an improvised litter. They were not accustomed to burdens, and the great elevation, no doubt, made it a trying business. So all I could do was to get myself strapped on the padded saddle of a camel, as soon as the going in the gorge became sufficiently safe for the animal under such a load. The constant jerks and swayings were most painful, and I shall not easily forget the sufferings of that day.

At Abdul-Ghafur-tam I found Ibrahim Beg with our ponies, and there I managed to have my camp-chair of Major Elliot's pattern made up into a sort of litter resting between two poles which were fastened to a pony in front and another behind. It cost no small effort to improvise sufficiently long poles out of the short pieces of bamboo which jointed served as our tent poles. Every mile or so the pieces lashed together would get loose or slide from the ponies' saddles, threatening to deposit me on the ground. But at least I could keep my feet high up on the felts and rugs made up into a foot-rest, and luckily the going in the broad Kara-kash Valley was easy.

There is no need to describe in detail this dolorous progress. Whatever the number of daily breakdowns I always felt grateful for my improvised litter, and even more grateful when at the end of the march I could be laid on firm ground. Half-way down to Portash, where I had previously ordered Tila Bai to join me with the heavy baggage, I was met by Muhammadju returning with heavy mail-bags brought across the Kara-koram from Ladak. The many letters from friends, now eagerly expecting me back in India and Europe, were cheering in spite of my crippled condition, and so also the presence of my trusted old follower who knew the Ladak route well and had something like genuine sympathy to offer. Lal Singh, Jasvant Singh, and he did all they could to alleviate my physical troubles. Portash was reached by September 27th, and there I had the satisfaction to see again my heavy caravan of antiques safely arrived across the Sanju Pass. Not a single case had suffered, in spite of the difficulties of the track and the exceptionally late flood in the gorges.

For two days I was kept hard at work on my camp-bed settling the accounts of Satip-aldi Beg and of our Khotan 'Kirakash.' The latter, in spite of the losses in ponies and donkeys, found themselves under the original terms amply rewarded for all the hardships they had shared with us. Their animals, too, had recovered their strength on the ample fodder rations I had given them as a present since we met the Kirghiz depot. I also made all needful arrangements for the further transport of my precious convoy of antiques, which was to move on camels across the Kara-koram and to be transferred beyond to yaks hired from Ladak for the difficult marches near and across the Sasser Glacier. The responsible task of seeing the whole of those fifty camel loads carried safely over the highest trade route of the world I entrusted to Rai Lal Singh, whose scrupulous care and untiring devotion I knew I could absolutely trust. One of Satip-aldi Beg's hardy Kirghiz had already a week before set out to carry news of my coming to Panimikh, the first Ladak village, and to summon yaks as well as the men who would be needed to assure safety to the loads in crossing the Sasser Glacier. Another of those indefatigable despatch-riders had since followed him with a letter reporting my mishap, and asking for medical help to be obtained, if possible, from the Moravian Mission at Leh.

On September 30th I myself set out from the Kara-kash Valley with the lightest possible baggage on ponies and only my few personal servants, in order to reach Leh as rapidly as the conditions of the difficult Kara-koram route, leading over passes of more than 18,000 feet and the troublesome Sasser glacier, would permit. Ibrahim Beg, my honest and energetic factotum from Keriya, to whom I said farewell here, had managed to hunt up from Kirghiz felt tents some staffs which somewhat improved the arrangement of poles required for the carriage of my improvised litter between ponies. By two forced marches I got myself carried to Sarigh-ot-darwaza, a point on the terribly bleak uplands where we struck the Kara-koram trade route. Then we followed the latter with its unending line of skeletons, sad witnesses of the constant succession of victims which the inclement physical conditions claim among the transport animals, and by October 3rd crossed the Kara-koram Pass, 18,687 feet above sea, and with it the frontier between China and India.

So far the marches, though long and very fatiguing to me in my helpless condition, had been practically free from natural obstacles except such as the high elevation and the total want of grazing for the animals offered. But after the camping-place of Burtze, which was reached on the following day, the track among the rocks of the Murghe defile became so difficult that it would have been quite impossible to get my gimcrack litter carried through on ponies. It was hence a great relief when, at the foot of the very first impasse, my sorry little caravan was met by a band of Tibetan coolies with which Lala Udho Das, the energetic and attentive Naib Tahsildar of Leh, had pushed across the Sasser. Without this timely help which Captain D. G. Oliver, of the Indian Political Department and British Joint Commissioner in Ladak, had provided, I could never have got myself carried in my litter over the ground before us—and I do not care to think now what sitting in a saddle would then have meant for me.

On October 7th I was taken over the glacier slopes and moraines of the Sasser Pass, the patient and good-natured Ladaki coolies doing their best to spare me painful tumbles on the ice and snow. But it was sad to think how a few weeks earlier I should have enjoyed such grand mountain scenery and such a glacier climb. Now the best I could do was to divert my thoughts, by reading, from the little miseries of the present and from worrying anxiety about what would become of my feet. I derived much pleasure in particular from the handy little volume of ' Selections from Erasmus,' which my dear friend Mr. P. S. Allen, of Merton College, Oxford, the editor of the great humanist's correspondence, had sent me as a forerunner of his *magnum opus*.

At last by the evening of October 8th, when descending towards Panimikh, the highest Ladak village on the Nubra River, I had the great relief of being met by the Rev. S. Schmitt, in charge of the hospital of the Moravian Mission at Leh. Though himself then still suffering from the after-effects of a serious illness, he had with kindest self-sacrifice hurried up by forced marches across the high Khardong Pass in order to bring me help. Having been trained as a medical missionary at that excellent institution, the Livingstone College in London, and provided with abundant surgical experience by his exacting but beneficent labours at Leh, he recognized at the first examination that the toes of my right foot had commenced to mortify and were more or less doomed. This was sad news, yet a relief from more serious apprehension. If only I could have obtained before the assurance that gangrene of this sort was not likely to spread! The injuries received by the toes of the left foot were far less serious and would cause no permanent loss.

Owing to my exhausted condition, due largely to the exertions and hardships which had preceded the accident and, no doubt, predisposed me for the latter by weakening my powers of resistance, my kindly Samaritan decided to postpone the operation necessary on my right foot until we reached Leh. But the fatigue of the four marches which brought us there was much relieved by his friendly ministrations and cheering company. I reached Leh on October 12th, having travelled nearly three hundred miles since my work closed at the foot of the Yangi Dawan.

Two days later Mr. Schmitt successfully effected the operation on my right foot, all the toes of which had to be amputated either completely or in their upper joints. His great kindness and that of his devoted helpmate and his fellow-missionaries provided me with much-needed comforts, while in the Agency building I found an elegantly furnished sick-room. From its veranda I caught glimpses of the picturesque castle and little town of Leh, lit up by autumnal sunshine in the midst of high barren ranges. It was a new and fascinating world to me, this corner of Western Tibet, and I much regretted that my glimpses of it were so exceedingly limited.

The wounds left after the amputation were very painful and healed with extreme slowness. The risk of finding the Zoji-la Pass on the route to Kashmir closed by snow urged an early departure from Leh if I were to reach India before next spring. But nearly three weeks passed before I was considered strong enough to face the fatigues of the fortnight's continuous travel down to Srinagar. It was some satisfaction that I could at least use this time for urgent writing tasks, including the arrangements for the safe onward progress of my archaeological collections. These were being carried down to Kashmir under Lal Singh's care, and were thence to do the long journey to London by cart, rail, and mail steamer under special safe-guards.

At last, by November 1st, I was able to say good-bye to Mr. Schmitt and the other members of that excellent Mission Station where so much good work is done to alleviate suffering and spread light among a race struggling with climatic and other hardships, and where I had received so much help and kindness. I had to be carried in my litter, being still unable to sit up or ride; and the long marches, mostly in desolate valleys swept by wintry winds, were very tiring to me. So it was a great comfort when on November 10th I had safely crossed the Zoji-la. This pass, though only 11,000 feet or so above the sea, is yet very awkward to cross when once snow has descended on its avalanche-swept defiles. Beyond I rejoiced again in sunny views of beloved Kashmir, though, alas! I had to rest content with being carried past the foot of my 'own' high Alpine Marg, the favourite scene for my labours during long happy summers.

At last, by November 13th, I reached Srinagar, where another long halt was imposed by the medical advice of my old mountaineering friend, Dr. Arthur Neve. He was able to confirm the assurance that my powers of walking and climbing would prove practically unimpaired, in spite of the loss of my toes, as soon as the wounds left by the partial amputation of them had healed. The long stay which I had to make at Srinagar under his orders in order to facilitate the process of healing was made pleasant and refreshing by the kind hospitality and attention I enjoyed on the part of my friends Captain Oliver and Captain Macpherson, the other Assistant Resident. In the genial surroundings provided by their comfortable house and the glories of a Kashmir autumn the multifarious labours of demobilizing my camping establishment and preparing final accounts could be pushed on with ease.

But my wounds, in spite of the most expert treatment, healed with tiresome slowness. What cheered me most during the seventeen days spent under that hospitable roof was a message from His Excellency the Viceroy. Kept informed from time to time of my doings by his Private Secretary, my old friend Colonel (now Sir James) Dunlop Smith, Lord Minto had followed my explorations and their results with kind and to me very encouraging interest. He was now pleased to convey to me, through Colonel Dunlop Smith, the anxiously awaited information that, in response to the proposals in the letter I had addressed to the Indian Government just a year before from Tun-huang concerning the elaboration of my scientific results, H.M. Secretary of State for India had agreed by cable to allow me to proceed on special duty to England along with my collections.

At last, towards the close of November, I could begin my first attempts at walking with crutches, and by December 1st start down on my way to India. My wounds had not yet completely healed. So the rest and care I could enjoy at Lahore under the hospitable roof of my old Punjab friend, Mr. E. D. Maclagan, was a great boon. There I was busily occupied with the final settlement of accounts for the Comptroller of India Treasuries and many other tasks. On my way to Calcutta, whither the need of various official interviews and a kind invitation to Government House called me, I was able to pay a flying visit to Dehra Dun, where the friendly help of Colonel S. Burrard, F.R.S., Superintendent of Trigonometrical Surveys, and now Surveyor-General of India, enabled me to settle details for the preparation and reproduction of the many map-sheets which were to embody the results of our surveys.

Muhammadju and Musa, the last of my Turki followers, had left me at Lahore to return next spring to their Yarkand home, with ample reward for their honest services. At Dehra Dun I had the great pleasure of being greeted again by my two highly efficient Indian helpmates, Rai Sahibs Lal Singh and Ram Singh, and by that honest gentlemanly Rajput, Mian Jasvant Singh, who had looked so well after their bodily needs. It was a real comfort to make sure that they were all to receive richly merited promotion in their Department.

During my few days' stay at Calcutta Lord Minto gave fresh proof of the personal interest with which he had followed my travels throughout, and of his benevolent thought for my Indian assistants. I could leave the Indian capital with the comforting assurance that, thanks to Lord Minto's personal interposition, poor Naik Ram Singh, whose helpless blind state had deeply moved me when I saw him again at Lahore, was soon to be granted a special pension far above the ordinary rates applicable to his rank and service.

To Rai Lal Singh, who had all through displayed zeal, energy, and utter indifference to hardships such as I had never seen equalled by any Indian, the Honours list of the New Year brought due official recognition by the award of the title of Rai Bahadur. Rai Ram Singh, the Surveyor, had before been awarded by the Royal Geographical Society a valuable prize in acknowledgment of the important topographical services he had rendered on successive expeditions. Nor was my excellent Chinese secretary forgotten, since the Indian Foreign Office, whose distinguished head, the Hon. Mr. H. Butler, had been made aware by me of Chiang-ssŭ-yeh's important services, arranged to present him with a valuable gold watch as a special mark of the Indian Government's gratitude.

On the day after Christmas, 1908, I was at last able to embark at Bombay for Europe. That very morning I had been obliged to part from 'Dash,' the last of my faithful travel companions, but, perhaps, the nearest to my heart, since the P. and O. Mail boat would not receive him amongst its passengers. However, he travelled quite safely, though alone, by another steamer, and in the end, after paying his penalty to 'civilization' by a four months' quarantine on the free shores of Britain, was joyfully restored to his master under Mr. P. S. Allen's hospitable roof at Oxford. The voyage home gave a short

and much-needed rest.   Under its influence and that of the
sea air the last of the wounds on my right foot, which had
still given me trouble at Calcutta, finally healed just before
I set foot for a brief halt in the city of Marco Polo.   Thus
by the time I reached London, after the middle of January,
I was able to walk without pain and to feel quite sure of
the day when I might climb again on the mountains.   But
it was to me an equally great satisfaction that all my cases
with antiques, close on a hundred in number, had just then
safely arrived there.

The return from a long journey like mine could not, I
well knew, mean rest, but only the prelude to labours in
some respects more important, and to me certainly more
arduous, than the work in the field.   The scientific results
achieved by my expedition would for the greatest and
most valuable part have been thrown away if all the exact
observations bearing on the physical conditions, past and
present, of the wide regions traversed ; on the ruins unearthed and surveyed ; on the antiquities and manuscript
remains which had been brought to light by thousands,
were not to be carefully recorded by myself and thus made
available for further researches.

It may give some idea of the tasks awaiting me if I
mention that our topographical surveys, now in course of
detailed publication by the Indian Trigonometrical Survey,
on the scale of four miles to the inch, fill ninety-four map-
sheets of the standard size, every one needing my repeated
careful revision in proof, and that the mere unpacking and
first arrangement of the thousands of archaeological objects
in basement rooms of the British Museum, which were
made available for what seemed like a temporary immure-
ment, took close on six months.   The decipherment and
publication of the manuscripts and documents, probably
over 14,000 in number and in about a dozen scripts and
languages, are bound for a long number of years to claim
the learned labours of quite a staff of Orientalist savants.
To select them and to organize their efforts, and those of
the many expert collaborators needed in other directions,
was by itself a heavy and responsible task.   Nor could
their labours be started in earnest until all facts bearing

on the origin, date, etc., of the finds, as observed by me on the spot, had been thoroughly sifted and placed at their disposal.

So with all these tasks and responsibilities before me, I had reason to feel grateful when the Government of India's generous proposal to allow me a period of two years and three months' 'deputation' in England for this purpose received the Secretary of State's sanction. Thanks to this consideration, my labours could proceed steadily both at the British Museum and at Oxford, where the kind hospitality of the Warden and Fellows of Merton College offered to me as peaceful a retreat for work as I could wish for in this ancient home of learning. I was thus assured of the chance of accomplishing what the results of this journey had imposed upon me as a duty to science. But when may I hope that the gate will open for work in those fields to which cherished plans have been calling me ever since my youth, and which still remain unexplored?

INDEX

NOTES.—TRANSCRIPTION. The spelling of Oriental names and terms other than Chinese in the text and Index conforms to the system of phonetic transliteration approved by the International Congress of Orientalists. No use, however, has been made of diacritical marks.

In the transcription of Chinese words the Wade system has been followed.

INDEX

'Inspection visits,' to garrison on Old Wall, ii. 148

Inspector-General of Education on North-West Frontier, i. 1

Iranian influence in Miran frescoes, i. 483, 487

Irises, i. 5, 10, 46, 100; ii. 158, 160, 162, 269

Iron nails and screws brought from India, i. 437

Iron-plated gate of castle at Chitral, i. 37

Irrigation : from canals, i. 103, 128, 137, 153, 154, 156, 253, 257-258; ii. 40-41, 75, 381, 414-415, 416, 429, 440; from 'Kara-su,' or springs, i. 104, 144, 157, 238, 253, 259, 308; ii. 273, 276, 426; from 'Karez' in Turfan, ii. 354-356, 361 ; in old times, i. 399; ii. 254

Ishidata, name of prince in Kharoshthi inscription on Miran fresco, i. 493

Islam Akhun, Niya villager, i. 272, 278, 279

Islam Beg, former Darogha, i. 168, 199, 203, 206, 218, 222, 265; host at Altunche, ii. 416

Islam, blacksmith, i. 367

Islam, Dak-man from Khotan, i. 505

Ismail, of Charchan, hunter and guide, i. 326, 327, 328, 329

Ivory die, ancient, i. 148

Jade axe-head, ancient, i. 416

Jade-diggers from Kumat, i. 223

'Jade Gate,' ancient Chinese frontier station, i. 513, 514, 515, 527; ii. 97, 106, 117, 118, 120, 122, 137, 147

Jaeger blanket, i. 384

Japanese, diggings by, ii. 375

Japanese war, echoes of, i. 95, 110, 118; ii. 18

Japanese wares at Su-chou, ii. 292

Jasvant Singh, Mian Rajput, cook to Surveyor, i. 9, 175, 365, 407; ii. 12, 401, 457, 484, 490

Jehu-lho, name of official in Tibetan document at Miran, i. 448

Jewelry, family, in house at Miragram, in Mastuj, i. 48

Jewelry, on Indian male figures in Miran frescoes, i. 482-483, 487, 488

Jigda, or Eleagnus trees, i. 103, 227, 230, 238, 259, 266, 315, 321

Johnson, Mr. J. de M., assistance of, i. XXIII

Johnson, Mr., surveyor, search for his route across Kun-lun Range to Khotan in 1865, i. 181, 186, 196, 198, 201, 204, 205 ; ii. 465, 467-470, 476, 479

Joyce, Mr. T. A., help of, i. xx

Juniper wood, or Archa, in Sarikol, i. 91, 92

K₁, mountain peak in Kun-lun Range, ii. 479

K₅, mountain peak above upper Yurung-kash Valley, i. 207, 208, 211

Kabul tent, i. 3

Kafirs, in Chitral, i. 27, 38-40; anthropological measurements of, i. 38-39 ; dancing by, i. 39-40

Kaghan, in Hazara, Alpine camp in, i. 2, 85

'Kaka-jade's town,' or 'Town of T'ang prince,' serrated range near Uch-Turfan, ii. 424

Kaks, or natural rock cisterns, in Kelpin hills, ii. 424, 426

Kalandars, or religious mendicants, i. 265

Kamarbaz, or professional gamblers, in Turkestan, i. 114

Kamghak, or thorny scrub plant in desert, ii. 405, 407

Kan-chou, halt at, ii. 332-335

Kan-chou River, ii. 328, 329, 331

Kansir, old fort in Wakhan, i. 70-71

Kao Hsien-chih, Chinese general of eighth century, in Mastuj and Wakhan, i. 52, 57, 58, 65, 69, 70, 72

Kao Ta-lao-ye, petty officer from An-hsi, ii. 248, 251

Kara-dong, excavations at, ii. 412

Kara-kash Town, near Khotan, i. 166-168

Kara-kash River, crossing of, near Khotan, i. 169 ; new canal along left bank, ii. 416; exploration of sources of, ii. 417, 456, 460, 465, 471, 472, 484-485

Kara-khoja, Uigur capital of Turfan, ruins at, ii. 359-361

Kara-koram Pass on route to Ladak, i. 10, 141, 145, 155, 158, 159; ii. 431, 434, 438, 471, 485-486

Kara-koshun, Loplik name for extant Lop-nor, i. 342, 356, 376, 442

Karanghu-tagh, valley and mountains in Kun-lun Range, i. 181, 197-212

Kara-ois = 'black huts,' felt tents of Taghliks, i. 199, 202

Kara-sai, excavations at, ii. 416

Kara-shahr, district and town, i. 434, 436, 500; excavation of old sites near; ii. 365-371

Kara-su = 'black water,' from springs, i. 104, 253, 308

Karaul Beg = 'chief of frontier guards,' in Wakhan, i. 62, 69, 70

Kar-dash Beg = 'Sir Snow-Friend.' *See* 'Dash'

Karez, or underground irrigation channels in Turfan, ii. 354-356, 361

Karghalik, oasis, i. 139-141

Karim Akhun, Surveyor's attendant, i. 437, 498

Kasim Akhun, hunter and guide, ii. 417, 420

INDEX

Palm-leaf MSS. in Sanskrit, from Miran,
i. 455; from Caves of Thousand Buddhas,
ii. 183, 211
Pamirs, or 'Roof of the World,' crossing
of, from Wakhan to Sarikol, i. 76-89
Pan Darin. *See* P'an Ta-jên
P'an Ta-jên, Tao-t'ai of Ak-su, his in-
fluential help, i. XVI, 133, 168, 332, 336;
ii. 8, 342, 365, 416; visit to, ii. 421-423
Panels, painted, i. 240; ii. 369, 413, 414
Panimikh, first village reached in Ladak,
ii. 485, 486
Panjkora valley, in Dir and Swat, i. 15-19
Panoramas. *See* Photographic panoramas
Pao-t'ai : mile-stone pillar, i. 130 ; measure
of distance, i. 157, 237 ; boundary pillar,
i. 138 ; survey mark, i. 179; ruined
tower, *passim*
Paper cast of Sanskrit inscription in
Chitral, i. 42
Paper documents, the earliest known, ii.
113-115 ; Tibetan, near Lop-nor, i. 352,
at Miran, i. 439, 441; Chinese, at Lop-nor
Site, i. 379, 383, 393-394 ; on Old Wall,
ii. 121 ; in Sogdian script, i. 394 ; ii. 113-
115
Paper money, ii. 70
Paper windows, of Chinese houses, ii. 11 ;
of Turki house, ii. 373
Pasa, yak-hunter and guide, in Kun-lun
Range, ii. 444-457
Pathan borderland, i. 12-25
Pathan dance, at Chitral, i. 36
Pathan traders, in Turkestan, i. 134, 168,
169, 319 ; ii. 38, 68
Pay-bills of soldiers on Old Wall, ii. 151
Peaches, i. 165, 177 ; ii. 158, 348
Pears, i. 45 ; ii. 158
Pei-shan desert, from An-hsi to Hami, ii.
335, 339-341
Pei-ta Ho, river, at Su-chou, ii. 285, 286,
297 ; in Richthofen Range, ii. 308, 312,
316, 324
Pelliot, M. Paul, his catalogue of Chinese
texts from Caves of Thousand Buddhas,
ii. 217-218, 219 ; his excavations at
Kuchar, ii. 375, 428
Pên Ta-jên, Amban of Yarkand, i. 132,
133
Peonies, ii. 287
Persepolitan style, of wood-carving, i.
410; of plaster columns at Miran, i. 453
Persian rock inscription in Chitral, i. 32
Peshawar, reception by Lord Minto at, i.
5-7
Photographic glass plates, i. 10
Photographic panoramas, i. 81, 180, 190,
208 ; ii. 270, 306-307, 308, 309, 311,
314-315, 322, 329, 330, 331, 443, 446,
447, 450, 454, 478-480
Photography under difficulties, i. 462-463,
493-494 ; ii. 225, 371, 443, 480

Phrygian caps in Miran frescoes, i. 473,
482, 484
Pichan oasis, ii. 353
Picketing posts and rope, ancient, ii. 98-99
Piedmont gravel, i. 103, 250, 318, 325,
348 ; ii. 257, 264
'Pigeons, Shrine of the,' i. 161, 163
Pigs at Tun-huang, ii. 38
Pigtail, ancient Tibetan, i. 442
Pile carpets, ancient, i. 275, 380, 381 ; ii.
159
Pilgrims to shrine of Imam Ja'far Sadik,
i. 266 ; to Caves of Thousand Buddhas,
ii. 159 ; to Mecca ; *see* Hajis
Pillars, wooden, with turned mouldings, i.
314, 410
Pink paper for Chinese correspondence, i.
144 ; ii. 38
Pir Bakhsh, Khan Sahib, Hospital Assist-
ant at Mastuj, i. 44, 47, 49
Pisha, valley in Kun-Lun Range, i. 205-
211
Plane-table, mapping with, i. 153, 175,
185, 186, 191, 326, 375, 504, 519 ; ii.
37, 333, 390, 410, 437, 446, 447, 474,
479, 480
Plane trees, or Chinars, i. 17, 28, 32, 37,
45
Plaster of Paris, Buddhist relievos in, ii.
416
Platforms in ancient houses, i. 277, 385,
392
Plums, i. 46, 48, 177 ; ii. 415
Poetry, Chinese, from Old Wall, ii. 153
Poisonous grass, on outer Kun-lun, i. 220;
on mountains near Su-chou, ii. 303
Polo at Chitral, i. 35-36
Polo ground at Reshun, in Chitral, i. 43
Polur, village and gorge, in Kun-lun Range,
ii. 440-445
Ponies, bought at Kashgar, i. 109 ; bought
at Yarkand, i. 131
Pools in the desert, ii. 420
Poplars, white, i. 97, 121, 129, 130, 139,
147, 148, 160, 230, 238, 259, 267 ; ii.
163, 293, 347
Poplars, wild. *See* Toghraks
Poppies in Dir, i. 18. *See also* Opium
Porcelain, its absence evidence for dating,
ii. 77
Port wine for Badakhshi pony, ii. 466
Portash, halting-place on upper Kara-kash,
ii. 484
'Post-registered' telegrams, *via* Bombay,
i. 47
Pothis, or MS. books, Brahmi, in 'un-
known' languages, i. 240 ; ii. 179, 183,
211 ; Sanskrit, i. 237, 240, 246, 455 ; ii.
179, 183 ; Sogdian, ii. 213 ; Tibetan,
i. 352, 441 ; ii. 184, 219
Pottery, hand-made, i. 365, 432
Pottery fragments. *See* Tati

Yü-tien, or Khotan, temple cave at Thousand Buddhas dedicated by Princess of, ii. 229

Yüz-bashi = 'head of hundred,' of Tagh-liks, i. 181, 199, 202, 203, 210, 212 ; of labourers, i. 415

Zahid Beg, Muhammadan trader at Tun-huang, ii. 18, 28, 42, 71

Zahid Beg, of Hami, ii. 342

Zailik, gorge in Kun-lun Range, with gold mines, ii. 445-449, 456

Zeus, on clay seal impression, i. 284

Ziarats, or Muhammadan shrines, in Swat, i. 16; in Chitral, i. 24, 25, 28; in Turkestan, i. 153, 267; ii. 425. *See also* Mazars

Zoji-la Pass, from Leh to Kashmir, crossing of, in litter, ii. 487, 488

THE END

A CATALOG OF SELECTED
DOVER BOOKS
IN ALL FIELDS OF INTEREST

A CATALOG OF SELECTED DOVER BOOKS IN ALL FIELDS OF INTEREST

DRAWINGS OF REMBRANDT, edited by Seymour Slive. Updated Lippmann, Hofstede de Groot edition, with definitive scholarly apparatus. All portraits, biblical sketches, landscapes, nudes. Oriental figures, classical studies, together with selection of work by followers. 550 illustrations. Total of 630pp. 9⅛ × 12¼.
21485-0, 21486-9 Pa., Two-vol. set $25.00

GHOST AND HORROR STORIES OF AMBROSE BIERCE, Ambrose Bierce. 24 tales vividly imagined, strangely prophetic, and decades ahead of their time in technical skill: "The Damned Thing," "An Inhabitant of Carcosa," "The Eyes of the Panther," "Moxon's Master," and 20 more. 199pp. 5⅜ × 8½. 20767-6 Pa. $3.95

ETHICAL WRITINGS OF MAIMONIDES, Maimonides. Most significant ethical works of great medieval sage, newly translated for utmost precision, readability. Laws Concerning Character Traits, Eight Chapters, more. 192pp. 5⅜ × 8½.
24522-5 Pa. $4.50

THE EXPLORATION OF THE COLORADO RIVER AND ITS CANYONS, J. W. Powell. Full text of Powell's 1,000-mile expedition down the fabled Colorado in 1869. Superb account of terrain, geology, vegetation, Indians, famine, mutiny, treacherous rapids, mighty canyons, during exploration of last unknown part of continental U.S. 400pp. 5⅜ × 8½. 20094-9 Pa. $6.95

HISTORY OF PHILOSOPHY, Julián Marías. Clearest one-volume history on the market. Every major philosopher and dozens of others, to Existentialism and later. 505pp. 5⅜ × 8½. 21739-6 Pa. $8.50

ALL ABOUT LIGHTNING, Martin A. Uman. Highly readable non-technical survey of nature and causes of lightning, thunderstorms, ball lightning, St. Elmo's Fire, much more. Illustrated. 192pp. 5⅜ × 8½. 25237-X Pa. $5.95

SAILING ALONE AROUND THE WORLD, Captain Joshua Slocum. First man to sail around the world, alone, in small boat. One of great feats of seamanship told in delightful manner. 67 illustrations. 294pp. 5⅜ × 8½. 20326-3 Pa. $4.50

LETTERS AND NOTES ON THE MANNERS, CUSTOMS AND CONDITIONS OF THE NORTH AMERICAN INDIANS, George Catlin. Classic account of life among Plains Indians: ceremonies, hunt, warfare, etc. 312 plates. 572pp. of text. 6⅛ × 9¼. 22118-0, 22119-9 Pa. Two-vol. set $15.90

ALASKA: The Harriman Expedition, 1899, John Burroughs, John Muir, et al. Informative, engrossing accounts of two-month, 9,000-mile expedition. Native peoples, wildlife, forests, geography, salmon industry, glaciers, more. Profusely illustrated. 240 black-and-white line drawings. 124 black-and-white photographs. 3 maps. Index. 576pp. 5⅜ × 8½. 25109-8 Pa. $11.95

CATALOG OF DOVER BOOKS

THE BOOK OF BEASTS: Being a Translation from a Latin Bestiary of the Twelfth Century, T. H. White. Wonderful catalog real and fanciful beasts: manticore, griffin, phoenix, amphivius, jaculus, many more. White's witty erudite commentary on scientific, historical aspects. Fascinating glimpse of medieval mind. Illustrated. 296pp. 5⅜ × 8¼. (Available in U.S. only) 24609-4 Pa. $5.95

FRANK LLOYD WRIGHT: ARCHITECTURE AND NATURE With 160 Illustrations, Donald Hoffmann. Profusely illustrated study of influence of nature—especially prairie—on Wright's designs for Fallingwater, Robie House, Guggenheim Museum, other masterpieces. 96pp. 9¼ × 10¾. 25098-9 Pa. $7.95

FRANK LLOYD WRIGHT'S FALLINGWATER, Donald Hoffmann. Wright's famous waterfall house: planning and construction of organic idea. History of site, owners, Wright's personal involvement. Photographs of various stages of building. Preface by Edgar Kaufmann, Jr. 100 illustrations. 112pp. 9¼ × 10. 23671-4 Pa. $7.95

YEARS WITH FRANK LLOYD WRIGHT: Apprentice to Genius, Edgar Tafel. Insightful memoir by a former apprentice presents a revealing portrait of Wright the man, the inspired teacher, the greatest American architect. 372 black-and-white illustrations. Preface. Index. vi + 228pp. 8¼ × 11. 24801-1 Pa. $9.95

THE STORY OF KING ARTHUR AND HIS KNIGHTS, Howard Pyle. Enchanting version of King Arthur fable has delighted generations with imaginative narratives of exciting adventures and unforgettable illustrations by the author. 41 illustrations. xviii + 313pp. 6⅛ × 9¼. 21445-1 Pa. $5.95

THE GODS OF THE EGYPTIANS, E. A. Wallis Budge. Thorough coverage of numerous gods of ancient Egypt by foremost Egyptologist. Information on evolution of cults, rites and gods; the cult of Osiris; the Book of the Dead and its rites; the sacred animals and birds; Heaven and Hell; and more. 956pp. 6⅛ × 9¼. 22055-9, 22056-7 Pa., Two-vol. set $20.00

A THEOLOGICO-POLITICAL TREATISE, Benedict Spinoza. Also contains unfinished *Political Treatise*. Great classic on religious liberty, theory of government on common consent. R. Elwes translation. Total of 421pp. 5⅜ × 8½. 20249-6 Pa. $6.95

INCIDENTS OF TRAVEL IN CENTRAL AMERICA, CHIAPAS, AND YUCATAN, John L. Stephens. Almost single-handed discovery of Maya culture; exploration of ruined cities, monuments, temples; customs of Indians. 115 drawings. 892pp. 5⅜ × 8½. 22404-X, 22405-8 Pa., Two-vol. set $15.90

LOS CAPRICHOS, Francisco Goya. 80 plates of wild, grotesque monsters and caricatures. Prado manuscript included. 183pp. 6⅜ × 9⅜. 22384-1 Pa. $4.95

AUTOBIOGRAPHY: The Story of My Experiments with Truth, Mohandas K. Gandhi. Not hagiography, but Gandhi in his own words. Boyhood, legal studies, purification, the growth of the Satyagraha (nonviolent protest) movement. Critical, inspiring work of the man who freed India. 480pp. 5⅜ × 8½. (Available in U.S. only) 24593-4 Pa. $6.95

ILLUSTRATED DICTIONARY OF HISTORIC ARCHITECTURE, edited by Cyril M. Harris. Extraordinary compendium of clear, concise definitions for over 5,000 important architectural terms complemented by over 2,000 line drawings. Covers full spectrum of architecture from ancient ruins to 20th-century Modernism. Preface. 592pp. 7½ × 9⅜. 24444-X Pa. $14.95

THE NIGHT BEFORE CHRISTMAS, Clement Moore. Full text, and woodcuts from original 1848 book. Also critical, historical material. 19 illustrations. 40pp. 4⅝ × 6. 22797-9 Pa. $2.25

THE LESSON OF JAPANESE ARCHITECTURE: 165 Photographs, Jiro Harada. Memorable gallery of 165 photographs taken in the 1930's of exquisite Japanese homes of the well-to-do and historic buildings. 13 line diagrams. 192pp. 8⅜ × 11¼. 24778-3 Pa. $8.95

THE AUTOBIOGRAPHY OF CHARLES DARWIN AND SELECTED LETTERS, edited by Francis Darwin. The fascinating life of eccentric genius composed of an intimate memoir by Darwin (intended for his children); commentary by his son, Francis; hundreds of fragments from notebooks, journals, papers; and letters to and from Lyell, Hooker, Huxley, Wallace and Henslow. xi + 365pp. 5⅜ × 8. 20479-0 Pa. $5.95

WONDERS OF THE SKY: Observing Rainbows, Comets, Eclipses, the Stars and Other Phenomena, Fred Schaaf. Charming, easy-to-read poetic guide to all manner of celestial events visible to the naked eye. Mock suns, glories, Belt of Venus, more. Illustrated. 299pp. 5¼ × 8¼. 24402-4 Pa. $7.95

BURNHAM'S CELESTIAL HANDBOOK, Robert Burnham, Jr. Thorough guide to the stars beyond our solar system. Exhaustive treatment. Alphabetical by constellation: Andromeda to Cetus in Vol. 1; Chamaeleon to Orion in Vol. 2; and Pavo to Vulpecula in Vol. 3. Hundreds of illustrations. Index in Vol. 3. 2,000pp. 6⅛ × 9¼. 23567-X, 23568-8, 23673-0 Pa., Three-vol. set $36.85

STAR NAMES: Their Lore and Meaning, Richard Hinckley Allen. Fascinating history of names various cultures have given to constellations and literary and folkloristic uses that have been made of stars. Indexes to subjects. Arabic and Greek names. Biblical references. Bibliography. 563pp. 5⅜ × 8½. 21079-0 Pa. $7.95

THIRTY YEARS THAT SHOOK PHYSICS: The Story of Quantum Theory, George Gamow. Lucid, accessible introduction to influential theory of energy and matter. Careful explanations of Dirac's anti-particles, Bohr's model of the atom, much more. 12 plates. Numerous drawings. 240pp. 5⅜ × 8½. 24895-X Pa. $4.95

CHINESE DOMESTIC FURNITURE IN PHOTOGRAPHS AND MEASURED DRAWINGS, Gustav Ecke. A rare volume, now affordably priced for antique collectors, furniture buffs and art historians. Detailed review of styles ranging from early Shang to late Ming. Unabridged republication. 161 black-and-white drawings, photos. Total of 224pp. 8⅜ × 11¼. (Available in U.S. only) 25171-3 Pa. $12.95

VINCENT VAN GOGH: A Biography, Julius Meier-Graefe. Dynamic, penetrating study of artist's life, relationship with brother, Theo, painting techniques, travels, more. Readable, engrossing. 160pp. 5⅜ × 8½. (Available in U.S. only) 25253-1 Pa. $3.95

HOW TO WRITE, Gertrude Stein. Gertrude Stein claimed anyone could understand her unconventional writing—here are clues to help. Fascinating improvisations, language experiments, explanations illuminate Stein's craft and the art of writing. Total of 414pp. 4⅝ × 6⅝. 23144-5 Pa. $5.95

ADVENTURES AT SEA IN THE GREAT AGE OF SAIL: Five Firsthand Narratives, edited by Elliot Snow. Rare true accounts of exploration, whaling, shipwreck, fierce natives, trade, shipboard life, more. 33 illustrations. Introduction. 353pp. 5⅜ × 8½. 25177-2 Pa. $7.95

THE HERBAL OR GENERAL HISTORY OF PLANTS, John Gerard. Classic descriptions of about 2,850 plants—with over 2,700 illustrations—includes Latin and English names, physical descriptions, varieties, time and place of growth, more. 2,706 illustrations. xlv + 1,678pp. 8½ × 12¼. 23147-X Cloth. $75.00

DOROTHY AND THE WIZARD IN OZ, L. Frank Baum. Dorothy and the Wizard visit the center of the Earth, where people are vegetables, glass houses grow and Oz characters reappear. Classic sequel to *Wizard of Oz*. 256pp. 5⅜ × 8.
24714-7 Pa. $4.95

SONGS OF EXPERIENCE: Facsimile Reproduction with 26 Plates in Full Color, William Blake. This facsimile of Blake's original "Illuminated Book" reproduces 26 full-color plates from a rare 1826 edition. Includes "The Tyger," "London," "Holy Thursday," and other immortal poems. 26 color plates. Printed text of poems. 48pp. 5¼ × 7. 24636-1 Pa. $3.50

SONGS OF INNOCENCE, William Blake. The first and most popular of Blake's famous "Illuminated Books," in a facsimile edition reproducing all 31 brightly colored plates. Additional printed text of each poem. 64pp. 5¼ × 7.
22764-2 Pa. $3.50

PRECIOUS STONES, Max Bauer. Classic, thorough study of diamonds, rubies, emeralds, garnets, etc.: physical character, occurrence, properties, use, similar topics. 20 plates, 8 in color. 94 figures. 659pp. 6⅛ × 9¼.
21910-0, 21911-9 Pa., Two-vol. set $14.90

ENCYCLOPEDIA OF VICTORIAN NEEDLEWORK, S. F. A. Caulfeild and Blanche Saward. Full, precise descriptions of stitches, techniques for dozens of needlecrafts—most exhaustive reference of its kind. Over 800 figures. Total of 679pp. 8⅛ × 11. Two volumes. Vol. 1 22800-2 Pa. $10.95
Vol. 2 22801-0 Pa. $10.95

THE MARVELOUS LAND OF OZ, L. Frank Baum. Second Oz book, the Scarecrow and Tin Woodman are back with hero named Tip, Oz magic. 136 illustrations. 287pp. 5⅜ × 8½. 20692-0 Pa. $5.95

WILD FOWL DECOYS, Joel Barber. Basic book on the subject, by foremost authority and collector. Reveals history of decoy making and rigging, place in American culture, different kinds of decoys, how to make them, and how to use them. 140 plates. 156pp. 7⅞ × 10¾. 20011-6 Pa. $7.95

HISTORY OF LACE, Mrs. Bury Palliser. Definitive, profusely illustrated chronicle of lace from earliest times to late 19th century. Laces of Italy, Greece, England, France, Belgium, etc. Landmark of needlework scholarship. 266 illustrations. 672pp. 6⅛ × 9¼. 24742-2 Pa. $14.95

CATALOG OF DOVER BOOKS

ILLUSTRATED GUIDE TO SHAKER FURNITURE, Robert Meader. All furniture and appurtenances, with much on unknown local styles. 235 photos. 146pp. 9 × 12. 22819-3 Pa. $7.95

WHALE SHIPS AND WHALING: A Pictorial Survey, George Francis Dow. Over 200 vintage engravings, drawings, photographs of barks, brigs, cutters, other vessels. Also harpoons, lances, whaling guns, many other artifacts. Comprehensive text by foremost authority. 207 black-and-white illustrations. 288pp. 6 × 9. 24808-9 Pa. $8.95

THE BERTRAMS, Anthony Trollope. Powerful portrayal of blind self-will and thwarted ambition includes one of Trollope's most heartrending love stories. 497pp. 5⅜ × 8½. 25119-5 Pa. $8.95

ADVENTURES WITH A HAND LENS, Richard Headstrom. Clearly written guide to observing and studying flowers and grasses, fish scales, moth and insect wings, egg cases, buds, feathers, seeds, leaf scars, moss, molds, ferns, common crystals, etc.—all with an ordinary, inexpensive magnifying glass. 209 exact line drawings aid in your discoveries. 220pp. 5⅜ × 8½. 23330-8 Pa. $3.95

RODIN ON ART AND ARTISTS, Auguste Rodin. Great sculptor's candid, wide-ranging comments on meaning of art; great artists; relation of sculpture to poetry, painting, music; philosophy of life, more. 76 superb black-and-white illustrations of Rodin's sculpture, drawings and prints. 119pp. 8⅜ × 11¼. 24487-3 Pa. $6.95

FIFTY CLASSIC FRENCH FILMS, 1912–1982: A Pictorial Record, Anthony Slide. Memorable stills from Grand Illusion, Beauty and the Beast, Hiroshima, Mon Amour, many more. Credits, plot synopses, reviews, etc. 160pp. 8¼ × 11. 25256-6 Pa. $11.95

THE PRINCIPLES OF PSYCHOLOGY, William James. Famous long course complete, unabridged. Stream of thought, time perception, memory, experimental methods; great work decades ahead of its time. 94 figures. 1,391pp. 5⅜ × 8½. 20381-6, 20382-4 Pa., Two-vol. set $19.90

BODIES IN A BOOKSHOP, R. T. Campbell. Challenging mystery of blackmail and murder with ingenious plot and superbly drawn characters. In the best tradition of British suspense fiction. 192pp. 5⅜ × 8½. 24720-1 Pa. $3.95

CALLAS: PORTRAIT OF A PRIMA DONNA, George Jellinek. Renowned commentator on the musical scene chronicles incredible career and life of the most controversial, fascinating, influential operatic personality of our time. 64 black-and-white photographs. 416pp. 5⅜ × 8¼. 25047-4 Pa. $7.95

GEOMETRY, RELATIVITY AND THE FOURTH DIMENSION, Rudolph Rucker. Exposition of fourth dimension, concepts of relativity as Flatland characters continue adventures. Popular, easily followed yet accurate, profound. 141 illustrations. 133pp. 5⅜ × 8½. 23400-2 Pa. $3.50

HOUSEHOLD STORIES BY THE BROTHERS GRIMM, with pictures by Walter Crane. 53 classic stories—Rumpelstiltskin, Rapunzel, Hansel and Gretel, the Fisherman and his Wife, Snow White, Tom Thumb, Sleeping Beauty, Cinderella, and so much more—lavishly illustrated with original 19th century drawings. 114 illustrations. x + 269pp. 5⅜ × 8½. 21080-4 Pa. $4.50

SUNDIALS, Albert Waugh. Far and away the best, most thorough coverage of ideas, mathematics concerned, types, construction, adjusting anywhere. Over 100 illustrations. 230pp. 5⅜ × 8½. 22947-5 Pa. $4.00

PICTURE HISTORY OF THE NORMANDIE: With 190 Illustrations, Frank O. Braynard. Full story of legendary French ocean liner: Art Deco interiors, design innovations, furnishings, celebrities, maiden voyage, tragic fire, much more. Extensive text. 144pp. 8⅜ × 11¾. 25257-4 Pa. $9.95

THE FIRST AMERICAN COOKBOOK: A Facsimile of "American Cookery," 1796, Amelia Simmons. Facsimile of the first American-written cookbook published in the United States contains authentic recipes for colonial favorites—pumpkin pudding, winter squash pudding, spruce beer, Indian slapjacks, and more. Introductory Essay and Glossary of colonial cooking terms. 80pp. 5⅜ × 8½. 24710-4 Pa. $3.50

101 PUZZLES IN THOUGHT AND LOGIC, C. R. Wylie, Jr. Solve murders and robberies, find out which fishermen are liars, how a blind man could possibly identify a color—purely by your own reasoning! 107pp. 5⅜ × 8½. 20367-0 Pa. $2.00

THE BOOK OF WORLD-FAMOUS MUSIC—CLASSICAL, POPULAR AND FOLK, James J. Fuld. Revised and enlarged republication of landmark work in musico-bibliography. Full information about nearly 1,000 songs and compositions including first lines of music and lyrics. New supplement. Index. 800pp. 5⅜ × 8¼. 24857-7 Pa. $14.95

ANTHROPOLOGY AND MODERN LIFE, Franz Boas. Great anthropologist's classic treatise on race and culture. Introduction by Ruth Bunzel. Only inexpensive paperback edition. 255pp. 5⅜ × 8½. 25245-0 Pa. $5.95

THE TALE OF PETER RABBIT, Beatrix Potter. The inimitable Peter's terrifying adventure in Mr. McGregor's garden, with all 27 wonderful, full-color Potter illustrations. 55pp. 4¼ × 5½. (Available in U.S. only) 22827-4 Pa. $1.75

THREE PROPHETIC SCIENCE FICTION NOVELS, H. G. Wells. *When the Sleeper Wakes, A Story of the Days to Come* and *The Time Machine* (full version). 335pp. 5⅜ × 8½. (Available in U.S. only) 20605-X Pa. $5.95

APICIUS COOKERY AND DINING IN IMPERIAL ROME, edited and translated by Joseph Dommers Vehling. Oldest known cookbook in existence offers readers a clear picture of what foods Romans ate, how they prepared them, etc. 49 illustrations. 301pp. 6⅛ × 9¼. 23563-7 Pa. $6.00

SHAKESPEARE LEXICON AND QUOTATION DICTIONARY, Alexander Schmidt. Full definitions, locations, shades of meaning of every word in plays and poems. More than 50,000 exact quotations. 1,485pp. 6½ × 9¼. 22726-X, 22727-8 Pa., Two-vol. set $27.90

THE WORLD'S GREAT SPEECHES, edited by Lewis Copeland and Lawrence W. Lamm. Vast collection of 278 speeches from Greeks to 1970. Powerful and effective models; unique look at history. 842pp. 5⅜ × 8½. 20468-5 Pa. $10.95

THE BLUE FAIRY BOOK, Andrew Lang. The first, most famous collection, with many familiar tales: Little Red Riding Hood, Aladdin and the Wonderful Lamp, Puss in Boots, Sleeping Beauty, Hansel and Gretel, Rumpelstiltskin; 37 in all. 138 illustrations. 390pp. 5⅜ × 8½.   21437-0 Pa. $5.95

THE STORY OF THE CHAMPIONS OF THE ROUND TABLE, Howard Pyle. Sir Launcelot, Sir Tristram and Sir Percival in spirited adventures of love and triumph retold in Pyle's inimitable style. 50 drawings, 31 full-page. xviii + 329pp. 6½ × 9¼.   21883-X Pa. $6.95

AUDUBON AND HIS JOURNALS, Maria Audubon. Unmatched two-volume portrait of the great artist, naturalist and author contains his journals, an excellent biography by his granddaughter, expert annotations by the noted ornithologist, Dr. Elliott Coues, and 37 superb illustrations. Total of 1,200pp. 5⅜ × 8.
Vol. I 25143-8 Pa. $8.95
Vol. II 25144-6 Pa. $8.95

GREAT DINOSAUR HUNTERS AND THEIR DISCOVERIES, Edwin H. Colbert. Fascinating, lavishly illustrated chronicle of dinosaur research, 1820's to 1960. Achievements of Cope, Marsh, Brown, Buckland, Mantell, Huxley, many others. 384pp. 5¼ × 8¼.   24701-5 Pa. $6.95

THE TASTEMAKERS, Russell Lynes. Informal, illustrated social history of American taste 1850's–1950's. First popularized categories Highbrow, Lowbrow, Middlebrow. 129 illustrations. New (1979) afterword. 384pp. 6 × 9.
23993-4 Pa. $6.95

DOUBLE CROSS PURPOSES, Ronald A. Knox. A treasure hunt in the Scottish Highlands, an old map, unidentified corpse, surprise discoveries keep reader guessing in this cleverly intricate tale of financial skullduggery. 2 black-and-white maps. 320pp. 5⅜ × 8½. (Available in U.S. only)   25032-6 Pa. $5.95

AUTHENTIC VICTORIAN DECORATION AND ORNAMENTATION IN FULL COLOR: 46 Plates from "Studies in Design," Christopher Dresser. Superb full-color lithographs reproduced from rare original portfolio of a major Victorian designer. 48pp. 9¼ × 12¼.   25083-0 Pa. $7.95

PRIMITIVE ART, Franz Boas. Remains the best text ever prepared on subject, thoroughly discussing Indian, African, Asian, Australian, and, especially, Northern American primitive art. Over 950 illustrations show ceramics, masks, totem poles, weapons, textiles, paintings, much more. 376pp. 5⅜ × 8.   20025-6 Pa. $6.95

SIDELIGHTS ON RELATIVITY, Albert Einstein. Unabridged republication of two lectures delivered by the great physicist in 1920–21. *Ether and Relativity* and *Geometry and Experience*. Elegant ideas in non-mathematical form, accessible to intelligent layman. vi + 56pp. 5⅜ × 8½.   24511-X Pa. $2.95

THE WIT AND HUMOR OF OSCAR WILDE, edited by Alvin Redman. More than 1,000 ripostes, paradoxes, wisecracks: Work is the curse of the drinking classes, I can resist everything except temptation, etc. 258pp. 5⅜ × 8½.   20602-5 Pa. $3.95

ADVENTURES WITH A MICROSCOPE, Richard Headstrom. 59 adventures with clothing fibers, protozoa, ferns and lichens, roots and leaves, much more. 142 illustrations. 232pp. 5⅜ × 8½.   23471-1 Pa. $3.95

CATALOG OF DOVER BOOKS

PLANTS OF THE BIBLE, Harold N. Moldenke and Alma L. Moldenke. Standard reference to all 230 plants mentioned in Scriptures. Latin name, biblical reference, uses, modern identity, much more. Unsurpassed encyclopedic resource for scholars, botanists, nature lovers, students of Bible. Bibliography. Indexes. 123 black-and-white illustrations. 384pp. 6 × 9. 25069-5 Pa. $8.95

FAMOUS AMERICAN WOMEN: A Biographical Dictionary from Colonial Times to the Present, Robert McHenry, ed. From Pocahontas to Rosa Parks, 1,035 distinguished American women documented in separate biographical entries. Accurate, up-to-date data, numerous categories, spans 400 years. Indices. 493pp. 6½ × 9¼. 24523-3 Pa. $9.95

THE FABULOUS INTERIORS OF THE GREAT OCEAN LINERS IN HISTORIC PHOTOGRAPHS, William H. Miller, Jr. Some 200 superb photographs capture exquisite interiors of world's great "floating palaces"—1890's to 1980's: *Titanic, Ile de France, Queen Elizabeth, United States, Europa,* more. Approx. 200 black-and-white photographs. Captions. Text. Introduction. 160pp. 8⅜ × 11¼. 24756-2 Pa. $9.95

THE GREAT LUXURY LINERS, 1927–1954: A Photographic Record, William H. Miller, Jr. Nostalgic tribute to heyday of ocean liners. 186 photos of Ile de France, Normandie, Leviathan, Queen Elizabeth, United States, many others. Interior and exterior views. Introduction. Captions. 160pp. 9 × 12. 24056-8 Pa. $9.95

A NATURAL HISTORY OF THE DUCKS, John Charles Phillips. Great landmark of ornithology offers complete detailed coverage of nearly 200 species and subspecies of ducks: gadwall, sheldrake, merganser, pintail, many more. 74 full-color plates, 102 black-and-white. Bibliography. Total of 1,920pp. 8⅜ × 11¼. 25141-1, 25142-X Cloth. Two-vol. set $100.00

THE SEAWEED HANDBOOK: An Illustrated Guide to Seaweeds from North Carolina to Canada, Thomas F. Lee. Concise reference covers 78 species. Scientific and common names, habitat, distribution, more. Finding keys for easy identification. 224pp. 5⅜ × 8½. 25215-9 Pa. $5.95

THE TEN BOOKS OF ARCHITECTURE: The 1755 Leoni Edition, Leon Battista Alberti. Rare classic helped introduce the glories of ancient architecture to the Renaissance. 68 black-and-white plates. 336pp. 8⅜ × 11¼. 25239-6 Pa. $14.95

MISS MACKENZIE, Anthony Trollope. Minor masterpieces by Victorian master unmasks many truths about life in 19th-century England. First inexpensive edition in years. 392pp. 5⅜ × 8½. 25201-9 Pa. $7.95

THE RIME OF THE ANCIENT MARINER, Gustave Doré, Samuel Taylor Coleridge. Dramatic engravings considered by many to be his greatest work. The terrifying space of the open sea, the storms and whirlpools of an unknown ocean, the ice of Antarctica, more—all rendered in a powerful, chilling manner. Full text. 38 plates. 77pp. 9¼ × 12. 22305-1 Pa. $4.95

THE EXPEDITIONS OF ZEBULON MONTGOMERY PIKE, Zebulon Montgomery Pike. Fascinating first-hand accounts (1805–6) of exploration of Mississippi River, Indian wars, capture by Spanish dragoons, much more. 1,088pp. 5⅜ × 8½. 25254-X, 25255-8 Pa. Two-vol. set $23.90

CATALOG OF DOVER BOOKS

A CONCISE HISTORY OF PHOTOGRAPHY: Third Revised Edition, Helmut Gernsheim. Best one-volume history—camera obscura, photochemistry, daguerreotypes, evolution of cameras, film, more. Also artistic aspects—landscape, portraits, fine art, etc. 281 black-and-white photographs. 26 in color. 176pp. 8⅜ × 11¼. 25128-4 Pa. $12.95

THE DORÉ BIBLE ILLUSTRATIONS, Gustave Doré. 241 detailed plates from the Bible: the Creation scenes, Adam and Eve, Flood, Babylon, battle sequences, life of Jesus, etc. Each plate is accompanied by the verses from the King James version of the Bible. 241pp. 9 × 12. 23004-X Pa. $8.95

HUGGER-MUGGER IN THE LOUVRE, Elliot Paul. Second Homer Evans mystery-comedy. Theft at the Louvre involves sleuth in hilarious, madcap caper. "A knockout."—Books. 336pp. 5⅜ × 8½. 25185-3 Pa. $5.95

FLATLAND, E. A. Abbott. Intriguing and enormously popular science-fiction classic explores the complexities of trying to survive as a two-dimensional being in a three-dimensional world. Amusingly illustrated by the author. 16 illustrations. 103pp. 5⅜ × 8½. 20001-9 Pa. $2.00

THE HISTORY OF THE LEWIS AND CLARK EXPEDITION, Meriwether Lewis and William Clark, edited by Elliott Coues. Classic edition of Lewis and Clark's day-by-day journals that later became the basis for U.S. claims to Oregon and the West. Accurate and invaluable geographical, botanical, biological, meteorological and anthropological material. Total of 1,508pp. 5⅜ × 8½. 21268-8, 21269-6, 21270-X Pa. Three-vol. set $25.50

LANGUAGE, TRUTH AND LOGIC, Alfred J. Ayer. Famous, clear introduction to Vienna, Cambridge schools of Logical Positivism. Role of philosophy, elimination of metaphysics, nature of analysis, etc. 160pp. 5⅜ × 8½. (Available in U.S. and Canada only) 20010-8 Pa. $2.95

MATHEMATICS FOR THE NONMATHEMATICIAN, Morris Kline. Detailed, college-level treatment of mathematics in cultural and historical context, with numerous exercises. For liberal arts students. Preface. Recommended Reading Lists. Tables. Index. Numerous black-and-white figures. xvi + 641pp. 5⅜ × 8½. 24823-2 Pa. $11.95

28 SCIENCE FICTION STORIES, H. G. Wells. Novels, *Star Begotten* and *Men Like Gods*, plus 26 short stories: "Empire of the Ants," "A Story of the Stone Age," "The Stolen Bacillus," "In the Abyss," etc. 915pp. 5⅜ × 8½. (Available in U.S. only) 20265-8 Cloth. $10.95

HANDBOOK OF PICTORIAL SYMBOLS, Rudolph Modley. 3,250 signs and symbols, many systems in full; official or heavy commercial use. Arranged by subject. Most in Pictorial Archive series. 143pp. 8⅛ × 11. 23357-X Pa. $5.95

INCIDENTS OF TRAVEL IN YUCATAN, John L. Stephens. Classic (1843) exploration of jungles of Yucatan, looking for evidences of Maya civilization. Travel adventures, Mexican and Indian culture, etc. Total of 669pp. 5⅜ × 8½. 20926-1, 20927-X Pa., Two-vol. set $9.90

DEGAS: An Intimate Portrait, Ambroise Vollard. Charming, anecdotal memoir by famous art dealer of one of the greatest 19th-century French painters. 14 black-and-white illustrations. Introduction by Harold L. Van Doren. 96pp. 5⅜ × 8½.
25131-4 Pa. $3.95

PERSONAL NARRATIVE OF A PILGRIMAGE TO ALMANDINAH AND MECCAH, Richard Burton. Great travel classic by remarkably colorful personality. Burton, disguised as a Moroccan, visited sacred shrines of Islam, narrowly escaping death. 47 illustrations. 959pp. 5⅜ × 8½. 21217-3, 21218-1 Pa., Two-vol. set $17.90

PHRASE AND WORD ORIGINS, A. H. Holt. Entertaining, reliable, modern study of more than 1,200 colorful words, phrases, origins and histories. Much unexpected information. 254pp. 5⅜ × 8½. 20758-7 Pa. $4.95

THE RED THUMB MARK, R. Austin Freeman. In this first Dr. Thorndyke case, the great scientific detective draws fascinating conclusions from the nature of a single fingerprint. Exciting story, authentic science. 320pp. 5⅜ × 8½. (Available in U.S. only) 25210-8 Pa. $5.95

AN EGYPTIAN HIEROGLYPHIC DICTIONARY, E. A. Wallis Budge. Monumental work containing about 25,000 words or terms that occur in texts ranging from 3000 B.C. to 600 A.D. Each entry consists of a transliteration of the word, the word in hieroglyphs, and the meaning in English. 1,314pp. 6⅞ × 10.
23615-3, 23616-1 Pa., Two-vol. set $27.90

THE COMPLEAT STRATEGYST: Being a Primer on the Theory of Games of Strategy, J. D. Williams. Highly entertaining classic describes, with many illustrated examples, how to select best strategies in conflict situations. Prefaces. Appendices. xvi + 268pp. 5⅜ × 8½. 25101-2 Pa. $5.95

THE ROAD TO OZ, L. Frank Baum. Dorothy meets the Shaggy Man, little Button-Bright and the Rainbow's beautiful daughter in this delightful trip to the magical Land of Oz. 272pp. 5⅜ × 8. 25208-6 Pa. $4.95

POINT AND LINE TO PLANE, Wassily Kandinsky. Seminal exposition of role of point, line, other elements in non-objective painting. Essential to understanding 20th-century art. 127 illustrations. 192pp. 6½ × 9¼. 23808-3 Pa. $4.50

LADY ANNA, Anthony Trollope. Moving chronicle of Countess Lovel's bitter struggle to win for herself and daughter Anna their rightful rank and fortune—perhaps at cost of sanity itself. 384pp. 5⅜ × 8½. 24669-8 Pa. $6.95

EGYPTIAN MAGIC, E. A. Wallis Budge. Sums up all that is known about magic in Ancient Egypt: the role of magic in controlling the gods, powerful amulets that warded off evil spirits, scarabs of immortality, use of wax images, formulas and spells, the secret name, much more. 253pp. 5⅜ × 8½. 22681-6 Pa. $4.00

THE DANCE OF SIVA, Ananda Coomaraswamy. Preeminent authority unfolds the vast metaphysic of India: the revelation of her art, conception of the universe, social organization, etc. 27 reproductions of art masterpieces. 192pp. 5⅜ × 8½.
24817-8 Pa. $5.95

CHRISTMAS CUSTOMS AND TRADITIONS, Clement A. Miles. Origin, evolution, significance of religious, secular practices. Caroling, gifts, yule logs, much more. Full, scholarly yet fascinating; non-sectarian. 400pp. 5⅜ × 8½.
23354-5 Pa. $6.50

THE HUMAN FIGURE IN MOTION, Eadweard Muybridge. More than 4,500 stopped-action photos, in action series, showing undraped men, women, children jumping, lying down, throwing, sitting, wrestling, carrying, etc. 390pp. 7⅞ × 10⅝.
20204-6 Cloth. $19.95

THE MAN WHO WAS THURSDAY, Gilbert Keith Chesterton. Witty, fast-paced novel about a club of anarchists in turn-of-the-century London. Brilliant social, religious, philosophical speculations. 128pp. 5⅜ × 8½. 25121-7 Pa. $3.95

A CEZANNE SKETCHBOOK: Figures, Portraits, Landscapes and Still Lifes, Paul Cezanne. Great artist experiments with tonal effects, light, mass, other qualities in over 100 drawings. A revealing view of developing master painter, precursor of Cubism. 102 black-and-white illustrations. 144pp. 8¾ × 6⅜. 24790-2 Pa. $5.95

AN ENCYCLOPEDIA OF BATTLES: Accounts of Over 1,560 Battles from 1479 B.C. to the Present, David Eggenberger. Presents essential details of every major battle in recorded history, from the first battle of Megiddo in 1479 B.C. to Grenada in 1984. List of Battle Maps. New Appendix covering the years 1967–1984. Index. 99 illustrations. 544pp. 6½ × 9¼. 24913-1 Pa. $14.95

AN ETYMOLOGICAL DICTIONARY OF MODERN ENGLISH, Ernest Weekley. Richest, fullest work, by foremost British lexicographer. Detailed word histories. Inexhaustible. Total of 856pp. 6½ × 9¼.
21873-2, 21874-0 Pa., Two-vol. set $17.00

WEBSTER'S AMERICAN MILITARY BIOGRAPHIES, edited by Robert McHenry. Over 1,000 figures who shaped 3 centuries of American military history. Detailed biographies of Nathan Hale, Douglas MacArthur, Mary Hallaren, others. Chronologies of engagements, more. Introduction. Addenda. 1,033 entries in alphabetical order. xi + 548pp. 6½ × 9¼. (Available in U.S. only)
24758-9 Pa. $11.95

LIFE IN ANCIENT EGYPT, Adolf Erman. Detailed older account, with much not in more recent books: domestic life, religion, magic, medicine, commerce, and whatever else needed for complete picture. Many illustrations. 597pp. 5⅜ × 8½.
22632-8 Pa. $8.50

HISTORIC COSTUME IN PICTURES, Braun & Schneider. Over 1,450 costumed figures shown, covering a wide variety of peoples: kings, emperors, nobles, priests, servants, soldiers, scholars, townsfolk, peasants, merchants, courtiers, cavaliers, and more. 256pp. 8⅜ × 11¼. 23150-X Pa. $7.95

THE NOTEBOOKS OF LEONARDO DA VINCI, edited by J. P. Richter. Extracts from manuscripts reveal great genius; on painting, sculpture, anatomy, sciences, geography, etc. Both Italian and English. 186 ms. pages reproduced, plus 500 additional drawings, including studies for *Last Supper, Sforza* monument, etc. 860pp. 7⅞ × 10¾. (Available in U.S. only) 22572-0, 22573-9 Pa., Two-vol. set $25.90

THE ART NOUVEAU STYLE BOOK OF ALPHONSE MUCHA: All 72 Plates from "Documents Decoratifs" in Original Color, Alphonse Mucha. Rare copyright-free design portfolio by high priest of Art Nouveau. Jewelry, wallpaper, stained glass, furniture, figure studies, plant and animal motifs, etc. Only complete one-volume edition. 80pp. 9⅜ × 12¼.   24044-4 Pa. $8.95

ANIMALS: 1,419 COPYRIGHT-FREE ILLUSTRATIONS OF MAMMALS, BIRDS, FISH, INSECTS, ETC., edited by Jim Harter. Clear wood engravings present, in extremely lifelike poses, over 1,000 species of animals. One of the most extensive pictorial sourcebooks of its kind. Captions. Index. 284pp. 9 × 12.
23766-4 Pa. $9.95

OBELISTS FLY HIGH, C. Daly King. Masterpiece of American detective fiction, long out of print, involves murder on a 1935 transcontinental flight—"a very thrilling story"—NY Times. Unabridged and unaltered republication of the edition published by William Collins Sons & Co. Ltd., London, 1935. 288pp. 5⅜ × 8½. (Available in U.S. only)   25036-9 Pa. $4.95

VICTORIAN AND EDWARDIAN FASHION: A Photographic Survey, Alison Gernsheim. First fashion history completely illustrated by contemporary photographs. Full text plus 235 photos, 1840–1914, in which many celebrities appear. 240pp. 6½ × 9¼.   24205-6 Pa. $6.00

THE ART OF THE FRENCH ILLUSTRATED BOOK, 1700–1914, Gordon N. Ray. Over 630 superb book illustrations by Fragonard, Delacroix, Daumier, Doré, Grandville, Manet, Mucha, Steinlen, Toulouse-Lautrec and many others. Preface. Introduction. 633 halftones. Indices of artists, authors & titles, binders and provenances. Appendices. Bibliography. 608pp. 8⅜ × 11¼.   25086-5 Pa. $24.95

THE WONDERFUL WIZARD OF OZ, L. Frank Baum. Facsimile in full color of America's finest children's classic. 143 illustrations by W. W. Denslow. 267pp. 5⅜ × 8½.   20691-2 Pa. $5.95

FRONTIERS OF MODERN PHYSICS: New Perspectives on Cosmology, Relativity, Black Holes and Extraterrestrial Intelligence, Tony Rothman, et al. For the intelligent layman. Subjects include: cosmological models of the universe; black holes; the neutrino; the search for extraterrestrial intelligence. Introduction. 46 black-and-white illustrations. 192pp. 5⅜ × 8½.   24587-X Pa. $6.95

THE FRIENDLY STARS, Martha Evans Martin & Donald Howard Menzel. Classic text marshalls the stars together in an engaging, non-technical survey, presenting them as sources of beauty in night sky. 23 illustrations. Foreword. 2 star charts. Index. 147pp. 5⅜ × 8½.   21099-5 Pa. $3.50

FADS AND FALLACIES IN THE NAME OF SCIENCE, Martin Gardner. Fair, witty appraisal of cranks, quacks, and quackeries of science and pseudoscience: hollow earth, Velikovsky, orgone energy, Dianetics, flying saucers, Bridey Murphy, food and medical fads, etc. Revised, expanded In the Name of Science. "A very able and even-tempered presentation."—The New Yorker. 363pp. 5⅜ × 8.
20394-8 Pa. $5.95

ANCIENT EGYPT: ITS CULTURE AND HISTORY, J. E Manchip White. From pre-dynastics through Ptolemies: society, history, political structure, religion, daily life, literature, cultural heritage. 48 plates. 217pp. 5⅜ × 8½.   22548-8 Pa. $4.95

SIR HARRY HOTSPUR OF HUMBLETHWAITE, Anthony Trollope. Incisive, unconventional psychological study of a conflict between a wealthy baronet, his idealistic daughter, and their scapegrace cousin. The 1870 novel in its first inexpensive edition in years. 250pp. 5⅜ × 8½. 24953-0 Pa. $4.95

LASERS AND HOLOGRAPHY, Winston E. Kock. Sound introduction to burgeoning field, expanded (1981) for second edition. Wave patterns, coherence, lasers, diffraction, zone plates, properties of holograms, recent advances. 84 illustrations. 160pp. 5⅜ × 8¼. (Except in United Kingdom) 24041-X Pa. $3.50

INTRODUCTION TO ARTIFICIAL INTELLIGENCE: SECOND, EN-LARGED EDITION, Philip C. Jackson, Jr. Comprehensive survey of artificial intelligence—the study of how machines (computers) can be made to act intelligently. Includes introductory and advanced material. Extensive notes updating the main text. 132 black-and-white illustrations. 512pp. 5⅜ × 8½. 24864-X Pa. $8.95

HISTORY OF INDIAN AND INDONESIAN ART, Ananda K. Coomaraswamy. Over 400 illustrations illuminate classic study of Indian art from earliest Harappa finds to early 20th century. Provides philosophical, religious and social insights. 304pp. 6⅜ × 9⅜. 25005-9 Pa. $8.95

THE GOLEM, Gustav Meyrink. Most famous supernatural novel in modern European literature, set in Ghetto of Old Prague around 1890. Compelling story of mystical experiences, strange transformations, profound terror. 13 black-and-white illustrations. 224pp. 5⅜ × 8½. (Available in U.S. only) 25025-3 Pa. $5.95

ARMADALE, Wilkie Collins. Third great mystery novel by the author of *The Woman in White* and *The Moonstone*. Original magazine version with 40 illustrations. 597pp. 5⅜ × 8½. 23429-0 Pa. $7.95

PICTORIAL ENCYCLOPEDIA OF HISTORIC ARCHITECTURAL PLANS, DETAILS AND ELEMENTS: With 1,880 Line Drawings of Arches, Domes, Doorways, Facades, Gables, Windows, etc., John Theodore Haneman. Sourcebook of inspiration for architects, designers, others. Bibliography. Captions. 141pp. 9 × 12. 24605-1 Pa. $6.95

BENCHLEY LOST AND FOUND, Robert Benchley. Finest humor from early 30's, about pet peeves, child psychologists, post office and others. Mostly unavailable elsewhere. 73 illustrations by Peter Arno and others. 183pp. 5⅜ × 8½. 22410-4 Pa. $3.95

ERTÉ GRAPHICS, Erté. Collection of striking color graphics: *Seasons, Alphabet, Numerals, Aces* and *Precious Stones*. 50 plates, including 4 on covers. 48pp. 9⅜ × 12¼. 23580-7 Pa. $6.95

THE JOURNAL OF HENRY D. THOREAU, edited by Bradford Torrey, F. H. Allen. Complete reprinting of 14 volumes, 1837–61, over two million words; the sourcebooks for *Walden*, etc. Definitive. All original sketches, plus 75 photographs. 1,804pp. 8½ × 12¼. 20312-3, 20313-1 Cloth., Two-vol. set $80.00

CASTLES: THEIR CONSTRUCTION AND HISTORY, Sidney Toy. Traces castle development from ancient roots. Nearly 200 photographs and drawings illustrate moats, keeps, baileys, many other features. Caernarvon, Dover Castles, Hadrian's Wall, Tower of London, dozens more. 256pp. 5⅜ × 8¼. 24898-4 Pa. $5.95

CATALOG OF DOVER BOOKS

AMERICAN CLIPPER SHIPS: 1833–1858, Octavius T. Howe & Frederick C. Matthews. Fully-illustrated, encyclopedic review of 352 clipper ships from the period of America's greatest maritime supremacy. Introduction. 109 halftones. 5 black-and-white line illustrations. Index. Total of 928pp. 5⅜ × 8½.
25115-2, 25116-0 Pa., Two-vol. set $17.90

TOWARDS A NEW ARCHITECTURE, Le Corbusier. Pioneering manifesto by great architect, near legendary founder of "International School." Technical and aesthetic theories, views on industry, economics, relation of form to function, "mass-production spirit," much more. Profusely illustrated. Unabridged translation of 13th French edition. Introduction by Frederick Etchells. 320pp. 6⅛ × 9¼. (Available in U.S. only)
25023-7 Pa. $8.95

THE BOOK OF KELLS, edited by Blanche Cirker. Inexpensive collection of 32 full-color, full-page plates from the greatest illuminated manuscript of the Middle Ages, painstakingly reproduced from rare facsimile edition. Publisher's Note. Captions. 32pp. 9⅜ × 12¼.
24345-1 Pa. $4.50

BEST SCIENCE FICTION STORIES OF H. G. WELLS, H. G. Wells. Full novel *The Invisible Man,* plus 17 short stories: "The Crystal Egg," "Aepyornis Island," "The Strange Orchid," etc. 303pp. 5⅜ × 8½. (Available in U.S. only)
21531-8 Pa. $4.95

AMERICAN SAILING SHIPS: Their Plans and History, Charles G. Davis. Photos, construction details of schooners, frigates, clippers, other sailcraft of 18th to early 20th centuries—plus entertaining discourse on design, rigging, nautical lore, much more. 137 black-and-white illustrations. 240pp. 6⅛ × 9¼.
24658-2 Pa. $5.95

ENTERTAINING MATHEMATICAL PUZZLES, Martin Gardner. Selection of author's favorite conundrums involving arithmetic, money, speed, etc., with lively commentary. Complete solutions. 112pp. 5⅜ × 8½.   25211-6 Pa. $2.95

THE WILL TO BELIEVE, HUMAN IMMORTALITY, William James. Two books bound together. Effect of irrational on logical, and arguments for human immortality. 402pp. 5⅜ × 8½.
20291-7 Pa. $7.50

THE HAUNTED MONASTERY and THE CHINESE MAZE MURDERS, Robert Van Gulik. 2 full novels by Van Gulik continue adventures of Judge Dee and his companions. An evil Taoist monastery, seemingly supernatural events; overgrown topiary maze that hides strange crimes. Set in 7th-century China. 27 illustrations. 328pp. 5⅜ × 8½.
23502-5 Pa. $5.00

CELEBRATED CASES OF JUDGE DEE (DEE GOONG AN), translated by Robert Van Gulik. Authentic 18th-century Chinese detective novel; Dee and associates solve three interlocked cases. Led to Van Gulik's own stories with same characters. Extensive introduction. 9 illustrations. 237pp. 5⅜ × 8½.
23337-5 Pa. $4.95

Prices subject to change without notice.

Available at your book dealer or write for free catalog to Dept. GI, Dover Publications, Inc., 31 East 2nd St., Mineola, N.Y. 11501. Dover publishes more than 175 books each year on science, elementary and advanced mathematics, biology, music, art, literary history, social sciences and other areas.